Career Development Practice in Canada

Career Development Practice in Canada

PERSPECTIVES, PRINCIPLES, AND PROFESSIONALISM

CANADIAN EDUCATION AND RESEARCH INSTITUTE FOR COUNSELLING
INSTITUT CANADIEN D'ÉDUCATION ET DE RECHERCHE EN ORIENTATION

Copyright © 2014 by CERIC Canadian Education and Research Institute for Counselling

Published in 2014 by
CERIC
18 Spadina Road
Suite 200
Toronto, ON M5R 2S7
Canada
www.ceric.ca

ISBN 978-0-9811652-3-3 (paperback)

ISBN 978-0-9811652-4-0 (ePDF)

ISBN 978-0-9811652-5-7 (ePUB)

Cataloguing-in-Publication Data available from Library
and Archives Canada.

Production Manager: Donald G. Bastian, www.bpsbooks.com
Cover: Daniel Crack, Kinetics Design, kdbooks.ca
Cover image: Shutterstock/Sergey Nivens
Text design and typesetting: Tannice Goddard, www.bookstopress.com

Table of Contents

Section 1: The Development of the Profession

one

two

Section 2: Basic Conceptual Frameworks of Career Development Practice

three

Section 3: The Nuts and Bolts of Career Development Practice

Section 4: Working With Diversity

Section 7: New Directions and Emerging Trends in Career Development Practice

Appendices

Analytical
Table of Contents

Section 1: The Development of the Profession

one

two

Section 2: Basic Conceptual Frameworks of Career Development Practice

five

Section 3: The Nuts and Bolts of Career Development Practice

seven

Section 4: Working With Diversity

ten

thirteen

Section 5: Navigating Developmental Tasks and Pathways

fourteen

Section 6: Specialties in the Profession

seventeen

Section 7: New Directions and Emerging Trends in Career Development Practice

twenty

Appendices

Appendix A

Appendix B

Appendix C

Foreword

It is a pleasure to see, in this comprehensive text *Career Development Practice in Canada: Perspectives, Principles, and Professionalism*, such a wide range of career development specialists addressing various facets of career development practice from a "Canadian" perspective. Many of the experts who have contributed to this text are recognized at both a national and international level for the significance of their work. Canada has a rich history of career development and with this supporting cast I am sure that the book will be of considerable interest to career development specialists in both Canada and other countries.

This text is uniquely Canadian in many respects. It addresses the emergence of career development in both English Canada and Québec. Considerable attention is also focused on diversity issues and the challenge of working in a multicultural context. Other uniquely Canadian perspectives relate to the *Canadian Standards and Guidelines for Career Development Practitioners* and the specific ways in which accreditation and professionalization has been developing within Canada.

In addition to the special focus on Canadian material, there also is some very helpful career development information about theory, ethics, social justice, ongoing evaluation, lifelong learning, and best practices. This is a textbook that addresses the integration of theory and practice, and provides many concrete examples of how career development ideas have been implemented.

The material in this book builds on the past but also pushes ahead to emerging trends, challenges, and future possibilities. There is a call to action and a highlighting of the need for collaborative community involvement in career development. This is a book that has relevance for a rapidly changing social and economic context.

I was particularly impressed by the structure and careful attention to learning objectives contained within each chapter. The material is organized in a practical manner that includes questions, reflections, definitions of terms, references, and considerable discussion and practical examples and activities. The authors have constructed a book that should be a good resource for anyone interested in furthering their knowledge of career development theory and practice.

The Canadian Education and Research Institute for Counselling (CERIC) should be commended for its financial support and encouragement in the development of this book. A number of meetings were held to establish the need for such a book, and there also was ongoing consultation with regard to structure and topics for inclusion. As mentioned earlier, a large number of notable Canadian authors have contributed to this resource and, ultimately, a very practical and informative book has been created.

The challenge for practitioners and educators will be to find ways to apply this wealth of information to today's situation, given the challenging times we live in and the increasingly complex context of our work. There is a great need for creativity and imaginative action. This book provides some solid foundational material and is a good starting point for moving forward.

> *Norman E. Amundson*, PhD
> Professor, Department of Educational and
> Counselling, Psychology, and Special Education,
> Faculty of Education, University of British Columbia

Acknowledgements

This textbook would not have been possible without the sustained encouragement and assistance of a number of people. In particular, we wish to acknowledge the generous assistance we received from the Canadian Education and Research Institute for Counselling (CERIC) in the completion of this project.

Our research assistants played a vital role in the editorial process. Special thanks go out to Allison Roest, who provided encouragement and good advice as she accessed various practitioners and academics in the area of career development across Canada to complete the needs assessment survey. We warmly acknowledge the diligent work of Lara Shepard, BA, who created the discussion topics and activities for students at the end of the chapters, found valuable websites, added nuggets of information, generated the glossaries, and verified APA style and references. We extend our deepest appreciation to Aaron Shepard, MFA, and Waylon Greggain, MEd, for their exceptional assistance with the review and formatting of chapters.

We would also like to express our deep gratitude to our academic institutions (University of Lethbridge and University of Manitoba) for their support, and finally our grantor (CERIC), which supported us throughout this project's development. Our thanks also to those working on the frontlines who contributed additional information. Most of all, we would like to express our heartfelt appreciation to the authors who have contributed to this book by sharing their insights and professional expertise with us.

Lastly, thank you to Gwen Harris for taking the book through the final editing process and steps to publication.

Blythe C. Shepard and Priya S. Mani

List of Contributors

Editors/Authors

Editors

Blythe C. Shepard, PhD, MA (Counselling), BA (Psychology), PDP (Education), is a Canadian of British and Mohawk ancestry (Mohawks of the Bay of Quinte) and an associate professor in Counselling Psychology at the University of Lethbridge. Blythe received her doctorate in Educational Psychology with a specialty in Counselling Psychology from the University of Victoria in 2002, where she continued as a faculty member and graduate advisor until 2008 in the Department of Educational Psychology and Leadership Studies. Her research and teaching foci include life-career development; rural youth transitions and rural women's career paths; counsellor training and identity; clinical supervision; child and adolescent mental health; and families living with children with Fetal Alcohol Spectrum Disorder (FASD). She is a recipient of the Canadian Counselling and Psychotherapy Association's (CCPA) Professional Contribution Award in recognition of outstanding promotion of the counselling profession in Canada. She has served on the BC Task Group responsible for the creation of entry to practice competencies for counsellors and co-chaired the National Symposium on Counsellor Mobility for three years (2008–2011). Blythe is currently (2013) the president of the Canadian Counselling and Psychotherapy Association (CCPA) and continues to advocate for the counselling and psychotherapy profession and the people it serves.

Priya S. Mani, PhD, is an associate professor at the University of Manitoba in the Faculty of Education. She is affiliated with the educational counselling program and teaches various courses at the postbaccalaureate and the graduate level, one of which is career development. Her research interest revolves around exploring the perception of supports, barriers, and different contexts that constrain and/or facilitate career development for Indo-Canadian young men and women. Specifically, she is interested in uncovering the career decision-making processes for these young adults who enter undergraduate professional degree programs. In 2008, she was invited to be part of a Canadian delegation specializing in psychology, affiliated with the Canadian Psychological Association, to meet in South Africa. There she had the opportunity to share her research findings and gain an international perspective on counsellors' understanding of diversity and career-counselling issues. One of her key publications is "South Asian Canadian Young Men and Women's Interest Development in Science: Perception of Contextual Influences," published in *The Canadian Journal of Family and Youth*, 3(1). She is a member of the Canadian Counselling and Psychotherapy Association and looks forward to seeing advances in the profession.

Authors

Nancy Arthur is a full professor and Canada Research Chair in Professional Education, Educational Studies in Counselling Psychology, at the Faculty of Education, University of Calgary. Nancy's teaching and research interests focus on multicultural counselling, career development, and international transitions. She has delivered keynote, workshop, and research presentations on these topics at local, national, and international conferences in more than 20 different countries. Nancy co-authored and co-edited the award-winning book *Culture-Infused Counselling*, co-edited *Case Incidents in Counseling for International Transitions*, and authored *Counseling International Students: Clients From Around the World*. Nancy is also a registered psychologist and works with clients in a private practice setting.

Lynne Bezanson, Sareena Hopkins, and Elaine O'Reilly are career development leaders, authors, researchers, and educators with the Canadian Career Development Foundation (CCDF). They have been instrumental in steering several of the career development transformations discussed in their chapter. CCDF directed the first two International Symposia on Career Development and Public Policy as well as the inaugural pan-Canadian Symposium on Career Development, Lifelong Learning, and Workforce Development. They have been actively involved in all subsequent International Symposia, as facilitators and/or members of the Canada Team. The International Symposia are now well-established forums for policy practice dialogue. CCDF was instrumental in the development of the *Canadian Standards and Guidelines for Career Development Practitioners* and the formation of the Canadian Research Working Group on Evidence-Based Practice in Career Development (CRWG).

CCDF is a founding member of the International Centre for Career Development and Public Policy and chairs the Canadian Council for Career Development (CCCD).

Sandra Boyd is a principal and career solutions lead in the Toronto head office of Knightsbridge. Sandra specializes in Career Management, Career Transition, and the Four Generations in the Workplace. As a member of the Knightsbridge team, Sandra brings extensive consulting experience to the practice, including coaching executives in career transition and providing ongoing career management strategies to individuals and corporations across Canada to ensure employee engagement. Sandra has successfully developed and co-leads the career-management practice at Knightsbridge. She has been instrumental in building the career-management framework and conducting extensive research. She is the author of the *The Hidden Job Market*, published by McGraw-Hill Ryerson, and co-author of *Flexible Thinker Guide to Extreme Career Performance*, published by Orange You Glad Publishing.

Jennifer Browne is the director of Career Development & Experiential Learning at Memorial University of Newfoundland. She holds a BA and an MEd in Postsecondary Education from Memorial University, with a focus on student services. She has worked in the area of career development in both community/non-profit and postsecondary settings. She has presented and written nationally and internationally, and has been an active board member with a number of professional organizations, including the Canadian Association of Career Educators and Employers (CACEE), Canadian Association of College and University Student Services (CACUSS), Atlantic Association of College and University Student Services (AACUSS), and Canadian Education and Research Institute for Counselling (CERIC).

Lisa Bylsma is a registered clinical counsellor on Vancouver Island. She currently works at Child & Youth Mental Health, part of the British Columbia Ministry of Children and Family Development. Lisa is interested in immigrant and refugee mental health and has completed research with new immigrants. She received her master's degree in Counselling Psychology from the University of Alberta in 2010.

Natasha Caverley holds a BA (with distinction) in Psychology, MEd in Counselling Psychology, and PhD in Organizational Studies from the University of Victoria. Natasha is a Canadian Certified Counsellor (CCC) through the Canadian Counselling and Psychotherapy Association. Since 1998, Natasha has held research and policy analyst as well as organizational development positions in Aboriginal, non-Aboriginal, and public service organizations specializing in community facilitation and troubleshooting, management, and organizational behaviour, including policy development, instrument design and analysis, and strategic planning. At present, Dr. Caverley is the president of Turtle Island Consulting Services Inc., located in North Saanich, British Columbia. To date, Natasha has written over 20 publications (nationally and internationally) in human resources management, counselling psychology, public administration, natural resource management, and indigenous studies. Natasha is Canadian of Irish, Jamaican, and Algonquin ancestry.

Sandra Collins is a registered psychologist and professor in the Graduate Centre for Applied Psychology, Faculty of Health Discipline, Athabasca University. Sandra's work in the area of distributed learning promotes access to educational and career advancement through the removal of barriers to graduate education. Her research, graduate curriculum development, and teaching has been on social justice, multi-cultural counselling, and career development, as well as distance and distributed learning. Sandra co-authored and co-edited the book *Culture-Infused Counselling*, which was awarded the Canadian Counselling and Psychotherapy Association 2006 book award. Sandra is the past-president of the Social Justice chapter of this national association.

Louis Cournoyer is a professor in Career Counselling for undergraduate and graduate programs in the field of career development at Université du Québec à Montréal. He also maintains a professional practice in career counselling, mainly as a supervisor for Career and Vocational Guidance Counsellors. His field of research includes career counselling practices in a variety of sectors (organizations, schools, employment centres, private practice, mental health, and physical rehabilitation).

Scott Fisher is a Certified Career Development Professional (CCDP) with extensive experience assisting internationally educated professionals in integrating into the Canadian job market. He is a member of the steering committee for the Canadian Council for Career Development (CCCD), board member of the Career Development Association of Alberta (CDAA), and past chair for the Standards and Certification Committee of the CDAA. Scott has actively participated in the Welcoming Communities Initiative project of the Social Science and Humanities Research Council (SSHRC) and is currently involved with the SSHRC-funded project Pathways to Prosperity. In terms of academic pursuits, Scott possesses postgraduate certificates in Psychological Measurement and Methodologies and Performance Management, and is currently in the process of completing a master's in the field of Industrial/Organizational (I/O) Psychology from Colorado State University.

Mark Franklin, MEd, PEng, CMF, is practice leader of CareerCycles. Mark and his team of associates have enriched the career well-being of 3,500+ clients. Mark developed the CareerCycles method of practice and trains career professionals nationally in the method, towards the Holistic Narrative Career Professional designation. He presents nationally and internationally (Cannexus, CACEE, CACUSS, CCPA, NCDA,

The Hague University) and produces and hosts the weekly Career Buzz radio show. Prior to leading CareerCycles, Mark worked as career counsellor at the University of Toronto and York University, redeploying many transferable skills from his earlier career in engineering and management consulting. Mark holds the Career Management Fellow designation through the Institute of Career Certification International. Mark's Career Statement and further information are available at <www.careercycles.com>.

Waylon D. Greggain, MEd, CCC, grew up in a small northern Saskatchewan town and moved to Calgary, Alberta, at the age of 18. Midway through his undergraduate program, he transferred to the University of Toronto, where he graduated with a Bachelor of Science in Psychology, along with minors in Sociology and Sexual Diversity Studies. He went on to complete a master of education degree in Counselling from the University of Northern British Columbia in Prince George, BC, and is currently a certified counsellor with the Canadian Counselling and Psychotherapy Association. Waylon has worked as a family counsellor in an elementary school and not-for-profit agencies. He has assisted Dr. Shepard in conducting community-based research in rural communities.

Bryan Hiebert is a professor emeritus of Education, University of Calgary, and adjunct professor in Educational Psychology and Leadership Studies at the University of Victoria. Dr. Hiebert co-chaired the first Canadian National Symposium on Evaluation in Career and Employment Counselling in 1994 and co-facilitated the first International Symposium on Career Development and Public Policy in 1999. In 2005, Dr. Hiebert was granted honorary life membership in the Alberta Teachers' Association Guidance Council in recognition of his contribution to guidance and counselling in Alberta. In 2007 he was awarded the Stu Conger Gold Medal and Diamond Pin for Leadership in Career Development. Dr. Hiebert is a member of the Canadian Working Group on Evidence-Based Practice in Career Development and part of the co-ordinating team for Prove It Works, an international initiative aimed at demonstrating the value of career development programs and services.

Stephen Hill is originally from England and has split his working life between there and Vancouver, Canada, combining international best practice from both places. Stephen's background and interest is "all about community." He offers support, ideas, and practical expertise in career development to communities. He has done this in a wide range of arenas including community centres, adventure playgrounds, inner city settlements, and woodwork training. In rural England, he even opened a café with a bicycle-hire operation in a railway station, providing a working example of both integrated transport and local food 20 years before the current locavore movement. Since 2003, Stephen, working mainly in Vancouver's Downtown Eastside, has used employment counselling as the opening for asking a simple question: "How can I help?"

Hany Ibrahim is a graduate of the Community Psychology master's program at Wilfrid Laurier University. She received her bachelor's degree in Psychology and Peace and Conflict Studies with an option in International Studies from the University of Waterloo. Her research interests include integration of newcomer students in education settings, disarmament of child soldiers, and immigration policies. In her master's thesis, Hany explored the academic and social integration challenges faced by refugee students in collaboration with a local public school board, which provided empirical data and facilitated changes that are gradually being implemented. Hany is privileged with an insider and outsider perspective on the issues affecting newcomers and refugees, and aspires to help equip those organizations and agencies working with them.

Phil Jarvis is director of Global Partnerships at Career Cruising. He supports communities, provinces, states, and countries implementing "whole-community" career and workforce development solutions. Career Cruising provides career exploration and planning resources to over 20,000 secondary and postsecondary schools, libraries, and employment support centers. As the author of CHOICES in the late 1970s, he was an early pioneer of computer-based career exploration and planning. He co-authored *Blueprint for Life/Work Designs* and co-created *The Real Game Series*. He has trained thousands of educators and workforce development personnel. Programs he authored or co-authored have helped millions of students in 15 countries transition from school to success.

Kathleen Johnston, MA, PHEc, CCC, RCC, has worked in the career development field for 25 years. She is currently the principal of KJ Consulting Services, a private career consulting company founded in 2003. Her business specializes in career counselling and executive career coaching for individuals, and career development consulting to improve employee engagement and retention for organizations. Kathleen has significant expertise related to women's careers. In 2010 she published a two-part book/journal series — *Ordinary Women, Extraordinary Lives: A Woman's Career Diary* and *A Woman's Career Legacy*. Kathleen has been a faculty member of Concordia University College's Career Development Diploma Program since 2004, where she currently teaches five courses. She is adjunct faculty with St. Stephen's College, Edmonton, serving as convenor of the Program Committee for the Master of Psychotherapy & Spirituality degree.

Jeffrey R. Landine is an assistant professor in the Faculty of Education at the University of New Brunswick. He has taught Counselling students at UNB for

15 years, in particular in the areas of Psychological Assessment and Counselling Ethics. He has worked as a counsellor in the public school system, with UNB's Counselling Services, and in private practice for 10 years.

Kerri McKinnon, MEd, BEd, BA, is executive director of University Relations and director of Career Development Programs at Concordia University College of Alberta in Edmonton. She has been responsible for career development programs at Concordia since 2006. Under her leadership, Concordia's Career Development Program continues to expand both in scope and enrollment. Kerri's background includes teaching at the high school level. She was directly responsible for successfully implementing an innovative and creative regional virtual learning program. A skilled speaker, Kerri has presented at a wide variety of venues. As executive director she is responsible for Concordia's enrollment management and marketing activities. She is nearing the completion of a Doctor of Management degree program.

Kris Magnusson is a professor (Counselling Psychology) and dean of the Faculty of Education at Simon Fraser University. Dr. Magnusson has been a featured speaker at local, national, and international conferences, has written several training manuals related to the practice of counselling, has been active in the design of innovative programs in career development, and was the 2006 recipient of the Stu Conger Award for Leadership in Career Development. He was a co-developer of Alberta's first dedicated program for the training of career development specialists, co-developed the MEd in Counselling Psychology at the University of Lethbridge, and was a founding member of the Campus Alberta Applied Psychology: Master of Counselling program. Dr. Magnusson is also a founding member of the Canadian Research Working Group on Evidence-Based Practice in Career Development, dedicated to improving the evidence base for the impact that career services have at individual, community, social, and economic levels.

Roberta A. Neault, president of Life Strategies Ltd., has recently completed a term as editor of the *Journal of Employment Counseling* (the journal of the USA-based National Employment Counseling Association). The final issue under her leadership was "Thoughts on Theories" — a compilation of current short articles from authors of many of the theories and models referenced in her chapter in this book. Dr. Neault is an award-winning career counsellor and counsellor-educator, and is recipient of the Gold Medal for Leadership in Career Development and the Stu Conger Award for Career Counselling and Career Development. Co-author of the Career Engagement model, Roberta has written many practical guides and workbooks for career practitioners and clients in transition. She currently divides her time between teaching, counselling/coaching, research, writing, and presentations within Canada and around the globe.

Geoffrey S. Peruniak is a professor in the Centre for Social Sciences, Athabasca University, Alberta. In 1994, he initiated, and now co-ordinates, a university certificate in career development. He has long been interested in a holistic approach to psychology. To that end, he has been involved in research and development in experiential learning for over 35 years. For the last 15 years he has been exploring how quality of life applies to career development. His book *A Quality of Life Approach to Career Development* was published by University of Toronto Press in 2010. Over the last 7 years, he has been studying quality of life in the professional development and experiential learning of career practitioners.

Deirdre A. Pickerell, PhD, CHRP, GCDF-I, has over 20 years of experience as a career development specialist, educator, and human resources professional. She has made significant differences within the field of career development — locally, nationally, and internationally — through innovative program design, leading-edge education for career practitioners, and inspiring facilitation and career coaching. In recognition of her work, Deirdre was honoured with a 2006 Award of Excellence, presented by the BC Human Resources Management Association. Deirdre inspires through her leadership and also through developing respectful relationships — as one student said, "You've never made me feel silly for asking questions and you've responded as though you have discerned wisdom in our comments that we weren't even aware of ..."

Seanna Quressette, MEd, has provided employment services for over 25 years in urban and rural settings to clients across inguistic, industrial, and economic spectra. Seanna has been training career development practitioners since 1999 and has been responsible for the design, development, and implementation of CDP curricula tied to the *Canadian Standards and Guidelines for Career Development Practitioners* since that time. She is the owner of Creating Intentional Change Inc., a company that provides career counselling services to individuals, training for career counsellors, and workshop and in-house training to the counselling industry. Seanna is also currently contract faculty in the Faculty of Child Family and Community Studies at Douglas College in Coquitlam, BC. Seanna received the 2011 Career Development Practitioner of the Year award from BCCDA for her contributions to the field. She has been published previously in the *Canadian Journal of Community Mental Health* and in the American Counseling Association publication *Vistas* (2010).

Lisa Russell has been immersed in the field of career development and experience-based learning at the postsecondary level for 12 years. In that time she has worked in frontline service delivery, management, and senior leadership. This experience has provided her with opportunities to see firsthand how the academic issues of career development at the postsecondary level play out in individual lives and stories. Her experiences have fuelled her passion for excellence, commitment to students, and relentless drive for enhancement and innovation. She holds a Bachelor of Arts (Honours) at Memorial University and a Master of Arts from Dalhousie University. She has presented on issues of career development locally and nationally and served as the associate editor of *The Canadian Journal of Career Development* from 2002 until 2010.

Kim Spurgeon, CEC, CMC, is a vice president at Knightsbridge who manages a team of consultants and oversees the financial operation of the Markham and Ottawa offices. She brings over 20 years of experience in human capital consulting. She is a certified coach who specializes in career management, career transition, and executive coaching. Kim's career has spanned private, public and not-for-profit sectors. She developed training curriculum for individuals developing skills as a career consultant. Kim has successfully developed and co-leads the career management practice at Knightsbridge and has been instrumental in building the career-management frameworks, conducting research, and expanding customer outreach. Kim has authored several articles and white papers on career management and engagement. Kim holds a Bachelor of Arts in Criminology from Simon Fraser University and a master's certificate in Executive Coaching, Royal Roads University. She also holds a certificate in Human Resources Management, is a member of the International Coach Federation, and is a Certified Management Consultant.

John Stewart is professor emeritus in the Faculty of Education at the University of New Brunswick. He received his EdD in Counselling Psychology from OISE in the University of Toronto. Prior to coming to the University of New Brunswick, he worked for 20 years in the public school system in Prince Edward Island as a teacher and school counsellor. At UNB, he taught courses in the Counselling program, particularly Counselling Theory, Vocational Development, and Assessment in Counselling. He has authored a number of articles dealing with vocational development and decision making. More recently, he wrote a book chapter on assessment from a contextual perspective. He has spent a number of winters in Bhutan as an educational consultant in school counselling. He has served as a director of a CIDA project for UNB, as a member the Standards and Guidelines Committee, as a member of the Board of Directors of the Canadian Counselling and Psychotherapy Association, and, currently, as a member of the Editorial Board of the *Canadian Journal for Counselling and Psychotherapy*.

Suzanne L. Stewart is a member of the Yellowknife Dene First Nation. She holds the Canada Research Chair in Aboriginal Homelessness and Life Transitions. She is a psychologist and an associate professor of Indigenous Healing in Counselling Psychology at OISE, University of Toronto. She also chairs the Indigenous

Education Network and is special advisor to the dean on Aboriginal Education. Research and teaching interests include Indigenous mental health and healing in psychology and education (homelessness, youth identity, and work-life transitions). As well she is the chair of the Aboriginal Psychology Section of the Canadian Psychology Association. She works within local Native communities and in her home territory and shares her experiences with regional, national, and international health and government organizations.

Stephen J. Sutherland is a consultant to the immigrant- and refugee-serving sector in Canada. He is founder and director of the Centre for Applied Settlement and Integration Studies. Stephen's research interests include issues faced by internationally educated professionals — particularly in fields that are regulated in Canada — and how the application of prior learning assessment and recognition models can assist newcomers in transitioning to successful careers in Canada. Stephen is a graduate of Trinity Western University's International Studies program and has worked for many years in support of the career development of newcomers to Canada and others with multiple barriers to employment.

Marilyn Van Norman, MA, first became interested in the history of Canadian career development when she was on the Advisory Board for the publication *Coming of Age: Counselling Canadians for Work in the Twentieth-Century*, funded by The Counselling Foundation of Canada. Currently she is the national co-ordinator of Innovation and Outreach for the Canadian Education and Research Institute for Counselling (CERIC). Marilyn has over 30 years of experience in career and student management services. Author of numerous articles and publications on career development, her book *Making It Work: Career Management for the New Workplace* was a Canadian bestseller. From 1987–2002, Marilyn was chair of the National Consultation on Career Development (NATCON). She was a founding board member of CERIC and has been a director and executive member of a number of national boards, including the Canadian Association of Career Educators and Employers (CACEE).

Beverley Walters, MA, has postsecondary credentials in Adult Education with a master's degree in Organizational Leadership from Royal Roads University. During her career she specialized in providing direction and training for members of management boards and staff professionals. In her role as an instructor, she developed and delivered organizational behaviour courses at the Northern Alberta Institute of Technology in Edmonton and at several public colleges and private vocational schools throughout Alberta and British Columbia. Beverley is the retired program manager for the Life Skills and Career Development Coach Diploma program offered through Bow Valley College in Calgary and currently works as a private consultant and human resources specialist. During her career, she authored several publications including *The*

Life Skills Coach Training Manual: A Guidebook for Trainers. The *Guidebook for Trainers* manual shaped the foundation for her chapter in this book.

Sophie C. Yohani, PhD, is a registered psychologist and an associate professor of Counselling Psychology at the University of Alberta. She is also director of the Counselling Centre's Clinical Services, a university-based community training centre for graduate students where she teaches graduate courses in Counselling Psychology. She maintains a research and practice interest in refugee and immigrant mental health and counselling, psychological trauma, and community-based therapy practices that promote hope and resilience.

Additional Contributors

Sharon Crozier, PhD, is Senior Counsellor Emeritus, University of Calgary. Sharon has been a registered psychologist for almost 30 years. She is now retired from the University of Calgary, where she worked as a senior counsellor and director of the counselling centre for many years with a focus on career/life planning. She enjoys counselling in a small private practice in Calgary.

Frank Deer, PhD, is an assistant professor in the Faculty of Education at the University of Manitoba and has conducted research in the area of employability among Aboriginal peoples in Manitoba.

Kathy Dokis-Ranney is the Principal of First Nation, Métis, and Inuit Education in the Rainbow District School Board, Sudbury Ontario.

Michael Herzog, MBA, created an online product called Essential Skills, which customizes job descriptions, skill gap reports, and training plans for individuals and groups that match training needs with Essential Skills learning materials.

Michael Huston, MA, is a registered psychologist with expertise in career counselling. He works at Student Counselling Services, Mount Royal University, Calgary.

Riz Ibrahim is vice president and general manager of the Canadian Education and Research Institute for Counselling (CERIC).

Gray Poehnell is an experienced author, trainer, and presenter who uses holistic approaches that cultivate hope, practical spirituality, creativity, imagination, and career integrity in order to make career success accessible to people, especially those who do not relate to mainstream approaches.

Sandra Salesas, MA, c.o., CCC, is a career counsellor at Commission Scolaire Marguerite Bourgeoys School Board. She has worked at the Minstère de l'Éducation (2005–2011) overseeing the development and implementation of the Guidance-Oriented Approach to Learning (GOAL).

Lara Shepard has a BA in Anthropology and Environmental Studies (University of Victoria). She contributed to the writing of the end pages of each chapter of this book. She has worked as a research assistant on research projects with families living with Fetal Alcohol Spectrum Disorder and with rural youth and life transitions.

Mark Slomp, MEd, is a counsellor at Counselling Services, University of Lethbridge. He also teaches a course in career development through the Faculty of Education.

Margaret Vennard is executive director at Career Transitions and a board member at Skills Canada Alberta.

Introduction

BLYTHE C. SHEPARD
University of Lethbridge
PRIYA S. MANI
University of Manitoba

The idea for this textbook grew out of the Advancement of Career Counsellor Education in Canada Think Tank held in Montréal in 2006. Funded by CERIC, the think tank consisted of educators across Canada who taught career counselling courses at the undergraduate and graduate levels at various postsecondary institutions. They soon identified the lack of an appropriate, Canadian-focused resource to inform their teaching practice as the greatest issue needing attention. A needs assessment by Dr. Natalie Popadiuk confirmed that a career counselling Canadian textbook was warranted and would contribute to best practice in teaching career development principles at the postsecondary level.

The decision was made to apply for CERIC funding in early 2009 to undertake two surveys and develop a textbook on Canadian perspectives of career development. We — Blythe Shepard and Priya Mani — took up the mission as co-editors. Dr. Mani's research focus has been career development and cultural diversity, and Dr. Shepard's studies have been centred on career development of rural populations.

The first survey sought to obtain from career educators, researchers, and practitioners in Canada a clear direction on the content and structure of the proposed textbook. In the fall of 2009, we sent a survey to 71 career educators, researchers, and practitioners inviting them to participate in developing a vision for a Canadian career development textbook. The response was outstanding. With this feedback, we generated an outline for the text and sent a second survey regarding the structure of the book. Respondents were generous in providing ideas for enhancing the content and flow of the book. They emphasized the importance of using Canadian statistics, identifying successful Canadian programs, describing key macro concepts, exploring social issues for special populations, and presenting theoretical frameworks to address diversity issues within a Canadian context.

The *Canadian Standards and Guidelines for Career Development Practitioners*, developed in 2004, are the guiding principles for this book. These professional competency statements not only provide quality assurance to the public and others in the industry, but also provide the foundation for designing training for career development practitioners.

The core themes in this textbook of professionalism, ethical practice, cultural-infusion, and social justice are consonant with the beliefs of the career educators, researchers, and practitioners who responded to our survey. Professionalism and professional identity were identified in Montréal as key to enhancing career development as a defined field of practice. Ethical practice and adherence to a code of ethics underpin the standards of integrity and professionalism in the field. This includes a requirement to increase one's multicultural competence in order to effect change at the professional level. Social justice has long been a core value in career development practice, and career practitioners as social agents are required to infuse the values of social justice into their work with individual clients and with the systems that influence service delivery.

Overall, our aim is to give the next generation of practitioners the understanding and tools to enhance opportunities for the poor and working class, and to promote social justice and systemic change for traditionally underserved populations in Canada. We also hope that this book will contribute to professionalism across the country and foster a sense of pride and intention in the choice to be a career development practitioner.

Section 1: The Development of the Profession

Not to know what happened before one was born is always to be a child.
— Cicero, 80 B.C.

In the first part of the book, we look at how economic processes and societal changes have affected the advancement of career practice in Canada over the past 100 years. "Historical Snapshots" surveys the history of career development in Canada, and the evolution of what constituted "best practices" for career practitioners. Career development in Canada first flourished in the province of Québec. The next chapter, "Career Counselling in Québec," examines the development and adoption of career development practices in that province over several decades.

The reader is urged to consider how the career practitioner's worldview is influenced by numerous factors, and how those views come to shape the training,

AN INTRODUCTION TO THE SECTIONS

SECTION 1:
*Development
of Profession*

1. Emergence of
   Career Development
2. Career Counselling
   in Québec

SECTION 2:
*Basic Conceptual
Frameworks*

3. Career Development
4. Diversity and Social
   Justice
5. Professional Ethics
6. Theoretical Foundations

SECTION 3:
*Nuts and Bolts of
Career Development*

7. Effective Client
   Relationships
8. Career Planning
9. Work Search Strategies

SECTION 4:
*Working
With Diversity*

10. Poverty
11. Immigrants
12. Refugees
13. Aboriginal Peoples

SECTION 5:
Tasks and Pathways

14. Career Development
    for Students
15. Postsecondary
    Practice
16. Lifelong Career
    Management

SECTION 6:
*Specialties
in the Profession*

17. Assessment
18. Career Cycles
19. Community Capacity
    Building

SECTION 7:
*Directions
and Trends*

20. Power of Evidence
21. Professionalization
22. Emerging Trends

APPENDIX A:
Code of Ethics

APPENDIX B:
*Professional
Resources for Career
Practitioners*

APPENDIX C:
*Primer on
Aboriginal Peoples
and Canadian Law*

practice, and engagement within the profession. By understanding the history of the profession and the changing role of the career practitioner over time, the reader will gain a greater perspective of issues affecting career development today.

Section 2: Basic Conceptual Frameworks of Career Development Practice

Because if you have a strong foundation like we have, then you can build or rebuild anything on it. But if you've got a weak foundation you can't build anything.
— Jack Scalia

Section 2 explores the fundamental principles that guide contemporary practices in career development. The first two chapters in this section explore the systematic underpinnings within society that impact people's careers.

In "Career Development: Key to Economic Development," we see the connection between achieving economic prosperity and deploying career management to make sure that talents are put to use.

The next chapter, "Diversity and Social Justice," positions cultural diversity and social justice as guiding concepts for understanding career development. Career development practitioners must be contextually sensitive to the influence that social systems have on diverse client groups: Individual career development cannot be understood if broader systemic contexts such as societal inequality and oppression are not recognized. The reader is encouraged to reflect on how social class intersects with culture and the impact it can have on the direction a career practitioner may take with a client.

Ethics codes, frameworks, and decision-making models are other key elements in career development practice. In "Professional Ethics, Role, and the Whole Person," we consider the interplay between context and what it means to engage in caring and principled actions that honour the self and the community. As practitioners, we are often so focused on helping others, we fail to care for, nourish, and replenish ourselves to allay job stress and professional burn-out. Self-care, including ongoing professional improvement, is an ethical imperative for career development practitioners in order to thrive in their work.

"Theoretical Foundations of Career Development" furnishes the reader with a framework and context for working with clients. When we work from a theoretical basis, we have a better understanding of how to use interventions and tools. With the ability to draw from a number of theories and models, we are better equipped to meet the particular needs of each client. No single theory of career development is comprehensive or complex enough to capture the needs of our culturally diverse clientele. As career practitioners, we also need to recognize and be aware of each theory's strengths, weaknesses, and inherent biases. A combination of career development theories, models, and strategies is necessary to work with clients in a holistic manner.

Section 3: The Nuts and Bolts of Career Development Practice

We feel "related" when we feel at one with another
(person or object) in some heartfelt way.
— Helen H. Perlman

The focus of Section 3 is on ways by which career development practitioners can develop helping relationships with their clients and counsel them in career awareness and career decision-making skills.

"Developing Effective Client Relationships" explains that engagement with clients involves creating a trusting or "mattering environment." Once trust is built with a client, the career practitioner can help the client gather information about current labour market trends, make plans, and develop skills to build a career.

One of the main messages in this section is that career planning is a lifelong activity. "Career Planning, Knowledge, and Skills" offers practical advice on collecting data and developing a career plan.

Finding work in today's competitive job market is challenging: Job seekers must learn to use proven job search methods described in "Work Search Strategies" to find meaningful employment that fits their needs.

Overall, this section outlines the three key elements of career development practice: (a) developing effective and caring client relationships; (b) helping clients with career exploration, planning, and decision making; and (c) equipping the client with job search skills suitable for unsettled times.

Section 4: Working With Diversity

Diversity ... is not casual liberal tolerance of anything not yourself.
It is not polite accommodation. Instead, diversity is, in action, the sometimes painful
awareness that other people, other races, other voices, other habits of mind have
as much integrity of being, as much claim on the world as you do ...
— William Chase

In this section, the reader will learn how to integrate the theoretical frameworks of Section 2 with "nuts and bolts" information in Section 3, and apply this understanding to helping clients of diverse backgrounds. The reader will become acquainted with the career development challenges and strengths of four underserved client populations: people of low socioeconomic status, immigrants, refugees, and Aboriginal peoples.

"Employment Counselling, and Poverty: A View From the Frontline in British Columbia" examines the conditions and consequences of poverty and unemployment.

"Immigrants in Canada: Contexts and Issues for Consideration" provides information about the history of the Canadian immigration system, characteristics of immigrants in Canada, and issues of importance for career and employment counsellors.

"Refugees in Canada: From Persecution to Preparedness" looks at issues that affect refugees in integrating into Canadian society and developing careers.

"Through an Aboriginal Lens: Exploring Career Development and Planning in Canada" gives the context, challenges, opportunities, and strategies for career development of Aboriginal peoples.

These four chapters will contribute to a better understanding of how to help individuals of different cultural and socioeconomic backgrounds develop their careers. This may involve identifying coping skills, addressing cognitive processes that shape their interactions within their environment, and/or working to change the environment and make systems more helpful or affirming. Paying attention to diversity issues in career development does not mean stereotyping people. Culturally competent practitioners must think outside their own cultural frames of reference when assisting people with career development.

Section 5: Navigating Developmental Tasks and Pathways

The purpose of learning is growth, and our minds, unlike our bodies,
can continue growing as we continue to live.
— Morris Adler

The three chapters in this section present career development as a lifelong process of managing learning and work; a process that begins in elementary school, expands in the high school and postsecondary years, and is adopted as a life skill thereafter.

We see in "Career Development for Students" and "The Practice of Postsecondary Career Development" that the objective of career development education is to provide children and young adults with the tools, resources, and opportunities to be self-directed in their work/life by making contributions that bring personal meaning and satisfaction to themselves and their community. By understanding the factors that contribute to successful learning environments at different stages of education, the reader will be able to assess programs and community-based actions undertaken to reach children, youth, and postsecondary students.

Adults and their needs for career-management skills is the subject of "Lifelong Career Management." The chapter equips readers with a toolbox of strategies to manage their careers across their lifespan.

Section 6: Specialties in the Profession

Before we choose our tools and techniques we must choose our dreams and values.
— Anonymous

The *Canadian Standards and Guidelines for Career Development Practitioners* identifies specializations within the practice of career development such as assessment, facilitating learning, career counselling, information management, work development, and building community capacity. These areas are considered specialties as they require additional training.

"Assessment in Career Guidance" considers the ethical principles in using assessment instruments, and offers guidance in the selection and use of instruments.

"CareerCycles: A Holistic and Narrative Method of Practice" describes a method of practice in which clients tell their career and life stories and transform the meaning from those stories into choices for their future.

"Community Capacity Building as a Model for Career Development Planning" is about using community capacity building to increase the capabilities of people to articulate and address issues and overcome barriers so that they can improve the quality of their lives.

These chapters provide the reader with a preview of the multifaceted nature of career development practice.

Section 7: New Directions and Emerging Trends in Career Development Practice

The future will be determined in part by happenings that are impossible to foresee;
it will also be influenced by trends that are now existent and observable.
— Emily Greene Balch

In this concluding section, some of the more pressing professional issues that career practitioners currently face are explored. Two of the most salient issues are the accountability of career practitioners and the efficacy of career services.

In "The Power of Evidence," an evaluation framework is presented that can be used to gather evidence that will substantiate the efficacy of career development services. In the appendices to that chapter, there are a number of assessment tools to measure outcomes that can document the impact of career development services. Assessment is important as outcomes have the potential to influence policy.

In "The Professionalization of Career Development in Canada in the 21st Century," our attention turns to transformations that are taking place in the career development sector in Canada and to some extent internationally. The authors discuss external influences on policy (i.e., outside-in transformations) as well as inside influences on practice (i.e., inside-out transformations). Here the focus is on the training and certification of career practitioners in order to ensure accountability to the public.

The book concludes with five "Emerging Trends" — namely: (a) newly recognized theories and models, (b) expanding roles of career development practitioners, (c) emerging work search strategies, (d) integrated employment services, and (e) the need for practitioners to work with all facets of Canadian society. The career development field continues to evolve, enabling practitioners to work in a variety of roles. These are exciting times for career development in Canada!

In the end, we hope that new questions will emerge for you as you read this book so that you might gain the self-awareness and skills to inspire others along their career path.

About the Chapters

The book has been designed to be a learning tool for students, a resource for educators, and a reference for career practitioners in the field.

Most chapters have the following:

1. Opening questions to orient the reader.
2. Learning objectives to guide the reader to the main learning points.
3. Stop-and-reflect moments to ponder and apply the material.
4. Glossary of key terms. Bolded words in the text are defined in the glossary at the end of the chapter.
5. References used in the chapter, often with links to a source on the Internet.
6. Discussion and activities for individuals and groups. Discussion topics may be general, relate to the career practitioner role, or ask for personal reflection.
7. Resources and supplementary readings. These include recommended websites, videos, and additional readings to fill out a subject area.

SECTION 1

The Development of the Profession

one

Historical Snapshots

The Emergence of
Career Development in Canada

MARILYN VAN NORMAN
Canadian Education and Research Institute for Counselling
BLYTHE C. SHEPARD
University of Lethbridge
PRIYA S. MANI
University of Manitoba

PRE-READING QUESTIONS

Give some thought to these questions before you read the chapter.

1. Vocational guidance was a precursor to career counselling and career development. When do you think vocational guidance began (mid-1900s, early 1900s, late 1800s) and under what circumstances? Who would seek out this guidance?

2. Interest in career development grew as Canada's economy became more complex and its workforce more diverse. What kinds of supports would be needed to develop the career development practice?

Introduction and Learning Objectives

This opening chapter reviews the history of career development in Canada. Our aim is to help practitioners comprehend changing views about work and a growing understanding of career interests, decision making, and career choices. The chapter tells the story through a series of snapshots of the emergence and growth of career development in Canada. The content is based in part on information from *A Coming of Age: Counselling Canadians for Work in the Twentieth Century* (The Counselling Foundation of Canada, 2002). These snapshots will show how career development in Canada has unfolded over the last century, the current professional issues in the field, and the importance of networks to the organizations that further professional growth and practice for career practitioners.

The specific learning objectives for this chapter are to:

1. Recognize key defining moments and turning points in the history of career development and career counselling in Canada.
2. Identify at different time periods how career practitioners worked with clients to help them make meaning in their lives.
3. Consider how work was defined by Canadians at different historical time periods.
4. Understand the scope of work of career practitioners at different time periods.
5. Understand the labour market trends that have influenced the field of career development.

❖ *Stop and Reflect*

Various historical snapshots are provided in the subsequent sections. As you read about each time period, consider views about career development and the role of the career development practitioner.

Early Career Development (1850–1910)

The story of vocational guidance from 1850 to 1910 is linked to the emergence of large commercial cities and an economy based on manufacturing and industry. From 1880 to 1902, the forces of industrialization, urbanization, and immigration propelled Canadian cities into modernity (The Counselling Foundation of Canada, 2002). The factory system of production was the major influence for the origins of career development as new innovations in energy production and technology were developed. The use of specialized machines required workers to have specific skills, and employers sought out people to perform a circumscribed set of tasks (Schmidt, 2008). The specialization of jobs in numerous occupations created a division of labour as these new jobs were grouped and clustered to form new "occupations" creating status and class differences (Miller & Form, 1964). Population grew rapidly in major cities as people, often lacking the skill sets needed, arrived to take up the new jobs. With this growth came higher numbers of unemployed people, poor working conditions in factories, delinquency, and an increase in crime (Miller & Form, 1964). Industrial growth also contributed to a factory mentality that disregarded individual rights, freedom, and human value (Schmidt, 2008).

In response to these conditions, educators and social activists formed groups and agencies to help workers make the transition from an agrarian to an industrial society and, where possible, support students and adults in their vocational aspirations (Schmidt, 2008).

Figure 1: Workers in a textile plant 1908. City of Toronto Archives.

The YMCA originated in 1844 in England to help young men in the cities develop a balanced life in body, mind, and spirit through religious and recreational programs. The first YMCA in North America opened in Montréal in 1851, and by 1900 there were 36 associations across Canada. The YMCA was the first to introduce guidance to young people in the form of character education, and vocational and education programming. (Hopkins, 1951; Winter, 2000).

During Victorian times, character traits that were valued and respected included self-restraint, industriousness, and a good work ethic (Winter, 2000). An individual's character became defined through work. Occupation was viewed as an outlet for self-expression as well as a way to assume an identity within a social class. The YMCA's notion of self-expression as a manner of building character echoed this sentiment and was used as a method to help the unemployed as well as the emerging middle class to discover their sense of identity (Hopkins, 1951; Winter, 2000). Emphasis on vocational guidance was an important response to industrialization.

In Canada, Etta St. John Wileman was a true pioneer in career development. A British expatriate and member of the staunchly conservative and Protestant Imperial Federation League (The Counselling Foundation of Canada, 2002, p. 13), Wileman was a strong advocate for Canadian employment services. She was horrified by the lack of effective government action in Canada. She believed passionately that work was a social obligation and lobbied politicians and business leaders to accept their responsibility for helping the unemployed. She argued that various societal

Figure 2: YMCA in Ottawa, 1910. Courtesy of Toronto Public Library.

barriers (e.g., gender, lack of Canadian work experience by immigrants, low proficiency in English) had a direct bearing on the unemployed. In this she was running counter to the prevailing feeling that those who wanted to work could do so. In reality, however, the economic downturn of 1907 had put thousands out of work through factory closings and a halt to construction work.

Some of the provinces began to address the issue. In 1911, Ontario opened a government labour employment bureau in Hamilton and another in Ottawa. A year later, in 1912, Québec created a system of government employment offices — the most advanced system in the country at the time. Wileman, who began her crusade in 1912, convinced Calgary's city council to create a civic employment office with her as manager. She was relentless in lobbying the federal government to create employment offices across the country in order to facilitate the movement of Canadians. The federal government was reluctant to do so but did create a Department of Employment Services in 1918 responsible for collecting employment data (Makarenko, 2009).

Wileman continued her advocacy for a federal system that would allow immigrants to move where the work was and direct much needed workers to factories to support the war effort. After the war she argued that returning veterans be provided assistance to find work. In 1918, Prime Minister Robert Borden's government, through an order in council, created the Employment Service Council of Canada.

Vocational guidance in Canada grew slowly. Education was a provincial responsibility and each province had its own take on its implementation. In the early days, vocational guidance was directed to those in technical schools. Wileman, with her vision and tenacity, lobbied for what is known today as career guidance and counselling in schools, and she was instrumental in providing labour market information to Canadians. Wileman believed in the importance of helping individuals find a fit between their abilities and available occupations.

In this, Wileman was strongly influenced by Frank Parsons (1854–1908), considered by many to be the father of vocational guidance in the United States. Parsons (1909) laid out in his book, *Choosing a Vocation*, a three-part framework for selecting a vocation that has continued relevance to today.

> In the wise choice of a vocation there are three broad factors: (1) a clear understanding of yourself, your attitudes, interests, ambitions, resources, limitations and their causes; (2) a knowledge of the requirements and conditions of success, advantages and disadvantages, compensation, opportunities and prospects in different lines of work; (c) true reasoning on the relations of these two groups of facts. (p. 5)

In 1912, Taylor Statten, the Boys' Work Secretary for the National YMCA offered advice similar to Parsons to the young men with whom he was working.

Emergence of Career Development (World War I and II)

Following World War I, Canada was faced with integrating returning soldiers into Canadian life while dealing with an economic recession (The Counselling Foundation of Canada, 2002). Little assistance was offered by the government. In 1919, to protest against working conditions and obtain collective bargaining rights, workers walked out in a massive six-week general strike in Winnipeg. Civil unrest spread quickly and sympathy strikes spread to Toronto, Vancouver, Edmonton, and Calgary.

The federal government introduced the 1918 Employment Officers Co-ordination Act, a federal-provincial cost-sharing program in which the federal government subsidized provincial employment offices (Pal, 1988). In addition, the federal government created the Department of Employment Services, which was mandated to provide employment data and advice. The creation of Employment Services represented an important first step in the Canadian government's view of unemployment as a more permanent and national issue.

Beginning in the late 1930s, the federal government initiated constitutional negotiations with the provinces to expand federal powers in the area of unemployment insurance. In 1940, Prime Minister William Lyon Mackenzie King succeeded in gaining unanimous provincial consent to introduce unemployment insurance. Following the Great Depression, unemployment was increasingly viewed as a social and involuntary phenomenon requiring concerted government action. The Employment Service was now operating as a network of provincial employment bureaus through which the federal government administered financial grants.

Programs for returning veterans were put in place through the newly established Department of Veterans Affairs. Approximately 200,000 veterans returned to their previous employers and another 150,000 used educational grants to attend university (The Counselling Foundation of Canada, 2002). The University of Toronto set up the Placement Centre under Col. Ken Bradford to help returning veterans find employment.

During the Great Depression, career counselling was provided by laypersons and social workers in community agencies and church basements. The words "career" and "counselling" at that point were never put together. The assistance provided reflected changing social, economic, and political realities and provided help in acquiring new skills. Community agencies, such as Goodwill Industries (1935) and Toronto's Woodgreen Community Centre (1937), joined the YMCA in providing assistance to unemployed people.

Between the two world wars, a mental health hygiene movement gained momentum in Canada that set the foundation for the counselling and vocational guidance movement. The program was originally developed to diagnose and treat mental illness with a focus on school age children and adolescents (Jasen, 2011). In 1918, Dr. Clarence Hincks helped organize the Canadian National Committee for Mental

Hygiene (CNCMH) and advocated that testing and advising and vocational information be offered in junior and senior high schools (Jasen, 2011; Marshall & Uhlemann, 1996). Eventually, the program extended to college and university settings and included a focus on psychiatric assessment for war veterans as well as the rest of the student population (Jasen, 2011). This program led to collaboration between mental health professionals in the community and the education system. In 1938, the CNCMH movement was defined as "applied psychology" and its growing recognition served as the catalyst for psychology professors across Canada to create the Canadian Psychological Association (CPA).

By the 1940s, guidance counselling became a formal part of the education system and provincial guidance associations began to appear. Among these were L'Association des orienteurs de la province de Québec and the Maritime Guidance Association. Overall, the advocacy efforts of the CNCMH were concerned with encouraging the federal and provincial governments to assume greater responsibility in the area of public health, and to redefine social problems (e.g., poverty, crime, and unemployment) as public health concerns (MacLennan, 1987).

Morgan Parmenter, a guidance counsellor at Toronto's Danforth Technical School, was frustrated by the lack of career information materials available to his students. He authored what he called "occupational monographs" to describe jobs available in the workplace. At the same time, Dr. Clarence Hincks, who was a strong advocate for vocational guidance for young men and for improvements in high school guidance, helped Parmenter create the Vocational Guidance Centre as a way to distribute his career information materials to other teachers. In 1943, Parmenter

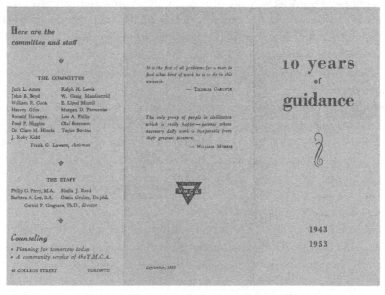

Figure 4: Brochure from YMCA, Toronto, Counselling Service 1953.

was appointed associate professor of guidance at the Ontario College of Education, taking the Vocational Guidance Centre with him. A year later, in 1944, the Ontario Department of Education appointed a director of guidance and encouraged school boards to appoint guidance officers in secondary schools. Other provinces soon followed suit.

In 1943, the Toronto YMCA, influenced by Dr. Hincks, established a counselling service for young men and youths. Dr. Gerald Cosgrave, a professor of psychology at the University of Toronto, joined as director of the Counselling Service. Frank G. Lawson, a Toronto businessman, who had been long involved with the YMCA, became the chair.

Lawson felt that young people needed assistance in three areas of their lives: (a) to discover the kind of work they were interested in and would enjoy; (b) to obtain the education and training to strengthen their abilities; and (c) to get help in dealing with negative attitudes that might otherwise hold them back. Cosgrove and Lawson worked together for 20 years at the helm of the Toronto YMCA Counselling Service.

A brochure from 1953 (Figure 4) lists the committee members and staff. The Counselling Service philosophy is expressed in the quotation from Thomas Carlyle: "It is the first of all problems for a man to find what kind of work he is to do in this universe."

Rise of Career Counselling (1950–1999)

Growth in Vocational Counselling

The postwar period saw the emergence of theorists such as Carl Rogers, Erik Erikson, and Abraham Maslow. Their theories departed from a focus on matching the individual to a job and instead sought a greater understanding of individual needs, preferences, and motivations. Donald Super, a key developmental psychologist, stressed the psychological nature of career choice across the lifespan of an individual. His research demonstrated that career was developmental in nature and that vocational choice involved self and occupational understanding. Consequently, during the 1940s and 1950s, the role of the school counsellor began to shift from one of fulfilling a guidance role to one of encompassing client-centered and individualized approaches in addressing the needs of students.

In the 1950s, universities showed little interest in funding career counselling programs or research initiatives: Québec was the exception, where Laval University initiated a three-year degree program in career counselling.

After World War II, counselling services were opened in universities to help returning veterans, and the University Advisory Services Association was formed. In 1949, the association expanded to include individuals working in student services personnel. This became the University Counselling and Placement Association (UCPA) and is now known as the Canadian Association of Career Educators and Employers (CACEE).

Upon retirement in 1955, Frank G. Lawson devoted more attention to promoting the counselling services he saw as essential for enabling people to do well in both their jobs and lives, and to contribute positively to the economy of the country. In 1959, Frank Lawson formed **The Counselling Foundation of Canada** and hired Gerald Cosgrave as its first executive director.

Figure 6: Gerald Cosgrave.

Figure 5: Frank G. Lawson.

In the 1960s, Frank Lawson, who had been unsuccessful in persuading the Psychology Department at the University of Toronto to introduce applied psychology, found a willing partner in Murray Ross, the newly appointed president of York University. Assisted by funds from The Counselling Foundation of Canada, York University added an applied psychology studies program at undergraduate and graduate levels. Further funding in the late 1970s enabled establishing the new Career Counselling Centre for assisting students in vocational choices.

In 1961, unemployment in Canada reached a postwar high of 7.1%. The economic rebound in growth in 1963 saw most of the unemployed returning to work. However, 30% of Canadians earned incomes that were low enough to be considered at the poverty level. Stuart (Stu) Conger, whose background included psychological counselling, training, human resources, and business, and who worked for the Department of Trade and Commerce, was invited by the federal government to provide ideas for the newly initiated War on Poverty Program. Conger proceeded to set up a series of experimental laboratories across the country "to invent new methods of counselling and training adults who were educationally disadvantaged" (The Counselling Foundation of Canada, 2002, p. 72). He created a program called New Start, which ran in six provinces. This initiative heralded the federal government as much more active in addressing workplace needs. Ross Ford, the director of the Technical and Vocational Branch, asked Conger to put together a team to develop a national position paper on career guidance in technical and vocational education. Stu Conger and Gerald Cosgrave authored a report in 1965 to support guidance services and to build awareness of the need to serve the Canadian labour market.

Postsecondary institutions across Canada responded to the demand of employers who wanted to hire professionally trained school counsellors and teachers trained in counselling by creating graduate programs in counselling. The University of British Columbia added graduate programs in educational psychology in 1965. McGill University began to offer courses in educational psychology around this time as well. By 1969, 14 postsecondary institutions had master's level programs in counselling delivered through faculties of education (Neault et al., 2012).

New counselling services were opened to provide career and employment counselling to youth in Ontario. The first Youth Employment Services (YES) office opened in Toronto in 1968. In the 1980s, this grew to a network of 50 youth employment counselling centres (YECCs) across Ontario, which worked with unemployed youth aged 16 to 24.

Figure 7: Youth Employment Services (YES) opened its first office in Toronto in 1968.

During the 1970s, The Counselling Foundation of Canada took an active role by providing funding to more than 20 Canadian universities to support their career services and applied psychology programs. Elizabeth McTavish became counselling director of the Foundation in 1974. Her knowledge of the theory and practice of career counselling along with her wide range of networks greatly enhanced the work of the Foundation. She may also have been one of the first in Canada to express concern about the need to increase the qualifications and skill level of counsellors.

Associations for Counselling Professionals

In response to the demand for trained school counsellors, the Canadian Guidance and Counselling Association (CGCA) was formed to serve counsellors who worked in the area of guidance and counselling, especially school counsellors, who made up the majority of members (Neault, Shepard, Benes, & Hopkins, 2012). The association changed its name twice — first to the Canadian Counselling Association and, in the 1990s, to the **Canadian Counselling and Psychotherapy Association (CCPA)**, its current name, to reflect the changing nature of the profession and the association's membership. Over this time, there was an increase in specialization and integration across professions and in the number of counselling-related associations across Canada. Some of the associations formed to support the needs of the many new professionals were the Canadian Association of Rehabilitation Professionals (renamed the Vocational Rehabilitation Association of Canada in 2003); the Applied Division of the Canadian Psychological Association; and the Ontario Association of Consultants, Counsellors, Psychometrists, and Psychotherapists (OACCPP).

In 1980, Stu Conger organized a joint conference in Ottawa of the Canadian Guidance and Counselling Association and the International Association for Education and Vocational Guidance (IAEVG). He decided to use some of the profits from this conference to create the Canadian Guidance and Counselling Foundation (CGCF) (later to become Canadian Career Development Foundation) to support research development and various special projects. This Foundation was instrumental in developing the CAMCRY program (described below).

National Conference on Career Development

The National Consultation on Career Development (NATCON) was founded in 1975 by the federal government, under Stu Conger's direction. It was an opportunity for professionals to come together to share ideas, information, and resources. In the first year, 20 people attended the NATCON conference. From 1987 to 2002, NATCON was part of a three-way partnership between Human Resources Development Canada, The Counselling Foundation of Canada, and the University of Toronto. Under this partnership, NATCON became the largest bilingual career development conference in the world. Between 2003 and 2012, NATCON was organized for a few years by the Canadian Career Consortium and later by the Conference Board of Canada. In 2012, NATCON was rebranded by the Conference Board of Canada and named Workforce One-Stop.

New Tools and Programs

Phil Jarvis, a researcher/writer working under Stu Conger in Ottawa's Occupational and Analysis branch, created CHOICES — Computerized Heuristic Occupational Information and Career Exploration System. CHOICES was a computerized occupational information tool designed to facilitate exploring career options. Several years later, CHOICES was sold to a private company and Jarvis joined the company to further develop the product.

During the 1980s, the federal government took advantage of the expertise of several top academics in the field such as Phil Patsula from the University of Ottawa, Norm Amundson and Bill Borgen from University of British Columbia, and Vance Peavy from the University of Victoria to develop competency-based training programs for government employees.

Federal Government Policies in the 1980s

The *Labour Market Development in the 1980s* report produced by the Task Force on Labour Market Development served as the blueprint for Employment and Immigration Canada in directing its policy and programs towards addressing skills shortages and training needs. An examination of demographic and employment trends, changing technology, and changing labour market demands formed the basis for the new National Training Act by which the federal government began to focus on industrial, on-the-job training. The National Training Act also created the Skills Growth Fund, a program for providing monies to the provinces for facilities and equipment to be used in training for jobs of national importance. Partnerships were formed with provincial ministries of education and private organizations to develop new tools to meet the diverse needs of society.

As well, labour market forecasting became part of the federal government policy. The federal government created the Canadian Occupational Projection System (COPS) as a vehicle for projecting supply and demand by sector and occupation across the country.

Classification of occupation-related statistics received more attention when Statistics Canada introduced the Standard Occupational Classification in 1980 using the categories from the Canadian Classification Dictionary of Occupations. Employment and Immigration Canada replaced the Canadian Classification with the National Occupational Classification in 1993 as the master taxonomy for organizing job titles into occupational groupings.

Students and Youth

By this time there were school-based counselling programs in all provinces. These programs focused on the areas of self-esteem, decision making, career exploration, and planning.

At the postsecondary level, York University, with funding from The Counselling Foundation of Canada, initiated two large research projects concerning students with learning disabilities and underachievers.

The Counselling Foundation of Canada also supported many community-based youth services in the years 1985 to 1994. Its support helped to found the Ontario Association of Youth Employment Centres (OAYEC) in 1987. The OAYEC handbook — *Community Career and Employment Counselling for Youth: Principles and Practice* — produced in 1994 provided a standardized approach to service delivery, as well as ideas and strategies for practitioners.

CAMCRY

In the late 1980s, career development in Canada really took root when Norman Amundson and William Borgen published their article, "The Dynamics of Unemployment," in which they revealed that many young people were not completing their education and were slipping through the cracks in the system. Students most affected were youth with special needs, those at-risk, and students that were underemployed (Hiebert, Jarvis, Benzanson, Ward, & Hern, 1992). Even students who decided to stay in school had a high degree of indecision and a low sense of purpose. Within this social climate, the Creation and Mobilization of Counselling Resources for Youth

(CAMCRY) initiative was conceived (CAMCRY; Hiebert et al., 1992).

CAMCRY was a program development and research initiative funded by Employment and Immigration Canada for $7.4 million and $8 million from universities, colleges, provincial governments, and businesses (Hiebert et al., 1992). The Canadian Guidance and Counselling Foundation (CGCF) co-ordinated this initiative with Stu Conger as the executive director. It was highly collaborative. Some projects supported professionals who worked with youth, and others focused on the youth themselves. Additionally, projects from this initiative required partnerships between educational institutions and community agencies. The career and occupational programs that researchers developed for specific groups of youth involved students, young offenders, teenage mothers, street kids, First Nations youth, and learning-disabled youth. This initiative produced 41 distinct projects at 18 postsecondary institutions across Canada and involved over 200 researchers (Hiebert, 1992). It also produced for the public resources in the form of print material, computer simulations, and videos.

Initially, funding was secure and development was ongoing, with centres of excellence being built across the country. But when Stu Conger retired as executive director of CGCF, funding for phase 3 of CAMCRY (the marketing of the products) was denied. CGCF had to decide whether to close its doors due to lack of federal funding or become a foundation. It chose the second. Under its new name, the Canadian Career Development Foundation became a grant-making entity, funding projects to advance career development and assist the profession.

Stay-in-School Program

During the 1990s, the Canadian economy was again in a deep recession. Youth unemployment became a key concern as about one third of Canada's youth was not graduating from secondary school (Lafleur, 1992). A Conference Board of Canada study entitled *Dropping Out: The Cost to Canada* (Lafleur, 1992) raised awareness among various stakeholders of the social and economic costs of youth not completing school. In response, the federal government initiated the Stay-in-School program to encourage young people to finish high school and acquire the skills needed for the labour force (Renihan et al., 1994). Career practitioners advocated strongly for collaboration among groups working with youth, development of best practices to prevent students from quitting, and education of the public on the importance of programs for lifelong learning. As a result of this initiative, a wide variety of programs for at-risk youth was developed.

Games and Online Tools

In the early 1980s, Québec developed a system for providing educational and vocational information to students. Through the work of Société GRICS, this has evolved into REPÈRES, a "cybercentre" with information and activities for personalized research into occupations and training. <http://reperes.qc.ca> (Société GRICS, n.d.)

In 1994, Bill Barry, from Newfoundland, set out to develop an engaging tool that would make learning about careers and work both fun and interesting. The result was *The Real Game* designed for 12- to 14-year-olds. *The Real Game Series* evolved into six internationally recognized career development programs and is seen as an effective classroom tool to aid in understanding career choice and development.

SPOTLIGHT: *THE REAL GAME SERIES*
by Phil Jarvis

The Real Game Series is a group learning program that engages students and young adults in career exploration and envisioning positive futures. In facilitator-led groups, players travel to the future and imagine their lives and careers in 5–10 years. They make lifestyle choices, budget money and time, and juggle work, home, and leisure responsibilities. They return to the present with new visions of the future they want to create for themselves, and become more intentional and purposeful in their learning and life choices. Developed in Canada, *The Real Game Series* is now used in schools and community settings around the world. For more information or to register for a free trial, visit <http://public.careercruising.com/us/en/products/cctherealgame/>.

- *Play Real Game: Living and Working in a Community* (Grades 3/4; Ages 8–10).
- *Make it Real Game: Working in a Small Company Engaged in International Business* (Grades 5/6; Ages 10–12).
- *The Real Game: Making Ends Meet and Prospering in Adult Life and Work* (Grades 7/9; Ages 11–15).
- *The Be Real Game: Balancing Work, Family, Leisure and Community and Preparing for the Transition from School to Career* (Grades 10+; Ages 15–25).
- *Real Times, Real Life: Finding Opportunity in Adversity and Learning to Successfully Manage Life and Career* (Adults).

In 1999, an online career guidance and planning system was introduced called Career Cruising. This online system includes self-assessment tools to determine skills and aptitudes, detailed occupational profiles, and tips for users regarding job interviews. Career Cruising was developed as a practical tool for helping individuals explore their education and training options, and was designed to help people build their own employment portfolios (LaGuardia, 2010).

Federal Government in the 1990s

In 1993, Conger, Hiebert, and Hong-Farrell (1993) conducted a national survey of career and employment counselling in Canada. Over 1,600 individuals comprised of counsellors, managers of career counselling centres, and employment counselling practitioners in community-based settings responded. The results of the survey represented a national snapshot of the career development climate.

- General attitudes reflected in the survey suggested the need to challenge societal beliefs and to emphasize that career-related problems need to be interpreted within the context of the individual's life.
- Career practitioners wanted more training and to be seen by the public as being an integral part of service delivery.
- A community capacity based approach was purported to be the preferred way to provide career service delivery. The Canadian Career Information Partnership (CCIP) was established to bring together provincial representatives to share ideas and materials related to youth and labour market issues.
- Additionally, a special department for youth issues was established within the federal employment bureaucracy and a five-year national strategy was launched. Career awareness and career choice materials were developed and distributed during a specified "Canada Career Week."

Human Resources Development Canada (HRDC) was formed in 1993, absorbing Employment and Immigration Canada. In 1995, HRDC provided equipment and staff for CanWorkNet to launch a national electronic database of career, employment, and labour market information resources. By 1998, Canada Work-InfoNet (later called CanWin) provided "hot links" to labour market information, Electronic Labour Exchange, Job Futures, and other career and job search related information including provincial WorkinfoNet sites (to be largely dismantled 10 to 15 years later).

In 1993, the internationally recognized National Occupational Classification (NOC) was developed by HRDC staff under the direction of Jo Ann Sobkow, Margaret Roberts, and the late Lionel Dixon. The new classification system supported the work of labour market analysts, researchers, counsellors, students, and educators in understanding the relationships between occupations.

CERIC: A New Institute for Counselling

Figure 8: CERIC banner for website in 2005.

The dream of an institute for counselling in Canada was first conceived by Frank Lawson and carried forward by Elizabeth McTavish as counselling director. But it wasn't until 2004 that the **Canadian Education and Research Institute for Counselling (CERIC)** was officially launched under The Counselling Foundation of Canada's executive director Jean Faulds. This launch followed several years of meetings and visioning by the founding board, led by Donald Lawson. CERIC is a charitable organization that advances education and research in career counselling and education. CERIC's vision has been to increase the economic and social wealth and productivity of Canadians through improved quality, effectiveness, and accessibility of counselling programs, especially in the areas of career counselling and education. CERIC has provided funding through project partnerships to a wide range of interesting and innovative projects across the country.

CERIC organized learning and professional development forums in Montréal and Vancouver in 2006, and in 2007, launched **Cannexus**, the organization's first bilingual National Career Development Conference. Now held every January in Ottawa, Cannexus promotes the exchange of information and innovative approaches for career development and counselling.

CERIC has produced a number of publications, including:

CERIC

by Riz Ibrahim

The Canadian Education and Research Institute for Counselling (CERIC) is a charitable organization dedicated to promoting career counselling–related research and professional development opportunities across Canada. Its pan-Canadian volunteer board of directors is broadly representative of the career-counselling field. CERIC funds both research as well as learning and professional development in Canada. Career professionals from all sectors and work/life settings benefit from the CERIC programs: contactpoint.ca/ orientation.ca online community hubs; *Careering* magazine, in print and digital formats; the national, bilingual Cannexus career development conference; the peer-reviewed *The Canadian Journal of Career Development* (CJCD); and a Graduate Student Engagement Program.
  See <www.ceric.ca>.

- *The Decade After High School: A Professional's Guide* and *A Decade After High School: A Parent's Guide* authored by Cathy Campbell, Michael Ungar, and Peggy Dutton, and

- *Good Work! Get a Great Job or Be Your Own Boss: A Young Person's Guide*, in addition to the Facilitator's Guide Companion Workbook by Nancy Schaefer.

CERIC AWARDS

by Riz Ibrahim

CERIC sponsors a number of awards and bursaries for students and professionals in the field, including:

- the Etta St. John Wileman Award, which recognizes and celebrates lifetime achievement in, and contributions to, career development;

- the Graduate Student Award, which is presented to select full-time graduate students to help them attend the Cannexus conference;

- the Elizabeth McTavish Bursary, which was established in honour of the late Elizabeth McTavish, counselling director of The Counselling Foundation of Canada, 1974–1995. Each year the Foundation awards selected applicants a bursary to support them in attending Cannexus.

CERIC engages full-time graduate students with an academic focus in career development in activities through its Graduate Student Engagement Program. Students are introduced to CERIC and its programs and may be asked to join one of CERIC's committees or write articles for one of CERIC's publications.

Professionalization and Development of Competencies

As early as 1987, career practitioners sought out increased professionalization across Canada. Québec published the first code of ethics for career counsellors in 1987. In 1997, the Canadian Career Development Foundation (CCDF) recognized the need to provide a national standard by which career development practitioners could unify the career development community. Such an initiative would also help shape the development of programs and training of career practitioners to ensure public accountability. A National Assembly on Career Development Guidelines was held and a National Steering Committee formed. CCDF realized that, if it worked in partnership with associations and practitioner groups, the standards and guidelines could be built from within the profession by the people who deliver career development services and programs. CCDF then initiated a series of regional consultations to explore the development of Standards and Guidelines for Career Development Practitioners in Canada.

The *Canadian Standards and Guidelines for Career Development Practitioners* (better known as the S&Gs) were formally published in 2003, revised in 2004, and have been recognized as an international model by the OECD. The S&Gs outline the competencies that service providers need to deliver comprehensive career services to clients. They have been used as the basis to establish a competency framework by the International Association for Educational and Vocational Guidance (IAEVG).

The S&Gs are organized into (a) core competencies (attitudes, skills, knowledge, and codes of ethical behaviour) that are relevant to all career practitioners; and (b) specialized competencies (assessment, community capacity building, work development, facilitating individual and group learning, and information and resource management) that are applicable to specific settings. Background material, consultation kits, and regular updates on the S&Gs are available on the *Canadian Standards and Guidelines for Career Development Practitioners* website (<http://career-dev -guidelines.org/>).

The **Blueprint for Life/Work Designs** was another initiative during the same period. Human resource specialists, counselling professionals, and educators from across Canada met to delineate the skills, knowledge, and attitudes — the competencies — that people need to have to succeed in career and in life. The participants drew on a similar project in the United States that produced the U.S. National Career Development Guidelines. Individuals can use the *Blueprint for Life/ Work Designs* to self-assess and manage their careers throughout their lives, and to find out about the career management competencies that they can expect to learn from a career development specialist. It's an equally important tool for career practitioners for developing products, guiding clients through a process, and assessing success.

Many organizations and people were involved in developing the Blueprint. Leading bodies were Canadian Career Information Partnership, Human Resources Development Canada, National Blueprint Advisory Group (1998 to 2002), and the National Life/Work Centre. Phil Jarvis co-authored the Blueprint with Dr. Dave Redekopp, when he was vice president at the National Life/Work Centre, and Lorraine Hache. Dr. Roberta Neault and Deirdre Pickerell developed the online training to guide people in using the Blueprint.

Career Practitioners in Canada

Career practitioners across Canada are still grappling with how they can define their profession and are taking collective action to address this issue. In 2008, executives of several provincial, territorial, and national career development professional associations and other interested international partners met to explore the possibility of developing a pan-Canadian career development body. In April 2009, a discussion paper was circulated to a wide network of career practitioners and leaders. After several meetings, the Canadian Council of Career Development Associations (CCCDA) was formed in March 2011 as an umbrella association for career development groups. By 2013, the association had become the Canadian Council for Career Development (CCCD) — also known as 3CD — with a mandate "to

Figure 9: Early postcard to promote the ContactPoint website.

Canadian Career Development Researcher Database

by Riz Ibrahim

CERIC developed the Canadian Career Development Researcher Database to answer the question: "Who is doing what research in Canada?" Canada has many leading researchers at universities and in community-based settings doing important work within the career development field. The database brings this rich information together in one easy-to-use online resource.

Researchers can use the database to identify potential academic and non-academic partners for future research projects. They can also use it to determine research already being done in Canada and how to best move this knowledge forward. The database is also of value to those seeking to learn about the latest research in any area of career development.

<http://www.ceric.ca/researchers>

strengthen the professional identity of all career development practitioners and to establish a coherent national voice on career and labour market development issues to influence policy and enhance service delivery for all Canadians" (<http://cccda.org/cccda/>). The Canadian Career Development Foundation (CCDF) chairs the CCCD Steering Committee.

The professionalism of career practitioners in Canada has been fostered for many years in Canada by ContactPoint (<http://www.contactpoint.ca>), an online resource site and community hub for professionals in the career development field. With funding from The Counselling Foundation of Canada, ContactPoint opened on the Web in 1997 as a place where professionals could access learning resources and share their experiences and expertise. OrientAction, ContactPoint's French-language sister site, was launched in 2003 and is a partnership with Société GRICS. Both ContactPoint and OrientAction are now services of CERIC.

For many years, ContactPoint and Orient-Action published *The Bulletin*, in English and French. This was replaced in January 2013 by the new print and digital magazine *Careering*. ContactPoint and OrientAction also host popular job boards.

The first issue of **The Canadian Journal of Career Development (CJCD)** (<http://www.cjcdonline.ca>) was published in 2004. CJCD is a free, peer-reviewed publication of multi-sectoral career-related academic research and exploration of best practices from Canada and around the world. The journal is published twice annually and accepts articles submitted by career development professionals. The CJCD began as a partnership project between ContactPoint and Memorial University of Newfoundland with the support of The Counselling Foundation of Canada. As of 2005, the professional journal came under the auspices of CERIC. The CJCD celebrated its 10th anniversary with the launch of a book entitled *A Multi-Sectoral Approach to Career Development: A Decade of Canadian Research* at the Cannexus 2012 conference.

While much progress has been made in the professionalism of Canadian career practitioners, more work needs to be done to firmly establish their identity. Burwell and Kalbfleisch (2007) created a Think Tank consisting of career educators and trainers across Canada to consider key aspects that would help in the advancement of career counsellor education in Canada. An important theme that emerged was the need to define the discipline's core and to develop a career development curriculum. A preliminary framework was developed to define the various roles, responsibilities, and educational levels needed for career practitioners in Canada with the intent of developing a national career development curriculum (Burwell, Kalbfleisch, & Woodside, 2010).

Conclusion

The major purpose of this chapter was to examine Canada's defining moments and involvement in the career development field. This chapter presents only a few snapshots and perspectives about the early beginning, rise, and emergence of career development in Canada. The snapshots provided of the many movements and key historical turning points over nearly six decades help us to gain insight into the current understanding of career development and the profession in addition to the challenges and obstacles Canadian career practitioners have faced. By exploring such an extensive timeframe, one can develop a greater appreciation of how the field of career development has come to be based on an ideology of humanitarianism and social justice. Career practitioners are required to take part in public policy development and to advocate for their unique services and skills. As this history of career development in Canada reveals, there have been many exciting and significant innovations in the field over the past century. Yet, in many ways career development is still in the midst of defining its identity and there are many more exciting advances to come.

References

Arthur, N., & Collins, S. (2010). Introduction to culture-infused counselling. In N. Arthur & S. Collins (Eds.), *Culture-infused counselling* (pp. 3–26). Calgary, AB: Counselling Concepts.

Blueprint for Life/Work Designs. (n.d.). Retrieved from <http://www.lifework.ca>.

Burwell, R., & Kalbfleisch, S. (2007). Deliberations on the future of career development education in Canada. *Canadian Journal of Career Development*, 6(1), 40–49.

Burwell, R., Kalbfleisch, S., & Woodside, J. (2010). A model for the education of career practitioners in Canada. *Canadian Journal of Career Development*, 9(1), 44–52.

Canadian Council of Career Development (CCCD). (n.d.). Retrieved from <http://cccda.org>.

Canadian Standards and Guidelines for Career Development Practitioners. (n.d.) Retrieved from <http://career-dev-guidelines.org/career_dev/>.

Conger, D. S., Hiebert, B., & Hong-Ferrell, E. (1993). *Career and employment counselling in Canada.* Ottawa, ON: Canadian Labour Force Development Board.

The Counselling Foundation of Canada. (2002). A coming of age: Counselling Canadians for work in the twentieth century. Toronto: Author. Retrieved from <http://www.counselling.net/jnew/index.php?option=com_content&view=article&id=75&Itemid=65>.

Gardner, H. (2002, February). Good work, well done: A psychological study. *The Chronicle of Higher Education.* Retrieved from <http://chronicle.com/weekly/v48/i24/24b00701.htm>.

Hiebert, B. (1992). CAMCRY: Innovations in career counselling. *Guidance and counselling*, 7(3), 6–16.

Hiebert, B., Bezanson, L. (1995). CAMCRY: An innovation in collaborative program development. *ERIC Digest.* Retrieved from <http://www.ericdigests.org/1997-2/camcry.htm>.

Hiebert, B., Jarvis, P. S., Bezanson, L., Ward, V., & Hern, J. (1992). CAMCRY: Meeting the needs of Canadian youth. In M. Van Norman (Ed.), *Natcon-18* (pp. 33–39). Toronto, ON: OISE Press.

Hopkins, C. H. (1951). *History of the Y.M.C.A. in North America.* New York, NY: Association Press.

Jasen, P. (2011). Student activism, mental health, and English-Canadian universities in the 1960s. *The Canadian Historical Review*, 92, 455–480. doi: 10.3138/chr.92.3.455

Lafleur, B. (1992). *Dropping out: The cost to Canada.* Ottawa, ON: The Conference Board of Canada.

LaGuardia, C. (2010). Career Cruising. *Library Journal*, 135(13), 108.

MacLennan, D. (1987). Beyond the asylum: Professionalization in the mental health hygiene movement in Canada, 1914–1928. *Canadian Bulletin of Medical History / Bulletin canadien d'histoire de la medicine*, 4, 7–23.

Makrrenko, J. (2009). Employment insurance in Canada: History, structure and issues. *MapleLeafWeb.* Retrieved from <http://www.mapleleafweb.com/features/employment-insurance-canada-history-structure-and-issues>.

Marshall, A., & Uhlemann, M. (1996). Counselling in Canada. In W. Evraiff (Ed.), *Counseling in Pacific Rim countries: Past-present-future* (pp. 17–30). San Mateo, CA: Lake Press.

Miller, D. C., & Form, W. H. (1962). *Industrial sociology: The sociology of work organizations.* (2nd ed.). New York, NY: Harper & Row.

Neault, R., Shepard, B., Benes, K., & Hopkins, S. (2012). Counseling in Canada: Coming of age. In T. Hohenshil, N. Amundson, & S. Niles (Eds.), *International Handbook of Counseling* (pp. 305–314). Alexandria, VA: American Counseling Association.

Pal, L. (1988). *State, class, and bureaucracy: Canadian unemployment insurance and public policy.* Montréal: McGill-Queen's University Press.

Parsons, F. (1909). *Choosing a vocation.* Boston, MA: Houghton Mifflin. Available online at <http://archive.org/details/choosingvocation00parsuoft>.

Renihan, F., Buller, E., Desharnais, W., Enns, R., Laferriere, T., & Therrien, L. (1994). *Taking stock: An assessment of the national stay-in-school initiative.* Hull, PQ: Human Resources Development Canada.

Schmidt, J. J. (2008). *Counseling in schools: Comprehensive programs of responsive services for all students* (5th ed.). Boston, MA: Allyn & Bacon.

Schulz, W. E., Sheppard, G. W., Lehr, R., & Shepard, B. (2006). *Counselling ethics: Issues and Cases.* Ottawa, ON: The Canadian Counselling Association.

Société GRICS (n.d.) REPÈRES. Retrieved from <http://reperes.qc.ca>.

Winter, T. (2000). Personality, character, and self-expression: The YMCA and the construction of manhood and class, 1877–1920. *Men and Masculinities, 2,* 272–285.

Young, R., & Lalande, V. (2011). Canadian counselling psychology: From defining moments to ways forward. *Canadian Psychology, 52,* 248–255. doi: 10.1037/a0025165

Glossary

Blueprint for Life/Work Designs is intended to: (a) map out the life/work competencies Canadians need to proactively manage their career building process from kindergarten to adulthood; (b) provide administrators and practitioners with a systematic process of developing, implementing, evaluating, and marketing career development programs or redesigning and enhancing existing programs; (c) enable researchers and practitioners to determine the extent to which clients/students have acquired competencies; (d) allow career resource developers to design products, programs, and services to address specific competencies and for users to identify appropriate resources; and (e) provide a *common language* across Canada for the outcomes of career development initiatives and activities in any setting. For more information visit: <http://206.191.51.163/blueprint/home.cfm>.

Canadian Council for Career Development (CCCD or 3CD) is a national advocacy organization that provides a voice for the career development profession. It promotes provincial and territorial collaboration on common issues such as certification, training, and practitioner mobility. 3CD has formed and oversees a Certification Group that brings together leaders from all provinces with the goal of sharing of best practices, consistency, and portability for certification programs and initiatives across Canada. <http://cccda.org>.

Canadian Counselling and Psychotherapy Association (CCPA) is a national bilingual association of professionally trained counsellors engaged in the helping professions. Since 1965, the Association has been providing leadership and promotion of the counselling profession. CCPA has several Chapters representing specialized interest groups in counselling, including a Career Development Chapter. The CCPA website is at <http://www.ccpa-accp.ca/en/>.

Canadian Education and Research Institute for Counselling (CERIC) is a charitable organization dedicated to promoting career counselling and professional career development in Canada through research and education. Its programs support career professionals from all sectors. These include the online community hubs ContactPoint and OrientAction, *Careering* magazine, the national conference Cannexus, *The Canadian Journal of Career Development* (CJCD), and a Graduate Student Engagement Program. <http://ceric.ca>.

The Canadian Journal of Career Development (CJCD) is a peer-reviewed publication of multi-sectoral career-related academic research and best practices from Canada. Visit <http://www.cjcdonline.ca>.

Canadian Standards and Guidelines for Career Development Practitioners **(S&Gs)** provide descriptions of the knowledge, skills, and attitudes that are essential to be an effective service provider. The S&Gs are a valuable resource for career development practice, professional development, human resource development, program development, and curriculum design. The S&Gs can be found at <http://career-dev-guidelines.org/career_dev/>.

Cannexus is a national career development conference designed to promote the exchange of information and explore innovative approaches in the areas of career counselling and career development. Visit <http://www.cannexus.ca>.

The Counselling Foundation of Canada is a family foundation established by Frank G. Lawson in 1959 to create and enrich career counselling programs and improve the technical skills of career counsellors. The object of the Foundation is to engage in charitable and educational activities for the benefit of people; thus enabling them to improve their lifestyles and make a more effective contribution to their communities. <http://www.counselling.net>.

Discussion and Activities

Discussion

1. How would you define career development? Give your rationale.

Personal Reflection

1. What do you see as the greatest challenges faced by the profession of career development practitioners?
2. What do you hope to accomplish in your career as a career development practitioner? What are some of your goals?
3. What organizations/associations would be the most relevant to you?
4. What "negative attitudes" might hold a young person back? Would these reactions be context sensitive? Would this change as the person grows older?

Career Practitioner Role

1. What does having a professional identity mean? What are the key elements which constitute a professional identity? Explain each element.

Activities

1. What career development associations are near you? Use the CCCD Directory of Members as a starting point for identifying associations that are located in your province or territory.
   <http://cccda.org/cccda/index.php/members/directory-of-members>

2. A musical journey over time: Explore popular song lyrics of various eras and consider the societal messages, social processes, and intergroup themes that might reflect the politics of the times, social, and economic conditions. (For example, consider the following songs: "YMCA" and "Macho Man" sung by the Village People, "R-E-S-P-E-C-T" by Aretha Franklin, or "The Wall" by Pink Floyd.)

Resources and Readings

Resources

Websites

Canadian Career Development Foundation (CCDF) <http://www.ccdf.ca>.
The Canadian Journal of Career Development <http://cjcdonline.ca/>.

Canadian Standards and Guidelines for Career Development Practitioners <http://
career-dev-guidelines.org/career_dev/>.
ContactPoint <http://www.contactpoint.ca/>.
International Association for Educational and Vocational Guidance (IAEVG)
<http://www.iaevg.org/iaevg/index.cfm?lang=2>.

Supplementary Readings

Canadian Career Development Foundation. (2005). The State of practice in Canada in
measuring career service impact: A CRWG report. <http://www.crwg-gdrc.ca/crwg
/index.php/research-projects/state-of-practice>.
The Counselling Foundation of Canada (2002). A Coming of Age: Counselling
Canadians for Work in the Twentieth Century. Available at
<http://www.counselling.net/jnew/index.php?option=com_content&view=
article&id=75&Itemid=65>.

two

Career Counselling in Québec

Its Evolution
and Future Outlook

LOUIS COURNOYER
Université du Québec à Montréal

Introduction and Learning Objectives

The profession of vocational and guidance counsellors has been practiced in Québec for over 70 years. Professional counsellors constantly support youth and adults in their efforts towards educational and professional (re)insertion, rehabilitation, and career (re)development in the sectors of education, employability, community, health and social services, and private and institutional practice. To date, only a few studies (Duval, 1995; Mellouki & Beauchemin, 1994a, 1994b) have recorded Québec's history of the profession. This chapter aims at a better understanding of the social and historical evolution of the vocational and guidance counselling profession in Québec.

The specific learning objectives for this chapter are to:

1. Recognize key defining moments and turning points in the profession of vocational and guidance counsellors in Québec.
2. Understand the scope of practice and regulation of the profession in Québec.
3. Identify change in the profession through different periods of educational and social reform.

Québec Today

Québec is the only province in Canada, and one of the few jurisdictions in the world, to regulate the title and various professional activities of vocational and guidance counsellors (Turcotte, 2004). The **Ordre des conseillers et des conseillères**

d'orientation du Québec (OCCOQ) works with universities offering undergraduate, graduate, or postgraduate specialized programs in vocational and guidance counselling, such as the Université Laval, Université Sherbrooke, McGill University, and Université du Québec (à Montréal). It also oversees entry into the profession and the competency of its members. According to Cuerrier and Locas (2004), there are approximately 2,500 vocational and guidance counsellors in Québec spread across several sectors of practice: education (45%), employment (20%), consulting firms (12%), public and semipublic organizations (4%), companies (2%), rehabilitation centres (2%), hospitals (1%), and in miscellaneous sectors (18%). Regardless of their area, counsellors' roles consist of:

> Assessing psychological functioning, personal resources and local conditions; working on identity issues and developing and maintaining active coping strategies for personal and professional choices throughout life; restoring social and professional independence and achieving career plans for human beings in interaction with their environment. (Government of Québec, 2009, p. 4).

In addition to the above, their role involves providing information services, health promotion, and prevention of suicide, disease, and accidents, as well as addressing social problems among individuals, families, and communities. Since the adoption of **Bill 21**, vocational and guidance counsellors may practice various regulated activities in terms of assessments conducted among clienteles deemed most vulnerable with respect to school and professional integration (Government of Québec, 2009). In this regard, vocational and guidance counsellors are now among those professionals recognized for their competency in managing the risk of harm and the autonomy and complexity of their practices. The responsibility that accompanies such recognition leads to some questioning of the practices and vision of vocational and guidance counsellors (Landry, 2004). Legault (2008) points out that adopting a new direction in a profession where activities are very diverse requires a period of constructing a common identity.

A Century of Vocational Counselling

1900–1920: Search for Suitability of Skills

Frank Parsons, considered the father of vocational and guidance counselling, proposed that counselling skills should involve:

(a) facilitation of self-understanding in terms of skills, abilities, interests, resources, and limitations;

(b) knowledge of the requirements and conditions for success, advantages and disadvantages of career options, working conditions, and employment prospects of various lines of work; and

(c) connection between self-awareness and knowledge of the labour market. (Zunker, 2002)

In the years following the publication of Parsons' *Choosing a Vocation*, vocational and guidance counsellors began showing up in Europe and the United States. These early counsellors were influenced by recent discoveries in differential psychology that involved measurements of individual capacities. In Canada, Manitoba took the first steps in 1912 to provide career information to graduates with liberal arts degrees (Mellouki & Beauchemin, 1994a).

In Québec from 1900 to 1920, the concept of career options was virtually non-existent among French Canadians, who were primarily destined for work in industrial settings or on the farm. The State entrusted the Church with providing education, and health and social services to the population (Lacoursière, Provencher, & Vaugeois, 2001). The situation was quite different, however, for the British anglophone minority that controlled the Québec economy.

1920–1940: The Embryonic Phase

In the aftermath of World War II, productivity-management systems associated with **Fordism** and **Taylorism** led some manufacturers to become interested in psychometric measurement of individual characteristics and abilities in order to improve worker performance in, and assignment to, various jobs (Anastasi, 1994; Guichard & Huteau, 2006). In Québec, vocational and guidance counsellors remained at the embryonic stage. Only a small fringe group in the "medical-pedagogical" field at the University of Montréal were interested in assessing skills and intelligence for the purpose of evaluating school or work potential (Mellouki & Beauchemin, 1994a).

During the Great Depression, lack of a genuine social safety net, or measures to promote employment or schooling for the working class, mobilized certain influential members of the French-Canadian upper-middle class, including professionals, and the clergy (Lacoursière et al., 2001). It was then that Fr. Wilfrid Éthier and Fr. Paul-Émile Farley quietly laid the first foundations for vocational and guidance counsellors in Québec, with the avowed purpose of improving economic prospects for the francophone majority (Mellouki & Beauchemin, 1994a).

1940–1960: Building the Foundations

During World War II, Canada and several other countries invested heavily in the production of psychometric instruments for the purposes of assigning various positions according to measures of intelligence and abilities. Meanwhile, Wilfrid Éthier continued his "guidance" mission by successively creating the first three institutes for training and practice in educational and vocational counselling. This first occurred in 1941 at L'institut canadien d'orientation scolaire et professionnelle (ICOP) in Montréal (Mellouki & Beauchemin, 1994a), where the first cohort of counsellors was trained in the latest knowledge in differential psychology, the use of psychometric tools, and the features of the labour market. A year later, in Québec City, Éthier founded a similar institute in collaboration with the leaders of Catholic Action and an insurance company (Mellouki & Beauchemin, 1994a). However, the Québec Institute was focused more on the different branches of psychology: experimental, childhood and adolescent, educational, commercial and industrial, pathological, and performance.

In 1943, the University of Ottawa opened the Centre d'Orientation scolaire et professionnelle. As noted in a speech by the director of the Montréal ICOP at the time, career guidance was clearly a tool for the national assertion of French Canadians: "Do we wish not to waste our talent and instead to work on making the most of our energies? Organize career guidance. That is what will greatly enable us to achieve economic conquest" (Mellouki & Beauchemin, 1994a, p. 221).

The first Association of Vocational and Guidance Counsellors in the province of Québec was launched in 1944 and immediately proposed a definition of the scope of its members' practice: "To guide individuals in choosing a profession and preparatory studies, so that a choice can be made on the basis of a systematic analysis and objective assessment of their abilities and interests" (Landry, 2004, p. 8).

Following World War II, the business, health, and education sectors began to rely on psychometrics developed by the armed forces (Savickas, 2000). Although the business world was to benefit from the services provided by educational institutions and counselling practices in Montréal and Québec City, the beginnings of counselling in the health sector were still challenging. In veterans hospitals, counsellors were faced with the medical model and the dilemma of trying to help patients on a professional level without being able to intervene in other spheres of the individual's life (Lecomte & Guillon, 2000). In the education sector, several activities staged throughout Québec illustrated the dynamism of counsellors: an annual counselling week, teacher training in counselling principles and methods, and specialist counselling in schools and communities (Mellouki & Beauchemin, 1994a). During the 1950s, psychological concepts evolved rapidly. Carl Rogers gained recognition for his innovative approach focused on the individual (Lecomte & Guillon, 2000). The schools of humanistic, cognitive, and developmental psychology all challenged behaviourist and psychoanalytical models.

Despite all this activity, Québec still invested little in education, creating a significant obstacle for its citizens. Québec was below the Canadian average for investment in education, and last in terms of graduation rates and attendance at all educational levels. It employed undereducated teachers, mismanaged the imminent arrival of thousands of teenage baby boomers in college, and lacked succession planning at the teacher level (Mellouki & Beauchemin, 1994a). Under pressure from influential members of the francophone community and the clergy, a subcommittee was formed in 1952 to review the education system. The objectives were to increase skilled labour training rates in higher education and in scientific, economic, and social career fields, and to assist educational decision makers to select the best candidates to successfully complete a classical, liberal education program (Mellouki & Beauchemin, 1994a). The importance of counselling was now more recognized than ever.

1960–1970: Opening Up to New Experiences

During the 1960s, the world was in a state of turmoil with conflicts, revolutions, and dreams. In Québec, the election of Jean Lesage with the slogan of *Maîtres chez nous!* unleashed nationalist passions in a French-Canadian population impatient for major reform (Lacoursière et al., 2001). In Western societies, developmental psychology appeared at this time. Its influences on intellectual development (e.g., Jean Piaget), psychosocial development (e.g., Erik Erickson), and the social and historical theories of Vygotski changed the dominant paradigms of differential psychology. Counselling became more receptive to understanding the learning process and the influence of an individual's social, cultural, and educational development (Patton & McMahon, 1999). Characteristics of stages or steps were seen as universal (Cournoyer, 2008; PaVie, 2003), and human potential was recalibrated in the light of social, economic, cultural, and historical conditions determining individual life paths (Evans & Furlong, 2000; Savickas, 2000). The works of two major theorists of vocational and guidance counselling, Donald E. Super and John L. Holland, were just beginning to have an impact (Bujold & Gingras, 2000).

The 1960s were marked by the publication of the *Parent Report* (Royal Commission of Inquiry in Education in Québec/Commission royale d'enquête sur l'enseignement dans la province de Québec, 1964), which proposed a major overhaul of the Québec education system and provided an important gateway for vocational and guidance counsellors. Elementary, secondary, and college levels now had to consider the student's evolution, development of skills, interests, and diverse life experiences, and to help students make informed choices by offering a clear assessment of their strengths and limitations. The responsibilities of vocational and guidance counsellors now extended to conducting assessments and screening students who were gifted or who had learning disabilities. Other responsibilities included: consulting with teachers and proposing or testing new teaching methods; establishing workshops for students requiring early graduation; participating in committees for training the labour force; retraining and accelerated training of specialists in new employment fields; assisting married women who were returning to work; hiring the elderly; and categorizing students with special needs. Vocational and guidance counsellors were now required to possess a four-year undergraduate degree.

The arrival of these new, more highly qualified experts threatened the teaching and other professional staff, who found their roles reduced (Mellouki & Beauchemin, 1994b). The general public still tended to see the vocational and guidance counsellor as a type of "fortune teller," someone who tells others what path to take towards the future, a view invariably accompanied by negative criticism about the lack of such powers.

1970–1980: Becoming Aware of Possibilities

The 1970s was the period when women made a massive entry into the labour market; when school boards and CEGEPs (Collèges d'enseignement général et professionnel or junior colleges) hired new vocational and guidance counsellors throughout the province; and when the economy of the province permitted individuals to envisage a personal career "plan." The international phenomenon of the youth counterculture influenced concepts of human development and career life. Self-actualization, creative potential, a focus on relationships, experimentation, and personal growth became important goals for many approaches in psychology (Lebourgeois, 1999) and consequently for vocational and guidance counsellors as well. Humanistic, existentialist, and gestalt approaches dominated Québec universities and psychotherapy training centres. Meanwhile, new research in the neurosciences was emerging, but would not be applied to counselling practices for several more years.

In Québec, a theoretical model known as *activation du développement vocationnel et personnel (ADVP)*, was developed (Pelletier, Noiseux, & Bujold, 1974). This cognitive and developmental model was to have a large influence following its implementation within career education courses in high school. Although perfectly in line with the intentions of the *Parent Report*, its implementation was too often assigned to non-specialist teachers looking to fill out their workload. In a very short time, students lost all interest, followed in turn by parents and the general public (Mellouki & Beauchemin, 1994b).

During this same period, psychosocial approaches and sociological perspectives in career development were adding to the knowledge base of vocational and guidance counsellors. These new concepts of counselling would find their place in the first "legal" field of practice for counsellors. Counsellors were tasked with helping individuals become aware of personal and community resources so that individuals could make informed and increasingly independent choices in regards to their education and career lives.

In fact, the government adopted a professional code (*code des professions*) in 1973 to ensure legislative and regulatory consistency in the exercise of professions related to risk of physical and psychological harm or to patrimonial integrity (Office des professions du Québec, n.d.). This meant the end of the concept of an association to protect the interests of vocational and guidance counsellors and introduced the idea of membership in a corporation (now a **Regulatory College**) authorized by legislation (Mellouki & Beauchemin, 1994b).

1980–1990: Adapting to Change

The economic crisis of 1982 resulted in massive layoffs of less educated, lower qualified workers. It became hard to find a job after the age of 45, just as it became difficult to integrate into the workforce if under the age of 25 and lacking experience. Employability development became a fruitful source of work for vocational and guidance counsellors. Practitioners were no longer working exclusively with the young, but also with adults seeking employment, workplace and highway accident victims, workers on employee assistance programs, as well as ever-increasing numbers of unemployed workers and welfare recipients. Vocational and guidance counsellors sought to improve the relationship that existed between themselves, their clients, and third-party funders. As a corollary, the community organizations sector focused on feminist and social justice approaches, while insurance companies and various agencies subsidizing vocational rehabilitation services entered the scene. Private counselling firms also increased in number, although most of the growth did not start until the mid-1990s. In the secondary education sector, Mellouki and Beauchemin (1994b) reported that, following the failure of the career education course and a series of education reforms that gave more power to teachers, the role of vocational and guidance counsellors in institutions diminished.

The era of health care management emerged in the United States and influenced governments and public institutions in Canada. From that point forward, the crucial question to deciding social policies in health, education, and employment would be "How can we do more with less?" Within this new paradigm of economic efficiency, humanist and gestalt systems lost much ground to short-term cognitive and behavioural models (Lebourgeois, 1999). This spirit of efficacy was evident in the new field of practice adopted by la Corporation des conseillers d'orientation professionnelle du Québec in 1982, which defined a professional as someone "who by means of appropriate methods and techniques, guides an individual in their career development, that is to say, personally and professionally… and …to establish and maintain a harmonious relationship between the individual and the world of work" (CPCOQ as cited in Landry, 2004, p. 8).

With the 1980s came the emergence of new conceptual models that were focused more on life transitions in adulthood, and based on Levinson's (1978) adult career development model and Schlossberg's (1981) life transitions model. In Québec, Riverin-Simard (1984) published a work on the different stages of work life. In addition, Spain and Bédard (1986) provided new insights into motivation and the decision process among Québec women. Lastly, Limoges (1987) proposed his lucky clover model, which explored different interdependent dimensions in employability development for job seekers. That same year, the first professional code of ethics was adopted, a master's degree became the minimum standard for admission to the profession, and the name of the Corporation was modified to include the feminine form for female counsellors (Matte, 2008).

1990–2000: Keeping Pace With Change

In the early 1990s, unemployment in Québec hovered between 10% and 15%. Social expenditures were rising while the population was aging, which meant that immigration and training the unemployed were seen as solutions for Québec's economic recovery. Two major events, the Estates-General on Education in 1995 and the Sommet du Québec et de la Jeunesse [Québec youth summit] in 1998, identified the need for more informational services for youth, as well as more educational, vocational, and guidance counsellors. This call to politicians resulted in the **Réseau des carrefours jeunesse-emploi (CJE)** [youth employment network], which included over one hundred organizations for youth aged 16 to 35 and was located in all regions of Québec. During this same time period, the Ministry of Education, Sports, and Leisure implemented a new approach to guidance, the Guidance Oriented Approach to Learning (GOAL). At the end of this decade, employment-related services were transferred from the federal government to the provinces.

This shift is associated with a decrease in counselling services provided by the government whose professional employees were covered by collective agreements, and an increase in outsourcing to community organizations, youth employment marketplaces, and private companies. New vocational and guidance counsellors entering the job market found their salaries and working conditions more insecure, and clienteles that were mostly poor, unstable, and vulnerable in terms of economic, educational, and psychological well-being. In 1993, vocational and guidance counsellors were accredited for family mediation and in 1994, the term "Corporation" was replaced by that of "ordre professionnel" (Matte, 2008).

The 1990s also saw an explosion of conceptual approaches to educational, vocational, and guidance counsellors. Although not entirely abandoned, positivist and objectivist approaches and trends gave way to more interpretive and postmodern perspectives (Savickas, 2000). Lecomte and Guillon (2000) note the emergence of non-linear, dynamic models. Introduction to "social" existence was accomplished through interactionist approaches (Patton & McMahon, 1999; Vondracek & Reitzle, 1998; Young, Valach, & Collin, 1996). Several studies were conducted on common indicators of effectiveness in counselling (Drapeau & Koerner, 2003), which influenced an emerging integration of concepts and tools from different approaches into one single model. In Québec, Bégin's (1990) psychogenic perspective challenged the many models of educational counselling taught and practiced by vocational and guidance counsellors. Cognitivist in approach and centred on identity development, Bégin proposed that intervention be focused on how individuals cognitively process different information resources.

2000–2010: Participating in Change

Between 1984 and 2003, the number of vocational and guidance counsellors who were members of the professional order increased from 1,255 to 2,235 (Cuerrier & Locas, 2004). The profile of members was completely transformed: Two thirds of members were now women; the education sector no longer comprised the majority of members; and clients increasingly consisted of under-educated adults with social and mental health problems. During the 2000s, Québec institutions in the education and employment fields developed a wide range of new programs and measures for the public and education sectors, including a guidance oriented approach to learning, personal career plans, skill assessments, government return-to-work support programs, and measures targeting adult education (Cournoyer, 2008). Hence, counselling is no longer just a matter of educational choice: It is more of a support system for career development throughout an individual's life (Cuerrier & Locas, 2004).

Two committees, le Groupe de travail ministériel sur les professions de la santé et des relations humaines [Ministerial Task Force on Health Professions and Human Relations] and the Comité d'experts–Modernisation de la pratique professionnelle en santé mentale et en relations humaines [Expert Committee — Modernization of professional practice in mental health and human relations] (2002), studied the modernization of human relations and mental health professions in order to better respond to growing public concern regarding the quality of services in these areas. This paved the way for the adoption of Bill 21 in 2009, which granted new reserved activities for vocational and guidance counsellors, as well as privileged access to qualifications for the practice of psychotherapy and the title of psychotherapist. This again remodeled the scope of practice to include:

> Assessing psychological functioning, individual resources and personal situation; intervening in issues of identity and developing and maintaining active coping strategies for personal and professional decisions throughout life; restoring social and professional independence and implementing career plans for individuals in interaction with their environment. Information, health promotion, prevention of illness and social problems, including suicide, are also part of professional practice among individuals, families and communities. (Government of Québec, 2009, p. 4)

These changes concur with Dubar and Tripier's (2003) understanding that "being a professional is much more than completing a program of academic training; it means being initiated into a role, embracing a vision both of the world and oneself in order to practice this role, being saturated in the culture, which implies a separation and a transformation of identity" (p. 101).

Summary

The profession of vocational and guidance counselling is over 70 years old. At its birth, it was linked to discoveries made in differential psychology in the early 20th century, especially in psychometric measurement. As it grew, a small group of Jesuits, with the backing of some of the French-Canadian élite, thought it important to develop training institutions and professional counselling practices to enhance the future prospects of the francophone community. As the counselling field matured, similar to Québec society, the profession became more confrontational in its demands for a social and political revolution within Québec institutions, leading to the **Quiet Revolution**.

Institutionally, and then legally after a few years, educational and professional counselling had the tools to assert itself and demonstrate its social relevance. Now established with professional status, vocational and guidance counsellors suddenly came up against a crisis that swamped the profession at the economic level in the form of economic recession and mass layoffs and in the sociopolitical sphere with the aftermath of the 1981 referendum and labour disputes between government and public sector employees. This transformed the structure and climate of operations in the employment and education sectors where most counsellors worked. The profession, therefore, had to rapidly adapt to the rise of **neo-liberalism** that had attacked its gains, requiring it to seek new areas of operation and concepts of intervention procedures.

As the years passed, life sped up, and with new technologies and new economic realities, professions intermingled and competed for the same types of services. More than ever, competency had to be both demonstrated and publicized to policy makers, employers, and the media. Amid the turmoil of these changes, Bill 21 arrived to reserve professional activities that vocational and guidance counsellors shared with a small group of professionals. Nevertheless, vocational and guidance counsellors were still seeking an identity. Even within the profession, they shared increasingly different systems of practice. Today, the focus is on defining and demonstrating the common, societal relevance of the profession.

Challenges to the Profession

The Challenge of Positioning

Given that counsellors are working more than ever in different employment sectors where they perform different practices and must deal with varied organizational standards and missions, it is important to consider commonalities. The scope of practice of the profession as stated by the Ordres des conseillers et conseillères d'orientation includes the assessment of psychological functioning, personal resources, and environmental conditions; identity development; the development and maintenance of active coping strategies in order to allow personal and professional choices throughout the lifespan; the restoration of socioprofessional autonomy; and the ability to make career plans.

How similar are the current practices of counsellors? Beyond ethical and legal obligations, to what or to whom do vocational and guidance counsellors owe their true allegiance — to their profession and professional order, or to their position within an organization? In other words, is the identity of the vocational and guidance counsellor today more functional than professional? Is it based on ethics or on the standards of the workplace?

The Challenge of Definition

The assessment of mental disorders is now a reserved act involving many different professions. Bill 21 reserves the title of psychotherapist and the practice of psychotherapy to authorized professionals such as psychologists, medical doctors, and psychotherapists who are permit holders. Bill 21 demands rigorous, specific, and comprehensive work on the part of vocational and guidance counsellors. How will guidance counsellors define their roles under the Bill? What are the acts which are reserved for or excluded from guidance counsellors? How will professionals and the public know the scopes of practice of each professional? Will Bill 21 move the profession of guidance counselling from a strengths-based, hope-based perspective to a deficit, medical model? Some individuals in the profession are concerned that educational counselling is destined to disappear or be overshadowed by remedial or rehabilitation counselling.

Cournoyer (2010) suggests that counsellors may take different perspectives: determinism (focusing on the factors, causes, and effects relating to the subjective and intersubjective experience of clients); phenomenological (focusing on the reality constructed by clients, consisting of themselves and their interactions with their environment); and interactionism (focusing on the cross-influences of transactions between individuals and their environment). According to Cournoyer, the approaches adopted by counsellors can bring different shades to their conceptions of their role and that of their clients during the counselling process.

The Challenge of Self-Assertion: "Social-Relationship Marketing"

Until 1973, the goal of career counselling associations was to establish the profession as one of the crucial steps for developing the educational and human potential of Québecers. In 1973, taking advantage of the status conferred in the aftermath of the *Parent Report*, the profession transitioned from advocating an "**associative model**" to an "**institutionalized model**" in which the government institutionalized the counsellors' professional activity through regulation. In an integrated or associative system, the development of the profession depended on the ability to manage change through periods of educational and social reform, economic growth and decline, budget provisions and cuts.

Vocational and guidance counsellors have worked mainly in public or semi-public companies where their job descriptions have been set by government policy. As the government was unable to sustain the funding of earlier years and when social needs are determined by the priorities of various health, social, and education services, counsellors moved to work in the private sector. The private sector is a marketplace of competing products and services, and is based on public demand and the ability of service providers to respond. Is this, therefore, the advent of a third development model for vocational and guidance counsellors, a type of sociorelational marketing?

Today, the market for professional services in education, employment, and mental health has become a business in which new competencies, ethical considerations, and business talent are required. Effective marketing and good relationships with various stakeholders are as important as the actual delivery of these services. Vocational and guidance counsellors have always managed to adapt in the face of societal change. How will counsellors meet the challenge of social-relationship marketing?

Moments of major progress recorded by the profession have mostly occurred when counsellors worked together and had confidence in their competencies. In a world of constantly escalating needs and opportunities, vocational and guidance counsellors are required to maintain a culture of continuous, lifelong learning through a variety of ways, such as special training, mentoring, peer counselling, group sharing of expertise, and clinical supervision. The history of vocational and guidance counsellors also demonstrates that major advances are possible when the profession embraces a culture of bottom-up change, in which its members (at the bottom) take up, maintain, and defend their interests even at the risk of disrupting institutions (at the upper level), including the government and even their own professional order. Asserting their social relevance in the workplace and in the community is an indisputable part of the counsellor's role.

As noted by Villeneuve (2005), it is also vital that counsellors grasp opportunities to play a counselling role in the community and in their immediate circle. They may do this by joining working committees and decision-making bodies; showing interest in working on urgent projects; seeking discussions with influential people on issues relating to counselling; taking part in round tables; mobilizing other actors around shared issues; providing policy opinions; and seeking an audience with different bodies and points of view. Practitioners should aim to demystify their role at the same time.

Counsellors must not only assert themselves where they are currently working, but must also look for opportunities and consider where their services would be relevant. Counsellors today may work with specialized mental health assessment, socioprofessional integration, recognition of prior learning, psychological health in the workplace, and psychoeducation via radio, television, print, and electronic media. They will also assist with second careers, coaching and training on-site, web-based vocational and guidance counselling, intercultural counselling, social justice, and advocacy. Seventy years after the founding of the profession, and nearly 40 years after its recognition as a regulated profession, it is time that the initial training of future vocational and guidance counsellors be provided by counsellors with several years of practice, in order to pass on their knowledge and experience and to ensure ethical and quality service.

Conclusion

The history of the profession of vocational and guidance counsellors in Québec is strongly linked to that of Québec society, and also to the history of French Canadians in general. For nearly half a century, the growth of the profession required transformative individuals, such as Father Wilfrid Éthier, who saw counselling as a tool to serve an entire people. During the years of great social change in the Quiet Revolution, vocational and guidance counsellors established themselves wherever individual, organizational, and social needs existed, and put themselves in proximity to the levers of power in society. Subsequently, counselling became institutionalized, which gave the profession a sheltered space to act, create, and maintain its gains. Today, vocational and guidance counsellors must seek inspiration in their past and draw lessons from their history in order to better define their future.

References

Anastasi, A. (1994). *Introduction à la psychométrie*. Montréal: Guérin Universitaire.
Begin, L. (1990). *Identité du moi: L'approche psychogénétique et ses applications*. Montréal:

Agence d'Arc.

Bujold, C., & Gingras, M. (2000). *Choix professionnel et développement de carrière. Théories et recherches* (2nd ed.). Boucherville, QC: Gaëtan Morin.

Comité d'experts — Modernisation de la pratique professionnelle en santé mentale et en relations humaines (2005). *Partageons nos compétences. Rapport du comité d'experts.* Québec, QC: Gouvernement of Québec.

Commission royale d'enquête sur l'enseignement dans la province de Québec. (1964). *L'orientation scolaire et professionnelle. Rapport Parent. Rapport de la Commission royale d'enquête sur l'enseignement dans la province de Québec*, Vol. 2, Chapter 4. Québec: Gouvernement du Québec.

Cournoyer, L. (2008). *L'évolution de la construction du projet professionnel chez les collégiennes et les collégiens lors des 18 premiers mois d'études collégiales: Le rôle des relations sociales* (Unpublished doctoral dissertation). Université de Sherbrooke, Sherbrooke, Québec.

Cournoyer, L. (2010, June 3). *Comment les conditions du milieu du client peuvent-elles être autre chose que l'arrière-plan de nos pratiques?* Presentation for the colloquium of the Ordre des conseillers et des conseillères d'orientation et des psychoéducateurs et des psychoéducatrices du Québec.

Cuerrier, C., & Locas, R. (2004). Portrait d'une profession aux caractéristiques changeantes. En pratique, 1, 10–11.

Drapeau, M., & Koerner, A. (2003, September). L'impact des techniques thérapeutiques. *Psychologie Québec*, 17–22.

Dubar, C., & Tripier, P. (2003). *Sociologie des professions.* Paris: Armand Collin.

Duval, R. (1995). *Les cheminements éducatifs de l'orientation et de la pédagogie de 1943 à 1993 à la Faculté des Sciences de l'Éducation de l'Université Laval.* Québec: Special issue.

Evans, K., & Furlong, A. (2000). Niches, transitions et trajectoires… De quelques théories et représentations des passages de la jeunesse. *Lien Social et Politiques, 43*, 41–48.

Government of Québec. (2009). *Bill 21: An Act to amend the Professional Code and other legislative provisions in the field of mental health and human relations.* Québec, QC: Government of Québec.

Groupe de travail ministériel sur les professions de la santé et des relations humaines (2002). *Deuxième rapport. Une vision renouvelée du système professionnel en santé et en relations humaines.* Québec: Government of Québec.

Guichard, J., & Huteau, M. (2006). *Psychologie de l'orientation.* Paris: Dunod.

Lacoursière, J. Provencher, J., & Vaugeois, D. (2001). *Canada Québec. Synthèse historique 1534–2000.* Montréal: Septentrion.

Landry, L. (2004). Le champ évocateur: un indice de l'évolution de la profession? In *L'Orientation: Une pratique en évolution.* En pratique, 1, 8–9.

Lebourgeois, C. (1999). Survol historique de la psychologie et de la psychothérapie existentielles-humanistes au Québec. *Revue Québécoise de Psychologie, 20*(2), 11–36.

Lecomte, C., & Guillon, V. (2000). Counselling personnel, counselling de carrière et psychothérapie. *L'orientation scolaire et professionnelle, 29*(1), 117–140.

Legault, G. (2008, June). *L'identité: Rôles, composantes et fonctions relationnelles.* Presentation for APEC Conference, Québec.

Limoges, J. (1987). *Trouver son travail.* Montréal: Fidès.

Levinson, D. J., with Darrow, C. N, Klein, E. B. & Levinson, M. (1978). *Seasons of a man's life.* New York, NY: Random House.

Matte, L. (2008). Une profession qui avance. *En pratique, 9*, 2.

Mellouki, M., & Beauchemin, M. (1994a). L'orientation scolaire et professionnelle au Québec. Émergence d'une profession, 1930–1960. *Revue d'histoire de l'Amérique française, 48*(2), 213–240.

Mellouki M., & Beauchemin M. (1994b). L'institutionnalisation, la crise et l'éclatement du champ de l'orientation scolaire et professionnelle au Québec (1960–1990). *L'Orientation Scolaire et Professionnelle, 23*, 465–480.

Office des professions du Québec (2010). Système professionnel. Québec: Office des professions. Retrieved from <http://www.opq.gouv.qc.ca/systeme-professionnel/>.

Patton, W., & McMahon, M. (1999). *Career development and systems theory: A new relationship.* Pacific Grove, CA: Brooks/Cole.

PaVie. (2003). *Trajectories, stages, transitions and events of the life course: Towards an interdisciplinary perspective.* Working paper for PaVie 2003 Research Colloquium, October 9–11. Lausanne and Geneva Universities: Centre lémanique d'étude des parcours et modes de vie.

Pelletier, D., Noiseux, G., & Bujold, C. (1974). *Développement vocationnel et croissance personnelle.* Montréal: McGraw-Hill.

Riverin-Simard, D. (1984). *Étapes de vie au travail.* Editions Saint Martin, Collection Edition Permanente.

Savickas, M. L. (2000). Renovating the psychology of careers for the twenty-first century. In A. Collin and R. A. Young (Eds.), *The future of careers* (pp. 53–68). Cambridge, England: Cambridge University Press.

Schlossberg, N. K. (1981). A model for analyzing human adaptation to transition. *Counseling Psychologist, 9*(2), 2–18.

Spain, A., & Bédard, L. (1986). Devenir parents: Les motivations et la décision de femmes québécoises et de leur conjoint. *L'orientation professionnelle, 21*(3), 48–69.

Turcotte, M. (2004). L'orientation au Québec et dans le monde. *En pratique, 1*, 12.

Villeneuve, C. (2005). Le rôle conseil: un rôle nécessaire et … profitable. *En pratique, 4*, 1.

Vondracek, F., & Reitzle, M. (1998). The viability of career maturity theory: A developmental-contextual perspective. *The Career Development Quarterly, 47*(1), 6–15.

Young, R. A., Valach, L., & Collin, A. (1996). A contextual explanation of career. In D. Brown, L. Brooks and Associates (Eds.), *Career choice and development* (3rd ed., pp. 477–512). San Francisco, CA: Jossey-Bass.

Zunker, V. G. (2002). *Career counseling: Applied concepts of life planning* (6th ed.). Pacific Grove, CA: Brooks/Cole.

Glossary

Associative model refers to the functional structures of relations between ideas, persons, and manners determined by members of a group and based on shared goals.

Bill 21 is the short name for An Act to amend the Professional Code and other legislative provisions in the field of mental health and human relations. Passed in 2009 in Québec and in force since June 2012, this law restricts the practice of professions in the field of mental health and human relations to members of professional orders. Guidance counselors (conseillers d'orientation) were among the professionals affected by this law, as were psychologists, nurses, social workers, marriage and family therapists, and psychoeducators.

Fordism and **Taylorism** are two related management theories of production efficiency. Fordism refers to increased productivity through the use of assembly lines and is named after Henry Ford who used it most famously for manufacturing cars. Taylorism is the factory management system developed by Frank W. Taylor's system for breaking a production process into small, repetitive tasks for greater labour efficiency.

Institutionalized model refers to the functional structures of relations between ideas, persons, and manners determined by a public and official bodies based on law.

Neo-liberalism involves the dominance of individualism and the marginalization of collectivism in society. Neo-liberalism can involve the loss of provincial and federal jurisdiction over institutions, which in turn can increase market competition with limited regulations in place to safeguard individuals.

L'Ordre des conseillers et conseillères d'orientation du Québec (a.k.a. the Order) or the College of Guidance Counselors in Québec (OCCOQ) protects the public in the quality of guidance services offered by its members by providing legal remedies. The College ensures the competence of those who join the Association and oversees the support of its members in maintaining and developing their professional skills. The Order decides on issues of public concern and offers a space for exchange, allowing members to improve their practice and participate in the development of their profession. The OCCOQ website is found at <http://www.orientation.qc.ca/>.

Quiet Revolution began in the 1960s and involved several series of changes regarding political, ideological, cultural, and social aspects of life for the French-speaking population of Québec that resulted in an intense and renewed nationalism.

Regulatory Colleges establish and administer a quality assurance program to promote high practice standards for a specific profession or discipline. The mandate of the college is to develop standards and procedures to regulate the practices of the professionals who are its members, with the overall goal of serving and protecting the public. Québec has four regulatory colleges that relate to counselling, one of which is the Ordre des conseillers et conseillères d'orientation du Québec.

Réseau des Carrefours jeunesse-emploi (CJE) or Youth Employment Marketplaces have the mission to inform, orient, counsel, and encourage youth in their search for a job. CJE tries to integrate youth into the marketplace; improve their living and working conditions; and help them look for a job, go back to school, or start a small business.

Discussion and Activities

Discussion

1. What are the key events in the history of vocational counselling in Québec?
2. What are the main issues regarding the future of the career counselling profession in Québec?

Activity

Compare the development of the profession in Québec to the rest of Canada. What are the similarities and differences?

SECTION 2

Basic Conceptual Frameworks of Career Development Practice

three

Career Development

Key to
Economic Development

PHIL JARVIS
Career Cruising

PRE-READING QUESTION

1. What is the difference between the new career management paradigm and the traditional vocational guidance paradigm?

Introduction and Learning Objectives

Despite growing workforce skill gaps, current processes to connect talent with opportunities remain inefficient. Too many students fail to see the relevance of their studies to future work roles. They do not know how to identify local employers who need their unique talents. Thus, they lack motivation to optimize learning opportunities that public education and local training providers offer. The fastest growing youth cohorts tend to be the least adequately served. At the same time, many adults find themselves in jobs in which they are not fully engaged. Too many are unemployed, underemployed, or marginalized. Employers don't have an efficient mechanism to identify future talent in their own community. They insist schools are producing graduates that lack essential employability and applied skills, character, and attitude. So employers cast their talent nets across the country and around the globe. Using ads, the Internet, and recruiters, they seek to find and relocate the talent they need. Employers are importing talent even though students are dropping

Phil Jarvis

out of school in the employer's community, and adults are yearning for meaningful opportunities at home. Of new employees who are enticed to come, many will move on to other employers in other communities. All in all, the process of matching talent to opportunity is hit-and-miss, and there are vast economic and human consequences.

After reading this chapter, you will:

1. Understand the economic consequences of inadequate career development.
2. Be knowledgeable as to how **demographic trends** contribute to Canada's economic challenges.
3. Be familiar with the differences between the industrial age career model and the new **career management paradigm**.
4. Appreciate how the *Blueprint for Life/Work Designs* can assist in matching talents with opportunity.
5. Be cognizant of alternatives that will increase the return on investment for governments and employers for individuals, families, communities, and the nation.

Leaks in the Talent Pipeline

The majority of secondary school students do not feel prepared for employment or for postsecondary studies (Talbot & Associates, 2006). According to the Lifelong Learning Strategy Report undertaken for the City of Vancouver by Talbot & Associates, only 30% of Grade 12 graduates attend colleges and universities in British Columbia and only 19% of them obtain a degree. As can be seen, the majority of students do not pursue postsecondary education. Given that 85% of new job openings will require education beyond a basic high school diploma (BC Ministry of Advanced Education and Human Resources Development Canada, 2003), students and their parents need to be better informed as to the educational requirements in the 21st century. Many students are bored and cynical about education, and one in five in Canada drop out before completing high school. Some groups fare worse than others. For example, the majority of Aboriginal students in Canada do not complete Grade 12 within six years of entering Grade 8 for the first time (Bowlby & McMullen, 2002).

The majority of high school graduates also do not have career goals to which they are emotionally committed. About a third of students enter university or college directly without clear workforce goals, hoping to discover their calling through further study. Too few students select apprenticeship, trades, or technology training to meet current and projected demand. Over one third of postsecondary students change programs or drop out by the end of their first year. Of those who graduate, 50% will not be in jobs directly related to their program of study two years after graduation (Centre for Education Statistics, Canada, 1997). Considering how badly our workforce now needs the right talent in the right place at the right time, today's "talent pipeline" has far too many leaks.

The issue of managing careers is not only a problem for young people; career management is a concern for adults as well. Many adults go through their entire working lives without ever making fully intentional, fully informed career choices. Many "land" jobs through happenstance rather than informed choice, and then spend 50% of their waking hours in work settings they do not like. In a Gallup survey, seven in ten adults (69%) reported that if they were starting their careers over, they would try to get more information about job and career options before they started working (Gallup Organization, 1999). In the same survey, more than five times as many people indicated that they entered the workforce by chance rather than by a choice influenced by a career development professional. While many people eventually find their way to satisfying and fulfilling work roles, many never do. Those who feel trapped in inappropriate work roles are less productive than their satisfied counterparts. The Gallup Organization estimates that as many as 25 million workers (19% of the workforce) are "actively disengaged" from their jobs, and that this is costing the U.S. economy $300 to 350 billion annually (Harter, 2001). The loss of productivity and the waste of human capital are palpable, whether they are measured in training costs or unrealized human potential.

Economic Consequences of Inadequate Career Development

Canada invests heavily to support individuals, groups, and regions in need, accepting higher taxes than many countries to "level the playing field" and to ensure a higher quality of life for more citizens. Even minimal losses on these huge investments cost governments, corporations, and communities dearly. Fallout from gaps between people's skills and the needs of the workplace reduces the return we rightly expect from our investment in education, health care, and social services. A workforce that is unmotivated, unskilled, or inadequately skilled, results in lost revenues for the government and affects the ability of some businesses to remain competitive in a global market.

Productivity

We are sitting on a huge potential boom in **productivity** — if we could just get the square pegs out of the round holes (Bronson, 2002, para. 5). According to a 2009 study by the Conference Board Research Group, only 45% of workers are satisfied with their work, down from 49% in 2008 (Stanglin, 2010). This is the lowest level ever recorded in the 22 years of studying this issue. The study suggests that the drop in worker happiness can be partly blamed on the worst **recession** since the 1930s, but in fact, worker dissatisfaction has been on the rise for two decades. Fewer workers find their jobs satisfying, creating a working environment that stifles innovation and negatively impacts competitiveness and productivity. A 1% increase in Canada's productivity would result in an increase of $13 billion in goods and services each year. Improving the mechanisms for job placement so that people were connected with work that truly suited their skills and personalities would have profound ramifications for businesses across Canada, and yield standard-of-living gains in communities from coast-to-coast.

Education

In the 2009 Programme for International Student Assessment study from the OECD (2010), Canadian students ranked in the top 5 of 32 countries for reading, mathematics, and science. Nonetheless, our education system is failing too many students. Many students are unclear as to why they must learn what they are being taught. Too many students change programs, underachieve, or drop out. Some extend their education because they are reluctant to enter the world of work. Few students fully understand the diversity of work roles that align with their academic skills. Many graduate with heavy student loan debt and unclear career prospects. Too few master the skills in career and life management they will need after graduation to become adept, confident, self-reliant, and resilient navigators in the constantly changing waters of the workplace and society. If more students saw the relevance of their classes to their adult lives, more would be motivated to perform at high levels, thus increasing the return on our massive investment in education.

The One-Percent Difference: Health, Social Services, Protection, and Corrections

Unemployed people or people in jobs they dislike are subject to increased stress, have increased likelihood of unhealthy lifestyles, and are more prone to substance and physical abuse. Good jobs foster good mental health, whereas poor jobs cause distress (Loscocco & Roschelle, 1991; Savickas, 2002). In a September 2002 Ipsos-Reid survey, one in six adults surveyed (17%) said there have been times they were under so much stress they considered suicide. The main causes of stress cited were work (43%) and finances (39%). It is estimated that workers with depression cost U.S. employers $44 billion yearly in lost productive time (Stewart, Ricci, Chee, Morganstein, & Lipton, 2003). About $122 billion was invested by all levels of government in Canada in 2009 on health care (Statistics Canada, 2009). If health expenditures were reduced by only 1% by helping more people find satisfying work, the potential savings would be over $1.2 billion each year. This would cover the salaries of an additional 15,000 teachers or counsellors or average annual tuition for over 120,000 undergraduate students.

Just over $190 billion was invested by all levels of government in Canada in 2009 on social services, including social assistance and welfare (Statistics Canada, 2009). Fewer recipients would need assistance if more had the skills to find and keep suitable work. A 1% improvement would save nearly $2 billion annually. Just under $51 billion was invested by all levels of government in Canada in 2009 on "protection of persons and property," including policing, prisons, and correctional services (Statistics Canada, 2009). A 1% improvement in the number of detainees who acquire career management/planning skills could save $510 million annually.

Over $585 billion was collected by all levels of government in Canada in 2009 in income taxes (individual and corporate), property taxes, consumption taxes, health premiums, social insurance contributions, and so on (Statistics Canada, 2009). If more Canadians were able to find suitable work, revenues would increase for all levels of government. A 1% increase in the number of Canadians paying taxes rather than drawing on entitlement programs would generate over $5.8 billion per year in government revenues each year. A 5% increase in employment would yield a $29 billion annual windfall for all levels of government.

Together, a 1% increase in government revenues and productivity, and a 1% decrease in social costs, represents over a $20 billion annual windfall for Canadian individuals, organizations, and communities. Again, to put this staggering number in perspective, this would cover the salaries of over 250,000 additional teachers or counsellors, or provide more learning resources and facilities, or cover the full tuition for over a million undergraduate and graduate students.

The economic consequences of having too many citizens unemployed, underemployed, or in jobs they dislike, are staggering. The human consequences are even higher. Too many Canadians are simply not enjoying satisfying, purposeful, and fulfilling lives because they have not found the right work. What's more, this is not just the individual's problem. Families, communities, and society in general all lose when individuals are unable, confidently and effectively, to manage their careers.

❖ *Stop and Reflect*
1. What are some of the economic consequences of having a large number of Canadians in "jobs they dislike"?
2. What is the role of the career practitioner in addressing the inadequate career development of Canadians?

Impact of Demographic Trends

Generational cohorts are groups of people who share birth years, history, and a collective personality as a result of their defining experiences. Generational profiles, while not infallible, help us to understand how the life experiences of a generation capture the attention and emotions of millions of individuals at a formative stage in their lives and ultimately affect personal core values. The historical, political, and social events experienced by generational cohorts that typically span 15 to 20 years help to define and shape their values, work ethics, attitudes towards authority, and professional aspirations (Cowin & Duchscher, 2004).

Members of the *Baby Boom Generation (boomers)* are between the ages of 51 and 68. Research highlights that employees in this generation want to be recognized for their deep experience and dedication to their careers, in the form of compensation and unique development opportunities (Howe & Strauss, 2000; Sessa, Kabacoff, Deal, & Brown, 2007). Boomers seek personal growth opportunities through varied and interesting work at this point in their careers.

Members of *Generation X (Gen-Xers)* are currently between the ages of 31 and 50 (born between 1961 and 1980) and are in the middle of their careers. Data suggests this generation greatly values stability and seeks balance between job and family demands (Howe & Strauss, 2000; Sessa et al., 2007). While Gen-Xers want to advance into senior leadership positions, the expected speed for advancement is less aggressive than among members of Generation Y.

Members of *Generation Y (Gen-Yers)*, who were born between the years of 1981 and 2000, are today between the ages of 11 and 30. Research (Howe & Strauss, 2000; Sessa et al., 2007) shows that this generation perceives work as an opportunity for personal development and growth. Generation Y greatly values a sense of work/life balance that enables opportunities to enjoy other life interests. Since this generation was born and influenced by the wired "24/7" world, data suggests Gen-Yers have low patience levels. This translates into the need for instant feedback and fast-paced career advancement.

Canada, like many industrialized countries, is approaching a demographic transition that will affect many aspects of its economy. The baby boom generation has had a substantial impact on the demographics of the nation's population over the past 60 years (Sauvé, 2012). Concerns have been raised in Canada that as the boomers leave the workplace there will be shortages in labour, skills, and knowledge.

This shortage will be compounded by fewer young people entering the workforce. Family size and fertility rate have been dropping. Family size has dropped to 2.5 in 2006 and overall fertility in Canada has declined to 1.61 children per family (Statistics Canada, 2012) as couples have children later. This is not sufficient to maintain the population.

It is worrying that the number of unskilled workers is growing. It is projected that by 2016, Canada will have 1,350,000 unskilled workers (about 8% of total workforce) in a country that can no longer absorb unskilled workers. In 2010, there were more than a million unfilled positions begging for skilled workers (Miner,

2010). Even factoring for immigration, the projected worker shortfall of close to 500,000 in 2011 will grow to close to three million in 2031.

It is getting more difficult for employers to find people with the knowledge, skills, and attitudes considered essential in the 21st-century workplace. These skills include commitment to lifelong learning, comfort with ever-changing technology, problem finding and solving, communication and collaboration, and appreciation for diverse cultures and people. "Canada is already facing a labour crunch as baby boomers retire, but that could turn into a labour crisis if the education system is not fixed" (Cappon, 2011).

Impact of Labour Market Trends

Massive weather systems occasionally converge in extraordinary ways and create a "perfect storm." Three labour force megatrends are now converging to create a perfect storm in the Canadian job market that will impact career prospects for decades to come: (a) the great recession, (b) up-skilling of jobs, and (c) unprepared workforce.

The global economy and communities across the country are weathering the worst economic downturn since the Great Depression nearly a century ago. Despite a combination of service cutbacks and massive economic stimulus, recovery from the great recession is slow and faltering, and the economy is vulnerable.

Accelerating technological advances have rendered many jobs obsolete, and there is an up-skilling of jobs in all sectors that has produced new types of jobs at an unimagined rate. More formal education, technical training, and "soft skills" are now demanded of workers in all job sectors, but especially in new and emerging career fields. It is estimated that 80% or more of all jobs available now and in the future require some form of formal postsecondary education or training, often with a focus on science, technology, engineering, and mathematics.

In raw numbers, Canada's biggest workforce challenge is upgrading the skills of current workers and adult job seekers. Few employers are investing adequately in employee career management and training. Workers themselves are also not investing adequately in upgrading their skills. If their employer provides inadequate opportunities for upgrading skills, few can quit work for an extended period to upgrade their skills.

There is inadequate support to help students. Without a vision of their future, many students fail to see personal relevance in their academic studies. Today's students will need higher levels of academic, technical and "soft" skills than any cohort before them. Much of our current and future workforce is at risk of becoming casualties of the looming perfect storm in the job market. A new paradigm of career navigation and workforce preparation is required.

Basic building blocks of this new paradigm of exemplary career navigation and workforce development resources already exist, but they tend to be used in a fragmented fashion, and are largely underutilized. Consensus on "best practices" suggests a core of five "foundational resources" that should be in place at all levels of education:

1. Experiential career learning programs at all school levels.
2. Comprehensive Internet-based career exploration and planning systems.
3. Electronic portfolio systems that follow students through education levels out into adulthood.
4. Online-course-planner systems linked to student information systems that enable students, teachers, and parents to collaborate in maintaining individual learning plans for all students.
5. Online-networking systems that connect students to adult job seekers and employers seeking immediate and future talent. These connections can result in immediate hires, as well as work experience, job shadowing, co-op, volunteerism, and part-time job opportunities that allow employers and students to "test the fit."

In the end, entire communities need to be mobilized to support these foundational career and workforce development resources.

In summary, technology has transformed work in all sectors into essentially two kinds of "knowledge-era" jobs: (a) new jobs generated to fill various labour needs recently created by technological advances; and (b) changing jobs — that is, traditional jobs that have evolved in response to new technology. Truck drivers, farmers, and fishermen, for instance, now need to be comfortable with laptops, the Internet, spreadsheets, GPS systems, and smart phones.

New jobs are emerging daily. No one can predict the full range and diversity of new jobs that will appear, even those in the next five years. We can speculate on some, like nano-mechanic, old-age wellness manager, memory augmentation surgeon, weather modification police, waste data handler, social networking worker, personal brander/communications advisor, and manager of a stem-cell bank (Gordon, 2009). What is certain is that the new job market will require higher and higher levels of knowledge and skills.

Immigration is not the solution. Competition among developed and developing countries for highly qualified immigrants, who come from countries that need their best talent more than we do, grows more intense each year. There is no scenario in which immigration alone can resolve our projected labour force talent gap. Clearly, we must seriously re-think our approaches to preparing all young people for success in work and life, and assist a great many more adults to "**up-skill**."

The good news is that there are, and will be for years to come, more than enough 21st-century jobs available for every Canadian who wants to work. However, most will have to up-skill to qualify for them. Moreover, we must dramatically increase labour force participation rates among traditionally under-represented, socially excluded groups such as Aboriginal peoples, lower socioeconomic groups, new immigrants, and the disabled.

A New Paradigm for Career Development

The traditional career-choice paradigm is not working for many Canadians. This paradigm expects youth, possibly with help from a counsellor, to make an informed, long-term career choice in middle or high school. Yet, few adults are doing the work they expected to be doing when they were in school. The evidence suggests that only a small minority of young people can identify a "calling" in secondary school, despite strong pressures to do so. Young people now entering the workforce are likely to have at least 10 to 15 jobs, in several occupations, and in multiple industry sectors during their working lives. How can they (and why would they) confidently answer the question, "What will you be when you grow up?"

The **industrial-age career-choice model** was about helping people make an informed, point-in-time, occupational choice, in the following manner:

1. Explore one's interests, aptitudes, personality, and values.
2. Determine a "best fit" occupation by matching personal traits to occupational factors.
3. Develop a plan to attain the prerequisite education and training.
4. Graduate, choose a secure job in a solid organization, climb the ladder.
5. Retire as young as possible on pension as a reward for decades of service.

Steps 1 through 3 apply in contemporary workplaces, although the terms work role, cluster or **industry sector** may be substituted for occupation. In knowledge societies, however, these steps are now recurrent, dramatically increasing the need for information and support services at all ages. Step 4, to obtain a secure job after graduating from university, is no longer assured. Even senior executives are not secure in their positions. Step 5, to retire, will only occur for those who learn and successfully apply personal financial planning skills. Increasingly, people either cannot or do not wish to stop working at a fixed age.

The career-choice paradigm emphasizes provision of career, learning, and labour market information to enable citizens to make appropriate career choices. Consequently, Canadians have access to world-class information resources from government and community agencies, industry sector councils, and private sector providers in print, video, and digital formats. Indeed, an OECD report on a survey of 36 countries noted that Canada is a global leader in the provision of labour market information (Sultana & Watts, 2004). Good information is essential, but is insufficient.

The new **career management paradigm** is not about making the right occupational choice. It is about equipping people with the competencies (skills, knowledge, attitudes, character, and emotional intelligence known as "soft skills") to make sound decisions about the myriad choices that adults face in every aspect of their lives, for the rest of their lives.

While technical and job-specific skills sufficed in the past, it is increasingly being accepted that the worker of the future will need a more comprehensive set of meta-competencies that are not occupation-specific and are transferable across all facets of life and work. The economic value, to the individual and the nation as a whole, of a workforce equipped with these meta-competencies cannot be underestimated and their development cannot be left to chance. (McMahon, Patton, & Tatham, 2003, p. 3)

The key to success in the workplace, and in life, is not finding the perfect job, friend, or life partner: it is becoming the best possible worker, friend, or life partner.

- In the career management paradigm the question, "What do you want to be when you … (grow up / graduate / lose your job, etc.)?" is replaced by the following: Who are you now, and what do you love to do?
- What are your unique assets, talents, skills, and predispositions?
- What evidence do you have that what you offer is special?
- What types of situations, people, environments, and roles appeal to you?
- What types of organizations or consumers need what you can offer?
- What innovative work arrangements will suit you and potential employers?
- What do you want to do first when you graduate? Then what?
- What competencies do you need to focus on to increase your options?
- What will success look and feel like?

The objective is to find satisfying work and construct a fulfilling career with purpose, meaning, and authenticity. Workers, more than ever, are seeking meaning, purpose, and opportunities for growth through their work. Dychtwald, Erickson, & Morison (2006) in their book, *How to Beat the Coming Shortage of Skills and Talent*, reported that work was most highly valued for reasons of personal development. Their survey results showed that: "'Work that enables me to learn, grow, and try new things' ranked third among ten basic elements of the employment deal … It ranked higher than more pay, more vacation, flexible schedule, flexible workplace, work that is personally stimulating, and even (by a small margin) a workplace that is enjoyable" (p. 161).

Competency Frameworks

Tests and computer systems will never fully answer people's life questions, and career professionals are not exclusively qualified to ask the questions. The **career management paradigm** puts control and responsibility in the hands of the individual — not in tests, computer systems, or specialists. To be fully in control of their own lives, people need to learn career management competencies just as they learn mathematics, science, language, or technical skills. Career management must be a lifelong learning process for everyone, rather than an occasional counselling process for the few who need help. Career practitioners and human resource specialists who understand the new paradigm become pivotal players in the paradigm shift in their organizations. They play vital coaching, mentoring, and co-ordinating roles, whereas those not attuned to the new paradigm are relegated to the periphery.

Two competency frameworks are needed to harmonize efforts to help citizens connect with opportunities, and employers connect with the talent they need. The first is a framework of the competencies that people need to find and keep good jobs, and to self-manage their careers. The second is a framework of the competencies that educators, career practitioners, and human resources specialists need in order to: (a) help youth and adults acquire those competencies; (b) help them connect with suitable learning and work opportunities; and (c) help employers connect with the talent they require.

The first was met through the *Blueprint for Life/Work Designs*, which was modeled on the National Career Development Guidelines (2004) developed by the U.S. National Occupational Information Coordinating Committee. Career and workforce development experts across Canada collaborated for several years in creating, testing, and implementing the Blueprint.

> The Blueprint is a national effort to outline the outcomes of quality career development programs and services. The Blueprint specifies what individuals can expect to learn from services at different developmental levels, ranging from elementary school, to secondary and adult populations. The Blueprint also has a strong focus on implementing career development programs and helping providers be clear about the outcomes actually achieved by specific programs. (ATEC, 2001, p. 7)

During the same timeframe, a National Steering Committee undertook to develop the *Canadian Standards and Guidelines for Career Development Practitioners* (S&Gs). This pan-Canadian initiative engaged professional associations of career and workforce development and human resource specialists at the national, provincial, territorial, and local levels, and from the public, private, and non-profit sectors. These dedicated volunteers detailed a framework of competencies that career development professionals need to have to help their clients succeed in career development. Several provinces have developed certification of career practitioners based on this national framework.

The Blueprint and the S&Gs have been adopted by other countries seeking to harmonize their talent-opportunity matching processes. Both were cited as model national infrastructure elements in an OECD report (as cited in Sultana & Watts, 2004) that examined promising practices in 36 countries.

Career practitioners, counsellors, educators, workforce developers, and human resource specialists all need programs and resources that are based on career management learning objectives and performance indicators in order to best help their clients. They need to assess the client's **prior learning and acquired knowledge** and their career management learning in order to select programs, resources, and services that will meet the client's actual needs or gaps. Using the Blueprint and the S&Gs, organizations in the career and workforce development "business" are able to develop new and more effective service delivery and accountability mechanisms.

Blueprint for Life/Work Designs

The Blueprint identifies core career management competencies with associated performance indicators at four levels across the lifespan. The core competencies are the basis upon which career management programs are designed. The performance indicators, which are organized by learning stages, are used to measure learning gains and demonstrate program effectiveness. The Blueprint competencies are arranged in three domains as seen in Table 1.

Included in these competencies are employability, emotional skills, and character traits employer groups find lacking in many prospective employees, particularly youth. In fact, work habits and attitudes so strongly influence early adult earnings that educational and training programs need to emphasize work behaviours as much as job skills (Savickas, 2002). Self-reliance grows out of the acquisition of these skills.

Traditional career development practices have focused largely on information acquisition (Competency 5) and job search (Competency 7). The assumption has been that with access to appropriate information along with the necessary guidance, people can choose the right occupation: They acquire the education and training and, with job search skills, find the right job.

The reality is that a person may fail even with good information and job search skills. This can happen if the person:

- expects to fail again (Competency 1),
- has poor communication and teamwork skills (Competency 2),
- complains about change rather than embracing it (Competency 3),

- is not open to learning and innovating (Competency 4),
- cannot balance life and work effectively (Competency 9).

(A) PERSONAL MANAGEMENT	(B) LEARNING AND WORK EXPLORATION	(C) LIFE/WORK BUILDING
1. Build and maintain a positive self-image.	4. Participate in lifelong learning that is supportive of life/work goals.	7. Secure, create, and/or maintain work.
2. Interact positively and effectively with others.	5. Locate and effectively use life/work information.	8. Make life/work-enhancing decisions.
3. Change and grow throughout one's life.	6. Understand the relationship between work and society/economy.	9. Maintain balanced life and work roles.
		10. Understand the changing nature of life and work roles.

Table 1: Blueprint Competencies.

If the person does land a job, chances are it will be short term. Moreover, a person lacking these competences will likely not find satisfaction and fulfillment in the job, and most likely not be highly productive.

Everything changes when career development becomes widely viewed as a quest to acquire and hone the competencies needed to construct a purposeful and fulfilling life, rather than a point-in-time choice of "the perfect career." Now we are helping young people connect with their passions and purpose and learn how to make the most of every day for the rest of their lives. Character traits such as respect, responsibility, honesty, integrity, empathy, fairness, initiative, perseverance, courage, optimism, and resilience become the foundational pieces, rather than career and labour market information, or tests. One cannot maintain a positive self-image (Competency 1) and earn genuine self-respect if one is dishonest, lacks integrity, and so on. One cannot interact positively and effectively with others for long without being empathetic and fair. One cannot change and grow (Competency 3) without courage and resilience. Helping students master these career and life building competencies will help them find and maintain jobs they find satisfying and fulfilling. It will also help them to be better friends, parents, and citizens. Economic success buys comfort, not genuine happiness. If the next generation of youth masters these competencies, the nation will enjoy not only increased economic prosperity, but a resurgence of the core human values and character upon which it was built.

The Blueprint recognizes that people at different ages and stages learn differently, and that even young children can learn and appreciate these competencies. In fact, attitudes towards work are formed early in life, so workforce and career management policy must take a developmental perspective. Vocational psychologists such as Donald Super, John Crites, Robert Gibbons, and Paul R. Lohnes have each concluded from their longitudinal studies that planful competence in early adolescence relates to more realistic educational and vocational choices, occupational success, and career progress (Savickas, 2002). For this reason, the core competencies are defined at four developmental levels:

1. Primary/elementary school.
2. Junior high/middle school.
3. High school.
4. Adult/Postsecondary.

To view the entire framework, with nearly 500 performance indicators sorted by developmental levels and learning stages, visit <http://blueprint4life.ca/competencies.cfm>.

Conclusion

Canada's education system is more successful than most in helping young people acquire academic and technical skills. It is less successful in equipping students with the competencies they need to navigate and manage their careers. Too few students see the relevance of school experience to their future and, thus, lack motivation to excel in school. In fact, school is their first job beyond home. It can be the perfect "starter job" in which they can acquire academic knowledge that will serve them well in the future, and hone the habits, skills, attitudes, and character needed for success in school and all future life roles.

With an increasing shortage of skills in the workforce, and too many adults working in positions that undervalue their talents, Canada is slipping in productivity and competitiveness. Employers urgently need to find employees with the right skills and, equally important, the right attitudes. While employers need more talent, too many young people and adults are languishing in unemployment, underemployment, and marginalization. New, more effective and efficient mechanisms are needed to connect talent with opportunities across Canada. The Blueprint can assist citizens to purposefully acquire career and life management competencies. The Standards and Guidelines ensure that professionals in education, training, and workforce development settings have the competencies they need to help individuals manage their career and life planning.

References

ATEC (2001). Canadian Standards and Guidelines for Career Development Snapshot 2001. Ottawa, ON: ATEC. Retrieved from http://onestep.on.ca/whatsnew/pdfs /Snapshot.doc>.

Blueprint for Life/Work Designs. (n.d.). Retrieved from <http://www.lifework.ca>.

Bowlby, J., & McMullen, K. (2002). At a crossroads: First results for the 18 to 20-year old cohort of the youth in transition survey [Statistics Canada Catalogue no. 81-591-XIE]. Ottawa, ON: Human Resources Development Canada and Statistics Canada. Retrieved from <http://www.statcan.gc.ca/pub/81-591-x/81-591-x2000001-eng.pdf>.

BC Ministry of Advanced Education and Human Resources Development Canada. (2003). Employment Outlook for British Columbia COPS BC Unique Scenario for 2003 to 2013. Retrieved from <http://s3.amazonaws.com/zanran_storage /www.llbc.leg.bc.ca/ContentPages/51221477.pdf>.

Bronson, P. (2002). What should I do with my life? The true story of people who answered the ultimate question. Retrieved from <http://www.fastcompany.com /45909/what-should-i-do-my-life>.

Cappon, J. (2011, Oct.). What is the future of learning in Canada? Canadian Council on Learning. Retrieved from <http://www.sfu.ca/sfunews/stories/2011 /what-is-the-future-of-learning-in-canada.html>.

Centre for Education Statistics, Canada. (1997). School leavers follow-up survey –1995. Ottawa, ON: Statistics Canada and Human Resources Development Canada. Retrieved from <http://data.library.utoronto.ca/datapub/codebooks/cstdli/sls/1995 /slfs95eguid.pdf>.

Cowin, L., & Duchscher, J. E. B. (2004). Multigenerational nurses in the workplace. Journal of Nursing Administration, 34(11), 1–9.

Dychtwald, K., Erickson, T. J., & Morison, R. (2006). Workforce crisis: How to beat the coming shortage of skills and talent. Boston, MA: Harvard Business School Press.

Gallup Organization. (1999). National survey of working America, 1999. Princeton, NJ: Author. Retrieved from <http://files.eric.ed.gov/fulltext/ED450212.pdf>.

Gordon, A. (2009, August 13). Jobs of the future: Science and technology enabled employment for 2020–2030. [Web log post.] Retrieved from <http://futuresavvy.net/2009/08/jobs-of-the-future-technology-enabled -employment-for-2020-2030/>.

Harter, J. (2001, March). Taking feedback to the bottom line. Gallup Management Journal. Retrieved from <http://gmj.gallup.com/archives/3/2001/issue.aspx>.

Howe, N., & Strauss, W. (2000). Millennials rising: The next great generation. New York, NY: Vintage.

Ipsos-Reid. (2002). Canadians and stress: A special report." Globe and Mail, September 2002.

Loscocco, K. A., & Roschelle, A. N. (1991). Influences on the quality of work and nonwork life: Two decades in review. *Journal of Vocational Behavior, 39*, 182–225.

McMahon, M., Patton, W., & Tatham, P. (2003). *Managing life, learning and work in the 21st Century. Issues informing the design of an Australian Blueprint for career development.* Perth: Miles Morgan Australia Pty Ltd. Retrieved from <http://www.blueprint.edu.au/Portals/0/resources/DL_life_learning_and_work.pdf>.

Miner, R. (2010, February). People without jobs, jobs without people. Ontario's labour market future. Retrieved from <http://www.collegesontario.org/research /research_reports/people-without-jobs-jobs-without-people-final.pdf>.

National Career Development Guidelines. (2004). The National Career Development Guidelines. Washington, D.C. Retrieved from <http://acrn.ovae.org/ncdg.htm>.

National Center for Education Statistics. (2002). *The Condition of Education 2002.* (NCES 2002-025). Washington, DC: U.S. Government Printing Office. Retrieved from <http://nces.ed.gov/pubsearch/pubsinfo.asp?pubid=2002025>.

National Steering Committee (2004). *Canadian standards and guidelines for career development practitioners.* Retrieved from <http://career-dev-guidelines.org /career_dev/>.

OECD (2010). PISA 2009 results: What students know and can do. Student performance in reading, mathematices and science (Vol. 1). Retrieved from <http://www.oecd.org/pisa/pisaproducts/48852548.pdf>.

Sauvé, R. (2012). Canada job trends update 2012 (11th ed.). Summerstown, ON: People Patterns Consulting.

Savickas, M. (2002). 14 facts career specialists could assert in debates about public policy Regarding workforce development and career guidance. *International Career Development Policy/Practice Symposium 2002.* Vancouver, May 2002.

Sessa, V. I., Kabacoff, R. I., Deal, J., & Brown, H. (2007). Generational differences in leader values and leadership behaviors. *Psychologist-Manager Journal, 10*, 47–74.

Stanglin, D. (2010, January 5). US job satisfaction falls to record low of 45%. *USA Today.* Retrieved from <http://content.usatoday.com/communities/ondeadline /post/2010/01/us-job-satisfaction-falls-to-record-low-of-45/1>.

Statistics Canada. (2012). Fifty years of families in Canada: 1961 to 2011. Families, households and marital status, 2011 Census of Population (Catalogue no. 98-312-X2011003). Ottawa, ON: Ministry of Industry. Retrieved from <http://www12.statcan.gc.ca/census-recensement/2011/as-sa/98-312-x /98-312-x2011003_1-eng.pdf>.

Stewart, W. F., Ricci, J. A., Chee, E., Morganstein, D., & Lipton, R. (2003). Lost productive time and cost due to common pain conditions in the US workforce. *JAMA: The Journal of the American Medical Association, 290*(18), 2443–2454. doi: 10.1001/jama.289.23.3135

Sultana, R. G., & Watts, A.G. (2004) Career guidance policies in 37 countries: Contrasts and common themes. *International Journal for Educational and Vocational Guidance, 4*, 105–122.

Talbot, J., & Associates (2006). Lifelong Learning Strategy for the City of Vancouver Discussion Document. Burnaby, BC. Retrieved from

<http://vancouverlearningcity.ca/images/uploads/Lifelong_Learning_Strategy_for_
the_City_of_Vancouver.pdf>.

Glossary

Career management paradigm recognizes that career development is a lifelong process
of knowledge and skills acquisition that reflect a continuum of learning and mastery.

Demographic trends describe the historical changes in demographics in a population
over time.

Generational cohorts are groups of people who share birth years, history, and a
collective personality as a result of their defining experiences.

Industrial-age career-choice model was based on helping people make an informed
occupational choice, by engaging in the following steps:

1. Exploring one's interests, aptitudes, values, et cetera (e.g., using tests and professional
   assistance).
2. Exploring the world of work and occupations.
3. Determining a "best fit" occupation by matching personal traits to occupational factors.
4. Developing a plan to obtain the prerequisite education and training.
5. Graduating and obtaining secure employment, climbing the ladder, et cetera.
6. Retiring as young as possible on pension as a reward for decades of work.

Industry sector refers to the goods-producing segment of an economy, including
agriculture, construction, fisheries, forestry, and manufacturing.

Prior learning and acquired knowledge is assessed through prior learning assessment
recognition (PLAR). PLAR is the process of identifying, assessing, and recognizing
skills, knowledge, or competencies that have been acquired through work
experience, unrecognized training, independent study, volunteer activities, and
hobbies. PLAR may be applied towards academic credit, requirement of a training
program, or for occupational certification.

Productivity is a measure of how efficiently goods and services are produced. It is
usually expressed as output per unit of labour.

Recession is a decline in activity across the economy lasting longer than a few months.
It is visible in industrial production, employment, real income, and wholesale-
retail trade. The technical indicator of a recession is two consecutive quarters of
negative economic growth as measured by a country's gross domestic product (GDP).

Up-skill refers to learning new skills.

Discussion and Activities

Discussion

Class Discussion Questions

1. How do career practitioners enhance and help their clients maintain employability in a turbulent and unpredictable economy? How can they help clients contend with a "boundaryless" and non-linear exploration?
2. Why must career practitioners continually redefine their own identity?

Personal Reflection Questions

1. In Canada, the labour force spans four generations to include the World War II Generation (born before 1946), the baby boomers (1946–1965), Generation X (1966–1980), and Generation Y or Millennials (1981–2000). Please read the descriptions of each generation as summarized at <http://www.catalyst.org/knowledge /generations-workplace-united-states-canada>.

    i.   What generation do you belong to? How well do the descriptions of that generation fit for you?
    ii. Do you think your generation's situation and concerns are similar to the ones experienced by your parents at your age? What are some of the similarities and differences?
    iii. What are some topics that people of different generations agree and disagree on?

2. We are all a product of the generation before us; that is, our behaviours and attitudes are strongly influenced by our parents. Consider the events and trends that occurred during the lives of your parents. How did their experience affect your ideas about the world of work and career planning?

Career Practitioner Role Questions

1. Career practitioners must learn new skills, stay aware of new trends in work and the economy, and provide expanded services geared towards those with patch-work careers, persons who work at several companies at the same time, retirees who need or want to continue employment, and workers who have not been able to accommodate themselves to these changing conditions. What other challenges do you see for career practitioners in this ever-changing world?
2. What skills will you need to work with the following groups: portfolio workers, youth, older adults, displaced workers?

Activities

Analysis of Strengths, Weaknesses, Opportunities, and Threats (SWOT)

SWOT analysis is a method to evaluate strengths and weaknesses of an organization, person, or project in meeting an objective; and to identify the threats and opportunities that might affect success. In this exercise, you will apply SWOT analysis to the career counselling profession. The matrix can be constructed quickly and will help you consider multiple viewpoints.

PERSONAL	Strengths	Weaknesses
	•	•
EXTERNAL ENVIRONMENT	Opportunities	Threats
	•	•

Strengths are characteristics that provide an advantage over others, and weaknesses are a disadvantage. From the external environment, there may be opportunities for new markets or jobs (as one example), and also threats due to competition, economy, legislation and other factors.

Use SWOT analysis to examine some of the global, national, and local issues that face us as a profession and as professionals. The following headings can be used as a guide:

- internal weaknesses of current career practice,
- internal strengths of current career practice,
- external threats to the profession,
- external opportunities to the profession.

Resources and Readings

Resources

Websites and Video Resources

Baran, D., & Baran, P. (2008). *Smart options plus*. National Life Work <http://www.lifework.ca/lifework/Media/SO+Brochure.pdf>.

Bartlett, S., & LeRose, M. (Directors). (2013). Generation jobless. In *Doc Zone*. Dreamfield Productions & CBC-TV. Available from <http://www.cbc.ca/doczone/episode/generation-jobless.html>.

Chan, Andy. (2013). *Career services must die: Andy Chan at TEDxLawrenceU*. [Video]. Available from <http://www.youtube.com/watch?v=6Tc6GHWPdMU>.

SPOTLIGHT: *CAREER CRUISING*
by Phil Jarvis

Career Cruising is a 100% Canadian-owned, Toronto-based organization, that provides career exploration software for helping people of all ages reach their goals. Its career resources are licensed by roughly 80% of all English-speaking secondary and postsecondary schools in Canada, and it is the first web resource to which most Canadian counsellors refer their students for exploring career options.

Career Cruising ccEngage Suite: description of products <http://public.career cruising.com/ca/en/products/>.

Career Cruising Blog <http://public.careercruising.com/us/en/blog/>.

The following are recommended:

- The Perfect Storm: 4 workforce megatrends you need to know about <http://public.careercruising.com/us/en/blog/bl/2012/02/the-perfect-storm-4-workforce-megatrends-you-need-to-know-about/>,
- Creating Pathways to Prosperity (category in weblog) <http://public.careercruising.com/us/en/blog/?category=Career%20Summits>.

People Right Careers (2010) *College-bound students face the perfect storm.* [Video]. Available from <http://www.youtube.com/watch?v=qZUZa7mRlI0>.

Harvard Graduate School of Education (2013, June 21.) Workshop: Effective career guidance: Developing a vision of what we can / must provide [Video.] Available from <http://www.youtube.com/watch?v=5qF1CtQe__U>.

Harvard Graduate School of Education, Creating Pathways to Prosperity Thoughtstream Site <http://sites.thoughtstream.ca/pathways/>.

National Career Development Association, NCDA Thoughtstream site <http://sites.thoughtstream.ca/ncda/>.

Symonds, B., Gysbers, N., Gabbard, P., & Feller, R. (2013, June 3). *Discussion with experts, addressing the challenges of career educators in North America* [Weblog post.] Retrieved from <https://public.careercruising.com/us/en/blog/bl/2013/06/a-discussion-with-experts-addressing-the-challenges-of-career-educators-in-north-america/>.

Wolfe, I. (n.d) *The Perfect Labor Storm* [Weblog]. Available at <http://www.perfectlaborstorm.com/>.

Supplementary Readings

Acker, C., & Rowen, N. (2012). Creating hope, opportunity, and results for disadvantaged youth. *The Canadian Journal of Career Development, 12*(1), 63–79.

Anders, L., & Adamuti-Trache, M. (2008). Life-course transitions, social class, and gender: A 15 year perspective of the lived lives of Canadian young adults. *Journal of Youth Studies, 11*(2), 115–145. doi: 10.1080/13676260701800753

Berger, J., & Baldwin, N. (2009). Student financial assistance in Canada: Past, present and future. In J. Berger, A. Motte & A. Parken (Eds.), *The Price of Knowledge: Access and Student Finance in Canada* (4th ed.). Montréal: Canadian Millennium Scholarship Foundation.

Finnie, R., Frenette, M., Mueller, R. E., & Sweetman, A. (2010). *Pursuing higher education in Canada: Economic, social, and policy dimensions.* Kingston, Ontario: McGill-Queen's University Press.

International Labour Organization. (2012). *The youth employment crisis: Time for action. Highlights of the 2012 ILC report.* Retrieved from ILC101-TRAITEXT-CEJ-2012-05-0056-1-En.docx/v2>.

McCrea Silva, M., & Phillips, S. M. (2007). *Trading up — high school and beyond: Five illustrative Canadian case studies.* Pathways to the Labour Market Series — No. 4. Ottawa, ON: Canadian Policy Research Networks.

Raymond, M. (2008). *High school drop-outs returning to school.* Ottawa, ON: Statistics Canada. Retrieved from <http://www.statcan.gc.ca/pub/81-595-m/81-595-m2008055-eng.pdf>.

Sandell, N. (2012), Atkinson Series: Career education lacking in Canada. *The Toronto Star.* Retrieved from <http://www.thestar.com/news/insight/2012/12/01/atkinson_series_career_education_lacking_in_canada.html>. (This is one of 13 excellent articles in this series.)

Schoon, I., & Silbereisen, R. K. (2009). Conceptualizing school-to-work transitions in context. In I. Schoon & R. K. Silbereisen (Eds.), *Transitions from school to work: Globalization, individualization, and patterns of diversity* (pp. 3–29). Cambridge, UK: Cambridge University Press.

Versnel, J., Deluca, N. L. H., Hill, A., & Chin, P. (2011). International and national factors affecting school to work transition for at-risk youth in Canada: An integrative review. *The Canadian Journal of Career Development, 10*(1), 21–31.

four

Diversity and Social Justice

Guiding Concepts for Career Development Practice

NANCY ARTHUR
University of Calgary
SANDRA COLLINS
Athabasca University

PRE-READING QUESTIONS

1. What does culture mean to you?
2. What does social justice mean to you?

Introduction and Learning Objectives

Vignette: Imagine

Imagine a world where every student had equal access to basic education, had supports to encourage academic success, and had resources to access higher education. Imagine a world where every child could live out the dream, "you can be whatever you want to be when you grow up." Imagine a world where gender, religion, social class, ability, ethnicity, sexual orientation, and/or age would not be a barrier for pursuing career opportunities. Imagine a world where people could do their jobs without concern about fitting in, without fear of exploitation, and with the same pay as their co-workers. Imagine a world where people had access to relevant career development services that took into account their values, their current needs, their views regarding work, and other roles in their lives. Imagine a world where professionals could address people's career development needs through interventions with individuals, but also make a positive difference by initiating systemic and social change.

Overview

Although the above statements may seem idealistic, they are intended to get you thinking about some of the key influences on people's career development and to encourage reflection on some of the opportunities and barriers that impact the lives of Canadians seeking to fulfill their educational and occupational goals. The purpose of this chapter is to position cultural diversity and **social justice** as guiding concepts for understanding career development. Although Canada is known around the world for its progressive policies on multiculturalism, there are notable differences between policies and practices. The lives of many Canadians are seriously impacted by whether or not they are members of dominant groups who have more economic and political power, by their access to economic and social resources such as education and employment, and by their capacity to access professional services (Arthur & Collins, 2010). As you review the content of this chapter as well as those of other chapters, we hope you will consider the influence of culture on career development and the roles that career development practitioners play in addressing social justice issues.

We begin with an exploration of the term "culture" as it relates to the identities and experiences of individuals and groups. We then take a look at the cultural context of Canada, examining the impact of culture on career development for particular non-dominant populations. This leads into a more detailed examination of how culture specifically impacts career development perspectives, resources and services, theories, and models. We emphasize the importance of infusing cultural awareness into all aspects of career development, which necessitates active change in current career practices. We end with an exploration of the implications of social justice for career development practices.

By the end of this chapter, our aim is that you succeed at the following learning objectives:

1. Define the meaning of culture and social justice.
2. Describe how culture influences career development.
3. Identify individual differences in educational and occupational attainment.
4. Explain the relationships between culture and social justice.
5. List common barriers for access to career development services.
6. Identify competencies required by career development practitioners.
7. Discuss levels of interventions that could be used to address social justice issues.

What Is Culture?

Vignette: Peter

Peter works in an employment agency where clients come from a variety of countries and cultures. He has been running workshops for his clients but notices that it is difficult for participants to talk openly about their career concerns, and he often wonders if they are getting much out of it. Some of the clients seem impatient when he takes the time to explain ideas related to career, career planning, and the decision-making process. Most of the questions that clients ask are focused on job searching. Peter wonders if he should educate the workshop participants about career planning or simply emphasize the job search process. He doesn't want to do this, but there is pressure from the agency director to show how the workshop connects to the agency mandate of job placement. He raises his concern with a trusted colleague who asks him more about the needs of clients who attend the workshop. They talk about the possible cultural influences on his clients' participation and how he could better tailor the workshop to address their short- and longer-term needs. Peter feels excited about this possibility but also a little confused about how to change his approach to meet the needs of clients from diverse cultural backgrounds.

In this section, we will explore the meaning of culture, cultural diversity, and cultural identities. As you read through this section, reflect on the vignette above and ask yourself how Peter's culture or the cultural identities of his clients might be impacting the success of his career development workshops.

The Meaning of Culture

Culture is a term that is part of everyday language, yet has various meanings. People often use the term to mean race or ethnicity. However, culture is not just one specific characteristic; it includes a range of factors and experiences that influence how people view themselves, how they view other people, and how they behave. Arthur and Collins (2010) outline several assumptions about culture:

1. Every individual is a cultural being.
2. Culture is learned and transmitted through social interactions and from generation to generation.
3. Culture is dynamic and changeable.

As practitioners, we are each unique cultural beings. We need to reflect on our own personal culture and understand who we are and what we bring to professional practice. This also means that we need to consider how our cultural background impacts the way we view other people. The second and third points emphasize how culture is transmitted through shared customs, values, and traditions (Sue & Sue, 1990). The emphasis on learning reinforces that culture is not fixed; our personal cultural identities change and evolve over time (Collins, 2010). In turn, through our life experiences, we integrate new understandings into how we define ourselves. These same basic assumptions apply to our work with clients. Every interaction requires us to appreciate the cultural identity of the other person. It is also our responsibility to learn about the cultural norms and practices of other people and to develop a better understanding about the influences of culture on their career development.

The Meaning of Cultural Diversity

We invite you to consider the following question: Whom do you think of when you use or hear the terms "culturally different" or "culturally diverse"? What are your first thoughts? What are the cultural characteristics that led you to consider them as culturally different from you? Is it country of origin? Is it visible differences, such as skin colour, sex, age, or ability? What about people whose differences might not be visible but are expressed through attitudes and behaviour? Your personal beliefs about culture may lead you to categorize other people on the basis of only one or two factors. We caution you about making assumptions based on group membership or perceived differences. Sometimes, the person who looks the least like you actually has the most in common with you, and vice versa!

The Meaning of Cultural Identity

When people have a similar cultural background of customs, values, and traditions — they are likely to have a similar worldview; when they have very different cultural backgrounds, their assumptions are more likely to be different (Pedersen & Ivey, 1993).

People's cultural identities are also a composite of their experiences. Two individuals from the same cultural community may define their own cultural identity very differently based on different experiences, affiliation with different cultural groups, or emergent aspects of their own identity, such as sexual orientation.

We see **cultural identity** as the unique composite of cultural influences (including gender, ethnicity, religion, age, sexual orientation, ability, socioeconomic status) that define each individual (Collins & Arthur, 2010). The factor most important in understanding the cultural identity of another person is how that person sees herself or himself (Collins, 2010). Career development practitioners must avoid cultural stereotypes and consider carefully the relevant cultural influences on each person's career development.

❖ *Stop and Reflect*

Questions on the Vignette
1.   How might Peter's cultural identity shape the lens through which he views the career development needs and priorities of his clients?
2.   What effect might his cultural lens have on the selection and effectiveness of the activities and processes he implements for his workshops?

The Canadian Context

This section provides an overview of Canada's population with some background information about selected populations. Please consider this information in the context of the previous definition of culture. Background knowledge about group membership may provide a potential starting point for cultural understanding; however, you must always explore an individual's unique worldview, experiences, and cultural identity to appreciate his or her idiosyncratic career development needs. We conclude with some further reflections on the implication of diverse cultural identities to career development.

Inuit, Métis, and First Nations Peoples

Canada is a nation that is founded on cultural plurality. According to the 2012 Census (Statistics Canada [SC], 2012), the population of Canada is approximately 34,880,500 people. When we refer to cultural diversity within the Canadian context, it is important to recognize the people who founded our country. The 2006 Census reported about 1.1 million as **Aboriginal peoples** — specifically, **Inuit, Métis**, and **Aboriginal** peoples. However, it is noteworthy that between 1996 and 2006, the Aboriginal populations grew by 45%, compared to 8% growth in the rest of the population (SC, 2008).

There are about 630 First Nations communities in Canada with First Nations constituting the largest indigenous group in Canada (Indian and Northern Affairs Canada, 2009). First Nations are culturally, linguistically, and geographically diverse peoples, residing in both their traditional territories and in rural and urban areas throughout Canada (Blue, Darou, & Ruano, 2010). First Nations peoples experience high rates of under-employment and unemployment in comparison to the dominant populations of Canada. The lingering effects of colonization, historical oppression, and differential rates of access to education and employment opportunities are all influential forces (Arthur & Collins, 2010). Focusing on education appears to be key to helping future generations achieve academic and work success (Offet-Gardner, 2010).

Immigrants and Refugees

Over the past 30 years Canada has become much more ethnically diverse due to shifting patterns in immigration and an increase in immigrants and **refugees** from new countries of origin. (Arthur, 2010). There have also been greater numbers of temporary foreign workers and students from other countries attending schools in Canada. Together, these groups resulted in more than 500,000 newcomers in 2008 (Citizenship and Immigration Canada [CIC], 2009a). Canada depends upon immigration as part of a national strategy to fulfill projections of labour market needs in the future. With an aging population, Canada needs more skilled labourers from other countries in order to prosper economically (Arthur, 2012).

As people with diverse cultural practices come to study, work, and live in Canada, it is incumbent on us to consider how effectively our career development practices and services address their needs. Many factors impact the career development and employment experiences of new Canadians. Newcomers require recognition of their foreign credentials and experience. They may encounter cultural differences in teaching and learning methods. The time it takes to be accepted by local communities, workforces, and organizations is a factor. Resources and supports for transition between the home country and Canada will differ among groups.

There is a tendency to consider immigrants and refugees as if they are a homogenous group. However, there are many factors premigration, such as educational attainment and availability of documentation, as well as postmigration, such as language capacity, recognition of foreign credentials, and experience, that impact their career development in a new country (Arthur, 2012). Involuntary relocation due to war or natural disasters results in unplanned career and life disruptions. Other career issues may begin to surface upon arrival in Canada at a time when securing education or employment is an urgent matter. Further issues may surface after a period of living, learning, or working in Canada. For example, immigrant youth are least likely to pursue postsecondary education, which has consequences for their short- and long-term career development (Bezanson et al., 2007). Secure employment is a major concern for family stability. There may also be role shifts and changing family dynamics, depending on which family members are successful in gaining employment (Arthur, Merali, & Djuraskovic, 2010).

Although the onus to adapt to Canadian society is often placed on immigrants, we need to consider if local communities, schools, and workplaces are sufficiently prepared to welcome and integrate people who choose Canada as their new home. The process of integration is not just the responsibility of newcomers, but a complex process shared with members of the receiving society, including career development professionals (Arthur, 2012).

Religious Diversity

One of the important aspects of cultural diversity in Canada is the increase in religious diversity. The non-Christian population continues to grow, particularly the number of people practising Muslim, Hindu, and Sikh religions (CIC, 2009b). In previous decades, religion might have been viewed as a personal or private matter. However, there is growing recognition that religious and spiritual beliefs play a strong role in shaping people's cultural worldview, including their perspectives on gender roles, personal values, and one's purpose in life. As we explore cultural influences on career development, the role of religion in people's lives should be considered a key area of influence.

Sexual Orientation

In exploring dimensions of cultural diversity, you are encouraged to look beyond Canada's increased ethnic diversity. For example, it is estimated that the population of people with **non-dominant sexual orientations** ranges between 3% and 10% of the population (Alderson, 2010). However, exact statistics are difficult to ascertain, as many members of the LGBT (lesbian, gay, bisexual, transgender) community feel that it is not socially acceptable to be public about their identity. The degree to which individuals feel that they can be open about their sexual orientation has implications for their career development (Degges-White & Shoffner, 2002). Workplace discrimination based on homophobic attitudes continues to impact hiring practices, as well as daily interactions with co-workers, employment benefits to same-sex partners, and the general sense of safety in the workplace (Collins & Oxenbury, 2010).

Ability

The dimensions of ability and disability have not received sufficient attention in the discussion of cultural influences on career development. The term "disability" is used to describe individuals with "a variety of distinct physical, intellectual, and emotional conditions" (Arthur & Collins, 2010, p. 33). It is often not ability, per se, that influences career opportunities; it is that other people's views stigmatize and position individuals as disabled, creating barriers to access and success. Although there is increased support for **persons with disabilities** in educational, social, and work environments, there continue to be major gaps in educational preparation and employment mobility which reduces their economic capacity and quality of life (Office of Disability Issues, 2002). Even though many accommodations have been made in workplaces for those with disabilities, much more could be done to fully recognize the capabilities of all people who could contribute to the Canadian labour force.

Socioeconomic Status and Social Class

There has been surprisingly little attention paid to socioeconomic status and social class (SESC) in the literature addressing career development within the Canadian context. Perhaps it is easier to point out living conditions or other factors associated with poverty in other countries, than it is to acknowledge the persistently high poverty rates in our own (Valetta, 2006). Approximately 5% of Canadians are classified as low income (SC, 2006). However, there are higher rates of poverty among single seniors, families led by single-mothers, members of visible minority groups, and people with disabilities (National Council of Welfare, 2006). Low-income Canadians face major barriers for economic and social mobility, which is strongly associated with determinants in physical and mental health (Pope & Arthur, 2009). The lower the socioeconomic status, the higher the incidence of health concerns. People's access to educational and employment opportunities is fundamentally tied to SESC. There are approximately 1.5 million Canadians who may be characterized as the **working poor**, people who work more than 910 hours per year, but whose income levels still fall below poverty cut-offs (Fleury & Fortin, 2004).

Implications of Diverse Cultural Identities

From our viewpoint, all clients have a cultural background that influences how they view themselves and their relationship to education, **work**, and other life roles. However, it is not their group membership, per se, that leads to career barriers or challenges; rather it is the way in which particular individuals or groups are positioned in our society that leads to conditions of oppression or marginalization, which in turn impact career development. It is paramount that we pay attention to which people or peoples are disproportionately disadvantaged in terms of educational and employment opportunities. It is also important to remember that people within each of these groups will have varied experiences, some more successful than others.

We caution you not to categorize people or assume understanding based on their group membership. This can lead to stereotyping and a failure to recognize the unique aspects of each individual's **cultural identity**. There are multiple dimensions that make up a person's cultural identity and the intersections of those factors are what make people unique (Collins, 2010). For example, gender may have a significant impact on career development, but how this plays out may be quite different depending on other cultural or contextual factors. Compare, for example, women who are raised in a middle-class household to women who arrived in Canada as refugees with little family support, or lesbians in a work environment where they feel unsafe about being out. Career practitioners need to balance a general knowledge about the cultural beliefs and practices of diverse populations with an assessment of each individual client's worldview and needs.

The bottom line is that everyone has a unique cultural identity. This identity may affect the ways in which we perceive ourselves and the ways in which we are perceived by others. These perceptions, in turn, can have a significant influence on career development. In the next section, we will consider the ways that our Canadian society affords some people more opportunities and resources than others, including access to educational and employment systems.

❖ *Stop and Reflect*

Questions on the Vignette

1. How might cultural diversity impact the willingness of participants to open up and share their perspectives and needs in the workshop?
2. What questions might Peter need to ask himself about the cultural identities of his clients to create content and processes that will meet their needs?

Culture and Career Development

Cultural influences are inextricably woven into people's career development in several ways. Culture may affect one's understanding of career and career development, the use of career development resources and services, the perceived availability of career resources and services, and the relevance and appropriateness of career theories and models. We discuss each of these in this section. We wrap up with a call to move from an understanding of cultural diversity to action that transforms career practices. Remember to return to the vignette to see what insight this discussion provides.

The Meaning of Career and Career Development

It is important to recognize that the terms **career** and **career development** may not have the same meaning for everyone. These terms need to be understood according to the historical and cultural influences that have led to contemporary definitions. "Career has been and is enmeshed in notions of work, employment, occupations, and jobs" (Young & Collin, 2004, p. 4). "The term career development is culturally constructed. For members of diverse cultural groups ... the term career may mean different things, if it holds significance at all" (Arthur, 2007). The term has been criticized for being an elitist concept based on the notion that people have free choice about self-expression through their work and other life roles (Arthur, Collins, McMahon, & Marshall, 2009). This may not be the experience of millions of people around the world who work to survive and for whom work is no more than a means to that end. Some authors have suggested that we should, instead, place the emphasis on the concept of "work" (Blustein, 2006, Blustein, Kenna, Gill, & DeVoy, 2008), because it has more universal relevance and applicability. It is important to consider whether our clients relate to the concepts of career and/or work as a meaningful construct in their lives (Richardson, 2009).

Use of Career Development Resources and Services

For many people, cultural beliefs may also impact whether or not they make use of professional services. There can be strong cultural norms about how future educational and vocational options are decided. Family members may be highly influential in decision making. Religion, gender roles, socioeconomic status, or ethnicity may either limit or expand the types of occupational and lifestyle choices viewed as acceptable (Arthur & Popadiuk, 2009). Family resources, either in the form of economic support or in terms of attitudes or beliefs, may be strong influences on the career pathways of children, youth, and adults. There may also be strong cultural beliefs about the acceptability of seeking help outside of the family or community. Discussing important issues about career or education with a stranger may, indeed, be a foreign idea!

Perceived Availability of Career Development Resources and Services

Beyond individual and family attitudes towards seeking help, the perceived availability of services is an important consideration. There is significant variability in the extent to which career development services are available, and in the design and delivery of those services in different countries around the world (Watts & Sultana, 2004). One of the biggest barriers to accessing career development services may be a lack of information about their availability and their relevance to an individual's education and employment planning needs. If the priority is accessing a living wage, then career-values assessment or career-life meaning may seem irrelevant.

When people do access services, they are looking for resources that are relevant to their situation. One key issue is the capacity of these services to address the needs of individuals from diverse cultural backgrounds (Arthur & Lalande, 2009). Although services offered to the general public may address common issues, such as job search, career planning, and decision making, they may neglect fundamental needs of clientele when cultural issues are not taken into consideration. The adage one-size-fits-all does not work when offering culturally responsive professional services. The design and delivery of programs must be matched with the unique needs of people who are living in our communities, and evaluation methods should be used to demonstrate how cultural diversity is incorporated (Arthur & Lalande, 2009).

Relevance and Appropriateness of Career Theories and Models

In order to offer culturally relevant professional services, it is important to consider the theories and models used as guides. A number of **cultural assumptions** are evident in theories and models of career development. The following have been adapted from Gysbers, Heppner, and Johnston (2009):

1. The assumption of **individualism** and **autonomy** — the individual makes choices that ultimately shape that person's destiny.
2. The assumption of **affluence** — the individual holds a certain amount of affluence, including financial resources.
3. The assumption of **opportunity** — the individual is in control of and can choose to strive towards selection, attainment, and ultimate satisfaction in career choices and in life.
4. The assumption of the **centrality** of work in people's lives — work plays a central and pivotal role in people's lives and in fulfilling personal identity.
5. The assumption of the **linearity**, **progressiveness**, and **rationality** of development — the individual's progress in the world can be described and decided upon in orderly, rational, and linear terms.

The examples of cultural assumptions illustrate how many of our theories and models of career interventions are based in a Western **worldview**. How well do these theories and models inform professional practice with populations whose values and cultural norms contrast the views of dominant culture in Canadian society? Applying such models without considering their cultural relevance to all people or peoples is **ethnocentric**; it reflects a false belief that the Western worldview is right and applies to everyone. As a result, the cultural validity of related programs and services is called into question. When career development practitioners select theories and models to guide their practices, they need to consider how effectively these models account for cultural influences on people's career planning and decision making and provide appropriate career-related interventions (Arthur & McMahon, 2005).

Moving Past Awareness to Action

So far in this chapter, we have highlighted two important steps for enhancing **cultural competence** in career practice:

1. Career practitioners must recognize cultural differences, often coined as **cultural sensitivity**.
2. Career practitioners must reflect on their own personal cultural background, assumptions, and cultural lenses.

However, simply recognizing diversity is not a sufficient base for competent professional practice. These steps remain at a relatively passive level, without **initiating action** to embrace diversity and to respond to career development needs from the client's point of view. As supported by the recent revisions to the *Canadian Standards and Guidelines for Career Development Practitioners* (National Steering Committee, 2004), a third step is required:

3.   Practitioners need to design and deliver effective interventions that take into account unique aspects of the other person's cultural worldview.

Practitioners need to develop the skills to move from a passive approach to actively incorporating the influences of cultural diversity into their practices with all clients. Above all, they need to infuse their work with an understanding of the effect of cultural influences on people's career development. The onus is on career practitioners to diversify their worldview, their understanding of people's career issues, and the types of interventions that they offer to support clients. Figure 1 provides an overview of the culture-infused counselling model of Arthur and Collins (2010), which focuses on development of specific knowledge, attitudes, and skills in three core-competency domains. For some clients, attention to multiple influences on cultural identity will be essential for building a culturally sensitive working alliance and designing culturally responsive career interventions.

CORE COMPETENCY DOMAINS	CULTURAL IDENTITY INFLUENCES						
	Ethnicity /Cultural Heritage	Gender	Sexual Orientation	Ability	Social Class	Religion	Age
Awareness of your own cultural identities and worldview							
Understanding of the cultural identities and worldview of your client(s)			• Attitudes and Beliefs • Knowledge				
Establishment of a culturally sensitive working alliance that supports social justice							

Figure 1: Assessing Cultural Identity Influences.

❖ *Stop and Reflect*

Questions on the Vignette

1. How might the meaning of career and/or work influence engagement of Peter's clients?
2. How might some of the assumptions common to the Western worldview be expressed through this workshop? What barriers to engagement might these create for clients?
3. What actions might Peter take to infuse his understanding of cultural diversity into his career practices in a way that transforms these practices for his clients?

Linking Culture and Social Justice

Many theories and models utilized by career counsellors were developed in a social context in which notions of career development were linear and progressive, and the world was characterized as stable and secure (Hudson, 1999; Savickas, 2003). However, clients who experience employment as chaotic, unpredictable, and/or unstable require career development interventions that address the environmental and social conditions that impact their lives. This requires us to carefully analyze our theories and methods of interventions in light of the realities of people who are marginalized in Canadian society. Rather than fitting people into existing practices, we need to consider how well our theories and interventions support the experiences of our clients. A major concern is that most interventions focus on working with individuals. To fully embrace cultural diversity, career practitioners require education about interventions to address organizational, systemic, or environmental change (Arthur, 2005). This final section of the chapter will explore the relationship between culture and social justice, examine some research on how career practitioners view social justice, and summarize the implications for career development practice.

Relationship Between Culture and Social Justice

We can no longer ignore the fact that the career development of people living in Canada is strongly influenced by the systems that surround them. We need to acknowledge systemic inequities and oppressive practices. The relationship between culture and social justice can be summed up in two key points (Stead, 2004):

1. Cultural affiliation provides some people with vocational privilege and better access to resources.
2. Cultural affiliation poses as a constraining force through which some people

are excluded from educational opportunities and access to a fuller range of occupational choices.

Some groups of people continue to face challenges with employment access, retention, and mobility. These include persons with disabilities, Aboriginal peoples, women, visible minorities, and other members of non-dominant populations (Arthur, Broadhead, Magnusson, & Redekopp, 2003).

Defining Social Justice

Social justice was foundational to occupation guidance at the beginning of this century (Parsons, 1909), and has recently resurfaced as a major theme in career development literature (e.g., Arthur, 2005; Fassinger & Gallor, 2006; Irving & Malik, 2005). Although the concept of social justice has stood the test of time, there are many different perspectives about how to define it. Arthur and colleagues (2009) highlight three core components of social justice relevant to the discussion of career development:

1. Fair and equitable distribution of resources and opportunities.
2. Direct action to ameliorate oppression and marginalization within society.
3. Full inclusion and participation of all members of society in a way that enables them to reach their potential. (p. 23)

It is important for career development practitioners to examine how their work may inadvertently support the status quo by focusing on helping clients to adapt to oppressive social and employment conditions. From a social justice perspective, career issues are influenced by both client factors and their surrounding environment and social structures. When clients' career issues are defined only as intrapersonal, there is a risk of blaming clients for their situations. We must consider the environmental and societal forces acting as systemic barriers to people's growth and development. People of different cultural backgrounds continue to be marginalized in society through discriminating social rewards and sanctions that determine who receives the better education and employment positions in our society.

Practitioner Views of Social Justice

Although there is a growing belief that social justice is an important aspect of career development, there are few examples to guide the incorporation of social justice into career-related interventions. To that end, we designed an exploratory study with career development practitioners in Canada to consider their views on social justice and how they incorporated social justice practices (Arthur et al., 2009;

Arthur, Collins, Marshall, & McMahon, 2013). It was found that practitioners associated social justice with advocacy, equity, fulfillment and personal potential, equal opportunities, inclusive practices, relevant client resources, education, improved policies, and the acknowledgement of contextual influences on people's career development. Furthermore, they believed that practitioners should consider possible social justice issues in their work with all clients. However, practitioners also identified gender, socioeconomic status, immigration, race, age, disability, sexual orientation, religion, and criminal record as specific cultural factors associated with more educational and employment disadvantages. Discrimination and other forms of oppression are often internalized negatively by clients and become significant barriers to their career development.

Implications for Career Development

Embracing social justice as a core value has significant implications for contemporary career development practices. A social justice lens requires more awareness of the cultural identities and contexts of their clients; consciousness of their own cultural identities and potential biases; understanding of the influences of social, economic, and political systems on career resources and opportunities; and an ability to move beyond the individual to target these contextual influences as part of career interventions.

Career practitioners require a deeper understanding of social justice concepts, and more education and training in how to translate that knowledge into both **micro** and **macro systems** interventions (Burwell, Kalbleisch, & Woodside, 2010). However, practitioners face certain barriers and conditions that undermine their efforts to incorporate social justice concepts into career development interventions (Arthur et al., 2009). These include, but are not limited to, lack of time and financial resources, support from supervisors, mandates of their work setting, insufficient training, lack of interest, doubts about trying to change the status quo, or fears regarding the potentially negative impact on their employment. Along with the barriers clients face, there are several organizational and structural barriers that need to be addressed. Career practitioners may benefit from additional training about how to influence the systems that not only impact their clients, but also the systems in which they work, in order to enact roles and interventions related to social justice.

❖ *Stop and Reflect*

Questions on the Vignette
1. What external, systemic factors might be affecting the career paths of clients that Peter is working with?

2.	Why might "job search" be a more important focus for these clients than "career" and "career decision making"?
3.	What actions might Peter take to explore the systemic barriers faced by these clients?
4.	What barriers might Peter himself face in shifting his focus towards social justice interventions?

Summary and Conclusion

We invite career practitioners in Canada to fully consider the contextual influences on people's lives. As noted in the discussion of social justice, it is important to frame people's career issues in light of the conditions and systems that surround them. Canadian society affords a wealth of resources in comparison to many other countries around the world. However, that does not eliminate our responsibility to look inward and see how the lives of many people in Canada are adversely impacted by unequal distribution and access to social and economic resources. Culture and social justice are inextricably linked to the provision of career development services. They influence the ways in which practitioners view both themselves and their clients and are key to the design and implementation of effective interventions on a range of levels, including individual, organizational, community, systems, and social change.

We introduced this chapter with a series of statements directed at imagining a world without sociocultural barriers, where individuals were given the necessary support to reach their academic and occupational potentials. In conclusion, we invite readers to consider ways of making those dreams a reality through professional practice.

Imagine a world where career practitioners embraced diversity, where honouring the cultural identities of their clients was part of everyday practice. Imagine working in ways that make a positive difference for clients through addressing the barriers that adversely impact the career development of many individuals in Canada.

We hope that readers can envision ways of incorporating these aspirations into their future roles as career development practitioners.

References

Alderson, K. (2010). From madness to mainstream: Counselling gay men today. In N. Arthur & S. Collins (Eds.), *Culture-infused counselling* (2nd ed., pp. 395–422). Calgary, AB: Counselling Concepts.
Arthur, N. (2005). Building from cultural diversity to social justice competencies in international standards for career development practitioners. *International Journal*

for Educational and Vocational Guidance, 5(2), 137–149. doi: 10.1007/s10775-005-8791-4

Arthur, N. (2007). Career planning and decision-making needs of international students. In M. Pope & H. Singaravelu (Eds.), *A handbook for counselling international students in the United States* (pp. 37–56). Alexandria, VA: American Counseling Association.

Arthur, N. (2012). Career development and international transitions. In M. McMahon & M. Watson (Eds.), *Career development: Global issues and challenges* (1st ed., pp. 93–110). Hauppauge, NY: Nova Science.

Arthur, N., Brodhead, M., Magnusson, K., & Redekopp, D. (2003). Employment equity career counselling in Canada. *Guidance & Counselling, 18*(2), 52–58.

Arthur, N., & Collins, S. (2010). Introduction to culture-infused counselling. In N. Arthur & S. Collins (Eds.), *Culture-infused counselling* (2nd ed., pp. 3–26). Calgary, AB: Counselling Concepts.

Arthur, N., Collins, S., McMahon, M., & Marshall, C. (2009). Career practitioners' views of social justice and barriers for practice. *Canadian Journal of Career Development, 8*(1), 22–31.

Arthur, N., Collins, S., Marshall, C., & McMahon, M. (2013). Social justice competencies and career development practices. *Canadian Journal of Counselling and Psychotherapy, 47*, 136–154.

Arthur, N., & Lalande, V. (2009). Diversity and social justice implications for outcome approaches to evaluation. *International Journal for the Advancement of Counselling, 31*(1), 1–16. doi: 10.1007/s10447-008-9063-z

Arthur, N., & McMahon, M. (2005). A systems theory framework for multicultural career counseling. *The Career Development Quarterly, 53*(3), 208–222.

Arthur, N., Merali, N., & Djuraskovic, I. (2010). Facilitating the journey between cultures: Counselling immigrants and refugees. In N. Arthur & S. Collins (Eds.), *Culture-infused counselling* (2nd ed., pp. 285–314). Calgary, AB: Counselling Concepts.

Arthur, N., & Popadiuk, N. (2010). A cultural formulation approach to counseling international students. *Journal of Career Development, 37*(1), 423–440. doi: 10.1177/0894845309345845

Bezanson, L., Arthur, N., Saunders, R., Hughes, D., Browne, V., Watts, T. et al. (2007, December). *Career development from under-represented to inclusive: Opening doors to post-secondary participation.* Research paper submitted to the Canadian Millennium Scholarship Foundation for the Neither a Moment nor a Mind to Waste International Symposium, Ottawa, ON.

Blue, A., Darou, W., & Ruano, C. (2010). Engaging the Elder within: Bridging and honouring the cultural spaces in counselling with First Nations. In N. Arthur & S. Collins (Eds.), *Culture-infused counselling* (2nd ed., pp. 259–284). Calgary, AB: Counselling Concepts.

Blustein, D. L. (2006). *The psychology of working.* Malwah, NJ: Lawrence Erlbaum Associates.

Blustein, D., Kenna, A., Gill, N., & DeVoy, J. (2008). The psychology of working: A new framework for counseling practice and public policy. *Counseling Psychology Quarterly, 56*, 294–308.

Burwell, R., Kalbfleisch, S., Woodside, J. (2010). A model for the education of career practitioners in Canada. *Canadian Journal of Career Development, 9*(1), 44–52.

Citizenship and Immigration Canada. (2009a). *News release: Canada welcomes a record high number of newcomers in 2008.* Retrieved from <http://www.cic.gc.ca/english /department/media/releases/2009/2009-02-20.asp>.

Citizenship and Immigration Canada. (2009b). *A survey of recent research on religious diversity and implications for multiculturalism policy.* Retrieved from <http:// publications.gc.ca/collections/collection_2009/policyresearch/CP12-1-10-2E.pdf>.

Collins, S. (2010). The complexity of identity: Appreciating multiplicity and intersectionality. In N. Arthur & S. Collins (Eds.), *Culture-infused counselling* (2nd ed., pp. 247–258). Calgary, AB: Counselling Concepts.

Collins, S., & Arthur, N. (2010). Self-awareness and awareness of client identities. In N. Arthur & S. Collins (Eds.). *Culture-infused counselling* (2nd ed., pp. 67–102). Calgary, AB: Counselling Concepts.

Collins, S., & Oxenbury, J. (2010). Affirming women who love women: Principles for counselling lesbians. In N. Arthur & S. Collins (Eds.), *Culture-infused counselling* (2nd ed., pp. 363–394). Calgary, AB: Counselling Concepts.

Degges-White, S., & Shoffner, M. F. (2002). Career counseling with lesbian clients: Using the theory of work adjustment as a framework. *The Career Development Quarterly, 51*, 87–96.

Fassinger, R. E., & Gallor, S. M. (2006). Tools for remodeling the masters' house: Advocacy and social justice in education and work. In R. L. Toporek, L. H. Gerstein, N. A. Fouad, G. Roysicar, & T. Israel (Eds.), *Handbook for social justice in counseling psychology: Leadership, vision, and action* (pp. 256–275). Thousand Oaks, CA: Sage.

Fleury, D., & Fortin, M. (2004). Canada's working poor. *Horizons, 7*(2), 51–57.

Hudson, F. M. (1999). The adult years: Mastering the art of self-renewal. San Francisco, CA: Jossey-Bass.

Gysbers, N. C., Heppner, M. J., & Johnston, J. A. (2009). *Career counseling: Processes, issues, and techniques* (3rd ed.). Alexandria, VA: American Counseling Association.

Indian and Northern Affairs Canada. (2009). First Nations. Retrieved from <http://www.aadnc-aandc.gc.ca/>.

Irving, B. A., & Malik, B. (Eds.). (2005). Critical reflections on career education and guidance: Promoting social justice within a global economy. Abingdon, Oxon: RoutledgeFalmer.

National Council of Welfare. (2006). *Poverty profile 2002 and 2003.* Ottawa, ON: Minister of Public Works and Government Services Canada. Retrieved from <http://publications.gc.ca/collections/Collection/SD25-1-2003E.pdf>.

National Steering Committee. (2004). *Canadian standards and guidelines for career development practitioners.* Retrieved from <http://career-dev-guidelines.org /career_dev/>.

Offet-Gardner, K. (2010, November). Education as the white buffalo. Paper presented at the inaugural Counselling Psychology Conference, Montréal, Québec.

Office of Disability Issues. (2002). Strategic plan 2002–2007: Leadership, engagement, results. Retrieved from <http://publications.gc.ca/collections/Collection/RH37-4-2-2002E.pdf>.

Parsons, F. (1909). *Choosing a vocation*. Boston, MA: Houghton-Mifflin.

Pedersen, P., & Ivey, A. (1993). *Culture-centered counseling and interviewing skills: A practical guide*. Westport, CT: Praeger.

Pope, J., & Arthur, N. (2009). Socioeconomic status and class: A challenge for the practice of Psychology in Canada. *Canadian Psychology, 50,* 55–65. doi: 10.1037/a0014222

Richardson, M. S. (2009). Another way to think about the work we do: Counselling for work and relationship. *International Journal for Educational and Vocational Guidance, 9*(2), 75-84. doi: 10.1007/s10775-009-9154-3

Savickas, M. L. (2003). Advancing the career counselling profession: Objectives and strategies for the next decade. *The Career Development Quarterly, 52,* 87–96.

Statistics Canada. (2006). *Persons in low income before tax (2000–2004)*. Statistics Canada Catalogue no. 75-202-X. Retrieved from <http://www.statcan.gc.ca/tables-tableaux/sum-som/l01/cst01/famil41f-eng.htm>.

Statistics Canada. (2008). *Aboriginal peoples in Canada in 2006: Inuit, Métis and First Nations, 2006 census: Findings*. Ottawa, ON: Government of Canada. Retrieved from <http://www12.statcan.ca/english/census06/analysis/aboriginal/index.cfm>.

Statistics Canada. (2012). *Summary table: Population by year, by province and territory*. Retrieved from <http://www.statcan.gc.ca/tables-tableaux/sum-som/l01/cst01/demo02a-eng.htm>.

Stead, G. (2004). Culture and career psychology: A social constructivist perspective. *Journal of Vocational Behavior, 64,* 389–406. doi: 10.1016/j.jvb.2003.12.006

Sue, D. W., & Sue, D. (1990). *Counseling the culturally different: Theory and practice*. New York, NY: Wiley.

Valetta, R. (2006). The ins and outs of poverty in advanced economies: Poverty dynamics in Canada, Germany, Great Britain, and the United States. *Review of Income and Wealth, 52,* 261–284. doi: 10.1111/j.1475-4991.2006.00187.x

Watts, A. G., & Sultana, R. G. (2004). Career guidance policies in 37 countries: Contrasts and common themes. *International Journal for Educational and Vocational Guidance, 4,* 105–122.

Young, R., & Collin, A., (2000). Introduction: framing the future of career. In A. Collin & R. Young (Eds.), *The future of career* (pp. 1–20). Cambridge, UK: Cambridge University Press.

Glossary

Aboriginal peoples is the term used to collectively describe three cultural groups of Aboriginal people: Inuit, Métis, and Indians (commonly referred to as First

Nations). Each group has distinct histories, languages, and social, cultural, and spiritual beliefs.

Career is a lifestyle concept that involves the sequence of work, learning, and leisure activities in which one engages throughout a lifetime. Careers are unique to each person and are dynamic and unfold throughout life. Careers include how persons balance their paid and unpaid work and personal life roles.

Career development is the lifelong process of managing learning, work, leisure, and transitions in order to move towards a personally determined and evolving preferred future.

Cultural assumptions in career theory:

- **individualism/autonomy**: assumption that the individual makes choices that ultimately shape his or her own destiny;
- **affluence**: assumption that the individual holds a certain amount of affluence, including financial resources;
- **opportunity**: assumption that the individual is in control and can choose to strive towards selection, attainment, and ultimate satisfaction in career choices and in life;
- **centrality**: assumption that work plays a central and pivotal role in people's lives and in fulfilling personal identity;
- **linearity**, **progressiveness**, and **rationality of development**: assumption that individual's progress in the world can be described and decided upon in orderly, rational, and linear terms.

Cultural competence is the set of skills, attitudes, behaviours, and policies that allow one to understand the cultural identities of one's clients, and to work effectively within and across different cultures.

Cultural identity is a term that refers to the unique composite of cultural factors (including gender, ethnicity, religion, age, sexual orientation, ability, and socio-economic status) that define each individual.

Cultural sensitivity refers to the awareness of the centrality of culture and cultural identity of both the counsellor and the client. It includes the recognition of cultural influences, differences in worldview, and potential personal biases.

Culture includes a range of factors and experiences that influence how people view themselves, how they view other people, and how they behave.

Ethnocentrism refers to the judgement of other cultures by the standards of one's own.

First Nations is the term used today instead of Indian. It refers to Status and Non-Status Aboriginal people in Canada. Status Indians are registered under the Indian Act, and Non-Status are not. Many communities also use the term "First Nation" in the name of their community. Currently, there are 615 First Nation communities, which represent more than 50 nations or cultural groups and 50 Aboriginal languages.

Immigrant refers to a person from another country who has migrated and permanently resides in Canada.

Initiating action is the act of embracing cultural diversity and responding to career development needs from the client's point of view. Practitioners must be able to design and deliver effective interventions that take into account the unique aspects of the client's cultural worldviews.

Inuit are Indigenous peoples that reside in the Arctic regions of Canada, Denmark, Russia, and the United States. In Arctic Canada, about 45,000 Inuit live in 53 communities in Nunatsiavut (Labrador), Nunavik (Northern Québec), Nunavut, and the Inuvialuit Settlement Region of the Northwest Territories. Each of these four Inuit groups has settled land claims. These Inuit regions cover one third of Canada's land mass.

Macro system is based on Bronfenbrenner's Ecological Systems Theory. Development reflects the influence of several environmental systems including the macro system that describes the culture in which individuals live. Cultural contexts include, for example, developing and industrialized countries, socioeconomic status, poverty, and ethnicity.

Métis are Aboriginal people who can trace their parentage to First Nations and European descent. Métis means a person who self-identifies as Métis, is of historic Métis Nation Ancestry, is distinct from other Aboriginal peoples, and is accepted by the Métis Nation.

Micro system is based on Bronfenbrenner's Ecological Systems Theory. Development reflects the influence of several environmental systems including the micro system or the setting in which the individual lives. These contexts include the person's family, peers, school, and neighborhood. It is in the micro system that the most direct interactions with social agents take place (e.g., with parents, peers, and teachers). The individual is not a passive recipient of experiences in these settings, but someone who helps to construct the settings.

Non-dominant sexual orientations are defined by the gender to which individuals are sexually attracted. Someone who is attracted primarily or exclusively to members of the same gender is characterized as gay, lesbian, or homosexual, though the latter word has largely fallen out of use. Someone who has strong, viable attraction for people of both genders is characterized as bisexual or pansexual.

Persons with disabilities refers to persons who identify themselves as experiencing difficulties in carrying out the activities of daily living or experience disadvantage in employment, and who may require some accommodation, because of a long-term or recurring physical or developmental condition.

Refugee refers to someone who faces persecution in their home country or the country where they normally live, or who would face persecution if they returned to that country. The United Nations (1967) defines refugee as any "person who owing to a well-founded fear of being persecuted for reasons of race, religion, nationality, membership of a particular social group, or political opinion, is outside the country of his nationality, and is unable to or, owing to such fear, is unwilling to avail himself of the protection of that country" (p. 2). Retrieved from <http://www2.ohchr.org/english/law/pdf/protocolrefugees.pdf>.

Social justice refers to the fair and equitable distribution of resources and opportunities; the direct action to ameliorate oppression and marginalization within society; and the full inclusion and participation of all members of society in a way that enables them to reach their potential.

Work is a set of activities with an intended set of outcomes, from which it is hoped that a person will derive personal satisfaction and contribute to some greater goal. Work is not necessarily tied to paid employment, but to meaningful and satisfying activities (e.g., volunteer work, hobbies).

Working poor is a term used to describe individuals and families who maintain regular employment (910 hours per year) but remain in relative poverty due to low levels of pay and dependent expenses.

Worldview is the way in which an individual perceives his or her world from philosophical, ethical, social, and moral contexts.

Discussion and Activities

Discussion

After reading the chapter, revisit your original responses to the pre-reading questions.

1. What does culture mean to you?
2. What does social justice mean to you?

Discussion Questions

1. How true do you think this statement is for children in Canada: "You can be whatever you want to be?" What might influence their realities as they try to live out this dream?
2. What are the potential implications of a mismatch between the worldview of career development practitioners and the worldview of clients?
3. What are the key competencies that you think career practitioners need in order to incorporate social justice into their roles?

Personal Reflections

1. What dimensions of culture are relevant for your personal identity? In which situations or relationships are some dimensions of your identity more prominent or visible than others? What leads you to shift how you present your identity in different situations?
2. In reflecting on your own career development, what influences have helped you to be successful? To what degree were those influences related to your personality or personal history, to your social or cultural context, or to broader community or societal factors?
3. In reflecting on your own career development, what personal and/or systemic barriers have you faced?
4. How have you approached your own career planning and decision making? Did you follow certain predetermined steps, or did chance other unforeseen events play a role? To what degree were these events influenced by cultural or social justice influences?
5. What influences did your family or other significant people in your life have for your career development? What academic programs or types of occupations were you encouraged or discouraged from pursuing? How did your family's views of gender roles, ability, socioeconomic status, or other cultural identity factors influence your choices?

Career Practitioner Role

1. When you were a child, what messages do you remember hearing about people from non-dominant cultural groups in Canada? What evidence was there to support those messages?
2. What personal biases or cultural lenses might influence your views of others and your views of career development practice? How open are you to examining these biases and embracing other perspectives? What makes you hesitant to engage in this self-examination and change?
3. What values related to cultural diversity and social justice resonated for you as you read this chapter? How might principles of social justice align with your worldview?

Activities

Thoughts on the Vignette

On reading the vignette about Peter, write down your initial impressions of the career practitioner, his client group, and potential issues that may arise for him and/or his clients. After reading the chapter, revisit the vignette and your initial responses and identify any blind spots or preconceived ideas. How might you view this scenario differently by applying a cultural identity and social justice lens?

Lifeline Activity

Create a visual map of your life path using significant memories or turning points from the past that have influenced your career development. You may choose an age range or a period of time instead of your entire lifeline. This activity is intended to increase awareness of the impact of past events and influences (e.g., context, family, social class, gender, etc.) on your choices and directions.

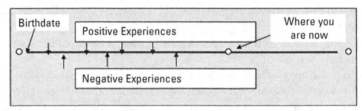

Figure 2: Visual Map of Life Path.

To construct your lifeline:

1. Draw a horizontal line across your paper.
2. Put a dot at each end of the line.
3. Over the left dot, place a zero. This dot represents your date of birth, so write your date of birth under this dot. The dot on the right represents the end of your life.
4. Now put a dot which indicates where you are right now on the line between birth and end of life.
5. Above the line, experiences that were positive, happy, or rewarding should be plotted chronologically. Below the line plot experiences in chronological order that were negative, unhappy, or painful.
6. The distance above or below the line indicates the degree of positive or negative impact or feeling.
7. Focus on experiences that have influenced who you are as a cultural being and the direction of your career development.
8. Try to write at least two or three positive and challenging events or experiences.
9. Label these events or experiences in such a way that you will be able to identify

them. One idea might be to use symbols to identify these different markers on the path.

10. Note the cultural factors that influenced this event or experience — for example, your own cultural identity, family or community influences, broader social contexts, et cetera.

Debriefing:

1. What patterns did you notice?
2. How is your present situation affected by the points along your path?
3. How much control have you had over the events in your life?
4. How did you manage to get through that challenging time in your life?
5. Were there any "allies" along the way?
6. What messages did you receive from important others in your life at that time?
7. What surprising thing have you learned about yourself and your lifepath in relation to influences of culture on your career development?
8. At what points did someone advocate for you or did you advocate for someone else?

Case Analysis

Create a client case taking two or three cultural factors mentioned in the chapter and imagining how they might impact the individual's career choices, resources, or opportunities. Map potential social justice issues that might affect this particular client. How might you work with this client in providing resources and supports?

Community Resources

Explore the social justice initiatives in your community. One way to do this is to interview someone who works at a career centre, an agency, a women's shelter, et cetera. Here are some potential interview questions to get you started:

- What does social justice mean to you?
- Can you give me an example of how you incorporate social justice into your work?
- What are some of the challenges in implementing a social justice framework?
- How has your understanding of social justice/advocacy changed over time?

Uncovering Blindspots

For this exercise, you should work in pairs or with a small group of other students in your class. One student should be the career practitioner and one should be the client. Start by role-playing a client session in which diversity is not focused on at all or is ignored. Then role-play the same session focusing on the same issues, but make diversity a central focus for the practitioner. You might want to switch roles for the second round. Discuss what it was like from both the practitioner's and the client's perspective in both scenarios.

Social Justice in Everyday Life

Sometimes social justice boils down to a simple action in everyday life. Describe a time when you did or said something that could be described as an act of social justice; for example, standing up for a friend or a principle that you strongly believe in. What were the outcomes of that simple action? What challenges or barriers did you encounter in carrying out this act? What did you learn about yourself, about social justice, and about advocacy?

Resources and Readings

Resources

Websites

Counsellors for Social Justice (Canada) <http://www.counsellorsforsocialjustice.ca
Synergos <http://www.synergos.org/>.
EdChange: Choosing Social Justice Activities <http://www.edchange.org/multicultural /activities/choosing.html>.
National Institute for Multicultural Competence <http://www.coedu.usf.edu/zalaquett /nimc/nimc.html>.
Social Justice Organizations <http://www.startguide.org/orgs/orgs06.html>.
Social Justice: A moral imperative for counsellors <http://counselingoutfitters.com /vistas/ACAPCD/ACAPCD-07.pdf>.
Social Justice Advocacy among Graduate Students <http://muse.jhu.edu/journals/csd /summary/v046/46.3nilsson.html>.
Teaching Tolerance Activities <http://www.tolerance.org/activities>
Economic and Social Justice: A Human Rights Perspective, by David Shiman: Part II Activities <http://www1.umn.edu/humanrts/edumat/hreduseries/tb1b/Section2/ index.htm>.

Videos on Social Issues

A Land called Paradise by Kareem Salana <https://www.youtube.com /watch?v=sbcmPe0z3Sc&list=PL6146946ABC5A8BA2>.
Democracy Now: website for the U.S. independent news program with international coverage <http://www.democracynow.org/>.

Supplementary Readings

Collins, S., & Arthur, N. (2010). Culture-infused counselling: A fresh look at a classic framework of multicultural counselling competencies. *Counselling Psychology Quarterly, 23* (2), 203–216. doi: 10.1080/09515071003798204

Lapour, A. S., & Heppner, M. J. (2009). Social class privilege and adolescent women's perceived career options. *Journal of Counseling Psychology, 56*(4), 477–494. doi: 10.1037/a0017268

Lee, C. (Ed.). (2007). *Counseling for social justice* (2nd ed.). Alexandria, VA: American Counseling Association.

Miller, M., & Sendrowitz, K. (2011). Counseling psychology trainees' social justice interest and commitment. *Journal of Counseling Psychology, 58* (2), 159–169. doi: 10.1037/a0022663

Ratts, M. J., & Hutchins, M. A. (2009). ACA advocacy competencies: Social justice advocacy at the client/student Level. *Journal of Counseling & Development, 87*(3), 269–275.

Ratts, M. J., Toporek, R. L., & Lewis, J. A. (Eds.). (2010). *ACA advocacy competencies: A social justice framework for counselors.* Alexandria, VA: American Counseling Association.

Toporek, R.L. (2006). An integrative approach for competencies: Career counseling, social justice advocacy and the multicultural counseling competencies. *Career Planning and Adult Development Journal, 21*(40), 34–50.

Toporek, R., Chope, R. C., Tripp, F., & Gluck, R. (2008). Everyday social justice: Applying advocacy competencies in career counseling practice, training, and policy. Retrieved from <http://online.sfsu.edu/~rtoporek/presentations/ncda%20 2008%20social%20justice.pdf>.

five

Professional Ethics, Role, and the Whole Person

GEOFFREY S. PERUNIAK
Athabasca University

PRE-READING QUESTION

1. What are your thoughts on the practical use of ethics?

Introduction and Learning Objectives

It is a common but misguided belief that all there is to practising professional **ethics** is to follow the ethical code of the particular association to which you belong is. There is much more to professional ethics than following a rulebook. In this chapter we look at some of these rules, and examine where they came from and why. There are primary and philosophical principles of ethics that impact us as citizens and whole persons before and after we become professionals. Ethical codes in professional associations are basically tools. It can happen that the rules in such codes are misinterpreted or distorted or given different priorities. It is one thing to talk about adhering to ethical codes, and quite another to actually follow them.

The first part of this chapter explores implications of professional ethics for career development practitioners. Our discussion begins with "Case 1: Moral Issues," an illustration of ethics based on a true story. General concepts and definitions of morality are introduced, as well as an evaluation of what it means to be a professional. We then examine key factors that frame how ethical questions are handled. Code of ethics is one major factor. A principle-based approach to decision making is applied to Case 1 using one of the codes of ethics. Other factors covered include private and public morality, social responsibility, professional dissent, and finally the role of personal character.

The second part of this chapter uses "Case 2: Professional Development" to highlight the often-overlooked and under-valued ethical principle of self-improvement. This approach to personal and professional improvement builds on local knowledge while minimizing costs. Case 2 is analyzed using a virtue-based approach to ethical decision making. Clearly, in a short chapter such as this, it is not possible to do justice to all the complex issues raised by professional ethics. It is hoped that all career practitioners will take at least one course in professional ethics.

After reading this chapter, you will:

1. Understand general ethical concepts including definitions of morality.
2. Recognize the importance of being a self-reflective career practitioner.
3. Be able to distinguish between a principle-based approach and a virtue-based approach to ethical decision making.
4. Utilize the steps in ethical decision making.
5. Have knowledge of the Code of Ethics for the *Canadian Standards and Guidelines for Career Development Practitioners*
6. Understand the importance of self-improvement as an ethical imperative.

Case 1: Moral Issues

Pat is an intelligent, 38-year-old woman living in a rural town. After high school, Pat worked with her husband in their real estate business. When the business went bankrupt and her husband left the marriage, she was suddenly financially broke, a single mother with a 5-year-old son. She applied for a career practitioner job and acquired it only recently. She needs this job, because paid work in town is not plentiful. "The good jobs, full-time with benefits, are all spoken for," she reports. Pat has a two-year business certificate from a college and several years of volunteer experience as the director of a local food bank.

In recent years, the provincial government had offloaded much of career services to the private sector. Pat works for Ted, a private contractor. Ted runs his career services business by securing contracts from various levels of government. Contracts usually run from year to year with no guarantee of renewal. Pat shares office space with two other women who provide administrative support for the project. She works full-time, being paid minimum wage with few benefits. "What really annoys me," says Pat, "is that Ted says that there is no money for professional development. I don't feel competent in my job. Sure, I can make my way through his manuals, but that and a two-year business certificate are not good enough for this job. I want some real training. Sometimes I feel like a fraud."

Ted had informed her that the number of clients seen per month is down; so, in addition to service provision, he is asking Pat to circulate through the town and "solicit" clients. This means trying to persuade clients to sign up for career services. Pat doesn't like this "hidden" part of her role. "I didn't sign up for this," she said. "I'm not going to go around trying to create a demand for my services. It just feels wrong in my gut." She expresses the added resentment that "Ted calls to check up on my numbers all the time. He's on vacation in Europe where he is travelling with his latest girlfriend. So here I am slogging away on minimum wage while he's off on his latest world cruise that I'm helping to fund!"

She may secure a future funding renewal if she recruits people, but that goes against her principle of doing what her job and her heart says — service provision. If she fails to recruit, Ted may fire her or she may lose her job because the funding agency doesn't renew the contract due to low client numbers. She could complain to a labour relations board, but that would likely end her chances for a job from Ted and any of his associates. What should Pat do?

General Concepts

Professional ethics often involves questions of morality to distinguish between right and wrong. **Moral issues** are about what values or whose values are to prevail in securing the rights and welfare of people, and in making the world a better place to live. Mautner (1966) explains that ethics comes from the Greek word *thos*, meaning "habit" or "custom," and he further characterizes ethics, as used in this chapter, as **normative ethics**:

> . . . rational inquiry into, or a theory of, the standards of right and wrong, good and bad, in respect of character and conduct, which ought to be accepted by a class of individuals.
>
> This class could be mankind at large, but we can also think of medical ethics, business ethics, et cetera, as a body of standards that the professionals in question ought to accept and observe.
>
> This kind of inquiry and the theory resulting from it . . . do not describe how people think or behave, but prescribe how people ought to think and behave. This is accordingly called normative ethics, since its main aim is to formulate valid norms of conduct and of evaluation of character. (p. 137)

Again, moral issues are about **values**. They are not necessarily about fact. The question of whether Pat should report Ted for pressuring her to "make up" clients is a moral issue. That Pat actually did report Ted is a matter of fact. Of course, facts contribute enormously to the making of moral decisions, but decisions about facts are not the same as decisions about moral issues.

What makes moral issues particularly difficult are the **value dilemmas** that they raise. The protection of one set of values necessarily precludes another value or set of values. To make no decision at all can result in a decision by default. If Pat ignores Ted on the recruitment issue, then Pat not only jeopardizes her pay cheque and her son's welfare, but also leaves herself open to being blacklisted as a trouble-maker. She might have a hard time getting another job in town. She also puts the renewal of the career services contract at risk and jeopardizes the jobs of her fellow employees. If she obeys Ted, then she stands to undermine her own credibility and that of the local career services office. She cannot easily opt out of a decision here. We will return to Pat later.

What makes morality even more complex is that every person is immersed in an unfolding history of **sociocultural heritage** that includes one's race, gender, and social class. Principles of right and wrong are handed down in this rich, social mosaic and we adopt or reject these principles on an individual basis. Many times we are not even aware of which principles of right or wrong we have adopted. This often makes it difficult to recognize that an **ethical conflict** even exists. That is why it is sometimes easier to see ethical breaches in someone else's behaviour than in our own.

Towards an Ideal Self-Reflective Practitioner

In this chapter we are not as concerned about obvious immoral activities, such as stealing or killing, as we are about the choices between sets of conflicting values. We are striving towards an ideal of a **self-reflective career practitioner**. Callahan (1988) described this ideal:

> An individual acts as an autonomous moral agent when he or she acts on the basis of principles which are not merely imposed from without (e.g., by peer pressure, by some authority) or which have been internalized as a matter of mere habit, but rather when those principles have been consciously evaluated and accepted by the individual as the correct principles to direct his or her behavior. The autonomous moral agent has a clear sense of why he or she acts as he or she does and deliberately accepts acting that way on the basis of a reasoned, reflective conviction that such action is morally right. . . [and] involves the movement be-yond conditioned or "knee-jerk" reactions and merely self-interested behaviors to principled action where acceptance of the principles governing one's behavior is the result of a careful reflection which takes into account the moral integrity of the agent and the rights and interests of others. (pp. 10–11)

There is an expectation that human service professionals, such as career practitioners, should be guided by ethical principles and be especially sensitive to moral issues, as clients may be fragile and vulnerable when accessing the services of a professional. But who are professionals, anyway?

The Profession

Career development is an emerging **profession** in English Canada (Burwell, Kalbfleisch, & Woodside, 2010; Kalbfleisch & Burwell, 2007). Professions usually require a code of ethics for their members. But what is it about a profession that it requires such a code? There is no one accepted definition of "profession," but Webster's International Dictionary (1986) gives many of the relevant characteristics:

> . . . a calling requiring specialized knowledge and often long and intensive
> preparation including instruction in skills and methods as well as the scien-
> tific, historical, or scholarly principles underlying such skills and methods,
> maintaining by force of organization or concerted opinion high standards of
> achievement and conduct, and committing its members to continued study
> and to a kind of work which has for its prime purpose the rendering of a public
> service. (p. 1811)

"Maintaining by force of organization or concerted opinion" might suggest an ethical code as a means for upholding high standards within the profession and protecting the interests of the clients and the public. A focus on intellectual development is also implied in the definition — in our case, this would be attention to career development theory and methods. Thus, a professional facilitates direction and growth, rather than producing relatively static things such as furniture or bricks. Another characteristic of a professional is the ability to work autonomously and use judgement when providing service. Of course, there is a wide range of autonomy in professions depending upon structures for oversight.

One further characteristic of a profession is that it tries to limit outsiders from providing the same service. In older, established professions such as medicine, there is a virtual monopoly over the provision of service. Membership in the profession is a privilege rather than a right. This means that the onus is on professionals to prove they are qualified to provide such services. Finally, professions are self-regulating to a large extent (Bayles, 1988). Self-regulation means that the government has granted a professional group the privilege and responsibility to regulate itself and to protect the public from harm by governing its members, including qualifying and disciplining, in a competent and reasoned manner.

The Resolution of Moral Questions

A number of factors affect how moral questions are identified and resolved. A code of ethical conduct for the profession is the first point of reference. Private and public morality, social responsibility, professional dissent, and personal character are other factors that will be discussed below.

Codes of Ethical Conduct

As mentioned, most professional associations have codes of ethics composed of principles for their members to follow. A principle is a "rule or code of usually good conduct by which one directs one's life or actions" (Webster's Third International Dictionary, 1986, p. 1803). For instance, the code of ethics for the *Canadian Standards and Guidelines for Career Development Practitioners* or S&Gs (National Steering Committee, 2004) outlines 17 principles that cover competency and conduct (9 principles), the practitioner-client relationship (6 principles), and consultation with other professionals (2 principles). The British Columbia Career Development Association's (BCCDA) code of ethics provides 13 principles for their members (BCCDA, 1996), with slightly different emphasis than the Canadian Standards. The code of ethics for the Career Development Association of Alberta (2009) has a set of 13 principles that again look different than the other two codes but cover much of the same territory — respect for the client, beneficence, non-malfeasance, and integrity.

SPOTLIGHT: *PRINCIPLES OF ETHICS*
by Lara Shepard

The Principles of Ethics represent goals that professionals aspire to. There are five fundamental principles that form the foundation of ethical codes:

1. *Autonomy*: Professionals have a duty to treat the client according to the client's desires, within the bounds of accepted treatment, and to protect the client's confidentiality.
2. *Non-maleficence*: Professionals have a duty to protect the client from harm.
3. *Beneficence*: Professionals have a duty to act for the benefit of others.
4. *Justice*: Professionals have a duty to be fair in their dealings with clients, colleagues and society.
5. *Fidelity*: Professionals have a duty to be honest and trustworthy in their dealings with people.

Principles can overlap each other as well as compete with each other for priority. Principles may at times need to be balanced against each other, but, otherwise, they are intended to act as a guide to practice.

Key Resources

- The *Canadian Standards and Guidelines for Career Development Practitioners*. The Standards and Guidelines <http://career-dev-guidelines.org/career_dev/index.php/the-standards-guidelines/the-sgs-at-a-glance>.
- British Columbia Career Development Association (BCCDA) Code of Ethics <http://www.bccda.org/codeOfEthics.cfm>.
- Career Development Association of Alberta (CDAA) Code of Ethics <http://www.careerdevelopment.ab.ca/Default.aspx?pageId=1184755>.

Implementing the Ethical Decision-Making Model

The *Canadian Standards and Guidelines for Career Development Practitioners'* Code of Ethics (National Steering Committee, 2004) includes a set of problem-solving steps in the resolution of an ethical dilemma called "Steps in Ethical Decision-Making" (see Appendix A). It may be helpful to apply the Code of Ethics to Case 1 to see how a principle-based method might work in practice. (Before proceeding, please review the principles of the code and the steps in Appendix A.)

1. The *first step* in the ethical decision-making method is to recognize that an ethical dilemma exists. Unfortunately, no rule tells us how to do this. Pat was troubled by Ted's directive to solicit clients for the business. Upon reflection, she was able to articulate: "I'm not going to go around trying to create a demand for my services. It just feels wrong in my gut."
2. The *second step* is to identify the ethical issues involved, the parties concerned, and the principles that apply from the Code of Ethics. Pat knew that her ethical issue involved herself, her boss, her clients, and the community-at-large. Pat reviewed each principle of the Code in light of her reluctance to solicit clients and could see her employer was in violation of four of the principles as follows:

    i. *Marketing* (Principle 1.e.) indicates that practitioners should "maintain high standards of integrity in all forms of advertising, communications, and solicitation and conduct business in a manner that enhances the field" (S&G's Code of Ethics, 2004, p. 131). We see from Pat's case that these high standards of integrity are compromised when she is expected to "raise" more clients. How far should she go in selling her services? Should she trick people into a service they have not asked for? This is a slippery slope. Also, this is not bread she is selling but a very personal activity.
    ii. *Relations With Institutions and Organizations* (Principle 1.f.) indicates that practitioners should "encourage organizations, institutions, customers and employers to operate in a manner that allows the career development

practitioner to provide service in accordance with the Code of Ethics" (p. 131). Again, there is reason for Pat to resist her employer's entreaties in this respect. Ted is pressuring Pat to break principles in the Code.

iii. *Integrity/Honesty/Objectivity* (Principle 2.a.) cautions practitioners to be "aware of their own personal values and issues and avoid bringing and/or imposing these on their clients" (p. 132). If Pat follows Ted's directive, it is clear that her own concerns about job security are conflicting with her professional conduct towards potential clients.

iv. *Conflict of Interest* (Principle 2.f.) advises that practitioners "do not exploit any relationship to further their personal, social, professional, political, or financial gains at the expense of their clients . . ." (p. 133). Once again, if Pat actively seeks out clients in the manner Ted suggests, she would be exploiting potential clients for financial gain, clearly a conflict of interest.

3. *Step 3* calls for an analysis of the risks and benefits of any proposed action. We did part of this analysis earlier in the chapter under "General Concepts," when we saw that there were drawbacks to following Ted's directions as well as real risks in not doing so. The risks involved the limited job opportunities in a small town and the need to put bread on the table. Pat first proposed talking to Ted about his directive and attempted to convince him to change it. If she was unsuccessful, then the next step might be to approach some of Ted's colleagues and friends in the hope that they could change his mind. If that proved unsuccessful, Pat believed that, although she might lose her job, jeopardize her future prospects, and place a strain on the family finances, her self-esteem and peace of mind demanded that Ted's directive be challenged.

4. *Step 4* is to take action and review the results with a view to making appropriate adjustments along the way. Pat tried talking to Ted to get him to change his mind. He refused. One adjustment she made then was to approach his colleagues, but they declined to interfere. Finally, Pat reported her boss to a legal body responsible for labour practices in the province, and at the same time initiated a search for new employment in the area.

5. Finally, *Step 5* asks the practitioner to review the whole episode and consider how to best prevent such an occurrence in the future. The review would also highlight what the practitioner had learned from the experience and how that learning would affect his or her future performance. In this case, Pat did not see how she could have prevented Ted from issuing his demands. On the other hand, she was proud that she recognized there was a problem and that she took action consistent with her values, even at the expense of her financial security. She recognized that without a union, she was on her own in this kind of situation. She would put more emphasis on seeking unionized work in the future.

Private and Public Morality

In addition to codes of ethics, private and public morality is a major factor in the identification and resolution of ethical questions. As multidimensional beings, we fulfill many roles in our lifetime. We can simultaneously be parent, child, spouse, executor of a will, neighbour, and citizen. The norms of **private morality** would usually apply across such roles. Private or individual morality is ordinary, everyday morality that applies to people within the social and historic norms of the culture, and relates to how we conduct ourselves in our relations with others. For instance, we know that it is wrong to steal, lie, cheat, and kill — these are norms that apply across all roles. However, there are some occupational roles that seem to have their own rules with respect to morality. If you are a judge, then you may send people to prison or even to death. A defence lawyer may try to trick an honest witness and defend a liar. These are not responsibilities given to the ordinary citizen. These are special occupational roles that confer special moral privileges. This is known as **public morality** (Nagel, 1988).

One of the big questions raised by private/individual versus public/occupational morality is the extent to which the latter can escape from the considerations of morality that apply to ordinary citizens. In other words, to what extent and under what conditions does public morality trump private morality? If you are a career practitioner then it is unlikely that this occupational role will shield you from the obligations of private morality. The role is only at the early stages of being professionalized in English Canada and it does not come with such power or responsibility to slip the normal bounds of private morality.

Social Responsibility and Professional Dissent

Sometimes there may be a social responsibility on the part of the professional to disagree with his or her employer. We saw this illustrated earlier with Pat. When, in what ways, and to what extent are the individuals within a corporation accountable for moral misdeeds committed by that organization? When is there an obligation on the professional to oppose official policy or practice of his or her organization?

Personal Character

There is a final factor that is involved in moral questions and that is the character and personality of the career practitioner. As May (1988) stated:

> The practitioner's perception of role, character, virtues and style can affect the problems he [or she] sees, the level at which he tackles them, the personal presence and bearing he brings to them, and the resources with which he survives moral crises to function another day. (p. 408)

This personal character factor yields a diversity of counsellor perspectives and has led to a virtue-based ethical approach to decision making in organizations such as the Canadian Counselling and Psychotherapy Association (Schulz, Sheppard, Lehr, & Shepard, 2006). Virtue-based approaches recognize that emotional and intuitive aspects of a counsellor's personality play an important role in decision making beyond the rational and cognitive elements of the principle-based approach discussed earlier for Pat's case. Case 2 will illustrate a virtue-based approach.

Furthermore, we differ in our capability for critical self-reflection when faced with moral crises of consciousness, dilemmas of confidentiality, or conflicts of interest. Also, the self is not static, and the ability of the self to change and grow must be considered.

Self-Improvement, Awareness, and Development

One of the tenets of professionalism is the practitioner's commitment to self-improvement. We recognize that learning needs continue regardless of the credential we have obtained. I believe that the continuing self-development of the practitioner is greatly underestimated in importance. For example, of the 72 ethical guidelines provided in the Canadian Counselling and Psychotherapy Association (CCPA) Code of Ethics (Schulz et al., 2006), only one directly addresses the professional and personal development of the practitioner. In the S&Gs' Code of Ethics, *Principle 1.b of "self-improvement"* is mainly aimed at the role and the field of practice, not the whole person: "Career development practitioners are committed to the principle of lifelong learning to maintain and improve both their professional growth and the development of the field in areas of knowledge, skills and competence" (p. 131).

This is not surprising since most codes of ethics are devoted to ensuring proper standards of practice, quality assurance, and an overarching emphasis on the clients and the service provided. While this emphasis is laudable and understandable in the professionalization of the field, it minimizes the role of self-develop-ment among the layers of rules and regulations. There is a singular lack of attention to the development of the whole person and his or her relationship to the professional role.

A large component of the career practitioner's time is spent in **experiential learning** both before and after the attainment of specific professional credentials. This type of learning is fundamental to the identity and essence of the whole person-practitioner. It is assumed here that what facilitates the person also facilitates the practitioner — that the practitioner is part of the whole person and best integrated as such. Furthermore, it is assumed that of the many elements of experiential learning, only some pertain directly to the practitioner role, but all may enhance insights and critical reflection of the whole person in a developmental progression towards points of view that are more inclusive, discriminating, permeable, and integrative of experiential learning (Mezirow, 1991, 2006).

Different roles sometimes call upon different aspects of the self to show up. Here, *role* is defined as "a function performed by someone or something in a particular situation, process, or operation" (Webster's International Dictionary, 1986). *Self* refers to "an aspect of one's personality predominant at a certain time or under certain conditions" (Webster's International Dictionary, 1986, p. 2059). Horowitz (2008) talked about how roles are adopted by a person in terms of that person's committee of selves and he asked, "Which self is the chair?" In other words, which of the many parts of your personality will assume leadership in this situation? He suggested that different selves emerge from different emotional states (e.g., the angry self, the self-righteous self), but they can also emerge from different roles (e.g., the judicial role, the daughter role, the office role, etc.). One challenge is to integrate these various selves so that they all contribute to one another, and ultimately to a lasting sense of fulfillment.

SPOTLIGHT: *BOUNDARIES*
by Waylon Greggain

Boundaries make the relationship professional and safe for the client, and set the parameters within which services are delivered. Professional boundaries typically include fee setting, length of a session, time of session, personal disclosure, limits regarding the use of touch, and the general tone of the professional relationship. In a more subtle fashion, the boundary can refer to the line between the self of the client and the self of the therapist.

The primary concern in establishing boundaries with each individual client must be the best interests of the client. Except for behaviours of a sexual nature or obvious conflict of interest activity, boundary considerations often are not clear-cut matters of right and wrong. Rather, they are dependent upon many factors and require careful thinking through all of the issues, always keeping in mind the best interests of the client. The practitioner has a fiduciary duty to act in the best interest of the client. Being ultimately responsible for managing boundary issues, the practitioner is accountable should violations occur. Given the power imbalance that is inherent in the professional/client relationship, clients may find it difficult to negotiate boundaries or to recognize or defend themselves against boundary violations. Clients, if unaware of the need for professional boundaries, might at times even initiate behaviour or make requests that could constitute boundary violations. (Herlihy & Corey, 2006)

Case 2: Professional Development

It has been said that necessity is the mother of invention. Such might apply to the following case. Career practitioners working in rural communities face a number of challenges in pursuit of professional development. First, there is often not enough money to cover travel, subsistence, accommodation, and professional fees to send rural practitioners to the city for training. To bring an expert from the city into the community is also expensive, with not enough practitioners in need of training to justify the costs. A regional approach would often attract more practitioners, but the problem of rural travel brings the discussion full circle (Dickson, Koons, McElligot, Peruniak, & Speers, 2007).

I have been a member of a local, rural professional development group for nine years. It was not what I had in mind when we started. In the spring of 2003, many government and non-government agencies in Alberta were challenged with limited resources. Services were being privatized. Staff and budget cuts had been ongoing for several years. Increased workloads were leading to high levels of stress and burn-out in career practitioners.

Building a Local Professional Development Network

Shaky Beginnings

The impetus for a local professional development network came from two career practitioners who felt we should be able to do professional development locally. We approached the provincial body of career practitioners about setting up a local chapter. Yes, there was start-up money, but everyone in the group had to belong to the provincial body and pay association dues. After several unsuccessful starts, we realized that people did not wish to pay dues and that to get a stable number of participants we could not insist that everyone be a formal career practitioner. We invited counsellors and other human service providers as well. We finally had a group of five regular members.

Our informal style — no formal agenda, no minutes, no chairperson — belied an implicit agenda of discovering what we were to be doing together. We grappled with what our professional development would look like. Ideas ranged from (a) developing a structural framework for assessing the possible negative side effects of human services through the work of John McKnight (1989), (b) developing a community manifesto, or (c) changing the mandate of a local human service provider. But something was wrong with all these ideas. One of the counsellors identified it: "I spend all day helping solve other people's problems. The last thing I need is to belong to a group that wants to solve more problems. Maybe problems are the problem."

Specifically, we realized that our preoccupation for solving other people's problems — external problems — prevented us from examining our own. No one had asked us to solve a "community" problem. It slowly began to dawn on us that we were the community. But how could we need help? After all, we were the professionals. We help others. To help ourselves is to admit that we need helping, not an easy admission when you are getting to know new colleagues. Besides, wasn't it selfish to serve ourselves first? How could we justify getting time off from work in order to meet? As it turned out, several of us could not. Therefore, we scheduled meetings after work.

Our early meetings examined the challenges each of us faced in our professional role. We looked at how our role could benefit from having our "whole self" come to work. We studied how so-called efficiencies in our respective workplaces cut a wedge between our role and our whole self. Numbers counted; creativity did not. Onnismaa (2004) discussed the impact of a disturbingly similar, business-like trend with counsellors — a marketing approach, superficial measures of client satisfaction, and quality that had come to mean only the absence of mistakes. We pondered how to respond. We shared perspectives. The insights that emerged became the impetus for our meetings. We legitimized, at least to ourselves, why what we were doing was valuable. For example, if we as professionals became burned-out, our contributions to our larger community would be diminished. This led us to see the strengthening of our professional resiliency as an appropriate professional development activity. Over the years, we have examined our own stories through topics such as barriers to communication, differences between listening and hearing, impacts of limited resources on staff, impacts of performance appraisals and wage disparity, importance of organizational culture, burn-out, and strategies for implementing change.

We became less concerned with trying to justify our activities to the workplace and more engrossed in how our larger self interacted with our role. We thought it was telling of the schism between role and person that our personal and professional insights would never appear on the annual performance assessment. For instance, several of our participants were able to identify that they were not happy in their present workplace, that it was constricting the development of their whole self, and affecting their work performance. Subsequently, they changed jobs. Other participants changed the way they reacted to workplace stressors. The identification and naming of various kinds of discontent may not hit the radar of a performance review but they have tremendous and long-term impact on who we are as persons. The following kinds of questions acted as stimulants in one of our early meetings:

1. Am I becoming someone I don't like?
2. Am I in a place I don't like?
3. Am I at the back of someone else's bus?
4. How did I get here?
5. What's the worst that can happen? Have I blown things out of proportion?

6. Is my anger [or other emotion] an early warning sign for me to look after myself?
7. Am I happy about how my various roles contribute to a fuller sense of self?

Eventually the group took as its purpose the finding, preserving, and enhancement of ourselves in our work role. In other words, our group explored ways to integrate our professional and career lives with our personal lives. In this sense, we were our own client first. We could see that our group sessions functioned as a form of restorative professional development.

Mechanics

As we went along, we uncovered important elements in this model of professional development. There was no plan. Group size varied from five to eight participants. Meetings were monthly. If most members felt that such a meeting was an added hassle for them that month, then we happily cancelled. We were trying to counter the trend of a prescribed, objective-driven work environment that fostered increased defensiveness and self-protection while limiting a sense of playfulness and openness.

When providing personal, narrative illustrations, special care must be taken to protect participant confidentiality, especially in a small community. Without those narrative illustrations, however, discussion gets bogged down in language meanings. A story gives us a common starting ground from which to raise relevant questions. Space in this chapter prevents a more detailed exposition of the dynamics of the group.

Cautions

This model is simply one example of professional development done in a rural locale, although it is applicable beyond a rural location. It is neither the best way nor the only way to pursue professional development in a local setting. This is not a new model and it shares many characteristics of Parker Palmer's clearance committees in which there is no judgement — only open, honest questions. (Palmer, 2004).

There are a number of limitations to this model. First, not everyone is interested in sharing their experience with others or in examining their beliefs introspectively. Second, there must be the possibility of a degree of trust emerging from the process if this model is to have a chance at success. Third, there must be some tolerance for ambiguity, especially at the beginning, for common interests and directions to emerge. Fourth, power relationships were equal in our group, with no member having their work boss present. Otherwise, a problem of conflicting interests might arise when personal, work-based examples were used to clarify thinking. Fifth, this group seemed to work best with five to eight members. After that, getting "air time" was a problem. Sixth, employers may not be supportive of this kind of model. If work is just about service to others or making money, then employers may not buy in. But if work also concerns the impact of quality of life, including worker participation, then this model may be appropriate (Lowe, 2000, Phillips, 2006). Finally, this model may work best when members come from a range of agencies rather than within a single agency. Not all employers tolerate criticism of their workplace. Because bureaucratic power is real, being too honest with people in the same organization might leave a worker vulnerable to repercussions.

Virtue-Based Ethical Decision-Making Approach: Application to Case 2

In Case 1 about a Moral Issue, the approach to decision making was based on principles: it was a rational, systematic, problem-solving, step-by-step analysis. For Case 2, Professional Development, we will show a **virtue-based approach** to decision making. A virtue-based approach recognizes that in addition to the rational mind there is an important role for emotions and intuitions. CCPA suggests that a series of questions be considered in a virtue-based approach (Schulz et al., 2006, pp. 339–340; Sheppard & Schulz, 2007, p. 4). Each question will be considered in turn with respect to Case 2 about the integrative model.

Question 1: What emotions and intuitions am I aware of as I consider this ethical dilemma, and what are they telling me to do?
Initially the practitioners were feeling beat up and burned-out. Of course, this basic truth did not emerge at first. Who would want to admit to such feelings among strangers? But with enough time and trust, we realized that we all were feeling undervalued and having a hard time reconciling our professional roles with our personal character. These feelings led to wanting to take charge of our own professional development by getting together locally with other practitioners who were similarly concerned.

Question 2: How can my values best show caring for the client in this situation?
Airlines tell us that in the event of a change of pressure and the appearance of oxygen masks, parents should place the masks on themselves before helping young children. Airlines recognize that to provide effective service for others we first need to look after ourselves first. In the local professional development network the clients were in fact us. By recognizing that we were experiencing a conflict between our work roles and our identity as whole persons, care was shown to our clients. In the helping services, it is sometimes hard for organizations, pressed as they are to be efficient, to recognize that in giving help to others there is a danger in neglecting the helper. Of course, unions have formed in reaction to this danger, but not everyone has access to a union and neither are unions completely trouble-free. In showing care for ourselves, we simultaneously show caring for our other clients by enabling ourselves to be the best we can be.

Question 3: How will my decision affect other relevant individuals in this ethical dilemma?
"Relevant individuals" in this case could include fellow employees, family members,

friends, and any others who are working with us. Obviously, finding a way out from feeling beaten up and burned-out would have a positive effect on our personal and professional relationships. This was certainly the premise on which we operated and which our experience confirmed.

Question 4: What decision would I feel best about publicizing?
Would we have acted differently under a wider, more public scrutiny? The choice was to take charge of our professional development or to remain unhappy and reactive in our various agencies. We would have felt good about publicizing our proactive stance.

Question 5: What decision would best define who I am as a person?
Again, we had a choice to remain silent and reactive or try to take charge. The whole point of exploring this model was to integrate our professional development with who we were as persons. Our decisions to get together, to allow enough time for a process to emerge, to see ourselves as our own clients, to opt out of formal structures and agendas, and to trust our whole self were all cumulative affirmations of who we were as persons. In retrospect, we gave ourselves permission, space, and time to discover who we were as people vis-à-vis our professional roles. As mentioned previously, several members changed their employment, not solely because of these talks, but in conjunction with them.

In summary, a virtue-based approach to ethical decision making seeks to uncover clues for making the right ethical choice from our emotional and intuitive life. It seems reasonable to expect that practitioners would use both principle-based and virtue-based ethical decision making to the extent that they supplement one another. Both approaches rest on a foundation of principles even though these principles differ in terms of what senses of the self are most valuable in making an ethical choice — analytic/rational for the principle-based approach and emotional/intuitive for the virtue-based approach.

Conclusion: Implications and Further Considerations for Career Practitioners

Part of the purpose of this chapter was to help situate practitioners with respect to ethics as citizens and as members of a profession, both of which are intertwined. Rote recognition of the ethical principles from a professional code is only the beginning. We need to understand that ethics are not simply an externally imposed set of rules, but come also from within the person through interpretation. Hence in this chapter there has been an emphasis on the personal and the ideal self-reflective practitioner.

Ethics may sound abstract but the effects are very concrete. What we believe to be right or wrong affects our roles, our relationships, and our very sense of self. Like gravity, ethics pervades our lives whether we're aware of it or not. This chapter has advocated for a practitioner who is willing to critically reflect on his or her beliefs of what is right and wrong in the course of assisting others on their journeys. Through such moral self-reflection, we honour the integrity of the service we provide and the role we adopt with the person we are becoming.

SPOTLIGHT: *A MODEL FOR ETHICAL DECISION MAKING*
by Seanna Quressette

Career development practitioners (CDPs) operate in a range of settings, funding structures, and circumstances. CDPs need both the knowledge of the S&Gs' Code of Ethics and the skills to apply the Code across a wide range of service platforms. In legislated counselling professions, skills in ethical decision making are gained through training and exposure to industry recognized codes of ethics, case study reviews, and supervision during ethical decision-making processes. At present, an informal survey of the Canadian career development training landscape shows an array of opportunities for CDPs to gain knowledge of the S&Gs' Code of Ethics through coursework, practical case applications within courses, and case studies. However, in order to advance the profession as a whole, there is a need for organizations and provincial associations to take up the challenge of building a framework for supervision of ethical practices.

Gray (2007) proposed a systemic approach to coaching supervision that has strong applicability to a wide range of CDP settings. We can see that this model includes the key components of the shifting CDP landscape in Canada. To translate this model to a Canadian CDP ethical decision-making skills setting, I propose the following understanding. These points are depicted in Figure 1:

1. The contracting circle represents the client-CDP ethical decision-making interaction.
2. Training methods represents the CDP ethics courses where knowledge, practice, and case study exposure is provided.
3. The evaluation circle represents the in-house review of ethical decision making (when CDPs consult with their immediate managers regarding ethical decisions).
4. The supervisory relationship circle represents a new relationship in the Canadian CDP landscape — that of professional CDP supervisor who sits outside the management relationship. This supervisory relationship could be fulfilled by certified CDPs with a reasonable length of client service experience and advanced training in both ethics and supervision skill.

Supervision is a key tenet of many human services professions. A major step forward in the field of career development practice in Canada would include a systemic approach to ethical decision-making supervision.

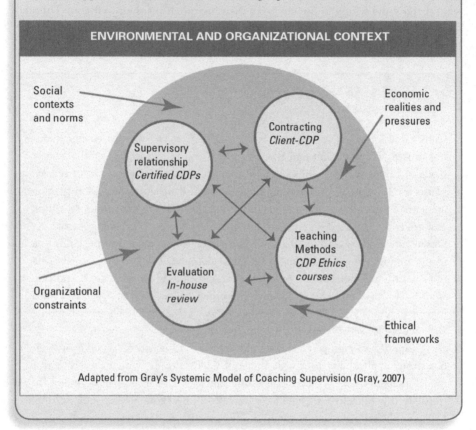

Adapted from Gray's Systemic Model of Coaching Supervision (Gray, 2007)

References

Bayles, M. D. (1988). The professions. In J. C. Callahan (Ed.), *Ethical issues in professional life* (pp. 27–30). New York, NY: Oxford University Press.

British Columbia Career Development Association. (1996). *Code of ethics.* Retrieved from <http://www.bccda.org/codeOfEthics.cfm>.

Burwell, R., Kalbfleisch, S., & Woodside, J. (2010). A model for the education of career practitioners in Canada. *Canadian Journal of Career Development, 9*(1), 44–52.

Callahan, J. C. (1988). Basics and background. In J. C. Callahan (Ed.), *Ethical issues in professional life* (pp. 3–25). New York, NY: Oxford University Press.

Career Development Association of Alberta (2009). *CCDP code of ethics.* Retrieved from <http://www.careerdevelopment.ab.ca/Default.aspx?pageId=1184755>.

Dickson, K., Koons, S., McElligot, J., Peruniak, G., & Speers, M. (2007). Reclaiming the self: An alternative model to professional development. In A. Smith (Ed.), *Building tomorrow today conference proceedings* (pp. 49–58). Edmonton, AB: Career Development Association of Alberta.

Gray, D. (2007). Towards a systemic model of coaching supervision: Some lessons from psychotherapeutic and counselling models. *Australian Psychologist, 42*(4), 300–309.

Herlihy, B., & Corey, G. (2006). *Boundary issues in counseling.* Alexandria, VA: American Counseling Association.

Horowitz, M. (2008). *A course in happiness: Mastering the 3 levels of self-understanding that lead to true and lasting contentment.* New York, NY: Penguin.

Kalbfleisch, S., & Burwell, R. (2007). Report on the Canadian career counsellor education survey. *Canadian Journal of Career Development, 6*(1), 4–20.

Lowe, G. S. (2000). *The quality of work: A people-centred agenda.* Don Mills, ON: Oxford University Press.

McKnight, J. (1989). Do no harm: Policy options that meet human needs. *Social Policy,* Summer, 5–14.

Mautner, T. (Ed.). (1996). *A dictionary of philosophy.* Oxford: Blackwell.

May, W. F. (1988). Professional virtue and self-regulation. In J. C. Callahan (Ed.), *Ethical issues in professional life* (pp. 408–421). New York, NY: Oxford University Press.

Mezirow, J. (1991). *Transformative dimensions of adult learning.* San Francisco, CA: Jossey-Bass.

Mezirow, J. (2006). An overview on transformative learning. In P. Sutherland & J. Crowther (Eds.), *Lifelong learning* (pp. 24–38). New York, NY: Routledge.

Nagel, T. (1988). Ruthlessness in public life. In J. C. Callahan (Ed.), *Ethical issues in professional life* (pp. 76–86). New York, NY: Oxford University Press.

National Steering Committee. (2004). *Canadian standards and guidelines for career development practitioners.* Ottawa, ON: National Steering Committee for Career Development Standards and Guidelines. Retrieved from <http://career-dev-guidelines.org/career_dev/>.

National Steering Committee. (2004). *Canadian standards and guidelines for career development practitioners. Code of ethics.* Retrieved from <http://career-dev -guidelines.org/career_dev/>.

Onnismaa, J. (2004). Ethics and professionalism in counselling, *Canadian Journal of Career Development, 3*(1), 43–48.

Palmer, P. J. (2004). *A hidden wholeness.* San Francisco, CA: Jossey-Bass.

Phillips, D. (2006). *Quality of life: Concept, policy and practice.* New York, NY: Routledge.

Schulz, W., Sheppard, G. W., Lehr, R., & Shepard, B. (2006). *Counselling ethics: Issues and cases.* Ottawa, ON: Canadian Counselling Association.

Sheppard, G., & Schulz, W. (2007). *Code of Ethics.* Ottawa, ON: Canadian Counselling and Psychotherapy Association. <http://www.ccpa-accp.ca/_documents/CodeofEthics_en_new.pdf>.

Webster's Third New International Dictionary. (1986). Springfield: Merriam-Webster.

Glossary

Ethical conflict occurs when two ethical principles demand opposite results in the same situation. Solving ethical conflicts may require establishing a hierarchy or priority of ethical principles, or examining the situation through another ethical system.

Ethics (or moral philosophy) is the systemization and defence of concepts of right and wrong behaviour (Adapted from *Internet Encyclopedia of Philosophy* <http://www.iep.utm.edu/ethics/>).

Experiential learning is inductive, action-oriented, and learner centred with emphasis on the process of learning rather than the product. Experiential learning is often viewed as a cyclic five-phase process where: (a) an activity occurs, (b) observations are shared, (c) patterns are determined, (d) inferences and principles are derived, and (e) learning is applied.

Moral issues are concerned with or relating to human behaviour, especially the distinction between good and bad or right and wrong behaviour.

Normative ethics are concerned with establishing norms, criteria, or standards that define principles of ethical behaviour by which professional practices might be guided or judged.

Profession is a calling requiring specialized knowledge and often long and intensive preparation, including instruction in skills and methods as well as the scientific, historical, or scholarly principles underlying such skills and methods. A profession is a group of people in a learned occupation, the members of which agree to abide by specified rules of conduct when practising the profession.

Private morality refers to conduct that is personal and free from government or societal concerns.

Public morality is a moral and ethical standard imposed by society.

Self-reflective career practitioners engage in active reflection to ensure their continuous development that in turn supports the growth, development, and learning of clients. It is believed that the ability to analyze one's own weaknesses and strengths while planning positive ways to enhance one's effectiveness provides the basis of skills to work effectively with clients.

Sociocultural heritage includes one's race, gender, and social class, encompassing both social and cultural values and practices.

Value dilemmas occur when one's beliefs or principles are in conflict with another set of beliefs.

Values are a broad range of beliefs or principles that are meaningful to a particular group or individual. Values are subjective and based on inner personal experience and occur at cultural and organizational levels.

Virtue-based approach is to work from the premise that a person will be caring and virtuous because it is the "right way" to be. The counsellor is an ethical agent who is able to make ethical decisions.

Discussion and Activities

Discussion Questions

1. What are your views of forming social relationships with your clients? What about after you have completed your professional relationship?
2. What unethical behaviours by your colleagues would you report, if any? How would you proceed?
3. In what circumstances would you break confidentiality? How can you inform clients about issues pertaining to confidentiality and the legal restrictions on it?
4. What is meant by informed consent? What rights do clients have when they meet with a career practitioner? Which rights are most important?

Personal Reflection

1. What kinds of barriers impede a practitioner's ability to recognize that an ethical conflict exists, as called for in Step 1 of the ethical decision-making model?
2. What early signs in the helping process indicate that a career practitioner needs to look after himself/herself?
3. Why is it so much easier to see ethical breaches in someone else's behaviour than our own?
4. Maintaining competency is a requirement of most professional bodies. How will you ensure that you meet this requirement?

Career Practitioner Role

1. What responsibilities do bureaucracies have to provide a healthy environment, free of unwarranted stress and burn-out for practitioners?
2. How can we as professionals help these bureaucracies live up to the aforementioned responsibility?

3. Why is relatively little attention paid to self-development in the professional codes of career practitioners?

Activities

Thinking About Pat

Use the Code of Ethics in Appendix A to identify a second ethical conflict for Pat in Case 1. Analyze the conflict using the set of ethical problem-solving steps as outlined in the chapter?

1. Which ethical conflict is of gravest severity? Why?
2. To what extent is context important to the adherence of ethical principles? For instance, Pat faced real hardship if she alienated her boss by refusing his directive. Should we cut her some slack? If so, how much?
3. Why could Ted not successfully argue, that like any good business person, he was just advertising his career development services in his directive to Pat? After all, to our knowledge he did not specify how she was to solicit clients.
4. Of what significance is Ted's personality in resolving the ethical conflict? Of what significance is Pat's personality?
5. Did Pat do the right thing by reporting her boss to the regulatory body? What other reasonable choices did she have?
6. How does Pat combine principle-based and virtue-based ethical decision-making approaches?

Scenario Analysis

You are a career practitioner in a small town. You work with four other practitioners at a small agency. Through your work with a client, you become aware that one of the other practitioners is engaging in what you consider to be unethical behaviour. You are able to confirm what the client has shared with you.

1. What course of action would you take?
2. Explain why you would take this particular course of action.
3. What ethical principle and what ethical standards in the *Canadian Standards and Guidelines for Career Development Practitioners'* Code of Ethics apply?

Resources and Readings

Resources

Websites

Canadian Counselling and Psychotherapy Association has several resources on ethics including the CCPA code of ethics, standards of practice, and ethics casebook. <http://www.ccpa-accp.ca/en/resources/>.

Videos

Zurinstitute. Part A. Introduction to Boundaries <http://www.youtube.com /watch?v=9G1_0alVkIc>.
Zurinstitute. Part E. Dual or Multiple Relationships in Psychotherapy <http://www.youtube.com/watch?v=Zc0XpuA_5cQ>.

Supplementary Readings

American Counselling Association, Ethics and Professional Standards <http://www.counseling.org/knowledge-center/ethics>
Bingham, R. P., & Wong, G. (2010). My life is a balance. ... In J. G. Ponterotto, J. M. Casas, L. A. Suzuki, & C. M. Alexander (Eds.), *Handbook of multicultural counseling* (pp. 19–25). Thousand Oaks, CA: Sage Publications.
Career Development Association of Alberta <http://www.careerdevelopment.ab.ca /Default.aspx?pageId=1184755>.
Edgar, K. (2013). Rebellion and the absurd: Camus's moral philosophy and ethical issues in career counseling. In C. Jungers & L. Gregoire (Eds.), *Counseling ethics. Philosophical and professional foundations* (pp. 279–301). New York, NY: Springer.
Ethics Resource Center. Introduction: An ethical decision-making model <http://www.ethics.org/resource/plus-decision-making-model>
Guindon, M. H. (2011). Ethics, social and cultural diversity, human growth and development, and career development. In M. H. Guindon (Ed.), *A counseling primer: an introduction to the profession* (pp. 49–65). New York, NY: Routledge.
National Career Development Association: Career Counseling Competencies. Available from <http://associationdatabase.com/aws/NCDA/pt/sd/news_ article/37798/_self/layout_ccmsearch/true>
National Career Development Association: Code of Ethics (Revised May 2007). Available from <http://associationdatabase.com/aws/NCDA/asset_manager/ get_file/3395>
Neault, R. (2009, Feb. 26). The ethics of advocacy: A Canadian perspective. Contact Point <http://contactpoint.ca/the-ethics-of-advocacy-a-canadian-perspective/>.

Patsiopoulos, A. T., & Buchanan, M. J. (2011). The practice of self-compassion in counseling: A narrative inquiry. *Professional Psychology: Research and Practice*, *42*(4), 301–307. doi: 10.1037/a0024482

six

Theoretical Foundations of Career Development

ROBERTA A. NEAULT
Life Strategies Ltd.

PRE-READING QUESTIONS

1. Consider your own career as you read this chapter. Which theories or models seem to fit your own career development? Which do not fit as well? Why?
2. Consider a client whose career path has been quite different from your own. Which theories or models seem to best fit him or her? Which do not fit as well? Why?

Introduction and Learning Objectives

Through reading, reflection, and responding to questions and activities in this chapter, students will:

1. Recognize the importance of gaining a theoretical understanding of career development.
2. Be equipped with a variety of traditional and emerging theories and models to support case conceptualization and interventions with diverse clients.
3. Understand careers from a variety of theoretical perspectives.
4. Gain the versatility needed to support the career development of all Canadians

— regardless of geographic region or individual characteristics.

5. Recognize and accommodate the impact of change and chance on career development.
6. Become familiar with Canadian contributions to career theories and models.

Overview

The role of work in people's lives has changed over generations. Similarly, theories of career development have changed to accommodate the diverse client base that counsellors currently serve. In this chapter, several career development theories and models are briefly introduced. Some will resonate with you more than others; however, all have been found useful for conceptualizing the career journeys of individuals and groups.

The *Canadian Standards and Guidelines for Career Development Practitioners* (National Steering Committee, 2004) specify core career development knowledge, including the ability to describe how human development models relate to career development (C3.1.1), major career development theories (C3.1.2), and how change and transition affect clients moving through the career process (C3.1.3). Although there are comprehensive textbooks available on career development theory, the goal of this chapter is to provide an overview that will inspire you to read more about the theories and models that seem to fit best for your clients.

Vignette

Kim lives in a rural community — about a two-hour drive from the nearest city. The local town has limited employers (a grocery store, bank, several restaurants, pub, coffee shop, medical clinic, and a few independently owned retail stores and salons). There is a mill, a mine just outside of town, and a small industrial park with a variety of businesses focused on services for local residents. Kim is on medical leave from the mine, recovering from a back injury, and won't be able to return to work.

As you read through this chapter, use various theories and models as frameworks for understanding Kim's current career situation. How might the theory or model you choose impact the kind of background information you consider important?

Introduction to Career Counselling Theories and Models

Theories help to explain why careers develop as they do, whereas **models** help show us how to work more effectively with our clients. This chapter briefly introduces some traditional and emerging theories and models that influence our understanding of career development.

Theories and models tend to reflect the eras in which they were introduced. In the early years of vocational psychology, for example, Parsons (1909) was tasked with matching individuals to jobs in the newly industrialized workplace. By the 1950s, Ginzberg and colleagues (Ginzberg, Ginsburg, Axelrad, & Herma, 1951), as well as Super (1957), were moving beyond job-matching to considering how career development was influenced by life stages and significant roles. In the 1970s and 1980s, theorists including Krumboltz (Krumboltz, Mitchell, & Jones, 1976) and Gottfredson (1981) were examining the impact of context and culture on career development. As post-modern reasoning emerged, many career theorists began to explore how to work collaboratively with clients to construct meaning (Cochran, 1997; Hansen, 2001; Peavy, 1997; Savickas, 1997; Young & Valach, 2004).

Many adults currently seeking career support are in the midst of major **life transitions**. Career practitioners will need theories of change and transition to help frame effective interventions for them (Bridges, 2009; Krumboltz, 2011; Schlossberg, 2011). Career theories and models emerging in the early years of the 21st century reflect the rapid shifts of our labour market and the cultural diversity of our clients (Bright & Pryor, 2011; Pope, 2011). In recent years, several Canadian researchers and theorists have made significant international contributions and this chapter will introduce some of their work (Amundson, 2009, 2011; Arthur & Collins, 2010; Cochran, 1997; Magnusson & Redekopp, 2011; Neault & Pickerell, 2011; Peavy, 1997; Peruniak, 2010; Young & Valach, 2011 — of these co-authors, Young is the Canadian). There has also been significant Canadian career development literature published in French and a few francophone authors have also published in English (e.g., Limoges, 2003; Riverin-Simard, 1995).

Theories and models are organized in this chapter into three major clusters.

1. Career Matching theories — focus on placing individuals into jobs.
2. Career Development theories — acknowledge different career issues and needs at various ages and stages of human development.
3. Career Responsiveness theories — recognize the complex interaction of diverse individuals finding and maintaining work in an ever-changing global economy.

All three types of theories influence our understanding of career issues that clients hope to resolve.

Career Matching Theories

Many career theories, particularly some of the earliest ones, focused on matching people to jobs. Sometimes referred to by critics as "test and tell" approaches, such theories help people choose careers by systematically comparing personal characteristics to job requirements or workplace roles.

Frank Parsons (1909) has long been recognized as the father of vocational guidance. In the early years of vocational counselling, Parsons was tasked with helping immigrants and young people to find work. To facilitate this process, he introduced a fundamental understanding of career choice that still influences our work today. There were three parts to Parsons' "trait-factor" framework: (a) self-understanding (e.g., abilities, interests, resources, limitations); (b) knowledge about the workplace (e.g., opportunities, compensation); and (c) understanding the relationship between these two factors (i.e., "true reasoning"). To extend the services provided by his organization, Parsons established the first training program for career and employment counsellors (Hartung & Blustein, 2002).

Parsons' contributions are still often cited. Hartung and Blustein (2002), for example, used his work in making a case for a return to the social justice roots of our field. Parsons' trait-factor focus is also foundational to many of today's career assessment tools, employee screening assessments, job development programs, and work placement initiatives. Tools like our **National Occupational Classification System** (NOC), for example, have been developed to support the career matching process.

Another theorist, Holland (1997), identified six distinct personality types (Realistic, Investigative, Artistic, Social, Enterprising, Conventional; RIASEC). Since it was first introduced in 1959, Holland's theory of person-environment fit has generated more research than any other in the field. Holland's six types can be arranged in a hexagon — such a distribution places Realistic, for example, directly opposite from Social, suggesting that there is little commonality between those two types. (See the spotlight on Holland's Theory of Vocational Types.)

Aside from rich descriptions of six personality types and corresponding work environments, Holland introduced the notions of congruence (i.e., the similarity between an individual's most preferred types and the work environment type), consistency (i.e., how similar an individual's two most preferred personality types are, as arranged on the hexagon), and differentiation (i.e., the degree of similarity or difference between an individual's highest and lowest type scores). Holland's theory is foundational to many of the career interest assessment tools in use today (e.g., Holland Self-Directed Search, Majors Career Exploration Survey, Strong Interest Inventory).

Identifying career goals and securing employment are two major areas of focus for many career programs and services in community-based settings, educational institutions, and even corporate career centres. Although career professionals have moved away from the test-and-tell approach of the last century, career matching theories are still relevant in helping individuals find career direction and are foundational to many of the computer or Internet-based career-planning programs (e.g., CHOICES, Career Cruising). It's not uncommon, however, for matching theories to be used in combination with the career development and career responsiveness theories presented in the following sections.

❖ *Stop and Reflect*

Thinking about the vignette, how might identifying Kim's traits and characteristics help to generate alternate career paths that involve less strenuous physical activity?

SPOTLIGHT: *HOLLAND'S THEORY OF VOCATIONAL TYPES*
by Lara Shepard

The basic premise of John Holland's Theory of Career Choice (RIASEC) is that our behaviours are determined by an interaction between personality and the characteristics of our environment. In choosing a career, individuals search for work environments that allow them to express their interests, skills, attitudes, and values. Therefore, work environments tend to become populated by individuals with related occupational personality types.

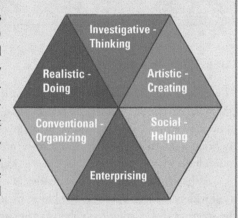

Holland's theory is centred on the notion that most people fit into one of six personality types:

1. Realistic: are good at working with tools, mechanical or electrical drawings, machines, or animals. This type often works outdoors (e.g., in construction).

2. Investigative: are precise, scientific, and intellectual. This personality type is good at understanding and solving science and math problems. They are open to new ideas and often have a wide range of interests.

3. Artistic: are creative, preferring to express themselves with ideas and materials. They enjoy ambiguous, unsystematic activities and work best in an aesthetically pleasing environment, responding positively to recognition. Vocations are in music, art, literature and drama.

4. Social: are drawn to working with, nurturing and helping others with their verbal, interpersonal, and educational skills. They like to inform, train, develop, cure, or enlighten others.

5. Enterprising: prefer competitive environments, leadership, influence, selling, and status. This type can be ambitious, energetic, and self-confident. Example professions include management, marketing, and sales person.

6. Conventional: are precise, rule-regulated, orderly, and unambiguous. This type can be conforming, efficient, practical, unimaginative, and inflexible. Example professions include accountant, clerk, and editor.

Just as there are six personality types, there are six basic types of work environments each directly related to a personality type. People who choose to work in an environment similar to their personality type are more likely to be successful and satisfied.

Career Development Theories

Theories of human development (e.g., Maslow, Skinner, and Erikson as cited in the S&Gs, C3.1.1; S&Gs, 2004) help to explain stages that humans go through in terms of basic needs, behaviours, and identity development. Similarly, career development theories help to explain typical career progression, as well as what happens to individuals when their anticipated career journey is interrupted.

Although there are several theories of career development, the best known and most widely used is Super's (1980) life-span life-space approach to careers. It is beyond the scope of this chapter to explain Super's approach in depth but his 14 propositions of career development are described in detail by Super, Savickas, and Super (1996).

Super, similar to the trait-factor theorists, acknowledged how individual differences impact career qualifications. However, different from the trait-factor theorists, Super added a focus on life stages, identifying a "maxi-cycle" through which most individuals progress sequentially from growth in the early years (aged 4 to 13) to disengagement in senior years (over 65). (See Figure 1.) Although typical ages can be assigned to each stage, Super recognized that life circumstances such as job loss may result in individuals revisiting earlier stages, a process he referred to as "mini-cycles."

Life Stage	Growth	Exploration	Establishment	Maintenance	Disengagement
Age	4–13	14–24	25–44	45–64	65+

Figure 1: Super's Life Stages.

Super was ahead of his time in recognizing the impact of environmental factors on career development (e.g., socioeconomic status of parents) and in introducing the notion of "career maturity" to explain why some individuals seem to cope better than others with career decision making and attachment to the workforce.

He also highlighted the importance or "salience" of a variety of life roles that he named child, student, leisurite, citizen, worker, homemaker, or parent. Super believed that the salience of roles changes across one's lifespan and that sometimes, work may not be the most important life role. This concept is essential for career counsellors to understand because life-role conflict is a career issue many Canadians face (Duxbury & Higgins, 2003; Neault, 2005).

The *Career Development Assessment and Counseling* model has its roots in Super's theory (C-DAC; Super et al., 1996). This model takes a developmental approach, beginning with an intake interview to identify the client's career concern(s). Next, the model proceeds through four phases: (a) systematically considering life- and work-role salience; (b) career development to date; (c) personal characteristics (including values, interests, and abilities); and (d) self-concepts and life themes. Formal and informal assessment data is then integrated with interview information to produce a comprehensive career narrative and the beginning of a collaborative career development plan. Many assessment tools have been developed to complement Super's theory, including the Adult Career Concerns Inventory (ACCI), Salience Inventory (SI), Career Development Inventory (CDI), and Work Values Inventory (WVI). Several of them are available through Vocopher, the learning "collaboratory" available online at <http://vocopher.com/>.

Career development theories such as Super's have particular relevance when counselling members of age-related cohorts (e.g., high school or college students, recent graduates, mid-career changers, or individuals contemplating retirement). The notion of "mini-cycles" is useful in normalizing the experience of individuals whose career trajectory has been temporarily or permanently disrupted (e.g., through job loss, injury, or returning to school as an adult). The construct of salience plays a particularly important role in understanding the career issues faced by single parents, dual career couples, mature students, people juggling work with community commitments or semi-professional sports careers, and adults faced with elder-care responsibilities.

A Canadian tool, the *Blueprint for Life/Work Designs* (Haché, Redekopp, & Jarvis, 2000) is a comprehensive framework for career counsellors, incorporating a developmental approach. Each of 11 competencies has different tasks across four developmental levels. The model also accounts for four stages of learning for each cell in the framework: acquisition, application, personalization, and actualization.

❖ *Stop and Reflect*

The vignette at the beginning of this chapter doesn't mention Kim's age or other life roles. How might age and life responsibilities beyond work impact Kim's career situation? How might you proceed if Kim were 23? 55? A mother of one preschooler? A father of three children in college? Juggling elder-care responsibilities?

Theories and Models for Career Responsiveness

Most of the newer theories and models acknowledge the interaction between individuals and their environments. The focus of career counselling in the 21st century is no longer solely on an individual's personal characteristics and goals. The term **career responsiveness** was originally introduced to describe effective career management in times of significant change and transition — "a proactive, yet adaptable, approach to navigating career journeys" (Neault, 2000, p. 7). Over the years, several metaphors have been used to illustrate career responsiveness (e.g., the Machu Picchu model, in Neault, 2000; kayaking vs. riding a log raft down a river, in Neault, 2002; and most recently, career flow, in Niles, Amundson, & Neault, 2011). The notion of career responsiveness seems to fit many current career theories and models and has been used as a framework for a special issue of the *Journal of Employment Counseling — Thoughts on Theories* (Neault, 2011).

Although introducing every recent or emerging theory is far beyond the scope of this chapter, as is covering any one of them in depth, a few examples will be used to illustrate the general direction that theories seem to be heading towards in the early decades of the 21st century. Themes include **cultural complexity**, change and transition, **collaborative meaning-making**, systems, workplace career development, and **quality of life**.

For the purpose of organizing this chapter, somewhat arbitrary divisions have been made between types of theories and models. However, many of the theories and models introduced could just as easily fit into a different subsection — such is the complexity of career counselling today.

At the end of each subsection, relevant Canadian contributions to theory will be highlighted. As this textbook is written in English, selected theories have been drawn primarily from English publications. It's important to acknowledge, however, that there is exceptional career-related research being conducted in French-speaking Canada and a few examples are included to inspire you to read more.

Cultural Complexity

It is now generally accepted that culture comprises far more than ethnicity; all counsellors and all clients are culturally diverse and bring cultural traditions, beliefs, values, and behaviours to their work together (Arthur & Collins, 2010). Several theoretical approaches facilitate career practitioners and counsellors to engage in culturally appropriate assessments and interventions. Leong and Lee (2006) introduced a *Cultural Accommodation Model* (CAM), identifying a three-step approach to counselling that includes (a) identifying cultural gaps in existing theory, (b) filling in those gaps with culturally specific constructs drawn from other sources, and (c) testing the culturally accommodated theory for incremental validity above the original theory. Pope (2011), in his *Career Counseling with Under-Served Populations* (CCUSP) model, has focused his attention on traditionally underserved populations. He presented a fascinating keynote address at Cannexus 2009 in Toronto, identifying 13 keys for successful career counselling with ethnic, racial, and sexual minorities.

Canadian authors Arthur and Collins (2010) have developed a *Culture-Infused Counselling Model*, comprising three essential components: (a) the counsellor's cultural self-awareness; (b) awareness of the client's cultural identities and worldview; and (c) establishing a culturally sensitive working alliance. Other Canadians have focused their attention on models and strategies to support Aboriginal career development (McCormick, Amundson, & Poehnell, 2002; Poehnell, Amundson, & McCormick, 2006); their *Guiding Circles* workbook and resources have been widely used in Aboriginal career programs and services throughout Canada and beyond.

Change and Transition

During periods of change and transformation, theories to help explain the transition process are important. Career practitioners use several such theories and models to guide their work. A few will be introduced here: *Bridges' Transition Model*, Schlossberg's *4S Model*, Porot's *One Step at a Time Model*, and Prochaska and DiClemente's *Stages of Change Model/Transtheoretical Model*. Riverin-Simard (1995), a Canadian, has also written extensively about career transitions, primarily in French.

Bridges' (2009) transition model identified several "zones." Those most relevant to career practitioners are the ending zone, the neutral zone, and the new beginning. In the ending zone, individuals have tasks to complete before they will reach a sense of closure after a change (e.g., after being laid off, the individual may need to sign a letter agreeing to accept a severance package, complete forms to apply for employment insurance, or empty out his or her office and return property that belongs to the organization). Between the ending and new beginning, individuals find themselves in the neutral zone — a place of uncertainty that has been compared to being "between trapezes" or "walking on quicksand." In the neutral zone, nothing seems stable or routine. It can be disconcerting, but it is also a creative time for hopes and dreams to surface. Eventually, individuals become established in the next phase of life — the new beginning. The individual may have started a new job or returned to school; new routines are established and life feels "normal" again.

Schlossberg's (2011) transition model helps to explain why some people navigate through the same transition very differently than others. She identifies "4 S's" that impact transition: situation, self, supports, and strategies. Her research has considered a wide range of transitions, including those that were anticipated, unanticipated, and what she terms as "non-events" (i.e., expected transitions that failed to occur, such as not receiving a long-awaited promotion or needing to postpone retirement). Career practitioners can help clients navigate transitions by considering their unique situation (e.g., health, significant others, location), self (e.g., inner strengths or challenges, optimism, resiliency), supports (e.g., social, financial), and coping strategies.

Porot's *One Step at a Time Model* (as cited in Bolles, 2011, p. 142) offers another useful way to conceptualize change. Porot acknowledged that making dramatic career changes is challenging. He recommended that individuals consider jobs as comprising two components (i.e., the job title and the field). Shifting only one of those elements at a time (e.g., changing job titles but staying in the same field, or applying for the same type of job in a different sector) can maximize one's chances of a successful transition.

Originally used in health behaviour change (e.g., drug and alcohol counselling), but now widely used within career services, Prochaska and DiClemente's (1982) *Transtheoretical Model of Change* acknowledged that change is a process. They identified that change readiness begins at a precontemplation stage and then moves through contemplation, planning, making the change, and maintaining, sustaining, or relapsing.

Riverin-Simard (1995) summarized her career transition model in an ERIC Digest. She emphasized that transitions:

- are continuous and cyclical;
- involve interaction between people and their environments, resulting in redefinition of relationships;
- require consideration of four dimensions (i.e., analogical, relational, organismic, transactional);
- are completed through analysis, recognizing relationships, preparation, achieving stability, and judging multiple inter-related factors.

These theories address the impact of change and transition on career development. The next section focuses on how career development practitioners and counsellors work together to conceptualize careers within such dynamic environments.

Collaborative Meaning-Making

Increasingly, individuals are being recognized as the experts on their own lives. Many current approaches to career counselling focus on collaborative meaning-making. Savickas (2011) encouraged counsellors to listen for a client's career story from multiple perspectives in order to offer an appropriate intervention. Such perspectives include the actor (i.e., who someone identifies with or resembles; what traits and characteristics are most pronounced), agent (i.e., how someone sets and seek goals), and author (i.e., how someone's identity is unique). Canadian Cochran (1997) also promoted a narrative approach to career counselling that focuses on composing narratives to articulate and understand the main character of a specific career plot.

Another Canadian, Peavy (1997), introduced *Sociodynamic Counselling*, a constructivist perspective, grounded in a philosophy of helping. Using this theory, career counsellors focus on four key factors:

1. Relationship — forming a strong co-operative alliance with the client;
2. Agency — facilitating the client's self-helpfulness;
3. Meaning-making — co-constructing an understanding of key elements of the career decision; and
4. Negotiation — constructing meaningful and realistic career plans.

Systemic Influences on Career Development

Another important approach to conceptualizing career development in the 21st century acknowledges the systemic interactions of individuals and their environments. Gottfredson's (1981) work on *Circumscription and Compromise* was one of the earliest attempts to conceptualize systemic influences on career development. Gottfredson described two key elements: *circumscription* (i.e., the process people use to systematically eliminate career possibilities, often due to what careers are perceived as available to their gender or class), and *compromise* (i.e., the ongoing process of adjusting career choices due to labour market realities, family responsibilities, and access to training).

Similarly, Krumboltz's (1996) early work, the *Learning Theory of Career Counseling*, acknowledged that career decision making is impacted by a complex combination of genetic endowment (e.g., sex, race, disabilities, and special talents), environment (e.g., socioeconomic status, access to education, family influences, culture, and shifts in the economy), formal and informal learning, and something he called "self-observation generalizations" (SOGs; i.e., the comparison of one's perceived abilities with an outside standard). More recently, Krumboltz (2009) has focused on the impact of happenstance on career development, refining his earlier work to become the *Happenstance Learning Theory*. To facilitate career development in the midst of uncertainty, Krumboltz emphasized four elements: (a) accepting that uncertainty is natural, (b) pursuing opportunities for learning, (c) actively creating chance, and (d) identifying, then overcoming, career barriers.

Social Cognitive Career Theory (Lent, Brown, & Hackett, 1994) was built upon Bandura's Social Cognitive foundations, incorporating a focus on such individual characteristics as culture and social context, gender, genetics, and life events. The theorists recognized the impact of individual beliefs on career choices, regardless of whether or not those beliefs were grounded in actual accomplishments, learning from others, cultural influences, or physiological responses to the situations they encountered.

SPOTLIGHT *ON HAPPENSTANCE*
by Lara Shepard

In recent years, Krumboltz has developed ideas around supporting (even encouraging) career indecision (Krumboltz & Levin, 2004). Indecision can be sensible and desirable as clients can create and benefit from unplanned events.

The National Guidance Research Forum summarized the key ideas and implications as follows:

- Open-mindedness should be celebrated, not discouraged.
- Benefits should be maximized from unplanned events.
- Lifelong learning is essential.

Some of the implications for practitioners from this new dimension of the theory are discussed and include:

- Career counselling should be a lifelong process, not a one-off event.
- The distinction between career counselling and personal counselling should disappear.
- "Transitional counselling" is a more appropriate term than career counselling.
- Professional training should be expanded to ensure practitioners are properly supported in this extended role.

Reference
Bimrose, Jenny. (2004) Learning theory of careers choice & counselling, National Guidance Research Forum. Retrieved from <http://www.guidance-research.org/EG/impprac/ImpP2/traditional/learning-theory/>.

Integrative Life Planning (Hansen, 2011) offers another holistic approach to conceptualizing career development. Embedded within an advocacy-based social justice perspective, Hansen has identified six critical life tasks: (1) finding work that needs doing; (2) attending to our physical, mental, and emotional health; (3) connecting family and work; (4) valuing pluralism and inclusiveness; (5) exploring spirituality and life purpose; and (6) managing personal transitions and organizational change.

Patton and McMahon (2006), in their *Systems Theory Framework* (STF) of career development, have addressed the dynamic and complex nature of career development through the idea of three interconnecting systems (i.e., individual, social, and

SPOTLIGHT: *Te Whare Tapa Wha* MODEL FOR HOLISTIC MENTAL HEALTH
by Seanna Quressette

Drawing on wellness traditions of the Maori in New Zealand, Dr. Mason Durie proposed the Te Whare Tapa Wha as a model for holistic mental health. The basic premise is that well-being is like a meeting house: In order for the house to stand strong each wall of the structure must be strong and balanced. In this metaphor the four walls of the house are: te taha hinengaro (psychological health), te taha wairua (spiritual health), te taha tinana (physical health), and te taha wh nau (family health). This framework invites career professionals to move outside the traditional mechanistic view of the individual with skills, attributes, interests, and values that match with labour market needs to a view where the individual is a dynamic, whole, strong structure that can be resilient to shifts in the landscape.

Te Whare Tapa Wha is an optimistic, strengths-based theory that allows for client experiences of success along broad life domains. "To increase the likelihood of making successful transitions, career education and guidance needs to build on clients' knowledge of themselves and their potential for development" (Careers New Zealand, 2012). Given the increasingly dynamic and global labour market, a theoretical frame that provides many options for strategy development and is applicable across a wide range of career development settings is a welcome addition to the career theory landscape.

Reference
Careers New Zeland (2012). Te Whare Tapa Wha. Retrieved from <http://www.careers.govt.NZ/educators-practitioners/career-paractice/career-theory-models/te-whare-tapa-wha/>.

environmental-societal). They've also highlighted several process influences (e.g., change over time, chance), emphasizing how ongoing interactions between systems and processes result in complex, ever-changing career development.

Another systems approach, the *Chaos Theory of Careers* (CTC), has been recently developed by Bright and Pryor (2011). Similar to other current theorists, they emphasize complexity, change, and chance, while acknowledging the importance of engaging individuals in "constructing" their careers. Borrowing from the original chaos theory, their work introduces to career development such terms as "attractors," "fractals," and "phase shifts" to help explain many of the career issues that individuals encounter in today's somewhat chaotic work environment.

Several Canadians have also taken systemic approaches to their work. *Action Theory* was developed by a Canadian, Young, and his co-author, Valach (Young &

Valach, 2004; 2011); it is grounded on the premise that career development is, in essence, an interaction between individual intention and social context. They focus on co-constructed "projects," recognize that the most effective career interventions may occur in natural settings such as the workplace or home, and welcome the involvement of the clients' significant others throughout the process. Similarly, Amundson's (2009) *Active Engagement Model* promotes taking career counselling out of sterile offices.

Two other Canadians, Magnusson and Redekopp (2011), have created a model of *Coherent Career Practice*. They have identified four core elements:

1. Career literacy (the fundamental skills, knowledge, and attitudes required to successfully manage one's career).
2. Career gumption (the energy and motivation to engage in career development activities).
3. Career context (the relationship between an individual's immediate environment and the larger world of work).
4. Career integrity (the balance between personal, social, economic, and community factors, that supports finding meaningful work).

Further expanding upon the systems theories, Canadians have led the way in highlighting the importance of hope and optimism to successful career development. Neault's (2002) research identified optimism as the single best predictor of career success and job satisfaction and, in the *Career Flow* model (Niles et al., 2011), hope is acknowledged as the centre of a career development system that involves the ongoing interaction of individuals with their environments. Similarly, Poehnell and Amundson (2011) have recently written about *hope-centred engagement*.

Career Development at Work

Clearly, one system that is inextricably connected to career development is the workplace. Some researchers have bridged the silos of career development and **human resource management** with a specific focus on career development within the workplace. Dawis and Lofquist (1984) introduced the *Theory of Work Adjustment* (TWA), which described the dynamic, ever-changing relationships between individuals and their environments. More recently, Canadian career and human resource consultant, Pickerell (Neault & Pickerell, 2011) identified four essential elements of employee engagement (i.e., alignment, contribution, commitment, and appreciation) and introduced career management as an employee engagement strategy.

Quality of Life

Building on the systems notion of the interaction of work with other life roles, several current theories and models address overall quality of life. Although not specific to career development, Csikszentmihalyi's (1997) work on *Flow* helps to explain "optimal experience" (i.e., when an individual is so absorbed in work, and it's going so well, that he or she loses track of time). Csikszentmihalyi found that optimal flow could be attributed to a good match between skills and challenge. For highly skilled individuals, too little challenge could result in boredom. On the other hand, individuals who lack sufficient skills to handle challenging situations are likely to feel overwhelmed and anxious. Both extremes (i.e., any significant mismatch between skills and challenge) could also result in apathy.

Influenced by Csikszentmihalyi's work and other positive psychologists, Niles and Amundson developed the *Career Flow Model* (Niles et al., 2011). Optimal career flow is grounded in hope and strategically aligned with environmental influences. Canadians Neault and Pickerell's (2011) *Career Engagement Model* similarly acknowledges the importance of aligning capacity (i.e., individual competencies and organizational resources) to challenge; too little challenge results in individuals feeling underutilized, too much challenge or too little capacity results in feeling overwhelmed, and extremes in both directions result in disengagement. Another Canadian author, Limoges (2003), has written extensively about work-life balance, or maintenance. He suggested that balance results from strategic decisions about what tasks, activities, or activities to hold on to and what to let go of.

Another Canadian, Peruniak (2010), has articulated a *Quality of Life Approach to Career Development*, warning that "quality of life has not yet captured the imagination of career development theorists but it is too important and central to our work to leave to the exclusive attention of other disciplines" (p. 192). He conceptualized quality of working life as influenced by numerous factors including job conditions, leadership, employability, and job security. However, he also recognized that, as a value-based construct, quality of life will be defined uniquely by each individual. All these approaches suggest that quality of life can be enhanced through strategic career and life management — taking on new challenges as skills develop and reducing challenges when resources are stretched too thin.

❖ Stop and Reflect

In the vignette at the beginning of this chapter, Kim's culture is not revealed. What cultural-related information would help you customize your support for Kim? How can taking a systems perspective help you understand Kim's career situation? Imagine if the best work opportunities for Kim require relocation — how might this impact quality of life (both Kim's and her significant others')?

Summary

Some of these theories and models may stand the test of time and, at some point, be referred to as influential. Others may just serve for today as current models illustrating effective approaches for working with clients.

Career theory will continue to be dynamic. We need new theories for exploring the unique social, cultural, and economic circumstances that form the context of our clients' lives and careers. Today is a time of unprecedented technological change, environmental crises, and global interconnectedness. Recent theories and models tend to acknowledge the impact of constant changes, how the meaning of career is co-constructed by individuals and their counsellors, and the central importance of strengthening hope.

Although each client's story will be unique, career practitioners can use theories and models to understand and explore the career issues that trouble their clients. Theories and models equip us with effective starting places to begin to understand what has already happened, what is happening now, and what needs to happen next. Working from a theoretical foundation removes the randomness of an atheoretical approach to career practice and increases our effectiveness as practitioners.

References

Amundson, N. E. (2009). *Active engagement* (2nd ed.). Richmond, BC: Ergon Communications.

Amundson, N. E. (2011). Active engagement and the use of metaphors in employment counseling. *Journal of Employment Counseling, 48*(4), 182–184.

Arthur, N., & Collins, S. (Eds.). (2010). *Culture-infused counselling: Celebrating the Canadian mosaic* (2nd ed.). Calgary, AB: Counselling Concepts.

Bolles, R. N. (2011). *What color is your parachute? A practical manual for job-hunters and career-changers*. Berkeley, CA: Ten Speed Press.

Bridges, W. (2009). *Managing transitions: Making the most of change* (3rd ed.). Jackson, TN: Da Capo Lifelong Books.

Bright, J. E. H., & Pryor, R. G. L. (2011). The chaos theory of careers. *Journal of Employment Counseling, 48*(4), 163–166

Cochran, L. (1997). *Career counseling: A narrative approach*. New York, NY: Sage.

Csikszentmihalyi, M. (1997). *Flow: The psychology of optimal experience*. New York, NY: Harper Perennial.

Dawis, R. V., & Lofquist, L. H. (1984). *Psychological theory of work adjustment: An individual-differences model and its applications*. Minneapolis, MN: University of Minnesota Press.

Duxbury, L., & Higgins, C. (2003). *Work-life conflict in Canada in the new millennium: A status report*. Ottawa, ON: Health Canada. Retrieved from

<http://publications.gc.ca/collections/Collection/H72-21-186-2003E.pdf>.

Ginzberg, E., Ginsburg, S. W., Axelrad, S., & Herma, J. L. (1951). Occupational choice: An approach to a general theory. New York, NY: Columbia University Press.

Gottfredson, L. S. (1981). Circumscription and compromise: A developmental theory of occupational aspirations. Journal of Counseling Psychology, 28(6), 545–579.

Haché, L., Redekopp, D. E., & Jarvis, P. S. (2000). Blueprint for life/work designs. Memramcook, NB: National Life/Work Centre. Retrieved from 206.191.51.163/blueprint/documents/BPFULLEDITION.doc

Hansen, L. S. (2001). Integrating work, family, and community through holistic life planning. Career Development Quarterly, 49(3), 261–274.

Hansen, S. (2011). Integrative life planning. Journal of Employment Counseling, 48(4), 167–169.

Hartung, P. J., & Blustein, D. L. (2002). Reason, intuition and social justice: Elaborating on Parsons' career decision-making model. Journal of Counseling and Development, 80(1), 41–47.

Holland, J. L. (1997). Making vocational choices: A theory of vocational personalities and work environments (3rd ed.). Lutz, FL: Psychological Assessment Resources.

Krumboltz, J. D. (1996). A learning theory of career counseling. In M. L. Savickas & W. B. Walsh (Eds.), Handbook of career counseling theory and practice (pp. 55–80). Palo Alto, CA: Davies-Black.

Krumboltz, J. D. (2009). The happenstance learning theory. Journal of Career Assessment, 17, 135–154. doi: 10.1177/1069072708328861

Krumboltz, J. D. (2011). Capitalizing on happenstance. Journal of Employment Counseling, 48(4), 156–158.

Krumboltz, J. D., Mitchell, A. M., & Jones, G. B. (1976). A social learning theory of career selection. The Counseling Psychologist, 6, 71–81.

Lent, R. W., Brown, S. D., & Hackett, C. (1994). Toward a unifying social cognitive theory of career and academic interest, choice and performance (Monograph). Journal of Vocational Behaviour, 45, 79–122.

Leong, F. T. L., & Lee, S. H. (2006). A cultural accommodation model of psychotherapy: Illustrated with the case of Asian-Americans. Psychotherapy: Theory, Research, Practice, and Training, 43, 410–423. doi: 10.1037/0033-3204.43.4.410

Limoges, J. (2003). A balanced work life: A matter of maintenance. Food for Thought, 11, 1–4. Retrieved from <http://www.iaevg.org/crc/files/Communication_Strategy_No. 11_Limoges740_2.pdf>.

McCormick, R., Amundson, N. E., & Poehnell, G. (2002). Guiding circles: An Aboriginal guide to finding career paths, Booklet 1: Understanding yourself. Saskatoon, SK: Aboriginal Human Resources Development Council of Canada.

Magnusson, K., & Redekopp, D. (2011). Coherent career practice. Journal of Employment Counseling, 48(4), 176–178.

National Steering Committee. (2004). Canadian standards and guidelines for career development practitioners. Retrieved from <http://career-dev-guidelines.org/career_dev/>.

Neault, R. A. (2000). Planning for serendipity? Career management for changing times. *NATCON 2000* <http://www.eric.ed.gov/ERICWebPortal /detail?accno=ED461076>.

Neault, R. A. (2002). Thriving in the new millennium: Career management in the changing world of work. *Canadian Journal of Career Development, 1*(1), 11–21. Retrieved from <http://ceric.ca/cjcd/archives/v1-n1/article2.pdf>.

Neault, R. (2005). That elusive work-life balance! *NATCON Papers.* Available: <http://www.natcon.org/archive/natcon/papers/natcon_papers_2005_e5.pdf>.

Neault, R. A. (2011). Thoughts on theories: Editorial. *Journal of Employment Counseling, 48*(4), 146–146.

Neault, R. A., & Pickerell, D. A. (2011). Career engagement: Bridging career counseling and employee engagement. *Journal of Employment Counseling, 48*(4),185–188.

Niles, S. G., Amundson, N. E., & Neault, R. A. (2011). *Career flow: A hope-centered approach to career development.* Upper Saddle River, NJ: Prentice Hall.

Parsons, F. (1909). *Choosing a vocation.* Boston, MA: Houghton Mifflin.

Patton, W., & McMahon, M. (2006). *Career development and systems theory: Connecting theory and practice* (2nd ed.). Rotterdam, NL: Sense Publishers.

Peavy, R. V. (1997). *Sociodynamic counselling: A constructivist perspective.* Victoria, BC: Trafford Publishers.

Peruniak, G. S. (2010). *A quality of life approach to career development.* Toronto, ON: University of Toronto Press.

Poehnell, G., & Amundson, N. E. (2011). *Hope-filled engagement: New possibilities in life/career counselling.* Richmond, BC: Ergon Communications.

Poehnell, G., Amundson, N. E., & McCormick, R. (2006). *Guiding circles: An Aboriginal guide to finding career paths, Booklet 2: Finding new possibilities.* Saskatoon, SK: Aboriginal Human Resources Development Council of Canada.

Pope, M. (2011). The career counseling with under-served populations model. *Journal of Employment Counseling, 48*(4), 153–155.

Prochaska, J. O., & DiClemente, C. C. (1982). Transtheoretical therapy: Toward a more integrative model of change. *Psychotherapy: Theory, Research and Practice, 19*(3), 276–288.

Riverin-Simard, D. (1995). Career transitions. *ERIC Digest.* Retrieved from <http://www.fse.ulaval.ca/danielle.riverin-simard/pdf/Career_transitions_ERIC_ Digest.pdf>.

Savickas, M. L. (1997). Constructivist career counseling: Models and methods. *Advances in Personal Construct Psychology, 4*(2), 149–182.

Savickas, M. L. (2011). *Career counseling.* Washington, DC: American Psychological Association.

Schlossberg, N. K. (2011). The challenge of change: The transition model and its applications. *Journal of Employment Counseling, 48*(4), 159–162.

Super, D. E. (1957). *The psychology of careers.* New York, NY: Harper and Row.

Super, D. E. (1980). A life-span, life-space approach to career development. *Journal of Vocational Behaviour, 16,* 282–298.

Super, D. E., Savickas, M. L., & Super, C. M. (1996). The life-span, life-space approach to careers. In D. Brown & L. Brooks (Eds.), *Career choice and development* (3rd ed., pp. 121–178). San Francisco, CA: Jossey-Bass.

Young, R. A., & Valach, L. (2004). The construction of career through goal-directed action. *Journal of Vocational Behavior, 64*, 499–514. doi: 10.1016/j.jvb.2003.12.012

Young, R. A., & Valach, L. (2011). Evaluating the processes and outcomes of vocational counselling: An action theory perspective. *L'Orientation Scolaire et Professionnelle, 38*, 281–306. doi: 10.4000/osp.1944

Glossary

Career responsiveness involves a constant interaction between individuals and their environments.

Collaborative meaning-making is a social activity that is conducted jointly by a community to generate a shared understanding of a process, outcome, and/or future goal.

Cultural complexity allows helpers to consider a number of dimensions that comprise an individual's understanding of cultural identity (gender, ethnicity, and age).

Human resource management (HRM) is the function within an organization that focuses on recruitment of, management of, and providing direction for the people who work in the organization. Human Resource Management is the organizational function that deals with issues related to people such as compensation, hiring, performance management, organization development, safety, wellness, benefits, employee motivation, communication, administration, and training.

Life transitions is both a process and a stage that occurs throughout our lives and is associated with a discontinuity with the past (e.g., the transition from high school to work).

A **model** symbolically represents a set of concepts or ideas which is created to depict relationships. Models are useful in showing the process or steps involved with working with clients.

National Occupational Classification (NOC) is a national, standardized reference on occupations in Canada. Over 30,000 job titles have been organized into 520 occupational group descriptions that can be used for defining and collecting statistics, managing information databases, analyzing labour market trends and extracting practical career-planning information. Also, it provides statisticians, labour market analysts, career counsellors, employers and individual job seekers a consistent way to collect data that describes and understands the nature of work. The NOC is updated according to five-year Census cycles, reflecting the evolution of the Canadian labour market.

Quality of life refers to individuals' perceptions of their position in life in the context of the culture and value systems in which they live and in relation to their goals, expectations, standards, and concerns. It is a broad ranging concept affected in a complex way by the person's physical health, psychological state, level of independence, social relationships, personal beliefs, and their relationship to salient features of their environment.

A **theory** is a set of interrelated concepts, which together create a systematic view of phenomena for the purpose of explaining or predicting.

Discussion and Activities

Discussion

Discussion Questions

1. Discuss the purpose of taking a theory-based approach to career services.
2. Compare and contrast one theory or model from each of the broad types introduced in this chapter: Career Matching, Career Development, and Career Responsiveness. Consider the years when each theory was first developed and the characteristics of the clients or students that the theory or model was likely based on. How do your selected theories or models fit for the clients you work with (or will work with) today?
3. Some program mandates fit more closely with one type of theory (e.g., age-related programs may take a developmental approach whereas return-to-work programs may focus on finding work that fits individual characteristics). Discuss how you could use theories and models to make a compelling case for changing some of your programs or services.

Personal Reflection

Briefly describe your own career development story, reflecting on how you got where you are today as a career practitioner. Consider how perceived gender roles, socioeconomic status, chance, interests, and failures have impacted your career. Identify themes and patterns within these factors. Apply insights from your career experiences to your work as a career practitioner. Assuming that other people may make career decisions in ways similar to you, what implications does this have for career practitioners? How can you more effectively facilitate your clients' career exploration?

Career Practitioner Role

Watch a movie such as *It's a Wonderful Life, Working Girl, Office Space, or the Pursuit of Happyness*. Take a theoretical approach (e.g., Social Cognitive Career Theory) and conceptualize the client's concerns, using the terms and concepts from the selected theory. What interventions might be helpful?

Activities

1. Reflect on the vignette provided at the beginning of this chapter.
   a) Choose one of the theoretical approaches to examine Kim's career dilemma. How does this theoretical perspective impact your understanding of the situation? What interventions might you choose to support Kim's next career steps?
   b) Choose a different theory or model to use with Kim. How does shifting your theoretical perspective impact your understanding of the career issues? What additional interventions does this new perspective suggest?
   c) Choose a third theory or model that seems relevant to Kim's situation. Does it bring other possible interventions to mind?
2. Reflect on your own career journey.
   a) Draw a lifeline to date, identifying at least five developmental milestones that impacted your career.
   b) Add contextual elements to your lifeline. What external factors have influenced your career journey?
   c) Identify at least three personal characteristics that have remained relatively constant throughout your career to date. What have you been known for, wherever you have worked?

Resources and Readings

Resources

Websites

Career theory and models <http://www2.careers.govt.nz/educators-practitioners /career-practice/career-theory-models/>.
Canadian Career Development Foundation (CCDF). E4. Understanding the career development big picture. *Big picture view of career development theory* <http://ccdf.ca/ccdf/NewCoach/english/ccoache/e4a_bp_theory.htm>.
Life Strategies. 10 Key Concepts in Career Theory <http://www.lifestrategies.ca /docs/10-Key-Concepts-in-Career-Theory.pdf>.

Supplementary Readings

Amundson, N. E. (2005). The potential impact of global changes in work for career theory and practice. *International Journal for Educational and Vocational Guidance*, 5, 91–99.

Bloch, D. P. (2005). Complexity, chaos, and nonlinear dynamics: A new perspective on career development theory. *The Career Development Quarterly*, 53, 194–207.

Bright, J. E. H., & Pryor, R. G. L. (2008). Shiftwork: A chaos theory of careers agenda for change in career counselling. *Australian Journal of Career Development*, 17(3), 63–72.

Bright, J. E. H, Pryor, R. G. L, Chan, E. W. M., & Rijanto, J. (2009). Chance events in career development: Influence, control and multiplicity. *Journal of Vocational Behavior*, 75(1), 14–25. doi: 10.1016/j.jvb.2009.02.007

Inkson, K., & Amundson, N. E. (2002). Career metaphors and their application in theory and counseling practice. *Journal of Employment Counseling*, 39, 98–108.

Savickas, M. (2005). The theory and practice of career construction. In S. D. Brown & R. W. Lent (Eds.), Career development and counseling: Putting theory and research to work (pp. 42–70). Hoboken, NJ: John Wiley & Sons.

SECTION 3

The Nuts and Bolts of Career Development Practice

seven

Developing Effective Client Relationships

BEVERLEY WALTERS
Alberta Institute for Life Skills, Literacy and Business Education

BLYTHE C. SHEPARD
University of Lethbridge

PRIYA S. MANI
University of Manitoba

PRE-READING QUESTIONS

1. What are the characteristics of an effective helping relationship?
2. What qualities do you think the career practitioner should have?

Introduction and Learning Objectives

At the heart of our expertise is awareness.
— Ronald R. Short

The focus of this chapter is to explore the importance of building and maintaining effective client relationships throughout the career-planning cycle. The chapter begins with an outline of the *Canadian Standards and Guidelines for Career Development Practitioners* (S&Gs) competencies related to effective communication and relationship building. Then, the philosophical ideas that influence the way career practitioners envision their relationships with clients are considered. In the next section, the primary needs of clients are summarized followed by an explanation of relationship building blocks. In the final sections of the chapter, challenges to active listening are explored as are ways to work with clients who are unwilling to engage in the relationship.

The following are the learning objectives:

1. Identify the S&G competencies in building effective client-practitioner relationships.
2. Understand philosophical ideas that form the basis for relationship building between the career practitioner and client.
3. Be knowledgeable about the primary needs of the client: inclusion, affection, and shared control.
4. Be familiar with the building blocks of the client-practitioner relationship.
5. Recognize three common challenges to active listening.
6. Consider barriers to client change.

The tools presented in the chapter are not intended to be "used on" clients. The intent of presenting these skills is to increase the practitioner's personal repertoire of skills so that they might position themselves "in" a client relationship with a keen *awareness of self*. Respect for the autonomy of the client including self-determination, providing career development services appropriate for the life circumstances and interests of the client, doing no harm to the client by maintaining a high level of self-awareness, and providing service to clients with competency and integrity are all part of the profession's ethical imperative. As Short (1998) states, "You will shift from managing others to managing yourself with others" (p. 31).

Competencies Required

The *Canadian Standards and Guidelines for Career Development Practitioners* (National Steering Committee, 2004) identify seven competencies that underpin an effective client career practitioner relationship. (<http://career-dev-guidelines.org/career_dev/>)

1. C2.2.1 Work with climate and context to enhance communication to support clients in a courteous, respectful, and authentic manner in order to create a **"mattering" environment**.
2. C2.2.2 Use a framework for verbal communication that promotes a co-operative and productive work environment and that validates a client's own beliefs, values, and opinions.
3. C2.2.4 Use effective listening skills to actively listen in a climate of confidence, openness, and safety in order to understand the client's world.
4. C2.2.5 Clarify and provide feedback to develop clients' abilities to self-assess and to support them in their growth and development.
5. C2.2.6 Establish and maintain collaborative work relationships by recognizing the importance of starting from the client's point of reference.
6. C2.3.1 Foster client self-reliance and self-management to encourage independence and self-directedness.

7. C2.3.2 Deal with reluctant clients by understanding the difference between a reluctant client and one who is simply not yet ready to take the appropriate steps.

The Foundation of the Client-Practitioner Relationship

The changing Canadian economy has resulted in an increased need for individuals to seek assistance with a wide variety of career-related issues. While clients commonly seek information regarding occupational skill development, further education, job search techniques, and job maintenance skills, they also need assistance with a declining standard of living, underemployment and unemployment, company downsizing, and the challenges in making decisions due to the shifting labour market (Larkin, LaPort, & Pines, 2007; Trevor & Nyberg, 2008).

One of the most difficult challenges faced by career practitioners is to encourage optimism and hope in the face of uncertainty (Niles, Neault, & Amundson, 2011). The level of optimism and hope in clients is the only significant predictor for both career success and job satisfaction. Clients often feel a certain level of vulnerability when sharing concerns with a career practitioner; therefore, creating an effective working relationship that fosters hope and optimism with a client requires a foundation built on trust and collaboration.

Career practitioners must take a position of "walking alongside" their clients, and work through issues and concerns in a collaborative and supportive manner. Any positioning of authority within the relationship should be due to subject-specific knowledge and not to status, role, or location in social life (Peavy, 2004). The career practitioner and client are experts in different fields of knowledge, each having something to offer, and each party entitled to respect. Individual differences that exist between the parties are to be explored and nurtured. From this framework, the career practitioner steps away from the self-presentation strategy of being perceived as the sole "expert" and presents a more human face to those they help (Peavy, 2004).

Yukl (2006), a leading writer on organizational leadership, believes that clients have three intra-interpersonal needs — inclusion, affection, and shared control — that must be met before the collective goals of the client and practitioner can be addressed. This shift will happen when clients feel safe and have confidence in the practitioner. "Supporting," Yukl (2006) noted, "includes a wide variety of behaviors that show consideration, acceptance and concern for the needs and feelings of other people" (p. 43).

According to Buber (1958), the issue that the client presents is perceived as the actual problem and is worked out through a relationship that is based on reciprocity (or mutuality), spontaneity, acceptance, and confirmation of the uniqueness of the other. Analysis of how individuals position themselves in relation to "the problem" challenges more traditional views of the career practitioner and offers new insights for career education and practice. From Buber's perspective, the career practitioner, like the client, discovers who he or she is in relation to the other. By seeing the situation from both sides, the career practitioner gains an understanding of the client, and is able to imagine the client's situation while maintaining personal perspective. The client is perceived as more than just the career issue that is presented, and is instead "encountered" as a whole person.

Amundson draws on the concept of "mattering" (Schlossberg, Lynch, & Chickering, 1989) in an effort to make clients feel welcome and important — that they matter. "Mattering" is expressed not just in words but through action. Clients can feel special when they are offered something to drink or are asked to choose which chair to sit on in the office. Within this milieu, the focus is on creating a warm and inviting climate and on giving clients the opportunity to fully tell their story.

Amundson, Harris-Bowlsbey, and Niles (2009) outline three levels of mattering: (a) visibility, (b) **active listening**, and (c) offering of help. *Visibility* implies that the client feels noticed. The expression of acknowledgement starts with the very first contact between career practitioner and client, and can set the tone for the rest of the sessions. The second level of mattering is to *actively listen* when the client describes the problem, thus confirming the importance of the client while providing emotional support. The opportunity for all parties to *offer and receive help* is the third level — it contributes to a sense that each person has something of value to offer. Generally, help is provided from the career practitioner to the client in the form of instrumental support (e.g., providing information, conducting assessments, and discussing the results with the client, etc.). However, clients integrated within a group career psycho-educational experience benefit from the opportunity to help other group members through sharing of personal experiences.

Peavy (2004) suggests that genuine, ethical helping should be offered under conditions of respect for the integrity and uniqueness of the individual. In Peavy's estimation, professional practitioners should make it their practice to:

- focus on alleviating the problem;
- assist individuals in identifying personal strengths and potential;
- improve clients' self-understanding;
- help individuals develop their capacities and strengthen their self-concept;
- increase their capacity to identify meaningful goals;
- recognize the range of choices available to clients;
- help clients to increase the skills needed to perform in the world of work.

The Client-Practitioner Relationship in Action

Relationship building is a two-way street. The helping relationship is not something practitioners "do" to clients; rather it is a process that practitioners and clients work through together. Tuning in to each other, is at the heart of relationship building. This awareness becomes the basis for an approach to counselling called "eyes out" — what do I need to learn about this person? — rather than "eyes in" — what knowledge and information can I bestow on this person? Try folding your arms across your chest as you would naturally. Then, uncross your arms and refold them with the opposite arm on top. You may discover that assuming this position is rather uncomfortable and unnatural. This is what it can be like when building rapport with a client.

Meeting the Client's Three Primary Needs

People need to be acknowledged to feel validated and that their problem matters. To validate someone doesn't mean agreeing with the person's feelings; it means acknowledging those feelings. Clients need to know that they can feel safe sharing their experiences and their feelings. You, as the practitioner, can show that you have been expecting the client and that you are devoting this time to the client's concerns. One way to show inclusion is to acknowledge the client with such welcoming comments as, "Thank you for coming in today," or "I hope you found our office without any difficulty."

Affection or recognizing the impact your personal style has on clients includes showing genuine care and concern for the situation. The "affect" you have on clients will be based on the congruency of your words and actions. If you express your concern and desire to support your clients, then you have an obligation to follow through with actions. The behaviours used to attend to clients should present the message that you are genuinely interested in them. The "affect" you have on clients is the "impact" they experience after meeting with you (intent + delivery = impact).

Practitioner motive(s) + actions = how the client has been affected by the practitioner.

To engage in authentic behaviour with clients means you put into words what you are experiencing as you work together. Actual understanding occurs when we suspend our own personal frame of reference and, through paraphrasing and empathy, show that we have taken into account what the other person means and feels from his or her frame of reference. "This is the most powerful thing you can do to have the leverage you are looking for to build client commitment" (Block, 2000, p. 37).

Shared control is built on meeting clients' needs for validation and affection. It refers to the collaborative nature of the relationship. It involves sharing the conversation in ways that may require practitioners to withhold their comments until clients have finished speaking. It can mean interjecting when clients' stories become cyclical; or, it can mean encouraging clients to say more. Practitioners are responsible for balancing the manner in which information is shared. This "co-operative" method ensures that the responsibility for outcomes of the session is shared between practitioners and the clients; that is, clients need to walk away intending to act upon what has been discussed. Practitioners, in addition, need to follow up on concerns and issues raised in the session. There are times when clients may want practitioners to give them answers and tell them what to do (e.g., Can you do the work for me?). In this case, practitioners will have to guide them towards finding most of these answers themselves. Practitioners might want to give suggestions; however, it is best to avoid giving "advice" to clients. The intent is to have clients act on their own self-directedness rather than on the direction of the professional (S&Gs C2.3.1).

Practitioners have the responsibility of developing rapport with clients. When the three primary needs of clients are met, a relationship bridge is built. Here is an equation for your consideration.

Inclusion (validation and acknowledgement of the client) + *Affection* (genuine care for the person and concern for their situation) + *Shared Control* (equal contribution to the process) = *Safety and Trust* for the client, thus building an effective client relationship.

Relationship Building Blocks

Active listening is often identified as an important interpersonal skill; an inability to listen well is certainly a deficiency. Active listening involves the listener clarifying and restating what the other person is saying. This process increases the listener's understanding of the other person, helps to clarify the client's thoughts, and shows that the listener is attentive to the client's viewpoint. This process stimulates an open exploration of ideas and feelings while establishing trust and rapport. Important to this process is the suspension of value judgements and total acceptance of the client's thoughts, ideas, and feelings. The listener clarifies information by reflecting back to the client what has been heard. The practitioner begins by looking at the person and fully focusing on what the client is saying. In your role as a practitioner, it is imperative that you listen with the intention of understanding as you build your relationship with the client (S&Gs C2.2.4).

There are five specific listening skills that make up the concept known as "attending behaviours" and are identified by the acronym *FIBER*.

F - Following
I - Equal I–Thou language
B - Body Language
E - Eye Contact
R - Relaxed Response

(F) Following

Clients know that practitioners are following them when both verbal and non-verbal responses are used in the listening process. Verbal encouragers should be employed with non-verbal prompts. This could involve using simple spoken terms like "Yes," "Uh huh," "Right," and "Hmmmmm." In addition, reflective listening, by which practitioners restate what clients have just shared (i.e., paraphrasing), demonstrates to clients that they have been heard and understood. When enough trust has been built, practitioners can add further points for clients to consider. Non-verbal listening involves looking appropriately and comfortably at the speaker. Head nods, smiles, and frowns — all are positive attending behaviours. A pleasant tone of voice that portrays concern for the other person's comfort is another attending behaviour. Practitioners' facial expressions mirror clients' words.

> ### Tips for Active Listening
> by Lara Shepard
>
> Active listening involves clarifying and restating what the other person is saying.
>
> 1. Listen to the emotions as well as the words.
> 2. Be sincerely interested in what the other person is talking about.
> 3. Restate what the person said.
> 4. Ask clarification questions once in a while.
> 5. Be aware of your own feelings and strong opinions.
> 6. If you have to state your views, say them only after you have listened.

(I) Equal I–Thou Language

I–Thou Equality is an attitudinal skill that involves "staying on the client's rock" when listening. The relationship is one of equality and balance and shows respect for others as equal human beings, even though the roles are different. Practitioners do not take over the conversation or the space through story-telling, or body posture, or by any questions or comments that might be inappropriately timed.

Empathic listening is perhaps the most important listening skill and involves remaining focused on clients at all times and providing safe and respectful environments by paraphrasing, clarifying, questioning, and remembering details of clients' stories.

(B) Body Language

Physical attending is the way practitioners use *body language* to communicate understanding to clients: square shoulders, an open posture, leaning slightly forward, making eye contact, and maintaining a relaxed position. The body must be quiet from the neck down avoiding any fidgeting behaviours. Practitioners' bodies are often synchronized with their clients; they may find that they automatically shift positions as their clients move.

(E) Eye Contact

Eye contact allows practitioners to let clients know they are "observing" what is being said and that they are not distracted by other movements such as someone walking by. However, adjustment is often necessary when listening to individuals whose cultural norms do not include direct eye contact. Eye contact is not staring or glaring; it encompasses observing faces of clients, reading their lips, viewing their expressions, and, when appropriate, making direct eye contact.

(R) Relaxed Response

A *relaxed response* indicates to clients that you have time to listen to them. Practitioners are quiet, still, and purposeful in their responses, responding in a relaxed manner that does not rush clients. Practitioners ensure that there are no interruptions and their body language shows that their focus is solely on their clients. Practitioners much learn to quiet down their own thinking in order to hear completely.

A process known as *tracking* is a great listening tool. Our minds can think more than twice as fast as people can speak. It is therefore necessary for us to repeat the client's words in our own head to avoid our own mind chatter from running ahead of clients, or drifting off into our own thoughts (Walters, 1992). Remember that people feel validated when they feel heard. Repeating the main point of their issue or concern lets them know their message was received. You might offer the following: "I understand you to say …", or "I'll summarize what you've said just to ensure I've heard it correctly."

What Not to Do — Blocks to Communication

by Lara Shepard

Active listening means not judging what is being said, and controlling the urge to provide information. Any of the following actions can stop communication dead in its tracks.

• "Why" questions, which tend to make people defensive.

• Quick reassurance, saying things like, "Don't worry about that."

• Advising — "I think the best thing for you is to move to assisted living."

• Digging for information and forcing someone to talk about something they would rather not talk about.

• Patronizing — "You poor thing, I know just how you feel."

• Preaching or lecturing — "You should" or "You shouldn't ..."

• Interrupting — May indicate that you are not interested in what someone is saying.

Stumbling Blocks to Active Listening

There can be several stumbling blocks to active listening: insufficient time, clients who are not sure of their career-related needs, and the inappropriate use of questions.

SPOTLIGHT: *ENGAGEMENT/INVITATIONAL SKILLS*
by Lara Shepard

Eye Contact
- Suggests that you are attending to what the other is saying.
- Should be natural and culturally appropriate.
- Is more likely to be modified when a break in discussion occurs or when either party is thinking.
- Can signal understanding and provide feedback.

Body Posture
- Should be natural, attentive, relaxed, and communicate interest.
- Gestures should be easy and natural.
- Facial expression should be appropriate to the material under discussion.

Verbal Responses
- Should be made in a warm and expressive tone, made at an appropriate pace, and communicate involvement.
- Should follow from the client's comments.
- Should relate to previous aspects of the client's story when the topic being discussed is exhaustive.
- Should be made with regard to both the verbal (content and tone) and the non-verbal (glances, gestures, and other physical reactions) behaviour and culture of the client.

Silence
- May occur, since clients need time to think.
- Can be a positive form of communication.
- Should not become excessive without an interviewer response.

From: Evans, D. R., Hearn, M. T., Uhlemann, M. R., & Ivey, A. E. (2004). *Essential interviewing: A programmed approach to effective communication* (6th ed.). Toronto, ON: Thomson & Brooks/Cole.

Insufficient Time

Lack of sufficient time to listen to a client's story is a common problem. Many organizations that employ career development practitioners are contracted by their provincial or federal governments to offer career development services. Unfortunately, the time a practitioner can spend with each client might be dictated by the terms of this contract. In these situations, it is necessary for the practitioner to inform the client, on the first visit, that additional appointments may be necessary.

Lack of Clarity

The second stumbling block is the client who, being unsure about the problem, describes the situation through many stories. It becomes the practitioner's task to figure out what concern the client wants to address. There may be an individual or cultural characteristic that predisposes the client to give a great deal of background information before making a request. In this situation, the FIBER concepts of Relaxed Response and Following provide appropriate responses. Let clients talk and, when you think you have heard the root of their concern, you will need to intervene (not interrupt) and state what you have heard. Then lead clients towards the next steps in problem solving and action orientation.

A Case Example

In this scenario, a recent immigrant described his work situation to the career practitioner.

Back home in my country, we have a lot of war and it is very hard to make a future for myself and my family. I have two brothers and a sister who are working in Canada now and I was sponsored by my brother to come here. He wanted me to have a better chance than I had back home. He told me that I could go to school to better my English and there were places that I could find work. My friend told me to come here. He came here last year and you helped him so he told me to come here. He speaks English very well. I know that I don't speak it that well. I need a job so I can support my family but I can't find a job because I don't speak English well. My wife stays home with my kids and she doesn't need English. My kids learn it in school.

The practitioner's intervention would be to say the following:

- I understand the many reasons you came to Canada and I'm glad to hear that you have had the support of family and friends since you arrived. (Validate)
- I just want to repeat what I've heard you say so I know I've understood you correctly. (Care for the Person)
- You would like to learn more English and you would like to work in Canada. (Concern for their Situation)
- What is more important for you right now? (Shared Control)
  — Do you want to go to school to learn English?
  — Do you want to find work right now?
  — Do you want a program that lets you learn English and helps you find a job?

In this scenario, the practitioner met the primary needs of the client: inclusion (validation), affection (genuine care for the person and concern for their situation), and shared control (questions posed by the practitioner to gain the client's perspective or answers).

As the time scheduled for a first meeting might be limited, the practitioner must acknowledge the client by listening to the story, while trying to identify the issue to be addressed, and then intervening with a supposition. Intervention is not an interruption of a client's story. The intervention is timed carefully to ensure the client does not get lost in the story, especially if unsure of how to ask for support. The practitioner gets a contextual picture of the client's circumstances and is then able to lead the client towards identifying specific issues.

Building the relationship is accomplished by the practitioner showing understanding for the client's circumstances. The practitioner listens with the intention of discovering the issue that needs to be addressed, and uses questions to determine if there is a shared understanding of the client's needs (S&Gs C2.2.1). Whereas empathy is the accurate understanding of the world from the client's perspective, **validation** is the active communication that the client's perspective is real. To validate means to confirm and to authenticate. The primary need of inclusion is expressed through validation. Listening with intention is validating to the client. Taking a genuine interest in a client by asking the critical questions that need to be answered is validating. The practitioner listens carefully to the client's point of view and realizes how much it is influencing the client's behaviour. The practitioner realizes that at some point this perspective may need to be confronted or challenged because it may be this outlook that is keeping the client stuck. Active listening and other relationship-building skills are supportive and encourage a client to open up, but it is by asking difficult questions that the client will begin to examine choices, feelings, and thoughts critically.

Use of Questions

Questions are a critical component of the interview: Well-phrased questions will build trust and gather information — the client may be encouraged to volunteer information and think about the issues; poorly phrased questions can quickly close down the conversation and damage the relationship. Questions are most valuable when they challenge the individual to think, organize, compare, relate, or draw conclusions. Well-formulated questions are almost guaranteed to stimulate mental activity and generate much useful information (S&Gs 1.4.2). Excessively long or poorly formulated questions may distract the client from listening, or worse, make the client feel interrogated and evaluated. Leading questions will be seen to be disguised attempts to push through the client's acceptance of the practitioner's agenda. The challenge is to know when to ask questions and which questions to ask.

Questions may be open ended (please tell me about), or closed (how old are you?). Both forms are useful for gathering information but the career practitioner must know when and how to use these.

An **open or open-ended question** allows freedom of expression and encourages the client to speak about the topic: it elicits more information than a closed question. An open question is used to gather lots of information and has no correct answer. As seen in Table 1 below, the question typically begins with who, what, where, when, and how.

TYPE OF QUESTION	TYPE OF ANSWER	EXAMPLE
Who	Answered with a person	Who is looking for work?
What	Identifies a list of one or more options	What kind of work are you looking for?
Where	Answered with a place or location	Where do you live?
When	Answered in time	When will you be ready to start work?
How	Identifies a process/procedure or a measurement in response to the question	How long have you looked for work?

Table 1: Types of Interview Questions.

A **closed question** is used to gather specific information and can normally be answered with a single word or a short phrase. Examples would include: Where do you work? Are you ready to stop doing that job now? Closed questions are good for collecting facts and short answers, and for bringing a talkative client back on track. Although useful for getting the facts straight, closed questions can have a dampening effect on the relationship as clients can feel that their job is to respond to the practitioner's questions rather than to tell their story.

Here are some guidelines for good questioning:

- Use open-ended fact-finding questions rather than closed questions that demand a yes or no answer. Where have you applied for work? versus, Have you applied for work?
- Use open-ended questions for information seeking rather than asking "why" questions that ask for the client's opinion. What skills do you have that match this job's description? versus, Why do you think you would be suitable for this job?
- Use open-ended questions to elicit information instead of direct (probing) questions: How many positions have you interviewed for? versus, Do you usually get an interview when you apply for a job?

You will note that closed-ended questions (such as those starting with the words "have you" and "do you") give a limited response. Closed-ended questions can be used to confirm information; however, they do not generate new information.

Why was not included on the list of critical elements of action inquiry for a very good reason. Why is considered a deficiency-based question, often requiring a justification from the client rather than an explanation. It is often misused or over-used and carries a negative impact for the client. Characteristics of "why" questions that form stumbling blocks to the relationship:

- WHY may pose a threat: Why did you leave your last job?
- WHY implies blame or wrong: Why didn't you call them to tell them you might be late for the appointment?
- WHY implies that there is an intention behind the question and the answer you get may not be truthful: Why were you not looking for work during the month of August?
- WHY puts people on the spot and individuals will often defer or avoid a why question: "Why didn't you include a cover letter?" "I don't know."

As you can see the why question can close conversations and can create a conflict between people because the question implies a big "I" and a little "thou."

If you want your questions to be answered factually and without ambiguity, it is important to choose your words carefully. People feel validated when they are asked questions that demonstrate someone is truly interested in them and are not just interrogating them. Identify the potential impact of your questions by distinguishing between the various types of questions as outlined in the previous paragraphs.

❖ *Stop and Reflect*
Reflect on the following quotations:

- *Asking the right questions takes as much skill as giving the right answers.* (Robert Half)
- *I love the early process of asking questions about a story and deciding which questions matter most.* (Diane Sawyer)
- *You've got to ask! Asking is, in my opinion, the world's most powerful — and neglected — secret to success and happiness.* (Percy Ross)

Working With Difficult Clients

Occasionally, despite a practitioner's best efforts, clients will fail to act in their best interests and respond negatively to all interventions. The behaviours displayed by these difficult clients are often collectively referred to as "resistance," or "a process of avoiding or diminishing the self-disclosing communication requested by the interviewer because of its capacity to make the interviewee uncomfortable or anxious" (Pope, 1979, p. 74). Resistance can interfere with the practitioner's perceived efficacy, impede client motivation, and undermine the ability of the client to change (Nystul, 2001).

It is important for practitioners to recognize the expectations clients have about seeking help. Unsure of what to expect, clients are asked to enter into a working relationship built on trust and intimacy with an individual they have just met. They must be ready to explore personal issues they might not have shared with even their closest friends and family. For some clients, the choice to seek help might not have been their own; they may have been coerced into it, and as a result they are not willing to fully commit themselves to the process.

There are several ways practitioners can work with a difficult or challenging client:

- Establish an amicable relationship from the beginning using the building blocks of the client-practitioner relationship outlined earlier in the chapter.
- Convey a tolerant, accepting attitude towards clients. A relaxed, non-defensive demeanour may help to put clients at ease and counteract resistance.
- Examine the equality of interpersonal responses or style. Avoid being critical, impatient, or overly directive. Practitioners should strive to be patient and supportive, and to have realistic flexible expectations of clients.
- Establish as much mutuality as possible. Effective practitioners will apply the principles of collaboration and reciprocity. They will appropriately model these principles for clients, while making role expectations clear.
- Help clients explore and find incentives for moving past their resistance. Sometimes it makes sense to acknowledge the resistance overtly and to paraphrase and restate both the feelings and words of the client.

Conclusion

The development of effective client relationships is a process rather than an end product that focuses on what happens while the relationship is taking place. Here is a review of the seven competencies explored in this chapter that underpin an effective client-practitioner relationship.

1. Use appropriate verbal and non-verbal techniques to meet the primary support needs of clients.
2. Actively listen with the intention to understand.
3. Design questions that will gather the information you need and require clients to reflect and respond.
4. Demonstrate professional ethics in your relationship with the client.
5. Support clients in a courteous, respectful, and authentic manner.
6. Encourage independence and self-directedness.
7. Recognize that each client has his or her own needs, goals, level of understanding, and awareness. Recognize the client's point of reference.

This chapter on developing effective client relationships opened with a quote by John Short: "At the heart of our expertise is awareness" (Short, 1998, p. 3). As a practitioner, you have an obligation to recognize the impact of your personal style on the clients you serve. Be aware that your personal values, beliefs, culture, and assumptions influence your relationship with a client. As a career development practitioner, you have a responsibility to serve clients with competence, integrity, and authenticity. Doing so ensures proficiency with the models and processes of career development, adherence to a Code of Ethics, and helps build client commitment.

References

Amundson, N. E., Harris-Bowlsbey, J., & Niles, S. G. (2009). *Essential elements of career counseling: Processes and techniques.* Saddle River, NJ: Pearson Education.

Block, P. (2000). *Flawless consulting: A guide to getting your expertise used* (2nd ed.). San Francisco, CA: Jossey-Bass

Buber, M. (1958). *I and thou* (2nd ed.). New York, NY: Charles Scribner's Sons.

Larkin, J. E., LaPort, K. A., & Pines, H. A. (2007). Job choice and career relevance for today's college students. *Journal of Employment Counseling, 35,* 98–113.

National Steering Committee for Career Development Guidelines. (2004). *Canadian standards and guidelines for career development practitioners.* Ottawa, ON: National Steering Committee for Career Development Standards and Guidelines. Retrieved from <http://career-dev-guidelines.org/career_dev/>.

Neault, R. A. (2001). *Beyond the basics: Real world skills for career practitioners.* Life Strategies Ltd. Retrieved from <http://www.lifestrategies.ca/resources/articles.cfm>.

Neault, R. A. (2002) Thriving in the new millennium: Career management in the changing world of work. *Canadian Journal of Career Development, 1*(1), 11–21.

Niles, S. G., Amundson, N. E., & Neault, R. A. (2011). *Career Flow: A hope-centered approach to career development.* Boston, MA: Pearson Education.

Nystul, M. S. (2001). Overcoming resistance through individual psychology and problem solving. *Journal of Individual Psychology, 58,* 182–189.

Peavy, V. R. (2004). Sociodynamic counseling: A practical approach to meaning making. Chargin Falls, Ohio: Tao Institute.

Pope, B. (1979). *The mental health interview.* New York, NY: Pergamon.

Pope, M., & Minor, C. W. (2000). *Volume 1: Experiential activities for teaching career counseling classes and for facilitating career groups.* Tulsa, Oklahoma: National Career Development Association.

Schlossberg, N. K., Lunch, A. Q., & Chickering, A. W. (1989). *Improving higher education environments for adults.* San Francisco, CA: Jossey-Bass.

Short, R. R. (1998). Learning in relationships: Foundations for personal and professional Success. Washington: Learning in Action Technologies.

Trevor, C. O., & Nyberg, A. J. (2008). Keeping your headcount when all about you are losing theirs: Downsizing turnover rates and the moderating role of HR practices. *Academy of Management Journal 51,* 259–276.

Walters, B. (1992). *The life skills coach training guide: A guidebook for trainers.* Copyright Registration No. 410545 (used by permission). Bow Valley College, Calgary, Alberta.

Yukl, G. (2006). *Leadership in organizations* (6th ed.). Upper Saddle River, NJ: Pearson Prentice.

Glossary

Active listening is a structured form of listening and responding that focuses the attention on the speaker. The listener must take care to attend to the speaker fully, and then repeats, in the listener's own words, what he or she thinks the speaker has said.

Affection is the genuineness, realness, or congruence that the practitioner brings to the relationship. The more the practitioner is "real" in the relationship, the greater is the likelihood that the client will change and grow in a constructive manner.

A **closed question** can be answered with either a single word or a short phrase. Closed questions are intended to give facts, are easy to answer, and keep control of the conversation with the questioner. Also referred to as **closed-ended question**.

Mattering environment is a climate where the client feels acknowledged, respected, and valued.

An **open question** is a question that is likely to receive a long answer. These types of questions ask the respondent to think and reflect, to give opinions and feelings, and they hand control of the conversation to the respondent. Also referred to as an **open-ended question**.

Shared control refers to the co-operative approach in the client-practitioner relationship. The practitioner considers the client as the expert on his or her life and as the practitioner's teacher. There is a sharing of time and space in the session, with the practitioner listening more than talking in the initial stages.

Validation is similar to mattering. The practitioner ensures that clients feel that they are important to the process and that their experiences, thoughts, and feelings are valued by the practitioner.

Discussion and Activities

Discussion

Class Discussion Questions

1. The following is a common career concern encountered by career practitioners. An ideal opportunity has been provided to you (guaranteed security, room for advancement, good benefits, great salary, lots of resources available to do your work, and the position matches your personal interests, qualifications, and training), but the dilemma is that you would need to relocate to a place far away and be immersed in a place that is culturally very different from your current home. Please break off into pairs in which one individual acts as the career practitioner and the second individual shares personal reasons for accepting or rejecting the job offer. Debriefing of the activity should centre on the complexities of making a career decision with a focus on the importance of self-awareness.
2. Brainstorm a list of competencies needed to form effective client relationships. Number these competencies from most to least important. Then, as a class share your answers and try to reach a consensus.

Personal Reflection Questions

1. Think of a time when you asked someone for help and the outcome was successful (from your point of view). What was helpful about the interaction?
2. Think of someone you really enjoy talking to. What are the qualities that make speaking to them so enjoyable?
3. What are some traits of active listening?

Career Practitioner Role Questions

All elements of communication, including listening, may be affected by barriers that impede the flow of conversation. The next time you engage in a conversation notice what gets in your way of actively listening. What strategies can you use to improve your listening ability?

Activities

1. Try your hand at answering these "why" questions. What are the challenges you encountered in attempting to answer the following questions?

    *   Why do we press the start button to turn off the computer?
    *   Why is the sky blue?
    *   Why do we put our suits in a garment bag and our garments in a suitcase?
    *   Why is it called quicksand if it sucks you down very slowly?

2. Role-playing conversations using the skills of effective listening:

    *   The "gossip" game involves a person telling one person a short story (three to four sentences that are written down); the listener then whispers the story to his neighbour, and this continues until the last person in the chain tells the story out loud. The object is to see how much the story is changed by the time the last person hears it. To demonstrate the benefits of effective listening, do the same activity with a different story but have the participants use good listening skills rather than whispering.
    *   Divide the group into pairs and have each pair select a listener and a speaker. The speaker is given a situation to talk about as the listener actively listens. After the speaker is done, the listener tries to rephrase the speech and offer solutions or feedback to the speaker. They can then review each other's performance and swap roles.

3. Leaders and Followers
    Ask everyone to find a partner in the room, preferably someone they don't know well. Have pairs decide who is A and who is B. Instruct the pairs to do the following:

    1. Face your partner with your palms open but not touching.
    2. When you say GO, A should begin to move and B will follow or mirror the movements of A. They are to move slowly and precisely, so that it will be hard to tell who is leading and who is following. They are to keep eye contact and to not look at the hands or any other part that is moving.
    3. When you say SWITCH, they are to change roles: B is the leader and A is the follower. This should be a fluid transition.

    Eventually there is no way to tell which player is leading the exercise. The focus is being shared rather than taken by one player or the other.

Resources and Readings

Resources

Web Resources

Active Listening

New Jersey Self-Help Group Clearinghouse. Improving your listening skills
<http://www.mededfund.org/NJgroups//Listening_Skills.pdf>.
MindTools. Mind Tools on Active Listening (2005) <http://www.mindtools.com
/CommSkll/Mind%20Tools%20Listening.pdf>.
The Careers Group. Listen very carefully <http://careersintheory.files.wordpress.com
/2009/09/types-of-listening.pdf>.

Communication Skills

Developing Effective Communication Skills <http://www.slideshare.net/nusantara99
/communication-skills-51895>.
New Conversations Initiative. The seven challenges workbook: Communication skills
for success at home & work <http://www.newconversations.net/>.

Counselling Skills

Life Strategies Ltd. Life Strategies articles <http://www.lifestrategies.ca/resources/
articles.cfm>.
The Careers Group. Past-Present-Future
<http://careersintheory.files.wordpress.com/2010/10/past-present-future.pdf>.
The Careers Group. The questioning type.
<http://careersintheory.files.wordpress.com/2009/10/questioningtype.pdf>.
The Life Role Development Group [website] <http://www.life-role.com/>.
Vance Peavy. Sociodynamic Counselling. A Constructivist Perspective [website]
<http://www.sociodynamic-constructivist-counselling.com/>.

Supplementary Readings

Bimrose, J. (2010). What do clients need and really want? In H. Reid (Ed.), *The
re-emergence of career: Challenges and opportunities* (pp. 9–14). Retrieved from
<http://www.canterbury.ac.uk/education/career-and-personal-development/docs/
ProfJennyBimroseKeyNote.pdf>.
Bimrose, J., & Hearne, L. (2012). Resilience and career adaptability: Qualitative studies
of adult career counseling. *Journal of Vocational Behavior*, 81(3), 338–344. doi:
10.1007/s10775-011-9191-6

Cardoso, P., & Moreira, J. M. (2009). Self-efficacy beliefs and the relation between career planning and perception of barriers. *International Journal for Educational and Vocational Guidance, 9*, 177–188. doi: 10.1007/s10775-009-9163-2

Chung, Y. B., & Gfroerer, M. C. A. (2003). Career coaching: Practice, training, professional, and ethical issues. *Career Development Quarterly, 52*(2), 141–152.

Douglas, F. (2011). Between a rock and a hard place: Career guidance practitioner resistance and the construction of professional identity. *International Journal for Educational and Vocational Guidance, 11*, 163–173. doi.org/10.1007/s10775-011-9205-4

Jones, G., & Gorell, R. (2012). *50 top tools for coaching: A complete tool kit for developing and empowering people.* London, UK: Kogan Page.

Masdonati, J., Massoudi, K., & Rossier, J. (2009). The effectiveness of career counseling and the impact of the working alliance. *Journal of career development, 36*(2), 182– 203. doi: 10.1177/0894845309340798

Neault, R. A., & Pickrell, D. A. (2011). Career engagement: bridging career counseling and employee engagement. *Journal of Employment Counseling, 48*(4), 185–188. doi: 10.1002/j.2161-1920.2011.tb01111.x

Olry-Louis, I., Brémond, C., & Pouliot, M. (2012). Confidence sharing in the vocational counselling interview: emergence and repercussions. *International Journal for Educational and Vocational Guidance, 12*(1), 47–65.

Shelly, M. (2008). GROWing your career conversations through coaching. *The Foundation Years, 4*(1), 47–48.

Westergaard, J. (2012). Career guidance and therapeutic counselling: sharing 'what works' in practice with young people. *British Journal of Guidance & Counselling, 40*(4), 327–339. doi: 10.1080/03069885.2012.687711

eight

Career Planning, Knowledge, and Skills

KERRI MCKINNON
KATHLEEN JOHNSTON
Concordia University College of Alberta

PRE-READING QUESTIONS

1. In thinking about your career path to this point, what has been your planning process?
2. Were you planful, impulsive, a procrastinator, or a fatalist?

Introduction and Learning Objectives

While it's true we cannot predict what the future has in store for us,
planning can increase the odds that our life will hold meaning. Career planning
can help create a personal vision of where we want to go with our working lives.
— Kathleen Johnston

This chapter is about the knowledge and skills required to create and implement career planning for life. An important reality in today's multifaceted world is that change is a constant. Career development professionals need to consider and understand the nature of change as they support individuals in creating sound career strategies. Accordingly, career planning in the 21st century requires that you:

- know yourself;
- understand how best to choose work that fits your unique essence and

strengths;
- know economic, occupational, and labour market trends;
- be adept at self-managing a career particularly when dealing with change and opportunity.

In this chapter, you will learn about **career planning** as an ongoing process through which an individual sets career goals and identifies the means to achieve them. It is through career planning that one evaluates abilities and interests, assesses values and personality, considers alternative career opportunities, establishes career goals, and plans practical developmental activities. The main components of career planning are self-discovery, researching occupations and the **labour market**, making career decisions, taking action, implementing **job search** skills, and developing and maintaining career management skills.

As you work through this chapter, consider the importance of understanding the career-planning process from the perspective of the professional career practitioner. As a starting point, we recommend that you begin a career-planning journal. Career practitioners are often challenged to consider the underlying values that can guide their practices with clients. Use this journal to record answers to questions as you read through the chapter; consider your perspectives both from the position of a client and of a practitioner; and highlight your assumptions and insights regarding each role. This journal will serve as a reflective tool that will shed light on your growth as a career development practitioner.

The learning objectives of this chapter are that you will be able to:

1. Appreciate the complexity and dynamic nature of selecting and managing a meaningful career path.
2. Understand the six components of the career-planning process.
3. Be able to define key labour market concepts and list main sources of labour market information.
4. Understand the skills involved in decision making, goal setting, action planning, and career management.

Career Planning

The more you practise career planning for yourself the better able you will be as a career practitioner to help the client. By considering the career-planning process from the client's standpoint you will gain in self-understanding and be able to lead the client through the process. Start by answering the questions in this section with yourself as the client to gain that perspective.

What Is Career Planning?

Making a plan for your career future involves understanding yourself, understanding the labour market, making informed decisions based on all relevant information, and, not the least, having a contingency plan to allow for change. In the 21st-century work world, it is imperative to know how to manage one's career continuously through all the stages of life. This means anticipating change and allowing for it in the plan.

Career planning can be a creative and dynamic process by which an individual develops a vision of work for the long term. The process helps people adapt to change, and deal with career challenges more expertly. But it's not easy to do alone: A professional career practitioner can help.

The following reflective questions are typically considered as part of the career-planning process and form the structure that guides a client through this process. Answer the following questions for yourself.

WHO AM I?
• What is my life purpose? When I reach the end of my life journey, what is it I hope to have accomplished?
• What are my unique talents, interests, values, characteristics, motivators, likes, and dislikes?
• What specific results do I want to achieve from my career?
• How might those outcomes change as I move through different life stages?

WHAT HAVE I DONE?
• What are my transferable skills?
• What education, training, knowledge, experience, and competencies do I have to offer?
• What is the most effective way to market myself in the world of work?

WHERE AM I GOING?
• What's my understanding of alternatives and options for my career path?
• What are my specific career goals (short, medium, and long term)?
• How do I make successful career transitions?
• How will I ensure that my career brings meaning to my life?

HOW WILL I GET THERE AND WHAT MIGHT GET IN THE WAY?
• What's my strategy for reaching the career goal(s) I have identified?
• What resources and strengths do I have to surmount obstacles and challenges?
• What support and networking resources are available to me?
• What ongoing career management strategies do I need?

Table 1: Questions for Career Planning.

❖ *Stop and Reflect*

Now that you have answered these questions for yourself, what challenges can you see facing clients in each of the steps outlined in the career-planning process?

Career-Planning Models

One of the many challenging aspects of career planning is in identifying and organizing information about yourself. Career-counselling professionals often approach this through the application of a model (see Chapter 6 on Theoretical Foundations of Career Development) or the use of a specific process. Several models have been developed in Canada.

- Bill O'Byrne (1998) developed the *Career Compass* model that focuses on four components: self-knowledge, development, social systems, and opportunity. Each component is broken down into sub-components for an easy-to-use practical tool.
- The *Five Critical Career Processes* model (Magnusson, 1992, 1995) includes: initiation, exploration, decision making, preparation, and implementation, with individuals moving back and forth through these processes as their circumstances change.
- The University of Waterloo's Career Development eManual is an online, self-help tool (<https://emanual.uwaterloo.ca>). Its six modules include self-assessment, research, career decision making, marketing one's self, work skills, and life/work planning.
- Norm Amundson's (2009) career counselling model as described in *Active Engagement* emphasizes the use of creativity, storytelling, questioning techniques, action strategies, and relationship building at the same time recognizing the need to integrate personal and career counselling.

Although each of these models uses different terminology and proposes different steps for the career-counselling process, they are similar in that they include self-discovery, research on occupational information, understanding the labour market, developing options and alternatives, goal setting, and strategies for achieving an outcome.

Components of Career Planning

Career planning is a dynamic process that can be learned by individuals. Through this process, a person creates a personal vision of what he or she hopes to achieve through meaningful work. The planning process requires an in-depth understanding of self in relation to vocation. It includes setting goals that will meet lifestyle needs, and providing for change and transition as one moves through life-cycle changes. Individuals become self-directed in the management of their career over their lifetime as well as at specific times when re-careering. It is now common for people to have four or five distinctly different careers during a lifetime.

The six-step career-planning process outlined in this chapter looks like the table below.

STEP	DESCRIPTION
6. Career Management Skills	Manage career continuously and plan for the next.
5. Action Plans	Create a road map from choosing an occupation to becoming employed in that occupation to reaching your long-term career goals.
4. Job Search Skills	Find suitable jobs by accessing formal and informal networks.
3. Decision-Making Skills	Identify the decision to be made, identify options, gather information, evaluate options to solve the problem, select the best option.
2. Occupational Information	Identify and explore career options.
1. Self-Discovery	Identify and understand your values, interests, skills, personal attributes, and personal mission.

Table 2: Six Steps to Career Planning.

1. Self-Discovery

The term **self-discovery** implies a reflective process of careful self-examination regarding something in particular, in this case, career planning. Through a self-discovery process, information will emerge that can be used for planning and decision making. There are many resources that can be applied in the self-discovery process. Although self-discovery suggests finding out about interests, things that interest you don't necessarily make the best careers. Interests are also influenced by opportunity and exposure and may be related to your comfort level and familiarity. Although interests, as well as skills, are important, they are only part of the picture. You must also gather information about other key factors such as your:

- personality type,
- work environment preferences,
- work and personal values and motivators,
- natural talents and competencies (strengths/weaknesses),
- learning style preferences,
- life purpose and lifestyle preferences,
- personal and family needs/factors,
- academic strengths.

In the self-discovery part of career planning, individuals must be prepared to do reflective work, research, and engage in self-clarity. Self-clarity is the process of doing the work to answer the questions about yourself (Niles, Amundson, & Neault, 2011).

> With effort, self-clarity emerges. In many ways, the process is similar to developing a photograph. That is, self-reflection is like entering the photographer's darkroom to do the work that results in a clear image (self-clarity). Ancient Greek philosopher Aristotle noted the importance of self-clarity when he emphasized the importance of "knowing thyself" to live life effectively. This advice is essential in managing your career effectively. Everything starts from the foundation of self-awareness. If you are clear about who you are, then you can use this important information to move forward systematically and intentionally in identifying and achieving your career goals…. Developing self-clarity will enable you to be the captain of your ship as opportunities and challenges are presented to you. (p. 19)

This self-discovery process needs to be repeated whenever the individual is faced with a career transition, or is experiencing an age or stage-of-life change. For tips on self-reflection, see Katharine Hansen's list available at <http://www.quintcareers. com/15_assessment_tips.html>.

❖ *Stop and Reflect*
How might your current personal and family factors impact your career options or choices?

2. Occupational Information

Consider your role as a developing career practitioner. What do you need to know or understand about occupational information in order to help your clients? Effective career planning involves research on **occupations** and job families. The latter are simply groups of occupations based upon skills, training, education, credentials, and work tasks. Canada's National Occupational Classification (NOC, 2011) provides a standard way of organizing labour market information through the use of a uniform language to describe the work performed by Canadians in the labour market. Examples of job families include community and social services, legal, computer and mathematical, personal care and service, and health care support, to name a few.

The more informed people are about occupational possibilities, the better able they will be to select the occupations with the highest degree of personal fit. A recent study of people in 150 countries discovered that career well-being is the most essential element to an individual's well-being. That research indicated that people who are thriving in their careers are more than twice as likely to be thriving overall in their lives (Rath & Harter, 2010).

Essential Skills

by Lara Shepard

Human Resources and Skills Development Canada launched the Essential Skills National Research project in 1994 to identify common skills across all occupations. Over 180 jobs were studied. It identified nine essential skills that are used in almost every occupation in a variety of ways and at varying levels of complexity: reading text, document use, numeracy, oral communication, writing, working with others, continuous learning, thinking skills, and computer use. These skills are the foundation for learning new skills, and allow people to adapt to the changing workplace. Profiles were developed to describe how each essential skill is used by various workers in a particular occupation.

View these at <http://www10.hrsdc.gc.ca/es/english/all_profiles.aspx>.

More information can be found at Employment and Social Development Canada <http://www.hrsdc.gc.ca/eng/jobs/les/index.shtml>.

❖ Stop and Reflect

As a career practitioner, do you know the kind of work activities that bring you the greatest amount of satisfaction? Think back over your lifetime and brainstorm a list of the kinds of tasks that you love so much that time passes by unnoticed.

Labour Market Information (LMI)

Labour market information (LMI) is body of knowledge and impressions gleaned from statistical data on the labour markets and analysis. It includes occupational or career information such as educational requirements, main duties, wage rates, the availability of workers, current employment trends, and the outlook for the position.

LMI provides such information as how many people have jobs in the manufacturing sector in comparison to the service sector. This information may include descriptions of industries, lists of companies for an industry, and importance of those companies to a community. LMI can also include the economic well-being and outlook for communities such as unemployment rates, the supply and demand for skilled workers, and the age, gender, and educational level of people in the community. As such, LMI assists career practitioners in identifying changes or trends that affect the world of work.

The labour market in Canada is diverse and extremely flexible in nature. Occupations are being created, changed, and eliminated faster than ever before. An overall understanding of labour market trends actually helps guide long-term career plans and determines specific career paths. Consider for a moment that many jobs that existed 10 to 15 years ago no longer exist. One example is the major change in the manufacturing industry. Many of the jobs for skilled workers in manufacturing have been reduced or eliminated in the past 15 years while there has been rapid growth in the service-producing sector. Some new specialties have opened too — behavioural geneticists being one example.

Schell, Follero-Pugh, and Lloyd (2010) discuss how the labour market is being affected by changing economics in Canada. Gone are the days where employees stay with one organization for 25+ years. Instead the new trend sees Canadians changing jobs every 3 years with a major occupational shift occurring every 5 years. This trend is increasingly true for individuals under the age of 40. This is a pattern that will continue through your career and in the careers of those you advise.

❖ *Stop and Reflect*
Take some time and consider how the manufacturing industry has been transformed over the past 5, 10, and 25 years.

Labour market trends are powerful tools professionals may use to help clients make decisions about future careers and career paths. Many career development practitioners tend to distinguish between career information and LMI. Career information is defined as information related to the world of work that can be useful in the process of career development and typically includes educational, occupational, and psychosocial information related to work. LMI, on the other hand, is rarely directly related to a clients' immediate occupational need. Overall, the LMI is useful in identifying opportunities in the job market, in understanding labour market conditions and trends, in predicting outlooks for various occupational groups based on a variety of factors (economic, demographic, social, and political, technology, and globalization), and in providing information to support informed employment and career decisions.

Supply and Demand

In the simplest form, the labour market can be explained by relating employment demand and supply to wages. Supply refers to the workforce and reflects the number of workers willing to work, whereas demand refers to the number of workers employers want to hire. For a specific wage level where demand for workers is equal to the supply, there will be no additional workers looking for jobs at that wage as well as no more job vacancies. In theory, this determines the number employed and the wage level in any workplace or a specific job.

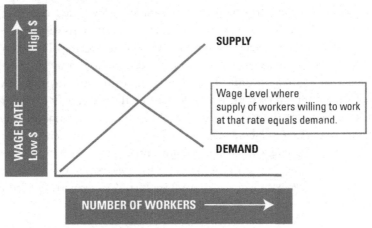

Figure 1: Supply and Demand for a Wage Level.

Segmentation

Skill segmentation refers to special labour markets that exist for specialized skills. Although supply theory regards workers as identical mass units of labour (i.e., the total number of hours of work workers can provide), the reality is that workers are very different, varying in terms of skills or occupation, geographic location, personality, and family dynamics. This means that labour markets are segmented. As a result, special labour markets exist for specialized skills, and various barriers are put up to keep unqualified workers out.

Geographic segmentation is the term used to define the geographic area where employers recruit workers for most occupations. This is typically the area within commuting distance of the location of the company. The labour market for most occupations is concentrated around a particular locale. The availability of jobs depends on the way an organization hires its workers. Organizations that fill vacancies primarily from inside the organization are considered "internal labour markets." Other organizations hire from outside, or the "external labour market." Keep in mind that no organization can operate as a purely internal labour market.

Primary vs. Secondary Labour Markets

Two separate labour markets are defined in the career development field. The "primary labour market" is defined as consisting of high-paying jobs, good working conditions, opportunities for promotion and training, and more employment stability. The "secondary labour market" is defined as consisting of low-paying jobs with high turnover, minimal job security, and often inconsistent personnel practices.

The economic downturn that began in 2008 resulted in a change in the way Canadians view the labour market. A prior upturn in the business cycle had improved profits in many organizations and increased demand for labour. However, when the economic crisis began, these organizations downsized operations and laid off workers. As the economy rebounded many organizations restructured such that they could increase productive outputs without increasing the size of their workforce. As a result, many workers who had been employed in primary labour markets found it extremely difficult to find meaningful employment. A large number of these employees took positions within the secondary labour market or in those occupations that tend to be located in the most competitive areas of the economy and are more labour intensive. These occupations tend to pay lower wages, be less secure in employment, be less unionized, and provide less opportunity for advancement. Some workers took up consulting work, contract employment, and other forms of self-employment, or were successful in formatting partnerships or doing job sharing.

❖ *Stop and Reflect*

Consider the last dramatic employment downturn. How was the geographic region you reside in impacted compared to others?

The Role of the Career Practitioner in Using Labour Market Information (LMI)

Career practitioners play a major role in assisting clients with the "when" and "how" of using LMI. In order to be effective, a career practitioner needs to have a thorough understanding of labour market trends and be comfortable with using the information with clients. They must be willing to keep up with the labour market information in their professional development activities. Career practitioners can remain current by subscribing to a selection of periodical publications, newsletters, journals, and publications that address labour market issues. The Conference Board of Canada is one source of publications on the impact of new technologies, employment practices, and major economic events. The publications that will be most useful to you will depend on the client population you serve. These publications should also keep current with circumstances that affect the labour market at local, provincial, and national levels. Catalogues, magazines, newspapers, brochures, phone books, and reports can also be valuable resources. Information on the labour force, help-wanted index, local government employment, pension plans, as well as resources from

Citizenship and Immigration Canada, Statistics Canada, and provincial government departments, should be available in offices where you work and on online. For example, the Alberta Learning Information Service (<www.alis.alberta.ca>) has put online such excellent resources as *Making Sense of Labour Market Information.*

Clients can find labour market information at multiple places including university career centres, public libraries, the Internet, and professional organizations. Despite the market situation of late, many job seekers use job boards to gather job and labour market information. With over 40,000 job board and employment websites available on the Internet, it is hard to know where to turn for accurate information. The most popular job boards in Canada include:

- Workopolis <http://www.workopolis.com>. Workopolis describes itself as the largest job board in Canada. It has career resources, job listings, and résumé submission.
- Monster.ca <http://www.monster.ca>. Formerly Monster Board Canada, this site provides a listing of job openings, employer profiles, résumé postings, and a career centre.
- Hot Jobs in Canada <http://www.hotjobscanada.ca/>.
- Service Canada Job Bank <http://www.jobbank.gc.ca/intro-eng.aspx>. Employers from across the country post listings of jobs and work or business opportunities.
- Public Service <http://jobs-emplois.gc.ca>. This site posts positions available within the federal government.

3. Decision Making, Goal Setting, and Action Plans

A third important factor in career planning is making career decisions, setting goals, and making action plans. The concept of a "job for life" belongs to a bygone era. Individuals can expect to be engaged in career decision making continuously in the dynamic work environment of the 21st century. To accommodate technology changes as well as socioeconomic changes — not to mention age and stage-of-life changes — individuals must be proactive about their careers.

Decision Making

Decision making can be a difficult process for some people. There are quick decisions that might be spontaneous and based on an opportunity that presents itself out of the blue. However, even when a career decision must be made quickly, it is wise to consider the long-term impact before implementation. The ability to consider the overall vision one holds for one's career can be most helpful.

❖ *Stop and Reflect*

How do you make a decision? Most people use a combination of styles with some styles being more practical than others. Read through the list below. Which styles describe the ways you make decisions?

- *Impulsive* — Spends little time considering alternatives; makes a decision at the last moment; dislikes making decisions; usually takes the first alternative available.
- *Intuitive* — Bases a decision on gut feelings that have not been verbalized. "It just feels right."
- *"What Do You Think?" Style* — Makes a decision based on the wishes of another person and goes along with the ideas or plans of someone else rather than making decision of their own. A person using this style generally doesn't trust his/her ability to make a decision.
- *Agonizing* — Involves much time and thought in gathering data and analyzing alternatives. The decision maker often gets lost in a pile of information and has trouble getting to the decision point.
- *Delaying* — Postpones thought and action on a problem until later. "I'll think about it tomorrow."
- *Fatalistic* — Leaves the decision to fate or the environment. "What will be, will be ..."
- *Paralytic* — Accepts the responsibility for making a decision, but then is unable to set the decision-making process in motion. "I know I should, but I just can't make this decision."
- *Planful* — Bases a decision on a rational approach with a balance between the cognitive and the emotional. People who use this style of decision obtain relevant information and clarify objectives before making decisions. They evaluate the cause and effect of their decisions before choosing and they usually choose something that seems comfortable and secure.

Steps to Career Decision Making

The format in Table 3 (*see* next page) is a planful, prescriptive model designed to lead problem solvers to the solution as efficiently as possible (Crozier, 2001).

Goal Setting

Goal setting is an important part of career planning and career management. Career goals provide the individual with a sense of direction and meaning. Career goals are not visions, hopes, dreams, or wishes. They are a defined method for getting to where you want to be in the future. When goals are directly connected to an individual's life purpose, they can become strong motivational factors. Ideally, career goals need to be aligned with an individual's strengths and values in order

STEP	DESCRIPTION
1. Reach a decision point.	A decision-making point is reached whenever you are required to make an important career decision.
2. Research.	Research yourself and your career. 1. Yourself: identify your interests, skills, values, temperament, and lifestyle factors. 2. Career: learn more about the educational programs and occupations you are most interested in pursuing. Once this research is complete, alternatives can be generated.
3. Evaluate alternatives and make a choice.	It is important to have more than one choice because choices allow you to develop a contingency plan in case things do not work out with your first choice.
4. Take action.	This step involves implementing one of your choices and using an action plan containing goals and timelines.
5. Review the decision and take action as necessary.	Career decisions should never be set in stone. You may need to make adjustments

Table 3: Steps to Career Decision Making.

to support the highest possible degree of personal satisfaction and engagement with their work.

Commitment to the completion of goals depends on (a) the importance of the outcome for the person, (b) personal belief that the goal is achievable, and (c) the extent to which others are involved. There are four types of goals:

1. Immediate: something small, simple, easy, that one can do in the next 24–48 hours.
2. Short term: things one can do over the next few days and weeks.
3. Medium term: things one can do over the next few weeks and months.
4. Long term: things one can do over the next few months up to five years.

It is important for career practitioners to consider client goals because they provide an important focus for the career-planning process. Monitoring client goals is also a way to measure and celebrate progress, and as well as to know when the practitioner-client work together is complete.

Career professionals working with individuals to set career goals must pay close attention to personality traits and the motivational levels of each individual. Understanding the beliefs held by the individual is an important place to start. For example:

- Do they believe goal setting will affect their future?
- Do they believe they are worthy of success?
- Do they fear failure based on previous experience?

The following provides a simple outline of the factors you may want to consider and identify when setting your career goals in a step-by-step format.

SETTING CAREER GOALS	
Points	*Description*
1. Career goal	Start by defining and writing down your goals in order of priority.
2. Benefits and advantages of reaching this goal	Listing these may help to motivate you. Be sure to include potential barriers to achieving your goals.
3. Key steps you need to take	Identifying these steps will help form your action plan.
4. Timeframe	Set target dates and deadlines.
5. Support and resources	What do you need from whom? Time, money, contacts?
6. Outcomes and reflection	Record, for future reference, whether you achieved the goal and what worked or did not work along the way.

Table 4: Setting Career Goals.

4. Job Search Skills

A fourth important factor in career planning is the development of specific job search skills. These are described in Chapter 9 on Work Search Strategies. Very briefly, the individual needs to have the skills and willingness to do the following:

1. Research the company.
2. Develop a networking plan.
3. Create a master résumé.
4. Design cover letters.
5. Prepare for interviews.
6. Negotiate job offers.

5. Action Plans

Once a career decision is made, individuals need to develop an action plan to help them achieve success in reaching their career goals. A SMART action plan includes: Specific, Measurable, Achievable, Realistic/Relevant, Time-specific goals (Doran, 1981).

Each career goal should be written down and allow for the inclusion of a detailed action plan for achievement. A workbook format can be used for easy reference, ongoing review, and revision. **Action planning** answers the following questions:

1. What specific steps do I need to take to achieve my goal?
2. Which of the steps are most urgent and which are less urgent?
3. What additional information, resources, or supports do I need?

The more specific the action plan, the more effective it will be in supporting goal achievement. The following table provides an example of an action plan related to a specific career goal.

FORMULATING AN ACTION PLAN			
Short-term Career Goal: Begin a Bachelor of Commerce Degree Program			
Action Steps	*Resources Needed*	*Completion Date*	*Done*
1. Complete university application and registration.	Check finances available with family and bank.	June 15	
2. Move into residence.	Make a list of items I will need to take and make arrangements to borrow truck.	August 15	
3. Complete course selection.	Seek the assistance of an academic advisor.	August 15	
4. Purchase books and materials.	See if I can purchase any from my new roommate.	September 1	

Table 5: Formulating an Action Plan.

Action plans are dynamic. They need to be responsive to the changes and demands of life. Ideally they enable personal reflection and the celebration of success. Whether they are quick or time consuming, effective career decisions require the use of analysis, critical thinking, good judgement, and strategy as well as consultation with key stakeholders, particularly family members. When asking clients to set career goals they must be able to identify the people, resources, or organizations that they will need to accomplish their goal.

6. Career Management Skills

The sixth critical factor in career planning is the concept of **personal career**

management skills. Education or training may prepare an individual for the job market from a technical viewpoint; however, the 21st-century work world requires much more than technical competence. In order to thrive in this diverse world, social attitudes need to reflect the demands of today. Within our communities and fields of expertise, changes are happening so fast that keeping up is almost impossible on our own.

Important factors for continuously directing and managing your career with intention include:

- developing a personal work ethic based on values and principles for authentic living;
- building an image competency;
- understanding how to communicate personal and professional strengths;
- establishing career mentors and supports;
- continually engaging in self-evaluation;
- engaging in ongoing professional development;
- adjusting to life-cycle stages.

Career practitioners play a vital role in supporting clients in applying personal career management skills to future career paths.

❖ *Stop and Reflect*

Consider your life as a case study. Use the list above as a guide and record your responses to questions such as: How would you describe your work ethic and the values that support it? Describe yourself in terms of being competent in the career you are considering for yourself. What are your strengths and how would you describe them to someone? Continue on creating your personal responses to the items on the list.

Establishing a Network

Career specialists understand the importance of having their clients establish and maintain networks to enhance their career-building activities. Networking is about making connections, developing leads, and building relationships with individuals and groups of people. The ability to network is crucial for most people to be successful in their career explorations. Networking is an opportunity to gather information, and research prospective employment opportunities. This is increasingly important according to Wright (2007), who suggests that over 75% of all available positions are found via the "hidden market." By hidden market we are talking about all the positions that organizations do not advertise. The key to finding a good job is your ability to market yourself from a stranger into a known commodity through networking.

Networking for employment can be considered a three-step process (as adapted from Guffey, Rhodes, & Rogin, 2011) whether using the traditional model or the online model for networking.

TRADITIONAL NETWORKING	ONLINE NETWORKING
Develop a list	**Join a networking group**
• Make lists of anyone you are interested in or who would be willing to talk to you regarding finding a job.	• Build a professional network by joining one or more online networks. LinkedIn is the leading network.
• Consider who can help you — family, former employers, colleagues, organizations you are a member of, former educators, neighbours, et cetera.	• Joining is easy: create a username and password, fill in a profile, and add business contacts.
• Consider university career centres and alumni offices.	• Some sites are fee-based. Find the one, whether free or fee, that best suits your need.
Make contact	**Participate**
• Arrange to meet with the people on your list. Depending on your comfort and knowledge of the individual, this can be done in person, on the phone, or informally via email.	• Participate in discussion groups, mailing lists, and social media. Find groups that have the expertise you need.
• Be professional, organized, and friendly and ask each person if they know anyone who might have an opening for an individual with your skill set.	• Find a relevant blog or Twitter feed for your career interest. Blogs and Twitter are very useful for networking and information sharing.
• Be prepared to highlight your skills and have a copy of your résumé available to share.	• Use Quintessential Careers as a starting point for networking tools <http://www.quintcareers.com>.
Follow up on your referrals	**Follow up on leads**
• Call the people you were referred to by your contacts.	• Use the connections you find to introduce yourself.

Table 6: Traditional and Online Networking.   (Continued on next page)

TRADITIONAL NETWORKING	ONLINE NETWORKING
Follow up on your referrals	*Use Twitter and blogs*
• You could say something like this: Hello, my name is Samantha Jones, a friend of _____. She suggested that I call you. I am looking for a position as_____, and she thought you might be able to steer me in the right direction.	• Use Quintessential Careers as a starting point for networking tools <http://www.quintcareers.com>.

Table 6 (continued): Traditional and Online Networking.

The Professional Career Practitioner

Life seldom runs along a predictable path. The economy, globalization, and company priorities require job skills and career plans that are flexible and adaptable to market needs. Therefore, in addition to guiding clients through the importance of networking, career specialists need to establish networks themselves for the purpose of assembling and using labour market and career information. Professional networking, community networking, and membership in professional associations are effective ways to stay current in the field.

Professional Networking

The professional networking is composed of individuals within departments and organizations whose primary role is to assemble and disseminate labour market information.

Beyond the Basics

by Deirdre Pickerell

Beyond the Basics: Real World Skills for Career Practitioners, published by Life Strategies, has tips and techniques for working with diverse clients. It is linked to the *Canadian Standards and Guidelines for Career Development Practitioners*. <http://www.lifestrategies.ca/store/proddetail.php?prod=BasicsPrint>.

• Each provincial government has designated departments that examine labour market information. Hotlines are available to provide you with appropriate contacts in your province or territory.

• Many municipalities gather information that can assist the business sector. This information is often available through the economic development officer in your community.

Of course there are always the hidden gems of labour market information (LMI) that are often overlooked. Liaison officers, counsellors, and university registrars can be valuable sources of LMI and are able to provide you with information regarding educational trends. These trends are often reflective of labour market needs and changing demographics.

Community Networking

Regardless of where you live in Canada, there are individuals who will have an understanding of the trends affecting the labour market. Consider individuals who are responsible for recruitment, government departments, schools, and career counselling agencies to get involved with regarding emerging trends.

Professional Associations

The third and final consideration for staying current is to belong to a career practitioner organization. These organizations can range in scope from a community network to provincial agencies or societies and national organizations. For more information on career-related professional associations, see Appendix B.

Staying Current

Some experts suggest that approximately 10 to 15% of your time should be spent on keeping current in your field. Staying current with labour market trends is especially challenging for the career practitioner as the labour market is in continual flux.

Two methods of monitoring and analyzing labour market trends include the Trend Evaluation and Monitoring Approach (TEAM) and Trend Tracking.

TEAM Approach. This approach is a method used to identify emerging issues and early signs of social, political, economic, and technological change. It is based on three levels of participation:

1. Volunteer Group of Monitors: The members of this group regularly review publications for articles suggesting changes that might affect the

CareerWise

by Riz Ibrahim

CareerWise in ContactPoint is a weekly roundup of news and views in the career development field. By putting together some of the most interesting articles on career counselling and career development each week, *CareerWise* aims to keep practitioners current, enrich their work — and save them time. Past issues are archived on the site. A French edition called *OrientAction en bref* is published biweekly. <http://contactpoint.ca/careerwise/>. ContactPoint and OrientAction are provided by the Canadian Education and Research Institute for Counselling (CERIC).

organization. Summaries of these articles are written and forwarded to the analysis team.

2. Analysis Team: A small group of people chosen for their diverse backgrounds and analytic skills meet regularly to try to put together the segments of information from the monitoring group to see how the information can be of benefit to the organization.

3. Senior Management Committee: The results of the analysis team's discussion are written up and sent to the senior management committee as well as to each of the volunteer monitors. The senior management committee reviews the material provided and decides which items will be brought to the attention of specific managers of the organization.

Tracking Trends. There is a multitude of labour market data available to researchers in Canada. Trend tracking is a way of systematically taking this information and turning it into usable and applied information. The minimum daily requirement for keeping up in one subject area is:

- reading the newspaper,
- watching or listening to a news show,
- reading a weekly news magazine,
- reading a monthly magazine in your own field of expertise,
- subscribing to relevant RSS feeds and content-curation services such as Academica and CareerWise.

We recommend incorporating trend tracking into your daily routine. By using information sources you have already identified, you are already tracking labour market trends!

Summary

Career planning is a dynamic process that helps individuals create a vision for their work future, to provide a process for adapting to change, and to prepare them for creating innovative career strategies and managing career decisions throughout all stages of their career journey. Labour market information, program requirements, occupational requirements, and many other aspects of career planning are constantly changing. As a result, it is more important than ever to remain up-to-date with the latest facts. Reading newspapers, reviewing websites, and staying in touch with one's networks are ways that ensure that the information used for making decisions is the most current and accurate available. Career development practitioners also need to stay current with emerging resources to make the time spent with your clients both effective and efficient.

References

Amundson, N. E. (2009). *Active engagement* (2nd ed.). Richmond, BC: Ergon Communications.

Crozier, S. (2001). Making a career decision. Retrieved from <http://www.ucalgary.ca /wellnesscentre/files/wellnesscentre/Making%20a%20Career%20Decision.pdf>.

Doran, G. T. (1981). There's a S.M.A.R.T. way to write management's goals and objectives. *Management Review, 70*(11), 35–36.

Guffey, M., Rhodes, K., & Rogin, P. (2011). *Business communications* (5th ed.). Mason, OH: Cengage Learning.

Hansen, K. (n.d.). *15 quick self-assessment tips*. Kettle Falls: Quintessential Careers. Retrieved from <http://www.quintcareers.com/15_assessment_tips.html>.

Magnusson, K. C. (1992). Five critical processes of career counseling. In M. Van Norman (Ed.), *National Consultation on Vocational Counseling Papers: 1992* (pp. 217–227). Toronto, ON: University of Toronto Press.

Magnusson, K. (1995). Five processes of career planning. Ottawa, ON: Canadian Guidance and Counseling Foundation. (ERIC Document Reproduction Service No. ED 404 581). Retrieved from <http://www.counseling.org/Resources/Library /ERIC%20Digests/95-065.pdf>.

National Occupational Classification. (2011). *About the NOC 2011*. Retrieved from <http://www5.hrsdc.gc.ca/noc/english/noc/2011/AboutNOC.aspx>.

Niles, S. G., Amundson, N. E., & Neault, R. A. (2011). *Career flow: A hope-centered approach to career development*. Boston, MA: Pearson Education.

O'Byrne, B. (1998). *Discovering futures: Featuring the Career Compass Model*. Toronto, ON: Guidance Centre, University of Toronto.

Rath, T., & Harter, J. (2010). *Wellbeing: The Five Essential Elements*. New York, NY: Gallup Press.

Schell, D., Follero-Pugh, F., & Lloyd, D. (2010). Making career sense of labour market information. Victoria, BC: ASPECT. Retrieved from <http://www.aspect.bc.ca /userfiles/file/publicfiles/MCSLMI_2010.pdf>.

Williams, P., & Lloyd, T. J. (2005). *Total life coaching*. New York, NY: W.W. Norton & Company, Inc.

Wright, D. (2007). No Canadian experience, eh? A career success guide for new immigrants. CreateSpace, a Division of Amazon.com.

Glossary

Action planning is a process that helps one focus his or her ideas and to decide what steps are needed to achieve a particular goal. It is a statement of what one wants to achieve over a period of time.

Career planning is an ongoing process through which a person sets career goals and identifies ways of achieving them. Through career planning, a person evaluates

his or her own abilities and interests, considers alternative career opportunities, establishes career goals, and plans practical developmental activities.

Decision making is the process of mapping the likely consequences of decisions, working out the importance of individual factors, and choosing the best course of action to take.

Goal setting is a two-part process of deciding what one wants to accomplish and then devising an action plan to achieve the result one desires.

Job search is the act of looking for employment.

Labour market is the arena where those who are in need of labour and those who can supply the labour come together. The market is in a constant state of flux, dependent on changing external influences.

Occupation is a group of similar jobs or types of work sharing similar skills, education, knowledge, and training.

Personal career management is the lifelong, self-monitored process of career planning that involves choosing and setting personal goals and formulating strategies for achieving them.

Self-discovery is the process of achieving understanding or knowledge of oneself.

Skill segmentation refers to dual labour markets, which consist of various sub-groups with little or no crossover capability. The labour markets are divided into the primary and secondary sectors. The primary sector generally contains the higher grade, higher status, and better paid jobs that require specific skills, with employers who offer the best terms and conditions. The secondary sector is characterized jobs which are mostly low-skilled and require relatively little training. There are few barriers to job mobility within the secondary sector.

Discussion and Activities

Discussion

How has the Web changed career planning and job searching for individuals and career practitioners? In your opinion, is the change positive or negative? Provide examples.

Personal Reflection Questions

Like the individuals we work with, career practitioners need to keep up-to-date on new strategies, exemplary practices and be aware of opportunities for professional growth. What steps will you take to stay current?

Career Practitioner's Role

1. List three professional associations that you could join. Explain the purpose of each.
2. Why is it important to intentionally manage one's career progress? What are some ideas you have for managing your career? What resources or support systems do you have at your disposal? If limited, how would you go about finding them?
3. Consider your role as a professional career practitioner. What issues might you face with clients as you engage them in the self-discovery process? What have you learned about yourself that will help or hinder your effectiveness as a career practitioner?

Activities

1. Review local labour market trends that appear to be impacting your role as a career practitioner. Consider the following questions:

   (a) Is this a one-time event/circumstance?
   (b) Is this a sequence of events/circumstances? And,
   (c) Do these events/circumstances have social, political, and/or economic significance?

   For each, write down the trend and identify the potential impact on yourself and your current role.
2. Compare the advantages and disadvantages of locating labour market and job listings from big board sites such as monster.ca.
3. Identify your talents, personality traits, interests, motivators, values, knowledge, skills, and experience relative to finding meaningful work. In an email to your instructor, describe what kind of career, company, position, and location would best fit with your self-analysis.
4. What type of salary can you expect for your chosen career? Visit Working in Canada at <http://www.workingincanada.gc.ca/> and select your occupation based on the kind of employment you are seeking now. If you live in Alberta, also visit the Alberta Learning Information Services (ALIS) website at <www.alis.alberta.ca> to compare provincial norms to the national rates.
5. Searching the job market: To keep current you will need to become familiar with the kinds of information available. Your task is to consider a position you would like to have and then clip or print potential job advertisement(s)/ announcement(s) from the following: (a) the classified section of a newspaper,

(b) a job board on the Web, (c) a company website, and (d) a professional association.

6. Case Study: As a career practitioner you are considering a one-year exchange with a practitioner in Winnipeg, Manitoba. Before you make the decision to move forward, you decide to apply your career management research and networking skills.

   (a) Write down some of the questions that you would have about:
      • the actual exchange,
      • the city of Winnipeg,
      • living/accommodations,
      • family needs/resources,
      • the job responsibilities,
      • the impact on your professional career.

   (b) Identify potential contacts that might be helpful in the transition (e.g., Winnipeg Chamber of Commerce).
   (c) Prepare five questions you would ask each of the potential contacts on your list.

Resources and Readings

Resources

Web Resources

Labour Market Information

Alberta Employment and Immigration (2009). Making Sense of Labour Market Information <http://alis.alberta.ca/pdf/cshop/LabourMarketInfo.pdf>.
British Columbia — Labour Market information <http://www.labourmarketservices.gov.bc.ca/labour_market_information.html>.
Human Resources and Skills Development Canada (HRDSC) — Labour Market Information <http://www.hrsdc.gc.ca/eng/jobs/lmi/publications/index.shtml>. "Labour Market Bulletins provide an analysis of the local labour market and an assessment of local employment-related events." HRSDC offices across Canada provide information such as local occupational and industrial trends, wage data, and training information. This information is also available through the HRDSC website.

WorkinfoNet — Directory to Resources

Alberta Learning Information Service <http://www.alis.gov.ab.ca> (English only)
Manitoba WorkInfoNet <http://mb.workinfonet.ca/> (English and French).

Ontario WorkInfoNet <http://www.onwin.ca> (English and French) — many
resources but some links may no longer be active.

Career Related

CareerWise from ContactPoint: Weekly roundup up news and views in the career
development field. <http://contactpoint.ca/careerwise/>.
Service Canada: Training and Careers <http://www.jobsetc.gc.ca/eng/>.
Links to tools for Career Navigator and Blueprint for Life/Work.
Alberta Learning Information Services: Self-Assessment Tools <http://alis.alberta.ca
/ec/cp/cpt/planning-tools.html>.
Careerinsite: career planning <https://careerinsite.alberta.ca/careerinsite.aspx>.
Ontario School Counsellors' Association has a page of self-assessment tools
<http://www.osca.ca/en/students/help-with-career-choices/self-assessment>.
Quintessential Careers (a plethora of articles and career tools on decision making)
<http://www.quintcareers.com/>.

Job Search Sites

National Job Bank <http://www.jobbank.gc.ca/>
Hot Jobs in Canada <http://www.hotjobscanada.ca>
Career builder <http://www. careerbuilder.com>
Monster <http://www.monster.ca>
Snag a Job <http://www.snagajob.com>

Decision Making

Decision-making Worksheet <https://career.berkeley.edu/plan/
DecisionMakingWorksheet.pdf>.
Make Decisions — Visualization Exercise <https://career.berkeley.edu/plan/
VisualizationExercise.stm>.
Career Decision making — University of Waterloo <http://www.careerservices.
uwaterloo.ca/resources/CareerDecisionMaking.pdf>.
Understand the what and how of making a career decision: Florida State University
<http://www.career.fsu.edu/techcenter/individual/index.html>.

Goal Setting

Goal-Buddy.com <http://www.goal-buddy.com/>.
Goal-setting Guide <http://www.goal-setting-guide.com/goal-setting-tutorials/smart-
goal-setting>.
University of Victoria. Motivation and Goal Setting Work Sheet <http://coun.uvic.
ca/learning/motivation/goals.html>.

Supplementary Readings

Bimrose, J., & Barnes, S. A. (2007). Navigating the labour market: Career decision making and the role of guidance. Coventry: Warwick Institute for Employment Research and Department for Education and Skills. Retrieved from <http://www2.warwick.ac.uk/fac/soc/ier/publications/2007/egreport08.pdf>.

Domene, J. F., Nee, J. J., Cavanaugh, A. K., McLelland, S., Stewart, B., Stephenson, M., Kauffman, B., Tse, C. K., & Young, R. A. (2012). Young adult couples transitioning to work: The intersection of career and relationship. *Journal of Vocational Behavior, 81*(1), 17–25. doi: 10.1016/j.jvb.2012.03.005

Gluszynski, T. (2011). *Educational pathways of youth in Manitoba impacts of exposure to career planning services and parental involvement in learning: an examination of data from the Youth in Transition Survey.* Winnipeg, MB: Manitoba Education, Citizenship and Youth.

Jarvis, P. S. (2003). Educators use career games to teach lifelong career management skills. Techniques, 79(1), 34–49.

Merina, R. (2007). Pathways from school to work: Can the competencies acquired in leisure activities improve the construction of pathways? *Journal of Education and Work, 20*(2), 139–159. doi: 10.1080/13639080701314696

Shaffer, M. A., Kraimer, M. L., Chen, Y., & Bolino, M. C. (2012). Choices, challenges, and career consequences of global work experiences. *Journal of Management, 38*(4), 1282–1327. doi: 10.1177/0149206312441834

Zikic, J., & Klehe, U. C. (2006). Job loss as a blessing in disguise: The role of career exploration and career planning in predicting reemployment quality. *Journal of Vocational Behavior, 69*(3), 391–409. doi:10.1016/j

nine

Work Search Stratgies

DEIRDRE A. PICKERELL
Life Strategies Ltd.

PRE-READING QUESTIONS

As you begin, reflect on your own work search experiences:
1. How did you find your last job?
2. How did you research the career development sector?
3. When was the last time you updated your résumé?

Introduction and Learning Objectives

An important part of the career development process involves understanding various work search strategies, including exploring the world of work, gaining relevant experience, identifying job leads, and preparing work search documents such as résumés and cover letters. Career practitioners, and their clients, need to understand the opportunities available now, trends for the future, and how to quickly and efficiently source relevant and accurate career information. Once career opportunities are identified, clients need to gain relevant experience (if they don't already have it), prepare their work search documents, and be ready for job interviews and negotiations.

At the end of this chapter, you will be able to help clients:

1. Be alert to employment trends and new job opportunities.
2. Develop options for gaining experience.

3. Be able to analyze their skills and values.
4. Build a career portfolio.
5. Use several methods for identifying job leads.
6. Create a master application form.
7. Develop an effective résumé.
8. Write persuasive cover letters.
9. Prepare for job interviews.
10. Be prepared to negotiate compensation.

Ten Components of Work Search Strategies

There are 10 key components to any work search strategy. Some components are the responsibility of the client, others the responsibility of the practitioner, and some are actioned by both. In the sections that follow, a brief summary of the 10 key components is provided.

1. Exploring Opportunities

The Canadian workplace is in a constant state of flux. Gone are many of the more traditional forms of employment that offered secure, long-term opportunities with one organization, along with medical and dental benefits, regular salary increases, and a pension. Today's workers may be self-employed, juggle multiple part-time jobs, or work virtually. There may be a small contingent of Canadians working for a multi-national corporation; many others will be employed in one of Canada's one million small businesses (Industry Canada, 2012).

Exploring opportunities focuses on learning about the world of work by asking: What jobs are available in my community today? What jobs will be available in the future? As a career practitioner you will have an important role in helping clients learn more about the type of work available, current employment trends, and prospects for the future. There is a wide-range of resources designed to assist you and your clients in researching career information and employment opportunities. Each province and territory has a website (or section of a website) that focuses on local labour market

Look Before You Leap: Self-Employment Survival Strategies

by Deirdre A. Pickerell

Self-employment is a growing trend in many sectors, and increasingly an option for career practitioners and counsellors. CERIC and Life Strategies Ltd. partnered on a Look Before You Leap project. The book *Look Before You Leap: Self-Employment Survival Strategies* is freely available at <http://issuu.com/ceric_ca/docs/look_before_you_leap_full_book_2011/1?e=2937234/3571913>.

information. This list is available at the end of the chapter. As with any research, check that the resources identified are relevant, reliable, and up to date.

2. Gaining Relevant Experience

Before making a firm commitment to enroll in an education program or to begin a focused job search, it may be important to gain relevant experience. This experience may be as brief as a visit to a job site while exploring work opportunities, or a longer commitment designed to develop required skills for a specific position. There are many ways for clients to gain relevant work experience, including volunteering, job shadowing, internships, and co-op terms.

Volunteering involves working without pay. Sometimes experience as a volunteer in an organization is a prerequisite for employment or for admission into an educational program. Clients should approach volunteering with the same level of professional commitment as they would paid employment. There are many benefits from volunteering:

- demonstrating skills and abilities to prospective employers,
- developing skills and knowledge,
- exploring and learning more about potential careers,
- giving back to the community,
- expanding professional networks.

When used as a work search strategy, clients should look for volunteer opportunities with organizations that match their career interests and values.

Job shadowing involves observing someone at work for a few hours or a few days. Some job shadowing is informal, such as simply observing people as they go about their tasks (e.g., restaurant server, bus driver, or teacher). A formal job shadow program allows clients to truly experience the position, ask questions, develop a relationship with the employer, and demonstrate skills and talents. When setting up a formal job shadow placement be sure to identify any workers' compensation or liability insurance requirements for your jurisdiction; that is, who covers your client should he/she suffer a workplace injury?

A work internship, practicum, or co-op term offers clients practical, hands-on experience in a specific job. These types of placements are usually unpaid, or paid below industry standard, and may last from one week to several months. Individuals are usually given the tasks and responsibilities of an employee in that same position with varying levels of supervision. Many such placements are completed as part of an educational program. *As with job shadowing, ensure clients are covered under workers' compensation and liability insurance.*

❖ *Stop and Reflect*

Workers' compensation programs are administered by provincial and territorial governments. As each geographical region may have different requirements, it will be important to contact the local office for information regarding coverage. See the following website for provincial links: <http://www.ccohs.ca/oshanswers/information /wcb_canada.html>.

3. Identifying Skills and Values

Once clients have explored the world of work and identified what type of position they might be interested in, they need to focus on their skills, interests, values, and personality, and think about how the sum of who they are connects to the work they are interested in doing. Amundson and Poehnell (2008) introduced The Wheel (Figure 1), a useful career-planning model that comprises eight areas to consider when contemplating career goals.

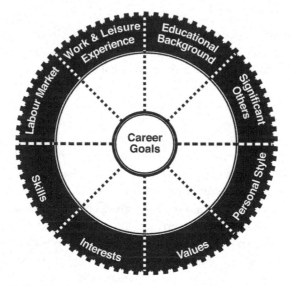

Figure 1: The Wheel. From N. Amundson & G. Poehnell, 2008, *Career Pathways* (2nd ed.). Richmond, BC: Ergon. Reproduced with permission.

The top half of The Wheel considers external factors (e.g., labour market or career opportunities, work experience, education, significant others, etc.), while the bottom relates to personal characteristics (e.g., skills, interests, values, style). The bottom half identifies what clients have to offer employers. Career assessments, whether formal psychometric tools (e.g., **Majors Personality Type Indicator** to measure personal style) or informal checklists (e.g., a proprietary tool developed by an organization for their clients), are a great way to quickly and efficiently identify a client's skills, interests, values, and personal style.

❖ *Did You Know?*
The Canadian government offers a series of career quizzes designed to link abilities, learning styles, and work values to various occupations. Check <http://www.jobsetc.gc.ca/toolbox/quizzes/quizzes_home.do> (requires registration).

Vignette: About Jason
Jason is 28 years old, single, and living in downtown Vancouver, BC. He recently completed his bachelor's degree in Computer Science at Dalhousie University, with a specialization in Graphics, Gaming, and Media. His degree program had a co-op component that allowed him to alternate study terms with paid, full-time employment. This created opportunities for Jason to apply his learning to real-world situations, gain valuable work experience, and build his career portfolio. Jason has come to Vancouver looking for employment as a video game designer.

Jason's Wheel would look like Table 1 below.

JASON'S PERSONAL CHARACTERISTICS	
Skills	Computer animation, various programs related to video game design, demonstrated ability to work under pressure, team player.
Values	Fast-paced environments, creative expression.
Personal Style	Outgoing, change-seeking, competitive.
EXTERNAL FACTORS	
Career Opportunities	Vancouver, BC, has a thriving video game design industry with some of the top firms (e.g., Electronic Arts) located in the Greater Vancouver area.
Work/Life Experiences	Won local and provincial arts awards; co-op terms provided valuable experience; has letters of reference from host employers.
Learning Experiences	Bachelor of Computer Science degree with a specialization in Graphics, Gaming, and Media.
Significant Others	Having recently relocated, Jason doesn't have any significant others in Vancouver but is developing a wide circle of friends.

Table 1: Jason's Completed Wheel.

❖ *Did You Know?*

- Amundson and Poehnell (1998, 2008) introduce The Wheel and provide some structure for moving through each of the eight sections in the two great resources, *Career Pathways* and *Career Pathways: Quick Trip*. Both are available from the publisher at <http://www.ergoncommunications.com/>.
- Check "10 Tips for Selecting Career Assessments" at <http://www.lifestrategies.ca/docs/10-Tips-for-selecting-assessments.pdf>.

4. Creating a Portfolio

A **career portfolio** is a collection of artifacts that demonstrate a client's unique skills and talents. Through their portfolio, clients can showcase their academic achievements, employment experience, accomplishments, skills, and awards. A portfolio might include:

- certificates, diplomas, transcripts,
- thank-you letters, accolades, awards,
- references from supervisors and clients,
- performance reviews / evaluations,
- résumé, biography, or brochure,
- work samples or photographs.

Even if never shown to a prospective employer, a career portfolio can provide the best method for storing career-related documents. The initial design and set-up of any portfolio will take time and effort but maintenance will be relatively simple. As each client is unique, each portfolio will also be unique in terms of its content; however, the overall structure can likely be similar. To begin, have clients gather and sort information into relevant themes (e.g., job descriptions, résumés, certificates, and reference letters). Then, have clients select a storage system such as an accordion file folder or binder with tabbed sections. Some clients may prefer to create and store their portfolios online. Online portfolios save paper, are environmentally friendly, and can support multi-media formats (e.g., videos, links to articles, and photographs). Clients have many options to choose from, including using sites designed specifically for portfolios (e.g., <http://

Guerrilla Marketing

by Lara Shepard

Guerrilla marketing is the use of unconventional tactics to get noticed and hired. It calls for energy, imagination, and creativity and requires one to thoroughly understand target employers, their products, and their competition, before approaching them for a job.

For more information read *Guerrilla Marketing for Job Hunters 3.0* by David Perry (<http://www.gm4jh.com/>) or listen to the audio Guerilla Job Search Secrets at <http://www.gm4jh.com/freecd/>.

www.carbonmade.com>), or creating a simple, user-friendly website where navigation relates to the sections of their portfolio.

As Jason is looking for work as a video game designer, an online portfolio is a great option. It will allow him to showcase school and work projects, demonstrate his design skills, and make effective use of available multi-media options. The following sites are examples of online portfolios by game designers: SSFusion (<http://ssfusion. com>), Devil's Garage (<http://www.devilsgarage.com/>), and Geneticeye (<http:// geneticeye-arts.com/>).

5. Identifying Job Leads

To identify job leads, clients often use online work search sites (see list at end of chapter; e.g., Monster.ca, Workopolis, Craigslist), and various newspapers that might advertise available positions. Other sources of leads might be government job banks, signs in windows, union halls, and even community bulletin boards. However, because all of these sources lead to advertised jobs, clients will need to compete with other job seekers.

As a career practitioner, try to help clients uncover the **hidden job market** (i.e., those jobs currently available, or about to become available, that aren't yet advertised). It is estimated that only about 10–25% of jobs are advertised, resulting in 75–90% being found through the hidden job market. As clients are likely to encounter less competition for unadvertised jobs, it is worth searching for them.

Networking is an important work search strategy and can be very useful in exploring the hidden job market. Networking is defined as "a proactive behaviour that helps develop one's relationship constellation with others who have the potential to assist them in their work or career" (Forret & Dougherty, 2004, p. 403). In working with clients, it is important to have them identify everyone who might be in their network (e.g., peers, family members, teachers, past employers, neighbours, professionals, and community leaders) regardless of whether or not they believe that contact will be able to help. Clients can use members of their network to learn more about a specific occupation or industry, to become connected with others who may offer assistance/advice, provide referrals, or act as references. Regardless of the method (e.g., phone, email, and/or career fair) it is important to ensure clients understand networking etiquette:

- keeping contacts informed of your skills, abilities, and education;
- being specific with your requests;
- nurturing your network;
- identifying what help you may be able to provide;
- going beyond "schmoozing" or collecting business cards — seeking to build relationships;
- thanking your contacts for any assistance provided.

Some clients might be interested in using social media (e.g., Facebook, LinkedIn) to network, identify job leads, and research potential employers. It is important, however, that clients follow some simple rules to ensure their use of social media doesn't harm future opportunities. At minimum, clients should set account privacy levels to the highest, most secure setting, upload only those photos suitable for prospective employers to view, and watch whom they accept as friends/contacts.

As Jason is new to Vancouver, he doesn't have many contacts in his network. To help explore the hidden job market, and to expand his network, Jason joins the International Game Developers Association's Vancouver chapter, regularly visits his local employment centre, and contacts relevant local organizations to request an informational interview. In preparing to cold call local employers, Jason first prepares a list of employers and key staff to contact. He then develops the following 30-second summary (also referred to as an "elevator pitch").

Hello, my name is Jason Matthews. I recently relocated to Vancouver after completing my bachelor's in Computer Science degree at Dalhousie University where I specialized in Graphics, Gaming, and Media. I am highly skilled in Maya, Z Brush, Nuke, and the full range of Adobe arts tools as demonstrated by my 3.8 GPA. I'm interested in learning more about the industry here in Vancouver and where you feel the industry is headed. I'd also love to learn more about what your organization is doing. Do you have time for an informational interview, either over the phone or in-person?

In supporting clients to create their elevator statement, it is a good idea to have one of your own as a sample. To begin, reflect on the points in the sample below:

Introduction:
Hi, my name is _____

Educational background:
This June, I'll be graduating from _____ university with a degree
in _____

Three or four key strengths to include:
accomplished facilitator – consistently evaluated at 4.5/5,
ability to provide exceptional client-centred career services,
certified Personality Dimensions™ facilitator.

Interest in the employer:
I see your team was recently honoured with the Career Development Award of Excellence. After reviewing your website I'm amazed at the breadth of work that you do.

Specific request:
Informational interview to learn more about your organization.

---

6. Creating a Master Application Form

Application forms are common screening tools that allow employers to gather consistent information from all job applicants. Although some employers use paper applications, many have transitioned to online versions. The key to successfully completing any application form is preparation. As most application forms will require the same information, it is relatively easy for clients to prepare in advance.

Most application forms have the following sections:

1. Contact information: generally full name, mailing address, phone number, and email. Clients should ensure their voicemail message and email address convey the right image. A silly phone greeting (e.g., "I listen to ABC Radio") or unprofessional email address (e.g., ilovedogs@email.com) may result in the employer screening them out. Clients can easily update their phone message and get a work-related email address through a free email service (e.g., GMail, Yahoo).
2. Employment history: clients can expect to provide job title, employer name, and dates (month and year) of their last three to five positions. Application forms may also ask for special duties/accomplishments, supervisor name, and contact information. Some forms will also ask the reason for leaving each prior position. This might be a difficult section for some clients, as the space provided may not allow for detailed explanations.
3. Education: similar to employment history, clients can expect to provide the course or program name, credential earned (e.g., certificate, degree), and dates (month and year). It is fine to list education as "in progress" or "22 credits towards bachelor's degree" for any education that has been started but not completed.
4. Relevant skills: some application forms will provide space to list skills. Many online application forms will ask for a skills summary or list of key words that allows employers to search their database of qualified applicants. In these instances, if key words are not listed, the application will not come up in a search.

Social insurance numbers, passport numbers, and similar personal information should never be requested on an application form. Coach your clients on appropriate ways to handle requests for sensitive information (i.e., it is okay to add a note stating social insurance number will be provided if hired). When completing any application form, clients should print neatly and follow all instructions, ensuring the information they have provided is legible and accurate. Any special requests (i.e., please attach your résumé) should also be accommodated. In instances where a client cannot complete an application form, it is best to take it away and return with all the necessary information.

Online application forms can be a bit challenging to complete due to time and space limitations, "required" fields that your client may prefer not to fill out, or drop down menus that do not quite fit. Coach clients to highlight, copy, and paste the online application into a Word document whenever possible. This process will allow them to save a record of their form, and also guard against losing everything they have typed due to an Internet interruption. Word will also highlight any obvious typing mistakes (i.e., spelling and grammatical errors) that clients may not notice when proofreading their submission. In choosing this method, however, clients must carefully check the completed online application as copying and pasting from Word to the Internet might insert unexpected codes or symbols.

7. Developing Effective Résumés

Résumés continue to be a crucial work search document. Yet, with many employers spending less than five seconds to initially screen a résumé, it is crucial for clients to prepare documents that are clear, compelling, and present only information the employer will want to know. Although there are several types of résumés, as noted in Table 2, it is important to help clients choose the format that will best highlight their knowledge, experience, and skills.

Most résumés will include the following sections:

1. Job/Career Objective: Following contact information, an objective is a simple statement that clarifies what job the candidate is seeking.
2. Profile or Career Highlights: Key accomplishments, skills, awards, and traits designed to grab the employer's attention.
3. Skills and Experience: Detailed list of skills and experience, called skill statements, usually sorted in clusters of similar skills (e.g., Administration, Facilitation, Computer). Every skill statement should be presented using the SAR format of situation — action — result (sometimes referred to as STAR format where T stands for task):

    a) *Situation* — the problem, challenge, or situation; may also include who was involved (i.e., client, co-worker, and customer) and how the problem surfaced.
    b) *Action* — the steps the client took to resolve the situation; may include who the client had to speak with.
    c) *Result* — outcome of the situation or what was accomplished; if the outcome wasn't positive, clients should focus on what they would do differently next time. The result is the key component of each SAR statement; examples include "increased sales by 15% in the 3rd quarter."

TYPE AND DESCRIPTION	ADVANTAGES	DISADVANTAGES
Chronological: lists most recent job experience first.	Highlights strong, consistent work history.	Highlights gaps in employment and irrelevant experience.
Functional or skills: strong section on skill.	Highlights strengths / hides weaknesses.	Employers may not like.
Combination: hybrid chronological and functional.	Highlights skills but presents details in chronological format.	Gaps in employment history are still apparent.

Table 2: Formats for Résumés.

4. Employment History: List of recent employment history in reverse chronological order (i.e., most recent first). Include job title, employer name, and dates. On some résumés, three to five key skills statements will be listed for each position.
5. Education: Relevant education listed in reverse chronological order.
6. Additional sections might include memberships in professional associations, volunteer activities, and hobbies or interests. In deciding what sections to put on a résumé, clients must ensure each statement adds value (i.e., the employer might not need to know your client likes to read mysteries). Clients should target each résumé to a specific position, rather than having one generic résumé they send to every employer. Résumés must never be sent out with inaccurate information or spelling/grammar errors. Each résumé should have an attractive format with no redundancy.

❖ *Did You Know?*
A wide range of résumé builders/templates are available online:

- The Resume Builder <www.theresumebuilder.com/>,
- How to Write a Resume.net <www.howtowritearesume.net>,
- Resume Builder Template.com <www.resumebuildertemplate.com>,
- Certified Résumé Strategist certification, available from Career Professionals of Canada; learn more at <http://www.careerprocanada.ca/>.

8. Writing Cover Letters

A targeted cover letter provides clients with an opportunity to introduce themselves to potential employers, offer information not contained in their résumé, highlight key skills and attributes, and show their interest in the position and the employer's organization. Cover letters should be clear, concise, and targeted to a specific position. Cover letters should follow a standard format:

1. The first paragraph should outline the reason for applying. It often describes how the applicant heard about the opening (i.e., via an advertisement or referral) and why he/she is interested in the position. This is an opportunity for the applicant to also demonstrate some knowledge about the organization. Inform your clients that it can be risky to mention a friend or colleague by name, in case that person is not respected by the employer. If the client is confident that his or her contact is in a position of respect, it can strengthen the cover letter. However, if there are any doubts, the client should avoid making that connection.

2. The second paragraph should provide a clear link between the job advertisement and the client's skills and experience. Ensure key points from the job ad or elements from the job description are sufficiently covered. Encourage clients to also highlight how the organization would benefit from hiring them.

3. The third and closing paragraph should express appreciation for the employer's time and attention, show interest in meeting the employer, and outline the best way to be reached. Encourage clients to follow up on their cover letters.

As with any business letter, cover letters must include contact information for both the sender (client) and receiver (employer). When addressing cover letters, ensure that the employer's name and title are correct. If a name is not available, *Dear Hiring Manager* would be more appropriate than *Dear Sir or Madam*. Encourage clients to produce cover letters with the same format or look as their résumés (e.g., font, colour, paper) to keep both documents consistent. Together, a résumé and cover letter represent a client's "personal brand" and allow his or her creativity to shine through. However, it is important to not sacrifice quality of content for a good "look."

When writing any document, clients should use active rather than passive voice (i.e., speak about things *they* did). It is also important to adopt a style that is clear, concise, and professional; to include only key points the employer might need to know; and to avoid unfamiliar words or technical jargon. For more tips on writing professional documents, see <http://www.lifestrategies.ca/docs/10-Tips-for-Writing-Professional-Documents.pdf>.

Most importantly, caution clients to proofread carefully for overall readability and proper grammar, spelling, and punctuation. Errors on work search documents may result in a qualified applicant being screened out. Career practitioners can play a huge role helping clients develop their work search documents and may include acting as proofreader or editor. For tips on editing professional documents see <http://www.lifestrategies.ca/docs/10-Tips-for-Editing-Professional-Documents.pdf>.

9. Preparing for Interviews

Job interviews can be stressful events for many clients. Career practitioners can help alleviate part of that stress by ensuring clients are well prepared for job interviews. To begin, clients need to know the different types of interviews they may experience. Table 3 below is an overview of the types of interviews. For more detailed information on the various types of interviews, please see Types of Resumes at JobSkills.info (<http://www.jobskills.info/resume_edge/types_of_interview.htm>).

TYPE OF INTERVIEW	DESCRIPTION
Screening	Brief Goal is to ensure candidate meets job's basic criteria
One-on-One Interview	Most common Involves one interviewer and one applicant
Panel or Committee Interview	More than one interviewer Each interviewer helps make the hiring decision
Group Interview	More than one candidate Might involve direct questions and group activities
Telephone Interview	Used to screen applicants, minimize interview costs, or bridge a distance gap
Informal Lunch/Coffee Interview	Often more casual than other types of interviews Candidate must manage eating and drinking
Stress	Seeks to measure candidate's ability to respond to stressful situations
Peer	Uses potential co-workers to interview candidate

Table 3: Steps to Career Decision Making.

Regardless of the type of interview, employers will often use a targeted behaviour approach, which is based on the belief that past behaviour can predict future behaviour. These types of questions ask interviewees to describe specific incidents or experiences. Targeted behavioural questions are very difficult to "fake," so clients should be encouraged to be well prepared and, if they truly haven't experienced the situation being discussed, to be honest with the employer. It is better to say *"I haven't had to deal with that type of situation, but believe I would_____."* Being prepared for interviews will help clients respond to these types of questions with confidence. To begin, clients can research the types of questions common to the job they are applying for (e.g., customer service positions might focus on dealing with customer complaints; sales positions might focus on strategies to increase sales). As clients prepare for interviews, it is important that they consider what types of questions they might wish to ask the employer. Ensure questions are appropriate to the interview stage (e.g., at first interview ask about job content/corporate culture, or upcoming projects; do not ask about salary, benefits, or vacation).

Clients also need to be aware that employers will sometimes ask illegal or unethical questions. These are questions that ask about race, ethnicity, gender, marital status, sexual preference, family status, age, and religious or political beliefs. Clients can choose to answer the question, which may make a good impression but leave them feeling violated. They can also choose to not answer, which may or may not impact their chance of getting the job. Clients could also redirect the question (e.g., "I think you may be asking about my availability for work in emergencies; we have an amazing support system within our extended family, so it's never an issue for me to adjust my hours as needed").

After the interview, clients should be encouraged to send a thank-you note to each interviewer. In 2009, Career Builder (www.careerbuilder.com) conducted a survey that found that "5 percent of hiring managers say they would not hire someone who failed to send a thank-you letter after the interview. Thirty-two percent say they would still consider the candidate, but would think less of him or her." For more tips of postinterview follow-up, please see <http://www.lifestrategies .ca/docs/10-Tips-for-Job-Interview-Follow-Up.pdf>.

❖ *Did You Know?*
Career Professionals of Canada offers certification as a Certified Interview Strategist. Learn more at <http://www.careerprocanada.ca/>.

10. Understanding Negotiation Strategies

Regardless of the position, clients should be prepared to speak to prospective employers regarding wages, benefits, and other work-related issues (e.g., tuition allowance, vacation, etc.). While negotiation might not always be possible (i.e., sometimes the employer's terms will be clear), it is important that clients carefully consider what they might need and/or want from a position. The first, and perhaps most important step, is to understand what the position is really worth. Ensure clients have researched:

- *Wages*: Use salary surveys and informational interviews to discover the salary range common to the position. Clients need to realize that education, years of experience, and location can make a big difference in wage rates (i.e., someone relatively new to a position or working in a rural community can probably expect to earn less than a someone with several years of experience working in downtown Toronto).

- *Benefits*: Extended health, dental, eye care, and a multitude of other benefits might be available. Larger employers can often offer more extensive options, due to volume cost savings, but many small employers have access to plans. Health and dental benefits might be very important to some clients (i.e., single parent with children), but not matter a great deal to others (i.e., individual who is covered under a spouse's plan). In exploring benefits, clients need to know if any part of the cost is recovered from the employee via payroll deductions.
- *Pension/RRSP*: Does the employer have an established pension or contribute to RRSPs on behalf of employees?
- *Vacation*: Each province or territory will have some form of legislation covering vacation time allowed. Clients can research what the minimum amount is in their region and use that as a guide when talking with employers.
- *Tuition allowance*: Does the employer support ongoing education, with either time off or some form of tuition reimbursement?

When comparing offers, clients should look at the total compensation package (i.e., wages plus benefits). In some cases, compensation packages can add up to several thousand dollars per year in non-cash items; or, conversely, add 15–30% of value to a base salary. Regardless of the total compensation, clients need to know (a) what wage they need to take home in order to make ends meet, and (b) what other benefits they consider "must haves."

Jason has established a realistic budget based on his rent, utilities, food, other personal items, transit costs, entertainment, and remaining student loans. At minimum, Jason needs to earn $2,800 per month, or $33,600 per year. When looking for work, Jason turns down any opportunity that comes in lower than that figure. While he recognizes the need to find work and the value of getting established, he also knows he has to earn enough to pay his bills.

Summary

Career practitioners have an important role to play in supporting clients with various work search strategies. Clients might need assistance researching occupational information, developing résumés, or preparing for interviews. Effective work search strategies can go a long way in helping to obtain a person's ideal job as well as build confidence in a job seeker's ability to find the job that fits. Although this chapter provided a brief overview of the 10 key components of work search strategies, career practitioners are encouraged to engage in additional research and learning in order to be well prepared to support clients as they prepare for the world of work.

Importance of Volunteering

by Lara Shepard

Volunteering is an excellent strategy for building skills, meeting people, contributing to the community, and extending a résumé. Non-profit organizations depend on volunteer help to survive and offer many opportunities in all manner of capacities. Many non-profits have lots of ideas that they would like to accomplish for the community but don't have the resources, which means that volunteers are often relied upon to make this happen.

Check Volunteer Canada (<http://www.volunteer.ca>).

References

Amundson, N. E., & Poehnell, G. R. (2008). *Career pathways* (3rd ed.). Richmond, BC: Ergon Communications.

Amundson, N.E., & Poehnell, G. R. (1998). *Career pathways: Quick trip*. Richmond, BC: Ergon Communications.

Forret, M. L., & Dougherty, T. W. (2004). Networking behaviors and career outcomes: Differences for men and women? *Journal of Organizational Behavior, 25*(3), 419–437. doi: 10.1002/job.253

Industry Canada. (2012). *Key small business statistics*. Public Works and Government Services Canada: Ottawa, ON. Retrieved from <http://www.ic.gc.ca/eic/site/061.nsf/eng/h_02711.html>

Glossary

Career portfolio is a collection of artifacts that demonstrate a client's unique skills and talents.

Hidden job market refers to job openings that are not advertised or publicly listed. It also applies to situations where a job can be created, adapted, or modified for particular individuals. The most effective means for accessing this market are by word of mouth, active networking, social online networking, and unsolicited approaches to potential employers.

Majors Personality Type Indicator is an assessment tool consisting of 52 items and is a self-scoring questionnaire. The Indicator is designed to uncover information on how clients make decisions, direct their energy, take in information, and how they orient themselves to their environment. The result is a four-letter personality type code based on Jungian Type Theory (16 Personality Types):
- Introvert-Extrovert,
- Sensing-Intuition,

- Thinking-Feeling,
- Judging-Perceiving.

Networking is a process in which the client develops long-term relationships with others for mutual benefit.

Volunteering involves performing a service without pay in order to obtain work experiences, learn new skills, meet people, contribute to community, and help those less fortunate.

Discussion and Activities

Discussion

Questions

1. Career planning starts with the questions: "Who am I?" "What do I want?" and 'What am I capable of?" An honest and thorough self-analysis will help you to decide which areas of the employment market you wish to explore. How can you assist a client through this process?
2. Imagine that a client comes into your agency and says that they are unhappy with their work. What types of activities might you engage in to help the client decide whether it is the work situation or the career the client has chosen?
3. What is the difference between a job search and a career change?

Personal Reflection Questions

1. Think back on how you have undertaken your own work search. Which of the 10 components of work search strategies would you say was the most important?
2. How did you ensure that you had right strategies in place to engage effectively in finding work? What tools would you have liked in your "toolkit"?

Career Practitioner Role Questions

1. What key networking strategies would be steps in the right direction for your gaining greater control of your career?
2. Research an industry or company in your city. Can you predict what lies ahead for the industry or company that you researched?

Activities

For the following activities, find a partner to take on the role of a client.

Exploring Opportunities

To help partners get started, send them on a webquest (i.e., a Web-based scavenger hunt) in which they do the following:

- select a job they wish to learn more about;
- find three separate sources of information to identify:
  — job duties/tasks (i.e., job description),
  — required education, certifications, or licenses,
  — wage range,
  — employment prospects/trends.

Building Your Network

To help classmates get started, have them engage in the following activities:

- create a list of all members of their network,
- identify three to five people they could ask for assistance,
- prepare a script for the initial contact,
- identify a relevant career fair or plan.

Developing a 30-Second Summary

Use the following to guide a classmate in developing a 30-second summary.

Introduction	
Relevant education	
3–4 Key strengths	
Goal	

SAR–Skills Statements

Write up your partner's skill/accomplishment statements in the SAR format:

What was the situation?	
What action did you take?	
What were the results?	

Establishing a Budget

Working with your partner, use the chart below to calculate monthly expenses/required income.

ITEM	COST PER MONTH
Shelter (i.e., rent, mortgage)	
Personal taxes (i.e., property tax if you own a home)	
Transportation (i.e., car payment, maintenance, and insurance or transit)	
Food	
Household operation (i.e., utilities, cable/Internet)	
Health care	
Recreation	
Clothing	
Other:	
Other:	
Other:	
Total monthly expenses:	

Resources and Readings

Resources
....

Web Resources

Government of Canada

Government of Canada Labour Market Information
    <http://www.servicecanada.gc.ca/eng/sc/lminfo/index.shtml>.
Government of Canada: Working in Canada <http://www.workingincanada.gc.ca/>.
The National Occupational Classification (NOC) tool that includes a self-directed
    tutorial <http://www5.hrsdc.gc.ca/noc/english/noc/2006/Tutorial.aspx> is a key
    resource for anyone who needs to explore work opportunities.

Provincial Labour Market Sites

Alberta Labour Market Information <http://eae.alberta.ca/labour-and-immigration
    /labour-market-information.aspx>.
Work BC <http://www.workbc.ca/>.
Manitoba Prospects <http://www.gov.mb.ca/tce/lmi/prospects/index.html>.
New Brunswick Post-Secondary Education, Training and Labour
    <http://www2.gnb.ca/content/gnb/en/departments/post-secondary_
    education_training_and_labour/Labour.html>.
    <http://www.gnb.ca/redirect/0105/0126/index.htm>.
Newfoundland and Labrador LMI Works <http://www.lmiworks.nl.ca/>.
Northwest Territories Career and Labour Market Information
    <http://www.ece.gov.nt.ca/advanced-education/career-and-employment
    /career-labour-market-information>.
Careers Nova Scotia <http://careers.novascotia.ca/>.
Ontario Job Futures <http://www.tcu.gov.on.ca/eng/labourmarket/>.
Saskatchewan NetWork <http://www.sasknetwork.gov.sk.ca/>.
Yukon WorkInfoNet <http://www.yuwin.ca/>.

Interview Skills

Interview Skills #5: The "STAR" Technique to Answer Behavioral Interview Questions
    <http://www.rightattitudes.com/2008/07/15/star-technique-answer-interview
    -questions/>.

For Practitioners

Can Learn <http://www.canlearn.ca>.

Circuit Coach, although focused on youth, includes fabulous information and ready-to-use workshops on a wide range of work search topics. Read more at <http://www.ccdf.ca/ccdf/NewCoach/english>.

ContactPoint <http://www.contactpoint.ca>.

Ontario School Counsellors' Association Resources <http://www.osca.ca/>.

Networking

Adams, J. (2011). Assessing the hidden job market: How to find a SME job. Career Options <http://www.careeroptionsmagazine.com/4999 /accessing-the-hidden-job-market-how-to-find-an-sme-job/>.

Portfolios

A Self-Managed Career Portfolio Guide <http://www.edu.gov.mb.ca/k12/docs /support/c_portfolio/index.html>.

Career portfolios: Telling your life/work story <http://www.blueprint4life.ca /blueprint/documents/BPAppE.pdf>.

Résumé Skills

Ten Tips for Crafting Compelling Résumés <http://www.lifestrategies.ca/docs/10-Tips-for-Crafting-Compelling-Resumes.pdf>.

Volunteering

Canadian Volunteering Contacts <http://www.canadiancareers.com /volunteering.html>.

Volunteer Canada <http://volunteer.ca>

Youth Canada <http://www.youth.gc.ca/eng/topics/jobs/volunteer.shtml>.

Work Search Sites

ALIS Career Shop <http://alis.alberta.ca/ep/careershop/main.html>.

Monster Job Search <http://www.monster.ca>

Job Bank <http://www.jobbank.gc.ca>.

Workopolis <http://www.workopolis.com/en/common/homepage.aspx>.

Youth Employment Strategy Programs <http://www.servicecanada.gc.ca/eng/epb/yi/yep/newprog/yesprograms.shtml>.

Supplementary Readings

Amundson, N. E. (2009). *Metaphor making: Your career, your life, your way*. Richmond, BC: Ergon Communications. Available at <http://www.ergoncommunications.com/>.

What Works: Career-Building Strategies for People from Diverse Groups

by Lara Shepard

What Works is an online publication available for free from the Alberta Learning Information Service. Chapters cover Aboriginal Peoples; Ex-Offenders; Gender; Immigrants; Older Workers; Persons With Developmental Disabilities; Persons With Learning Disabilities; Persons With Low Income; Persons With Mental Health Disabilities; Sexual Minorities; and Youth.
<http://alis.alberta.ca/ep/careershop/showproduct.html?DisplayCode=PRODUCT&EntityKey=6100>

A book, with accompanying card sort, introduces 40 metaphors for counsellors to use with clients — both individuals and groups — who are looking for work.

Amundson, N. E., & Poehnell, G. R. (2001). *Career Crossroads: A personal career positioning system.* Richmond, BC: Ergon Communications. Available at <http://www.ergoncommunications.com/>. This workbook guides readers through a series of steps related to managing their careers. Readers will explore options, evaluate current work and future possibilities, and consider whether to stay on their current career path or transition to something new.

Amundson, N., Poehnell, G., & Pattern, M. (2005). *Careerscope: Looking in, looking out, looking around.* Richmond, BC: Ergon Communications. Available at <http://www.ergoncommunications.com/>.

McCormick, R., Amundson, N. E., & Poehnell, G. R. (2002). *Guiding circles: An Aboriginal guide to finding career paths.* Richmond, BC: Ergon Communications. Available at <http://www.ergoncommunications.com/>. Similar to the popular Career Pathways book, but based on Aboriginal traditions and wisdom.

Neault, R. (2006). *Career strategies for a lifetime of success.* Coquitlam, BC: Life Strategies. Consists of six modules (also sold separately as e-books), including:

- Time to Reflect: Understanding Yourself,
- Time to Explore: Understanding the Workplace,
- Time to Choose: Identifying Career Possibilities,
- Time to Prepare: Developing Portfolios, Résumés, and Interview Skills,
- Time for Action: Successful Marketing Strategies,
- Time to Look Ahead: Proactive Career Management.

For adults of all ages, this workbook contains invaluable tips for successfully managing careers. Available at <https://www.lifestrategies.ca/store/proddetail.php?prod=Strategies>.

Niles, S. G., Amundson, N. E., & Neault, R. (2011). *Career flow: A hope-centered approach to career development.* Upper Saddle River, NJ: Prentice Hall. Using a "career flow" metaphor, the authors outline several strategies for addressing career challenges in the 21st century.

O'Byrne, B. (1998). Discovering futures: Featuring the Career Compass Model. Toronto, ON: Guidance Centre.

SECTION 4

Working With Diversity

ten

Employment Counselling and Poverty

A View From the Frontline in British Columbia

STEPHEN HILL
Employment Counsellor

PRE-READING QUESTIONS

1. What are the reasons for poverty in a rich, industrialized country?
2. What makes a person or family considered "poor"? What income level or lack of income is involved?
3. To what extent do you think it is possible to eliminate poverty?
4. Are people poor because they are unemployed, or are people unemployed because they are poor?

Introduction and Learning Objectives

The other day I was walking from the bus stop to where I work as an Employment Counsellor in the Downtown Eastside of Vancouver, BC. On the corner a man stood with both a battered Tim Horton's cup to collect spare change and several packs of counterfeit cigarettes tucked under his arm. Alternating pitches between "spare change" and "cigarettes, cigarettes" most passersby did just that. One elderly woman dropped a quarter into the repurposed coffee cup. As I approach, Bill looks up and gives me a cheery "Stephen!" We agree it's a beautiful morning, and as I move to leave, Bill asks, "Are we still on for 9:30?" I tell him we are. We have an appointment to talk about finding work, emailing résumés, and whether the training we looked at last time might be available to Bill, existing on welfare of $610 a month. This is employment counselling with people who are "living" in poverty, and it is a world away from career counselling, career exploration, or theories of employment models.

The W for Vancouver's iconic Woodwards department store becomes the background for a poem: "You'll never live like Common People do, You'll never do whatever common people do, You'll never fail like common people, You'll never watch your life slide out of view." (From the song, "Common People" by Pulp, 1995.)

Figure 1: Photo of W with poem. Courtesy of Stephen Hill.

Despite the fact that Canada has one of the highest standards of living among all the developed nations, and has been voted numerous times in recent years by the United Nations as one of the best countries in the world in which to live, poverty is prevalent in Canada today (Mikkonen & Raphael, 2010). Chronic poverty results from the cumulative impact of discrimination, risk, vulnerability, and exclusion across the life-cycle and between generations. Multiple social and cultural factors, such as ethnicity, gender, physical disability, and mental health can determine an individual's vulnerability. This chapter outlines the cycle of poverty and the impact it has on the lives of unemployed people, their search for work from a social justice framework, and the role of the career practitioner in helping to break the cycle. "Poverty of ideas" will be explored in order to examine different ways of conceptualizing poverty and taking social action.

The learning objectives of this chapter are:

1. Define poverty and identify measures of poverty.
2. List and describe the categories of poverty.
3. Understand the various terms used in accessing social services.
4. Describe the cycle of poverty and the impact it has on working lives.
5. Explain the role of the career practitioner as an agent of social justice.
6. Describe various community and national social justice initiatives.

Poverty and Unemployment, Unemployment and Poverty
It would be nice if the poor were to get even half of the money
that is spent in studying them.
— Bill Vaughan

People who are unemployed often become more fearful and anxious as their financial resources dwindle and social connections weaken. Individuals who are also reliant on welfare have a second set of damaging problems to cope with: the shame, humiliation, and inadequacy of the welfare system.

What Is Poverty?

On the surface, being poor describes someone who doesn't have enough money. Nobel laureate Amartya Sen (1983) views poverty as that standard of living at which one cannot "achieve adequate participation in communal activities ... and be free from public shame from failure to satisfy conventions" (p. 167). The United Nations (2001) defines poverty as: "A human condition characterized by sustained or chronic deprivation of the resources, capabilities, choices, security and power necessary for the enjoyment of an adequate standard of living and other civil, cultural, economic, political and social rights" (n.p.). Common to both definitions is "a sense of what is decent" (Shillington, Lasota, & Shantz, 2009, p. 2) or acceptable, in guaranteeing the general welfare of all individuals.

Canada has no official definition of poverty, no official method of measuring poverty, and no official set of poverty lines. Various measures of poverty exist, including: (a) low income cut-offs (LICO); (b) low income measures (LIM); (c) market basket measures (MBM); and (d) basic needs poverty measures. These terms are defined below (Shillington et al., 2009; Statistics Canada, 2010).

- **Low Income Cut-Offs** (LICO): A calculated income threshold that takes into account the amount of income a family spends on the necessities, food, shelter, and clothing. For example, cost of necessities as a percentage of income may be 20 percentage points higher for poor families as for the average Canadian family.
- **Low Income Measures** (LIM): 50% of national median income adjusted for family size.
- **Market Basket Measures** (MBM): Cost of a basket of goods and services sufficient for a standard of living.
- **Basic Needs Measures** (BNM): Cost of a basket of goods needed to meet the basic physical needs for long-term survival.

Adjustments are typically made to these measures to account for variables such as family size and composition, location (i.e., urban/rural categories or city), and changes in living standards or price levels (Shillington et al., 2009). What is missing here is the human element. These measures are used by provincial and federal governments to categorize those who are living in poverty from those who aren't, and pay little attention to the individual.

A more humane gauge is the Ontario Deprivation Measure (Tamarack, n.d.). A "deprivation index" is a list of items or activities considered essential for a standard of living above the poverty level (given current social and economic conditions) but which poor people are unlikely to be able to afford. The intent of the index is to distinguish the poor from the non-poor. This poverty measure was developed through partnership of the Ontario Government, the Daily Bread Food Bank, the Caledon Institute of Social Policy, and Statistics Canada. It is the first deprivation index developed in North America (Matern, Mendelson, & Oliphant, 2009).

According to researchers (Matern et al., 2009), the deprivation index: (a) reflects the real-life experiences of the poor; (b) paints an authentic picture of poverty to the public; (c) is inclusive of other dimensions of poverty beyond income (e.g., social isolation); and (d) complements existing income measures.

Coming to Terms With Poverty

National Council of Welfare (2007) has estimated that over 15% of Canadians are living in poverty (about 4.9 million people). Child poverty rates are highest among new Canadians, Aboriginal peoples, and single parent households headed by women. When it comes to the material welfare of our nation's children, Canada now ranks a dismal 17th out of 24 high-income countries as evaluated by UNICEF (Adamson, 2010). The face of poverty differs across communities, particularly in the various regions in Canada.

Social welfare in Canada includes all government programs designed to give assistance to citizens outside of what the market provides. The Canadian social safety net includes a broad spectrum of programs. Under Canada's federal system, social programs are largely the responsibility of provinces. However, the federal government has charge over the employment insurance program.

In order to understand poverty and the implications of being poor, one has to have a firm grip on the various terms used.

The **minimum wage** is a provincial legally imposed lower limit on wage rates. For example, the minimum wage in British Columbia is $8.75 per hour,; and in Ontario is $10.25 per hour (both set in 2011).

A **living wage** is a level of hourly pay that enables a full-time worker to have enough to meet basic needs and build some savings for the future. This newer concept is based on the local cost-of-living and takes into account specific factors, with rent being the biggest single cost. In British Columbia, the Canadian Centre for Policy Alternatives (2013) calculated the 2013 living wage for a family in Metro Vancouver at $19.62 / hour. Several community organizations support the Living Wage for Families campaign whose slogan is "Work should lift you out of poverty, not keep you there." The living-wage measure includes other benefits such as medical services plan, matched RRSPs, a company bus pass, and other in-kind payments that contribute to the overall value of being employed.

Employment Insurance (EI) is a national program to assist Canadians who have lost their jobs or aren't able to work for other reasons. Canadian workers pay into a central fund that they may temporarily draw on if later they lose their job. The amount a person receives and for how long varies with previous salary, length of time at the job, and the unemployment rate in their area. Canadians who are sick, pregnant, or caring for a newborn or adopted child, as well as those who must care for a family member who is seriously ill with a significant risk of death, may also be assisted by Employment Insurance (Service Canada, 2013).

> ### Are You Living in Poverty?
> by Stephen Hill
>
> This easy-to-use calculator from A Living Wage for Families will show you if a person is being paid a living wage: <http://livingwageforfamilies.ca/calculator/>.

Hardship Assistance is a support and shelter allowance in British Columbia provided to persons who are not otherwise eligible for income assistance. A person who receives hardship assistance may have to repay the money to the Ministry of Social Development (<http://www.eia.gov.bc.ca/factsheets/2004/hardship.htm>).

Social Assistance is available in all provinces but the programs carry different names: "social assistance," "income support," "income assistance," and "welfare assistance." They are all popularly known as "welfare." The purpose is to alleviate extreme poverty by providing a monthly payment to people with little or no income. The rules for eligibility and the amount given vary widely among the provinces. For example, in British Columbia the following terms and categories are used:

1. **Income Assistance** is a basic monthly support and shelter allowance provided under the Employment and Assistance Act (EAA). People in poverty, without "good" work track records, savings, or family resources, are the frequent recipients in a recession.

   Income-assistance benefits for BC families have not kept pace with inflation. In one of its last reports before being cut in the federal budget in 2012, the National Council of Welfare (2010) reported that between 1998 and 2008, inflation-adjusted annual income-assistance benefits in BC fell by $449 for a lone parent with one child, and by $1,474 for a couple with two children. The inadequacy of income assistance is revealed in the increase in the number of individuals assisted by food banks which has risen from 67,237 in 2001 to 96,150 in 2012 (First Call: BC Child and Youth Advocacy Coalition, 2012).

2. **Disability Assistance** is a slightly higher, but still modest, monthly support and shelter allowance provided in British Columbia under the Employment and Assistance for Persons with Disabilities Act (EAPWDA) to those who meet the definition of person with disabilities (Klein & Pulkingham, 2008).

3. **Persons with Persistent Multiple Barriers (PPMB) assistance** is another program in British Columbia. This is intended to help those people facing many obstacles to employment, referred to as "multi-barriered." Those designated as "Persons with Persistent Multiple Barriers" do not receive more money; this assistance simply gives a temporary reprieve to individuals from not having to prove they are actively seeking work.

Imagine waking up each morning knowing that you have been so described. Much of my work is about diluting or countering the effects of this stigmatizing language and categorization on my clients' mental health, morale, and hope.

Categories of Poverty

Definitions of poverty can only be understood in relation to particular social, cultural, and historical contexts. Definitions are political and socially defined and as such have often been the source of controversy. There is no single "correct" definition. In Canada, Cabaj (2004) has developed a poverty matrix that identifies categories of people who are at risk of living in poverty.

At-Risk are those who are currently not poor, but are vulnerable to experiencing poverty in the near to medium future. Demographic groups that often fall into this category are young people struggling in school, people approaching retirement with little to modest savings or pension plans, people with mental disabilities, and persons working in struggling industries, businesses, sectors, or jobs (e.g., commercial fishery, downsizing corporations, etc.).

Working Poor (or Waged Poor) are individuals who are working in full-time, part-time, or seasonal jobs that pay poorly and provide few, if any, benefits. Workers receive inadequate wages and may lack the job stability to maintain themselves at a decent standard of living. Demographic groups that tend to fall into this category include youth, persons with high school education, single parents, older workers, seasonal workers, and immigrants.

Temporarily Unemployed are those individuals who are normally gainfully employed, often with good wages, but are temporarily unemployed due to a lay-off or firing, or because they have left a job voluntarily. Demographic groups that have a higher than normal incidence of temporary unemployment include those returning to school from the workforce, older workers transitioning to new employment due to a lay-off, seasonal workers, and women on maternity leave.

Persistently Unemployed are those who have trouble securing and maintaining paid work and often find themselves unemployed and frequently in need of social assistance. Demographic groups that experience higher than average rates of persistent unemployment include youth entering the job market, people involved in the criminal justice system, people with physical disabilities, people experiencing mental illness, Aboriginal peoples, and those without a high school education.

Dependent Poor are those who are unable to work and whose major source of income is from savings or government income support. There are several demographic groups more likely to be viewed as dependent poor. These include retired persons living on a fixed income, persons on long-term disability pensions, single parents, Aboriginal peoples, immigrants, and students.

Homeless tend to be individuals who have sporadic income that is insufficient to pay for basic food, shelter, and clothing. Historically, persons with mental illness and young people have a higher than average risk for homelessness. More recently, fully employed persons in major cities where rent is high and vacancy rates low (e.g., Calgary, Victoria, Vancouver) may be homeless while they look for accommodation.

Surviving (on) Welfare

And Number 2: You have the right to food money
Providing of course you
Don't mind a little
Investigation, humiliation
And if you cross your fingers
Rehabilitation
Know your rights
These are your rights
— From "Know Your Rights" by The Clash

How do Bill and others in his situation survive on welfare and at the same time try to find work? The $610 per month that Bill receives is based on $375 for shelter and $235 for "supports." Supports consist of everything that everyday life requires — food, tea or coffee, bus tickets, toilet paper, razor blades, toothpaste, a pen, a notebook, all for around $7.73 per day. Bill can't find a room at $375; instead he pays $435 for his room. The extra $60 a month comes out of his $235 support

Figure 2: A shopping cart is a common tool for carrying your belongings when you are homeless. Courtesy of Stephen Hill.

money, leaving him with just $5.75 per day for living expenses.

If Bill finds work for a few days, he must report it to the B.C. Ministry of Social Development and Social Innovation which will reduce his welfare cheque by the amount he earns. For example, if he earns $400, his next welfare cheque will be $210, which forces him to find a few more days work to survive, and so on — a vicious cycle.

The Cycle of Punishment and Reward: To Encourage the Others

Dans ce pays-ci, il est bon de tuer de temps en temps un amiral pour encourager les autres.[*]
— From Voltaire's *Candide*

In British Columbia, only those who have status as people with disabilities or multiple barriers are permitted to keep any earnings. The earnings exemption for people with disabilities is $500. However, only a minority in this category are able to work. Currently, British Columbia is the only province in Canada that does not allow welfare recipients to keep some of the money they earn, although other provinces have restrictions on the amount of earnings allowed. All provinces force people to cash in retirement savings plans or other savings, and to drain their bank accounts to almost nothing as a condition for applying for welfare. In British Columbia, individuals are only allowed to have $500 in the bank. This severely limits the resources available to secure employment. I recently spoke to a carpenter who had been told that he had to sell his hand tools, worth about $1,500, before he could receive welfare. How do you find work as a carpenter without tools?

Applebaum (2001) aimed to understand how perceptions of the poor affect policy decisions and found that liberal policies were more likely to be recommended when the target group was perceived as deserving rather than as undeserving. The deserving poor were viewed as the very old, sick, or severely disabled. And the undeserving poor were those capable of working.

To request welfare, applicants must reveal bank accounts to strangers, stand in line, often outside in public view, to see a worker at the Ministry office, and sign declarations of poverty. Those in the "expected to work" category will be sent, not voluntarily, to an employment service of some kind with no thought or consideration of an applicant's job skills, aptitudes, mental health issues, and so forth. Applicants will be expected to apply for a certain number of jobs per week or month and to keep records of these applications. It is not surprising that some people on income assistance

---

[*] *"In this country, it is wise to kill an admiral from time to time to encourage the others."*

resort to panhandling, survival sex, or various illegal activities, or stay in abusive relationships. These points show the various ways in which society pays for the failings of the welfare system.

The reality is that someone has to appear to apply for jobs they don't want, won't get, or can't find. From an employment counselling perspective, this deeply damaging dance crushes an unemployed person's dignity. Much of my frontline work addresses the effects of the damage inflicted by welfare.

Figure 3: Shopping cart has a plaque with the words, "Paying with Interac Debit Just Feels Right." Clearly, this photo is not what Interac services intended. Courtesy of Stephen Hill.

Tales From the Frontline

I sit here at my TV lost in this little dirty underground welfare room. I turn away
as a pizza commercail comes on, get up like off of fly paper from my garbage
bin La Z -Boy. I look into the rooms' full size frigde, discovering only sad
lonely 3 day old Kraft Dinner, stail brown bread and penut butter.
— Henry Doyle (*Megaphone*, April 2010)

Where to Start?

The core work of employment counselling varies little between different segments of society, whether rich or poor. When working with skilled professionals and trades people, for example, you are helping people who are dealing with the depressing and anxious effects of unemployment. However, as an employment counsellor working with disenfranchised and marginalized people living in poverty you may be confronted with the issue of your own loyalty and fealty to the system. Most employment programs, even those run by non-profit agencies, can trace their funding back to the very levels of government that run the employment insurance and welfare systems. Yet much of your work with people living in poverty will be spent trying to get the most out of the system — advocating for someone who is being wrongly denied benefits, working outside the system or bypassing it (e.g., tracking down work clothing from a local charity or finding free personal grooming services). Effective work with people in poverty demands that we offer more than apologies for the system.

Figure 4: The homeless person's camp is not the sort of camping that's on sale. Courtesy of Stephen Hill.

❖ *Stop and Reflect*
When you are providing employment counselling, who are you working for? Is it the government, the unemployed person in front of you, the taxpayers, or your own employer?

Ignoring the "Hierarchy of Needs"

Almost all counselling and helping courses teach Abraham Maslow's theory of hierarchy of needs (e.g., Betz, 1982; Kenrick, Griskevicius, Neuberg, & Schaller, 2010).

Basic needs are at the lowest levels of the pyramid, and more complex needs are located at the top. At the bottom of the pyramid are basic physical requirements including the need for food, water, sleep, and warmth. When these lower-level needs have been met, individuals can move on to the next level of needs for safety and security. Further up the pyramid are more psychological and social needs such as love, friendship, intimacy, and the need for personal esteem and feelings of accomplishment. At the top of the pyramid is the process of growing and developing as a person to achieve individual potential or self-actualization. Upper levels of the hierarchy are deemed irrelevant by the welfare system.

In working with people affected by poverty you will break the integrity of this hierarchy every single day. No doubt the providers of welfare across Canada believe that they have taken care of the basic needs; however, this is not the case. A good suggestion when working with people affected by poverty is to ask them the question: "Is it recent, is it temporary, or is it a lifelong experience?"

As an employment counsellor working with the impoverished, you will coach someone on interview techniques who has not eaten for 24 hours. You will celebrate a client's new job offer, knowing that Mohsen will have to walk 30 blocks to work and back as he does not have the money for bus tickets, and he does not fall into the "right" category to be entitled to help to buy them. You will go to ridiculous lengths to provide food for Frank during his first two weeks at work until he receives his first paycheque. Frank has been using the food bank and other food lines to

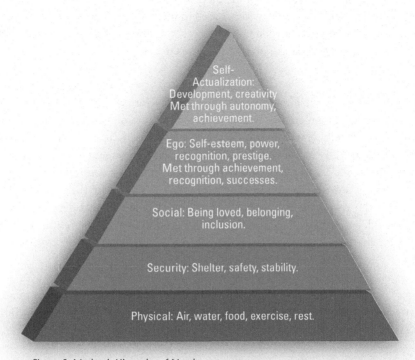

Figure 5: Maslow's Hierarchy of Needs.

feed himself while he's been on welfare, but these services are offered during the day when he will now be working. You will work hard to connect Jay to that chef job he wants and is absolutely qualified to apply for, hoping that he won't still be sleeping in the local park when the colder weather comes, and that he can still get free showers every day so he smells fresh when showing up to cook.

Tips for Employment Counselling

I quickly learned three key things as an employment counsellor working in a predominately poor neighbourhood. First, leave your ego at the door; it's not the effect on you but the effect you have that's important. Second, dismiss any thoughts of whether the client is at fault. Finally, realize that the system is badly set up to help poor people, and that there is an element of punishment within the system that conflicts with your wish to help.

Get Out

Get out of the office and meet people on the street, their streets, in their community spaces. This does not mean chasing a person down the street, but it does mean being visible and available. Some counselling models that are associated with more formal counselling practices (but are sometimes used to inform our work) advise against this and say that to acknowledge a client outside the "counselling setting" (i.e., your office where you have control) is inappropriate. This is nonsense.

Get In

Genuine community attachment is not "outreach." Outreach — often an expected part of employment programs — can often mean handing out business cards and making light, casual connections to other services in the neighbourhood where you work. For example, I am fully involved in several arts and social justice groups in my work neighbourhood. I see this as an extension of my work that contributes to my credibility. It is not a cynical, planned strategy to satisfy "the funder" (i.e., the word used to describe the government money that most employment services depend upon) or to look good, but rather a natural extension of genuine care and interest in the affairs and well-being of the community in which I work and for whom I work.

Get Experience

It's very useful for practical reasons and to build credibility that you have a range of experience. If you are new to the field, you may not yet have the range of work or life experience to be effective.

Be Available

You can indicate to clients that you are available and willing to help them in the way you address them (Laird, 2009). Use sentences such as these:

- Let me help you.
- I can give you all the time you need.
- Let's figure this out.
- Whatever the issue is, I'll help you get it resolved.
- It's very important to me that you are satisfied with what happens here.
- You are unique. I'm happy to adapt things for you.
- I really want you to feel that this is a community and that you belong here.
- When things don't work so well, we fix them together.
- I take my role, and yours, very seriously.
- I will stay with this until we find a resolution.

Use Humour

I use humour every day in my work. This does not mean off-colour jokes (though they can have their place!) or making light of bad situations, but simply giving the gift of a smile or a laugh. How people respond to humour is a useful indicator of their mood and personality. Gentle teasing is a way of showing you care about them and establishing common ground.

Stay Current

It is essential to be aware of local events in addition to job fairs, arts and culture and recreational activities, discussions, activist meetings, and talks at the local library. Be prepared to talk about life, news, interests, politics, art, current affairs, sporting events and more. Read the local news every morning.

Acquire Local Knowledge

Having personal experience and familiarity with resources and places you can suggest people go to for additional help, support, or resources is crucial. Personally, I will not refer anyone to any service I have not visited and approved of myself.

Mind Your language

"Said, Meant, Heard, Felt" — Stephen Hill

Examine the following statements:

- "I'm going to send you for training ..."
- "I can offer you training ..."
- "I'm referring you to ... for training ..."
- "Go see my buddy, Lana; she'll set you up. You go up the stairs and there's a blue door on the right ..."
- "Oh, while we are at it, I've got some time; let me grab my coat and I'll introduce you to Lana ..."

> ### Handy in Your Desk Drawer
> by Stephen Hill
>
> - razor blades,
> - tampons,
> - toothpaste,
> - toothbrushes,
> - shampoo,
> - combs,
> - socks,
> - stamps,
> - condoms.

All the sentences listed above may mean the same but the nuances range from command and control to genuine knowledge, commitment, and caring. "How can I help?" is a phrase to use at each meeting with an unemployed person. The question forces you to be able to respond usefully to every answer they provide.

Keep Resources and Supports at Your Fingertips:

- sources of housing and free food;
- training opportunities;
- health care and dental care facilities;
- access to mental health, addiction, and battered women's services, and to post-traumatic stress disorder specialists;

- location of free work clothing, showers, laundry, and bus tickets.

The relationship you build with people living in poverty is the foundation for all the work you do. This relationship looks a bit different from what you might expect as it requires more personal and authentic investment on the part of the helper.

A Poverty of Ideas?

When I give food to the poor, they call me a saint.
When I ask why the poor have no food, they call me a communist.
— Archibishop Dom Helder Camara

I realize that the picture I paint of a system that is broken and that damages those it is designed to aid is rather bleak. Here, I want to introduce some hopeful ideas and actions, all of which take a radical stance and use creativity to tackle both the effects and causes of poverty in Canada. Some are grand, all-encompassing ideas; others are small, local neighbourhood initiatives.

Mincom

Minimum Income or Mincom (Forget, 2008) was the name of an experiment in the town of Dauphin, Manitoba that was conducted in the mid-1970s, where every adult citizen was given a guaranteed income. The study and its findings were revisited in 2008 by Dr. Evelyn L. Forget of the University of Manitoba. The study was designed to test the prevalent idea, still so engrained in our society today, that people are inherently lazy. Did Mincom encourage people to be "lazy bums"? Well, the unemployment rate did alter slightly. Yes, a few people chose not to work, such as mothers staying home to raise their children. The divorce rate went up slightly as women gained financial independence and were able to leave unhappy marriages. Dr. Forget found that along with the positive mental health results, teenagers stayed in school longer, likely because their families were assured of a minimum income. The long-term health and social effects would be dramatically different for somebody who completed Grade 12 compared with someone who did not finish high school.

For some individuals, whose families were promised income security, the health and social consequences may have lasted much longer than the experiment. For example, adolescents of the families in the study appear to have been able to graduate from high school rather than entering the labour force earlier or working on family farms, in comparison with their contemporaries elsewhere in rural Manitoba who seemed to follow earlier patterns of leaving school before graduation. The life chances of adolescents in the experimental site may have been permanently altered and, although more tenuous, their own children may have benefited from the better economic outcomes of their parents.

The Equality Trust

The Equality Trust Canada (<http://equalitytrust.ca>) advocates for income equality. Like the parent organization, The Equality Trust in the UK, it works to make people aware of the harm done by large inequalities in income. Richard Wilkinson and Kate Pickett were co-founders of the UK organization. Their book, *The Spirit Level: Why More Equal Societies Almost Always Do Better*, published in 2009, demonstrated, through analysis of international data, the connection between inequalities and a spectrum of social conditions. These range from obesity to trust, from the number of patents per capita to life expectancy. The clear finding was that it is not the wealth of a population that is most important but the spread of wealth within the population.

In 2010, Richard Wilkinson came to British Columbia to speak at Simon Fraser University and at the Downtown Eastside Carnegie Centre, across the street from where I work, in Vancouver. His audience at the centre was mainly people who were homeless and affected daily by the inequalities he highlighted. It was refreshing to see an academic practising what he preached. He began by acknowledging that he was about to say what most in the room already knew from personal experience — inequality is damaging. When asked by a member of the audience whether he thought change was possible he said: "We are meant to live in a democracy. This doesn't mean we continue to allow the top 1% to get what they want" (Personal communication, December 13, 2010).

Small Is Beautiful

Living off the poverty grid demands alternative currencies. Alternative currencies include bottles and cans for recycling, saleable items found in dumpsters, calendars and magazines for sale — usually produced by non-profit organizations. In Vancouver, we have United We Can for recycling and two publishing projects: *Megaphone* and *Hope in Shadows*.

"Binning" or making money by collecting resalable items from dumpsters has been turned into a major project by the perfectly named United We Can. Hundreds of people show up each day with shopping carts, strollers, or garbage bags full of cans and bottles and anything else that has a recycling fee attached to them. The cash they receive helps to supplement welfare benefits.

United We Can has recently expanded into growing vegetables and herbs in raised beds, a project known as SoleFood. Unused parking lots and the flat roofs of supportive buildings provide jobs for local residents and tap into the popular **locavore movement**.

Megaphone is a fortnightly magazine that is sold by licensed vendors. The vendors buy each copy for 50 cents and then sell them for a cover price of two dollars though some purchasers choose to pay more. The articles are written by both local residents and well-known authors. At least one vendor now lives off the system and is self-sufficient through only sales of *Megaphone*.

Hope in Shadows is a program that involves handing out cameras to local Downtown Eastside residents who take pictures of their community, places, and people. Some photographs are touching and gentle, others more gritty and political. A judged selection process is used to choose the 13 photographs (one per month and one for the front cover) to be featured in the calendar. Local vendors, often including the photographers themselves, then buy the calendars for $10 and sell them for $20.

SPOTLIGHT: *CITY LINKS*
by Lara Shepard

In Calgary, City Links offers a safe and supportive work environment where those individuals who encounter employment barriers can receive paid work experience, work skills training, and vocational counselling. For example, workers are trained to help low-income seniors to live safely and securely in their homes. There is no charge for this service and clients are provided with basic yard care, snow removal, house cleaning, painting, and minor repairs. The City Links Program has been around for over 40 years, in various formats, and is partially funded by Alberta Employment and Immigration. For more information, go to: <http://www.calgary.ca/CSPS/CNS/Pages/Seniors/City-Links /About-City-Links.aspx>.

Summary

If you have a passion for social justice, not as a theory but something you simply have to put into practice by taking action, then being an employment counsellor for people living in poverty is a calling, not a job. It can be bleak. Some of the people you meet and the stories you hear will stay with you forever. I am asked about burn-out and how I stay fresh. Personally, I stay strong by remaining relentlessly current, and grasping the creative new initiatives for a nationwide change of attitude towards the treatment of people living in poverty.

If Senator Hugh Segal (2010) is right and we really have an opportunity in the next 5 years to make radical change, then a hopeful picture remains possible. Imagine if we could guarantee everyone $20,000 a year.

- Welfare? Gone.
- Employment insurance? Gone.
- Food banks? Gone.
- 75% of non-profits who exist to prop up or supplement the current broken system? Gone.
- The stress and tension and humiliation of the current poverty machine? Gone.
- But in the meantime, Bill still needs my unwavering support.

References

Adamson, P. (2010). The children left behind: A league table of inequality in child well-being in the world's rich countries. Innocenti Report Card 9. United Nations Children's Fund. Retrieved from <http://www.unicef-irc.org/publications/619>. <https://webexchange.uleth.ca/owa/redir. aspx?C = 23266890f34348d89871994cd97db5fc&URL=http%3a%2f%2fintraspec .ca%2fpovertyCanada_news-and-reports.php>.

Applebaum, L. D. (2001). The influence of perceived deservingness on policy decisions regarding aid to the poor. *Political Psychology, 22*(3), 419–442. doi: 10.1111/0162-895X.00248

Betz, N. (1982). Need fulfillment in the career development of women. *Journal of Vocational Behavior, 20,* 53–66. doi:10.1016/0001-8791(82)90063-X

Cabaj, M. (2004). *The poverty matrix: Understanding poverty in your community: A tool for vibrant communities* (2nd ed.). Waterloo, ON: Tamarack — An Institute for Community Engagement. Retrieved from <http://tamarackcommunity.ca/ downloads/tools/poverty_matrix2e.pdf>.

Canadian Centre for Policy Alternatives. (2013). *2013 living wage calculation: Costs of raising a family in Metro Vancouver rising faster than inflation.* Retrieved from <http://www.policyalternatives.ca/newsroom/news-releases /2013-living-wage-calculation-costs-raising-family-metro-vancouver-rising-fast>.

Clash. (n.d.). *Know your rights.* Retrieved from <http://www.plyrics.com/lyrics/clash /knowyourrights.html>.

Doyle, H. (April 2, 2010). Rooming House Blues. In MEGAPHONE, *Word on the Street, 50.* Retrieved from <http://www.megaphonemagazine.com/> and <http://wastelandjournalschapters.wordpress.com/>.

First Call: BC Child and Youth Advocacy Coalition. (2012). 2012 Child Poverty Report Card. Vancouver, BC: Author. Retrieved from <http://www.firstcallbc.org /pdfs/EconomicEquality/First%20Call%20BC%20Child%20Poverty% 20Report%20Card%202012.pdf>.

Forget, E. (2008). *The town with no poverty: A history of the North American guaranteed annual income social experiments.* Winnipeg: Community Health

Sciences, Faculty of Medicine University of Manitoba.
<http://economix.fr/pdf/seminaires/H2S/forget.pdf>.

Kenrick, D. T., Griskevicius, V., Neuberg, S. L., & Schaller, M. (2010). Renovating
the pyramid of needs: Contemporary extensions build upon ancient foundations.
Perspectives on Psychological Science, 5, 292–314. doi:10.1177/1745691610369469

Klein, S., & Pulkingham, J. (2008). *Living on welfare in BC. Experiences of longer-term
"expected to work" recipients*. Canadian Centre for Policy Alternatives (CCPA).
Retrieved from <http://www.policyalternatives.ca/sites/default/files/uploads/
publications/BC_Office_Pubs/bc_2008/bc_LoW_full_web.pdf>.

Laird, R. (2009). Statements to work in whenever possible. Retrieved from
<http://www.rosslaird.com/blog/mentorship-language/>.

Matern, R., Mendelson, M., & Oliphant, M. (2009). Developing a deprivation index:
The research process. Toronto, ON: Daily Bread Food Bank and the Caledon
Institute of Social Policy. Retrieved from <http://www.caledoninst.org
/Publications/PDF/836ENG.pdf>.

Mikkonen, J., & Raphael, D. (2010). *Social determinants of health: The Canadian facts*.
Retrieved from <http://www.thecanadianfacts.org/>.

National Council of Welfare. (2007). *Solving poverty: Four cornerstones of a workable
national strategy for Canada*, 127 (Cat. No. HS4-31/2007E-PDF). Ottawa, ON:
Author. Retrieved from <http://publications.gc.ca/collections/Collection
/HS4-31-2007E.pdf>.

National Council of Welfare. (2010). Welfare incomes. Ottawa, ON: National Council
on Welfare. Retrieved from <http://publications.gc.ca/collections/collection_2011
/cnb-ncw/HS51-1-2009-eng.pdf>.

Segal, Senator Hugh. (2010, May 6). *Guaranteed Annual Income, Part 1*. Retrieved
from <http://www.youtube.com/watch?v=IdmeOseNuwE>.

Sen, A. (1983). "Poor, relatively speaking." *Oxford Economic Papers, New Series,
35*(2), 153–169. Retrieved from <http://links.jstor.org/sici?sici=00307653%281983
07%292%3A35%3A2%3C153%3APRS%3E2.0.CO%3B2-1>.

Service Canada (2013). *Employment Insurance*. Retrieved from
<http://www.servicecanada.gc.ca/eng/sc/ei/index.shtml>.

Shillington, R., Lasota, M., & Shantz, L. (2009). *The meaning of poverty: Working
paper No. 1*. Retrieved from <http://metcalffoundation.com/wp-content/
uploads/2011/05/fog-working-paper-01.pdf>.

Statistics Canada (2010). Low income lines, 2008–2009. Retrieved from
<http://www.statcan.gc.ca/pub/75f0002m/75f0002m2010005-eng.pdf>.

Tamarack. (n.d). *Measuring poverty: Ontario's deprivation index*. Retrieved from
<http://tamarackcommunity.ca/g3s61_VC_2010a.html>.

United Nations. (2001, April 23 — May11). Substantive issues arising in the
implementation of the international covenant on economic, social, and
cultural rights: Poverty and the international covenant on economic, social,
and cultural rights. Geneva, SUI: Committee on Economic, Social and Cultural
Rights. Retrieved from <http://www.unhchr.ch/tbs/doc.nsf/0
/518e88bfb89822c9c1256a4e004df048?Opendocument>.

Vaughan, B. (n.d.). *Brainy quote*. Retrieved from
    <http://www.brainyquote.com/quotes/authors/b/bill_vaughan.html>.
Wilkinson, R. (2010, December 13). *The age of unequals: An evening with Richard
    Wilkinson*. Retrieved from <http://www.youtube.com/watch?v=jxBSKLxt3Wc>.
Wilkinson, R., & Pickett, K. (2009). *The spirit level*. London: Penguin Books.

Glossary

Basic Needs Measures (BNM) is the cut-off point based on the cost of a basket of goods needed to meet the basic physical needs for long-term survival.

Disability Assistance is a monthly support and shelter allowance provided under the Employment and Assistance for Persons with Disabilities Act to those who meet the definition of "person with disabilities."

Employment Insurance (EI) is a national program for Canadian workers who are laid off. Canadian workers pay into a central fund that contributors can temporarily draw on if later they are unable to work.

Hardship Assistance is a support and shelter allowance provided to persons who are not otherwise eligible for income assistance. A person who receives hardship assistance accrues a debt owing to the government.

Income Assistance is a basic monthly support and shelter allowance provided under the Employment and Assistance Act (EAA).

Living wage is a level of hourly pay which enables someone working full time to have enough to meet their basic needs and build some savings for the future. This newer concept is based on the local cost of living and takes into account specific factors of these local conditions with rent being the biggest single cost.

Locavore movement was first used on World Environment Day 2005 as a way to describe the now increasingly popular practice of eating foods harvested from within a local area, usually within a 100-mile radius.

Low Income Cut-Offs (LICO) are incomes set where families are spending a substantial share of their incomes on necessities, for example 20% higher than the Canadian norm.

Low Income Measures (LIM) is 50% of the national median income adjusted for family size.

Market Basket Measures (MBM) is based on the cost of a basket of goods and services sufficient for a standard of living "between the poles of subsistence and social inclusion."

Minimum wage is a provincially imposed lower limit on wage rates.

Persons with Persistent Multiple Barriers (PPMB) refers to people who are facing multiple barriers to employment. This assistance gives temporary reprieve from not having to prove that they are actively seeking work.

Social assistance is also known as "income support," "income assistance," and "welfare assistance." These programs are intended to alleviate extreme poverty by providing a monthly payment to people with little or no income.

Discussion and Activities

Discussion

Discussion Questions

1. Julie is on welfare and she often mentions that she struggles to get enough to eat and has to spend several hours a day lining up at food banks and soup kitchens. You are working with Julie on her résumé, and you smell alcohol on her breath.

    -   Does this mean that Julie has a drinking problem?
    -   Does it change your view of her?
    -   Does it mean that she is not good with money?
    -   Does it change your view of how realistic her job search is?

2. Born Poor versus Becoming Poor

    -   Does someone who grew up in poverty, and who is still poor, find it easier or more difficult than someone who was wealthy, and who is now poor?
    -   If a previously wealthy person became poor through addiction, how would this change your view of that person?
    -   If a rich woman lost her wealth through ill health, how would this change your view of her situation?

3. "Poverty Pimps" and "Povertarians"

    -   Poverty Pimps and Povertarians are the disparaging descriptions of people who work in poor areas of town, are not poor themselves, nor live in the area where they work. These are workers for government or non-profit who "live on the backs of the poor."
    -   How would you counter this charge?

- Should only local people help others especially in poor neighbourhoods?
- Should local people have priority when helping agencies are hiring?

Personal Reflections

1. Reflect on your reasons for wanting to become a career practitioner. What are your expectations about your role? How does this vision fit with working with marginalized and stigmatized populations?
2. Given the challenges in negotiating systems and advocating on behalf of clients, how will you keep yourself healthy when working within this environment?

Career Practitioner Role

1. Over the course of two weeks, as a class, collect from the Web or newspaper articles that highlight issues related to poverty and employment. What are some of the themes that emerge?
2. You will sometimes hear that career practitioners become over-involved with clients and some may suggest that it is important to keep a distance. What limits do you think career practitioners should set in their relationship with clients? Does having limits mean that you do not care about your clients? Refer to ethical guidelines about practitioner-client relationships. How might current ethical guidelines form a barrier in working with marginalized populations?

Activities

Stepping Out of Your Comfort Zone

Visit several of your local community services in a lower income part of your town or city:

- What do these services look like and feel like? Do they feel safe, welcoming, and respectful? What is your feeling at first contact?
- Visit your local social assistance/welfare office. What does it look like, and feel like? How are people treated?
- Where do poor people congregate in your town or city? Visit and observe.
- What surprised you most about your experiences?

Welfare in Your Province (Research Activity)

- What is the social assistance/welfare rate in your province?
- How much is dedicated to shelter and how much to other supports?
- Can someone on assistance earn any money without it being cut dollar for dollar from their support cheque?
- How many people (not a percentage) depend on welfare in your province or local community?

- Is there sufficient housing in your town or city, and do the rates match the shelter portion of the welfare cheque?
- Now that you have explored social assistance in your province, cross-compare to other provinces.

Case Studies

To explore case studies, read the publication by Seth Klein and Jane Pulkingham (2008), entitled *Living on Welfare in BC: Experiences of Longer-Term "Expected to Work" recipients*. Available at <http://www.policyalternatives.ca/sites/default/files /uploads/publications/BC_Office_Pubs/bc_2008/bc_LoW_summary_web.pdf>.

Read the cases of John and Lorraine. Choose one to explore.

1. What are three central issues that need to be addressed?
2. What theoretical approach might you draw on in working with this client?
3. As a career practitioner what would you do? Why?
4. What types of information/resources do you think would benefit this client?
5. What kinds of employment might be suitable?
6. What are other, more counselling-related (mental health) issues that could be addressed?

Explore Some Alternatives to Regular Employment in Your Neighbourhood.

These do not have to be top-heavy, ponderous operations. Their success is based on small startup costs and the requirement of few human and other resources.

- With your classmates, brainstorm possible alternative employment initiatives.
- How would you go about starting up such an initiative? How would this initiative assist those who live in poverty?
- Perhaps it's time to gather some friends together and start an alternative employment opportunity.

Strategies and Interventions

"A low-income senior citizen on a fixed income experiences different barriers to economic self-sufficiency than a young person that struggles to obtain a well-paying, steady job. Similarly, the strategies used to reduce poverty among homeless residents will differ markedly from those used to improve the circumstances of people working in low paying jobs" (Cabaj, 2004, p. 1).

Brainstorm strategies you might use with the different groups. What are the similarities and differences in strategies/interventions? Information on using a poverty matrix can be found at the following link: <http://tamarackcommunity.ca/downloads/ tools/poverty_matrix2e.pdf>.

Resources and Readings

Resources

Canadian Council on Social Development (CCSD)
CCSD has the most thorough statistics on urban poverty, broken down by demographic
group as well as by employment status. Retrieved from
<http://www.ccsd.ca/facts.html>.

Statistics Canada
Many Canadian communities have created local consortiums to purchase Statistics
Canada census data in order to produce more detailed local profiles of poverty
than the general urban profiles created by the Canadian Council on Social
Development. They generally use this information to break down the frequency
and depth of poverty for different demographic groups and neighbourhoods.
<http://www12.statcan.ca/english/profil01/PlaceSearchForm1.cfm>.

Supporting Communities Partnership Initiative (SCPI)
Communities accessing federal SCPI funds will have completed research on the
number of homeless in their city, often broken down by demographic group.
<http://www21.hrdc-drhc.gc.ca/home/index_e.asp>.

Videos
CBC radio and TV archives have an excellent collection of pieces on employment,
unemployment, social policy, and more. Especially recommended is one on "The
Exhaustees" about people who have run out of Employment Insurance, and one on
"The Pogey Police." Pogey is a uniquely Canadian term for Employment Insurance.

- Economy & Business: employment <http://archives.cbc.ca/economy_business
/employment/>.
- Gainfully Unemployed <http://www.cbc.ca/archives/categories
/economy-business/employment/on-the-dole-employment-insurance-in-canada
/gainfully-unemployed.html>.
- CBC Radio One: A special edition on Poverty in Canada. We are the 10%:
Poverty in Canada. Retrieved from <http://www.cbc.ca/thecurrent/episode
/2011/12/02/a-special-edition-on-poverty-in-canada/>.
- CBC Radio One: The Current, a CBC morning radio program of ideas and
perspectives that often concern social issues. Episode segments are available as
podcasts <http://www.cbc.ca/thecurrent/episode/>.

Supplementary Readings

Ball, D. P. (2013, June 20). Study details Canada's "perfect storm" housing problem:
Eroding incomes and plunging rental stock leave 380,600 households in "severe"

need. *The Tyee*. Retrieved from <http://thetyee.ca/News/2013/06/20/Canada-Housing-Problem-Study/>.

Dietitians of Canada, BC Region & the Community Nutritionists Council of BC. (2011). *Cost of eating in British Columbia 2011*. Retrieved from <http://www.dietitians.ca/Downloadable-Content/Public/CostofEatingBC2011_FINAL.aspx>.

Forget, E. (2008). *The town with no poverty: A history of the North American Guaranteed Annual Income social experiments*. Winnipeg: Community Health Sciences, Faculty of Medicine University of Manitoba. Retrieved from <http://economix.fr/pdf/seminaires/H2S/forget.pdf>.

Hawkins, R. & Kim, E. (2013). The socio-economic empowerment assessment: Addressing poverty and economic distress in clients. *Clinical Social Work Journal, 2012*, 40(2), 194–202. doi: 10.1007/s10615-011-0335-4

Smith, L., Li, V., Dykema, S., Hamlet, D., & Shellman, A. (2013). "Honoring somebody that society doesn't honor": Therapists working in the context of poverty. *Journal of Clinical Psychology*, 69(2), 138–151. doi: 10.1002/jclp.21953

The Standing Senate Committee on Social Affairs, Science, and Technology. (2009). *In from the margins: A call to action on poverty, housing and homelessness*. Report from the Subcommittee on Cities. Ottawa, ON: Author. Retrieved from <http://www.parl.gc.ca/Content/SEN/Committee/402/citi/rep/rep02dec09-e.pdf>.

Walberg, R., & Mrozek, A. (2009). *Private choices, public costs: How failing families cost us all*. Ottawa, ON: Institute of Marriage and Family Canada. <http://www.mercatornet.com/articles/view/families_matters>.

eleven

Immigrants in Canada

Contexts and Issues
for Consideration

LISA BYLSMA
Nanaimo, British Columbia

SOPHIE C. YOHANI
University of Alberta

PRE-READING QUESTION

A lack of Canadian work experience is one of the main obstacles in securing employment for immigrants in Canada. How can career practitioners facilitate this for their immigrant clients?

Introduction and Learning Objectives

This chapter provides information about the history of the Canadian immigration system, characteristics of **immigrants** in Canada, and issues of importance for career and employment counsellors working with immigrants.

Newcomers to Canada originate from all over the world and settle as temporary or permanent residents. During the mid- to late-20th century most immigrants came from the United Kingdom and Europe. Changes in immigration policy after 1976 to encourage skilled workers and others who qualified as "economic class" led to a shift to migrants from Asia and the Middle East forming the majority. Career practitioners and employment counsellors need to understand the demographic and geographic trends of immigration to Canada in their consideration of Canada's very diverse labour market, and to appreciate the challenges and difficulties immigrants face as they settle in Canada. These experiences are likely to affect the careers and employment of the immigrants.

At the conclusion of this chapter, you will be able to:

1. Describe the categories or classes of immigrants in Canada.
2. Understand the challenges immigrants face and the impact on their career and employment.
3. Summarize the four strategies newcomers use in interacting with Canadian culture.
4. Recognize the barriers for immigrating professionals to successful employment in their fields.
5. Comprehend how social justice issues impact immigrant employment experiences.

History of Canada's Immigration System

Canada has taken many different approaches to immigration since the 18th century. The Immigration Act (1869) and Dominion Land Act (1872) were the original frameworks for attracting migrants to Canada predominantly from Great Britain, Continental Europe, and the United States. Since World War II, Canada has adopted an increasingly expansionist immigration policy (Reitz, 2001). The stated purpose of immigration policy has been mainly to stimulate economic growth. For many years immigrants from Britain, the United States, and Europe were favoured because they were Caucasian, a practice later judged to be discriminatory (Omidvar & Richmond, 2003). In 1967, the Canadian government introduced a points system whereby applicants received points for attributes such as education, skills, and ability to work in Canada's official languages (Reitz, 2001). The points system is still used, albeit with numerous revisions. Currently, the points system is designed to select "the best and brightest" individuals for migration to Canada (Omidvar & Richmond, 2003).

With the Immigration Act of 1976, three broad classes of immigrants were created: independents, selected through the points system based partially on skills; a family class for reuniting families; and humanitarian for refugees. A business class was added in the 1980s to attract investors and entrepreneurs. The Immigration and Refugee Protection Act of 2001 replaced the 1976 Act and refined the criteria for acceptance into the economic class for skilled and business immigrants (Marenko, 2010). The intention was to facilitate entry of skilled individuals who could adapt more readily to the Canadian labour market. Today, immigrants are being accepted more for education, skills, and entrepreneurial potential and less for family reasons. This economic class of "independents" now makes up more that 60% of admissions.

After the 1970s, as a result of these changes in policy, the principal **source countries** of immigrants became Asia, Africa, the Middle East, Latin America, and the Caribbean (Omidvar & Richmond, 2003). Under the new business class, many wealthy immigrants from Hong Kong brought billions of dollars of investment, mainly to the Vancouver area, in the 1980s. During the 1980s and 1990s, well-educated professionals from Africa immigrated to Canada. Other African immigrants immigrated to Canada under refugee status.

❖ *Stop and Reflect*

How important is fairness in the process of making immigration decisions? For instance, should there be a right of appeal from a negative decision?

Should family reunification considerations overcome economic interests when selecting immigrants? For instance, should Canada exclude a close family member who has a disability from immigrating because the disability may pose an added cost to our publicly funded health or social services system?

Characteristics of Immigrants to Canada

People emigrate for a variety of reasons. Conditions in countries of origin, such as security risks and lack of employment, may create **push factors**. On the other hand, there are also **pull factors** that lead to migration, including opportunities to advance careers and to live and raise a family in a different political and social environment. Individuals migrating to Canada have a variety of temporary and permanent options.

Temporary Residence: Objectives and Classes

A **temporary resident** is someone whose entry into Canada involves a short-term stay, such as being admitted briefly as a visitor (citizens of certain countries must have a visa to visit or transit Canada), obtaining a work visa and finding temporary employment, or acquiring a student visa and attending a Canadian school (Figure 1). A new visa to allow parents and grandparents of Canadian citizens and permanent residents to visit was added in December 2011. Being granted temporary residence does not guarantee permanent residency — applying for permanent residency is a separate process.

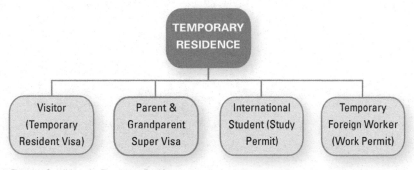

Figure 1: Conditions for Temporary Residence.

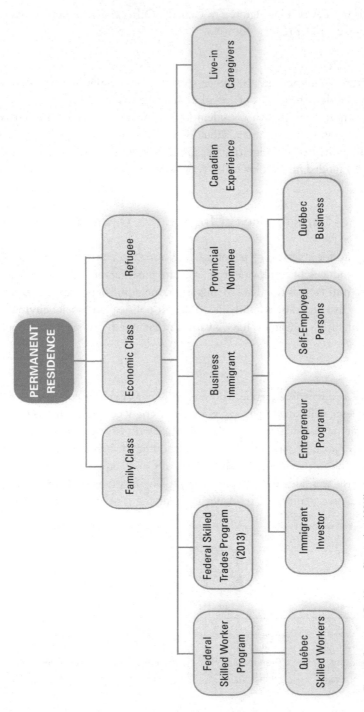

Figure 2: Permanent Residency Classes (as of 2013).

Permanent Residence: Classes

Canada offers individuals who wish to move permanently to Canada three broad categories for acceptance: family class — to be reunited with family members; refugee — for humanitarian reasons; and the economic class — for employment based on skills and business offering (CIC, 2005; Reitz, 2001). A **permanent resident** may work for any organization in Canada. (See Figure 2 above.)

Family Class

Family-class immigrants are individuals who are reuniting with close family members already established in Canada (CIC, 2005). Individuals can be sponsored by a close family member who is a permanent resident or Canadian citizen and who has committed to providing financial support during the settlement of the applicant.

Refugees

Refugees are individuals needing protection, and who fear returning to their home country. Small numbers of immigrants can also be admitted as "other immigrants," a grouping that includes various special categories created for humanitarian and public policy reasons.

Economic Class

The economic class consists of several programs: the Federal Skilled Worker Program, the new Federal Skilled Trades Program, the Business Immigrant Program, the Provincial Nominee Program, and the Canadian Experience Class. Economic immigrants as a whole are admitted based on the likelihood of success in the Canadian labour market or in business (CIC, 2011).

- To be selected through the **Federal Skilled Worker Program** immigrants must have the education, experience, and abilities that will enable them to become financially established in Canada. Skilled worker immigrants and professionals wanting to settle in Québec must apply through an independent class known as Québec-selected skilled workers. This is because Québec establishes its own immigration requirements and selection process under the Canada-Québec Accord on Immigration (Gouvernement du Québec, 2000).
- In January 2013 the Federal Skilled Trades Program started to accept applicants with specific skills in the trades (and adequate English-language skills) to fill known labour shortages.
- The **Business Immigrant Program** was designed to attract experienced business people who will support the development of the Canadian economy. On July 1, 2011, the Business Immigrant Program was subdivided

to include the **Immigrant Investor Program**, the **Entrepreneur Program**, and the **Self-Employed Persons Program**.

— Investors are required to have a personal net worth of $1.6 million and invest $800,000.
— The Entrepreneur Program was designed to attract experienced business people who will own and manage businesses.
— The Self-Employed Persons Program seeks to attract individuals who have the intention and ability to become self-employed in Canada. In particular, self-employed persons are required to contribute to Canada's cultural, athletic, or agricultural sectors. For example, they may work as music teachers, artists, coaches/trainers, or farmers.
— Québec has its own program for selecting investors, entrepreneurs, and self-employed persons.

• **Provincial Nominee Program** by which a province or territory (except Québec or Nunavut) can nominate individuals with particular education, experience, and skills to meet specific local labour market needs.
• In 2008, the **Canadian Experience Class** was added to enable temporary foreign workers and international students living in Canada who have skilled work experience in Canada to become permanent residents.

Live-in Caregivers are foreign workers who have come to Canada to care for children, the elderly, or the disabled under a work permit. After two years they may apply for permanent residency.

Distribution of Classes

Since the year 2000, Canada has granted permanent residency to between 220,000 to 280,000 individuals each year (CIC, 2012). In 2012, Family-class immigrants made up about one quarter of all newcomers to Canada; economic-class immigrants were 82% of all newcomers, refugees constituted 9% of the newcomers; and the remaining 3% was made up of "other immigrants" (e.g., humanitarian and compassionate cases; see Figure 3).

During the same time period, skilled workers, along with their spouses and dependents, made up 57% of all economic class immigrants and 35% of all new permanent residents. The number of family-class immigrants has been fairly constant at around 65,000 in 2003 and 2012, while economic-class immigrants have increased (CIC, 2012).

Since the policy changes in 1967 that eliminated the preference for American and Western European immigrants, there has been a considerable shift in the source countries for newcomers (Omidvar & Richmond, 2003). Although there is relative consistency in the top-source countries from year-to-year, there have also been some

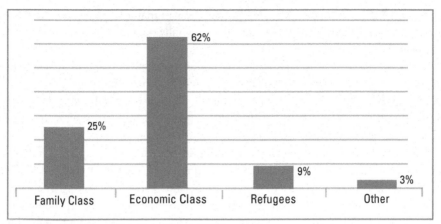

Figure 3: Immigration to Canada by Class in 2012.

large shifts, likely brought about by political factors. Hong Kong, for example, was the top source country in 1997, but the 46th in 2007 (CIC, 2009). In 2007, the top 10 sources, accounting for 52% of new permanent residents, were China, India, the Philippines, the United States, Pakistan, the United Kingdom, Iran, the Republic of Korea, France, and Columbia (CIC, 2009). In 2012, China, Philippines, India, and Pakistan made up 44 % of the total (CIC, 2012). From 2003 onwards, the majority of immigrants to Canada has originated from Asian nations.

Settlement Location

The vast majority of immigrants settle in Canada's three largest cities, Toronto, Vancouver, and Montréal (CIC, 2005). Between 1996 and 2001, 73% settled in these "big three" cities, whereas only 27% of the Canadian-born population resides in these cities. Figures from 2011 showed that 63.4% of Canada's immigrant population lived in Toronto, Vancouver, or Montréal, with Toronto having the largest share (37.4%) (Statistics Canada, 2013). There is some differential distribution, with immigrants from Western Europe and the United States more likely to settle in smaller cities and other areas of Canada compared to immigrants from other countries. Generally speaking, newcomers tend to settle in a location where they have friends and/or relatives (Statistics Canada, 2005a).

Age, Gender, and Religion

Almost one half (47%) of immigrants arriving between 1996 and 2001 were between the ages of 25 and 44, whereas only 30% of the Canadian-born population fell within this age group (CIC, 2005). The Longitudinal Survey of Immigrants to Canada (LSIC), which surveyed about two thirds (169,400) of newcomers arriving from

October 2000 to September 2001, found that the vast majority of new skilled worker immigrants were between 25 to 44 years old, especially the principal applicants (89%; Statistics Canada, 2005a).

The overall gender distribution of newcomers to Canada is approximately equal to the Canadian-born population, with just over one half of all immigrants being women (CIC, 2012). Based on LSIC findings, 77% of principal applicants in the skilled worker category are male, and 75% of spouses and dependents of skilled workers are female (Statistics Canada, 2005a).

In terms of religion, while Christianity is still the most common religious affiliation of newcomers (43%), there were significantly higher proportions of Muslim (18%), Hindu (6%), Buddhist (4%), and Sikh (5%) affiliations among immigrants arriving between 1996 and 2001. In comparison to the Canadian-born population, non-Christian affiliations are represented by 1% or less of the population (CIC, 2005).

Education

Levels of education differ significantly between immigrants and the Canadian-born. Twenty-one percent (21%) of all immigrants and 36% of those who immigrated between 1996 and 2001 have obtained a university degree, compared to 14% of the Canadian-born population (CIC, 2005). In 2012, 20.1% of immigrants 15 years or older had a bachelor's degree or above, and 37.8% of the principal applicants in the economic class (CIC, 2012). Although part of the difference in educational attainment can be attributed to rising education levels over time, immigrants as a whole are more educated than the Canadian-born population.

Migrant Personality

Boneva and Frieze (2001) proposed that individuals who choose to immigrate tend to display particular personality traits and values, known as the "**migrant personality**," which distinguishes them from those who prefer to stay in their home country. Those who choose to leave tend to be more work oriented, have higher achievement and **power motivations**, and have lower affiliation motivation and family orientation. The finding that language proficiency and youth are two of the most important factors in the economic success of immigrants seems to fit with the personality traits identified by Boneva and Frieze, especially in terms of career orientation and **achievement motivation**.

The migrant personality characteristics may apply for the skilled workers and economic classes, but may not be the case for other categories of immigrants. Refugees, for example, are motivated by the need to ensure the safety and survival of their families.

❖ *Stop and Reflect*

1. Consider the differences and similarities between a temporary and permanent migrant to Canada. How might the similarities and differences between the two types of migrants affect the approach taken in offering career services?
2. Given that approximately 50% of immigrants to Canada are between the ages of 25 and 44 years, what are the implications for career work?
3. What are some push and pull factors in migration that may influence career decisions for immigrants?

Challenges Immigrants Face That Affect Career and Employment

Immigrants to Canada of all types and countries of origin have some common challenges and experiences. These pertain to (a) the phases of settlement, (b) the process of acculturation and adaptation, (c) language issues, and (d) the impact of the point system on employment success. Practitioners who work with newcomers need to be aware of these experiences and challenges, and how they may impact career and employment.

Phases of Settlement

Immigration is a series of steps beginning with the move to Canada, obtaining employment, and joining in social and political participation (McIsaac, 2003).

According to Mwarigha (2002), there are three major stages of settlement: initial, middle, and final. The initial stage of settlement begins with meeting immediate needs, including food, clothing, shelter, orientation, and initial language instruction. Newcomers are helped by settlement agencies, cultural communities, and their families and friends. In the middle stage of settlement, immigrants require assistance with accessing employment, education, health care, housing, legal assistance, and advanced language instruction. The goal of the final stage of settlement is equal participation in Canada's economic, cultural, social, and political life.

Mwarigha (2002) argues that immigrants benefit most from services in the first two stages of settlement. Although the most barriers to settlement occur in the second stage, most programs focus on meeting immigrants' needs during the first stage (Mwarigha, 2002). Unfortunately there is a lack of understanding of immigration as a process and of the varying needs of immigrants as they move through the three stages.

Acculturation and Adaptation

Acculturation and **adaptation** are unavoidable aspects of the immigration experience. Berry (2001) describes acculturation as the process that occurs when cultural groups come into contact with each other and the resulting effect of the interaction on primarily the non-dominant group. Adaptation refers to changes that occur as an individual or group responds to external demands from the new culture (Berry, 2003). Adaptation may involve changing to blend in with the environment or attempting to change the environment (Berry, 2003). Cultural adjustment can be scary and destabilizing for newcomers, particularly if many of the norms and expectations are very different from the culture in their home country. Immigrants often fear losing their cultural identity, customs, and language (Arthur & Merali, 2005).

According to Berry (2003), newcomers to Canada must decide on the amount of contact they will have with other cultures, and how much of their own culture they want to retain. The strategies newcomers utilize can take four different forms:

1. Separation (i.e., avoiding interaction with other cultures and total maintenance of one's original culture).
2. Assimilation (i.e., frequent interaction with other cultures and loss of one's original culture).
3. Marginalization (i.e., avoiding interaction with other cultures and loss of one's original culture).
4. Integration (i.e., frequent interaction with other cultures and maintenance of one's original culture).

The strategy of integration, also known as biculturalism, is linked to positive adjustment, adaptation, and good mental health outcomes. However, integration also requires that certain conditions exist in the host society, such as the shared value of cultural diversity, low levels of prejudice, and a sense of attachment to the host society among all groups and individuals (Berry, 2003).

Language Issues

The ability to speak an official language is widely considered one of the most important predictors of successful economic and social integration (Tolley, 2003). Language issues can be a major barrier for immigrants (Aycan & Berry, 1996; Lee & Westwood, 1996). As well, language difficulties can contribute to higher accident rates where the workplace is more hazardous (Health Canada, 1999). In a survey of immigrants six months after their arrival in Canada, almost all skilled worker principal applicants (99%) reported they were able to speak English and/or French (Statistics Canada, 2005a). However, 13% of skilled worker principal applicants cited language barriers as a serious problem when trying to find employment, which may suggest their official language skills were not fully developed. Furthermore, language instruction tends to focus on vocabulary for conversational language rather than the technical language skills that are required by skilled workers. This situation further limits the opportunities for highly educated immigrants to obtain appropriate language training that could increase their chances for employment.

Points System and the Provincial Nomination System

The points system was initially adopted to maximize the likelihood of immigrants obtaining employment (Reitz, 2001). The underlying assumption of this initiative was that gainfully employed immigrants were most likely to result in a positive economic, social, cultural, and political impact. Although the points system has resulted in dramatically raising the skill level of newcomers, the employment success of new immigrants has been declining in recent years (Reitz, 2001). The inherent paradox for skilled workers has been pointed out repeatedly (Khan, 2007; Tang, Oatley, & Toner, 2007). As Tang and colleagues (2007) commented, "The system by which economic immigrants are treated in Canada is inherently unfair, in that the same foreign education and work experience that are judged to be sufficient to permit migration are insufficient to access professional work" (p. 288).

Obtaining work in Canada is often difficult for immigrants because they lack prerequisite Canadian work experience (McIsaac, 2003). Skilled worker principal applicants most frequently cited lack of Canadian work experience as the most serious problem they encountered as they sought employment (Statistics Canada, 2005b). Therefore, immigrants can face the classic catch-22 in finding a job: They seek jobs in order to obtain Canadian experience, but their lack of Canadian experience is cited as the reason they cannot get a job (Arthur & Merali, 2005; Khan, 2007).

Foreign Qualifications Recognition

Lack of acceptance or recognition of their foreign work experience or qualifications is cited as the second most frequent problem by skilled workers (Statistics Canada, 2005b). Immigrants are unable to determine the status of their credentials until they arrive in Canada (Khan, 2007; McIsaac, 2003). Foreign education has been increasingly devalued, resulting in a shift in perception about immigrant education and skills (Reitz, 2001). Research has shown that education and work experience attained abroad are considerably discounted in the Canadian labour market (Alboim, Finnie, & Meng, 2005; Reitz, 2001). Khan (2007) argued that "credentials are an instrument used by the dominant class to restrict access, privileges and opportunities for the subordinate classes" (p. 64).

Many professions in Canada, such as medicine, engineering, and teaching, are regulated by professional self-regulating bodies that stipulate the requirements individuals must meet to be part of the professional body and practise in the profession. The requirements are generally designed with the assumption that individuals have received their education in Canada. Since many professional bodies are not well equipped to appropriately evaluate foreign education and credentials, this tends to result in a devaluation of foreign qualifications. Many immigrants require additional years of education to meet certification standards to work in their profession in Canada (Aycan & Berry, 1996). Those individuals who want to make up for educational "deficiencies" may find it difficult to acquire the appropriate education and/or experience. For example, Peirol (1996) reported that foreign-trained medical doctors must write licensing exams and complete an internship in order to become licensed in Ontario. Although every Ontario medical school graduate is guaranteed an internship after passing the licensing exams, only 24 of up to 500 foreign-trained physicians were able to participate in such internships each year.

Professional immigrants routinely face these types of difficulties as they attempt to work in their premigration occupation, regardless of the reputation of their educational program, years of experience, and premigration standing in the field. It is not uncommon to hear stories of immigrants who were well-respected practitioners in their field, yet unable to work in their profession in Canada (Choudry, Hanley, Jordan, Shragge, & Stiegman, 2009). It is not only immigrants who suffer as a result — Canada loses by failing to utilize the skills and knowledge of its new citizens. If the foreign education and **credentials** of immigrants were recognized, between $3.4 and $5 billion would be added to the Canadian economy every year (Conference Board of Canada, 2004).

A newcomer's self-worth is often tied to occupational status (Canadian Task Force on Mental Health, 1988). The various delays encountered in returning to the workforce may lead to a loss of skills and decreasing confidence in abilities. If immigrants choose to continue in their premigration occupation, they are often faced with the reality of retraining, which may mean virtually starting over (Adamuti-Trache & Sweet, 2005). This can be frightening, confusing, and overwhelming, particularly for older immigrants (Lee & Westwood, 1996). If immigrants are not integrated into their premigration profession within three years of arriving, they are unlikely to return to it at all (Galabuzzi, 2005).

Employment Experiences: A Question of Social Justice

Since 1975 there has been a steady decline in the employment status and earnings of immigrants (Reitz, 2001). Several years after their arrival, immigrants in the past were able to match or even surpass the earnings of their Canadian-born peers (McIsaac, 2003). However, it appears that this is no longer the case, as more recent cohorts of immigrants have struggled to keep pace, even several years after migration (Schellenberg & Hou, 2005). In addition, other indicators of economic well-being, such as unemployment and poverty levels, paint a similarly bleak picture (Reitz, 2001).

Unemployment and **underemployment** are major concerns of immigrants (Galabuzzi, 2005). The unemployment rate of immigrants has gradually increased, and the gap between the unemployment rates of the Canadian-born compared to immigrants is continually widening (McIsaac, 2003). Six months after arrival, 75% of skilled worker principal applicants indicated having problems finding employment (Bergeron & Potter, 2006). In 2007, the unemployment rate among working-age immigrants was 6.6%, compared to the rate of 4.6% among Canadian-born individuals (Statistics Canada, 2008).

The discrepancy is more striking when comparing university-educated immigrants and Canadian-born individuals. In 2006, the unemployment rate among immigrants who immigrated in the previous five years with a university degree was 11.4%, nearly four times the rate of 2.9% for Canadian-born individuals with university education (Statistics Canada, 2007).

Underemployment is more difficult to measure, but one indicator is to compare the level of education required for a job to the individual's level of education. Almost three quarters (73%) of Canadian-born individuals with a university education are employed in a job requiring that level of education, compared to just over half (51%) of university-educated immigrants who arrived between 1996 and 2001 (CIC, 2005). Grant and Nadin (2007) reported that many skilled worker immigrants from Asia and Africa were unable to obtain employment equivalent to their premigration occupation. As a result, these individuals were often underemployed and had to volunteer and/ or upgrade their training. Six months after arriving, two thirds of employed skilled worker principal applicants were not working in their intended occupation (Statistics Canada, 2005a).

Supporting Employers Embracing Diversity (SEED)

by Lara Shepard

SEED is a diversity program to enhance cultural diversity in the workplace. Its HR Toolkit "offers support services to employers in activities related to recruitment planning, training and workforce maintenance."

SEED offers ideas and approaches to employers for solving diversity issues. SEED also facilitates collaborations between management, Human Resources, and employees.

SEED website has a complete virtual guide to diversity management: <http://www.embracingdiversity.ca/>.

Immigrants face a paradox in obtaining work, in that they may be considered underqualified for high-level positions because of a lack of Canadian work experience, language barriers, or other reasons; however, they are also not hired in lower-level positions because they are considered overqualified (Arthur & Merali, 2005). This paradox, among other reasons, has resulted in disproportionate numbers of immigrants in low-paying, part-time, temporary, insecure, high-risk employment with poor working conditions (Galabuzzi, 2005). While some immigrants do obtain gainful employment, university-educated immigrants are vastly over-represented in low-skill occupations such as taxi drivers, security guards, and janitors (McIsaac, 2003) and high-risk occupations such as those in the manufacturing and construction industries

(Health Canada, 1999). The marginal status of immigrants in the workforce also makes them prone to exploitation (Canadian Task Force on Mental Health, 1988).

According to Citizenship and Immigration Canada (2005), the education of recent immigrants has not been fully utilized. Despite rising education levels among immigrants over the years, the gap between the wages of immigrants and Canadian-born individuals is ever widening, including immigrants with university education and knowledge of an official language (McIsaac, 2003). Data indicates that between 1980 and 2000, the income of recent male immigrants dropped 7%, whereas incomes increased by 7% for Canadian-born males (Galabuzzi, 2005). For university-educated immigrants, the drop in earnings was even greater at 13%. In 2000, individuals who immigrated between 1986 and 1995 earned about 80% of the Canadian-born worker's average income, while individuals who immigrated between 1996 and 1999 only earned about 70% (CIC, 2005).

Unstable, low-paying employment tends to result in financial struggles among immigrants who are consistently overrepresented among the poor (Kazemipur & Halli, 2001). Skilled-worker immigrant women frequently indicate financial strain as a major difficulty (Tang et al., 2007). Financial pressures may lead immigrants to take jobs for which they are highly overqualified. Clearly, this represents a circular problem.

Employment tends to be a good indicator of overall immigrant adjustment (McIsaac, 2003). Participation in the Canadian labour market is essential for immigrants to successfully integrate, to feel a sense of belonging, and to form their identity within the Canadian context (Galabuzzi, 2005). The employment-related experiences of immigrants are predictive of adaptation and psychological well-being (Aycan & Berry, 1996). More specifically, immigrants' unemployment has been associated with feelings of alienation, acculturative stress, adaptation problems, negative self-concept, anger, frustration, chronic stress, and other health problems (Aycan & Berry, 1996; Canadian Task Force on Mental Health, 1988; Grant & Nadin, 2007; Health Canada, 1999; Omidvar & Richmond, 2003). These findings indicate that employment offers purpose, status, and identity, and helps individuals establish social relationships (Aycan & Berry, 1996). Thus, because social interaction plays a vital role in helping immigrants adapt to Canadian society, unemployment hinders the process of acculturation. Conversely, when immigrants' employment status and income improves, it tends to lead to a greater sense of competence, success, and improved social interaction.

Expectations Meet Reality

Often a primary reason for immigrating is to improve employment opportunities (Boneva & Frieze, 2001). It can be very destabilizing to the individual when these expectations are not met. Research has indicated a link between mental health and the congruence of expectations and reality, either positively associated with life satisfaction, or negatively associated with depression (Murphy & Mahalingam, 2006). Unmet expectations "results in frustration, alienation from a familiar working environment, erosion of skills, and ultimate loss of human potential to the Canadian economy" (Canadian Task Force on Mental Health, 1988, p. 30).

The immigration process can be hard on the individual who is expected to make many adjustments. People may suffer immense disappointment when expectations and dreams are obstructed. Hopes and expectations may help motivate some immigrants to quickly adjust to their new surroundings (Lee & Westwood, 1996). However, individuals often find adjusting to Canadian culture and employment more difficult than they anticipated. Immigrants who have difficulties in the adjustment process may, in turn, experience a sense of inadequacy (Lee & Westwood, 1996). While immigrants may anticipate short-term unemployment or underemployment, longer-term unemployment and underemployment tend to have a greater detrimental impact (Health Canada, 1999).

Khan and Watson (2005) proposed a four-stage model to encapsulate the immigration experiences of skilled Pakistani women in Canada. In *Stage One, Seeking a Better Future*, participants identified their premigration dreams, hopes, and goals. *Stage Two, Confronting Reality*, describes how, shortly after immigrating, the women were forced to confront the reality of their situation and their limited options. Overall, the women described a severe discrepancy between premigration hopes and postmigration experiences, with some individuals reporting that they felt misled. Individuals lost financial stability, professional status, and self-confidence, and felt uprooted, and without support. In *Stage Three, Grieving and Mourning*, individuals discussed anger and frustration with their current situation, as well as homesickness, family problems, and culture shock. *Stage Four, Adjusting*, included a sense of appreciation for parts of Canadian life and society such as free education and health care. As well, participants' plans to upgrade their education in Canada increased their feelings of hope for the future.

Racism and Discrimination

Immigrants to Canada during the past 30 years are far more likely to be visible minorities. Of those who arrived in the 1990s, 73% were visible minorities (McIsaac, 2003). The cross-cultural adjustment of newcomers to Canada is greatly affected by the attitudes of individuals already residing in Canada, especially when newcomers are perceived as competition for limited jobs (Lee & Westwood, 1996; Palmer, 1996). Research suggests that, controlling for education, gender, and language ability, visible minority immigrants tend to earn less than non-visible minority immigrants (Adamuti-Trache & Sweet, 2005).

While immigrants are consistently overrepresented among individuals of low economic status in Canada, visible minority immigrants tend to be the poorest group (Kazemipur & Halli, 2001). Further, poverty rates are higher among immigrants compared to non-immigrants of the same ethnic origin (Kazemipur & Halli, 2001). These findings indicate systemic discrimination based on both race and immigration status. In addition, skilled worker immigrants reported feeling discriminated against by Canadian employers (Grant & Nadin, 2007). Research has also established a link between perceived discrimination and depression (Noh, Beiser, Kaspar, Hou, & Rummens, 1999). Conversely, Aycan and Berry (1996) noted that some immigrants may blame failure to obtain employment on discrimination as a coping strategy. For career practitioners, understanding the reality and detrimental effects of discrimination as a barrier to finding employment is an important factor in career and employment counselling with this population.

Feelings of Loss

Feelings of loss frequently accompany major changes in the lives of immigrants. When individuals move to Canada, the losses they experience can outweigh the positives they gain. According to Lee and Westwood (1996), difficulties with recognition of credentials and finding employment frequently lead to feelings of loss. They explain that "being lumped with other unskilled workers is extremely disheartening to immigrants who are accustomed to maintaining professional identities" (p. 35). Skilled immigrants can also face loss of professional identity due to the devaluation of their foreign credentials. Additionally, the social and professional networks that once validated their professional identities cease to exist. After arriving in Canada, immigrants may find themselves a minority for the first time, losing their dominant-group status. Other significant losses include financial stability, lifestyle, professional status, culture, social support, and self-confidence (Khan & Watson, 2005).

Physical and Mental Health

The immigration screening process tends to result in what has been termed the "healthy immigrant effect" (Health Canada, 1999). Despite the superior health of newcomers on arrival, immigrant health generally begins to decline. This decline has been linked in part to various barriers to accessing health care, including language and culture (Kramer, Tracy, & Ivey, 1999). The experience of immigration also seems to have negative effects on the health of newcomers, with Health Canada (1999) stating that "sufficient research was found to warrant inclusion of the experience of immigration itself as a central determinant of health for recent immigrants" (p. 28). The stressors of immigration may be one reason for the deteriorating health of immigrants (Khan & Watson, 2005) as the mental health of immigrants, when excluding refugees, has been found to be equal to that of Canadians (Health Canada, 1999). Unemployment, however, seems to be related to a decline in immigrant mental health (Health Canada, 1999). Likewise, employment-related concerns and financial difficulties have been linked with mental health concerns among Chinese immigrant women (Tang et al., 2007).

Gender Issues

Adjustment difficulties are common among immigrant women. This group may be considered "triple disadvantaged" as a result of being women, immigrants, and often minorities (Wittebrood & Robertson, 1991). They frequently end up working in poorly paid, low-status jobs. Overall, immigrant women are more likely to be unemployed or underemployed than Canadian women (CIC, 2005; Health Canada, 1999). Khan and Watson (2005) found that immigration tended to negatively impact families, with marriages in particular weakening under the stress of Canadian settlement.

Immigrant women may work in order to allow their husbands to complete the education needed to obtain gainful employment (Worswick, 1996). Because the earnings contributions of immigrant wives are important to the family, the immigration process may challenge previously held gender-role expectations for some newcomers (Dion & Dion, 2001). For example, women who were not employed in their home countries may develop a shift in attitudes and expectations as a result of employment experiences in Canada. As a result, immigrant families may need to renegotiate gender-related roles; particularly when both partners are employed. Um and Dancy (1999) showed that women who were unable to renegotiate gender-roles were more likely to be depressed than those who did so successfully.

❖ *Stop and Reflect*
1.   Given the changing ethno-cultural make up of immigrants to Canada, what can career practitioners do to ensure they are well prepared to work with immigrants?
2.   What role can career practitioners play in raising awareness regarding the barriers to employment that immigrants may face in Canada?

Summary

Immigrants to Canada come from over 200 countries, with the Asia Pacific region as the largest source at close to 50%. In the last decade, the largest proportion (roughly 60%) of new permanent residents has immigrated via the economic class and they mostly settle in large urban centres. Most skilled worker immigrants are between 25 and 44 years of age and tend to be highly educated and career driven.

The demographic and geographic trends in Canadian immigration have relevance to the career development profession. Specifically, they highlight the increasing diversity of employees in the workplace and the need for understanding the settlement and integration challenges and opportunities faced by immigrants.

As immigrants settle in Canada, they encounter a variety of challenges, such as adjusting to a new culture, discrimination, and loss. They may have to learn a new language or improve their language proficiency. Employment is crucial to successful settlement, but many immigrants, including skilled worker immigrants, encounter difficulty in obtaining suitable employment. A lack of Canadian work experience is one of the main obstacles in securing employment. Another barrier is the lack of recognition of individuals' foreign education and work experience, which often complicates the transition into their premigration professions. Immigrants frequently experience feelings of loss during settlement and problems obtaining suitable employment can exacerbate these feelings. Immigrant women and couples may encounter additional problems after relocating, such as having to renegotiate gender-roles. For some immigrants, the multitude of challenges and stressors during settlement results in declining physical and mental health. In the end, career practitioners need to be aware and understanding of the issues immigrants face when settling in Canada in order to offer this population more effective supports and services.

References

Adamuti-Trache, M., & Sweet, R. (2005). Exploring the relationship between educational credentials and the earnings of immigrants. *Canadian Studies in Population, 32*, 177–201. Retrieved from <http://www.canpopsoc.org/journal/CSPv32n2p177.pdf>.

Alboim, N., Finnie, R., & Meng, R. (2005). The discounting of immigrants' skills in Canada: Evidence and policy recommendations. *IRPP Choices, 11*(2), 1–26.

Arthur, N., & Merali, N. (2005). Counselling immigrants and refugees. In N. Arthur & S. Collins (Eds.), *Culture-infused counselling: Celebrating the Canadian mosaic* (pp. 331–360). Calgary, AB: Counselling Concepts.

Aycan, Z., & Berry, J. W. (1996). Impact of employment-related experiences on immigrants' psychological well-being and adaptation to Canada. *Canadian Journal of Behavioural Science, 28*, 240–251. doi: 10.1037/0008-400X.28.3.240

Bergeron, J., & Potter, S. (2006, Spring). Family members and relatives: An important resource for newcomers' settlement? *Canadian Issues*, 76–80.

Berry, J. W. (2001). A psychology of immigration. *Journal of Social Issues, 57*, 615–631. doi: 10.1111/0022-4537.00231

Berry, J. W. (2003). Conceptual approaches to acculturation. In K. M. Chun, P. B. Organista, & G. Marin (Eds.), *Acculturation: Advances in theory, measurement, and applied research* (pp. 17–38). Washington, DC: American Psychological Association.

Boneva, B. S., & Frieze, I. H. (2001). Toward a concept of a migrant personality. *Journal of Social Issues*, 57, 477–491. doi: 10.1111/0022-4537.00224

Canadian Task Force on Mental Health. (1988). *After the door has been opened: Mental health issues affecting immigrants and refugees in Canada*. Ottawa, ON: Author.

Choudry, A., Hanley, J., Jordan, S., Shragge, E., & Stiegman, M. (2009). *Fight back: Workplace justice for immigrants*. Winnipeg, MB: Fernwood Publishing.

Citizenship and Immigration Canada. (CIC). (2005). *Recent immigrants in metropolitan areas*: Canada (Cat. No. MP22-20E/1-2005E-PDF). Ottawa, ON: Strategic Research and Statistics. Available at <http://www.cic.gc.ca/english/resources/research/census2001/canada/partb.asp#b4b>.

Citizenship and Immigration Canada (CIC). (2011) *Strategic Outcomes and Program Activity Architecture: Program Activity 1.1 — Permanent Economic Residents.* <http://www.cic.gc.ca/english/department/paa/2011/activity-11.asp>.

Citizenship and Immigration Canada. (CIC). (2012). *Facts and figures: Immigration overview — permanent and temporary residents* (Cat. No. Ci1-8/2012E-PDF). Ottawa, ON: Research and Evaluation Branch. <http://www.cic.gc.ca/english/pdf/research-stats/facts2012.pdf>.

Conference Board of Canada. (2004). *Performance and potential 2004–2005: How can Canada prosper in tomorrow's world?* Ottawa, ON: Author.

Dion, K. K., & Dion, K. L. (2001). Gender and cultural adaptation in immigrant families. *Journal of Social Issues*, 57, 511–521. doi: 10.1111/0022-4537.00226

Galabuzzi, G. (2005, Spring). Factors affecting the social economic status of Canadians in the new millennium. *Canadian Issues*, 53–57.

Gouvernement du Québec (2000). Canada–Québec accord relating to immigration and temporary admissions of aliens. Ministère des Relations avec les citoyens et de l'Immigration. Retrieved from <http://www.micc.gouv.qc.ca/publications/pdf/Accord_canada_Québec immigration_anglais.pdf>.

Grant, P. R., & Nadin, S. (2007). The credentialing problems of foreign trained personnel from Asia and Africa intending to make their home in Canada: A social psychological perspective. *Journal of International Migration and Integration*, 8, 141–162. doi: 10.1007/s12134-007-0011-2

Health Canada. (1999). *Canadian research on immigration and health: An overview.* Ottawa, ON: Minister of Health.

Kazemipur, A., & Halli, S. S. (2001). The changing colour of poverty in Canada. *The Canadian Review of Sociology and Anthropology*, 28, 217–238.

Khan, C. (2007, Spring). The closed door: Credentialized society and immigrant experiences. *Canadian Issues*, 63–66.

Khan, S., & Watson, J. C. (2005). The Canadian immigration experiences of Pakistani women: Dreams confront reality. *Counselling Psychology Quarterly*, 18, 307–317. doi: 10.1080/09515070500386026

Kramer, E. J., Tracy, L. C., & Ivey, S. L. (1999). Demographics, definitions, and data limitations. In E. J. Kramer, S. L. Ivey, & Y. Ying, (Eds.), *Immigrant women's health: Problems and solutions* (pp. 3–18). San Francisco, CA: Jossey-Bass.

Lee, G., & Westwood, M. J. (1996). Cross-cultural adjustment issues faced by immigrant professionals. *Journal of Employment Counseling, 33*, 29–42.

McIsaac, E. (2003, May). Immigrants in Canadian cities: Census 2001 — What do the data tell us? *Policy Options*, 58–63. Retrieved from <http://maytree.com/PDF_Files/SummaryImmigrantsInCanadianCities2003.pdf>.

Markenko, J. (2010). Immigration policy in Canada: History, administration, and debates. *Maple Leaf Web*. Retrieved from <http://www.mapleleafweb.com/features/immigration-policy-canada-history-administration-and-debates>.

Murphy, E. J., & Mahalingam, R. (2006). Perceived congruence between expectations and outcomes: Implications for mental health among Caribbean immigrants. *American Journal of Orthopsychiatry, 76*, 120–127. doi: 10.1037/0002-9432.76.1.120

Mwarigha, M. S. (2002). *Towards a framework for local responsibility: Taking action to end the current limbo in immigrant settlement — Toronto*. Toronto, ON: The Maytree Foundation.

Noh, S., Beiser, M., Kaspar, V., Hou, F., & Rummens, J. (1999). Perceived racial discrimination, depression, and coping: A study of Southeast Asian refugees in Canada. *Journal of Health and Social Behavior, 40*, 193–207. doi: 10.2307/2676348

Omidvar, R., & Richmond, T. (2003). *Immigrant settlement and social inclusion in Canada*. Toronto, ON: Laidlaw Foundation.

Palmer, D. L. (1996). Determinants of Canadian attitudes toward immigration: More than just racism? *Canadian Journal of Behavioural Science, 28*, 180–192. doi: 10.1037/0008-400X.28.3.180

Peirol, P. (1996, November 19). Skilled immigrants meet job barriers: More trained people than ever are coming in but bureaucrats are not ready to handle them. *The Globe and Mail*, p. A1.

Reitz, J. G. (2001). Immigrant success in the knowledge economy: Institutional change and the immigrant experience in Canada, 1971–1995. *Journal of Social Issues, 57*, 579–613.

Schellenberg, G., & Hou, F. (2005, Spring). The economic well-being of recent immigrants to Canada. *Canadian Issues*, 49–52.

Statistics Canada. (2005a). Longitudinal survey of immigrants to Canada: A portrait of early settlement experiences (Catalogue No. 89-614-XIE). Ottawa, ON: Minister of Industry. <http://publications.gc.ca/Collection/Statcan/89-614-XIE/89-614-XIE2005001.pdf>.

Statistics Canada. (2005b). Longitudinal survey of immigrants to Canada: Progress and challenges of new immigrants in the workforce (Catalogue No. 89-615-XIE). Ottawa, ON: Minister of Industry. <http://publications.gc.ca/Collection/Statcan/89-615-XIE/89-615-XIE2005001.pdf>.

Statistics Canada. (2007, September 10). Canada's immigrant labour market. *The Daily*. Retrieved from <http://www.statcan.gc.ca/daily-quotidien/070910/dq070910a-eng.htm>.

Statistics Canada. (2008, May 13). Canada's immigrant labour market. *The Daily*.

Retrieved from <http://www.statcan.gc.ca/daily-quotidien/080513/dq080513a-eng.htm>.

Statistics Canada (2013). Immigration and ethnocultural diversity in Canada. *National Household Survey 2011*. Retrieved from <http://www12.statcan.gc.ca/nhs-enm/2011/as-sa/99-010-x/99-010-x2011001-eng.cfm>.

Tang, T. N., Oatley, K., & Toner, B. B. (2007). Impact of life events and difficulties on the mental health of Chinese immigrant women. *Journal of Immigrant and Minority Health*, 9, 281–290. doi: 10.1007/s10903-007-9042-1

Tolley, E. (2003). The skilled worker class: Selection criteria in the Immigration and Refugee Protection Act. *Metropolis Policy Brief*, 1, 1–8.

Um, C. C., & Dancy, B. L. (1999). Relationship between coping strategies and depression among employed Korean immigrant wives. *Issues in Mental Health Nursing*, 20, 485–494. doi: 10.1080/016128499248457

Wittebrood, G., & Robertson, S. (1991). Canadian immigrant women in transition. *Canadian Journal of Counselling*, 25, 170–182.

Worswick, C. (1996). Immigrant families in the Canadian labour market. *Canadian Public Policy*, 22, 378–396. Retrieved from <http://economics.ca/cgi/jab?journal=cpp&view=v22n4/CPPv22n4p378.pdf>.

Glossary

Acculturation is the process of cultural and psychological change following contact between cultural groups and their individual members. The acculturation process implies mutual influence between members of the two cultures or groups.

Achievement motivation is the drive to pursue and attain goals. An individual with achievement motivation wishes to achieve objectives and advance up on the ladder of success. Here, accomplishment is important for its own sake and not for the rewards that accompany it.

Adaptation involves psychological adjustment and social adjustment and refers to the success of adapting to a new culture by participating in the local culture, learning the language, making friends, and enjoying life.

Affiliation motivation is the need for relationships and to relate socially with people. Persons with affiliation motivation perform work better when they are complimented for their favourable attitudes and co-operation.

Business Immigrant Program follows the principles of a mentor-mentee relationship to help newcomers from different cultural backgrounds integrate into the business community. Experienced professionals from the local business community will be matched with immigrant entrepreneurs.

Canadian Experience Class was introduced as an immigration class in 2008 to allow temporary foreign workers or recently graduated international students working in Canada to apply for permanent residence.

Credentials typically refer to formal learning and education (e.g., professional designation, degree, or diploma) required for regulated professions (e.g., engineering, trades, and medicine). However, this emphasis on formal learning has resulted in non-regulated occupations being largely overlooked.

Entrepreneur Program seeks to attract people with business experience who have the intention and ability to actively manage a Canadian business that will positively impact the Canadian economy and create employment opportunities for Canadian residents.

Federal Skilled Worker Program selects immigrants as permanent residents based on their education, work experience, knowledge of English and/or French, and other criteria that have been shown to help them become economically established in Canada.

Immigrant Investor Program seeks experienced business people to invest in Canada's economy and become permanent residents. Investors must show that they have business experience, have a minimum net worth of C$1,600,000 that was obtained legally, and invest $800,000 into the Canadian economy.

Immigrants choose to leave their countries of their own free will to make a new life elsewhere. They can return to their home country at any time and count on protection from that country's government.

Migrant personality refers to specific traits, values, and a set of motives that characterize the personality of people who desire to immigrate versus people who are willing to stay in their native country. Those who want to resettle in another country have higher achievement and power motivation but lower affiliation motivation.

A **permanent resident** is a person who has been allowed to enter Canada as a resident, but has not become a Canadian citizen. People seeking to immigrate to Canada on a long-term basis may apply for permanent residence.

Power motivation is the drive to influence people and change situations. Power motivated people wish to create an impact on their organization and are willing to take risks to do so.

Provincial Nominee Program is a program for those persons who immigrate to Canada and have the skills, education, and work experience needed to make an immediate economic contribution to the nominating province or territory. They are ready to establish themselves successfully as permanent residents of Canada.

Pull factors and **push factors** refer to the motives to migrate. Incentives that attract people away are known as pull factors, while circumstances encouraging a person to leave are known as push factors. Push factors include not enough jobs, few opportunities, famine/drought, loss of wealth, poor medical care, and other unfavourable conditions. Pull factors might be job opportunities, better living conditions, political and/or religious freedom, better medical care, security, and other advantages.

Self-Employed Persons Program is aimed at applicants who demonstrate that they have relevant artistic or athletic experience that will allow them to be self-employed and make a significant contribution to the cultural and sporting life of Canada. Relevant experience consists of at least two years of experience of self-employment in the arts or athletics, or participation at a world-class level in art, culture, recreation, or sport activities, as listed by Citizenship and Immigration Canada.

Source countries are the countries that the immigrant and refugees left to come to Canada.

Temporary resident is a person who has permission to remain in Canada on a temporary basis. This category includes visitors such as tourists, people visiting family, or people attending meetings or conferences, and temporary workers including seasonal workers and students.

Underemployment refers to being employed at work that does not permit full use of one's skills and abilities. This could mean working fewer hours than desired, doing jobs that require less skill, and working less intensively than able or willing to work.

Discussion and Activities

Discussion

Class Discussion Questions

It is important that career practitioners take care to not only educate immigrants about Canadian norms and customs, but also to facilitate discussions about the immigrants' cultural norms with regards to the job search process, culture of work, communication, and interpersonal relationships. Discuss.

Personal Reflection Questions

1. Read Roberta Neault's article, entitled *The Immigrant/Expatriate/Repatriate Experience: International Work in a Global Economy*, retrieved from <http://www .counseling.org/resources/library/vistas/2007-V-online-MSWord-files /Neault.pdf>.

   The author uses the term "global careerists." What does she mean by the term? What are the unique career challenges they face? How can career practitioners provide the unique support required by global careerists?
2. What skills, tools, or knowledge do you need in order to enhance your impact as a career practitioner working with immigrant clients?

Career Practitioner Role Questions

1. Career practitioners should be knowledgeable about premigration and postmigration challenges that impact immigrants' psychosocial adjustment to a new culture. What are some of the premigration issues faced by immigrants? What are some of the postmigration challenges? Why is it important for career practitioners to collaborate and work in interdisciplinary teams to assist with the complex premigration and postmigration issues that impact immigrants' psychosocial adjustment and adaptation?
2. Immigrants face numerous political, social, and systematic obstacles as a result of migrating to a different country. It is essential that career practitioners work with immigrant clients to promote fair and equal treatment and equivalent access to resources and opportunities. What are some steps that you can take to incorporate culturally responsive approaches, social justice, human rights, and cultural empowerment into your practice?
3. Explore the program "The Skills Connect for Immigrants Program," which is open to all unemployed or underemployed recent immigrants who have at least intermediate English language skills (<http://www.mosaicbc.com /employment-programs/working/skills-connect-immigrants-program>). What skills will you need to develop to help a client like Alena profiled on the website?

Activities

1. Imagine that you are working with an immigrant who feels that there is no hope in obtaining employment. As you work with this client you realize that you and the client are too focused on limitations and challenges. You decide to focus on the client's assets. What types of assets would many immigrants have? To start you off: Many new Canadians speak a number of other languages.
2. Interview a career practitioner who works with recent arrivals to Canada. What are some career strategies used when working with new immigrants?
3. Interview an immigrant to Canada. Ask for a description of the world he/she came

from — for example, family, community, or school — and ask how this world has shaped his/her dreams and aspirations.

Resources and Readings

Resources

Websites

British Columbia. Skills connect for immigrants. <http://www.welcomebc.ca/skillsconnect>.

Citizenship and Immigration Canada. (2010). *Planning to work in Canada? An essential workbook for newcomers* (Cat. No.: Ci4-10/2011E-PDF). Ottawa, ON: Minister of Public Works and Government Services Canada. This workbook is for people who are considering moving to Canada or who have recently arrived. The book helps new immigrants gather information about living and working in Canada. <http://www.credentials.gc.ca/immigrants/workbook/index.asp>.

Geert Hofstede Cultural Dimensions. Looks at how cultural values influence the workplace in Canada. <http://geert-hofstede.com/canada.html>.

Ontario WorkinfoNet. *Newcomers/Immigrants.* <http://www.onwin.ca/english/index.cfm?fuseaction=user_group&usergroup=2>.

University of British Columbia. *Certificate in Immigration: Laws, Policies and Procedures.* <http://cstudies.ubc.ca/immigration-professional/certificate-in-immigration-laws-policies-procedures/>.

The Centre for Intercultural Communication (CIC) offers programs and services to develop intercultural awareness, understanding, and skills for today's increasingly global academic and business environments. <http://cstudies.ubc.ca/intercultural-communication-diversity-and-immigration/>.

Video

Working in Canada. *Building futures in Canada 14/20: Immigrants and newcomers,* This video profiles the stories of 20 newcomers and immigrants to Canada who talk about why they chose Canada, where they decided to settle, the challenges they faced, the sources of help they received, and so on. <http://www.youtube.com/watch?v=wJWDqGckPl0>.

Supplementary Readings

Alberta Employment and Immigration. (2010). *What works? Career-building strategies for diverse groups: A counsellor resource. Immigrants.* Retrieved from <http://alis.alberta.ca/pdf/cshop/whatworks/ww_immigrants.pdf>.

Alboim. N., & Cohl, K. (2007). *Centres of expertise in immigration integration: An expanded role for colleges and institutes in immigration integration.* Retrieved from <http://www.accc.ca/ftp/briefs-memoires/200704-ImmigrantCentres.pdf>.

Guo, S. (2003). New citizenship learning: A place where workplace learning starts. Edmonton, AB: University of Alberta. Retrieved from <http://www.wln.ualberta.ca/en/Events/Archives/~/media/wln/Documents/Events/Conference_docs/ConferenceProceedings2003pt1.pdf>.

OECD. (2012). *Untapped skills: Realising the potential of immigrant students.* OECD Publishing. Retrieved from <http://www.oecd.org/edu/Untapped%20Skills.pdf>.

Sharaf, M. F. (2013). Job-education mismatch and its impact on the earnings of immigrants: Evidence from recent arrivals to Canada. *ISRN Economics,* 2013.doi.org/10.1155/2013/452358 Retrieved from <http://www.hindawi.com/isrn/economics/2013/452358/ref/>.

Stewart, J. (2003). Liberalizing workplace education for recent immigrants. *Proceedings of the changing face of work and learning conference.* Edmonton, AB: University of Alberta. Retrieved from <http://www.wln.ualberta.ca/en/Events/Archives/~/media/wln/Documents/Events/Conference_docs/Proceedings2003pt2.pdf>.

Yap, M. (2010). The intersection of gender & race: Effects on the incidence of promotions. *Canadian Journal of Career Development, 9*(2), 22–33. <http://ceric.ca/cjcd/current/v9-n2/article3.pdf>.

twelve

Refugees in Canada

From Persecution to Preparedness

STEPHEN J. SUTHERLAND
Centre for Applied Settlement and Integration Studies
HANY IBRAHIM
Ottawa, Ontario

PRE-READING QUESTIONS

The United Nations (1967) defines a refugee as a person who,

owing to a well-founded fear of being persecuted for reasons of race, religion, nationality, membership of a particular social group, or political opinion, is outside the country of his nationality, and is unable to or, owing to such fear, is unwilling to avail himself of the protection of that country. (UNHCR, n.d.)

1. What do you think are some of the barriers to accessing employment services for refugee communities?
2. What ideas do you have for improving access to employment services for refugees and their families?

Introduction and Learning Objectives

Refugees and immigrants to Canada, although they may share many characteristics, are quite distinct as groups and have different challenges. As described in Chapter 11, immigrants come to Canada to gain employment as skilled workers or professionals, to reunite with family, or because they have an entrepreneurial ability to contribute to Canada. Refugees, on the other hand, come to Canada because they are fleeing persecution in their home country, and may have no ties whatsoever to Canada prior to their arrival.

Refugees have many of the same issues related to the settlement and integration as immigrants. These include language proficiency, **prior learning** and employment experience (including foreign credential recognition), and **intercultural competence** (Sutherland, Conrad, Wheller, & Wadhwa, 2011). However, practitioners who work with refugees identify several issues that tend to apply more specifically to refugees and have an impact on their successful integration, particularly in the area of career development (Valenzuela, personal communication, December 1, 2010). These include mental health issues, addictions, ongoing socioethnic division and discrimination, and potential obligations to human smugglers who may have brought the refugee to Canada. This chapter will address these specific issues, but it is important to keep in mind that most issues relating to immigrants will likely apply to refugees as well.

At the end of this chapter, you will have gained a better understanding of:

1. The basics of the Canadian refugee system.
2. The differences between sponsored refugees and refugee claimants.
3. The primary mental health issues most commonly faced by refugees.
4. The ethno-cultural complexities that refugee clients may encounter upon arrival in Canada.
5. The importance of a holistic approach to refugee client services.

The Canadian Refugee System

Citizenship and Immigration Canada (CIC) defines **refugees** as people in or outside of Canada "who fear returning to their home country" due to a threat of torture, a risk to their life, or a risk of cruel and unusual treatment or punishment (CIC, 2010a). CIC (2013b) describes Canada as a compassionate country that takes seriously its responsibility towards refugees, and notes that since 2006 the Canadian government has maintained the highest sustained levels of immigration in Canadian history.

> Our compassion and fairness are a source of great pride for Canadians. These values are at the core of our domestic refugee protection system and our resettlement program.... Canada operates a global resettlement program which, in 2009 alone, resettled refugees from over 70 different nationalities. There are about 10.5 million refugees in the world today. Every year, approximately 20 countries resettle about 100,000 refugees. From that number, Canada annually resettles 10,000 to 12,000, or one out of every 10 refugees resettled globally. (CIC, 2010b, para.1)

Refugee applications are submitted to the Immigration and Refugee Board (IRB). The number of applicants in a year fluctuates as does the acceptance rate: 43,996 applied in 2000 of which 48% were accepted; in 2011, the number declined to 24,981 with only 38% acceptance (University of Ottawa, 2013).

In 2006, Mexico, China and Pakistan were the top three source countries for refugee claimants (CIC, 2012). As Roma people sought refuge following Canada's lifting of the visa requirement for Czech visitors, applications from that country rose to 813 in 2008. This increase made the Czech Republic the seventh-largest source of refugee claimants in 2009, and led Immigration Minister Jason Kenney to call on "the Czech government to crack down on unscrupulous operators believed to be behind a massive surge in the number of refugee claimants arriving at Canadian airports from that country" (O'Neil, 2009). The Canadian government introduced controversial new visa requirements for Mexican and Czech nationals to reduce the number of refugee claimants from those countries (CBC News, 2009). This did stem the flow of new claims but soon after there was a similar growth in claims from Roma people originating in Hungary (CIC, 2013c).

TOP THREE SOURCE COUNTRIES FOR REFUGEE CLAIMANTS TO CANADA		
Source: Citizenship and Immigration Canada: Canada — Refugee claimants present on December 1 by top source countries <http://www.cic.gc.ca/english/resources/statistics/facts2012/temporary/26.asp>.		
2006	2008	2012
Mexico 10,030	Mexico 18,340	Mexico 7,944
China 6,278	Haiti 9,243	China 7,032
Columbia 4,086	China 6,437	Hungary 6,957

Table 1: Top Three Source Countries for Refugee Claimants to Canada.

The Protecting Canada's Immigration System Act of 2012 made further changes to the asylum system to discourage applicants from countries considered safe — known as "designated countries of origin" (DCO). In May 2013, there were 37 countries on the list — much of Europe, some Middle East, the United States, Australia, and South Korea. These are considered to be democracies; that is, the country has an independent judiciary and human rights are protected. Refugee applicants from these countries are less likely to be admitted. This has effectively blocked the Roma from Hungary and other eastern European countries.

The length of time it takes to process an application has been a troublesome problem. Under the new Balanced Refugee Reform Act, which went into effect in June 2012, the CIC hoped to reduce the time it takes to finalize a "bona fide" refugee claim to 45 days for some countries (216 for others; Johnson, 2012).

The Canadian refugee system involves a certain amount of complexity with which career practitioners may wish to familiarize themselves via the Citizenship and Immigration Canada website at <http://www.cic.gc.ca/english/refugees/>.

Types of Refugees

Potential refugee clients can be broadly categorized as sponsored refugees and refugee claimants.

The Speak English Café

by Stephen J. Sutherland

The Speak English Café, operated by the Mennonite Coalition for Refugee Support in Kitchener, Ontario, provides refugees and newcomers with a supportive space to practise speaking English. The Café was given its name because of the importance it places on a relaxed atmosphere. Its purpose is to assist refugee claimants and other newcomers with language acquisition, while also building relationships. It began in 2002 with the help of students from Wilfrid Laurier University. Today, the Speak English Café builds community among refugees and Canadians alike by providing an inclusive space for conversations and learning to take place. One volunteer participant describes her experience at the Café: "I am happy with my personal, intellectual, and emotional growth, wanting to continue helping people like myself. I came disoriented in practising English, but I am improving with the participation and help."

For more information go to <http://www.mcrs.ca/programs/speak-english-cafe>.

Sponsored Refugees

Sponsored refugees arrive in Canada through a process referred to as **resettlement**. Citizenship and Immigration Canada relies on the United Nations High Commissioner for Refugees (UNHCR), other referral organizations, and private sponsorship groups to identify and refer refugees for resettlement in Canada. Many refugees selected through the government-funded Resettlement Assistance Program are from refugee camps.

Private sponsors are groups or corporations that have signed an agreement with Canada's Minister of Citizenship and Immigration (CIC, 2010c). In this agreement, they promise to provide funds and carry out certain duties to support refugees to Canada they have sponsored (United Nations, 1951, p. 16).

Sponsored refugees receive their refugee status prior to their arrival in Canada and are eligible for the same settlement supports that are offered to landed immigrants. These individuals do not require special permission to work or study, and can be referred to the same programs and services to which immigrants have access and that have been discussed in the previous chapter.

Refugee Claimants

Refugee claimants have already arrived in Canada but have yet to complete the application and approval process with Citizenship and Immigration Canada. These claimants may be **convention refugees** or **persons in need of protection**. Convention refugees are people who are outside their home country, or the country where they normally live, and who are unwilling to return because of a well-founded fear of persecution based on race, religion, political opinion, nationality, or membership in a particular social group, such as women or people of a particular sexual orientation. A person in need of protection is a person whose removal to their home country, or to the country in which they normally live, would subject them personally to a danger of torture, a risk to their life, or a risk of cruel and unusual treatment or punishment (CIC, 2008).

Refugee claimants require a **work permit** in order to obtain employment in Canada. They may receive a social insurance number (SIN), but it will begin with the number "9," indicating their non-permanent status in Canada. A **study permit** is not required for enrolling in English-as-a-Second-Language (ESL) classes; however, all other education can be taken only after a study permit is obtained. Refugee claimants are not eligible for the Language Instruction for Newcomers (LINC) program (Valenzuela, personal communication, December 1, 2010).

Human Smuggling

A large number of refugee claimants arriving in Canada do so by paying human smugglers to bring them (Macklin, 2005). Once established in the country and having secured jobs, there is the potential that obligations to smugglers will undermine their ability to make a living wage.

People who arrive by boat to seek asylum take risks. They sometimes give their savings to agents they don't know and board an unsafe vessel with an unknown destination. When they arrive in Canada, the **asylum seekers** along with their agents may be detained at length by the Canadian Borders Services Agency under the Immigration and Refugee Protection Act of 2001.

> "I know some people who took a boat to Canada," said one Sri Lankan man [who had made it as far as Thailand], whose wife was arrested and has been detained for months. "I support them getting to safety, but we cannot do that. Most of us living here can barely afford to keep an apartment. We cannot afford to pay for the boat trip." (Mullen, 2011, p. 1)

The Canadian government has tried to discourage "irregular mass arrivals" of boatloads of refugees through changes in the 2012 Protecting Canada's Immigration

System Act and the earlier Balanced Refugee Reform Act of 2010. Penalties for smugglers were substantially increased. Measures were also introduced to make this method less attractive to the migrants. The new provisions permit the Minister of Citizenship and Immigration to designate a group of migrants as "designated foreign nationals" to be detained until the claims are reviewed (CIC, 2013a).

Until 2012, under a long-standing program called the Interim Federal Health Program, the federal government provided basic health care, dental and vision care, medications, and medical devices as needed to refugee claimants until they became eligible for coverage under provincial health care. However, under the new government plan, some refugee claimants are only entitled to urgent care; others can be denied all care unless they have a disease that would be a risk to the public, such as tuberculosis.

Smuggled refugees can find themselves in a terrible dilemma when they arrive in Canada. An example would be the highly publicized arrival of 492 Sri Lankan refugee claimants in August 2010 aboard the MV Sun Sea that was intercepted off the coast of British Columbia by the Canadian navy. Major Canadian newspapers reported on the circumstances surrounding the transport, interception, and detention of the refugee claimants aboard the ship.

> The evidence is shedding new light on the bold migrant smuggling operation that has cost taxpayers $25-million and led the government to draft a new anti-human smuggling law ... As many as 45 smuggling agents were involved, posted at key locations along the smuggling route ... offering passage to the West — for a price. The fee varied but most paid $20,000 to $30,000. The agents collected a deposit of as little as 10%. The rest was to be paid in Canada, where the migrants were assured they would be wealthy. "We know that there are three or four syndicates, each of which had developed an area of expertise in smuggling contraband" said Jason Kenney, Canada's Minister of Citizenship and Immigration ... "If a syndicate sends someone to Canada that has an outstanding debt of $40,000, they need heavies on this side to collect on the de facto loan." (Bell, 2011)

It is reasonable to assume that financial obligations to human smugglers will significantly hinder the successful settlement of refugees in these situations. In particular, a large portion of a refugee's potential employment or other income will likely go to paying this debt, resulting in a level of poverty that does not necessarily correspond with their employment or income status. These potential issues should be important to career practitioners, who must consider the possibility that the income these clients earn may not go to meet their own needs and those of their families, and weigh that against the employment decisions made by their refugee clients.

There is also the potential for considerable stress, anxiety, and fear related to the pressure and threats of violence that refugees may face from the smugglers — either personally, or directed at family back home (Hainsworth, 2010). An added worry is that, in an effort to repay quickly, refugees might be (and sometimes are) subjected to the additional victimization of **human trafficking**, and either forced to commit crimes or be put to work by the smugglers in illegal and degrading activities in order to pay back the debt (Royal Canadian Mounted Police, 2010).

For refugee claimants who have arrived as a result of **human smuggling**, there are significant challenges once their settlement process begins. As well as a very large debt to smugglers, other barriers to their successful integration may include arriving with little or no money, illnesses requiring expensive medication, and a potentially long wait to even have their asylum claims heard. The Immigration and Refugee Board can only hear up to 25,000 asylum claims per year: By the end of 2009, the backlog of refugee claims had reached 61,000. Unsuccessful claimants can end up spending years in Canada before all possible appeals are exhausted (Thompson, 2011).

Mental Health and Addictions Among the Refugee Population

Individuals from refugee backgrounds may have experienced persecution, physical and emotional trauma, **forced migration** in their country of origin, and social exclusion and discrimination in the country of their resettlement (Murray, Davidson, & Schweitzer, 2010). Such incidences experienced by refugees differ from those of voluntary migrants and predispose many of them to symptoms of psychological disturbance prior to and following resettlement (Murray et al., 2010). Forced migration, traumatic events, resettlement in unfamiliar environments (Fazel, Wheeler, & Danesh, 2005), and unmet expectations in Canada (Simich, Este, & Hamilton, 2010) place refugees at higher risk for psychiatric morbidity and mental distress, including **post-traumatic stress disorder** (PTSD) and **major depressive disorder**. A global review of social factors associated with poor mental health among refugees found that poorer mental health outcomes were experienced by refugees living in institutional accommodations and experiencing restricted economic opportunity (Porter & Haslam 2005) — conditions that apply to most resettled refugee populations (Simich et al., 2010).

Mental health concerns are common among the refugee population, and studies have shown that individuals with higher rates of trauma, such as those experienced by the refugee population, have corresponding increases in severity of mental health symptoms, such as symptoms of PTSD (Murray et al., 2010). PTSD, depression, and **addiction** are particular areas of concern. Career practitioners can benefit from research-supported suggestions for approaching this population in a manner that will provide them with the most appropriate and effective service.

Post-Traumatic Stress Disorder (PTSD)

While mental health concerns vary among refugees — as experiences and exposure to trauma are idiosyncratically unique to each individual — one of the more commonly observed issues is PTSD. PTSD is a type of anxiety disorder that is developed after exposure to a psychologically traumatizing event, characterized by periodic flashbacks, and/or nightmares of the traumatic incident, hyper vigilance, and avoidance of stimuli associated with the trauma (Fazel et al., 2005).

Traumatic events such as human rights violations, civil conflicts, torture, and forced displacement may increase the likelihood of the diagnosis among refugees. Fazel and colleagues (2005) found that refugees in Western countries could be 10 times more likely than the age-matched general population to have PTSD. However, **prevalence** rates for PTSD vary widely, as the rate and severity of PTSD is directly proportional to the number of traumatic events experienced (Kozariæ-Kovaèiæ, Ljubin, & Grappe, 2000). Studies found prevalence rates to vary from 0% in conflict-affected regions such as Iran to 99% in Sierra Leone (Steel et al., 2009), with an overall rough estimate that 10% of refugees have PTSD (Fazel et al., 2005). In summary, refugees show greater levels of psychological disturbance than the general population (Fazel et al., 2005; Porter & Haslam, 2005), including higher rates of PTSD and major depressive disorder.

Contributing Factors

Significant exposure to torture, trauma, and loss during the immigration process elevate the risk of mental health concerns such as PTSD among refugees (Murray et al., 2010; Porter & Haslam, 2005). There are three phases through which refugees pass that are equally important when considering the likelihood of this disorder. The first is the **premigration phase**, characterized by social instability and a lack of security in one's country, which forces one to flee and seek refuge in some place safer. The second, or postmigration phase, begins when individuals have relocated and found a place to settle. The settlement phase is the last of the three and is identified as the time when refugees begin to adapt to their new environment. While practitioners will likely encounter clients at the **postmigration or settlement phases**, it is important to understand the implied risks to mental well-being inherent in each migration phase.

❖ Stop and Reflect

How could client experiences from the immigration process affect the relationship between refugees and practitioners?

Depression

In addition to post-traumatic stress disorder, depression is another significant mental health concern among refugees. Depression and major depressive disorder refer to the same condition; however, the former will be used here as it is a more general and less clinical term than the latter. Depression is generally characterized by low self-esteem, depressed mood, and loss of interest and pleasure in normally enjoyable activities. Although prevalence rates of depression vary among refugees, individuals who experience economic hardship are between 2.6 and 3.9 times more likely to experience loss of sleep, constant strain, unhappiness, depression, and bad memories, compared to individuals who do not experience hardship (Simich et al., 2006).

Contributing Factors

A refugee's chance of depression may be increased by such factors as time spent in a **refugee camp**, change in social status, economic hardship during resettlement, and discrimination upon settling (Maximova & Krahn, 2010). Maximova and Krahn (2010) found that time spent in a refugee camp was associated with a greater decline in mental health status. This may be due to poor living conditions and other trauma associated with living in refugee camps.

Change in social status among refugees was also found to play a role in determining the likelihood of having depression. For example, Maximova and Krahn (2010) found that refugees who had held professional or managerial jobs, or had completed a university degree in their home country, experienced a greater decline in mental and physical health upon resettlement.

Perceived economic hardship was also associated with greater declines in health (Maximova & Krahn, 2010). The reason for psychological distress was not simply economic hardship per se, but rather how it diminished one's ability to fulfill obligations to family in Canada and those still at risk in the homeland or refugee camps (Simich et al., 2006).

Discrimination was also identified as a contributing factor for depression. Refugees who reported experiencing **racial discrimination** had higher depression levels than their counterparts who reported no such experiences (Noh, Beiser, Kaspar, Hou, & Rummens, 1999).

In summary, there is a wide variety of contributing factors to depression among refugee clients. Career practitioners may want to be particularly aware of the mental distress that can be caused by a client's inability to fully participate in the labour market due to certain barriers, such as language difficulties, lack of Canadian work experience and/or job search skills, or issues with his or her foreign credentials being recognized in Canada. Moreover, obligations to support family in Canada or back home can place additional stress on a client and further exacerbate depression.

❖ *Stop and Reflect*

If low motivation and low self-esteem are symptoms of depression, how might these symptoms impact the effectiveness of interventions that a career practitioner considers for a refugee client?

Addictions

Among refugees, addiction — or, the physical and psychological dependence on a substance — is typically the product of the hardship and challenges endured throughout their lives, as opposed to the cause of this hardship (Kozariæ-Kovaèiæ et al., 2000). Addiction can vary from maladaptive patterns of alcohol and drug use, to abnormal activities that lead to significant impairment and/or distress.

Although limited research exists on the relationship between addiction and refugees, studies that do address this connection estimate that 60 to 80% of refugees with PTSD also have a concomitant alcohol or drug addiction, and that alcoholism is the most common co-diagnosis of PTSD (Kozariæ-Kovaèiæ et al., 2000). For adult males, an increase in alcohol dependence was associated with current PTSD, and comorbidity rates were dramatically higher in men than in women (69.6% vs. 11.7%). It should also be noted that within the co-morbidity group, men reported a higher number of war-related traumas (Kozariæ-Kovaèiæ et al., 2000), which could explain the difference in prevalence between genders. In other words, war-related traumas that contribute to the development of PTSD may also lead to alcohol or drug addiction.

Contributing Factors

There may be countless reasons as to why or how one can become dependent on a particular substance, but it can be said that addictions are both valid and logical responses to the injuries inflicted on an individual, and may serve as a form of self-medication or tension reduction. The mental health symptoms caused by trauma-related distress continuously stimulate the addiction compulsion, and the addictive behaviours then generate further mental distress (Miller, 2002).

General Observations

While refugees may have increased chances of post-traumatic stress disorder, depression, and addiction, professionals working with this population should be aware of the limitations of the existing research, and remain sensitive to the cultural and idiosyncratic differences between individuals. Prevalence rates of the above disorders vary, and depend on the extent and exposure to trauma, as well as the length of resettlement. The extent of premigration trauma exposure may explain some of the variations in PTSD rates across refugee studies. Just as Kozariæ-Kovaèiæ and colleagues (2000) found gender differences in war-related trauma, the degree and extent of exposure to conflict may have different impacts and outcomes on individuals. Similarly, the length of resettlement of refugees may also be a factor in the variability in rates of PTSD and other relevant disorders. The longer an individual spends in a refugee camp, struggles during resettlement, and is separated from loved ones, the more likely he or she will experience symptoms of the mentioned disorders. There may also be cultural differences in how an individual shows symptoms that should be taken into consideration when working with refugee clients. Therefore, while the refugee population may have an increased chance of PTSD, and depression, it does not imply that every client will have symptoms or have experienced similar situations to similar degrees.

How Career Practitioners Can Approach Mental Health Issues

Mental health symptoms among refugees appear to have a curvilinear pattern — symptoms increase during the initial stages of resettlement then gradually decline over time (Beiser, 1988; Tran, Manalo, & Nguyen, 2007). Of course, this depends on the circumstances experienced during resettlement and the type of support received. According to the literature (Beiser & Hou, 2006; Noh et al., 1999), economic difficulties, discrimination, and language issues are among the most significant challenges to well-being. Therefore, if refugees overcome these obstacles, they are more likely to experience fewer mental health challenges. Other factors associated with greater improvements in mental and physical health statuses are employment and sufficient access to settlement services during the first year in Canada (Maximova & Krahn, 2010). In light of this unique set of challenges, there is an ongoing need for information on existing mental health and psycho-educational interventions with refugee clients, and a need to assess the effectiveness of these interventions in reducing the symptoms of psychological trauma, as well as their ability to enhance the qualities of psychological and social well-being (Murray et al., 2010).

In order for professionals to provide the most effective and appropriate service to refugees, they must adopt a **holistic perspective**, engage in a non-medical/social approach, and provide services tailored to the client's unique strengths and needs (Murray et al., 2010). A holistic approach allows one to see the client as an individual with multiple perspectives and experiences. The professional is able to consider many different aspects, social and personal, of the client's life, and to understand cultural differences in meaning — all in order to foster culture-specific methods of coping and responding to adversity (Murray et al., 2010). A holistic understanding of an individual is a better base for shaping an appropriate service for that client, especially one that takes systemic factors into account, such as the client's experience as a member of a family.

Professionals working with refugees should attempt to steer away from the standard biomedical approach that views them as individuals with problems who need medical treatment. In more cases than not, they need social care rather than medical treatment (Bala, 2005; Ekblad & Jaranson, 2004; Mollica, 2002; Simich et al., 2010; Watters, 2001). Even researchers, service providers, and professionals who work with refugees have begun to shift their emphasis away from treating the experiences of trauma and the symptoms of PTSD, towards fostering strength, capacity, and resilience among individuals and communities (Papadopoulos, 2007).

Fleeing persecution and navigating the immigration process adds challenges and barriers for refugees that immigrants are less likely to face. Some refugees may be vulnerable to exploitation and abuse. Issues such as human smuggling and trafficking are far too common in cases of refugee resettlement, and arriving in a new country does not necessarily mean freedom from the persecution faced at home. One would hope that arriving in Canada and leaving persecution behind would set the stage for personal and interpersonal well-being; however, as the next section discusses, refugees may continue to face similar difficulty as newcomers to Canada.

❖ *Stop and Reflect*
What are some of the resources available in your community that might be appropriate referral opportunities for refugee clients struggling with mental health or addiction concerns?

Ethno-Cultural Division and Ongoing Persecution

Practitioners have taken particular note of the way in which refugees are received by immigrants of the same nationality, ethnicity, clan or tribe (Valenzuela, personal communication, December 1, 2010). They identify challenges faced by refugees who encounter **ethno-cultural divisions** that are similar to the ones they fled in their home country. This potential for ongoing division has particular relevance to career practitioners who may be counting on ethnic or cultural communities to provide a certain amount of settlement support for their clients.

Much study has gone into those issues related to refugees engaging with their new host culture, but less so with the challenges they face within their ethnic culture. At issue is the question of whether refugees, while attempting to settle in communities of immigrants from their own country, find that inter-ethnic discrimination and oppression from home has followed them here.

The literature indicates the potential for ongoing discrimination (or the perception of discrimination) to occur. A study of refugees who originally settled in cities in Alberta in the 1990s found that a substantial number relocated after a period of time. The reasons ranged from inadequate services, to better opportunities for employment and education, to the cold climate. But among them was the statement: "inter-ethnic hostilities within the immigrant community from the former Yugoslavia" (Krahn, Derwing, & Abu-Laban, 2003).

Quantitative studies are limited, but there are indications that some refugees find themselves no better off than they were before arriving in Canada. For instance, Yohani and Hagen (2010) looked at refugee women who were survivors of war-related rape. The authors cite a number of reasons for such women not seeking out the services that they need in order to cope with the PTSD and other conditions associated with their horrific experiences.

> Lack of language specific services makes it difficult for survivors to: (a) explain what happened to them in a second or third language, *(b) trust revealing their story in front of an interpreter from the same cultural background* (emphasis added), and (c) understand minor differences in dialect between interpreting services. (Yohani & Hagen, 2010, p. 212)

The same study also noted that the cultural meanings, roles, and beliefs that brought trauma in the old country are maintained and enforced among the same ethnic groups now in Canada.

> [W]omen assuming positions of subservience in relationships may not question sexual assault. In this context, *survivors can be blamed for speaking up, or turn the blame on themselves, for not acting appropriately.* Cultural and religious values of sexual purity and fidelity of women can make it hard for survivors to accept what has happened and disclose their experience to others. (Yohani & Hagen, 2010, p. 213)

A review of relevant literature (Gray & Elliott, 2001) reveals that refugees do not always find their own ethnic community to be a source of support. Writers such as Wahlbeck (1998) and Steen (1993) point to the need for strong ethnic communities as a source of support for resettled refugees, particularly in terms of integrating into society and finding employment. However, refugees are often unable to establish strong and united ethnic communities in their new country, because old political allegiances continue to influence and divide refugee communities. McSpadden and Moussa (1993) identified such political divisions as barriers to building a strong community in the case of Ethiopian/Eritrean refugees.

Although focused on the needs of refugees to New Zealand, Gray and Elliott (2001) drew widely from international literature and found that the needs of refugees settling in New Zealand often paralleled those of refugees taking up residence in other countries, including Canada. It is probably safe to say that, in dealing with the many needs of refugees, care must be taken to determine whether a newcomer's integration challenges have to do only with the Canadian culture, or whether the existing ethnic culture is creating its own barriers to successful resettlement.

Conclusion

Canada remains a major destination for refugees. The Government of Canada, through the Department of Citizenship and Immigration and the Immigration and Refugee Board, adjudicates thousands of applications per year. Those who are approved have access to a large variety of programs and services to assist them in their settlement and integration pursuits. A smaller number of programs and services are available to claimants already in Canada who are awaiting a decision on their application.

Although refugees and immigrants share a great number of similarities and face similar challenges upon entering Canada, refugees do find themselves with additional challenges due to the nature of their path to Canada. The tumultuous circumstances from which they have fled can result in mental health issues and addiction. Once in Canada, they may find that established immigrants from their ethno-cultural communities can perpetuate the persecution and discrimination that they sought to leave behind. For those refugees whose path to Canada has involved human smuggling, the added challenge of having obligations to terrorist groups or organized criminals may result in additional barriers to successful settlement and integration.

It is important for career practitioners to recognize these unique challenges as being different from immigrant clients, and be prepared to shape their interventions accordingly. Resources that are available to immigrants are not necessarily available to refugee claimants, either due to funding limitations or because of real or perceived ethno-cultural divisions that can discourage refugees from accessing certain resources meant to assist them. Finally, issues related to mental health and addictions may provide a significant barrier to refugees and, in combination with the variety of concerns discussed in this chapter, may require the career practitioner to take a holistic approach in dealing with the counselling and case management of their refugee clients.

References

Bala, J. (2005). Beyond the personal pain: Integrating social and political concerns in therapy with refugees. In D. Ingleby (Ed.), *Forced migration and mental health: Rethinking the care of refugees and displaced persons* (pp. 169–182). New York, NY: Springer.

Beiser, M. (1988). Influences of time, ethnicity, and attachment on depression in Southeast Asian refugees. American Journal of Psychiatry, 145, 46–51.

Beiser, M., & Huo, F. (2006). Ethnic identity, resettlement stress and depressive affect among Southeast Asian refugees in Canada. *Social Science & Medicine, 63*, 137–150. doi: 10.1016/j.socscimed.2005.12.002

Bell, S. (2011, February 14). Shedding light on the Sun Sea. *The National Post*, pp. A1, A6.

CBC News. (2009, July 14). *Canada defends visa change for Mexicans, Czechs.* Retrieved from <http://www.cbc.ca/news/world/story/2009/07/14/czech-visas-mexico.html>.

Citizenship and Immigration Canada. (CIC). (2008, October 24). *Refugee claims in Canada — who can apply?* Retrieved from <http://www.cic.gc.ca/english/refugees /inside/apply-who.asp>.

Citizenship and Immigration Canada. (CIC). (2010a, August 09). *The refugee system.* Retrieved from <http://www.cic.gc.ca/english/refugees/index.asp>.

Citizenship and Immigration Canada. (CIC). (2010b, August 6). *The refugee system in Canada.* Retrieved <http://www.cic.gc.ca/english/refugees/canada.asp>.

Citizenship and Immigration Canada. (CIC). (2010c, June 3). *Resettlement from outside Canada.* Retrieved from <http://www.cic.gc.ca/english/refugees/outside /index.asp>.

Citizenship and Immigration Canada. (CIC). (2012). *Facts and figures 2012 — immigration overview: Permanent and temporary residents.* Retrieved from <http://www.cic.gc.ca/english/resources/statistics/facts2012/temporary/26.asp>.

Citizenship and Immigration Canada. (CIC). (2013a). *New measures to crack down on human smuggling.* Retrieved from <http://www.cic.gc.ca/english/refugees /reform-smuggling.asp

Citizenship and Immigration Canada. (CIC). (2013b). News release: *Improving the citizenship application process.* Retrieved from <http://www.cic.gc.ca/english /department/media/releases/2013/2013-06-03a.asp>.

Citizenship and Immigration Canada. (CIC). (2013c). *Protecting Canada's immigration system.* Retrieved from <http://www.cic.gc.ca/english/refugees/reform.asp>.

Ekblad, S., & Jaranson, J. M. (2004). Psychosocial rehabilitation. In J.P. Wilson and B. Drozdek, (Eds.), *Broken spirits: The treatment of traumatized asylum seekers, refugees, war & torture victims* (pp. 609–636). Hove: Brunner-Routledge.

Fazel, M., Wheeler, J., & Danesh, J. (2005). Prevalence of serious mental disorder in 7000 refugees resettled in western countries: A systematic review. *Lancet, 365,* 1309–1314. doi: 10.1016/S0140-6736(05)61027-6

Gray, A., & Elliott, S. (2001). *Refugee voices.* New Zealand Immigration Service. Retrieved from <http://www.dol.govt.nz/research/migration/refugees/refugeevoices /RefugeeVoicesLiteratureReview.pdf>.

Hainsworth, J. (2010, August 13). Shipload of Sri Lanka refugees docks near Vancouver while wary Canadians eye refugee claims. *Associated Press.* Retrieved from <http://www.cleveland.com/world/index.ssf/2010/08/post_51.html>.

Johnson, Ian. (2012). Human smuggling and trafficking big business in Canada. CBC News. <http://www.cbc.ca/news/canada/story/2012/03/28 /f-human-smuggling-overview.html>.

Kozariæ-Kovaèiæ, D., Ljubin, T., & Grappe, M. (2000). Comorbidity of posttraumatic stress disorder and alcohol dependence in displaced persons. *Croatian Medical Journal, 41*(2), 173–178.

Krahn, H., Derwing, T. M., & Abu-Laban, B. (2003). *The retention of newcomers in second and third-tier cities in Canada.* University of Alberta. Edmonton, AB: PCERII Working Paper Series.

Macklin, A. (2005). Disappearing refugees: Reflections on the Canada–US safe third country agreement. *Columbia Human Rights Law Review*, 36, 365–426.

McSpadden, L. A., & Moussa, H. (1993). I have a name: The gender dynamics in asylum and in resettlement of Ethiopian and Eritrean refugees in North America. *Journal of Refugee Studies* 6(3), 203–225.

Maximova, K., & Krahn, H. (2010). Health status of refugees settled in Alberta: Changes since arrival. *Canadian Journal of Public Health*, 101(4), 322–326.

Miller, D. (2002). Addictions and trauma recovery: An integrated approach. *Psychiatric Quarterly*, 73(2), 157–170. doi: 10.1023/A:1015011929171

Mollica, F. (2002). Science-based policy for psychosocial interventions in refugee camps: A Cambodian example. *Journal of Nervous and Mental Disease*, 19(3), 158.

Mullen, M. (2011, January 13). *Thailand: Living day to day in limbo*. Retrieved from Jesuit Refugee Service <http://www.jrs.net/spotlight_detail?TN =DTN-20110113022723>.

Murray, E., Davidson, G., & Schweitzer, R. (2010). Review of refugee mental health interventions following resettlement: Best practices and recommendations. *American Journal of Orthopsychiatry*, 80(4), 576–585. doi: 10.1111/j.1939-0025.2010.01062.x

Noh, S., Beiser, M., Kaspar, V., Hou, F., & Rummens J. (1999). Perceived racial discrimination, depression, and coping: A study of Southeast Asian refugees in Canada. *Journal of Health & Social Behaviour*, 40, 193–207.

O'Neil, P. (2009, July 2). *Canada to reinstate visa requirements for Czechs*. Retrieved from <http://www.canada.com/Canada+reinstate+visa+requirement+Czechs /1752224/story.html>.

Papadopoulos, R. K. (2007). Refugees, trauma and adversity-activated development. *European Journal of Psychotherapy and Counselling*, 9, 301–312. doi: 10.1080/13642530701496930

Porter, M., & Haslam, N. (2005). Pre-displacement and post-displacement factors associated with mental health of refugees and internally displaced persons: A meta-analysis. *Journal of the American Medical Association*, 294, 602–612. doi: 10.1001/jama.294.5.602

Royal Canadian Mounted Police. (2010, October 12). *Frequently asked questions on human trafficking*. Retrieved from <http://www.rcmp-grc.gc.ca/ht-tp /q-a-trafficking-traite-eng.htm#5>.

Simich, L., Este, D., & Hamilton, H. (2010). Meanings of home and mental well-being among Sudanese Refugees in Canada. *Ethnicity & Health*, 15(2), 199–212. doi: 10.1080/13557851003615560

Steel, Z., Chey, T., Silove, D., Marnane, C., Bryant, R., & van Ommeren, M. (2009). Association of torture and other potentially traumatic events with mental health outcomes among populations exposed to mass conflict and displacement: A systematic review and meta-analysis. *Journal of the American Medical Association. Special Issue: Violence and human rights*, 302(5), 537–549. doi: 10.1001/ jama.2009.1132

Steen, A. (1993). *Varieties of the Tamil refugee experience in Denmark and England.* Copenhagen: University of Copenhagen/Danish Centre for Human Rights.

Sutherland, S. J., Conrad, D., Wheller, M. S., & Wadhwa, T. (2011). Approaches to portfolio development and applications for immigrants in a social work context. *Canadian Social Work. Special Issue: Immigration and Settlement.*

Thompson, E. (2011, February 16). Canada's refugee system is broken: Kenney. *Toronto Sun.* Retrieved from <http://www.torontosun.com/news/canada/2009/10/06/11325076-sun.html>.

Tran, T. V., Manalo, V., & Nguyen, V. T. D. (2007). Nonlinear relationship between length of residence and depression in a community-based sample of Vietnamese Americans. *International Journal of Social Psychiatry, 53,* 85–94. doi: 10.1177/0020764007075025

United Nations. (1951). *Convention and protocol relating to the status of refugees.* New York, NY: United Nations Publications.

UNHCR — The UN Refugee Agency (n.d). *Refugees.* Retrieved from <http://www.unhcr.org/pages/49c3646c125.html>.

University of Ottawa (2013). By the numbers: Refugee statistics, 2012. *Info Sheet,* May 17(8). Retrieved from <http://www.cdp-hrc.uottawa.ca/projects/refugee-forum/projects/Statistics.php>.

Wahlbeck, O. R. (1998). Community work and exile politics: Kurdish refugee associations in London. *Journal of Refugee Studies, 11*(3), 215–230. doi: 10.1093/jrs/11.3.215

Watters, C. (2001). Emerging paradigms in the mental health care of refugees. *Social Science & Medicine, 52,* 1709–1718.

Yohani, S. C., & Hagen, K. T. (2010). Refugee women survivors of war-related sexualised violence: A multicultural framework for service provision in resettlement countries. *Intervention, 8*(3), 207–222. doi: 10.1097/WTF.0b013e328341665c

Glossary

Addiction is defined as the continued use of a mood-altering substance or behaviour despite harmful and adverse consequences. There are many types of addictions ranging from gambling, to sex, to drugs, and alcohol.

Asylum seekers apply for admission under the standard definition of a refugee, as laid out by the United Nations, that they fear persecution at home based on factors such as race, religion, politics, or membership in a persecuted group.

A convention refugee is a person who meets the definition of a refugee contained in the 1951 United Nations Convention Relating to the Status of Refugees. In general, it is someone who has left his or her home country, has a well-founded fear of persecution based on race, religion, nationality, political opinion, or membership in a particular social group, and because of that fear is unable or unwilling to seek protection in his or her home country.

Ethno-cultural divisions are social divisions created by differences in nationality, ethnicity, clan, or tribe. For refugees or immigrants these divisions are similar to the ones they faced in their home country.

Forced migration refers to coerced movement of people — refugees, people displaced by conflict, disasters, or projects.

A holistic perspective ensures that services are offered in an inclusive manner, respectful of and sensitive to diversity. Service providers take account of the complex, multifaceted, interrelated dimensions of settlement and integration.

Human smuggling is the illegal transportation of people into another country. The migrants pay the smugglers to get them to the destination and are free from their smugglers upon arrival.

Human trafficking is trade in humans for enslavement of exploitation typically for labour, sex, or organs. What sometimes begins as smuggling can end up as exploitation and trafficking, but not all trafficking involves crossing borders.

Intercultural competence refers to someone having understanding, knowledge, and comfort in interacting with other cultures.

Major depressive disorder is characterized by one or more major depressive episodes defined as at least 2 weeks of depressed mood or loss of interest in usual activities accompanied by at least four additional symptoms of depression.

A person in need of protection is a person who, if removed to his or her home country, would be placed in great danger — possibly of torture, death, or cruel and unusual treatment or punishment.

Postmigration phase or settlement phase is defined as the absorption of the immigrant within the social and cultural framework of the new society. Social and cultural rules and new roles may be learned at this stage.

Post-traumatic stress disorder (PTSD) is a condition that can develop as a result of being exposed to an extremely traumatic stressor that involves feeling intense fear, helplessness, or horror. The disorder may be particularly severe or long-lasting when the stressor is of human design (e.g., torture, rape, etc.), and trust is lost.

Premigration phase involves the decision and preparation to move.

Prevalence refers to a sum of instances of a particular disease within the given population at a certain point in time.

Prior learning is a process that encompasses what a person knows and can do. This includes formal, informal, non-formal, and experiential learning.

Racial discrimination is discriminatory behaviour towards another based on race, ancestry, ethnicity, et cetera.

A **refugee camp** is a temporary settlement built to receive refugees. Hundreds of thousands of people may live in any one single camp. Usually they are built and run by a government, the United Nations, international organizations, or non-governmental organizations (NGOs).

Refugees are people who are forced to leave their home country to seek protection in another country.

A **study permit** is the official document issued by an officer that allows a person who is not a Canadian citizen or a permanent resident to study in Canada.

Work permits in Canada consist of work visas and employment authorizations. A work permit is a document issued by officials of the Canadian government that allows a foreign individual to work at a specific job for a specific employer.

Discussion and Activities

Discussion

Discussion Questions

1. What are the mental health issues for refugees, including refugee youth, in their countries of resettlement?
2. On what should career guidance education programs focus in order to help refugee youth succeed in resettlement over the long term?
3. Demographic research shows that most immigrants and refugees eventually gravitate towards Toronto, Montréal, and Vancouver, where there are large refugee and immigrant-based communities (Statistics Canada, 2005). This is probably an indication of the fact that refugees and immigrants draw strength and sustenance from large diasporic communities in these large cities as opposed to smaller towns and territories. According to Gray and Elliott (2001), not all refugees find that their ethnic community provides support. Give possible reasons for this finding.
4. Complete a review of services that exist in your community to address mental

health concerns for refugees. What types of mental health issues are common among refugees in Canada?

Personal Reflection Questions

1. Refugees may face a number of discriminatory attitudes in the Canadian labour market. How might you unintentionally contribute to this discriminatory attitude?
2. The word "stigma" is an ancient Greek term that once referred to the prick marks that people would inflict upon their slaves to demonstrate ownership. Today, stigma refers to the invisible prick mark that symbolizes society's discomfort with mental health issues. The stigma associated with mental health problems can often result in stereotyping, fear, embarrassment, anger, avoidance, and discrimination. What is a mental health issue? How comfortable are you working with individuals with mental health issues?

Career Practitioner's Role

1. One measure of success for refugees is the development of livelihood rebuilding strategies. Make a list of rebuilding strategies that you would consider essential. (e.g., establishing safety for the family, etc.).
2. Understandably, most refugees want to get into the labour market as soon as they can, in work that reflects their experience and qualifications. But even when they do find the ideal job, they will need to learn to manage their career in their new country. Consider the elements of career planning: self-discovery, researching occupational information including the labour market, implementing job search skills, engaging in decision making, taking action, and developing and maintaining career management skills. How will this process be similar to and different from Canadian-born clients?

Activities

Interview an individual who came to Canada as a refugee and who has transitioned to full-time work in Canada. Introduce yourself and indicate where you were born. Below are some suggested interview questions. Brainstorm other ideas with your classmates.

- How long have you been in Canada?
- What is the work that you are doing now? What does that work involve?
- How did you find out about this work? Why did you decide to do this work? What interests you most about this work? Have you had any other work or jobs?
- What do you like the most about your work? What do you like the least about your work?
- What were the biggest challenges you faced in finding work in Canada?

- How similar is the work you are doing in Canada to what you did in your home country?

Resources and Readings

Resources

Websites/Videos

Albany Volunteers and Refugees Find Common Ground in Soccer: <http://www.refugees.org/refugee-voices/refugee-resettlement /finding-common-ground-in.html>.
Burmese Refugees Recover from Addiction with DARE Network <http://www.youtube.com/watch?v=h6zVDYI9aUc>.
Canadian Centre for Refugee Employment <http://refugeeemployment.org/>
Canadian Council for Refugees <http://ccrweb.ca/>
Iraqi Refugees to Canada <http://www.youtube.com/watch?v=UYtDk5KQED4 &feature=related>.
Refugee Issues <http://www.youtube.com/watch?v=6PoWrFmH-c0&feature=related>.
The UN Refugee Agency Canada (UNHCR) <http://www.unhcr.ca/>.

Supplementary Readings

Abraham, D., & Rahman, S. (2008). The community interpreter: A critical link between clients and service providers. In S. Guruge & E. Collins (Eds.), *Working with immigrant women: Issues and strategies for mental health professionals* (pp. 103–118). Toronto, ON: Centre for Addiction and Mental Health.

Ager, A., Malcolm, M., Sadollah, S., & May, F. (2002). Community contact and mental health amongst socially isolated refugees in Edinburgh. *Journal of Refugee Studies, 15*(1), 71–79.

Affiliation of Multicultural Societies and Services Agencies of B.C. (AMSSA). (2013). *Info Sheet on Refugees.* Retrieved from <http://www.amssa.org/files/Info_Sheet/ AMSSA%20Info%20Sheet%20Issue%208%20-%20Final.pdf>.

DeVoretz D., Beiser M., & Pivenko S. (2005). The economic experience of refugees in Canada. *Homeland wanted: Interdisciplinary perspectives on the refugee resettlement in the West.* New York, NY: Nova Science Publishers.

Ehnholt, K., & Yule, W. (2006). Practitioner review: Assessment and treatment of refugee children and adolescents who have experienced war-related trauma. Journal of Child Psychology and Psychiatry and Allied Disciplines, 47, 1197–1210.

Fangen, K. (2006). Humiliation experienced by Somali refugees in Norway. *Journal of Refugee Studies, 19*(1), 69–93.

Grossman, J., & Liang, B. (2008). Discrimination distress among Chinese American adolescents. *Journal of Youth and Adolescence, 37*, 1–11.

Kanu, Y. (2008). Educational needs and barriers for African refugee students in Manitoba. *Canadian Journal of Education, 31*(4), 915–940. Retrieved from <http://www.csse-scee.ca/CJE/Articles/FullText/CJE31-4/CJE31-4-Kanu.pdf>.

Marshall, G., Schell, T., Elliott, M., Berthold, M., & Chun, C. (2005). Mental health of Cambodian refugees 2 decades after resettlement in the United States. *Journal of the American Medical Association, 294*, 571–579.

Pittaway, E., & Bartolomei, L. (2001). Refugees, race, and gender: The multiple discrimination against refugee women. *Refuge: Canada's Periodical on Refugees, 19*(6), 21–32.

Renaud, J., Piche, V., & Godin, J. (2003). "One's bad and the other one's worse": Differences in economic integration between asylum seekers and refugees selected abroad. *Canadian Ethnic Studies, 35*(2), 86–99.

Sowey, H. (2005). *Are refugees at increased risk of substance misuse?* Drug and Alcohol Multicultural Education Centre. Retrieved from <http://www.damec.org.au /downloads/Refugee_Drug_Alcohol_Vulnerability.pdf>.

Vasilevska, B. (2010). *Refugee mental health practices internationally: A review of the literature and implications for a Canadian study.* Centre for Addiction and Mental Health. Retrieved from <http://www.ahrni-irras.ca/index.php?option =com_sobipro&task=download.file&fid=269.8184&sid=102&Itemid=115>.

Wethington, H., Hahn, R., Fuqua-Whitley, D., Sipe, T., Crosby, A., Johnson, R., ... Chattodhyay, S. (2008). The effectiveness of interventions to reduce psychological harm from traumatic events among children and adolescents: A systematic review. *American Journal of Preventive Medicine, 35*(3), 287–313.

World Health Organization. (2009). Mental health of refugees, internally displaced persons and other populations affected by conflict. *Humanitarian Health Action* Retrieved from <http://www.who.int/hac/techguidance/pht /mental_health_refugees/en/>.

WRHA Research & Evaluation Unit (2010, November). Health of immigrants and refugees in the Winnipeg Health Region: A community health assessment resource for health services planning. *Focused Community Health Assessment Report (2010-001).* Retrieved from <http://www.wrha.mb.ca/research/cha/files /ImmRefug_PART01.pdf>.

thirteen

Through an Aboriginal Lens

Exploring Career Development and Planning in Canada

NATASHA CAVERLEY
Turtle Island Consulting Services Inc.

SUZANNE STEWART
Ontario Institute for Studies in Eduction

BLYTHE C. SHEPARD
University of Lethbridge

PRE-READING QUESTIONS

1. What is your personal level of awareness regarding key issues currently facing Aboriginal peoples in Canada?
2. What historical effects have Canadian legislation and policies had on Aboriginal peoples in Canada?
3. What type of career resources and supports are you aware of that are designed specifically for Aboriginal peoples?

Introduction

We hold it within our capacity to ensure that the next generation of Aboriginal Canadians become a generation of real and lasting change, the generation that stays in school, the generation that is given the tools to succeed, the generation that breaks the cycle of poverty, that writes the great music, that paints the great paintings, that discovers the secrets of science and builds the great companies. That's what this is all about.
— Excerpt from a speech delivered by former Prime Minister Paul Martin at the Inclusion Works '10 Conference (Aboriginal Human Resource Council, 2010, p. 6)

In Canada, career development and planning programs must be poised to respond to individuals' employment needs and current labour market changes. It is important to recognize that individuals have unique interests and sociocultural backgrounds.

Career development and planning programs have, and will continue to play, an important role in providing people with customized and **culturally congruent resources** that: (a) aid in the school-to-workplace transition, and (b) prepare current and future workers to proactively respond to employers' needs. For Aboriginal peoples in Canada, the concepts of career development and education, which includes formal Western-based education and **localized knowledge**, are integral parts of both individual and societal change.

According to the 2011 National Household Survey, 1,400,685 Canadians identified themselves as Aboriginal (i.e., self-identified as being First Nations, Métis, or Inuit). This represented 4.3% of the total Canadian population (Statistics Canada, 2013). From 2006 to 2011, the Aboriginal population increased by 20.1%, while the non-Aboriginal population grew by 5.2% (Statistics Canada, 2013). Aboriginal peoples represent the fastest-growing population in Canada. Though challenges (e.g., low labour force representation, socioeconomic hardships, discrimination, and low educational attainment) do exist for Aboriginal people in the labour market, strengths-based career development and planning strategies can greatly assist in meeting their personal career needs in a culturally congruent manner. The potential exists for Aboriginal peoples to provide the next generation of **human capital** in Canada.

We start the chapter by establishing the Aboriginal context for understanding career development and planning in Canada. This includes defining Aboriginal peoples and describing their cultural identities. (For a historical perspective on the legislation affecting Aboriginal peoples in Canada, see Appendix C). We then highlight major challenges that impact and influence career development and planning. Next, we focus on the strengths that exist — emphasizing opportunities for bringing together both traditional and Western ways of understanding the career journey. Finally, we examine career development strategies that can aid career practitioners, educators, and employers in effectively working with various groups in the Aboriginal population. Brief case study overviews and Aboriginal-specific career development resources are provided at the end of the chapter.

After reading this chapter, you will be able to:

1. Define the various groups that comprise the Aboriginal population in Canada.
2. Identify major challenges that affect Aboriginal peoples in advancing their career development and planning endeavours.
3. Explore the relationship between Aboriginal traditions, strengths, and career identity.
4. Describe culturally congruent career development strategies for Aboriginal peoples.

The Cultural Context:
Aboriginal Identities, Values, and Ways of Knowing

The number of Aboriginal persons residing in **urban** areas in Canada continues to grow. In 2006, 54% of the Aboriginal population in Canada lived in urban areas — an increase from 50% in 1996, with Winnipeg, Edmonton, Vancouver, Toronto, Calgary, Saskatoon, and Regina having the largest number (Statistics Canada, 2008).

This is a young population. According to 2011 National Household Survey data (see Table 1), the median age of individuals who identified themselves as Aboriginal was 28 years, compared to 41 years for non-Aboriginal people. In 2011, 46% of the Aboriginal population in Canada consisted of children and youth aged 24 years or younger, compared with 29.5% of the non-Aboriginal population (Statistics Canada, 2013). For years, policy makers have grappled with the increase in the number of Aboriginal youth, as many reserves in remote areas face high rates of school dropout and unemployment.

2011 NATIONAL HOUSEHOLD SURVEY	ABORIGINAL	NON-ABORIGINAL
Median age	28	41
Younger than 24	46%	29.5%

Table 1: Age Distribution of Aboriginal Peoples 2011 (Statistics Canada, 2013).

Being of Aboriginal ancestry ourselves, the authors can affirm that traditional ways of knowing are of equal weight and complement non-Aboriginal (or Western) counselling and development practices. Also, we recognize the diversity of **socio-cultural values** and worldview perspectives that exist across Canada's Aboriginal population of First Nations (Status and Non-Status Indians), Métis, and Inuit: Aboriginal people in these sub-groups do have distinct cultural perspectives and beliefs relative to their particular family lineage and community connections.

Unless specified, the information and resources presented in this chapter can be applied generally to all Aboriginal people of Canada. Finally, the authors have endeavoured to provide a snapshot of the diverse range of practices and associated case study briefs of career development and planning "in action." However, this is not an exhaustive list of Aboriginal resources.

Defining the Aboriginal Population

First Nations

They are the First Peoples of Canada, both Status and Non-Status. Status (or registered) Indians are individuals who are registered according to the Indian Act and are members of a band (i.e., First Nations community). Status Indians receive supports and related services (e.g., housing and financial assistance for postsecondary education) from Aboriginal Affairs and Northern Development Canada (AANDC). Non-Status Indians are individuals who are not recognized as Indians under the Indian Act.

At present, there are over 600 First Nations communities in Canada representing more than 50 Nations and language groups (Assembly of First Nations, 2012). A smaller proportion of First Nations people live on a **reserve** (38%) than off-reserve (62%) according to the 2011 National Household Survey.

Métis

Métis people are individuals possessing both First Nations and European ancestry and whose homeland encompasses parts of present-day Ontario, British Columbia, the Northwest Territories, Alberta, Saskatchewan, and Manitoba (Ahearn, 2005; Métis National Council, 2013). Historically, Métis people were "boundary walkers" and "natural negotiators" who worked with both European settlers and First Nations people and typically through the Hudson's Bay Company. As interracial marriages flourished between First Nations and Europeans, a distinct culture of the Métis people emerged that was a fusion of French, English, and First Nations influences. Métis people were important players in opening Western North America to exploration, the fur trade, and European settlements. The traditional language spoken by Métis people is Michif (Métis National Council, 2013). In 2006, the fastest growing Aboriginal group in Canada was the Métis (Statistics Canada, 2008).

Inuit

The Inuit are the Aboriginal people of Canada's Arctic who reside mainly in Northern Labrador (Nunatsiavut), Northern Québec (Nunavik), Nunavut, and the Northwest Territories. These geographic areas comprise approximately 40% of Canada's total land mass (Inuit Tapiriit Kanatami, 2012). The traditional language of Inuit people is Inuktitut. The Inuit population had a median age of 23 years, lower than the median of 28 for all three Aboriginal groups (Statistics Canada, 2013).

Honouring Aboriginal Cultures and Values

Aboriginal Engagement in Economic and Career Development

Aboriginal engagement in local, regional, provincial/territorial, and national economies is not a recent phenomenon. Wild harvesting, gathering, hunting, fishing, forestry, entrepreneurship, and trading have and continue to be primary economic development activities and career avenues for many Aboriginal communities.

Traditional economic and career activities are mainly aimed at satisfying important social, cultural, and nutritional needs, as well as the economic needs of families, households, and communities (Nuttall, 2005).

In general, Aboriginal peoples in Canada have worldviews that embrace a holistic approach to economic and career development. In contrast to a strictly profit-driven approach to life, the Aboriginal holistic approach respects sociocultural, spiritual, and ecological interests alongside the financial drivers in local Aboriginal communities (e.g., First Nations Mountain Pine Beetle Initiative, 2007). Successful economic and career development means preserving traditional cultural values, such as the interconnectedness of all living things, and sustainability for future generations. This may mean that some Aboriginal communities will forfeit short-term monetary gain for sociocultural interests to move ahead with a holistic approach to economic and career advancement.

Aboriginal Identities

James Frideres (1998) in *Aboriginal Peoples in Canada: Contemporary Conflicts* described three concepts of **Aboriginal identity**.

- Traditional Aboriginal people are those who adhere to and are guided by the teachings of Elders and Knowledge Keepers in their communities.
- Non-traditional Aboriginal people are those individuals who either align their behaviours, beliefs and lifestyles to mainstream culture or who feel displaced or alienated from their Aboriginal ancestry.
- Neo-traditional Aboriginal people are those who integrate their traditional practices with mainstream beliefs.

Cultural Values

In general, cultural values represent guiding principles, ideals, aspirations, and beliefs that serve as a foundation as to how Aboriginal people live and work in their communities. Cultural values often manifest themselves in local traditions, governance, language, institutions, and protocols that are major pillars in Aboriginal society. There is often a close relationship between knowing one's Aboriginal cultural values and leading a healthy lifestyle — connecting with one's values and traditional lands as a means of managing physical, mental, and spiritual ailments such as intergenerational trauma due to **colonization**, addiction, and sociocultural disruption (Duran, 2006; France, McCormick & Rodriguez, 2004; Stewart, Reeves, Mohanty, & Syrette, 2011). Some key Aboriginal cultural values include, but are not limited to those described below:

- *Respect for the teachings of Elders and Knowledge Keepers*
  The traditional teachings (shared through observations, stories, cere-monies, and prayers) of Elders and Knowledge Keepers reflect local and culturally specific knowledge that Aboriginal people pass on from one generation to the next. Traditional teachings aid in developing world-view perspectives on social, physical/spiritual issues, and practices, all of which serve as core aspects of developing one's self-identity. Traditional knowledge is localized to a given culture or society and tends to be closely linked to survival. It often provides a basis for local decision making in such areas as education, and health and wellness. (Battiste & Henderson, 2000; Sillitoe, 2002a, 2002b)
- *Importance of listening*
  Active listening involves awareness and recognition of historical teach-ings from previous generations. The stories, teachings, and songs are often fundamental aspects of one's lifestyle and are an integral part of the oral tradition by which values, ideals, and knowledge are shared in households and communities.
- *Connectedness of all living things*
  In general, the Aboriginal peoples are viewed as the caretakers of the land, water, air, and other living beings and hold the belief that every-thing has spirit. There exists interdependence and interrelationships among all people and the environment. Coupled with this value, there is recognition that group needs prevail over individual ones to maintain this balance and harmony (France et al., 2004).
- *The role of family*
  For many Aboriginal individuals, the connection to family, including extended family, is important in career development and planning. Social support is not limited to direct connections by blood and ancestral link-ages; it also includes acceptance, encouragement, reassurance, and vali-dation by all those in the community. An individual's family shapes and influences identity development and lays the groundwork for socialization and emotional support.

By taking these worldviews and shared interests into consideration, one can recognize the need to include and respect local cultures, languages, aspirations, tra-ditions, and history for each of the three Aboriginal peoples and their respective communities. Doing so will effectively identify economic and career development needs when designing collaborative initiatives with strategic partners (i.e., other Aboriginal communities and organizations; municipal, provincial, territorial, and federal governments; academia; and industry).

Societal and Organizational Challenges:
Current Barriers to Career Development

Career development is a central component to building a sustainable, local, and dedicated Aboriginal workforce. For Aboriginal communities, improved career and economic development prospects not only generate increased income in local communities but also promote greater independence and improved quality of life (Hanselmann, 2003; Mendelson, 2004; Papillon & Cosentino, 2004). However, in spite of the demographic strengths noted earlier of a young and growing Aboriginal population, nearly intractable societal and economic challenges exist. Problems of high unemployment rates, low wages, and low educational attainment are pervasive. Further, there is a serious lack of culturally congruent workplace resources pertaining to career development and employment.

Unemployment and Labour Force Representation

Based on 2006 Census data, Human Resources and Skills Development Canada (2010) reported that the national rate of unemployment for Aboriginal people in Canada was 14.8%; for non-Aboriginal people the rate was 6.1% (see Table 2). Aboriginal youth between the ages of 15 to 24 had unemployment rates ranging from 12% to over 20% depending on the provincial or territorial location. In comparison, the average unemployment rate for non-Aboriginal youth in Canada was 6%. Therefore, Aboriginal youth are two to three times more likely to be unemployed than their non-Aboriginal counterparts. The Government of Canada has viewed Aboriginal unemployment as a major concern. In response, equity policies have been adopted to address the recruitment, development, and retention of Aboriginal workers; however, these have not been enough to address this systemic problem (Dwyer, 2003).

2006 EMPLOYMENT DATA	ABORIGINAL	NON-ABORIGINAL
National rate of unemployment (2006)	14.8%	6.1%
Ages 15 to 24 (2006)	12 to 20%	6%
Participation in workforce (2010)	62.6%	67.1%
Employed or seeking employment ages 15 to 24 (2010)	57%	64.8%

Table 2: Aboriginal Employment Data (HRSDC, 2006).

After the Canadian labour market downturn in the fall of 2008, employment declined by 7% for Aboriginal people in 2009 and 2010 — particularly in private sector occupations such as trades, transport, sales, and manufacturing. In 2010, 62.6% of the Aboriginal population participated in the labour force, compared to 67.1% of the non-Aboriginal population. In that same year, 57.0% of Aboriginal youth (ages 15 to 24 years) were either employed or seeking employment compared to 64.8% of their non-Aboriginal counterparts. The labour market downturn coupled with systemic low labour force representation by Aboriginal people further widened the socioeconomic gap (e.g., employment rates, education levels, etc.) between Canada's Aboriginal and non-Aboriginal populations (Usalcas, 2011).

Socioeconomic Hardships

In 2005, Aboriginal people between 25 and 54 years of age earned a median income of $22,366.00 per year compared to the Canadian median income of $33,394.00 (Statistics Canada, 2012). As shown in Figure 1, median income for the Aboriginal sub-groups was: Métis at $27,728.00, Inuit at $24,782.00, and First Nations at $19,114.00. Off-reserve First Nations people had a median income of approximately $22,500.00, while on-reserve First Nations people earned a median income of just over $14,000.00 (Statistics Canada, 2012).

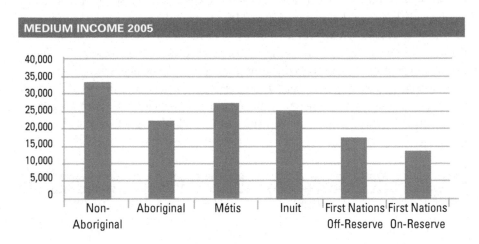

Figure 1: Median Income for Aboriginal Peoples 2005 (Statistics Canada, 2012).

The obstacles to the overall economic and career development success of Aboriginal people go well beyond unemployment to include overcrowding, lack of affordable housing, poverty, physical and mental health problems, high suicide rates, historical and intergenerational trauma (e.g., the Indian Residential School Programs), and substance abuse (Government of Canada, 1996; Kunin, 2009; St. Germain and Sibbeston, 2007). According to the **Treaty** Commission in British

Columbia, "Life under the Indian Act has meant no life at all. They are the casualties of marginalization and neglect. Many have died too young" (BC Treaty Commission, 2007, p. 13).

Cultural Losses

Another major challenge in advancing career development and planning initiatives that are culturally congruent is that much of the localized knowledge that remains in Aboriginal communities is held by a small number of people (typically Elders) and is in jeopardy of being lost forever (First Peoples' Heritage, Language and Culture Council, 2010). Because of the gradual loss of traditional languages and localized knowledge in Aboriginal communities due to colonization and assimilation initiatives, there has been less sharing of traditional knowledge with younger generations. As localized knowledge tends to be passed down orally from generation to generation, there is a risk of this knowledge source becoming extinct if pertinent information, strategies, and skills are not shared and subsequently documented with each younger generation (Battiste & Henderson, 2000). For example, according to the 2006 Census,

> (W)hile the Inuktitut language remains strong overall (69% of Inuit could speak Inuktitut), knowledge and use are declining. Inuit are less likely to speak it as their main language at home — 50% in 2006 down from 58% in 1996. In addition, smaller percentages of Inuit are reporting Inuktitut as their mother tongue and a declining percentage can speak it well enough to have a conversation. (Statistics Canada, 2008, p. 7)

Of those Aboriginal communities who are carrying out traditional knowledge research in order to protect and revitalize their distinct languages and cultural practices, there is growing concern about intellectual property of local knowledge — ownership of exclusive rights of cultural practices, resources, and property. Historically, cultural property (including traditional knowledge) has been taken from Aboriginal people without informed consent or compensation. In addition, there is concern that research in Aboriginal communities may lead to commodifying and revealing traditional knowledge to those who could potentially misuse this cultural property (Battiste & Henderson, 2000).

Education

Thomas Berger (2006) stated that "you can't speak of employment without speaking of education" (p. 47). Education levels for Aboriginal people remain below that of non-Aboriginal people, particularly for higher knowledge and skill-based occupations. Wilson and MacDonald (2010) identified a very large gap by which only 8% of

Aboriginal people obtained an undergraduate or higher degree compared with 23% of non-Aboriginals. Education and employment are directly related; as the amount of education people have increases, so do their opportunities for employment (Betz, 2006). Given this relationship, the statistics regarding educational attainment for Aboriginal people as a whole in Canada do not bode well for their career attainment and success.

As shown in Table 3, the 2006 Census shows that 34% of Aboriginal people aged 20 years and older had not graduated from secondary school, and for those who lived on a reserve, 50% of the students did not finish high school (Statistics Canada, 2006b).

The gap in university graduates is also widening. In 2001, 6% of Aboriginal individuals aged 25 to 64 completed some form of university education compared to 20% of the non-Aboriginal population. Both percentages were higher in 2006, but Aboriginal grew only to 8% and non-Aborginal rose to 23%. (Statistics Canada, 2006b).

EDUCATION 2006	ABORIGINAL	NON-ABORIGINAL
Had not graduated from secondary school (25 to 64 years and older)	34%	15%
Postsecondary graduates (trade, diploma, degree)	44%	61%
Undergraduate university degree or higher	8%	23%

Table 3: Education Rates in 2006 (Statistics Canada, 2006b).

These statistics reflect the limited access to education and the consequent limitations for career development and career outcomes. Battiste (1998) explains this disparity in education as resulting from the colonial experience, which has left generations of Aboriginal people and communities with multiple healing issues, limited access to health care and education, and in a state of economic marginalization.

Organizational Development

Some employers, practitioners, and educators continue to have difficulty working with Aboriginal people in a culturally congruent manner (i.e., acknowledging and respecting various Aboriginal cultures and traditions in relation to career development and planning). Findings from O'Donnell and Ballardin (2006) pointed to inadequate access to career-planning information (e.g., types of careers available in the public and private sectors, current job vacancies, and key skills needed in today's labour market) as a major obstacle for Aboriginal job seekers. More likely than not, employers also lack adequate resources and support networks to make Aboriginal employees feel welcomed and included in the workplace.

In addition to adopting postsecondary training, workshops, and adult education training programs, Aboriginal communities need to build organizational capacity at the local level. This means empowering the communities in developing core competencies, organizational structures, and incentives that make effective use of skills in promoting the concepts of economic and career development (Kumar, 2006). If organizations do not have the capacity to effectively use the skills developed by Aboriginal peoples, the newly acquired skills tend to disappear.

Cross-Cultural Relations

Researchers such as Gone (2004) have suggested that employing a Western paradigm is a form of colonial oppression and discrimination whereby Western ideologies and related points of view are imposed on Aboriginal peoples rather than integrating Aboriginal ways of knowing into various facets of life (e.g., economic, employment and career development). Although there has been some legislative action (in the areas of human rights, employment standards and employment equity) and accompanying workplace policies and procedures have been implemented in various work settings, discrimination continues to exist in today's society. Discrimination often manifests itself in overt racism, ignorance of customs and practices, and stereotyping or racial profiling based on misinterpretations of Aboriginal identities, lifestyles, and cultural values.

One example is the perception that Aboriginal people are not productive members of Canada's economy and labour force. In 2001, according to the Canadian Labour and Business Council's (CLBC) Viewpoints Survey, only 13% of business leaders and 21% of labour leaders surveyed thought that hiring more Aboriginal workers would help the company meet skill and labour shortages. These national findings appear to reflect a lack of awareness regarding Aboriginal people's skills and an unfavourable view by employers of Aboriginal people's workforce capabilities (Canadian Labour and Business Council, 2001; Lamontagne, 2004).

According to Stewart and colleagues (2011), many young people experience discrimination and racism when working outside of the Aboriginal sector. For example, some Aboriginal youth report that they would often hide their true ancestry in order to protect themselves from ill treatment and disparaging remarks, and to gain a sense of emotional and physical safety in their place of work. Others, in university or workplaces, felt they were treated unfairly (i.e., being singled out as the voice of all Aboriginal people, working beyond their job description, or working for unfair wages) due to their identity as an Aboriginal person (Stewart & Reeves 2009; Stewart et al., 2011).

Oteenow Training & Employment Centre

by Priya S. Mani

Oteenow Training and Employment Centre is located in Edmonton, Alberta, and has been serving the community since 1992. The organization offers various employment and training programs to First Nations and Inuit people in Alberta. The mandate of the organization is to help individuals find meaningful work and to become self-reliant. <http://oteenow.com/>

Funding

Limitations on both human capital (i.e., career opportunities) and financial resources create barriers for Aboriginal people to fully engage in economic and career development in Canadian society. Until government policy makers (provincial, federal, and Aboriginal) collectively work together and commit to designing national Aboriginal career development strategies (including linkages to education, economic development, and skills training with multi-year funding models), programs and related curricula will be short term and ineffective and will only aid in widening the socioeconomic divide between Aboriginal and non-Aboriginal populations in Canada.

Career Development Approaches and Supports

Career development requires the same rigour and attention as any other human resources management or organizational development activity. If well managed, career development and planning can deliver the right people with the right competencies at the right time, enabling organizations to deliver on their mandate, objectives, and outcomes. Accessing general employment and education supports such as academic and vocational services is not a problem for many Aboriginal youth, especially those residing in urban areas (Stewart & Reeves, 2009; Stewart et al., 2011). However, what does appear to be lacking are employment opportunities, vocational training, and postsecondary supports that are specifically geared towards the needs of Aboriginal youth. Stewart and Reeves (2009) and Stewart et al. (2011) show that while there may be an availability of some employment opportunities and employment programs developed for Aboriginal people, these opportunities remain unknown to many and are therefore inaccessible (especially if there is no access to information and other resources at school).

The career development approaches and supports presented in this section highlight general culturally compatible strategies and customized approaches for various segments of the Aboriginal population in Canada. Though not exhaustive in nature, these approaches and supports begin the process of awareness and recognition, and hopefully implementation of strategies that are congruent with Aboriginal people's career context and needs during their life journey.

Guiding Circles

Guiding Circles is an Aboriginal career tool that blends current career development knowledge with traditional Aboriginal perspectives and values to assist people to discover and value their identity as they craft their life/career journey. Gray Poehnell (Métis), Norm Amundson, and Rod McCormick (Mohawk) authored the initial programs and partnered with the Aboriginal Human Resource Council for publishing and marketing. Since 2003, Gray Poehnell has trained thousands of life/career practitioners in this approach in workshops across Canada, Australia, and elsewhere. His most recent book, *Hope-Filled Engagement*, sets forth the primary concepts and tools of the approach.

SPOTLIGHT: *HOPE-FILLED ENGAGEMENT AND GUIDING CIRCLES*
by Gray Poehnell

Hope-Filled Engagement and Guiding Circles are a positive illustration of the contribution that Aboriginal values and perspectives can bring to the career field. They address many personal and career issues that others are struggling with; many even in the mainstream are looking for practical answers to issues of creativity, spirituality, connectedness, community, values, and life balance. Many people, such as the young, immigrants, the disabled, and even some mainstream, also have difficulty relating to the traditional career approaches. Guiding Circles has been effectively used not only with Aboriginal people in urban and reservation contexts but also with a wide range of people (young and old, the disabled, immigrants, professionals) in a wide range of contexts such as schools, colleges/universities, employment centres, reservations, and correctional institutions. Awareness of the breadth of Hope-Filled Engagement's application can assist in normalizing some of the struggles of Aboriginal peoples while bringing a sense of renewed pride in their own values and culture.

References
- McCormick, R., Amundson, N. E., & Poehnell, G. (2002). *Guiding circles: An Aboriginal guide to finding career paths, Booklet 1: Understanding yourself.* Saskatoon, SK: Aboriginal Human Resources Development Council and Ergon Communications.
- Poehnell, G., Amundson, N., & McCormick, R. (2006). *Guiding circles: An Aboriginal guide to finding career paths, Booklet 2: Finding new possibilities.* Saskatoon, SK: Aboriginal Human Resource Council and Ergon Communications.

In an increasingly diverse world, it is essential that life/career practitioners expand their toolkit of tools and processes to embrace the diversity of people whom they seek to assist. Guiding Circles is an inclusive approach that supplements traditional career development approaches by making careers accessible to people who do not relate well to traditional career processes and language because their life journeys have been different from the traditional mainstream. It is a holistic approach that embraces practical creativity, spirituality, connectedness, community, values, and life balance. Lastly, it is a hope-filled approach that seeks to create an environment of hope, especially for people who believe that they have no hope.

The program has two parts:

1. Step 1, *Understanding Yourself*, assists people in discovering and valuing who they are. People learn to identify and tell their life stories, to do positive focused self-reflection, and to connect their personal discoveries to their world (including families, communities, school, and work).
2. Step 2, *Finding New Possibilities*, utilizes the discoveries from people's life stories to generate and explore realistic career alternatives and then make effective career decisions in association with the significant people in their lives.

Social Networking and Liaising

In today's digital age, social networking via Twitter, Facebook, and LinkedIn offers diversified access to career resources and supports for Aboriginal peoples. By connecting with educators, career specialists, employers, and role models in an online environment, individuals may tap into the hidden job market — establishing contacts and related organizational networks for recruitment and job search purposes.

Offline, Aboriginal-employee networks are typically based on a collaborative and united effort by various parties to (a) identify employment opportunities for Aboriginal job seekers in a particular jurisdiction, (b) develop support systems for Aboriginal employees to meet and share experiences, and/or (c) connect Aboriginal employees and non-Aboriginal employers to discuss methods and strategies for improving recruitment, training, career development, and promotion/advancement opportunities.

Aboriginal Government Employees' Network

Established in 1992, the Aboriginal Government Employees' Network (AGEN) is dedicated to promoting a supportive environment for Aboriginal employees in the workplace and raising awareness about Aboriginal issues. Key activities of AGEN are liaising with provincial government departments and unions, facilitating discussion on barriers to employment in government departments, and providing a support mechanism for Aboriginal employees (Aboriginal Government Employees' Network, 2012a).

Royal Eagles
Since 1990, the Royal Bank of Canada (RBC) has provided Aboriginal employees with opportunities to establish local networking and mentoring for fellow RBC Aboriginal employees. Royal Eagle members meet as a national group to share best practices and strategies for ensuring that RBC is inclusive and an Aboriginal-friendly workplace. In addition, Royal Eagles mentor Aboriginal youth as part of the Stay-in-School Program, co-ordinate annual celebration activities for National Aboriginal Day (June 21), and support local Aboriginal communities through various outreach initiatives (Royal Bank of Canada, 2012).

Job Autobiography

In a career counselling setting, a job autobiography provides an opportunity for Aboriginal clients to list jobs (paid and volunteer) that they have held. Clients reflect upon why they took the job and why they left, and what they liked and disliked about each job. Through the autobiographical process, career practitioners elicit themes, patterns, implicit values, beliefs, and assumptions in clients' narratives that they are hearing (e.g., enjoys new situations and the influence of pleasing others, etc.). As a career development tool, the job autobiography brings clients' personal experiences to the sessions and enhances their awareness of their decision-making strategies in the career/job arena. Career practitioners interact with their clients to facilitate the storytelling process by clarifying and exploring in-depth areas of significance.

Possible Selves

This technique/approach involves career practitioners working with their clients to discuss their possible selves: (a) what they hope for, (b) what their desired future states are, and (c) what are possible feared future outcomes (Shepard & Quressette, 2010). The possible selves of individuals tend to be based on the available social and cultural roles present in their environment. Possible selves have a concrete impact on how people initiate and structure their actions, both in realizing positive possible selves and in preventing realization of negative possible selves (i.e., "I think I am most able to be, I think that ... could happen").

Life Mapping

Life mapping is a career-counselling tool that is useful in understanding someone's context (e.g., cultural context for an Aboriginal client). Practitioners ask their clients to map important influences in their lives, or values that are important to them in their world (Shepard, 2004). Afterwards, practitioners draw connections between different aspects of their clients' maps to identify worldviews, cultural values, and

CAREERS Aboriginal Youth Initiative

by Lara Shepard

CAREERS is designed to bring career education and workplace learning opportunities to Aboriginal youth across Alberta. The Aboriginal Youth Initiative (AYI) assists young Aboriginal Albertans in completing high school equipped with career development experiences. AYI promotes a stay-in-school message, provides career awareness through workshops, and co-ordinates hands-on internship opportunities. CAREERS is composed of an Aboriginal team who work directly in Aboriginal communities to facilitate learning and training opportunities. Elders, band councils, parents, industry, and the education community welcome and support CAREERS' work.

For more information, see <http://www.nextgen.org/employers/hire-a-student/aboriginal-initiatives>.

beliefs in relation to self-identity (including career self-identity).

Dependable Strengths

This is a technique that practitioners can utilize to help clients uncover the strengths and assets that they may have minimized, taken for granted, or been entirely unaware of (Haldane, 1989). A "dependable strength" is a skill, talent, or quality that has been developed over a lifetime, from childhood to the present. Practitioners engage in dialogue with clients to determine "when clients did something well, when they enjoyed doing an activity or skill and felt proud of it."

Aboriginal Youth (25 Years of Age and Younger)

Targeted career development strategies and campaigns for Aboriginal youth help to promote the value of learning/skills development from kindergarten to postsecondary education, and promote the value of higher education and its relationship to career success in various industries. Gaiko, Wikle, and Kavanaugh (1999) point out that education and career development promotion need to be directed towards Aboriginal youth and their families. The families of Aboriginal youths provide a key support mechanism for them in achieving success in school and subsequently transitioning from school to employment (Gaiko et al., 1999).

Educational Achievement

In addition to guiding and developing Aboriginal peoples in the current workforce, it is equally important to promote the value of education to the next generation of workers. Some employers are leading the way by providing scholarships and grants to Aboriginal students. SaskTel (a Saskatchewan telecommunications company), for example, offers the Aboriginal Youth Awards of Excellence to Aboriginal youth (aged 13–19) in recognition for their outstanding achievement in 10 categories ranging from leadership and education to community services and technology/science (SaskTel, 2012). Cameco Corporation, a private sector uranium company in Saskatoon, offers the Bernard Michel Scholarship to provide a renewable $5,000 scholarship over four years to a Saskatchewan Aboriginal student enrolled in a geology, toxicology, chemistry, or geography program at the University of Saskatchewan (Cameco Corporation, 2012). Syncrude, a private sector crude oil producer, confers the Rod Hyde Aboriginal Award to an Aboriginal student from the Municipality of Wood Buffalo who is pursuing studies in fields such as sports, recreation, or education (Syncrude Canada Limited, 2012).

Indspire Awards
by Lara Shepard

Formerly known as the National Aboriginal Achievement Awards, the Indspire Awards are presented annually to 14 Aboriginal professionals and youth from across Canada in recognition of outstanding accomplishments in careers ranging from health, public service and arts/culture to education and law/justice. One of the key aspects of the Indspire Awards is to provide Aboriginal youth with role models of First Nations, Métis, or Inuit ancestry by showcasing their career accomplishments and their journey towards success.

For more information, visit Indspire at <www.indspire.ca>.

Modeling and Mentoring

Modeling (the act of emulating specific behaviours and/or social roles of another person who is a source of inspiration and motivation) is well documented in the career development literature as a key to success for individuals of all cultures. For Aboriginal populations in Canada, there is greater need for supports of this nature due to the lack of existing models that are directly applicable to Aboriginal people. For many Aboriginal people, their social support networks of mothers, partners, friends, and educators help to keep them motivated to continue with their program of study. Research shows (McCormick, 1997; Stewart & Reeves, 2009; Stewart et al., 2011) that many Aboriginal youth feel that inspiration and support from their families underpin their connection with their specific Aboriginal culture. As these young people define themselves, they will need positive career-related role models to help direct them towards the required competencies for various professions.

Researchers have begun to look at Aboriginal youth and the factors that determine their career opportunities. Stewart and colleagues (2011) completed a study that looked at the employment experiences of Aboriginal youth in downtown Toronto, in order to understand career development for urban Aboriginal youth. The youth who participated in this study reported that career supports and services often existed in their communities but were difficult to access if certain criteria could not be met, such as being a student enrolled in full-time studies in a postsecondary institution or being in receipt of some form of social assistance.

The Aboriginal Government Employees' Network (AGEN) Speakers Bureau in Saskatchewan (or Pîkiskwêwak) provides opportunities for Aboriginal employees in the public service and **Crown** corporations to speak with Aboriginal youth to encourage them to stay in school and understand the variety of career opportunities available to them in the Saskatchewan public service. In addition to providing Aboriginal youth with valuable career information, the Speakers' Bureau representatives serve as role models in their respective communities. Typically, AGEN Speakers Bureau representatives speak to students about their personal histories, career paths, and how they have integrated their Aboriginal cultures into their workplaces (Aboriginal Government Employees' Network, 2012b).

Future Bound: A Lifeworks Expedition Workshop for Rural Youth (Shepard, 2010) was designed by rural youth to address their unique needs. Participants had difficulty in integrating the available career information in ways meaningful to their particular life situations, and observed that resources and information needed to be relevant for youth living in small communities with limited services. Youth also identified positively with their rural community, feeling intimate ties to those they lived close to. Sense of place, proximity to nature, and relationships within the community were strong themes in the interviews. Sense of place, then, became a strong determinant in life-career decision making. Integrating lifestyle and career information in personally relevant ways was achieved in the workshop through the process of circling back, revisiting, and building upon activities and work done in previous loops using a hiking metaphor.

Work Experience Programs

Work experience programs (e.g., internships and summer employment programs) provide Aboriginal youth and postsecondary students with opportunities to apply their skills and gain work experience. In addition, work experience programs expose Aboriginal youth to the diversity of careers in several organizations and occupations. Cross-training to expand competencies also allows individuals who have already mastered one set of skills to become proficient in another.

Case Study Brief: The Aboriginal Internship Program —
Government of British Columbia
From 2007 to present, the Government of British Columbia (BC) has implemented a one-year paid internship for Aboriginal youth residing in BC who are 29 years of age or younger. The internship program provides experiential-based learning experiences for Aboriginal youth. It includes a placement for nine months in a government ministry, followed by a three-month internship at an Aboriginal organization. Job placements can range from policy development and community engagement to research analysis and negotiations.

The major goals of the program are to: (a) develop leadership skills; (b) encourage Aboriginal youth to consider employment in the BC public service or in Aboriginal organizations; (c) enhance relationships between the provincial government and Aboriginal organizations; and (d) aid in decreasing the socio-economic gap between Aboriginal people and non-Aboriginal people in BC.

Interns receive career development resources and associated cultural supports from the internship program staff (consisting of a program lead, co-ordinator, and administrator). Also, supervisors and mentors are available from the government and Aboriginal organizations to coach and guide the interns throughout their career development journey. From 2007–2011, 86 Aboriginal youth completed the Aboriginal Youth Internship Program.

For more information about this program, visit <http://www.gov.bc.ca/arr/social/fcf/ayip.html>. (Source: Government of British Columbia, 2012)

Aboriginal Women

Aboriginal women are disadvantaged in the workplace and labour force by all the traditional social and systemic barriers affecting women as well as by all the racial and geographical barriers affecting the broader Aboriginal population. All too often, Aboriginal women are among the working poor or the unemployed (Kenny, 2002; Levesque et al., 2001). Women are often denied skills training from their employers because they hold part-time or other non-standard employment (e.g., temporary or seasonal employment; Kenny, 2002; Levesque et al., 2001). Given the escalating costs in education, some Aboriginal women may not be able to participate in training opportunities outside of their workplaces as a means of enhancing their skills, abilities, and knowledge. Wilson and MacDonald (2010) noted that other socioeconomic hardships facing Aboriginal women include high rates of victimization and violent crimes (e.g., domestic abuse), single parenthood, and reliance on government transfers (e.g., income assistance, welfare, disability payments, etc.).

The Urban Aboriginal Peoples Study

by Lara Shepard

The *Urban Aboriginal Peoples Study* (UAPS) Study sought to understand and document the identities, experiences, and goals of urban Aboriginal people, recognized as an important and rapidly growing segment of the Canadian population. The study was guided by the Advisory Circle of Aboriginal people, and conducted by the Environics Institute. Aboriginal people's unique perspectives are an important part of the national discourse and provide new areas of inquiry about factors that are currently leading Aboriginal people towards success, autonomy, and cultural confidence.

For more information, go to <http://uaps.ca/>.

As a means of mitigating some of these various barriers to career development and planning, organizations such as Aboriginal Affairs and Northern Development Canada, and Vancity Credit Union are tailoring their social and financial supports to address Aboriginal women's needs.

Aboriginal Affairs and Northern Development Canada (2013) developed *Journey to Success: Aboriginal Women's Business Planning Guide*. This guide provides information about entrepreneurship from the perspective of Aboriginal business women; and was developed from consultations with Aboriginal women across Canada who were entrepreneurs and/or representatives from Aboriginal women's organizations.

Vancity Credit Union located in Vancouver, BC, was the administrator for the Women Entrepreneurs, Financing Opportunties for Growth (WE-FOG) project from 2011–2013. The purpose of the project was to help Aboriginal and newcomer women in building their own businesses. The project is intended to assist Vancity in reviewing its own practices and raise awareness about barriers (Vancity Community Foundation, 2013).

Aboriginal Adults and Urban Aboriginal Peoples

To address the unique issues facing urban Aboriginal peoples, the Government of Canada developed the Urban Aboriginal Strategy (UAS). Developed in 1997, the UAS is a community-based initiative to address socioeconomic hardships (e.g., securing meaningful and sustainable employment, accessing quality education, etc.) facing Aboriginal people living in 13 designated urban centres, among them Vancouver, Calgary, Saskatoon, Winnipeg, and Toronto. Through the UAS, the Government of Canada partners with the private sector, provincial and municipal governments, the community, and Aboriginal organizations to support projects that respond to local priorities, including urban Aboriginal learning and urban Aboriginal family, health, and wellness. National priority areas include: (a) improving life skills; (b) promoting job training; (c) skills and entrepreneurship; and (d) supporting Aboriginal women, children, and families (Aboriginal Affairs and Northern Development Canada, 2012).

Case Study Brief: The Institute for Integrative Science & Health
"Science can be defined in many different ways depending on who is doing the defining. But one thing that is certain is that 'science' is culturally relative. In other words, what is considered science is dependent on the culture /worldview/paradigm of the definer." (Excerpt from Leroy Little Bear in *Native Science: Natural Laws of Interdependence* [Cajete, 2000, p. ix].)

The Institute for Integrative Science & Health' (<http://www.integrativescience.ca/>) provided a postsecondary, scientific learning environment for students, educators, and researchers who are interested in advancing **integrative science** — a harmonization and bringing together of indigenous and **Western science**. From 2006–2013, the Institute utilized multidisciplinary approaches culturally compatible with Aboriginal ways of knowing, in particular, Mi'kmaw language and knowledge, and promoted authentic participation with Aboriginal people. Regrettably, upon the retirement of its founder, Dr. Cheryl Bartlett, the Institute closed June 2013. (Institute for Integrative Science & Health, 2013)

First Nations People on Reserve

Results of the study by Stewart et al. (2011) described barriers associated with accessing and maintaining work in Aboriginal organizations both on-reserve and in urban areas. Concerning First Nations people on reserve, participants spoke of the importance of having the status of a "community insider" in order to gain employment in this sector. Researchers noted: "…'outsiders' faced barriers such as nepotism and hiring within circles of friends and family; if one is outside of such circles, there can often be challenges to gaining entry into these types of work opportunities" (p. 40). Another barrier is that many jobs are held by non-Aboriginal people who often have high levels of postsecondary education and related work experience, though they may lack the cultural understanding and sensitivities to effectively carry out the job in a sustainable and culturally congruent manner.

Through bilateral Labour Market Agreements (LMAs), Aboriginal-specific career strategies and programs were brokered between Human Resources and Skills Development Canada (renamed Employment and Social Development Canada in 2013) and provincial and territorial governments. The purpose was to help unemployed or underemployed Aboriginal youth, Aboriginal peoples with disabilities, and Aboriginal peoples in urban centres. These programs provide financial, social, and technical supports for people transitioning from pre-employment skills training to sustainable employment. Notable strategies and programs include, but are not limited to, the Aboriginal Skills and Employment Training Strategy (ASETS) and the Aboriginal Training for Employment Program (ATEP).

Community-Owned Businesses

The Osoyoos Indian Band in British Columbia is one of three First Nations in Canada to receive certification from the First Nation Financial Management Board (FMB).

Certification from the FMB provides a signal of the health of a First Nation's financial management system and fiscal performance. It is part of the regulatory regime established by the First Nations Fiscal and Statistical Management Act (FSMA) that enables First Nations to raise money to build new infrastructure and attract more public and private sector development on reserves.

Senkulmen Business Park is a 10-year plan to develop 112 acres for light indus-trial use. It will eventually accommodate up to 40 business tenants and create upwards of 1,000 new manufacturing and supporting jobs in the region.

Other major capital projects underway include the Canyon Desert Resort, a 350-unit residential and vacation resort development in Oliver and a 44-residence unit located at the Band's Nk'Mip Resort in Osoyoos (<http://oibdc.ca/2012/01/indian-band-raising-its-profile/>).

Small Business Entrepreneurs

Entrepreneurship is a human, creative act that builds something of value from practically nothing. It is the pursuit of opportunity regardless of the resources, or lack of resources, at hand. It requires a vision and the passion and commitment to lead others in the pursuit of that vision. It also requires a willingness to take calculated risks. (Timmons, 2000, p. 14)

According to Statistics Canada (2006a), in 1981 there were 7,485 self-employed Aboriginal persons. By 2001, that number surpassed 27,000 and continues to grow. While many entrepreneurs pursue more traditional businesses such as fishing, trapping, farming, and the construction trades, Aboriginal entrepreneurs now own businesses in the areas of software design, tourism, the arts, and health care. Small business provides First Nation peoples and communities with the means to become self-determining and free from corporate and governmental control, manipulation, and exploitation. Communities with more resources and experience with governance can provide stable footing for potential entrepreneurs.

Aboriginal peoples represent a significant potential workforce available to replace aging Canadian workers who are currently entering into retirement. They also offer unique skills and knowledge in the Canadian labour market. For example, Aboriginal leaders can enhance collaborative partnerships between local Aboriginal communities (both in urban and rural settings) and employers — taking the form of providing insights into entrepreneurship, joint ventures, and niche market opportunities for goods and services that have not been fully realized in the broader marketplace (Hanselmann, 2003; Lamontagne, 2004). Dwyer (2003) acknowledges the benefits of an Aboriginal leadership style in the workplace, in particular one that values collectivism, co-operation, group cohesiveness, and consensus-based decision making — many of which are becoming key organizational competencies in today's workforce.

Case Study Brief: Community Wildfire Training and Employment Program for First Nations People in the Shuswap Nation Tribal Council Area

The BC First Nations Forestry Council (FNFC), in partnership with Community Futures Development Corporation of the Central Interior First Nations (CFDC of CIFN) and the First Nations' Emergency Services Society (FNESS) designed and implemented an Aboriginal Training for Employment Program (ATEP) specializing in community wildfire protection. Funded by the British Columbia Ministry of Advanced Education, this program was composed of on-campus and distance education, including on-site and field-based learning experiences. Journaling was utilized to supplement the classroom and field work, which afforded participants an opportunity to track their personal career journey and progression throughout the program. Participants' journal entries were shared and discussed in one-to-one sessions between facilitators/trainers and participants, which allowed participants to reflect on their personal learning experiences, thereby facilitating a storytelling process to clarify and explore individual learner's career journeys.

Within this framework, the following approaches were utilized:

1. Storytelling and oral dialogue, which ensured that a culturally congruent learning atmosphere was created to foster success for participants.
2. Multiple "classrooms" to provide training that reflected traditional Aboriginal ethics of respect and care in the management and protection of forests, grasslands, community members, and wilderness resources.
3. Existing pre-employment courses supplemented (where appropriate) with traditional knowledge or related cultural teachings via guest speakers (e.g., local Elders and Aboriginal community protection specialists), videos, and texts.

These supports and resources reflected the local and culturally specific knowledge of First Nations people. (Source: FNFC, CFCD of CIFN, & FNESS, 2012)

Since the implementation of this initiative, FNESS has continued its wildland firefighting skills training and employment work through subsequent ATEPs in the Lillooet Tribal Council area (in collaboration with CFDC of CIFN) and Carrier Sekani Tribal Council area (in collaboration with the Aboriginal Business and Community Development Centre and the First Nations Technology Council).

Implications for Career Practitioners, Employers, and Educators

The role of social justice and culture is becoming more recognized in career development and planning. Multicultural teaching, counselling, and organizational development strategies are needed as fundamental resources and supports for our diverse Canadian population. When working with Aboriginal peoples, the following considerations should be observed:

For Career Practitioners

- Be aware of personal attitudes, conditioning, and beliefs involving acceptance, understanding, and the accommodation of cultures that are different from one's own cultural heritage. (Torres, Howard-Hamilton & Cooper, 2003)
- Develop thorough knowledge of individual and systemic discrimination of Aboriginal peoples.
- Have thorough knowledge of the meaning of Aboriginal cultures, including an openness to learn about the beliefs and practices of Aboriginal spirituality.
- Commit to being a lifetime learner of cross-cultural issues (informal and/or formal training) in order to recognize personal feelings of defensiveness, resistance, mistrust, and vulnerability regarding ethnicity.
- Be comfortable with and be able to listen to silence as well as the words.
- Build rapport as a counsellor to establish trust by being consistent, straightforward, genuine, and honest.
- Be in the session and in the moment by listening and not jumping to conclusions and judgements. As a practitioner, gently challenge or provide options where possible.
- Be aware that direct/experiential learning takes precedence over theoretical learning.

For Educators

- Invite local and visiting Elders, consultants and/or Knowledge Keepers to be part of classroom discussions/presentations and include the use of Aboriginal stories and film within the learning environment.
- Recognize that traditional career development, lifespan, education, and personality theories are typically based on mono-cultural experiences. Failure to recognize the limitations of these traditional Western-based theories may create situations where an Aboriginal person's behaviours and perspectives are perceived as symptoms of a disorder as opposed to strengths-based attributes.

For Employers

- Organizations across all sectors and industries need to design and implement sustainable Aboriginal employment strategies by (a) setting aside designated funding and resources (i.e., human and technical resources) for Aboriginal-specific human resources management programs and practices (i.e., recruitment and career development activities); and (b) aligning key competencies, skills training, and career development initiatives that support existing and future labour market needs.
- Design targeted recruitment strategies for Aboriginal peoples, in general, and for each of the three groups (First Nations, Métis, and Inuit). In order to engage Aboriginal people in today's workforce, employers need a comprehensive targeted recruitment strategy to identify where Aboriginal job seekers go to find job postings and career information (e.g., Aboriginal radio, Aboriginal television programs, local newspapers, magazines, community newsletters, etc.).
- Identify the company's **succession planning** needs and advise the Aboriginal communities of these needs. By understanding employers' succession planning needs, Aboriginal communities can begin training and career development programs to meet current and future labour market demands across various occupations in management, science, and technology.
- Do more Aboriginal awareness training so that non-Aboriginal people can learn about Aboriginal cultures, traditions, and histories. Training programs of this nature present an opportunity for Aboriginal staff and non-Aboriginal employers to learn more about one another, discover ways to effectively communicate, and work together in their organizations and the broader society.

For career practitioners, educators, and employers, there is a continuing need to implement career strategies and practices that reflect the diversity of our society. In working with Aboriginal peoples, career practitioners, educators, and employers must recognize the barriers that face this population, yet at the same time have respect and sensitivity to transform these challenges into opportunities through participation in meaningful education and subsequent employment in Canada's labour force.

Conclusion

Aboriginal peoples have had to overcome numerous hardships and challenges that have affected their career life paths. Career practitioners must assist clients in drawing from their cultural strengths to facilitate their career development. The success of Aboriginal peoples continues to grow as they strive for higher levels of education and employment. Career practitioners, educators, and employers can support this growth by taking time to get to know Aboriginal people and becoming aware of Aboriginal cultures. Moreover, career practitioners should maintain a list of culturally congruent resources and supports to aid Aboriginal clients in developing their careers now and in the future.

References

Aboriginal Affairs and Northern Development Canada. (2012). *Urban Aboriginal strategy*. Ottawa, ON: Author. Retrieved from <http://www.aadnc-aandc.gc.ca/eng/1100100014277>.

Aboriginal Affairs and Northern Development Canada. (2013). *Journey to success: Aboriginal Women's business planning guide*. Retrieved from <http://www.equaywuk.ca/HomeBusiness/Journey%20to%20Success%20-%20Aboriginal%20Women%27s%20Business.pdf>.

Aboriginal Government Employees' Network. (2012a). *Aboriginal Government Employees' Network: About us*. Retrieved from <http://www.saskagen.com/>.

Aboriginal Government Employees' Network. (2012b). *Pîkiskwêwak*. Retrieved from <http://www.agen.sk.ca/info.shtml>.

Aboriginal Human Resource Council (2010). *Inclusion Works '10 Report*. Saskatoon, SK: Aboriginal Human Resource Council. Retrieved from <http://www.aboriginalhr.ca/en/inclusion10>.

Ahearn, J. (2005). *Indigenous peoples of the West Kootenays: A resource guide for students and teachers*. Nelson, BC: School District #8 (Kootenay Lake).

Assembly of First Nations. (2012). Our story. Retrieved from <http://www.afn.ca/index.php/en/about-afn/our-story>.

Battiste, M. (1998). Enabling the autumn seed: Toward decolonized approach to Aboriginal, knowledge, language and education. Canadian Journal of Native Education, 22(1), 16–27.

Battiste, M., & Henderson, J. Y. (2000). *Protecting indigenous knowledge and heritage: A global challenge*. Saskatoon, SK: Purich Publishing.

Berger, T. R. (2006). *Nunavut land claims agreement implementation contract negotiations for the second planning period 2003–2013: Conciliator's final report*. Vancouver, BC: Berger and Company. Retrieved from <http://www.aadnc-aandc.gc.ca/eng/1100100030982/1100100030985>.

Betz, N. E. (2006). Basic issues and concepts in the career development and counselling for women. In W. B. Walsh & M. J. Heppner (Eds.), *Handbook of career counselling for women* (2nd ed., pp. 45–7). Mahwah, NJ: Lawrence Erlbaum Associates.

British Columbia First Nations Forestry Council, Community Futures Development Corporation of Central Interior First Nations & First Nations' Emergency Services Society. (2012). *Final report prepared for Ministry of Advanced Education and Labour*

Market Development: Aboriginal training for employment program. Vancouver, BC: Authors.

British Columbia Treaty Commission. (2007). *Treaty commission annual report 2006.* Vancouver, BC: BC Treaty Commission.

Cajete, G. (2000). *Native science: Natural laws of interdependence.* Sante Fe, New Mexico: Clear Light Publishers.

Cameco Corporation. (2012). Scholarships. Retrieved from <http://www.cameco.com/responsibility/scholarships/>.

Canadian Labour and Business Council. (2001). *Make skills a national priority: Consultations by the Canadian Labour and Business Centre.* Ottawa, ON: CLBC.

Duran, E. (2006). *Healing the soul wound.* New York, NY: Teachers College, Columbia University.

Dwyer, R. J. (2003). Career progression factors of the Aboriginal executives in the Canada federal public service. *Journal of Management Development, 22*(10), 881–889.

First Nations Mountain Pine Beetle Initiative. (2007). *A strategy for developing a sustainable economy.* First Nations Mountain Pine Beetle Initiative, Prince George, BC.

First Peoples' Heritage, Language and Culture Council. (2010). *Report on the status of BC First Nations language.* Brentwood Bay, BC: Author.

France, M. H., McCormick, R., & Rodriguez, M. C. (2004). The "red road": Culture, spirituality and the sacred hoop. In M. H. France, M. C. Rodriguez, & G. G. Hett (Eds.), *Diversity, culture and counselling: A Canadian perspective* (Chapter 20). Calgary, AB: Detselig Enterprises.

Frideres, J. (1998). *Aboriginal peoples in Canada: Contemporary conflicts.* Scarborough, ON: Prentice Hall Allyn and Bacon Canada.

Gaiko, S. S., Wikle, M., & Kavanaugh, R. R. (1999). An employment program to preserve the Native American culture. *Innovations in Education and Training International, 36*(2), 161–168.

Gone, J. P. (2004). Mental health services for Native Americans in the 21st century. United States. Professional Psychology: Research and Practice, 35(1), 10–18.

Government of British Columbia. (2012). *Aboriginal Youth internship program.* Retrieved from <http://www.gov.bc.ca/arr/social/fcf/ayip.html>.

Government of Canada. (1996). *Highlights from the report of the Royal Commission on Aboriginal peoples.* Ottawa, ON: Author. Retrieved from <http://www.aadnc-aandc.gc.ca/eng/1100100014597/1100100014637>.

Haldane, B. (1989). *The dependable strengths articulation process: How it works.* Seattle, WA: College of Education, University of Washington. Retrieved from <http://www.dependablestrengths.org/>.

Hanselmann, C. (2003). *Shared responsibility: Final report and recommendations of the urban Aboriginal initiative: A western cities project report.* Calgary, AB: Canada West Foundation.

Human Resources and Skills Development Canada. (2010). *Canadians in context:*

Aboriginal population. Retrieved from <http://www4.hrsdc.gc.ca
/.3ndic.1t.4r@-eng.jsp?iid=36>.

Institute for Integrative Science & Health. (2013). *About the institute.* Retrieved from
<http://www.integrativescience.ca/About/>.

Inuit Tapiriit Kanatami. (2012). About ITK. Retrieved from <http://www.itk.ca/page
/about-itk>.

Kenny, C. (2002). *North American Indian, Métis and Inuit women speak about culture,
education and work.* Retrieved from <http://publications.gc.ca/collections
/Collection/SW21-90-2001E.pdf>.

Kumar, J. (2006). *First Nations capacity development for agriculture programs.*
Unpublished manuscript.

Kunin, R. 2009. *Economic development issues for rural communities in the four western
provinces: 2010–2015–2020.* Canada West Foundation, Vancouver, BC.

Lamontagne, F. (2004). The Aboriginal workforce: *What lies ahead: CLBC commentary.*
Retrieved from <http://www.clbc.ca/files/Reports
/Aboriginal_Commentary_piece.pdf>.

Levesque, C., Trudeau, N., Bacon, J., Montpetit, C., Cheezo, M., Lamontagne, M., &
Wawanoloath, C. S. (2001). *Aboriginal women and jobs: Challenges and issues for
employability programs in Québec.* Retrieved from <http://publications.gc.ca
/collections/Collection/SW21-75-2001E.pdf>.

McCormick, R. (1997). Healing through interdependence: The role of connecting
in First Nations healing practices. *Canadian Journal of Counselling, 31*(3),
172–184.

Mendelson, M. (2004). *Aboriginal People in Canada's Labour Market: Work and
Unemployment, Today and Tomorrow.* Ottawa, ON: Caledon Institute of Social
Policy.

Métis National Council. (2013). The Métis Nation. Retrieved from
<http://www.metisnation.ca/index.php/who-are-the-metis>.

Nuttall, M. (2005). Hunting, herding, fishing and gathering: Indigenous peoples and
renewable resource use in the Arctic. *Arctic Climate Impact Assessment: Scientific
Report.* New York Cambridge University Press.

O'Donnell, V., & Ballardin, A. (2006). *Aboriginal peoples Survey 2001 — provincial
and territorial reports: Off-reserve Aboriginal Population.* Ottawa, ON: Statistics
Canada.

Papillon, M., & Cosentino, G. (2004). *Lessons from abroad: Towards a new social model
for Canada's Aboriginal Peoples.* Canadian Policy Research Networks Inc.

Royal Bank of Canada. (2012). *Royal Eagles: Promoting Aboriginal culture at RBC.*
Retrieved from <http://www.rbcroyalbank.com/commercial/aboriginal
/royal-eagles.html>.

St. Germain, P. C., & Sibbeston, N. (2007). Sharing Canada's prosperity: A hand
up, not a handout. *Special study on the involvement of Aboriginal communities and
businesses in economic development activities in Canada.* Ottawa, ON: Standing
Senate Committee on Aboriginal People.

SaskTel. (2012). *SaskTel Aboriginal Youth awards of excellence.* Retrieved from

<http://www.sasktel.com/about-us/community-involvement
/aboriginal-youth-awards-of-excellence/>.

Shepard, B. (2004). In search of self: A qualitative study of the life-career development of rural young women. *Canadian Journal of Counselling, 38*(2), 75–90.

Shepard, B. (2010). *Future bound: A lifeworks expedition workshop for rural youth.* Self-published. Retrieved from <http://www.pathstothefuture.com/>.

Shepard, B., & Quressette, S. (2010). Possible selves mapping intervention: Rural women and beyond. In G. R. Wolz, J. C. Bluer, & R. K. Yep (Eds.), *Ideas and research you can use, Vistas 2010.* American Counseling Association.

Sillitoe, P. (2002a). *Participant observation to participatory development: Making anthropology work.* In P. Sillitoe, A. Bicker, & J. Pottier (Eds.), Participating in development: Approaches to indigenous knowledge (Chapter 1). New York, NY: Routledge.

Sillitoe, P. (2002b). Globalizing indigenous knowledge. In P. Sillitoe, A. Bicker, & J. Pottier (Eds.), *Participating in development: Approaches to indigenous knowledge* (Chapter 6). New York, NY: Routledge.

Statistics Canada. (2006a). *Aboriginal entrepreneurs.* Retrieved from <http://www41.statcan.gc.ca/2006/2239/ceb2239_002-eng.htm>.

Statistics Canada. (2006b). *Educational portrait of Canada, 2006 Census.* Ottawa, ON: Author. <http://www12.statcan.ca/census-recensement/2006/as-sa/97-560 /pdf/97-560-XIE2006001.pdf>.

Statistics Canada. (2008). *Aboriginal peoples in Canada in 2006: Inuit, Métis, and First Nations, 2006 Census.* Ottawa, ON: Author. <http://www12.statcan.ca /census-recensement/2006/as-sa/97-558/pdf/97-558-XIE2006001.pdf>.

Statistics Canada. (2012). *Chart 11 median total income in 2005 by Aboriginal identity, population aged 25 to 54.* Retrieved from <http://www.statcan.gc.ca/pub /89-645-x/2010001/c-g/c-g011-eng.htm>.

Statistics Canada. (2013). *Aboriginal peoples in Canada: First Nations people, Métis and Inuit, National household survey, 2011.* Ottawa, ON: Author. <http://www.statcan.gc.ca/daily-quotidien/130508/dq130508a-eng.htm>.

Stewart S., & Reeves, A. (2009, January). *Decolonizing graduate school: Exploring the successes of Indigenous graduate students in Canada.* Paper presented at the Hawaii International Conference on Education, Honolulu, HI.

Stewart, S., Reeves, A., Mohanty, S., & Syrette, J. (2011, June) *Indigenous mental health: Career and education as part of overall healing.* Paper presented at the Canadian Psychological Association Convention in Toronto, ON.

Syncrude Canada Limited. (2012). *Syncrude awards and scholarships.* Retrieved from <http://www.syncrude.ca/users/folder.asp?FolderID=7802>.

Timmons, J. A. (2000). The entrepreneurial mind. In P. Lambing & C. R. Kuehl (Eds.), *Entrepreneurship* (2nd ed.). Toronto, ON: Prentice-Hall Canada Inc.

Torres, V., Howard-Hamilton, M. F., & Cooper, D. L. (2003). *Identity development of diverse populations: Implications for teaching and administration in higher education* (6th ed.). San Francisco, CA: Jossey-Bass.

Usalcas, J. (2011). *Aboriginal people and the labour market: Estimates from the labour force survey, 2008–2010.* Ottawa, ON: Statistics Canada.

Vancity Community Foundation (2013). *Women entrepreneurs, financing opportunities for growth (WE-FOG) project.* Retrieved from <http://www.vancitycommunityfoundation.ca/s/projects_and_partnerships.asp ?ReportID=472346>.

Wilson, D., & MacDonald, D. (April 2010). *The income gap between Aboriginal peoples and the rest of Canada.* Ottawa, ON: Canadian Centre for Policy Alternatives.

Glossary

Aboriginal identity is an indicator of a person's affiliation with an Aboriginal group that is North American Indian, Métis, or Inuit.

Colonization was the deliberate attempt by Canadian governments to destroy Indigenous institutions of family, religious belief systems, tribal affiliation, customs, and traditional ways of life through enacted and enforced legal sanctions. Colonization is marked by cultural assimilation and destruction tactics in the form of residential schools, removal of Indigenous groups from ancestral lands, and cultural genocide.

Crown refers to all provincial and federal government departments, ministries and agencies, including all government employees that carry out work on behalf of the government.

Culturally congruent resources include water, plants, people, and animals.

Elder is any person recognized by the Aboriginal community as having knowledge and understanding of the traditional culture of the community, including spiritual and social practices. Knowledge and wisdom, coupled with the recognition and respect of the people of the Nation, are key characteristics of an Elder.

Human capital is investment undertaken by employees in the form of their knowledge, skills, capabilities, and experience within a given profession and/or organization.

Integrative science is an approach to recognizing and utilizing the complementing strengths of indigenous and Western science. For example, understanding basic relationships, patterns, and cycles in the world; embracing curiosity about the natural world and careful observation to acquire scientific knowledge; ensuring that scientific knowledge contributes to the community; and appropriate technologies that must be developed to meet societal needs while simultaneously protecting the environment.

Knowledge Keeper is any person recognized by the Aboriginal community as having knowledge and understanding of the traditional culture of the community, including spiritual and social practices. Knowledge Keepers are identified based on the community's respect for them and peer recognition for their depth and breadth of localized knowledge.

Localized knowledge is the knowledge that Aboriginal people have gained through generations of social, physical, and spiritual understanding of the world around them, traditional lands, and associated practical experience. Such knowledge can be localized and specific to certain communities, families, and even individuals.

Reserves are lands set apart for the use and benefit of a band and for which the legal title rests with the Crown of Canada through the Indian Act. The federal government has primary jurisdiction over these lands and the people living on them.

Sociocultural values are the guiding principles, ideals, aspirations, and beliefs that serve as a foundation in how Aboriginal peoples (as individuals and as a group) carry out work in their respective Nations. Cultural values manifest themselves in local traditions, institutions, and protocols that are major pillars that define the given Aboriginal society.

Succession planning is an organizational planning process that ensures continuity of leadership and core staff skills by identifying, developing and replacing key people (in mission-critical positions) over time.

Treaty is a legal document that was signed with Indian bands and various British colonial, and later Canadian governments, before and after Confederation in 1867. No two treaties are identical, but they usually provide certain rights, including annual payments for ammunition and annuities, clothing every three years, hunting and fishing rights, reserve lands, and other entitlements. In signing a treaty, the Indian bands surrendered their prior rights, titles, and privileges to the designated lands.

Urban refers to large cities or census metropolitan areas.

Western science is a system of knowledge that relies on certain laws that are established to understand phenomena in the world around us. The process of the scientific method begins with an observation followed by a prediction or hypothesis, which is then tested. Depending on the test results, the hypothesis can become a scientific theory or "truth" about the world.

Discussion and Activities

Discussion

Discussion Questions

1. Poverty, ill health, educational failure, family violence, and other problems reinforce one another to create a circle of disadvantage — where family violence leads to educational failure, which leads to poverty, which leads to ill health and back to violence. All these conditions must be considered when working with some Aboriginal clients. How can you work with Aboriginal individuals who are struggling to improve their lives while re-discovering their traditional values after years of oppression and possible trauma? What approaches can you take as a career practitioner?
2. The following seven good life teachings are values/principles that are central to the Anishinabek: respect, love, bravery, wisdom, humility, honesty, and truth. How would you use these values in working with Aboriginal clients? <http://www.edu.gov.on.ca/eng/literacynumeracy/inspire/research/Toulouse.pdf>.

Career Practitioner Role

1. An effective strengths-based approach involves asking questions to prompt client identification of strengths. Because self-esteem and self-confidence are, in many cases, challenging to Aboriginal clients, what sorts of questions might you ask?
    Think about:

    *   survival questions,
    *   support questions,
    *   possibility questions,
    *   esteem questions,
    *   exception questions.

    Visit the website <http://www.discoveringstrengths.com/>.
2. As a prospective career practitioner in a community-based setting, what do you see as the challenge of integrating aspects pertaining to spirituality within your practice?
3. What do you see as essential qualities of a career practitioner who works with Aboriginal people?

Personal Reflection

In your opinion, to what extent should career practitioners adopt an "ahistorical" (i.e., a lack of attention to social and cultural contexts) or a "historical" approach to the integration of Aboriginal history when developing career interventions or initiatives for their clients?

Activities

1. The Ontario National Literacy Coalition (ONLC) worked with the Ontario Ministry of Training, Colleges and Universities to create a new position entitled "Native Literacy Practitioner."

    The practitioner standards model development project, prepared by Kate Thompson for ONLC, identifies the training requirements of a Native literacy practitioner and suggests ways to assess the required skills and knowledge.

    Review this report at <http://en.copian.ca/library/research/practstn /practstn.pdf>.

    Form groups to discuss the initiative proposed in the report.

2. Give groups of two or three students a newspaper article on a current life-career issue facing Aboriginal people. Each group is asked to summarize their article and provide a handout of the summary to each class member prior to their panel presentation. Each group is asked to creatively present their information and ask for audience participation in a 15-minute period. For example, you could debate the issue from two different points of view and then give time for the audience to ask questions. The guiding principle is that you make the presentation informative and interesting to your audience.

    Examples:

    - violence against Aboriginal girls and women;
    - finding ways to move forward on First Nations ownership of First Nations education;
    - lack of sports funding for Aboriginal communities;
    - intergenerational effects of the residential school experience;
    - lack of learning enrichment initiatives outside of the formal educational system (e.g., mentorship programs, summer camps, transitional services for students and families, and leadership programs);
    - families living in poverty.

3. Imagine that you are working as a career practitioner at a college that has a large number of Aboriginal students in attendance. You are asked by administration to develop an Aboriginal career centre. You decide to include the following career-planning services:

    - **Self-Assessment**, or a profile of interests, skills and abilities, personal preferences, and important values. You will provide different resources including two assessment inventories. Explain what resources might be appropriate for your clientele?
    - **Exploring Your Options**, or resources that provide more information on educational programs, different occupations, and careers paths of interest. What types of online and print resources might be appropriate?

- **Re-evaluating Your Direction**. Many students decide to change their major or career direction after completing a few courses. Given the value of hands-on, experiential learning in many Aboriginal cultures, how might you assist students to explore or "test the waters" in their different interest areas?
- **Employment and Job Search Coaching**. How might you assist Aboriginal students find out more information about employment opportunities? How could you involve the Aboriginal community?

4. The process of being mentored is a valued aspect of Aboriginal communities. You have a number of clients who have identified a need to increase their business skills in order to move their business to the next level. You decide to ask the Aboriginal Healing Foundation of Canada (<http://www.ahf.ca/>) for funding to develop a program to provide Aboriginal business persons with a mentoring experience that guides and supports them as they identify and pursue their business goals. In your proposal, you are asked to identify the benefits to the Aboriginal entrepreneur and the benefits to the mentor. What do you say?

Resources

Web Resources on Building a Business

Aboriginal Business Guide <http://v1.canadabusiness.mb.ca/home_page/guides /aboriginal_business_infoguide/>.
Aboriginal Entrepreneurs <http://www41.statcan.gc.ca/2006/2239 /ceb2239_002-eng.htm>.
Aboriginal Entrepreneurship Branch Overview <http://www.designingnations.com /wp-content/uploads/JG2012-Feb-Ab-Entrepreneurship.pdf>.
First Nation Small Business and Entrepreneurship in Canada <http://fngovernance.org /ncfng_research/warren_weir.pdf>.
IdeaConnector Network <http://www.ideaconnector.net/aboriginal-entrepreneurs/>.
Starting a Business — for Aboriginal peoples <http://www.servicecanada.gc.ca/eng /audiences/aboriginal/business.shtml>.

SECTION 5

Navigating Developmental Tasks and Pathways

fourteen

Career Development for Students

Elementary to High School

BLYTHE C. SHEPARD
University of Lethbridge
PRIYA S. MANI
University of Manitoba

PRE-READING QUESTIONS

1. At what grade levels do you think students need to engage in career awareness, career exploration, and career planning?
2. What do you see as the role of parents in guiding their children towards a career?

Introduction and Learning Objectives

In a time of ever-changing patterns of work and education, students must have access to career education that equips them to plan and manage their learning and career pathways. Although **career education** should be aimed at a student's stage of development, a comprehensive career education program typically consists of the following components:

- self-awareness to help students identify their personal attributes;
- opportunity awareness to involve students in investigating, exploring, and experiencing the work world and the various pathways within it;
- decision learning to enhance informed decision making and planning;
- transition planning to develop skills for students to effectively move into new situations.

In a Canadian study of career development practices in the public school system (Malatest & Associates Ltd., 2009) one third of **school guidance counsellors** stated that their schools did not offer mandatory courses in career education. Mandatory programs were mainly at high schools, and usually one semester in length. Further, only one third of guidance counsellors reported that their schools offered career education workshops to parents or guardians, despite the influence that parents and guardians have in their children's education and career pathways (Bernes & Magnusson, 2004). Given the number of tasks required of guidance counsellors in schools and the very high ratio of students to counsellors (Malatest & Associates, 2009), "it has become the shared responsibility of all K–12 educators, parents/guardians and the communities" (p. v) to ensure that all students have the skills to make informed decisions about their futures and to pursue their interests and aptitudes.

The subject matter that teachers are required to convey to their students is staggering. One approach for adding career development curriculum to class time would be to "infuse" or integrate material with other subjects; for example, teach résumé preparation in an English class (Bernes & Magnusson, 2004; Borgen & Hiebert, 2006). Career education and guidance can be an integral part of school life when a wide range of people are involved. These include teachers, school staff, people assisting with extracurricular activities, parents and guardians, as well as community leaders.

After studying this chapter, you should be able to:

1. Outline the stages of career development as presented by career theorists.
2. Describe the typical structure of career development programs in schools.
3. Provide some developmentally appropriate career activities at the elementary, middle, and high school level.

Career Development Theory and Design

The elementary school years are not too early to begin to achieve a vision of what one desires to do in life contributing to the world of work.
— M Ediger (Ediger, 2000, p. 3)

Schools provide a unique and significant context for promoting the educational and vocational development of students. Most research on career guidance in schools has focused on discrete age groups, with a heavy emphasis on how to enrich the learning and work experiences of the high school student. But career development is a lifelong process that can begin even earlier. When elementary and middle school students do not receive career development instruction, they may enter high school feeling unprepared for making career decisions and/or entering the world of work (Gray, 2009).

Career education and related activities in the elementary years focus on (a) developing learning/social skills (a sense of social responsibility and career planning); (b) understanding the concepts of lifelong learning (interpersonal relationships and career planning); and (c) applying this learning to their lives and work in the school and the community (Walls, 2000).

Theorists

Although career theorists have not emphasized the importance of childhood career development, Donald Super (1990) realized that it is during childhood that crucial career-related concepts and attitudes are shaped. Theories of career development provide practitioners with some guidance in understanding the career paths of elementary-aged children. For example, Ginzberg, Ginsburg, Alexrad, and Herma (1951) emphasized that vocational behaviour has its roots in early childhood and develops through "fantasy" stages in childhood to "realistic" stages in late adolescence, when particular occupational choices are specified and crystallized. Children in the fantasy stage (aged 6 to 11) make choices without considering the actions needed to accomplish the goal. At about age 11, in the "tentative" stage, children begin to base their occupational choices on interests, and are aware that these interests may change and that, in the future, their choices could be different.

Gottfredson (1981) based her theory on the importance of self-concept in vocational development and explains that people pursue occupations that are congruent with their images of themselves. Gottfredson described a four-stage model of career development. The first stage, "orientation to size and power," typically occurs from ages 3 to 5. During this stage children develop the ability to picture themselves in adult roles. During the second stage, "orientation to sex roles," children between the ages of 6 and 8 start to expand their knowledge of careers beyond those they see in their family to those to which they have frequently been exposed. Sex-typing of occupations becomes highly influential. Orientation to "social valuation," the third stage, occurs from about ages 9 to 13. Children become aware of the existence of different socioeconomic levels and realize that high-status jobs typically require increased educational requirements. In the final stage, "orientation to internal, unique self," adolescents are able to describe their idealistic and realistic career aspirations.

Donald Super's (1990) developmental approach emphasized nine concepts that he believed to contribute to career awareness and decision making: curiosity, exploration, information, key figures or role models, interests, locus of control, time perspective (how the past, present, and future can be used to plan future events), self-concept, and planfulness. Super's main contribution to career education was his emphasis on the role of the self-concept in career development.

Schools and colleges therefore need to develop and carry out educational programs which have as their objectives: the development of adequate self-concepts in students, the orientation of students in the world of work, the translation of these self-concepts into occupational terms, and the testing of these vocational self-concepts against the realities of occupations. (Super, 1957, p. 310)

Super depicted the various phases of career development based on an individual's life stage. In the **growth stage** (ages 4 to 13), the main tasks are to develop a positive self-concept and build positive relationships with others. The **exploration stage** (ages 14 to 24) is about identifying opportunities for self-fulfillment given personal attributes. These opportunities may take many forms including summer jobs, co-op placements, or volunteer work.

Three Stages

Within the school system, career planning and development programs are roughly based on Super's ideas on stages: career awareness (kindergarten to Grade 6); career exploration (middle schools typically over two to three grades (Grades 6, 7, and 8, depending on the province), and career preparation (Grades 9 to 12). Guidance programs are typically built around this structure and more emphasis is placed on one of the three sub-organizers at different developmental levels. However, it is understood that career development is an ongoing cycle of awareness, exploration, and preparation.

KINDERGARTEN TO GRADE 6	GRADES 6 TO 8	GRADES 9 TO 12
Career Awareness	Career Exploration	Career Preparation
Elementary School	Middle School	High School

Table 1: Stages in Career Development: Kindergarten to Grade 12.

Career Awareness

In this stage during the elementary grades, children describe various opportunities, options, and roles that interest them in their communities, family, and the world of work. They use adult role models and other resources to learn about different occupations and gain awareness of the importance of personal responsibility and good work habits. Children develop awareness of how people work together, and depend on each other, to accomplish work in their community. The focus is on developing a sense of competence, promoting self-awareness, developing personal skills, contributing to the world around them (e.g., through their chores), linking interests to future activities, expanding options, and exploring roles.

Career Exploration

Career exploration helps young people learn about the wide variety of careers available to them, as well as the types of jobs that might best fit their skills, interests, and abilities. Extracurricular activities and volunteering contribute to the development of career management competencies. Under direction of their parents and school counsellors, they choose programs, classes, and work experiences to take in high school that will teach them skills needed to enter the workforce. The focus is on (a) building their awareness of their strengths and interests; (b) developing transferable skills in research, goal setting, evaluating options, and decision making; (c) linking abilities to future activities; (d) expanding options; (e) experiencing roles; and (f) engaging in initial career-planning skill development. As youth succeed in the exploration phase, they develop a sense of autonomy and of being in control of the present and even, to some degree, the future. Exploration also leads to the development of new interests. This is a time for learning how to access resources to achieve goals and to develop skills for making career decisions. Part of the career exploration phase is the identification of key figures, people who serve in some way as role models.

Career Preparation

At this level, high school students apply knowledge of their personal interests, strengths, abilities, and accomplishments to choosing and planning a post-secondary education or career path. In some schools, students develop a three- or four-year plan that assists them in relating their career interests and post-secondary education aspirations to academic and co-curricular achievements. This plan of action is updated annually and provides tentative career goals, identifies the courses that are required to achieve that goal, and reinforces the commitment and responsibility of the student to take charge of his or her career. This written document is developed jointly by the student, parents, and counsellors and can be stored in the student's career portfolio. The focus is on helping the young person integrate values, interests, and abilities into career planning, and perceive a greater range of options. Through the exercises, the student builds career-related skills, cultivates a positive work attitude, and demonstrates planning and decision-making abilities.

Blueprint for Life/Work Designs

The *Blueprint for Life/Work Designs* (2000) presents competencies and indicators that can be used as a general framework for schools establishing or redesigning a K–12 career development program. The Blueprint provides planning, development/redesign, and implementation activities. It lays out three areas of competence, each with a set of competencies. These are listed below.

Personal Management
1. Build a positive self-image while discovering its influence on self and others.
2. Develop abilities for building positive relationships in one's life.
3. Discover that change and growth are part of life.

Learning and Work Exploration
4. Discover lifelong learning and its contributions to one's life and work.
5. Discover and understand life/work information.
6. Discover how work contributes to individuals and the community.

Life/Work Development
7. Explore effective work strategies.
8. Explore and improve decision making.
9. Explore and understand the interrelationship of life role(s).
10. Discover the nature of life/work roles.
11. Explore the underlying concepts of the life/work building process.

The 11 competencies represent the basic skills and attitudes that children and adolescents need as they begin the process of developing an educational plan for academic growth and career development.

In addition to understanding the Blueprint competencies, guidance counsellors can build curriculum and activities on the "High Five" messages of career development (Redekopp, Day, & Robb, 1995).

1. *Change is constant*: Cultivate an attitude of "positive uncertainty" (Gelatt, 1989) or a curiosity about what opportunities will arise as a result.
2. *Follow your heart*: When change is constant, relatively stable guideposts become all the more important. The "heart" is the set of characteristics that include values, beliefs, and interests. Skills, knowledge, and attitudes are simply tools that allow the path to be followed.
3. *Focus on the journey*: Career development is not about making the right decision about a job ("What should I be?"); it is the understanding that every decision is a career development decision ("What do I want to be doing now and in the future?"). Setting goals is important, but don't forget to live in, learn from, and enjoy the present.
4. *Stay learning*: If change is constant then learning will need to be constant. Opportunities for learning are everywhere, but to make the most of these opportunities it is important for people to know how to pursue and track their learning experiences.
5. *Build relationships*: Community is important and others around us have already had experiences that can support our learning.

Career Education in Elementary School Years

In the following sections we assume an "integrative lifespan perspective" as we follow Baha, a fictional young girl, through her school years from elementary grades to completion of high school.

Baha arrived in Canada from India seven years ago. Her mother and father are very anxious that she does well in school and learns about opportunities in Canada. Baha enjoys all of her classes and has a small circle of friends. Her father has his own business and her mother is staying at home to raise Baha's two younger sisters. Her school creates and supports a career development climate including infusion throughout curricula. Teaching objectives in Grades 1 and 2 at her school have students learn about different jobs and how they are important in their community.

In the primary grades, Baha increased her self-awareness and awareness of others as she did her household chores and school work. She interviewed her parents about their favourite school subjects, careers they thought about when they were young, those who helped them make their career decisions, what they like and don't like about their work, and the skills that they learned in elementary school that they use in their work and home lives.

Knowing that parents play an influential role in their children's career plans, the school sent brochures with ideas on how Baha's parents could help her learn valuable career and life skills. Elementary school programs can assist students in creating connections between their academic studies and actual life situations (Magnuson & Starr, 2000), particularly when teachers have specific training in career planning (Slomp, Bernes, & Gunn, 2012). Baha's teachers and school counsellor used career education principles to stress the significance of school subjects. For example, in social studies, she gained understanding about other countries, languages, cultures, and the aspects of living in a global marketplace. She discovered how science is involved in distinct industries, such as food, media, agricultural, and automotive. Her teachers read books on various careers and the class took a field trip to observe the variety of businesses in their community and the workers involved. In her Grade 4 class, her teacher presented a strengths-based career classroom guidance unit to help Baha progress through steps to identify her personal strengths, make the link between classroom learning and potential careers, explore a variety of careers, and discuss how gender and race might influence career choices (Augst & Akos, 2012).

Baha particularly enjoyed *The Play Real Game*, (Career Cruising, n.d.), in which the class took on adult work roles, earned and spent money, chose a home, and created a town in the classroom! In teacher-led groups, students travelled to the future and imagined their lives and careers in 5–10 years. As Baha moves on to middle school, she has already been exposed to learning activities that are helping her to develop a positive self-image, build positive relationships, and understand the importance of lifelong learning. She has seen a range of life/work roles and appreciates how work benefits individuals and their community.

There are benefits to addressing the career needs of students as early as possible. Studies have shown cases of students becoming psychologically disengaged from school as early as third and sixth grade (Balfanz, Herzog, & MacIver, 2007; Looker, 2002), and of students becoming academically and socially disengaged during their middle school years (Looker, 2002). This underscores the importance of engaging young students from the beginning, motivating them academically and encouraging them to stay in school.

Career Education in Middle School

Baha is excited, but nervous, about entering middle school. She will have to adjust to a larger class size, contend with a more competitive environment and different grading and testing practices, and learn more challenging course material. Baha is hoping that she will learn how to select courses that will lay the foundation for her high school and post-high-school plans because she is feeling a bit directionless. Baha's parents are putting pressure on her to make a career decision before entering high school. The parents are eager to attend the parent–student career workshop offered by the school district.

The transition to middle school is marked by several changes in educational expectations and practices. In most elementary schools, children belong to a single classroom with classmates through the term and one or two teachers. When students reach middle schools, however, they must interact with more peers, more teachers, and with intensified expectations for both performance and individual responsibility. Social, developmental, and academic experiences are affected, requiring them to adjust to new settings, structures, and expectations (Tilleczek & Ferguson, 2007). All of this occurs at a time when they are also experiencing a host of changes associated with the transition from childhood to adolescence. Their attentions turn to exercising independence and developing strong relationships with peers. The atmosphere at home may become strained as both parents and children struggle with redefining roles and relationships. This complicated period of transition has often been associated with a decline in academic achievement, performance motivation, and self-perceptions (Lohaus, Ev-Elban, Ball, & Klein-Hessling, 2004). It is a time when young adolescents are most likely to experiment with risky behaviours. It is also the point at which children begin to make pivotal decisions regarding their academic and career choices — precisely at a time when they may be distracted or turned off by academic endeavours.

Certainly sociodemographic variables such as parental income, rural living, physical disabilities, single parent families, low academic performance, and negative attitudes about education contribute to being disengaged at the middle school level and not finishing high school. As an example, in British Columbia high school completion rates for all students is 80.3%, but only 54.1% for Aboriginal students (Ministry of Advanced Education, 2011). Knowing the factors that influence career progress of middle school students is important as it may help teachers and guidance counsellors keep students in school, and provide them with more purpose by establishing a linkage between their schooling experiences and employment.

During middle school the focus is on career exploration, where students seek out information on various occupations and identify their personal interests, values, and skills. Specifically, career development focuses on (a) understanding the concepts of lifelong learning, interpersonal relationships, and career planning; (b) developing learning and social skills, a sense of social responsibility, and the ability to formulate and pursue educational and career goals; and (c) applying this learning to their lives and work in the school and the community. Students are also taught ways to manage life transitions including the one from middle to high school.

Career Education in High School

Baha finds the transition to high school to be relatively smooth as she has been prepared by her school guidance counsellor for this next step. Baha knows the career cluster or distinct grouping of occupations that most interests her (i.e., business, marketing, and management). She is concerned about which specific courses she will need in order to go on to a postsecondary institution after graduation. She hopes that she can gain some experience in her area of interest before graduating from high school.

Expansion of postsecondary options and multiple work alternatives available to high school students in the 21st century makes career-planning and postsecondary choices more complex (Patton & McMahon, 2006; Truong, 2011). However, many students are leaving high school without the skills they need to make postsecondary plans (Code, Bernes, & Gunn, 2006). Employers believe that high schools do not teach the information and skills needed in the workplace, and that students do not link coursework to life beyond high school (Magnifico, 2007). To help students along their desired career paths, it is important that career guidance practice in schools integrates the developmental needs of high school students in conjunction with the changing expectations encountered in the workplace (Bernes & Magnusson, 2004; Borgen & Hiebert, 2006; Government of Alberta, 2012; Truong, 2011).

As students transition into high school, they focus more directly on the task of identifying occupational preferences, clarifying career choices, and developing skills in career planning. **Career maturity** is demonstrated by high school students when they do the following:

- show they understand the importance of narrowing career interests as a basis for post-high-school planning;
- identify one or more tentative career interests after an objective evaluation of their likes, dislikes, and aptitudes;
- engage in various activities within and outside the school environment to verify these choices;
- use their outside and within school experiences to help inform making post-high-school decisions;
- explore alternatives and plans for preparing to pursue these interests after high school. (Gray, 2009)

To raise their career maturity, high school students need to engage in career exploration that encompasses experiences within the school and outside. Work experience programs, volunteer requirements, co-op programs, and youth apprenticeship programs can provide the type of experience to prepare students for success beyond high school.

In Baha's school, counsellors help students develop career maturity and make tentative decisions regarding their career interests, rather than pushing them to select particular jobs or careers. Baha uses a student-learning career planner to help her learn about and apply the career-planning process and the principles considered important for career planning. Baha is fortunate that the school she attends has mapped out career-related programs and services to ensure that the programs meet the needs of every student. The programs and courses ensure that every student has access to personal career advice and coaching, is provided with opportunities to reflect on and consider their options and opportunities (both formal and informal learning experiences), and is exposed to career-related activities including how to write résumés.

Her high school has a work-experience component built into the program that provides students experiential learning opportunities outside of the school environment. Engaging in work experience will allow her to discover or confirm her career interests and aptitudes as well as further develop her career planning and employability skills. In addition, Baha will be required to develop an **e-portfolio** in which she can record her strengths, competencies, and accomplishments, and collect such materials as résumés, application forms, correspondence with businesses, and examples of job interview questions and responses. Baha is told that her portfolio must be presented in a way similar to how she would present it to a job interviewer (Bloxom et al., 2008).

In Grade 9, Baha takes part in the *Take Our Kids to Work*™ event. Annually, more than 200,000 Grade 9 students and over 75,000 businesses and organizations nationwide participate in Take Our Kids to Work Day. Baha was excited to go with her dad to his place of business and learn about the various aspects from accounting to product promotion. In reflecting on this experience, Baha had a better apprecia-

SPOTLIGHT: *CHINOOK REGIONAL FOUNDATION FOR CAREER TRANSITION*
by Margaret Vennard

Remember when you were in school and how many times people asked what you were going to do? Figuring out the answer can be a daunting task.

Chinook Regional Foundation for Career Transitions was formed to support the career development process for secondary students in southern Alberta. Six core school divisions along with several private schools partnered with Alberta Human Services, Lethbridge College, the University of Lethbridge, local business, and industry to support students making career decisions. Over 9,000 students from 50 schools have access to the career services provided by Career Transitions.

The staff of five provides a diverse menu of services ranging from regional skills competitions, divisional career events, school workshops, classroom presentations, and parent information nights. All of the career development programs are group-based and designed to engage youth in self-awareness and career path investigation. The power of partnership means programs that would be overwhelming for a single teacher to implement can be co-ordinated through Career Transitions to the benefit of all school partners.

More information is available at <http://www.careersteps.ca>.

tion of her dad's role in making a living and supporting his family. She believed that by understanding her father's job, she could make more informed decisions about her own future. Over the summer, she also went with her mother to her place of work in a long-term care home.

Baha found Career Cruising, an online career guidance website, to be very user friendly and helpful. Career Cruising <http://careercruising.com> has career assessment tools, over 550 occupational profiles, comprehensive postsecondary information, an employment section with a job search tool, student/client portfolios with résumé builders, and administrative tools.

The Youth Canada site (<http://www.youthcanada.ca/>) was also useful and very practical. Developed by two Vancouver high school students, Alex Shipillo and Michael Gelbart in 2006, the site provides a database for every program, competition, and conference for Canadian high school students and has articles on topics such as scholarships, postsecondary education, volunteering, enrichment opportunities, and so on.

Some of Baha's friends are undecided as to what to do at the end of high school and

Stories of Transition: What Happens in the Decade After High School

by Lara Shepard

The transition from high school into further education and employment is a bewildering process for many young people and their parents. Funded by CERIC, the Stories of Transition Project examined the educational and occupational pathways that high school students took after graduation and the factors that helped or hindered in the process.

The two publications — *The Decade After High School: A Professional's Guide and The Decade After High School: A Parent's Guide* — are available from CERIC <http://www.ceric.ca/?q=en/node/136>.

want to postpone continued study in order to explore areas of work that may be of interest to them. The school counsellor provides them with tips on how to plan for a successful "gap" year. A **gap year** can provide students with experiences that help them gain more insight into themselves and their career goals. For others, a break from studying will renew their enthusiasm for their studies. Students can gain real-world understanding of their classroom-based learning while taking time away from school, and they can earn money for tuition and other expenses prior to attending postsecondary education (Tropey, 2009).

Baha knows that not all her peers want to complete high school. Her school has implemented the innovative and much-acclaimed Pathways to Education program to encourage students in lower income neighbourhoods to finish high school and continue at a postsecondary school. Volunteer teacher candidates, university students, and older high school students tutor and mentor the students in Grades 9 to 12 so that they can achieve academically. The program offers some financial supports in the form of bus tickets and lunch vouchers. As a financial incentive, students graduating from the program are awarded a scholarship of up to $4,000 to continue in postsecondary education or training.

Pathways to Education was developed at The Regent Park Community Health Centre in Toronto in 2001 (with funding assistance from The Counselling Foundation of Canada) to address the high dropout rates and dismally poor future for young people in the low-income housing community of Regent Park. In 2007, the Pathways to Education Program received the Ruth Atkinson Hindmarsh Award, in recognition of its success in helping young people in Toronto do better in school and in replicating this program in other low-income communities in Canada (Pathways to Education, 2013). Over the first 10 years of the program, the high school dropout rate in Regent Park declined by over 70%, and postsecondary attendance grew from 20% to 80% (Pathways to Education, n.d.).

The completion of secondary school serves as a major transition point for many young adults (Arnett, 2007). In a 15-year longitudinal study that examined the educational and career pathways of high school students in British Columbia,

Andres and Adamuti-Trache (2008) found that participants did not progress linearly from high school to postsecondary education and then to work and other life-sphere activities. In fact, very few students followed a traditional route through the system, and trajectories became increasingly less traditional as students made their way through the postsecondary system. Gender, postsecondary completion status, parental education, and geographic region all contributed to the nature of each participant's trajectory.

At this transition point, Baha will need to contemplate the various educational pathways that exist for her, any of which will define her entry into young adulthood. These pathways may include: (a) employment; (b) a commerce program at a university; (c) an academic program at a community college that grants credits that are transferable to a university; and (d) a small business program at a community college that would lead to a certificate or diploma.

Today's 17-year-old secondary school student living in Canada can expect to participate in approximately three years of postsecondary education; and 10% to 20% of all young adults will participate in some form of education until their late 20s (Organisation for Economic Co-operation and Development [OECD], 2006). Bell and O'Reilly (2008) showed in their study of school-to-work-transition that the journey takes longer today (on average 8 years to complete compared to 6 years

---

SPOTLIGHT: *A NEW APPROACH TO CAREER DEVELOPMENT IN QUÉBEC*
by Sandra Salesas

In 1998, the Québec Ministry of Education, Sports, and Leisure implemented a new curriculum focusing on learning outcomes and cross-curricular competencies. In parallel, the Ministry introduced the Guidance-Oriented Approach to Learning (GOAL), which aims at infusing components of career development into subject areas. For example, a teacher may cover the job interview in an English class. Through experiential learning, students learn to make meaningful connections between school and work. The career counsellor, together with teachers and other professionals, work as a team in creating individualized units of learning and activities that encourage students to reflect on their talents and aspirations, and to explore different career possibilities. Thus, GOAL mobilizes all members of the school community to engage in guidance-oriented activities starting from elementary to the end of secondary school and even college.

As of 2012, GOAL is widely known and implemented in many high schools, Collèges d'enseignement général et professionnel (CEGEP), and universities. It is a culture that elicits partners to work together in order to ensure student success and meaningful connections.

20 years ago), and that pursuing further education is needed to facilitate entry into the workforce. Baha will need to consider the amount of time she is willing to invest in her education prior to working, the financial investment needed to complete particular programs, and employment prospects upon graduating.

Institutions have designed programs that are more flexible and accommodate students' life-needs. Schools make it easier for students to complete their studies while also balancing work and family responsibilities.

❖ *Stop and Reflect*

1. After Baha finishes high school, what type of trajectories in education and lifestyle can you imagine for her? Would you see it as an uninterrupted journey to a career, a circuitous one, or prolonged? What processes could be involved in the transition when considering different lifestyle trajectories? Identify individuals who might be perceived as important people in Baha's life who might impede or act as a support in the process.

2. How do the various educational and lifestyle trajectories that you considered for Baha reflect occupational status and gender-related aspects?

CAREER TREK (WINNIPEG)

by Priya S. Mani

Career Trek is a not-for-profit organization that provides programming for youth (Grade 5 through 9) from marginalized communities. The objective is to educate students and their families about postsecondary career options. Each year selected schools and community groups nominate candidates to participate. Career Trek runs from October to April with participants rotating through four to eight career modules at the University of Manitoba, the University of Winnipeg, and Red River College. Every five weeks students move to a new set of departments /faculties where participants learn about admission requirements, career trajectories, and personal/social skill development.

To find out more, go to Career Trek <http://www.careertrek.ca>.

Some of Baha's classmates are introduced to *Career Trek*, innovative educational programming for young people Grades 5 through 9 who come from traditionally marginalized communities such as adolescent parents, Aboriginal youth, and youth who have been assessed as at-risk for leaving school because of family stress, poverty, and other social-emotional issues. Career Trek's objective is to educate students and their families about staying in school, to inspire students to continue on to postsecondary education, and to provide hands-on career exploration (see Career Trek sidebar).

Other children identified as at-risk in her school are invited to take part in *Gameworks*, which encourages young people to exercise and utilize their creativity while working towards a real-life goal in a collaborative environment. During the building activity, team members experience firsthand how co-operation is essential to completing a project (see Gameworks sidebar on the next page).

Speakers — men and women in a wide variety of careers and from various ethnic groups — are invited to School Career Day (Rivera & Schaefer, 2009). Students talk with the guest speakers and learn from their personal and professional experiences in the field. Prior to career day, the students prepare various questions to ask the speakers in consultation with their home room teacher or the school counsellor. After the event, students report back to their home room or to the school counsellor on what they took away from the experience and what they learned about various careers.

In her social studies class, Baha developed a **community genogram**, a mapping activity in which she represented her community and the resources and supports within it. She learned about **role models** and was able to identify several from her life. Her class engages in the *Make It Real Game* (Career Cruising, n.d.), which shows students how their school courses, social life, work, and community experience contribute to the many opportunities open to them. Students examine their own aptitudes and interests and are able to test real-world decisions in a safe environment.

Recognizing that secure parent-child relationships and high parental involvement are associated with progress in career decision making (Young, Valach, & Marshall, 2007), the school counsellors developed a series of two-hour parent-child workshops on career development. The workshops were based on the publications, *Career Coaching Your Teens: A Guide for Parents* (Government of Alberta, 2008); *A Career Development Resource for Parents: Helping Parents Explore the Role of Coach and Ally* (Canada Career

---

SPOTLIGHT: *TRANSITIONING TO POSTSECONDARY*
by Kathy Dokis-Ranney

The Ontario Ministry of Education funds dual credit programs to enable students to complete secondary school and continue to postsecondary education or apprenticeship training.

Cambrian College in partnership with the Rainbow District School Board and the Sudbury Catholic District School Board offers a dual-credit program. There "the Dual Credit program is intended to encourage secondary school students to complete their secondary school education and to consider continuing on to post-secondary education; the program provides opportunities to explore career prospects; and it ensures a successful transition to College and apprenticeship programs." (<http://www.cambriancollege.ca/Programs/Pages/ProgramsDualCredit.aspx>)

For students interested in apprenticeship, the Ontario Youth Apprenticeship Program (OYAP) offers the Co-operative Education program to Grades 11 and 12 students by which students may start training in a skilled trade while completing an Ontario Secondary School Diploma. (<http://www.oyap.com>)

GAMEWORKS

by Lara Shepard

Gameworks is a "social board room" website where youth can build board games and take part in contests. Participants form teams to work on building a board game from conception to final packaging. Gameworks encourages participants to utilize their creativity while working towards a real life goal in a collaborative environment. Practicing negotiation, conducting research, and experiencing the pitfalls and successes of the choices they have made, youth realize that their needs can be met with the help of others. Participants receive a stronger learning experience by researching themes deeply and incorporating them into the concept of the game.

See <http://goratemygame.com/>.

Information Partnership, 2006); *Lasting Gifts: Helping Parents to Become Allies in Career Development* Workshop Series (CCDF, 2004); and *WorkBC Parents' Guide: A Career Development Resource for Parents to Support Teens* (Ministry of Advanced Education and Labour Market Development, 2008). Baha's parents learned various ways to assist their daughter in (a) discovering her career passion, (b) choosing the right career path, (c) selecting the type of training or education that would be appropriate post-high-school, and (d) accessing the best sources for informed and accurate advice. After attending the workshops, they could see the benefits of allowing Baha some time to discover those passions and had some ideas as to how to facilitate the process. They encouraged her to try new things, such as getting involved in other extracurricular activities, volunteering at a home for seniors, and job shadowing a friend who worked at the cancer clinic.

Career education in middle school is aimed at helping students become more self-aware and relate their growing knowledge of self to educational and occupational possibilities (Gray, 2009). Interests, skills, and values can be assessed informally or formally to provide a framework to help organize information about oneself and the world of work (Gray, 2009). Developing occupational lists could be a starting point for discussing the kinds of academic skills needed to pursue various career paths and to discover what career choices exist.

Junior high school students in Southern Alberta who completed the Comprehensive Career Needs Survey (Bardick, Bernes, Magnusson, & Witko, 2004) indicated that career planning was important to them. The researchers point out that career planning at this life stage could "increase students' awareness of the relevance of career decision making and influence their willingness to explore possible options, rather than putting off career planning until they are forced to make a decision" (p. 113). An unexpected finding of the study showed that students at this age tended to rely on their parents and friends rather than the school counsellor for assistance with career planning. Training parents to assist their children with career-related decision making is important in order for them to provide the needed encouragement and direction. A balance between familial and external supports may encourage young people to explore career options and increase their confidence in making career decisions (Bardick et al., 2004).

Disadvantaged Students

Research has demonstrated the negative effects of poverty on youth (Shookner, 2002; TkMC, 2006). There is also evidence for the existence of certain protective factors that shield students from these effects and that guidance counsellors can use in the planning and implementation of career interventions. For example, Lee (1999) found that supportive adult relationships were instrumental in boosting the self-confidence of economically disadvantaged students, thereby enabling them to achieve greater academic and career success.

Aiding students to persist in school requires having teachers who are emotionally supportive and who believe the student can achieve academically (Samuel, Sondergeld, Fischer, & Patterson, 2011). Guidance counsellors are also in a position to establish consistent relationships with students by collaborating or creating mentoring opportunities in students' lives. While education can help individuals break the cycle of poverty, these students and families may need extra support and encouragement to ensure that they have equal access and an opportunity to succeed. Factors such as lack of support, contextual and structural barriers, socioeconomic status, and gender role-stereotypes can impede a student's ability to pursue their goals and aspirations.

For Baha, the guidance counsellor might be interested in exploring ideas about future opportunities, options available to her, and what may be considered appropriate careers in terms of her cultural/societal values and expectations. Baha may also be provided with information about current national employment trends and resources available (e.g., financial aid and scholarships) to assist her in developing a broader framework of possibilities from which to consider options. The guidance counsellor could also reach out to the community and ask women in business to share their personal career stories to help Baha navigate different career pathways and address her hopes and fears. Additionally, the guidance counsellor could offer a parent workshop geared towards helping parents understand how parents can support their children as they make the transition from secondary school to the world of work or postsecondary education. The guidance counsellor and her family might also review Baha's career portfolio with her. The portfolio would be a rich resource reflective of her development and growth and could assist her in deciding on an educational pathway and in later preparing a personal and professional statement for employment or postsecondary applications.

❖ Stop and Reflect

1. Baha is torn between working in the family business, which is what she thinks her parents wish her to do, or leaving her parents to study at university. As a

CAREERS: The Next Generation Health Services Youth Initiative

by Lara Shepard

CAREERS partners with Alberta Health and Wellness and Alberta Health Services to offer high school students internship opportunities at health facilities. The goal is to attract young talent to hard-to-fill health occupations. The CAREERS Summer Internship program invites Grade 11 students to explore a health-related career and develop employability skills. During the summer, students work with a health services provider for about 6 weeks and earn one high school credit for every 25 hours worked. Most employers offer a salary or an honorarium. Some participating health service providers offer a second summer internship for Grade 12 students.

See <http://www.nextgen.org>.

career guidance practitioner, how would you help her navigate her dilemma?

2. Is the nature of the transition process different for high school students entering different kinds of institutions (universities, vocational colleges, technical training institutes, community colleges, nursing schools, research laboratories, centres of excellence, and distance learning centres)? Do you believe that the transition process to different forms of postsecondary education requires a redefinition of self and values for Baha?

Community Engagement

Societal and personal bias influences the way in which stakeholders talk about the academic and vocational options available to students and how students perceive those options and occupations. The past two decades have seen a range of reforms aimed at the high school level regarding the issue of curricular tracking and addressing the vocational and academic divide (Rose, 2008). One manner in which high schools can address this divide is by integrating academic and vocational education for both streams of students, thus providing students with a richer range of options for careers or education. In British Columbia, the Ministry of Education has mandated that secondary students participate in some form of community involvement for a set number of hours as part of their high school graduation requirements. By establishing local partnerships between schools, postsecondary institutions, colleges, and employers, schools can offer vocational and educational training opportunities to help increase the career pathways for students to consider (Taylor, 2007).

Community building within and outside of school can create situations in which young people are more successful in career development tasks. Research suggests that structured community-based experiences are critical developmental pathways through which young people can develop lifelong learning skills and become self-directed, socially competent, caring, and successful young adults (Larson, 2000). Structured activities such as service and civic activities, youth organizations like Girl

Scouts or Boy Scouts, and participating in a sport have been shown to help young people develop initiative and follow-through (Lapan, 2004). Community-school partnerships that provide career development opportunities for young people, such as work-based and service learning, help to introduce young people to broader career pathways.

Community engagement involves many stakeholders. Even financially disadvantaged communities have resources that can be used to support students. These might be elders, ethnic communities, church groups, sports organizations, businesses, and employers who can also serve as mentors and help students with their transition from school to employment or postsecondary education. Working from a strengths-based approach, school career counsellors can identify these potential supports and work with them in the best interest of the students and their community (Levin, 2011).

Conclusion

Career development of students should be a major mission of all schools — a process too important to be only a by-product of scattered learning and activities that are inherently uneven from student to student. Career development in the schools should (a) be planned, (b) have content derived from research and theory, (c) be systematically executed, and (d) use methods that are relevant to the developmental levels of students throughout elementary, middle, and senior high schools. Career choices determine how we spend much of our lives and the contributions we make to our families, communities, and society. In order to make the best possible career choices, students need a strong foundation of learning, self-awareness, career exploration, work search, and transition skills. Career development acts as this foundation.

References

Andres, L., & Adamuti-Trache, M. (2008). Life-course transitions, social class, and gender: A 15-year perspective of the lived lives of Canadian young adults. *Journal of Youth Studies, 11*(2), 115–145. doi: 10.1080/13676260701800753

Arnett, J. J. (2007). *Adolescence and emerging adulthood: A cultural approach.* Boston, MA: Pearson.

Augst, K., & Akos, P. (2008). *With all your power, what will you do? A strengths-based career unit for elementary students.* National Career Development Association. Retrieved from <http://ncda.org/aws/NCDA/pt/sd/news_article/5482/_PARENT /layout_details_cc/false>.

Balfanz, R, Herzog, L., & MacIver, D. J. (2007). Preventing school disengagement and keeping students on the Graduation path in urban middle-grades schools: early identification and effective Interventions. *Educational Psychologist, 42,* 223–235.

Bardick, A. D., Bernes, K. B., Magnusson, K. C., & Witko, K. D. (2004). Junior high career planning: What students want. *Canadian Journal of Counselling, 38*(2), 104–117.

Bell, D., & O'Reilly, E. (2008). *Making bridges visible: An inventory of innovative, effective or promising Canadian school-to-work transition practices, programs and policies.* Ottawa: Canadian Council on Learning. Retrieved from <http://www.ccl-cca.ca/pdfs/WLKC/CCDFENMakingBridgesVisibleFINAL.pdf>.

Bernes, K., & Magnusson, K. (2004). Building future career development programs for adolescents. *NATCON Papers 2004.* Les actes de la CONAT. Retrieved from <http://contactpoint.ca/wp-content/uploads/2013/01/pdf-04-11.pdf>.

Bloxom, J. M., Bernes, K. B., Magnusson, K. C., Gunn, T. T., Bardick, A. D., Orr, D. T., & McKnight, K. M. (2008). Grade 12 student career needs and perception of the effectiveness of career development services within high schools. *Canadian Journal of Counselling, 42*(2), 79–100. Retrieved from <http://files.eric.ed.gov/fulltext/EJ796324.pdf>.

Borgen, W., & Hiebert, B. (2006). Career guidance and counselling for youth: What adolescents and young adults are telling us. *International Journal for the Advancement of Counselling, 28,* 389–400.

Canada Career Information Partnership. (2006). *A career development resource for parents: Helping parents explore the role of coach and ally.* Author. Retrieved from <http://www.ccdf.ca/ccdf/wp-content/uploads/2010/12/a_career_development_resource_for_parents_e.pdf>.

Canadian Career Development Foundation. (2004). *Lasting gifts: Parents, Teens, and the Career Journey.* Ottawa, ON: Author. Retrieved from <http://www.ccdf.ca/ccdf/index.php/training/training-materials>.

Career Cruising. (n.d.) ccTheRealGame. Retrieved from <http://public.careercruising.com/us/en/products/cctherealgame/features/>.

Code, M. N., Bernes, K. B., & Gunn, T. (2006). Adolescents' perceptions of career concern: Student discouragement in career development. *Canadian Journal of Counselling, 40,* 160–174.

Ediger, M. (2000). *Vocational education in the elementary school.* (ED 442979). Opinion Papers. Retrieved from <http://www.eric.ed.gov/ERICWebPortal/search/detailmini.jsp?_nfpb=true&_&ERICExtSearch_SearchValue_0=ED442979&ERICExtSearch_SearchType_0=no&accno=ED442979>.

Gelatt, H. B. (1989). Positive uncertainty: A new decision-making framework for counseling. *Journal of Counseling Psychology, 36*(2), 252–256.

Ginzberg, E., Ginsburg, S. W., Axelrad, S., & Herma, J. L. (1951). Occupational choice: An approach to a general theory. New York, NY: Columbia University Press.

Gottfredson, L. S. (1981). Circumscription and compromise: A developmental theory of occupational aspirations. *Journal of Counseling Psychology Monograph, 28,*

545–579. Retrieved from <http://www.udel.edu/educ/gottfredson/reprints
/1981CCtheory.pdf>.

Government of Alberta. (2008). *Career coaching your teens: A guide for parents.* Alberta
Employment and Immigration. Retrieved from <http://www.alis.alberta.ca/pdf
/cshop/careercoach.pdf>.

Government of Alberta. (2012). *My choices, my work, my life.* Edmonton, AB:
AB Human Services. Retrieved from <http://alis.alberta.ca/pdf/cshop/
mychoicesmyworkmylife.pdf>.

Gray, K. (2009). *Getting real: Helping teens find their future.* Thousand Oaks, CA:
Corwin/Sage Press.

Lapan, R. T. (2004). Career development across the K–16 years: Bridging the present
to satisfying and successful futures. Alexandria, VA: American Counseling
Association.

Larson, R. W. (2000). Toward a psychology of positive youth development. *American
Psychologist, 55,* 170–183.

Lee, J. (1999). The positive effects of mentoring economically disadvantaged students.
Professional school counseling, 2, 172–179.

Levin, B. (2011). What schools can do for children in poverty. M.A.S.S. *Journal,
12*(2), 10–15.

Lohaus, A., Ev-Elban, C., Ball, J., & Klein-Hessling, L. (2004). School transition from
elementary to secondary school: Changes in psychological adjustment. *Educational
Psychology, 24,* 161–174.

Looker, E. D. (2002). *Why don't they go on? Factors affecting the decisions of
Canadian youth not to pursue post-secondary education.* Montréal, PQ: Canadian
Millennium Scholarship Foundation.

Magnifico, A. (2007, Nov/Dec). Bridging the relevancy gap: Employers, educators, and
high school students need to connect. *Teach,* 14–15.

Magnuson, C. S., & Starr, M. F. (2000). How early is too early to begin life career
planning? The importance of the elementary school years. *Journal of Career
Development, 27,* 89–101.

Malatest and Associates Ltd. (2009). *Pan- Canadian study of career development practices
in K–12 public schools.* Montréal: Canada Millennium Scholarship Foundation.
Retrieved from <http://www.malatest.com/CMSF%20Time-Motion
%20Report%202010-04-07.pdf>.

Ministry of Advanced Education. (2011). *STP fast facts.* Author. Retrieved from
<http://www.aved.gov.bc.ca/student_transitions/documents/stp_fast_facts.pdf>.

Ministry of Advanced Education and Labour Market Development. (2008). WorkBC
parents' guide: A career development resource for parents to support teens.
Victoria, BC: Author. Retrieved from <http://www.workbc.ca/Documents/Docs
/WorkBC_ParentGuide.pdf>.

National Life/Work Centre. (2000). *Blueprint for Life/Work Designs.* Memramcook,
NB: Author. Retrieved from <www.blueprint4life.ca>.

Organisation for Economic Co-operation and Development (OECD, 2006). *Education
at a glance: OECD Indicators.* Paris: OECD. doi: org/10.1787/eag-2011-en.

Retrieved from <http://www.oecd.org/education/skills-beyond-school /48631582.pdf>.

Pathways to Education. (n.d). *The pathways model.* Retrieved from <http://www.pathwaystoeducation.ca/about-us/pathways-model>.

Pathways to Education. (2013). *Awards and recognition.* Retrieved from <http://www.pathwaystoeducation.ca/en/results/awards-and-recognition>.

Patton, W., & McMahon, M. (2006). The systems theory framework of career development and counseling: Connecting theory and practice. *International Journal for the Advancement of Counseling, 28,* 153–166.

Redekopp, D. E., Day, B., & Robb, M. (1995). The *"high five"* of career development. ERIC/CASS Digest No. 95-64.

Rivera, L. M., & Schaefer, M. B. (2009). The career institute: A collaborative career development program for traditionally underserved secondary (6–12) school students. *Journal of Career Development, 35,* 406–426.

Rose, M. (2008). Intelligence, knowledge, and the hand/brain divide. *Phi Delta Kappan, 89*(9), 632–639.

Samuel, A., Sondergeld, T., Fischer, J., & Patterson, N. (2011). The secondary school pipeline: Longitudinal indicators of resilience and resistance in urban schools under reform. (Czech). *High School Journal, 94*(3), 95–118.

Shookner, M. (2002). *An inclusion lens for Atlantic Canada: Looking at social and economic exclusion and inclusion.* Health Canada, Atlantic Regional Office.

Slomp, M., Bernes, K. B., & Gunn, T. M. (2012). Integrating career development into school based curriculum: Preliminary results of an innovative teacher training program. In R. Shea & R. Joy (Eds.), *A multi-sectoral approach to career development: A decade of Canadian research* (pp. 444–461). Retrieved from <http://ceric.ca/cjcd/book/CJCD10thAnniversaryFullBook.pdf>.

Super, D. (1957). *The psychology of careers.* New York, NY: Harper & Row.

Super, D. E. (1990). A life-span, life-space approach to career development. In D. Brown, L. Brooks & Associates (Eds.), *Career choice and development* (2nd ed., pp. 197–261). San Francisco, CA: Jossey-Bass.

Taylor, A. (2007). Pathways for youth to the labour market: An overview of high school initiatives. Ottawa, ON: Canadian Council on Learning.

Tilleczek, K., & Ferguson, B. (2007). *Transitions and pathways from elementary to secondary school: A review of selected literature.* Toronto, ON: Ministry of Education. Retrieved from <http://www.edu.gov.on.ca/eng/teachers/studentsuccess /transitionliterature.pdf>.

TkMC. (2006). *Socioeconomic disadvantage: Health and education outcomes for school-aged children and youth.* Alberta Coalition for Healthy School Communities. Retrieved from <http://www.achsc.org/download/ACHSC%20Background %20Paper_SES_Health_Educ_SCY%28June%2015,06%29.pdf>.

Tropey, E. M. (2009). Time off, with a plan. *Occupational Outlook Quarterly, 1,* 26–33.

Truong, H. Q. T. (2011). High school career education: Policy and practice. *Canadian Journal of Educational Administration and Policy, 123,* 1–28.

Walls, R. T. (2000). Vocational cognition: Accuracy of 3rd, 6th, 9th, and 12th grade students. *Journal of Vocational Behavior, 56,* 137–144.

Young, R. A., Valach, L., & Marshall, S. K. (2007). Parents and adolescents co-constructing career. In V. Shorikov & W. Patton (Eds.), *Career development in childhood and adolescence* (pp. 277–295). Rotterdam, The Netherlands: Sense Publishers.

Youth Canada (n.d.). *Canada's top resources for high school students.* Impact Entrepreneurship Group. Retrieved from <http://www.youthcanada.ca/>.

Glossary

Career education is the curricula and programs that provide information and experiences that help students make meaningful career and education decisions. It facilitates adaptability in students and helps them make meaningful linkages between general education and work-life roles.

Career maturity expresses an individual's readiness to make educational and vocational choices including planfulness or time perspective, exploration, information, decision making, and reality orientation.

Community genogram is a versatile, graphic tool that places emphasis on the positive strengths and resources that can be brought to bear in examining the potential supports within one's community and culture, as well as family.

E-portfolio, also known as an **electronic portfolio** or **digital portfolio**, is a collection of electronic evidence assembled and managed by a user, usually on the Web. Such electronic evidence may include inputted text, electronic files, images, multimedia, blog entries, and hyperlinks. E-portfolios are both demonstrations of the user's abilities and platforms for self-expression, and, if they are online, can be maintained dynamically over time.

Exploration stage occurs during ages 15–20. The individual "tries things out" through classes, work experience, and/or hobbies. They collect relevant information and related skill development.

Gap year is associated with taking time out to travel between life stages. It refers to a period of time in which students disengage from curricular education and undertake non-curricular activities, such as travel, volunteering, or work.

Growth stage occurs from birth to age 14. The individual forms a self-concept, develops capacities, attitudes, interests, and needs, and forms a general understanding of the world of work.

Role models are people whom other individuals aspire to be like, either in the present or in the future. A role model may be someone you know and interact with on a regular basis, or someone you have never met, such as a celebrity.

School guidance counsellors are professionals who offer academic, career, university/college or postsecondary, social advice, and guidance to children in Grades K through 12.

Student-learning career planner is used as part of students' career planning. Students build a career "toolkit" to make career decisions and implement plans for further learning or workplace entry.

Discussion and Activities

Discussion

Discussion Questions

1. What are the developmental milestones that children and youth contend with? How does an understanding of developmental milestones help us to create appropriate career resources for children and youth?
2. What do you believe should be the focus of career school guidance programs in order to best support children and youth?
3. Career development principles are often integrated into a school's core curriculum so that career education does not become one more course for teachers to instruct. What external or internal resources would you draw upon to foster the integration of career development as a school-wide initiative? Discuss the possible policy implications for integrating career development as part of the school curriculum and the impact it may have on the future training of career school guidance counsellors.

Career Practitioner Role

1. What does career readiness and maturity mean at different stages of development?
2. As a prospective career guidance practitioner in the schools, what do you see as challenges in integrating career interventions into regular school subjects? How might you work with the community and local businesses to develop a community-based school program?
3. At each of the three school levels, what types of experiential learning activities would you implement to promote student engagement and achievement with students who appear to be at-risk or off-track?
4. As a career guidance counsellor in the school, how would you encourage the unique strengths and abilities of children and/or youth, and encourage hope and optimism for their future?

Personal Reflection

1. In your opinion, what can schools or faculties of education do to enhance career practitioners' sense of efficacy for integrating career interventions and programs within the school?
2. What would you do to enhance your sense of efficacy and your capacity as a career practitioner to integrate developmentally appropriate career development practices into a school setting?
3. Briefly examine the various career interventions described in this chapter. List the interventions that you consider the easiest to implement and those that you would consider the hardest. What steps would you take to learn more about the career interventions that you find most challenging to implement?
4. What external influences/messages have constrained or facilitated your navigation of various educational transitions and how has that contributed to your understanding of career development? What internal influences/messages have constrained or facilitated your management of various educational transitions that influenced your career identity? What strategies did you use or develop at different time periods to manage various transitions?
5. What do you hope to accomplish when working with students, parents, and people in your community as a career school guidance practitioner?

Activities

1. **Create a virtual career centre for students or parents.**
   For this exercise, you will work with a small group of students in your class. Each group will be responsible for creating a virtual career centre that could be implemented within a school. The small group will need to determine the school level for which they will be aiming their virtual career centre (elementary, middle, or the secondary level) and the client group (students or parents). Please draw on career development theories as you consider which activities and resources you will include (e.g., what Internet sources might you use, provide links to websites and consider guidelines for evaluating and selecting websites for inclusion). How might you use social media in your centre? What printables might be available for your clientele (parents or students)?
2. **Movie analysis of Billy Elliott**
   Billy Elliott is the story of a young boy and his dream of being a ballet dancer. His relentless pursuit of this goal allows him to overcome his economic hardship, societal pressures to conform to gender role expectations, and parental caution of the danger of pursuing his dreams. He confronts each obstacle with self-determination and accesses support along the way. As you view this movie please consider how the following themes unfold:
   1. Becoming your own person.
   2. Setting personal goals and planning for your future.
   3. Following a new-found dream.

4. Being self-determined.
5. Persevering.
6. Overcoming obstacles and substantial odds.

Resources and Readings

Resources

General

Bridges Transition Inc., a XAP Corporation company, offers education and planning tools for elementary, middle, and high school students. Choices Explorer is one of the products. In Canada <http://www.bridges.com/cdn/home.html>.

Career Cruising has several software products for students to use in exploring careers. One of these is ccTheRealGame <http://public.careercruising.com>.

Career Exploration and Experiential Learning Fact Sheet <http://www.ontla.on.ca /library/repository/mon/22000/283680.pdf>

The Learning Partnership, Take Our Kids to Work <http://www.thelearningpartnership.ca/Page.aspx?pid=250>

National Life/Work Centre. Blueprint for Life/Work Designs <www.blueprint4life.ca>

The Real Game Series. Main page is <http://public.careercruising.com/us/en/products/ cctherealgame/features/>. The following urls provide excellent background and historical information on *The Real Game Series*: <http://www.realgame.ca> (Canada), <http://www.realgame.org> (U.S.), <http://www.realgame.com> (International)

Career Resources

British Columbia

Health and Career Education Integrated Resource Package <http://www.bced.gov.bc.ca/ irp/pdfs/health_career_education/2006hcek7.pdf>.

School District No 69 Qualicum <http://www.sd69.bc.ca/Programs-services/EducationPrograms/CEP/Pages/default. aspx>.

Alberta

Alberta Learning Information Service (ALIS) <http://alis.alberta.ca/>. Site has a brochure on Resources for the Classroom <http://alis.alberta.ca/pdf /PSWRnews /classroom.pdf>.

Career Development Association of Alberta <http://www.careerdevelopment.ab.ca/>.

Government of Alberta Education. Career and Technology studies <http://education. alberta.ca/teachers/program/cts/program-of-studies.aspx>.

Saskatchewan
Career Education: Core Learning Resources
<https://www.edonline.sk.ca/bbcswebdav/library/resources/english/Core
/Grade%206-9/Career%20Education/career_ed_7_core_resources.pdf>.

Manitoba
Career Development <http://www.edu.gov.mb.ca/k12/cur/cardev/index.html>.
Manitoba Education, Citizenship and Youth: Career Development, Kindergarten to
Grade 12 <www.edu.gov.mb.ca/k12/cur/cardev/resources.html>.
Manitoba Education, Citizenship and Youth (2005) Focus on the Future: Career
Planning Begins at Home. Winnipeg, MB <http://www.edu.gov.mb.ca/k12/docs/
support/c_plan_home/c_plan_home.pdf>.

Ontario
Ontario Ministry of Education <http://www.psbnet.ca/eng/schools/sjw
/secondary_program.html>.
Ottawa-Carleton District School Board: Cooperative and Career Education
<http://www.ocdsb.ca/programs/sec/Pages/CooperativeEducation.aspx>.

Supplementary Readings

Beaucher, C. (2008). Aspirations and career plans of young people: The question of
meaning with the coming of the relationship to knowledge. *ContactPoint*, 5(2), 6–7.
Domene, J. F., Arim, R. G., & Young, R. A. (2007). Gender and career development
projects in early adolescence: Similarities and differences between mother and
mother/daughter dyads. *Qualitative Research in Psychology*, 4, 1007–1126.
Hooley, T, Watts, A. G., Sultana, R. G., & Siobhan, N. (2013). The Blueprint
framework for career management skills: A critical exploration. *British Journal of
Guidance and Counselling*, 41(2), 117–131. doi: 10.1080/03069885.2012.739374
LeBreton, D., Gingras, M., & Leclerc, G. (2008). *Template life/career for French
elementary schools*. New Brunswick: Department of Education of New Brunswick.
46 pages.
Nazli, S. (2007). Career development in primary school children. *Career Development
International*, 12(5), 446–462.
Porfeli, E. J., & Vondracek, F. W. (2007). *Career development in childhood and adolescents*
(pp. 143–168). Rotterdam: Sense Publisher.
Shepard, B. (2010). *Future bound: A lifeworks expedition workshop for rural youth*.
Self-published. Webpage: <http://www.pathstothefuture.com/>.
Shepard, B. (2011). Mapping: A resource-oriented approach for adolescent clients. In
G. R. Wolz, J. C. Bluer, & R. K. Yep (Eds.), *Ideas and research you can use*, Vistas
2011 (Article 92). American Counseling Association.
Young, R. A., Valach, L., Ball, J., Turkel, H., & Wong, Y. S. (2003). The family career
development project in Chinese Canadian families. *Journal of Vocational Behavior*,
62, 287–304.

fifteen

The Practice of Postsecondary Career Development

JENNIFER BROWNE
LISA RUSSELL
Memorial University

PRE-READING QUESTIONS

Reflect on your experiences at the career centre at the postsecondary school (college or university) you are currently attending (or may have attended in the past). What services have been most useful? What was not useful and why? If you have not used the career centre, provide reasons for not seeking assistance and support.

Introduction and Learning Objectives

In 2010, with almost 1.2 million students studying degree programs on Canadian campuses (twice that of 1980), the numbers of students attending postsecondary education in Canada had never been higher (AUCC, 2011). It has been well demonstrated that men and women with a higher education are more likely to have a higher income and are less likely to have long periods of unemployment or experience disruptions in the labour market (AUCC, 2011). Given that those with higher education tend to have more employment success and access to more diverse opportunities in the Canadian job market, it is not surprising the numbers of individuals participating in postsecondary education has grown. While the numbers are high, that does not mean postsecondary students have an easy time deciding on a career path. Career centres on campus originally created to assist returning World

War II veterans find employment have evolved significantly and been tasked with providing a variety of supports and services to assist with the career-planning process and the transition to work (Shea, 2010).

There is significant pressure on young people as they enter postsecondary education to establish their academic career. Students are expected to have a major/minor chosen and a career path identified very early in their academic studies.

Given the cost of education and the uncertainty of economic times, and the fact that many students know little about their interests and strengths, it is understandable that this situation can cause anxiety for students. Research indicates that uncertainty about career goals can be a significant contributor to student attrition (Hull-Blanks et al., 2005; Fouad et al., 2006). Students with identified goals, on the other hand, are more likely to persevere and remain in school (Tinto, 1993).

Entering postsecondary education is a time of significant transition for young people. Career services on campus are an essential support service for providing students with guidance, information, resources, and opportunities. Career counsellors and practitioners work with students to ensure that they are skilled in informed decision making and will be successful in transitioning from school to work. The work of the career practitioners is varied, important, and rewarding. They impart skills such as developing effective résumés, and guide students in examining and resolving key identity questions and in navigating academic programs.

In this chapter you will:

1. Understand the role of career development in postsecondary education.
2. Learn about the services provided on postsecondary campuses.
3. Learn how to provide career counselling/advising for diverse populations.
4. Learn more about the transition from postsecondary to the world of work.
5. Explore a day in the life of practitioners in the field.
6. Find out about trends in postsecondary career development.

Theories That Have Shaped Career Development

How we spend our days is how we spend our lives.
— Annie Dillard

There is no shortage of theories to assist career practitioners in understanding the process clients go through as they travel their career path. The field of career development emerged after World War II with the influx of returning veterans seeking employment and many enrolling in postsecondary education. Career development theories evolved along with the practice (Swanson & Gore, 2000). There were numerous theories developed over the last half-century in the area of vocational psychology. Among them were trait-and-factor/matching, developmental, constructivist career theory, social learning theory, and integrative approaches (Herr & Cramer, 1996). Some of the most referenced and widely applied career development theories are briefly summarized below. A more in-depth review of the theoretical foundations of career development can be found in Chapter 6, Theoretical Foundations of Career Development.

- For over 50 years, John Holland's theory of how personality types play a critical role in one's choice of careers has been one of the most widely studied. Holland works from the premise that heredity and environment strongly influence one's personality type. His theory of career choice highlights six personality types: realistic, investigative, artistic, social, enterprising, and conventional, with each linking to a group of occupations or environments. (Holland, 1966, 1985)
- Donald Super's development approach recognizes the interaction between personal and environmental variables and acknowledges where people are in their lives, and the roles they play (Super, 1951, 1953, 1963). The life-career rain-bow lays out five life stages (growth, exploration, establishment, maintenance, and disengagement) and nine roles (child, student, leisurite, citizen, parent, spouse, homemaker, worker, pensioner) that people play, some simultaneously, during their lives. People make career decisions based on a variety of factors arising from that context. (Herr, Cramer, & Niles, 2004)
- Assumptions underlying the constructivist career development model (Super, Savickas, & Super, 1996) are that people cannot be separated from their environments. According to these theorists, there are no absolutes; human behaviour can only be understood in the context in which it occurs. Individuals are viewed as active creators of themselves and their environments. From this postmodern perspective, if individuals actively participate in the creation of their own reality, then it follows that individuals create their own personal story in relation to their experiences. The use of language and dialogue is fundamental to the creation of meaning and knowledge for the personal story. When the personal story is uncovered, a new reality is constructed through dialogue between the client and the practitioner, a process referred to as co-construction.
- John Krumboltz's (2009) work on planned happenstance challenges the intention and planning on which much career theory is built. He posits the notion that indecision is sensible and desirable and that benefits can accrue from unplanned chance events.
- A relatively new focus in career development is on work-integrated learning (WIL), a theory that focuses on preparing graduates to meet the needs

of employers and ensuring they are equipped to successfully transition to the world of work. (Freudenberg, Brimble, & Cameron, 2010)

Ensuring students have opportunities to apply the theories learned in the classroom is not a new phenomenon. Co-operative education, which combines classroom education with practical work experience, has existed in Canada since 1957 and is an example of integrated and experiential learning (Lebold, Pullin, & Wilson, 1990).

Other forms of experiential education include part-time employment, volunteer work, and service learning, both curricular and co-curricular. These learning-on-the-job activities are highly valued by employers, and students are encouraged to obtain practical work experience while pursuing their education.

Mon Webfolio

by Riz Ibrahim

Mon Webfolio [My Webfolio] is a web service developed by Université Laval's Service de Placement [Employment Service of the University of Laval] to encourage its students to reflect on career-related questions to help guide them to the most suitable career outcomes. Webfolio helps students set goals, develop plans, and learn about the labour market. It is available at 1,150 institutions in Québec, including all CEGEPs and high schools as well as many career and employment assistance agencies and adult-focused career centers.

French: <https://webfolio.spla.ulaval.ca/>. The English-language version is available at individual institutions.

Université Laval is currently developing an entrepreurship module that it expects to include in the Webfolio in 2014 to support those interested in starting their own ventures.

Career Services Checklist and Opportunities

Career centres at universities and colleges offer an array of services that go beyond providing information on developing effective cover letters and résumés. They also offer a variety of programming to enhance student learning and awareness of their values, skills, and strengths. The metamorphosis from **placement** offices to the diverse programming and functions they provide today is an indicator of the evolution of the field itself.

Types of Career Services

Services vary depending on the campus. However, career centres generally provide the following services to students and, in many cases, to alumni (Herr, Cramer, & Niles, 2004; Shea, 2010):

- career counselling/advising;
- career information on various careers and educational offerings;
- job postings for part-time, full-time, summer employment;
- services for employers including job

postings, interview scheduling, space, career fairs;

- career and personality assessments;
- labour market information;
- workshops for résumé and cover letter, curriculum vitae creation, networking, job search, use of social media, dining etiquette, et cetera;
- experiential learning opportunities: volunteer opportunities, service learning, internships, work/study abroad;
- innovative programming focused on specific student populations such as students who have children, international students, discipline related, et cetera.

Many of these services are provided face-to-face. However, more and more services are being delivered on the Web, resulting in some loss in direct interaction with students. Websites have made job postings, employer profiles, educational opportunities, and other resources more accessible for the end user.

Ensuring first-year students are aware of the campus career centre is essential. Attracting them to Career Services early in their university career ensures they are aware of the services available to them and increases the likelihood that they will make use of these services. While some enter school with clear career goals in mind, many do not, and those who do may change their minds. Students without career goals tend to have higher levels of anxiety and are at greater risk of not completing their education; therefore connecting these students to the appropriate supports through career services is crucial (Fouad et al., 2006). Talking to a career counsellor or practitioner can help a student develop individualized and effective strategies for career planning, identify various barriers, and reduce anxiety.

Career Development and Experiential Learning at Memorial University

by Jennifer Browne and Lisa Russell

Career Development and Experiential Learning is a leader and innovator of career programs and services. The primary goal is to prepare students for work, provide experiential learning opportunities, connect students with employers, and provide resources for career exploration through a multidisciplinary team of career planners, advisors, administrative staff, and peer educators. They offer Memorial students and alumni help with work and volunteer experience, career exploration programs, résumé and cover letter critiques, career consultations, information sessions, career resource library, and LabNet computers.

Visit <http://www.mun.ca/cdel/career/>.

❖ *Stop and Reflect*
Reflect back to when you were leaving high school and think about what you wanted to be at that time in your life. Are you doing that today? What happened along the way that may have changed your mind?

School-to-Work Transition

Career services also play a significant role in students transitioning from postsecondary to the world of work. Successfully transitioning from school to work is a process that is dependent on a number of complex factors, as well as characteristics of the individual (Herr & Cramer, 1996). Astin (1993) found students in the 1990s placed a greater emphasis on careerism and on being prepared to enter the workforce than previous generations did. This notion of **careerism** has continued to be a dominant theme over the past two decades with the majority of students identifying their main purpose for attending higher education as a way to gain meaningful employment (Herr et al., 2004).

Employers also have high expectations for university and college graduates. Employers spend a great deal of time and resources on hiring the right candidate and expect graduates to be articulate and aware of their skills and strengths. In the development and delivery of career services, career centres need to consider a variety of factors which include taking account of the current economic climate, creating opportunities for networking, and developing partnerships with stakeholders. Today's graduates face stiff competition and, in certain regions and disciplines, limited employment opportunities. Career centres must arrange opportunities for students and employers to engage in a variety of settings beyond traditional career fairs. These include inviting employers to participate in career seminars or workshops and creating opportunities for students to receive mentoring in their field by participating in experiential opportunities (such as internships and overseas work experience). Partnerships between the postsecondary institution and various organizations help in providing these experiential opportunities. These partnerships can also lead to opportunities for students and graduates to gain financial assistance (i.e., wage subsidies and funding for employment programs). Another outcome can be creative programming, such as curricular or co-curricular **service learning**, that engages the community and faculty members.

Certification, Education, and a Day in the Life

Over the past 10 years, there has been a move to greater professionalization of career development practitioners with more attention given to educational preparation. The level of education required to work in the field may vary depending on region or organization. Many employers, particularly those in postsecondary settings, require of their counsellors a minimum of a master's degree in counselling or a related field. For community agencies, the minimum requirement is a degree in the humanities or social sciences, and some courses in career development will be helpful. In a survey of 1,013 career service professionals in 2011, 38% indicated their highest educational attainment as a bachelor's degree, while 44% indicated the completion of a master's degree (CERIC, 2011).

Typically, a "day in the life" of a career counsellor or practitioner is invested in providing direct services to students and alumni. One-on-one appointments or group work make up most of the interactions in a postsecondary setting. The career needs of students and alumni can be diverse, and it is helpful to be aware of special student groups when addressing specific concerns. Adult learners, single parents, international students, graduate students, LGBTQ students (lesbian, gay, bisexual, transgendered, and queer), students with disabilities, and many other groups require counsellors to address a variety of needs and concerns.

Career practitioners are often involved in creating programing for both individual and small groups, and, at times, may facilitate services to larger groups.

SPOTLIGHT: *FINDING YOUR CAREER PASSION*
by Michael Huston and Sharon Crozier

Do you want to be able to say, "Time just slipped by at work, I was having so much fun"? Many postsecondary students are looking to find their passion! Research shows a positive correlation between students' sense of "calling" and choice-work salience (Duffy & Sedlacek, 2007).

"Finding Your Career Passion" is a three-hour workshop for students who are confused about school and work options, worried about their indecision and the time and money they might be wasting. The workshop provides a chance to discover personally relevant career information. The workshop's prime intervention is reflective self-assessment, where students gather and organize information about their goals, inspirations, interests, values, and talents. We also ask about their natural abilities (the things they do well that are easy and/or effortless for them), emphasizing the concept of Flow (Csikszentmihalyi, 1990). Creative approaches, such as guided visualization (self-documentaries of their success in different areas) combined with asking quick response questions such as "What would you do if you knew you would not fail?", "What is the most important thing to you that you're not spending enough time doing right now?", and "What would you choose to do if all your potential life/career paths paid the same?" are helpful for reflection.

We discuss inspiration (when they want to do someone else's work) as reflections of their own interest, values, ability, and potential; finding opportunities to express interests (doing things one likes to do); and values (doing things one cares about); as well as explore matching occupations. We expand their understanding of a range of majors and occupations, noting that confidence about their career choices depends on it.

These may be short workshops such as for résumé and cover letter writing, or longer run programs for career exploration and planning. By putting together small groups to explore career opportunities, the career practitioner may encourage greater student involvement. The career practitioner might also develop mentoring and career-related programs specific to certain faculties or disciplines. By building in components that allow reflection, the practitioner provides the students opportunities to learn from each other and to share their experiences as they discover more about themselves and their career aspirations. Career practitioners receive a great deal of satisfaction from assisting students in setting their goals, taking the steps to succeed, finding their passion and embarking on a career path.

Demand for the services of a career practitioner can only go up. An Ipsos Reid study funded by CERIC indicated 71% of adults in Canada wished they had received more professional career-planning assistance than they did (Ipsos Reid, April 30, 2007). Through the career centre today's postsecondary students can get that assistance.

Special Populations

Within the postsecondary environment there are numerous special populations of students to be considered when planning activities, developing programming, or training staff. Students with disabilities, international students, Aboriginal students, and LGBTQ students are all significant populations in the postsecondary environment to whom career centres must be prepared to respond. Unfortunately, there is limited research on the career development needs of these groups. It is known that these students experience a high prevalence of stigma. Criticism has long been directed at career development theory for its lack of applicability to diverse populations and the lack of research on the needs of diverse groups (Arthur & Popadiuk, 2010; Watson, 2006). While there may be some similarities between these groups, there are also differences. There is also great variability within each group that cannot be overlooked by practitioners in their interactions with individual students.

Students With Disabilities

As a result of changes following the passage of the Canadian Charter of Rights and Freedoms in 1980, schools and school boards across Canada are required to provide the supports necessary for students with identified disabilities (Harrison, Larochette, & Nichols, 2007). They may have learning disabilities, physical disabilities, or be coping with mental illness. As more students with disabilities achieve success in the K–12 school system, more will graduate to the postsecondary level. Most postsecondary institutions have responded by creating dedicated services for students with special needs, including specially targeted career services. Some individuals with disabilities will succeed in the competitive work world without additional assistance from career services staff; however, others will require more in-depth interventions. Overall, employment prospects for individuals with disabilities are less positive compared to students without disabilities. One study showed that 33% of those with disabilities who were able to work were unemployed compared to 2.5% for those without disabilities (Roessler, Hennessey, & Rumrill, 2007). From a career-planning point of view, it is better to help the student seek the best fit between the disability and the options for education and career (Hardy, Cox & Klas, 1996). At the postsecondary level, most services that are available depend on self-identification by the student. Thus the delivery of service is triggered by the student's identification of his or her particular needs.

International Students

The rapid increase in the number of international students has led to the development of targeted support services and programming for this special population. It is important to note that all international students, regardless of country of origin, face challenges in the career context (Yang, Wong, Hwang, & Heppner, 2002) ranging from the logistics of proper documentation, to a lack of awareness about the Canadian cultural contexts concerning careers and employment, and to a complete lack of Canadian work experience. Career practitioners can provide support for students on issues such as racism, discrimination, pressure from families, as well as on dealing with their particular student context. The legal processes that delineate avenues of work experience for international students (i.e., off campus work permits and study permits) often means they tend to seek assistance early and in great numbers.

Programs and interventions aimed specifically at international students can serve as an initial point of connection. This makes it easier for career services staff to connect with these students and inform them of any other services that are available. Staff may need some cultural context training and preparation in delivering services to this population (Arthur & Popadiuk, 2010). Memorial University in Newfoundland recognized this and opened a Professional Skills Development Program to help international students prepare for professional employment.

Some international students will be interested in remaining in their country of study (Dyer & Lu, 2010). Students who want to work in Canada will need to learn about the key components for job competition success in the Canadian context.

SPOTLIGHT: *PROFESSIONAL SKILLS DEVELOPMENT PROGRAM OF MEMORIAL UNIVERSITY*
by Jennifer Browne and Lisa Russell

Memorial University runs a Professional Skills Development Program for international students. There are eight weekly in-class workshop sessions. Additionally, students are required to do the following: one volunteering experience beginning at week 3 and two networking sessions occurring after week 4, submission of a revised résumé and cover letter, and completion of a mock interview. Students must attend/complete all elements to get their "certificate" of completion awarded at the closing ceremony.

Session 1	What is the Professional Skills Development Program for international students? What resources can help me on campus?
Session 2	What skills can I offer an employer as an international student?
Session 3	How do I write an effective résumé and cover letter?
Session 4	Understanding the Canadian job search process.
Session 5	How are Canadian interviews different than international interviews? Tips on having a successful interview (mock interview).
Session 6	Social media and e-portfolios.
Session 7	Intercultural communication and the job search in Canada — understanding Canadian employment culture and workplace etiquette.
Session 8	Workplace etiquette. Final wrap-up of sessions and discussion.

<http://www.mun.ca/isa/employment/psdp.php>

Aboriginal Students

Aboriginal students face many of the same types of barriers as other minority groups. There are limited research findings and career theories that can serve to inform practitioners when working with Aboriginal students (Young, Marshall, & Valach, 2007). Young and colleagues also noted that there is a "disconnect" for

Aboriginal youth between schooling and the process of becoming adults. Although major educational gains have been made, Aboriginal students still face racism, institutional barriers, and cultural divisions that make the education system an undesirable and hostile place. Values and cultural background differ for Aboriginal students, who hold more collectivist values compared to the individualist values of Canadian society (Young et al., 2007; Schissel & Wotherspoon, 2003). These conditions can impede the student's success at school and result in the person being unprepared for the labour force (Schissel & Wotherspoon, 2003).

Aboriginal students are largely clustered in the fields of education, social and behavioural sciences, and business (AUCC, 2011). Occupational role models, particularly from non-traditional occupations, can provide a helpful vision of career success for this population (Herr et al., 2004). Given the lack of culturally sensitive assessment tools for choosing occupations, practitioners must be mindful of the limitations of those tools when working with Aboriginal students.

LGBTQ Students

Career development issues for LGBTQ students have received more attention since the early 1990s as more scholarly investigations and explorations of this population have been undertaken (Schneider & Dimito, 2010). Given the effect of the LGBTQ identity on so many other aspects of an individual's life it is not surprising that effects are seen in a career context as well. Those factors can include a lack of LGBTQ role models across a range of careers, which can inhibit the ability of students to see themselves in a particular career. LGBTQ students may also have concerns about discrimination and stereotyping within a hiring context (Herr et al., 2004; Schneider & Dimito, 2010). Schneider and Dimito (2010), in their examination of LGBTQ individuals and factors influencing career decision making, confirmed that identification as an LGBTQ individual did influence academic and career choices. Furthermore, given that the postsecondary environment in general is more liberal than the rest of society, LGBTQ students, while comfortable and welcomed within the postsecondary environment, often seek out additional preparation aroundthe transition from university or college into the workplace. Key to effectively working with this population is having sensitive career services personnel who can communicate empathically and respectfully with this population.

❖ *Stop and Reflect*
Imagine you are an individual from one of the special populations outlined above. How would you see the world of employment and your place in it? What are some of the differences?

Jennifer Browne, Lisa Russell

Trends and Challenges

A number of emerging trends and developments are presenting challenges as well as opportunities to the field of career development at the postsecondary level. Issues around certification/professionalization of the field, integrated approaches at the postsecondary level, and financial and assessment demands are all changing the landscape of postsecondary career development in ways difficult to fully predict. However, each of these changes provides opportunity for career development to achieve greater influence and recognition as an important element in the successful education of postsecondary students.

Certification and Professionalization

In 1999, the first draft of the *Canadian Standards and Guidelines for Career Practitioners* was released. It was a significant effort to "professionalize" the practice of career development in Canada. While not confined to the postsecondary career environment, the increasing emphasis on core competencies and standards of practice and education is being felt within the career centres at the postsecondary level as institutions attempt to ensure that outcomes match stated goals (Hung, 2002; Shea, 2010).

A framework for the education of career practitioners in Canada, developed in 2010, identified and defined five core functions of the field: career advising, career educating, **career counselling**, **career coaching**, and career consulting (Burwell, Kalbfleisch, & Woodside, 2010). These functions were considered to be the main activities that career practitioners engaged in while working with clients on career or employment matters. Additionally, five leadership functions integral to the field's performance and advancement were also identified: innovation, education, supervision of practice, systematic change, and management. The framework is intended to promote professionalism in the field, to enhance professional identity, and to increase consumer education and confidence in the services provided. (See videos listed in Resources.)

While the field continues to evolve, there is little question that university career centres will have to be aware of the pressures around certification and professionalization. Career services staff are typically interdisciplinary in their education and experience and, consequently, are a rich resource for students to call upon for guidance (Shea, 2010). Different provinces are at different stages in determining standards for career development and this too will impact the operations of postsecondary career services.

Shea (2010) identifies five primary national organizations that support professionals in career and employment:

1. Canadian Association of Career Educators and Employers (CACEE).
2. Student Affairs and Services Association (SASA).
3. Canadian University and College Counselling Association (CUCCA).
4. Canadian Education and Research Institute for Counselling (CERIC).
5. Canadian Association for Co-operative Education (CAFCE).

Note that SASA and CUCCA are both divisions of the Canadian Association of College and University Services (CACUSS).

Many provinces have established provincial associations that offer networking and professional development. Educational programs, including diplomas and certificates, are cropping up all over the country in a variety of delivery methods and types.

Integrated Approach to Learning

A recent trend for institutions across Canada is what is known as an integrated approach, referred to as work-integrated learning (WIL). The approach has been linked to efforts related to the retention and success of students (Hull-Blanks et al., 2005). This approach to career-focused education includes theoretical forms of learning that are appropriate for technical/professional qualifications, problem-based learning (PBL), project-based learning (PBL), and work-based learning (WBL). There is an emphasis on the integrative aspects of all these types of learning. WIL is an educational approach that aligns academic and workplace practices for the mutual benefit of students and workplaces.

In Ontario, work-integrated learning was strongly endorsed by institutional, employer, and community partners as an important element of the overall student experience, and was perceived as offering a range of benefits to students, including:

- career exploration, career clarity, and improved prospects for employment;
- opportunity to apply theory to practice in real workplace and community settings;
- development of marketable, workplace skills. (Sattler, 2011, p. 5)

Ideally, students should have the opportunity to participate in some form of WIL during their program, for example:

- professional practice/work placements;
- industry projects performed at the university or in a workplace;
- industry experience where students engage as employees in a work environment to meet practical experience requirements specified by professional or industry bodies;

- volunteer work for organizations such as not-for-profit organizations;
- learning activities within virtual and simulated work environments allowing the development and application of work-related skills and knowledge.

In addition to offering career development information, many career centres across Canada now offer programs to help students gain and build experience (Shea, 2010). Experience-based activities can take the form of co-operative education where work terms alternate with academic terms or where a service-learning approach program integrates classroom instruction with community service.

Measuring Outcomes

These changes are partially linked to the increased focus on measuring retention, results, and outcomes discussed below. Universities and colleges across Canada are greatly challenged by fiscal constraints. In an era of increasingly scarce dollars for postsecondary education, institutions are searching for savings and efficiencies. The pressure for career development offices to demonstrate the effectiveness of their programming and interventions is increasing as institutions grapple with shrinking government support and increased expectations of students.

The evolution of postsecondary students as consumers has been underway for some time, but has certainly accelerated as the amount of money students pay in tuition has soared. As consumers, students want to ensure that they "get what they pay for." In trying to respond to those demands, as well as to determine their own funding priorities, institutions are seeking to identify the outcomes for the services and interventions that are offered. "Demonstrated" outcomes, other than placement rates, have not traditionally been a priority for this human service area. People realize now that the transition to work from a postsecondary environment is a process and not an event (Finnie, 2000). Placement rate, which has been the traditional indicator, is limited in usefulness. It would be better to have longer-term indicators that are connected to job attainment and income. These indicators improve for graduates at their second- and five-year mark of employment. The career centre will need to demonstrate its role in the achievements of graduates two to five years later.

Recently, new means of establishing learning benchmarks and assessment regimes have been gaining in popularity. The work of Keeling, Wall, Underhile, and Dungy (2008), in the area of assessment and the use of learning outcomes, has influenced the program offerings of many institutions across Canada as career centres attempt to itemize and quantify the learning that is occurring. The 2012 CERIC project with the University Career Centre Metrics Working Group created a customized online resource, "Career Centre Evaluation: A Practitioner Guide" (<http://ceric.ca/careercentreevaluation/>), that is designed to be used by practitioners at the career centre level. In June 2012, the project received the 2012

Excellence in Innovation Award by the Canadian Association of Career Educators and Employers (CACEE). CACEE, as a national organization, provides professional networking and development opportunities, information, advice, and other services to employers and career service professionals. The guide will help university career centres better evaluate the impact of their activities.

Conclusion

Career counsellors and practitioners on postsecondary campuses play a pivotal role in the success of many students. Recognition of career development as a field of study, issues related to professionalism in the field, and the complex issues attached to career counselling are becoming clearer as the profession evolves. Since its humble beginnings as placement offices, career services at universities and colleges now provide a kaleidoscope of offerings well beyond résumé-writing workshops and job postings. Experiential learning and mentoring programs that involve students working with governments, agencies, community groups, and various employers have diversified the role of career professionals. The integrated learning programs that career practitioners/counsellors create and deliver have expanded the opportunities available to the students and alumni who utilize their school's career centre and resources.

References

Arthur, N., & Popadiuk, N. (2010). A cultural approach to career counseling with international students. *Journal of Career Development, 37*(1), 423–440.

The Association of Universities and Colleges of Canada (AUCC). (2011). *Trends in higher education: Vol. 1 — Enrolment.* Ottawa, ON: Author. Retrieved from <https://www.aucc.ca/media-room/publications /trends-in-higher-education-volume-1-enrolment/>.

Astin, A. W. (1993). *What matters in college? Four critical years revisited.* San Francisco, CA: Jossey-Bass.

Burwell, R., Kalbfleisch, S., & Woodside, J. (2010). A model for the education of career practitioners in Canada. *Canadian Journal of Career Development, 9*(1), 44–52.

CERIC Survey of Career Service Professionals. (2011). *Canadian education and research institute for counselling.* Retrieved from <http://ceric.ca/files/survey /SURVEY%20OF%20CAREER%20SERVICE%20PROFESSIONALS %20HIGHLIGHTS%20REPORT.pdf>.

Csikszentmihalyi, M. (1990). *Flow: The psychology of optimal experience.* New York, NY: Harper and Row.

Duffy, R. D., & Sedlacek, W. E. (2007). The presence of and search for a calling:

Connections to career development. *Journal of Vocational Behavior, 70,* 590–601.

Dyer, S., & Lu, F. (2010). Chinese born International students' transition experiences from study to work in New Zealand. *Australian Journal of Career Development, 19*(2), 23–30.

Fouad, N. A., Guillen, A., Harris-Hodge, E., Henry, C., Novakovic, A., & Terry, S. (2006). Need, awareness and use of career services for college students. *Journal of Career Assessment, 14*(4), 407–420.

Finnie, R. (2000). From school to work: The evolution of early labour market outcomes of Canadian postsecondary graduates. *Canadian Public Policy, 26*(2), 197–224.

Freudenberg, B., Brimble, M., & Cameron, C. (2010). Where there is a WIL there is a way. *Higher Education Research and Development, 26*(5), 575–588.

Hardy-Cox, D., & Klas, L. D. (1996). Students with learning disabilities in Canadian colleges and universities: A primer for service provision. *Journal of Learning Disabilities, 29*(1), 93–97.

Harrison, A. G., Larochette, A. C., & Nichols, E. (2007). Students with learning disabilities in postsecondary education: Selected initial characteristics. *Exceptionality Education Canada, 17,* 135–154.

Herr, E. L., & Cramer, S. H (1996). *Career guidance and counseling through the lifespan* (5th ed.). New York, NY: HarperCollins.

Herr, E. L., Cramer, S. H., & Niles, S. G. (2004). *Career guidance and counseling through the lifespan.* New York, NY: Pearson Education.

Holland, J. (1966). *The psychology of vocational choice: A theory of vocational personalities and work environments.* Waltham, MA: Blaisdell.

Holland, J. (1985). *Making vocational choices: A theory of vocational personalities and work environments.* Englewood Cliffs, NJ: Prentice-Hall.

Hull-Blanks, E., Robinson-Kurpuis, S. R., Befort, C., Sollenberger, S., Foley Nicpon, M., & Huser, L. (2005). Career goals and retention-related factors among college freshman. *Journal of Career Development, 32*(1), 16–30.

Hung, J. (2002). A career development course for academic credit: An outcome analysis. *The Canadian Journal of Career Development, 1*(1), 15–23.

Ipsos Reid Poll. (2007). *Given the chance to start over, most (71%) would get more professional career planning.* Toronto, ON. Canadian Education and Research Institute for Counselling. Retrieved from <http://www.ceric.ca/files/environics /Ipsos%20Reid-CERIC%20Factum%202007.pdf>.

Keeling, R. P., Wall, A., Underhile, R., & Dungy, G. J. (2008). *Assessment reconsidered: Institutional effectiveness for student success.* Washington, DC: National Association of Student Personnel Administrators.

Krumboltz, J. D. (2009). The happenstance learning theory. *Journal of Career Assessment, 17*(2), 135–154.

Lebold, I. A. T., Pullin, R. A., & Wilson, J. C. (1990). Cooperative education in Canada. *Journal of Co-operative Education and Internships, 26,* 7–13.

Roessler, R., Hennessey, M., & Rumrill, P. (2007). Strategies for improving career services for postsecondary students with disabilities: Results of a focus group study of key stakeholders. *Career Development for Exceptional Individuals, 30*(3), 158–170.

Sattler, P. (2011). Work-integrated learning in Ontario's postsecondary sector. Toronto, ON: Higher Education Quality Council of Ontario. Retrieved from <http://heqco.ca/SiteCollectionDocuments/WIL1E.pdf>.

Schissel, B., & Wotherspoon, T. (2003). *The legacy of school for Aboriginal people: Education, oppression and emancipation.* Don Mills, ON: Oxford University Press.

Schneider, M., & Dimito, A. (2010). Factors influencing the career and academic choices of lesbian, gay, bisexual and transgender people. *Journal of Homosexuality, 57,* 138–149.

Shea, R. (2010). Career and employment services. In D. Hardy-Cox & C. Strange (Eds.), *Achieving student success: Effective student services in Canadian higher education* (pp. 141–152). Montréal, QC: McGill-Queen's University Press.

Super, D. E. (1951). Vocational adjustment: Implementing a self-concept. *Occupations, 30,* 88–92.

Super, D. E. (1953). A theory of vocational development. *American Psychologist, 8,* 185–190.

Super, D. E. (1963). Self-concepts in vocational development. In D. E. Super (Ed.), *Career development: Self-concept theory* (pp. 1–16). New York, NY: College Entrance Examination Board.

Super, D. E., Savickas, M. L., & Super, C. M. (1996). The life-span, life-space approach to careers. In D. Brown, L. Brooks, & Associates (Eds.), *Career choice and development* (3rd ed., pp. 121–178). San Francisco, CA: Jossey-Bass.

Swanson, J. L., & Gore, P. A. (2000). Advances in vocational psychology theory and research. In S. D. Brown & R.W. Lent (Eds.), *Handbook of counselling psychology* (3rd ed., pp. 233–269). New York, NY: John Wiley.

Tinto, V. (1993). *Leaving college and rethinking the causes and cures of student attrition.* Chicago, IL: University of Chicago Press.

Watson, M. B. (2006). Voices off: Reconstructing career theory and practice for cultural diversity. *Australian Journal of Career Development, 15*(3), 47–53.

Yang, E., Wong, S. C., Hwang, M., & Heppner, M. J. (2002). Widening our global view: The development of career counselling services for international students. *Journal of Career Development, 28*(3), 203–213.

Young, R. A., Marshall, S. K., & Valach, L. (2007). Making career theories more culturally sensitive: Implications for counseling. *The Career Development Quarterly, 56*(1), 4–18.

Glossary

Career coaching is a relatively new and emerging form of career assistance and is often provided to motivate the student to navigate the practical complexities of their career journey.

Career counselling requires a master's degree in counselling or a closely related field to assist postsecondary students to assess their skills, values, and interests.

Careerism is the overwhelming desire or urge to advance one's own career or social status, usually at the expense of other personal interests or social growth.

Placement is the act of connecting students to employment opportunities. This could be part-time, summer, or full-time opportunities.

Service learning integrates community services activities with learning. Curricular service learning is to have community service as part of the course. Students apply the lessons of the classroom to the service activity, and bring back to the classroom reflection and experience. Co-curricular service learning is done in conjunction with a club or organization and is separate from a classroom.

Discussion and Activities

Discussion

Discussion Questions

1. Both young and older adults have a variety of educational options open to them once they enter a postsecondary institution. Choosing from the options available can be exciting and difficult. What types of educational information would you encourage a student to seek out when making scholastic choices? (e.g., factors to consider include the academic record of the individual, the ability of the student to finance their education, and the wishes of the student)
2. How can postsecondary institutions facilitate helping students integrate formal education with real-world experiential experiences prior to graduation?
3. What are some of the issues that confront career practitioners at the postsecondary institution as they plan programs for students?
4. Michael Huston and Sharon Crozier described a program created for postsecondary students to help them find their career passion (see Spotlight earlier in this chapter). In small groups, discuss your views and different feelings that arise when you read the following statement: "*Many postsecondary students are looking to find their passion, feeling that if they could figure out what it is, everything else would fall into place.*"

Personal Reflection

1. In your opinion, what type of financial and non-financial supports and barriers would impact a student's experience at the postsecondary level? Financial barriers include inadequate financial resources, or the need to work to pay for higher

education. Non-financial barriers include personal factors such as a lack of self-confidence and motivation, lower high school grades, lower levels of parental education and parental expectations, and institutional factors such as a lack of understanding of culture on campus.

2. What can postsecondary institutions do to build in more supports for students?
3. What would you hope to accomplish when working with postsecondary students, as a career practitioner?

Career Practitioner Role

1. What does experiential and informal learning mean? How does this impact mature students at the postsecondary level?
2. As a prospective career practitioner in postsecondary settings, what further information would you like to learn about to help develop your role?
3. At the postsecondary level, what types of postsecondary school-community partnerships would you like to see developed?
4. As a career practitioner in a postsecondary institution, what would you consider to be the key factors that impact the persistence and completion among under-represented learners? What possible barriers could exist for participation and completion of programs?

Activities

1. In small groups, create plans for a career workshop to address a specific student population. Ideas to consider for student groups include (but are not limited to): mature students, international students, Aboriginal students, students enrolled in professional degree programs who are preparing for entry to an internship, and a thesis completion support group for graduate students.

2. Movie Analysis: Students view the movie "Educating Rita" and consider the role of formal educational and informal or experiential learning and the impact it has on Rita as a learner. Discuss the following questions:

    (a) Describe Rita's self-concept and sense of identity, offering examples of how she sees herself and how she portrays herself to others.
    (b) Describe Rita's approach to conflict management, focusing on how she treats different people in different ways.
    (c) Is Rita's educational success worth the interpersonal costs that she incurs?
    (d) What does it mean to gain an "education" and to be "educated"?

3. Scenario: Position as Associate Director

Congratulations! You have studied hard and just graduated from a Canadian postsecondary institution. It has been a challenging educational journey, you have studied at both university and college, but you have survived, some might say thrived. During your time in school you have also spent time working and have now applied for a position as Associate Director of a postsecondary career centre in Atlantic Canada. Much to your surprise you have received an interview and are now preparing for the interview! They have sent you the questions in advance so that you can prepare.

Interviewer Questions:
1. Given the knowledge gleaned from your course in career development, what do you think are the critical components of a university career centre?
2. What methods would you use to deliver the critical themes within the career components highlighted above?
3. As the new associate director of career services and given your own experience in postsecondary studies, what do you think are the new challenges and opportunities ahead?

Resources and Readings

Resources

Websites

Canadian Association of Career Educators and Employers (CACEE) is a national non-profit partnership of employer recruiters and career services professionals whose mission is to provide authoritative information, advice, professional development opportunities and other services to employers, career services professionals, and students. <http://www.cacee.ca>.

Canadian Association for College and University Student Services (CACUSS) is a professional, bilingual association representing and serving staff in Student Affairs and Services in Canadian postsecondary institutions. <http://www.cacuss.ca>

Canadian Association for Co-operative Education (CAFCE) fosters and advances postsecondary co-operative education in Canada <http://www.cafce.ca>.

The Canadian Journal of Career Development (CJCD) <http://www.cjcdonline.ca>.

Frontline Partner with Youth Network (FPYN) <http://fpyn.ca/>.

Life-Role Development Group <http://www.life-role.com/>.

Services for Youth — Government of Canada <http://www.youth.gc.ca/eng/home.shtml>.

University of Victoria Career Services <http://www.careerservices.uvic.ca/>.

University of Waterloo Career Resources Manual <http://www.careerservices.uwaterloo.ca/>.

Resources

Assessment of Campus Career Centres <http://ceric.ca/careercentreevaluation/> *Career Centre Evaluation: A Practitioner Guide* is a customized online resource to help university career centres think about and design effective evaluation strategies. This resource looks at how five different career centres have tried to understand the components of evaluation and how they have developed tools to use in their settings.

This guide covers such topics as:

- choosing an evaluation framework and approach;
- scaling the approach to the needs of your centres;
- creating timelines and implementing evaluation activities;
- reporting and using evaluation results for quality improvement, influencing, and marketing.

Each career centre will have its own evaluation interests and priorities — by providing case studies of the experiences at several offices, along with a variety of tools and templates, this guide informs how evaluation may be adapted to the unique needs of your particular centre.

A Model for the Education and Training of Career Practitioners in Canada, CERIC. Gathers in one place a directory of programs, video of the framework, interactive PDF of the framework, and the journal article <http://www.ceric.ca/?q=en/node/155>.

National Occupational Classification 2011, Human Resources and Skills Development Canada <http://www.hrsdc.gc.ca/eng/jobs/lmi/noc/index.shtml#tab2>.

Portfolios: Don't Leave Home Without One <http://www.amby.com/kimeldorf/portfolio/p_mk.11.html>.

Supplementary Readings

Amundson, N. E., Borgen, W. A., Iaquinta, M., Butterfield, L. D., & Koert, E. (2010). Career decisions from the decider's perspective. *Career Development Quarterly, 58,* 336–351. Retrieved from <http://associationdatabase.com/aws/NCDA/pt/sp/cdquarterly>.

Burtnett, F. (2010). *Bound-for-career guidebook: A student guide to career exploration, decision making, and the job search.* Toronto, ON: Rowman and Littlefield.

Domene, J. F., Nee, J. J., Cavanaugh, A. K., McLelland, S., Stewart, B., Stephenson, M., Kauffman, B., Tse, C. K., & Young, R. A. (2012). Young adult couples transitioning to work: The intersection of career and relationship. *Journal of Vocational Behavior, 81*(1), 17–25. doi: 10.1016/j.jvb.2012.03.005

Greenhaus, J. H., Callanan, G. A., & Godshalk, V. M. (2010). *Career management.* Thousand Oaks, CA: Sage.

Grossman, K. W. (2012). *Technology job hunt handbook: Career management for technical professionals*. New York, NY: Apress.

Harrington, B. (2007). *Career management & work-life integration: Using self-assessment to navigate contemporary careers*. Los Angeles, CA: Sage.

Kaye, B. & Winkle-Giulioni, J. (2012). *Help them grow or watch them go: Career conversations employees want*. Williston, VT: Berrett-Koehler Publishers.

Kroth, M. S. (2009). *Career development basics*. Alexandria, VA: ASTD Press.

Kummerow, J. M. (2000). *New directions in career planning and the workplace: Practical strategies for career management professionals*. Palo Alto, CA: Davies-Black.

Lepa, B. & Boris, K. (2012). Graduates beliefs about career management. *Indusrija, 40*(2), 175–187. doi: 005. 966:37.048.3

Osoian, C., Zaharie, M., & Miron, A. (2011). Career management tools: Curriculum vitae design. *Managerial Challenges of the Contemporary Society, 2*, 210–213.

Richardson, M. (2009). Another way to think about the work we do: Counselling for work and relationship. *International Journal for Educational and Vocational Guidance, 9*, 75–84. doi: 10.1007/s10775-009-9154-3

Savickas, M. L., Nota, L., Rossier, J., Dauwalder, J., Duarte, M. E., Guichard, J., et al. (2009). Life designing: A paradigm for career construction in the 21st century. *Journal of Vocational Behavior, 75*(3), 239–250. doi: 10.1016/j.jvb.2009.04.004

Young, R. A., Valach, L., Marshall, S. K., Domene, J. F., Graham, M. D., & Zaidman-Zait, A. (2010). *Transition to adulthood: Action, projects and counseling*. New York, NY: Springer.

sixteen

Lifelong Career Management

SANDRA BOYD
KIM SPURGEON
Knightsbridge

PRE-READING QUESTIONS

1. Today's world of work is unrecognizable from the workplace of only a few years ago. What changes can you identify and what is the impact of those changes on employees?
2. What strategies and approaches can career practitioners use with clients to help them better manage their careers?

Introduction and Learning Objectives

Several factors have come together over the past decade to impact how we manage our careers. Canadian organizations are grappling with changing workforce demographics, increasing workforce diversity, new technologies, and the creation of **knowledge workers** (Florida, 2002). Besides the threat of outsourcing of jobs, **globalization** has also brought global labour markets, global collaborations, globally distributed work teams, and the global competition for talent. Increasingly workers are faced with changes to employment that are beyond their individual control. However, career development practitioners suggest that individuals can and ought to manage their lives and work to stay employable.

In this era, careers may involve employment in different types of work and with different employers. Career advancement has become characterized by job enrichment instead of promotions. Today, individuals are responsible for their own careers, as opposed to relying on the organizations where they work. As part of this responsibility, individuals are advised to assess their strengths and weaknesses and to identify employment trends in relation to jobs available and the employment outlook for that field. In other words, individuals need to prepare themselves with skills and knowledge for current and future career moves. Career management is really a lifelong career-planning process that involves choosing and setting personal goals, and formulating strategies for achieving them. It requires an analysis of changes in the job environment and an ability to adapt to meet the changing needs of organizations. Given the organizational changes that have occurred in recent years (downsizing, decentralization, cost-reduction, IT innovation, and per-formance-related measurement — to name a few), a positive framework is required for approaching the future.

In this chapter you will learn five simple steps to managing your career over a lifetime, regardless of the ups and downs of the corporate world. The focus is on understanding that one's marketability is as important as employability. This chapter is written in a way to directly engage you, the reader, in examining and exploring aspects of managing your own career. Career practitioners are encouraged to answer questions and take part in activities as if they themselves were the client. Practitioners need to have developed career management skills before they are able to instill those skills in others.

After reading this chapter, you should be able to:

1. Understand the career partnership approach.
2. Apply the five steps to managing one's career.
3. Put into practice career management strategies.

Values and Beliefs About Work

In this section two vignettes will be used to show how our beliefs and values influence our understanding of career success. The vignettes provide examples of how today's marketplace requires workers to be fluid and adaptable. Traditional ideas of work-life balance, retirement at age 65, or career movement as upward are being challenged.

Vignette 1: Being Laid Off

Sue is a first-generation Canadian of Asian heritage. Her parents told her that it was important for her to have a university education as it was the key to success and job security. "My father also told me, if you have a degree you will always have a job. I did all the right things — went to university for business, found a job with a large company, and stayed. I received five promotions in 10 years. To my family I was a huge success. However, I was given my walking papers and a package three weeks after celebrating my 10th anniversary and nine months after my most recent promotion. The department was being eliminated and they did not have another position for me. My father asked me what I did wrong.

Sue is no different than many employees. Our beliefs and values are formed by the advice and guidance that adults of influence pass on to us. Some of us are told education is the key for success; others are told to work for a large company, the government or a bank, and the expected result is a job for life. However, in today's very volatile marketplace of new businesses, **downsizing**, globalization, and much more, there is no one ingredient for success. You need to apply a number of strategies and approaches to ensure your marketability. You are the only person who can secure lifetime employment.

❖ *Stop and Reflect*
Is it realistic for Sue to believe that because she received her degree in 2004 she is owed a position for life?

- What was the first piece of advice your parents/adults gave you about working?
- Do you know if your beliefs are in line with the expectations of the workplace?
- Are your beliefs relevant? What challenges will they potentially create for your career in the future?

The true test of your belief and if it still holds up in today's workplace is to ask "would you give this advice to the next generation?"

Careers — Then

Through most of the 1900s, career direction was ultimately determined by the corporation you worked for. Organizations were rigidly structured and provided the individual very little flexibility. The following are aspects of this rigid structure:

- traditional hierarchy of management levels;
- well-defined paths for promotion;
- people tend to stay in the same job (or position), doing the same work, for a very long time;
- emphasis is on work, with little regard for a work-life balance;

- narrow definition of success;
- view that the company will look after the careers of its employees;
- expectation that the employee will retire at a set date.

For some people, the traditional organization affords clear goals for advancement and promotion. However, for many, career success is no longer defined this way.

Defining Your Success

❖ Stop and Reflect

What is your definition of success? Is it money, the position, or being recognized for a job well done?

It is important to take the time to evaluate and reflect on your definition of success. You will need to adjust your definition as circumstances in your life change (marriage, children, taking care of aging parents, being downsized, etc.). What factors you should consider when choosing a career will be dependent on your definition of success.

Vignette 2: Defining Success

Ahalya took the time to redefine success during a period of transition and was shocked to find out that the reason she was currently feeling like a failure at work had nothing to do with her performance and everything to do with how she was defining job success. Ahalya had been a star performer from the time she graduated. Her managers would always rate her at an "exceeds expectations" level in her job. However, during the past two years she was given a "meets expectations" rating by her manager. This evaluation was devastating to her. After attending a career-coaching session she realized she needed to rethink her expectations of performance and success for this period of her life.

Her father had been diagnosed with dementia and her mother was critically ill. Her ability to perform at the previous level was not possible with the emotional and physical toll both illnesses were taking on her life, not to mention the fact that she now spent a good deal of time in hospitals. She could no longer put in the hours nor did she have the time to participate in new strategic-initiative projects at her company. When she came to terms with adjusting her expectations and what success looked like in her life at the present time, she was able to feel proud of how she had handled both her work and her personal life.

❖ Stop and Reflect

Take the time to write down what your definition of success is today and ensure that you re-evaluate every two to three years or if your life circumstances change.

Careers — Now

In today's marketplace, careers are fluid and continuously changing. We no longer have to climb the ladder or stay put in one spot in an organization. The choices can be endless to match the many ages and stages of our lives. This means as employees, we are more empowered today than at any time in the history of the corporate workplace. We need to understand how to navigate this new world of work and learn to align and integrate our careers and work life with our personal life so that we can feel successful in both.

Career Fluidity

Being fluid in your career is like driving a car: You look in the rear-view mirror to see where you've been, and you look ahead to see where you are going. Career fluidity involves being adaptable to the changes and realities of the workplace. This is illustrated in Figure 1, Career Fluidity, below.

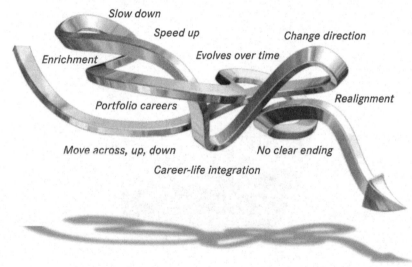

Figure 1: Career Fluidity — Copyright © Knightsbridge.

- Careers today are all about being fluid (or adaptable) in the face of rapidly changing environments, matrix organization structures where employees report across departments or functions, flatter hierarchies, and global reach. People continue to "evolve" their careers by moving up in an organization, across, and even down. A successful career doesn't mean the only option is upward. People may choose a lateral or junior role to get experience in new areas of a business.

- It's not about work-life balance but career-life integration.
- People don't have to retire at age 65; they may continue to work or even make career changes. We are seeing the evolution of portfolio careers and job seekers working multiple part-time jobs.
- Career direction and options are endless; we set our own direction.

Three-Way Partnership (Knightsbridge Model)

You are not on your own. When it comes to your career journey, companies do want to help their employees. Companies that invest in career management improve

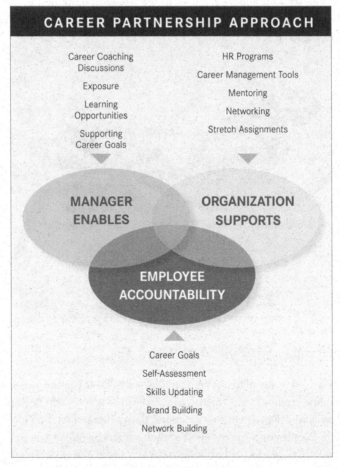

Figure 2: Knightsbridge Model. Copyright © Knightsbridge.

their employee retention and engagement rates. In a world where companies are competing for key talent on a global level, it is in their best interest to ensure that employees are supported in navigating the complexity of corporations both big and small. The benefits of career management go beyond improving engagement and retention for businesses. In a Knightsbridge career management survey done in 2009, 83% of respondents agreed that career management plays a critical role in achieving the organization's business objectives. Supporting employees in managing their careers is one way for an organization to ensure that employees are engaged.

Many companies are adapting the career partnership approach as shown in Figure 2.

In a career partnership approach (Knightsbridge, 2013a), three different factors come together to form a holistic and integrated approach to career management: (1) manager-enabled supports, (2) organization supports, and (3) employee account-ability. Managers, by providing learning opportunities and supporting career goals, help to empower their employees and further their career development. The organization, for its part, has a duty to help develop employees' career-management skills through human resources programs, mentoring, and networking. Lastly, the employees themselves must be accountable for their own development through self-assessment, skills updating, and setting career goals. When these three work together, employees become more engaged and retention improves.

Vignette 3: Being Engaged

Alba has worked as an engineer with her company for over five years and is part of Generation Y. In those five years, she has been promoted on two occasions, had the opportunity to work on key projects with senior executives, and was chosen to co-lead a team to develop an innovative approach to recruiting university students with the vice president of Human Resources. She attributes her early success to her attitude and ability to reach out across the company to key stakeholders to let them know of her interest in being mentored and having an opportunity to work with them. Alba explains the cost has been longer hours than many of her workers are willing to invest. Alba knows this will have to change when she and her husband have their first child. "My ability to work these crazy hours will change, but I want everyone around me to know that I am passionate about my work and that will not change because I have a child," she says. Alba expects that her employer will be flexible with work arrangements by allowing her to work from her home office. Her strategy is working and her employer sees her as a highly engaged employee.

Alba is the perfect example of an employee taking an active role in her career to ensure she is positioning herself as a person who is fully engaged in her work and the company. Alba is also taking a strategic approach to the future by ensuring she makes an impact on colleagues and senior management before she goes into the next stage of her life.

Many organizations seek to create **organization-manager-employee partnerships** to promote career ownership and accountability. In the future, employees will be encouraged to take charge of their career, with the manager and the organization providing the support and resources. It is no longer acceptable for employees to sit back and wait for the tap on their shoulder to join a team, seek out a promotion, or be asked if they want mentoring or training.

Employers must generate a culture of meaningful career development, stressing that growth can come from **horizontal or lateral movement, stretch assignments**, mentoring programs and training.

Employees need to show up and be present in their work and ask how they can contribute to the success of the company. Employees need to take the time to understand the vision and strategy of the company and work to ensure they are contributing to corporate and department business goals. In turn, the company will help employees with personal growth and career success. Career success today is partly defined by "**discretionary effort**" and going the extra mile to contribute to the business.

A Place for Quality of Life in Career Development
by Geoff Peruniak

Quality of life is the ongoing creation of an enduring state of well-being over the realms of a person's life experience and lifetime (Peruniak, 2010). Quality of life is heavily influenced by our structures of belief that originate from our sociocultural heritage; our immediate reference groups including family and community; and from our class, gender, and race. The career practitioner helps clients tune into their beliefs, acknowledge the ones that are helpful, and change the ones that are dysfunctional. This puts the onus on the practitioner to tune into their own beliefs first.

Five Steps to Managing Your Career

The following five steps to managing your career will help you strategize a vision for your career.

MANAGING YOUR CAREER
1. Gain insight about yourself
2. Identify your value proposition — how your strengths can add value to the organization.
3. Develop your "brand" — a vision that will enhance your marketability in the workplace.
4. Build your network.
5. Share your goals.

Table 2: Managing Your Career. Copyright © Knightsbridge.

By the end of this section you will be equipped with a "toolbox" of simple and practical strategies to take charge of your career.

Step 1: Gain Insight

Opening Story

Bruce has been working as a marketing manager for a tier-1 consumer-packaged-goods company for the last five years. He has performed his job effectively but has found it to be a struggle and not very stimulating. He really likes the company but doesn't know what other jobs are available. He knows he has the skills and the experience to do the job, but he no longer looks forward to going to work. During a career conversation with his manager, it became apparent that Bruce didn't really know what he likes to do in terms of work. He wasn't able to articulate his interests and skills and what factors were important in a job. His manager asked him some great questions to which he was unable to provide answers. Bruce came to the conclusion that he would like a new position but needed to determine what was important to him in terms of work, values, and interests. Because Bruce did not know where to start, a friend suggested he talk to a career coach to begin the process of assessing his skills, interests, and abilities to determine the nature of his next job.

Assess and Evaluate

Successful career management is founded on truly knowing yourself. The first step is to assess and evaluate yourself fully. Be realistic in analyzing and reviewing: (a) your interests, (b) motivators, (c) accomplishments, (d) strengths, (e) development gaps, and (f) hard and soft skills. This is an introspective look at what interests and motivates you, the strengths you bring to your work, your limitations or development needs, your career accomplishments, and your future goals.

Depending on your job or your profession, you will need to ensure that both your **hard and soft skills** are in demand and of value to the organization and/or marketplace. Taking the time to identify the skills for which companies in your industry are recruiting is one way of understanding the areas where you may need to invest time and/or money. This is a journey that never stops, even when you finish school or master skills. You will always have to re-evaluate to ensure that your skills are up-to-date and in demand. You will have to take the time to understand not only what the company you work for values, but what the job market considers as valuable. On an ongoing basis, you should speak to recruiters and review job boards. If you are currently working, take time to learn about your company's competitors — what type of skills and attributes do they require from their employees?

Four key methods will help you gain the insight about yourself needed to manage your career: (a) conduct self-assessments; (b) get feedback from teachers, friends, work colleagues, and parents; (c) draw on past performance reviews; and (d) keep a journal of your accomplishments.

You should be revisiting these methods at least once a year and also during times of transition within the company or in the marketplace, or during times you do not feel aligned with your work. If the organizational structure of the company changes and you find yourself reporting to a new manager, you will have an opportunity to review your skills and attributes based on what the new boss determines is needed for the business. Business restructuring, mergers, and acquisitions will also give you the opportunity to research what the new expectations are for employees. The ever-changing workplace (new technologies and processes, emerging markets and businesses) requires that you keep your skills and motivators in line with these shifting expectations. During times when you feel you are not aligned to your work, you need to reconnect with what is important to you and what drives and inspires you.

Keep an Accomplishment Journal

Every year just before her evaluation with her manager, Shawn would scramble to recall what it was she had been working so hard on, what projects she had completed, and what were her major accomplishments. "I would try to remember all this the night before I had my yearly evaluation. I would always ask myself how I could be working so hard and not remember what I was doing and what the result of it was to the company and my manager. At one point my manager became irritated with me and tried to explain the importance of being able to state my contributions to the organization. My explanation was I had been working so hard I did not have time to think about what I had accomplished over the last year. The reality check came when my manager asked if I was applying for the customer service manager position and, if so, what accomplishments I would mention during the interview. He was also quick to point out the other person who wanted the promotion was an outstanding self-promoter and could easily and effortlessly articulate all he had accomplished for the business in the last year. That was the motivation I needed to start documenting my accomplishments."

In an accomplishment journal you should record and measure the following on a regular basis: (a) specific accomplishments, (b) important projects, (c) notable recognition or examples where you exceeded expectations, and (d) particular activities outside your job description.

Questions to Help Identify Accomplishments
Did you:

- Identify a problem in your department or company that had been over-looked?
- Help to improve productivity?
- Take the initiative to improve something or respond to an immediate need?
- Solve a particularly difficult customer problem or identify a new need?
- Save your department or company money?

- Implement or improve a new system or procedure in your department or company?
- Present any new ideas that were put into effect?
- Undertake an assignment or project that was not part of your job, just because you were intrigued by the problem?

When you are composing your accomplishment journal, it is important to have old résumés, performance reviews, and job descriptions around you. Ask yourself the questions above as a starting point and remember to think of accomplishments from the viewpoint of the impact they had on you or other individuals, teams, the organization and/or the customer.

❖ Challenge Action Result (CAR) Exercise

Use the CAR formula of Challenge, Action, and Result to help you gather all the information you can about the problem. What was the challenge or problem; what action did you take to resolve it; and what was the result of your action?

Story: The Million-Dollar Customer

Challenge: Mikyla was a sales representative for a large retailer. Her team was in jeopardy of losing a million-dollar account. The customer said he was unhappy with how his firm was being treated and threatened to take his business elsewhere.

Action: As the junior person on the account team, Mikyla didn't think she would have much influence with the customer but she did know him and had established some rapport. Mikyla asked to meet with him. Her goal was to truly understand the customer's concerns. In their meeting, the customer told her that he was disappointed at how his firm was being pressured to pay an invoice, especially considering the amount of business they provided to the retailer. Mikyla took the time to explain how important his firm's account was to her company and they arrived at a win-win solution for the payment of outstanding invoices.

Result: The customer agreed to stay with her company and acknowledged that he was looking for more personal attention and someone who would listen to their concerns. In the end, this customer stayed with their organization and Mikyla became the account lead for this million-dollar account.

Step 2: Express Your Value Proposition

Opening Story

When Mandeep started his search for his first full-time position after finishing university, he was at a loss as to what his **value proposition** was to the job market. "I could not think of anything that I had done that would be a significant benefit to a full-time position in the

YOUR VALUE PROPOSITION

Circle your level of agreement with each of the statements from strongly disagree (1) to strongly agree (5). Add the circled items in the columns. Determine your total score and use the evaluation guide to interpret.

Legend: 1 = strongly disagree; 2 = agree; 3 = neutral; 4 = agree; 5 = strongly agree.

I know what values are most important to me.	1	2	3	4	5
I am clear on what tasks/projects I find most and least interesting.	1	2	3	4	5
I can clearly articulate examples to support my three greatest strengths.	1	2	3	4	5
I would feel prepared to sell myself at a job interview tomorrow.	1	2	3	4	5
I could confidently articulate my greatest accomplishments over the last year with my manager at a performance review.	1	2	3	4	5
I understand what has contributed to my career successes and failures in the past.	1	2	3	4	5
I am aware of what my areas of development are.	1	2	3	4	5
I know what kind of experiences or exposure I need to gain in order to grow in my career.	1	2	3	4	5
I regularly seek feedback from others to ensure my self-perceptions are in line with how others see me.	1	2	3	4	5
I keep track of my accomplishments on an ongoing basis.	1	2	3	4	5
Column Totals					
Total of Columns					

Evaluate Your Total Score

40–50: It looks like you have a solid understanding of your work environment and how you can fit within it to add your value. Keep your eye on the horizon to ensure you maintain that understanding.

25–39: It looks like you have given your value proposition some consideration but could benefit from making sure you're crystal clear on what you have to offer. Review your lowest-ranked responses to prioritize which items to action plan.

10–24: It looks like you're not quite ready to express your value. You may wish to do some more assessment work in order to gain further insights and also conduct research with others who know you so that you can express your value more clearly.

Tip: Ask yourself – what are the top three areas that require focus and improvement?

Table 3: Your Value Proposition. Copyright © Knightsbridge.

financial or banking industries. I had only done some unrelated part-time jobs, two student co-ops, and volunteer work for various organizations." With the help of his career advisor, Mandeep became aware that he did indeed have a value proposition. Over the last five years he had worked part time in a well-known retail store serving customers, handling cash, and organizing employee schedules. Acting as interim manager Mandeep had also volunteered at a number of charities. At one, he organized, with his fellow students, a two-week trip to Haiti to help build houses. Mandeep headed up the excursion, managed a budget of $30,000, and was also in charge of the fundraising committee. He completed two co-ops at a small brokerage firm that required him to review corporate stock trends and create weekly update reports for stockbrokers. Mandeep demonstrated a number of skills and attributes, including leadership, team work, budgeting, customer service, organizing, and analyzing information. Mandeep was astonished at all he had accomplished. This new awareness helped him feel confident in his ability to articulate his value proposition.

Know Your Value-Add

How well do you know your value proposition? Use Table 3 to rate your value proposition.

In articulating your value proposition, there are two key areas to consider: You need to understand your interests, skills, and knowledge, and you need to recognize customer, organizational, and team needs. Know how you personally contribute to team and department goals as well as how proficient you are at meeting customer expectations.

Once you understand yourself, look at your external environment. Research the current and future talent needs of the job market. What talent do companies need right now? What does the future look like in the corporate world? What will managers expect from employees?

You will also have to think of goals of the team and of the organization. What are the organization's goals, strategies, and vision? What are the organization's current challenges in the marketplace?

SWOT Exercise

SWOT Analysis (Strengths, Weaknesses, Opportunities, and Threats) is a tool that organizations use to concisely analyze the critical factors in their current business environment. Doing your own personal SWOT analysis (see Table 4) will give you insight into who you are, how you operate, what is standing in your way, and where you can grow. Keeping your SWOT analysis up to date will help you:

1. Recognize the areas where you excel.
2. Reveal gaps in your skills or knowledge.
3. Uncover opportunities to step up your game.
4. Anticipate threats to your career success.

	STRENGTHS	WEAKNESSES
Internal	What are you particularly good at? • differentiated skills • distinct knowledge • unique perspective • valuable relationships What would others say about your strengths?	What are the areas where you most need to improve or grow? What are the most important skill gaps you want to fill? What would others say about your weaknesses?
	OPPORTUNITIES	THREATS
External	How could you leverage your strengths better? Where can you make a difference in our organization? What opportunities await someone with your skills? What is going on in the economy that might require skills for future of a business?	What poses a risk to your own career development? What threats exist either internally or externally to your organization? How do they impact your career?

Table 4: SWOT Analysis.

Step 3: Develop Your Brand

Opening Story

Alex had been working for a large financial institution for three years as a human resources consultant. This was her first position after completing her master's degree and she was determined to be a rising star. Everything was going well until the day her manager gave her some very devastating feedback during a meeting. "My manager explained that I was being perceived as 'high maintenance' by the senior HR team and business leaders we support. It was the last thing I expected to hear and not the brand I wanted to convey." Her manager explained that she was very pleased with Alex's quality of work, attitude, critical thinking, decision making, and project co-ordination. The feedback and perception of high maintenance came from the simple fact that when she was given a project by senior managers in her client group, Alex would constantly check in with the managers, asking questions, probing for additional detail on what to do and how to do it. The result was that she was seen as a person who could not make decisions on her own, needed a large amount of hand holding, and was not confident in her abilities to manage the project. One manager explained that for the amount of time she spent guiding Alex, giving her feedback on every little decision and answering daily questions, she could have handled *the project on her own. Alex was also told by her manager that one individual said she would not use Alex again as it was too much work to have her manage a project.*

Alex thought that by being this detailed, asking questions and checking in with the managers daily, she was being diligent. Alex worked with her manager to shift how people perceived her and change her approach to managing projects. She was now on her way to again being regarded as a high-potential employee at her company.

Brand Discussion

Brands are designed to communicate a message: They are a critical component of marketing, and affect how clients or customers perceive a product or service. Branding should convey ideas of value, quality, and overall reliability of the organization and its products. The development of a brand is an important part of the marketing process and becomes central in promoting a consistent message to clients and customers about the nature of an organization or product. A brand is a "name, term, sign, symbol or design, or a combination of them intended to identify the goods and services of one seller or group of sellers and to differentiate them from those of other sellers" (Rowley, 2006, p. 418). To impart this powerful message, brands consist of a shorthand expression in the form of a name, term, design, and/or symbol that fully represents the organization's personality, image, core competencies, and characteristics. A brand, ultimately, is a promise to the customer, facilitating trust and maintaining a loyal customer base. A successful brand should:

- deliver the message clearly,
- confirm your credibility,
- connect to your market,
- motivate the buyer,
- create user loyalty.

Having a Personal Brand Is Not Optional

The following are qualities that are crucial to the success of your "brand" or reputation regardless of the level of position or the type of profession you choose.

- **Credentials** are your "résumé" and include your education and background experiences. You can strategically build your credentials to prepare you for opportunities. Credentials are also about your skills and competencies. Do people perceive you as having the right skills to do what you're doing?
- **Track record,** or your record of past successes, contributes to your credibility. Ask yourself if you are seen as a good risk. Remember that not everyone will be familiar with your track record, especially as you move within a company or pursue a position with a new company. Look for

opportunities to make your wins more visible to your audience. Do you have a reputation for following through on assignments?

- *Being authentic* is revealed in what you say and what you do. It means speaking truthfully, accepting failure, apologizing when mistakes are made, and behaving ethically. People respond to authenticity in others with more openness because they know what they can expect from them, and know they can trust them.
- *Demonstrating respect* involves hearing others' perspectives, really listening, and adapting based on what you hear.
- *Earning trust* is about being credible to others. There are different levels of trust: trust that you will do your job effectively; trust that you will not mislead others; trust that your motives are genuine; and trust that you will not hurt others. Trust is an outcome of authenticity.
- *Building relationships* means developing rapport with others. As you advance in an organization, your relationships with your colleagues and peers become increasingly important as you work more with other people to complete projects rather than on your own. The more relationships you can build within your organization, the more likely you will have people who will help you achieve your goals.

Brand Exercise

Credibility takes time to establish. You build credibility through what you do day-to-day and through your attitude. Arriving at work late frequently will have a negative effect on credibility. Being on time for work and meetings will demonstrate that you are reliable. Consider how each of the following activities or attitudes can impact how your supervisor and co-workers will view you.

- your initiative,
- your ability to work (collaborate) with others,
- what you say and how you say it,
- productivity,
- flexibility,
- your thoroughness,
- your responsiveness,
- participation in meetings,
- how you present yourself,
- openness to new ideas.

Define Your Brand

We all have a personal brand, whether we are aware of it or not, of who we are and what we are known for. To make sure the right people know the right things about you, it's important to think about, manage, and clearly articulate your brand. It may be time to consider re-branding yourself if you want to be known for something new.

- Who are you? Your personality, style, values, interests?

- Who is your target audience? Who values your expertise? What do they need from you?
- What is your key service offering? What expertise do you provide? What unique perspective or approach do you offer?
- What makes you unique?

❖ *Stop and Reflect*
1. What are you known for?
2. What do you want to be known for?
3. What is your vision for yourself?

Step 4: Build Your Network

The currency of real networking is not greed but generosity.
— Keith Ferrazzi

Opening Story

Todd graduated in 2010 with a college diploma in computer technology and has a solid two years of work experience with an insurance company in IT. His goal was to become an IT consultant with a professional-services firm. After six months of researching the top three companies in the consulting field, watching for new postings on the job boards, and applying to recruiters, he was getting nowhere. "I spoke to one recruiter and she advised me to start networking with people I know and go on LinkedIn to connect with people who worked at the companies I targeted. I started with LinkedIn and found two people I knew working for these companies. One was a person I went to high school with and the other was a woman in my mom's book club. When I reached out to them they agreed to help me. I was not comfortable with contacting people I didn't know; however, one night when I was out with friends for dinner I told everyone at the table that I was looking for a job and I named the three companies I was interested in working for. A friend's boyfriend told me his sister worked in the human resources department of one of the companies. He provided an introduction to his sister. A week later I had an interview and within two months I started my new position."

Networking Is About Investing in Future Possibilities

Networking is the key to success wherever you are. This is a skill in which you need to invest. That may mean attending workshops or reading books to acquire the proper tools to build a network of contacts. Many books, articles, recruiters, and human resources professionals will tell you that over 60% of jobs come through making contacts. Social networking sites like LinkedIn and Facebook are very helpful, but you also need to be able to meet and talk with people face-to-face and over the phone. By making contacts you are informed of possibilities and you develop connections as you move from one position to the next in a company. Generally networks can contribute to building your professional knowledge. In a company, interacting with others can help you to navigate complex organizational structures to acquire resources for projects and information. It is important to develop a style and comfort level that suits you. This can be done by gaining as much information and knowledge on networking as possible so that you can learn this valuable skill set.

❖ *Stop and Reflect*
1. When you think of networking, how you do feel?
2. What do you see as the benefits of networking?
3. What do you see as the negatives to networking?

Defining Networking
Many networking concerns come from a misconception of what networking is and isn't. Networking is building relationships and involves a very simple process:

Conversations > Information > Opportunities

Networking is developing and maintaining a line of communication with people you know, or would like to know, for the purpose of getting and sharing information for mutual benefit. Be mindful that different people can help in different ways — don't make assumptions.

Networking is not ...	**Networking is ...**
• manipulative,	• planned,
• "schmoozing,"	• purposeful,
• unplanned,	• ongoing,
• asking for a job!	• reciprocal.

Assess: How Strong Is Your Network?
In order to assess the strength of your network, you need to consider diversity, weak ties, hubs, and bridges (Hansen, 2009).

Your network should be diverse and include people of different skills and expertise, in various geographical locations, and in varied business units/levels. Rather than aiming for a massive network, focus on building an efficient one. This requires knowing people with different skills and viewpoints. They should be different from you, of course, but also different from one another.

Build *weak* ties, not strong ones. This might seem counterintuitive. After all, wouldn't your closest friends — your strongest ties — help you the most? But remember, strong ties are the people you already know well and talk to frequently. A strong tie is probably someone who knows many of the same people you do, whereas a weak tie forms a bridge to a new people who can provide you with new information. To keep a weak tie, you only need to contact them a couple of times a month.

When facing a problem at work, most of us will ask a close contact for help. Because we tend to befriend people at our own level, our closest contacts are unlikely to know more than we do. Instead, identify the *hubs* or those people who are already great organizational networkers and ask them to connect you to someone who knows more. Hubs tend to be long-tenured people who've worked on a variety of teams and projects.

Lastly, seek out *bridges* by finding those who seem to know everyone — they will often know someone who can help you.

How Strong is Your Network?
Rate the state of your current network using Table 5.

Networking Tips
1. Go to work events and challenge yourself to meet new people.
2. Get to know the "influencers" in your company/association/alumni.
3. Join relevant organizations and gain access to their membership.
4. Establish/maintain your online profiles.
5. Attend and/or speak at conferences and seminars.
6. Volunteer within your professional or personal community.
7. Record the names of everyone you know and take the time to keep in touch
8. Join networking groups.
9. Become a member of industry associations, business networking groups, rotary clubs, school alumni, et cetera.
10. Keep in touch with people you have previously worked with (many companies have "former employee alumni").
11. Help people along the way. The individual who is great at networking is always willing to give out more information than they will ever receive.

The Eight Deadly Sins of Networking (Messmer, 1999)
1. Making promises you know you are incapable of keeping.
2. Making promises you're capable of keeping but failing to keep them.
3. Having a hidden agenda. For example, you call someone and announce you have a question you want answered when what you really want is a favour.
4. Using someone's name as a door opener without first clearing it with the person whose name you are using.
5. Not being considerate — that is not taking into account when you ask someone for help how difficult it may be for them to provide that help and being resentful when they don't respond quickly enough.
6. Discussing business at inappropriate times, such as at a wedding or sports event

HOW STRONG IS YOUR NETWORK?

Circle your level of agreement with each of the statements below using the following key:

Legend: 1 = strongly disagree; 2 = agree; 3 = neutral; 4 = agree; 5 = strongly agree.

CAN YOU SAY?		SCORE			
Diversity					
I have many different types of connections in my network with:					
✓ Different skills/areas of expertise.	1	2	3	4	5
✓ Access to different technologies.	1	2	3	4	5
✓ Different geographies.	1	2	3	4	5
✓ Different business units.	1	2	3	4	5
✓ Different organizational levels.	1	2	3	4	5
I regularly reach out to people outside of my group to diversify my network.	1	2	3	4	5
Weak Ties					
I have many people in my network that I would describe as "acquaintances."	1	2	3	4	5
I periodically reach out to these connections in order to sustain the tie (through a quick email or by forwarding an article of interest, just to name a few examples).	1	2	3	4	5
I have hubs within my network who seem to know everyone and everything.	1	2	3	4	5
I give back to these people periodically.	1	2	3	4	5
I have many bridges within my network.	1	2	3	4	5
I give back to these people periodically.	1	2	3	4	5
Column Totals					
Total of Columns					

Evaluate Your Total Score

What are the top three areas that require focus and improvement?

1. _____

2. _____

3. _____

See the previous page for networking tips to support your actions.

Table 5: How Strong is Your Network? Copyright © Knightsbridge.

where the other person is doing his best to forget about business.

7.   Not showing your appreciation when someone has done you a favour.

8.   Putting persistent pressure on people who've agreed to help you.

Step 5: Share Goals

Opening Story

At 26, Rochelle was determined to be a success at the pharmaceutical firm where she has been working for the last 5 years. Rochelle started in finance, then moved to marketing and for the last year has been in administration. In the last 3 months, she had applied for two positions and had been turned down for both. After the second, she requested a meeting with the human resources manager and asked her for feedback. It was explained that both managers who interviewed her felt she lacked clarity in her career path and had no real goals. "I was told that I left the impression that I just wanted to jump from job to job without any specific goal and was not clear about the reason. Upon reflection, I came to the conclusion that I had not linked my career path with my skills, passion, or readiness for movement. I felt that if I was not happy or challenged it must be time to move, and if I was moving from job to job I would appear successful. Instead, I created confusion for myself and everyone else." Rochelle made the decision to sit down to determine her career goals and aspirations and then share this with her manager before making her next move. Her manager was able to help her gain insight into what action steps she needed to take before she made her next move.

You are now ready to set career goals. Begin this process by first thinking through what you would like next at this stage of your career (e.g., deciding on a career, finding a position, promotion, lateral move, enrichment, support, or new direction) and then ask yourself these key questions:

- What is the next logical upward move?
- What are some lateral or cross-functional moves?
- How can I enrich my current role?
- Where can I get mentoring, training, or assignments that would stretch me more in my area of interest?
- What would be a new career path?

For each possibility, ask yourself …

- Am I ready? If not, when will I be?
- What are the skills, knowledge, or experience required to make me ready?
- What are the benefits of doing this? What are the obstacles, risks, or tradeoffs?

Recall your strengths and opportunities you identified in steps 1 and 2 — gain insight and express value. Consider the different career opportunities available to you. Begin to focus your thinking on how you could leverage your strengths to deliver greater value and achieve new levels of professional satisfaction in the future. Identify the gap between where you are today and your image of your future. Focus your thinking on a few priorities that are of highest impact for you and the organization.

Set SMART Goals

As you set short- and long-term career goals, review in light of SMART goals and activities to evaluate whether you are achieving them. The acronym SMART stands for:

S = Specific
M = Measureable
A = Achievable
R = Relevant
T = Time-bound

Sharing Your Goals

You will be more successful in your career goals if you enlist the support of those around you — friends, colleagues, and leaders can help you here, so you need to be sure to:

1. Frame the conversation.
2. Discuss current role or position in your career journey.
3. Share career goals.
4. Ask for feedback and support.
5. Determine next steps.
6. And lastly, demonstrate to others how you plan to help yourself.

Be Prepared for Questions From Your Manager

The role of your manager or mentor is to have constructive career-coaching conversations with you. Expect your mentor to ask questions to help you move forward towards your goals. Before meeting consider how you will answer some of these common questions, so that you can make the most out of your manager's time. Being prepared will also demonstrate your commitment towards achieving your goals.

- What are your career goals?
- Where do you see yourself in 5 years?
- What interests you in this position?

- What strengths would you bring to the position?
- How could you build on your existing strengths?
- How could I assist you in the next 6–12 months to gain the additional experience you require for this position?
- What do you see as potential roadblocks to achieving your goal?

❖ *Stop and Reflect*
Action Plan for Managing Your Career

Because acting on your career goals is critical to achieving them, we've developed a template (Table 6) to help you take action to strategically manage your career. You may want to go back to those ideas you wrote down earlier, and write down one SMART goal for each step in the five-step process.

WHAT ARE YOU DOING TO:	ACTION STEP	TIMEFRAME	RESOURCES NEEDED
1. Gain Insight			
2. Express Value			
3. Develop Brand			
4. Build Network			
5. Share Goals			

Table 6: Action Plan Form. Copyright © Knightsbridge.

Summary

In a world of unprecedented change, career development has become a process of managing, learning, training, and working throughout the lifespan. The topics covered in this chapter provide strategies for taking an active and purposeful approach to one's career.

References

Florida, R. (2002). *The rise of the creative class*. New York, NY: Basic Books.

Hansen, M. (2009). *Collaboration: How leaders avoid the traps, create unity and reap big results*. Harvard, MA: Harvard Business Press Books.

Knightsbridge. (2013a). *Career management*. Retrieved from <http://www.knightsbridge.com/en/Optimize/CareerManagement.aspx>

Knightsbridge. (2013b). *Human capital solutions*. Retrieved from <http://www.knightsbridge.com/>

Messmer, M. (1999). *Job hunting for dummies* (2nd ed.). Foster City, CA: IDG Books Worldwide, Inc.

Rowley, J. (2006). *Information marketing*. Burlington, VT: Ashgate Publishing Company.

Glossary

Branding is a name, term, sign, symbol, design, or a combination of these developed to identify and differentiate the goods and services of one organization from those of other organizations.

Discretionary effort is the difference in the level of effort one is capable of bringing to an activity or a task versus the effort required to simply get by or make do.

Downsizing is the permanent reduction in an organization's workforce. Downsizing occurs when management seeks to "streamline" a company through corporate restructuring in order to increase profit and maximize efficiency. It may also result from a merger of two companies, or when a company cuts a product line or service.

Globalization commonly refers to the spread and connectedness of production, communication, and technologies across the world. That spread has involved the interlacing of economic and cultural activity. The speed of communication and exchange, the complexity and size of the networks involved, and the sheer volume of trade, interaction and risk give what we now label as "globalization" a powerful and potentially damaging force.

Hard skills are quantifiable accomplishments gained through experience and education. Examples include speaking a foreign language, typing speed, a degree, and proficiency in computer programming.

Horizontal or lateral movement involves a change to another functional area without necessary undergoing a change in status or salary. Lateral moves are fast becoming a way of demonstrating adaptive abilities and broadening skills, learning about other areas of the organization, and developing new talents.

Knowledge workers have high degrees of expertise, education, or experience, and the primary purpose of their jobs involves the creation, distribution, or application of knowledge.

Organization/manager/employee partnerships promote ownership and accountability. Career development, for example, is a partnership between employees, managers, and organizational leaders, therefore managers and organizational leaders must commit to employee development.

Portfolio careers are a non-traditional approach to jobs, the job market, and career management. The term "portfolio career" is attributed to the British management expert Charles Handy who predicted that the model of having a full-time job working for one employer would not endure. Instead, he envisioned a model in which an individual works for multiple employers, sometimes simultaneously, performing a series of short-term assignments. In this new model, everyone would be self-employed and responsible for planning and managing his/her own career.

Soft skills are largely intangible and represent personality traits and interpersonal skills. Examples include organizational skills; reliable, motivated and committed; a team player.

Stretch assignment is a task or project that you perform within your non-profit role that goes beyond your job description, challenges your current skills, and requires you to learn one or more new skills.

Value proposition is a business or marketing statement that summarizes why a consumer should buy a product or use a service. This statement should convince a potential consumer that one particular product or service will add more value or better solve a problem than other similar offerings.

Discussion and Activities

Discussion

1. Building and maintaining a high-profile professional stature in the careers community as a career management specialist requires a unique portfolio of qualifications. What special talents, personal qualities, skills, et cetera, would be beneficial in this specialty area?
2. What do each of the "high five" principles mean to you as you work towards your goal as a career practitioner?

   1. Change is constant.

2. Encourage the heart.
3. Focus on the journey.
4. Learning is ongoing.
5. Build relationships.

Activities

Checkpoint Activity

This exercise is intended to be completed at least annually in order to learn more about what you bring to the table and what you are looking for in the next steps of your career.

Who are you?

- What are your personal characteristics and traits?
- What do you value?
- What interests you?
- What does your ideal "day off from work" look like?

What do you have?

- What knowledge, skills, and abilities do you have?
- What is your educational background? What certifications do you have or professional development completed?
- Most importantly, what have you done with the skills, knowledge, ability, and education you have?

Where are you going?

- What are your goals in the next six months? In the next year? 3 years? 5 years?
- What are you going to do when you get there?
- How will you use your newest opportunity to help you meet your ultimate career goals?
- What projects are you going to seek out?
- What people are you going to try and meet and for what purpose (mentoring, networking)?
- How can you tailor this latest opportunity to ensure you are gaining the necessary skills for your next career step?

Career management "plans" can seem daunting. However, all of us have time, once a year, to ask some career-related questions. We can take the time to assess the answers, realize how they changed from the prior year, and determine the steps that can change our career path to meet our current needs and goals.

Personal Mission Statement Exercise

A personal mission statement addresses three questions:

1. What is my life about?
2. What do I stand for?
3. What action am I taking to live what my life is about and what I stand for?

A useful mission statement should include two pieces: what you wish to accomplish and contribute, and who you want to be — the character strengths and qualities you wish to develop.

(a) Describe your ideal day. This is not about being practical. It is designed to include as many sides of you and of your enthusiasms as possible: creative, competent, artistic, introverted, extroverted, athletic, playful, nurturing, contemplative.

(b) Imagine that it is your 35th or 50th birthday (or another milestone in your life). You have been asked by national print media to write a press release about your achievements. Consider what you would want your family, friends, and co-workers in your profession and in your community to say about you. What difference would you like to have made in their lives? How do you want to be remembered? This is designed to inventory your actions and accomplishments in all areas of your life.

Resources and Readings

Resources

Websites

Career Management
Straby, Rob. (2007) Discover the "High 5" of strategic career management today
    <http://www.slideshare.net/rstraby/5-principles-of-career-management>.

Supplementary Readings

Amundson, N. E., Borgen, W. A., Iaquinta, M., Butterfield, L. D., & Koert, E. (2010).
    Career decisions from the decider's perspective. *Career Development Quarterly*,
    5 (8), 336–351. Retrieved from <http://associationdatabase.com/aws/NCDA/pt/sp
    /cdquarterly>.
Bezanson, L., Hopkins, S. (2012) *Fragile or strong? Career management in
    Canada & Internationally*. Retrieved from <http://careercycles.com

/fragile-or-strong-career-management-in-canada-and-internationally>.

Burtnett, F. (2010). *Bound-for-career guidebook: A student guide to career exploration, decision making, and the job search.* Toronto, ON: Rowman and Littlefield.

Greenhaus, J. H., Callanan, G. A., & Godshalk, V. M. (2010). *Career management.* Thousand Oaks, CA: Sage.

Harrington, B. (2007). *Career management and work-life integration: Using self-assessment to navigate contemporary careers.* Los Angeles, CA: Sage.

Lalande, V., Borgen, B., Butterfield, L. (2009). *Career conversations: Employee workbook.* Ottawa, ON: CRWGDRC. Retrieved from <http://www.crwg-gdrc.ca/crwg /wp-content/uploads/2010/10/Tool-2-1-CC-Employee-Workbook.pdf>.

Neault, R.A. (2001). *Beyond the basics: Real world skills for career practitioners.* Coquitlam, B.C.: Life Strategies Ltd.

Neault, R.A. (2002). Thriving in the new millennium: Career management in the changing world of work. *The Canadian Journal of Career Development, 1*(1), 11–21. Retrieved from <http://ceric.ca/cjcd/archives/v1-n1/article2.pdf>.

Rosenberg, M., & Boyd, S. (2005). *A flexible thinker guide to extreme career performance.* Brooklyn, NY: Orange You Glad Inc.

Ryan, R. (2006). *Soaring on your strengths: Discover, use, and brand your best self for career success.* New York, NY: Penguin Books.

Schnabel, L. (2012). *Career branding buzz: What is your impact?* Retrieved from <http://www.torontojobs.ca/en/html/career_resources/articles /The_Career_Branding_Buzz.html>.

Wellness Models

Myers, J. E., & Sweeney, T. J. (Eds.). (2005a). *Counseling for wellness: Theory, research, and practice.* Alexandria, VA: American Counseling Association.

Myers, J. E., & Sweeney, T. J. (2005b). The indivisible self: An evidence based model of wellness (reprint). *The Journal of Individual Psychology, 61*(3), 269–279.

Myers, J. E., & Sweeney, T. J. (2008). Wellness counseling: The evidence base for practice. *Journal of Counseling and Human Development, 86,* 482–493.

Myers, J. E., Sweeney, T. J., & Witmer, J. M. (2000). The wheel of wellness: A holistic model for treatment planning. *Journal of Counseling & Development, 78,* 251–266.

SECTION 6

Specialties in the Profession

seventeen

Assessment in Career Guidance

JEFFREY LANDINE

JOHN STEWART
University of New Brunswick

PRE-READING QUESTIONS

1. Have you ever taken a standardized test?
2. What did you like or dislike about the experience?
3. Do you think you would use assessment instruments as a career practitioner? Why? Why not?

Introduction and Learning Objectives

The use of assessment instruments has been connected with career counselling since its beginning (Peterson & Gonzalez, 2005; Peterson & Nisenholz, 1999; Whiston, 2009). Instruments such as rating scales, tests, and inventories assess a number of career-related constructs, including skills, **abilities**, **aptitudes**, **values**, **interests**, **personality**, achievement, and cultural variables (Zunker, 2006). When these constructs are measured by such instruments, clients gain a greater self-understanding that helps them make realistic and satisfying educational and vocational choices (Herr, Cramer, & Niles, 2004). The results of such instruments can provide an individual with a number of alternatives and options to consider, and the motivation to further explore the decision-making process (Swanson & Fouad, 2010).

Assessment is much more than giving an individual a test (Neukrug & Fawcett, 2010; Peterson & Gonzalez, 2005; Stewart, 2010). Instead, assessment procedures involve, "exploring client information and concerns using a range of devices, such as norm-referenced tests, interviews, observations, and informal procedures" (Sattler, 2008, p. 5). These procedures might include a combination of formal or informal tests, interview data, or external reports like grades or work performance appraisals. Tests or instruments refer to the means used to obtain client information such as the Strong Interest Inventory, or the Myers-Briggs Type Indicator, both of which will be described later in the chapter. These assessment procedures help avoid the inherent pitfalls of the "test-and-tell" approach (Andersen & Vandehey, 2006).

After reading this chapter you will:

1. Comprehend the ethical principles involved in assessment practices.
2. Have knowledge of the range of career assessment instruments available to meet the needs of career practitioners and their clients.
3. Understand how to choose assessment instruments.
4. Understand the difference between formal and informal assessment tools.

We anticipate that readers will obtain an understanding of standardized tests as they engage in professional practice. It is beyond the scope of this chapter to provide all the information needed to use these instruments appropriately. This requires further training and education. Instead, we take a conceptual approach; that is, we hope that readers will develop an appropriate understanding of central concepts around standardized tests in order to use these instruments in an ethical and professional manner.

The chapter is divided into two major sections: the first part is about assessment issues and factors that can influence the choice of instruments practitioners use with particular clients, and the second part focuses on the instruments themselves.

Ethical Principles and Assessment Practice

Career practitioners are guided by principles laid out in codes of ethics, such as those articulated in the *Canadian Standards and Guidelines for Career Development Practitioners* (National Steering Committee, 2004). One of the overarching principles is that career practitioners practise within the limits of their competence. Typically, competence is achieved in preservice or in-service education programs. When selecting instruments, career practitioners choose the ones they have been educated to administer, score, and interpret, and those that show appropriate levels of validity and reliability. Before administering any instrument, career practitioners familiarize their clients with the purposes and benefits of assessment. When working with clients belonging to a minority group, career practitioners select standardized instruments based on the degree of similarity between their client and the characteristics of the group used to standardize the instrument (Arthur & Collins, 2010). Additionally, they interpret test results with caution, and consider issues like age, ethnicity, language, disability, gender, sexual orientation, religious affiliation, history, and socioeconomic status. Lastly, regardless of client characteristics, career practitioners consider the rights of their clients when explaining informed consent for testing. They are careful to use language that clients understand when discussing the results of assessment procedures, they ensure the confidentiality of results, and obtain client consent for their release.

Overall, these ethical principles establish the standards within which career practitioners choose assessment instruments and deliver professional services. These standards require practitioners to (a) be aware of the benefits and pitfalls of testing; (b) understand how tests are constructed, administered, scored, and interpreted; (c) determine the validity and reliability of instruments; (d) understand how diversity characteristics may influence test results; and, (e) be conscious of a client's right to informed consent and confidentiality. By informed, we mean the practitioner must help clients increase their readiness for writing assessment tests by familiarizing them with the test format and the questions that will be asked, the length of time involved, the cost of testing, and the skills needed to complete the testing process. The career practitioner is also responsible for administering, scoring, interpreting, and explaining the test results to clients in a respectful manner. All of the practitioner's decisions require caution and must be based on the best interests of his or her client. When the content and **norms** are not applicable to a client due to issues like ethnicity, language, sexual orientation, or gender, career practitioners may choose to not use formal assessment procedures.

Selecting and Administering a Good Test

Assessment is always conducted for a specific purpose, for example, to provide career guidance to clients and to help individuals choose occupations in which they are likely to be successful and satisfied.

There are several factors to consider when choosing tests and assessments. The ideal assessment instrument is reliable, fair, valid, and cost-effective. It is important that the instrument be of appropriate length and suitable for the individual's needs. As well, the test administrator must have the qualification to administer the test, find it easy to administer, and produce results that the administrator finds easy to understand. Test publishers often provide information on these factors on their websites (e.g., CPP's Strong Interest Inventory <https://www.cpp.com/products/strong/index.aspx>) or in technical manuals (e.g., ACR Interest Inventory Technical Manual <http://www.act.org/research/researchers/pdf/ACTInterestInventoryTechnicalManual.pdf>). In selecting an appropriate assessment, do the following:

1. Assist clients to clarify their goals.
2. Select those instruments that best help clients achieve their goals.
3. Locate and evaluate technical information about possible instruments.
4. Check the **validity, reliability, cross-cultural fairness**, and practicality of the possible instruments.
5. Consider all information and choose instruments judiciously.

Are You Qualified?

Appropriate, ethical use of testing tools requires general knowledge of tests and their applications and limitations. All practitioners, when using a test for the first time in their practice, need to be thoroughly familiar with the manual and to use the test they've chosen in a supervised field setting. Many assessments are sold only to professionals who are appropriately trained to administer, score, and interpret such tests and inventories. Assessments are designated as either A, B, or C level, and require different qualifications for purchase as outlined in the table.

ASSESSMENT LEVELS	DESCRIPTION
A-level assessments	Include self-assessments and do not require specific education or training to purchase or use (e.g., card sorts, some interest inventories, etc.).
B-level assessments	Require special certification or courses in assessment and training or supervision in the administration and interpretation of the instruments used (e.g., Myers-Briggs Type Indicator®).
C-level assessments	Include assessments typically used by psychologists such as I.Q. tests or neuro-psychological tests (e.g., MMPI, WAIS, etc.).

Table 1: Assessment Levels.

Selecting Assessment Instruments

Career practitioners consider a number of factors before they make decisions regarding the instrument(s) they might use (Neukrug & Fawcett, 2010; Swanson & Fouad, 2010). They think about the purpose of the assessment, the psychometric properties of the instrument(s), and a number of social variables that may influence the assessment results.

Purpose of Assessment

An important place to begin the discussion on selecting assessment instruments is with clients and their reasons for seeking help. Career practitioners use a variety of assessment approaches that are either formal (structured) or informal (unstructured; Neukrug & Fawcett, 2010). Formal approaches involve using a preexisting set of questions to collect information, while informal ones involve asking questions that arise from clients' responses. All tests, for example, are considered a structured approach because they have preexisting questions to which clients respond. Depending on the client, a career practitioner might choose to use an informal approach, such as a career fantasy activity or a card sort, in order to accommodate issues around education, ethnicity, and/or language proficiency.

Assessment results can be helpful to clients in a variety of ways (Andersen & Vandehey, 2006; Herr et al., 2004; Peterson & Gonzalez, 2005; Swanson & Fouad, 2010). The results suggest occupations and motivate clients to explore vocational options. They may help clarify **vocational interests**, confirm possible existing options, and/or predict satisfaction with possible future vocational choices. For example, the results of the Strong Interest Inventory provide a number of vocational options that are based on the similarity between a client's expressed interests and those of workers in particular occupations. Finally, assessment results may help clients understand issues that surround the decision-making process such as barriers to vocational choice or a lack of vocational identity. The results of My Vocational Situation may help to clarify both these issues for clients. These assessment instruments are described later in this chapter.

Psychometric Properties

Once the decision has been made to use an assessment instrument, career practitioners choose the instrument that will provide the most accurate information in response to the clients' concerns and goals. Career practitioners choose instruments that produce consistent scores and accurately measure constructs (Andersen & Vandehey, 2006; Sattler, 2008; Swanson & Fouad, 2010). In terms of choosing the best standardized instruments, two central concerns are validity and reliability (Anastasi & Urbina, 1997; Whiston, 2009).

Validity is concerned with what an instrument intends to measure and how well it accomplishes this intention; and **reliability** concerns the constancy of results from the instrument when repeated measures are taken. Reliability is an important prerequisite to determining an instrument's validity (Whiston, 2009). Both assess the sampling techniques used to "norm the instrument" (Anastasi & Urbina, 1997; Sattler, 2008; Whiston, 2009).

Sampling techniques help career practitioners determine the suitability of the instrument for their particular clients. Career practitioners obtain this psychometric information from a variety of sources, including technical and administration manuals produced by the test developers and the *Buros Mental Measurement Yearbook*, which provides a more objective report on the properties of instruments in print. Career practitioners take into account factors like validity, reliability, and sampling techniques when making decisions about which instruments to use in their practice.

Social Contexts

Culture and social diversity are two other variables career practitioners consider when deciding which instruments they will choose (Evans, 2008). Due to standardization procedures, assessment instruments may not always measure a particular client's characteristics objectively. Cultural factors like gender, sexual orientation, socioeconomic status, and geographic location (e.g., rural versus urban) may bias the results. All standardized assessment instruments assume that the test-taker has had an equal chance to experience all the activities that are queried in the instrument (Whiston, 2009). For example, if an interest inventory reflects mostly male experiences, the results may be biased for females. These circumstances do not mean that a career practitioner should not use such instruments. It simply means that practitioners do not interpret test scores in isolation but collect multiple data and use this comprehensive method to make decisions.

While test developers attempt to develop instruments that are fair and representative of regional demographics, it is reasonable to say that all tests are biased to some degree and that career practitioners should make the effort to minimize these biases as much as possible (Brown, 2007). Therefore, it behooves career practitioners to acquire knowledge of specific client variables and current research results when using career assessment instruments (Whiston, 2009).

An underresearched area now coming to the fore is a client's sexual orientation. For example, lesbian, gay, bisexual, transgendered, and questioning/queer (LGBTQ) clients may not have crystallized their sexual orientation. LGBTQ youth can be distracted from typical career development tasks because they are busy dealing with identity issues connected to their sexual orientation (Schmidt & Nilsson, 2006).

Language and cultural barriers may make it difficult to administer the test and share the results with the client. Since most career assessment instruments are printed in English, ethnic minority group members need to demonstrate high levels of English language proficiency in order to accurately interpret assessment instruments. Sometimes it may be appropriate to have an interpreter work with the career counsellor to help clients understand what is being asked of them, and to present the outcomes of the assessment (Sattler, 2008). Other clients, such as those who contend with illiteracy, may also benefit from alternative arrangements. For example, a client with a reading disability may need to hear the questions and be given more time.

Career practitioners seek to know and understand the uniqueness of their clients and the implications of that uniqueness. When interpreting the results of career assessment instruments, they also consider their clients' living environments. The results of a **career maturity** inventory, for example, may be influenced by a client's lack of knowledge and exposure to occupations and their inability to plan how to achieve their occupational aspirations due to their rural background or environment (Shepard, 2004).

Traditional approaches to career assessment expect the individual to make the decisions, and do not involve family or community in the process. First Nations people, for example, value connectedness and community (McCormick & Amundson, 1997). Consequently, most career assessment instruments may not be applicable. Neumann, McCormick, Amundson, and McLean (2000) found that "the input of family and community members in the career-planning process further strengthens the connectedness with greater sources of influence which play important roles in the guidance and well-being of Aboriginal First Nations people" (p. 182).

Assessment Instruments

Assessment instruments provide decision makers with information about components of their **self-system** and may point out barriers that influence their ability to choose an occupation.

In the first instance, assessment ideally addresses all aspects of the individual, such as interests, personality variables, values, abilities, aptitudes, and achievements. In doing so, assessment instruments prove particularly useful in the development of self-awareness as part of the career decision-making process. The information they provide may help identify problems or barriers, or close the knowledge gap between a client's self and potential occupations.

In the second instance, assessment may be used to identify barriers and/or problems influencing the readiness to make vocational decisions (Brown, 2012). Potential barriers might include career maturity or readiness. For example, first-year university students often experience career indecision as a result of a lack of **career readiness** (Morgan & Ness, 2003). By understanding the reasons behind their indecision, clients can begin to further their career development.

Types of Formal Assessment Instruments

In the review of assessment instruments below, we begin with instruments that measure individual traits such as interests, personality, values, and abilities, followed by a discussion of instruments that are diagnostic in nature and measure career maturity, career readiness, and career decision-making difficulties (personality trait assessment). The section ends with a discussion of computer-based assessments for charting career development growth, occupational selection, and informal assessments.

Assessing Interests

In career assessment, vocational interests are the most frequently assessed construct used to match an individual with occupations (Brown & Lent, 2005). John Holland and E. K. Strong Jr. have made substantial contributions to the definition and assessment of interests, particularly in relation to choice of and satisfaction with an occupation (Brown & Lent, 2005). Interests can promote self-awareness and stimulate exploration of additional occupational possibilities.

Table 2 describes the leading tools for personal interest inventories.

Inventory	STRONG INTEREST INVENTORY (SII) E. K. Strong, Jr., Jo-Ida C. Nansen, and David P. Campbell <https://www.cpp.com/products/strong/index.aspx>
Measures	Measures how personality is related to interests and level of interest on each of the six Holland Codes.
Population	Designed for individuals aged 14 and above.
Reliability & Validity	High reliability. Normed recently on 2,250 individuals (50% men, 50% women), selected from more than 20,000 respondents (Jenkins, 2009). Sample is generally representative of the racial and ethnic makeup of the U.S. workforce.
Inventory	JACKSON VOCATIONAL INTEREST SURVEY (JVIS) Douglas N. Jackson <http://www.jvis.com/>
Measures	Measures respondents' similarity to 17 university subject majors and 32 occupational group clusters rather than specific majors and occupations.
Population	High school and adult populations (14 and older) with educational and career planning, either individually or in group settings.
Reliability & Validity	Adequate validity and reliability for measuring occupational interests (Sanford-Moore, 2009). Norm sample consisted of 1,750 males and 1,750 females in Canada and the United States (1999) of which 2,380 were secondary school students and 1,120 were adults.
Inventory	SELF-DIRECTED SEARCH (SDS) John Holland <http://www.self-directed-search.com/>
Measures	Based upon Holland's theory that people are most satisfied in work environments that reinforce their personalities, the SDS categorizes people as one of six personality types. Results provide a three- or two-letter personal code that is used with the Occupations Finder or Majors Finder to locate a career or educational pathway of interest.

Inventory	SELF-DIRECTED SEARCH (SDS) (Cont'd) *John Holland* <http://www.self-directed-search.com/>
Population	Self-administered, self-scored, and self-interpreted. Two forms are available: Form R for high school students, college students, and adults and Form E for adults and older adolescents with lower educational levels (fourth grade reading level).
Reliability & Validity	The assessment itself is not standardized but norms exist for the codes. It is the most widely used career interest inventory in the world and has been adapted in over 25 countries (Ciechalski, 2009).

Table 2: Instruments for Personal Interest Inventories.

Assessing Personality Traits

In career counselling, personality assessment plays a key role in providing information that enables individuals to choose the occupations most likely to bring them fulfillment. For example, individuals described as extroverted tend to select occupations that provide regular opportunities for interaction with people. At the same time, **personality traits** can impact the process of career exploration itself. For example, the trait of being open to new experiences would suggest a proclivity for exploring new occupational experiences. While the following personality inventories may be based on differing theoretical foundations, they provide information on the individual's self-system that is helpful in the career exploration process. Additionally, the following instruments in Table 3 were designed to measure normal personality traits as opposed to problematic ones.

Inventory	MYERS-BRIGGS TYPE INVENTORY (MBTI) *Katharine Briggs and Isabel Briggs Myers* <http://www.myersbriggs.org/my-mbti-personality-type/>
Measures	Based on Jung's theory, the MBTI measures four aspects of personality: extroversion/introversion, sensation/intuition, thinking/feeling, and judging/perceiving. Involves responding to 93 forced-choice items to produce a Personality Type that is denoted by four letters (e.g., ENTP: extroverted, intuitive, thinking, perceiving).
Population	Suitable for individuals aged 14 and up.
Reliability & Validity	Norms are based on results from a broad, nationally representative sample of 3,009 people in the U.S. High levels of internal consistency and test-retest reliability are deceiving. Mastrangelo (2009) cautions practitioners to avoid an overly simplistic acceptance of occupations that are based on one pole of each dichotomy as opposed to a holistic view of the type.

Inventory	REVISED NEO PERSONALITY INVENTORY (NEO PI-R) Paul Costa Jr. and Robert McCrae <http://www.sigmaassessmentsystems.com/assessments/neopir.asp>
Measures	Assessment of personality based on the Five-Factor model — Neuroticism, Extroversion, Openness to experience, Agreeableness, Conscientiousness. Measures interpersonal, motivational, emotional, and attitudinal styles.
Population	Adolescents and adults, aged 17 and beyond.
Reliability & Validity	Scores are compared to a population sample of 1,301 (797 males and 353 females) ranging in age from 18 to 68. High levels of reliability and validity; however, there are concerns around problematic wording, which is particularly difficult for individuals for whom English is not the first language (Stebleton, 2009).
Inventory	WORK PERSONALITY INDEX (WPI) Donald Macnab and Shawn Bakker <http://www.psychometrics.com/docs/wpi-m.pdf>
Measures	WPI is an extensive model of 17 traits that describe how individuals work with others, approach their tasks, solve problems, manage change, and deal with stress. Scores measure the following constructs: personal drive, interpersonal style, thinking style, work style, dealing with pressure and stress.
Population	Individuals 18 years of age and up.
Reliability & Validity	Good construct validity but no studies reporting test-retest reliability or predictive validity (Carlson, 2010). Standardized on a relatively large sample of over 8,000 people, from which a matched sample of 3,000 males and 3,000 females were selected to create North American norms.

Table 3: Instruments for Assessing Personality Traits.

Assessing Values

Work values are central to our understanding of the reasons why people work (Brown & Lent, 2005). Most theorists assume that values are implicit in an individual's career choice and work behaviour. Additionally, work values address the manner in which individuals are socialized for work, and the ways in which work categories are designated. For example, occupations in the helping category reflect humanitarian values. In addition, most instruments measuring values assess a common pool of work values, such as income, achievement, independence, creativity, lifestyle, and prestige (Super, 1995). Instruments for assessing values are described in Table 4.

Inventory	CAREER VALUES SCALE (CVS)
	Macnab, Bakker, and Fitzsimmons
	Sample <http://www.psychometrics.com/docs/cvs_report.pdf> and <http://www.psychometrics.com/docs/cvs_m.pdf>
Measures	Provides a measure of intrinsic values inherent in the activity, for example, the degree to which abilities are utilized; and extrinsic values – the outcomes of the activity, for example, economic rewards.
Population	High school, university, and adult populations. Appropriate for individual and group administration. Written at an eighth grade level.
Reliability & Validity	The CVS is built on earlier work on values, specifically, on the research of Donald Super. The CVS was standardized on a large sample of over 28,000 people. From this group a matched sample of 7,000 males and 7,000 females were selected to create North American norms.
Inventory	VALUES CARD SORT (VCS)
	Richard Knowdell
	<http://www.careernetwork.org/career_assessment_instr.html>
Measures	Semi-formal assessment instrument used to identify and clarify career values. The cards sample 54 career-related value preferences. Examples of the values measured on the cards include job tranquility, creative expression, and status.
Population	Adolescents and adults.
Reliability & Validity	Client is very aware of the results as the client engages in the process of sorting the cards. The results are never a surprise and clients agree that they offer accurate descriptions.

Table 4: Instruments for Assessing Values.

Aptitudes and Abilities

Abilities and aptitudes refer to an individual's capacity to perform a task. They may be measured effectively with objective tests and by self-estimates. Both constructs predict success in the work environment (Brown & Lent, 2005). Table 5 lists instruments for assessing abilities and aptitudes.

Inventory	MULTI-DIMENSIONAL APTITUDE BATTERY-II (MAB-II) *Douglas N. Jackson* <http://www.sigmaassessmentsystems.com/resources/presentations/mab.pdf>
Measures	Assesses both aptitudes and general intelligence. The 10 sub-tests are assessed. Results include scores on the sub-tests and total scores for verbal, performance, and full-scale intelligence.
Population	Administered individually or in groups to persons aged 16 and up.
Reliability & Validity	Strong total score reliability and validity data. A group-based, general screening tool. Norms are available for nine different age groups, derived from a sample population of 1,600 (800 male and 800 female) from the U.S. and Canada.
Inventory	DIFFERENTIAL APTITUDE TEST, CANADIAN EDITION (DAT) *G. K. Bennett, H. G. Seashore, and A. G. Wesman* <http://www.creativeorgdesign.com/tests_page.htm?id=84>
Measures	Measures eight areas of abilities related to occupational performance. Provides an index of scholastic ability. Results assist students in selecting appropriate school courses and exploring career paths.
Population	Respondents in Grades 7–12 (Form A) and adults (Form B) answer multiple-choice questions in eight areas with a time limit for each area.
Reliability & Validity	Demonstrates high levels of content validity, face validity, and readability (Nelley, 2009). Suitable for group administration. Test items are representative of Canadian students in community colleges and universities, geographic regions, and types of school (e.g., private or public). Originally normed on 170,000 students.
Inventory	GENERAL APTITUDE TEST BATTERY (GATB) *Human Resources Development Canada* <http://www.assess.nelson.com/group/gp-gatb.html> <http://www.applicanttesting.com/pdf/confirmGATB.pdf>
Measures	Measures nine distinct aptitudes relevant to occupations: • general learning ability, • verbal aptitude, • numerical aptitude, • spatial aptitude, • form perception, • clerical perception, • motor co-ordination, • finger dexterity, and manual dexterity.
Population	Suitable for Grade 9 to adult.

Inventory	GENERAL APTITUDE TEST BATTERY (GATB) (Cont'd) *Human Resources Development Canada* <http://www.assess.nelson.com/group/gp-gatb.html> <http://www.applicanttesting.com/pdf/confirmGATB.pdf>
Reliability & Validity	Test results can be matched to aptitude levels appearing in the National Occupational Classification (NOC). The GATB (1986) can also be used in conjunction with interest levels found in the Canadian Work Preference Inventory (CWPI). The GATB includes Canadian norms from a population of 1,000 workers in 460 occupations (Spreen & Strauss, 1998).

Table 5: Assessing Abilities and Aptitudes Instruments.

Assessing Career Choice Problems

Diagnostic instruments are often employed to assess career development problems such as career maturity/readiness, career decision-making difficulties and barriers, and occupational information deficits. The increased recognition of the impact of these barriers at all stages of career development has led to the development and use of these instruments in both applied practice and research (Isaacson & Brown, 1997). Table 6 describes several instruments for career choice.

Inventory	CAREER DECISION SCALE (CDS) *Samuel Osipow* <http://www.creativeorgdesign.com/tests_page.htm?id=333&title=Career_Decision_Scale_%28CDS%29>
Measures	Identifies specific sources or antecedents of career indecision. Consists of 18 items to which individuals respond on a 4-point Likert scale ("Exactly like me" to "Not at all like me"). A 19th open-ended item allows respondents to clarify or provide additional information about their career decision making.
Population	Developed for students 14 to 23 years of age.
Reliability & Validity	Demonstrates strong test-retest reliability and validity (Harmon, 2010). The CDS manual provides normative data for high school and college students. Limited norms for adult college women and continuing education students.

Inventory	CAREER DECISION-MAKING DIFFICULTIES QUESTIONNAIRE (CDDQ) *Itamar Gati, Mina Krausz, & Samuel Osipow* <http://kivunim.huji.ac.il/eng-quest/cddq/cddq_main.html>
Measures	Based on a theoretical taxonomy of difficulties encountered in the career decision-making process. Difficulties are divided into two groups: those that exist prior to the process (e.g., low readiness due to a lack of motivation), and those that occur during the process (e.g., lack of information about self and occupations).
Population	There are no age limits.
Reliability & Validity	A relatively new instrument that may be useful in attempting to understand the multi-dimensionality of career indecisiveness. Empirical structure was found to be similar or identical to that proposed by the theoretical model. A clear distinction was found between difficulties that arise before the process and difficulties that arise during it, and between difficulties involving a lack of information and those connected with using the information, among the 10 proposed difficulty categories. (Gati, Saka, & Mayer, 2000)
Inventory	MY VOCATIONAL SITUATION (MVS) *John Holland, Denise Daiger, and Paul Power* Adapted version: <http://cms.bsu.edu/CampusLife/CounselingCenter/careerassess/TaketheSurvey.aspx>
Measures	Identifies difficulties people have in vocational decision making resulting from issues related to vocational identity, occupational information, and career barriers. The test consists of 26 items requiring a true/false or yes/no response.
Population	Ages 16 through adulthood.
Reliability & Validity	A relatively simple vocational assessment tool (self-administered and hand-scored). Sensitive to many aspects of psychological well-being. Norms derived from a sample of 16- to 69-year-old Americans in high school, college, and business.

Table 6: Career Choice Instruments.

Computer-Based Assessments

Computer-based comprehensive assessments, though expensive, have played an increasingly significant role in the delivery of career information to a diverse range of clients. One of their advantages is the ability to provide access to assessment instruments that measure traits in a number of areas addressed above. Because most paper-and-pencil tests can be adapted to a computer-based format, these systems are increasingly being used in educational institutions where the number of clients is large and time is a factor. However, one of the most significant disadvantages typically cited is the lack of opportunity to discuss results with a practitioner to prevent misunderstandings related to the information gathered.

Inventory	CHOICES (COMPUTER HEURISTIC OCCUPATIONAL INFORMATION AND CAREER EXPLORATION SYSTEM) <http://www.bridges.com/us/prodnserv/choicesexplorer_hs /index.html>
Measures	Aimed towards accessing information. Recent versions have numerous aspects of career exploration, including assessments of interests, aptitudes, and work values, as well as basic, workplace, and transferable skills.
	Close to 1,000 NOC career profiles and over 200 career videos are available in the database with information about the following: Description of Typical Tasks, Field of Work, Education Requirements, Job Requirements, Occupational Outlook, Earnings, and Website Connections to related organizations.
	Factors include interests, aptitudes, education, skills, and earnings that can assist in narrowing an extensive list of occupations. University and college database allows easy exploration of more than 1,000 educational institutions.
	A Planning Tools component assists with the process of creating an electronic portfolio.
Population	Software programs are available for elementary, middle, and high schools, universities and colleges, and career agencies in the U.S. and Canada.

Inventory	CAREER CRUISING (U.S. AND CANADIAN VERSIONS) <http://www.careercruising.com/>
Measures	Interests, skills, and learning style assessments help narrow the list of educational and occupational options. Includes job description, working conditions, earnings, education and training requirements, links to related college and university programs, sample career paths, related jobs, and multimedia interviews of people working in the individual occupation.
	The Career Cruising portfolio system allows individuals to store information and make use of numerical and descriptive data gathered in the career exploration process. Options are available for job search and résumé development, as well as direct connections to job-hunt sites.
Population	Products are available for students and people of all ages.

Table 7: Computer-Based Assessment.

Informal Assessment Methods

There are countless informal assessment tools (including card sorts, values and skills checklists, and interviews) that can be used for making decisions and expanding self-awareness. Informal measures may involve: (a) having clients tell their career life story and reflect on their successes and failures; (b) asking clients to draw a life line dotted with important career decisions and concentric life roles; or (c) projective-type activities, such as open-stem descriptive statements like: *I am most happy when …*, or *At work I tend to be…*

Clients may be drawn to informal tools because they appear less technical and more accessible, and are helpful in exploring rather than focusing on occupational options. Some clients have had unpleasant experiences with standardized tests, especially those with "right" or "wrong" answers. The practitioner can be creative in developing activities that fit with clients' needs and goals. However, informal assessment techniques have some disadvantages, such as the lack of standardization, poor technical rigour in reliability and validity although they may have **face validity**, and lack of a norm group against which to compare the clients' responses.

Genograms

Genograms were originally developed for use in family therapy. Adapted to career counselling, genograms can provide a graphic representation of the careers of family members, which may aid in understanding the context of an individual's career patterns and goals. For more details about creating genograms, please see:

- Example of a career genogram <http://www.virtualhabitats.com/Students /CareerCounselorWebquest/Genogram.pdf>.
- What is a Career Counselling Genogram? <http://work.chron.com/career-counseling-genogram-18191.html>.

Mind Mapping

Mind mapping is a creative, non-linear means of using words and images to assess the past and plan for the future. The creation of an occupation mind map can contribute to career goal development. For more information, please see:

- Mind Mapping software <http://www.novamind.com/planning /career-planning.php>.
- Mind Mapping for Career Success <http://conferences.alia.org.au /newlibrarian2004/zobjects/presymppapers/HarrisWebsitepaperFinal.pdf>.

Pattern Identification Exercises

Pattern Identification Exercises (PIE) have been used effectively in both individual and group career counselling (Amundson & Cochran, 1984). PIE starts with past experiences and seeks to identify, through in-depth questioning, personal patterns that are of relevance in establishing career aspirations. Examples of using PIE include in-depth exploration of success stories (including the Circle of Strength). Another type of qualitative assessment measure is the *Individual Style Survey*, which involves choosing self-descriptors from a list of characteristics and incorporating others' opinions along with your own self-assessment of personality style. Niles, Amundson, and Neault (2011) work through the steps of this type of survey in their book *Career Flow*.

Behavioural Observation Checklists

Behavioural observation checklists allow for a structured observation and assessment of behaviour skills important to the career process or a particular occupation. These assessments help to identify deficits (or strengths) in an individual's career-related behaviour. *Skill checklists* frequently make use of lists of skills and competencies and ask individuals to assess themselves against the criteria, considering whether they would like to use the skill on a job and how good they are at it.

SPOTLIGHT: *WHAT ASSESSMENT PROCESSES, MODELS, AND TOOLS ARE BEING USED?*
by Jeffrey Landine and John Stewart

A plethora of assessments, models, and tools are available for use in the field. However, the issue of not using a "one-size-fits-all" approach is a salient one as some practitioners report using the same assessment tool for a wide range of purposes. Although such use could be considered innovative, without empirical evidence to validate such use, it is risky. Similarly, reports of specific assessments being used with diverse populations (e.g., Aboriginal, immigrants, youth, etc.) have been made for which no research is available to confirm validity, reliability, or Canadian norms.

According to the Forum of Labour Market Ministers' report on *Use of Assessment Processes, Models, and Tools in Career Development Services*, the most commonly reported assessments used are:

- Intelligence/aptitude/skills: General Aptitude Test Battery (GATB); Test of Workplace Essential Skills (TOWES).
- Interest: Career Decision-Making System (CDMS); Self-Directed Search (SDS); Strong Interest Inventory (SII); Career Occupational Preference System Interest Inventory (COPS).
- Personality: Myers-Briggs Type Indicator (MBTI); Personality Dimensions; True Colors; TypeFocus.
- Values: Career Values Scale; Knowdell Values Cards.
- Employment readiness: Barriers to Employment Success Inventory (BESI); Job Search Attitude Inventory (JSAI); Employment Readiness Scale (ERS).
- Informal tools: Guiding Circles (specifically for Aboriginal clients).
- Computer-based tools: Career Cruising; CHOICES.

Roberta Neault found a bias among career practitioners favouring interest assessments in career decision making over other factors like employment barriers. Surprisingly, the practitioner's level of education was not found to be related to the type of assessment chosen, despite the extra training required to implement standardized tests. Across Canada, career planning and exploration assessments are used three times more often than measurements of program effectiveness, client change, or screenings for program readiness. The assessment process still needs to be fully embraced as a major contributor to establishing career services as an evidence-based practice.

- Neault, R. (2009). *Use of assessment processes, models, and tools in career development services* (Final Report). Coquitlam, BC: Life Strategies. Available from <http://www.flmm-fmmt.ca>.

Projective Techniques

Projective techniques are often unstructured tasks or ambiguous stimuli that are presented with the expectation that individuals will express needs, experiences, inner states, and thought processes. *Metaphors and symbols* can be used as a framework to help individuals think about their career in a unique manner (Amundson, 2010; Gysbers & Moore, 1987).

Audiovisual Feedback

Finally, *audiovisual feedback* provides the client with specific examples (either live or on audiotape or videotape) of themselves (or a model) performing selected skills that need to be learned. This is often followed by encouragement to rehearse or practise behaviours that have been modeled and role-played.

Conclusion

Assessment is a key component in the practice of career development and is used to provide and/or narrow a number of possible occupations as well as to identify interfering variables that confound the career development process. Practitioners who use career assessment instruments have a responsibility to understand the technical aspects of all instruments used whether formal or informal. Regardless of their type, these instruments emerge within a theoretical context and/or model that will guide their use.

Given the complex and changing nature of current demographics, test results need to be interpreted within the life-space of the individual. Since instruments were developed to measure constructs for the majority of the population, there are limitations when these instruments are used with individuals from minority groups. With such a variety of instruments available to augment their services, career practitioners need to keep abreast of instruments as they are developed, and consider their suitability for use with their clients. Above all, practitioners need to use instruments that have current norms and research to support their claims so that they provide clients with reliable information. Proper and thorough assessment gives clients the best possible chance of career success.

References

Amundson, N. E. (2010). *Metaphor making: Your career, your life, your way.* Richmond, BC: Ergon Communications.

Amundson, N. E., & Cochran, L. (1984). Analyzing experiences using an adaptation of an heuristic model. *Canadian Practitioner, 18*, 183–186.

Anastasi, A., & Urbiune, S. (1997). *Psychological testing* (7th ed.). Upper Saddle River, NJ: Prentice Hall.

Andersen, P., & Vandehey, M. (2006). *Career counseling and development in a global economy*. Boston, MA: Houghton Mifflin Company.

Arthur, N., & Collins, S. (Eds.). (2010). *Culture-infused counselling* (2nd ed.). Calgary, AB: Counselling Concepts.

Brown, D. (2012). *Career information, career counseling, and career development* (10th ed.).Toronto, ON: Prentice Hall.

Brown, S. D., & Lent, R. W. (2005). *Career development and counselling: Putting theory and research to work*. Hoboken, NJ: John Wiley & Sons.

Campbell, D. (1974). *If you don't know where you're going, you'll probably end up somewhere else*. Allen, TX: Tabor Publishing.

Carlson, J. F. (2010). Work Personality Index. In R. A. Spies & B. S. Plake (Eds.), *The sixteenth mental measurements yearbook*. Lincoln, NE: University of Nebraska Press.

Ciechalski, J. C. (2009). Self-Directed Search Career Explorer: (SDS-CE). In E. A. Whitfield, R. W. Feller, & C. Wood (Eds.), *A counselor's guide to career assessment instruments* (5th ed., pp. 302–308). Broken Arrow, OK: National Career Development Association.

Evans, K. (2008). *Gaining cultural competence in career counseling*. Boston, MA: Houghton Mifflin Company.

Gati, I., Saka, N., & Mayer, Y. (2000). Career counseling using the internet: Future directions. *Hayiutz Hachinuchi, 9*, 88–110 (In Hebrew).

Gysbers, N. C., & Moore, E. J. (1987). Career counseling: Skills and techniques for practitioners. New Jersey: Prentice-Hall.

Harmon, L. W. (2010). Career Decision Scale. In J. V. Mitchell Jr. (Ed.), *The ninth mental measurements yearbook*. Lincoln, NE: University of Nebraska Press.

Herr, E. L., Cramer, S. H., & Niles, S. G. (2004). *Career guidance and counselling through the lifespan: Systematic approaches*. (6th ed.) Toronto, ON: Pearson Education.

Isaacson, L. E., & Brown, D. (2007). *Career information, career counseling, and career development* (6th ed.). Toronto, ON: Allyn & Bacon.

Jenkins, J. (2009). Strong Interest Inventory assessment tool. In E. A. Whitfield, R. W. Feller, & C. Wood (Eds.), *A counselor's guide to career assessment instruments* (5th ed., pp. 309–319). Broken Arrow, OK: National Career Development Association.

Mastrangelo, P. M. (2009). Myers-Briggs Type Indicator (MBTI). In E. A. Whitfield, R. W. Feller, & C. Wood (Eds.), *A counselor's guide to career assessment instruments* (5th ed., pp. 400–406). Broken Arrow, OK: National Career Development Association.

McCormick, R. M., & Amundson, N. E. (1997). A career-life planning model for First Nations people. *Journal of Employment Counseling, 34*, 171–179.

Morgan, T., & Ness, D. (2003), Career decision making difficulties of first year students.

The Canadian Journal of Career Development, 2, 33–37.

National Steering Committee. (2004). *Canadian standards and guidelines for career development practitioners: Code of ethics.* Retrieved from <http://career-dev-guidelines.org/career_dev/>.

Neault, R. (2009). *Use of assessment processes, models, and tools in career development services* (Final Report). Coquitlam, BC: Life Strategies. Retrieved from <http://www.flmm-fmmt.ca/CMFiles/FLMM%20Archive%20-%20Document%20Archive/Use%20of%20Assesment%20Process%20Models%20and%20Tools/Assessment%20Project%20Final%20Report.pdf>.

Nelley, K. N. (2009). Differential Aptitude Tests (DAT) & Career Interest Inventory (CII). In E. A. Whitfield, R. W. Feller, & C. Wood (Eds.), *A counselor's guide to career assessment instruments* (5th ed., pp. 127–136). Broken Arrow, OK: National Career Development Association.

Neukrug, E. S., & Fawcett, R. C. (2010). *Essentials of testing & assessment: A practical guide for counselors, social workers, and psychologists* (2nd ed.). Belmont, CA: Brooks/Cole, Cengage Learning.

Neumann, H., McCormick, R. M., Amundson, N. E., & McLean, H. B. (2000). Career counselling for First Nations youth: Applying the First Nations career-life planning model. *Canadian Journal of Counselling, 34*(3), 172–185.

Niles, S. G., Amundson, N. E., & Neault, R. A. (2011). *Career flow: A hope-centered approach to career development.* Boston, MA: Pearson Education.

Peterson, N., & Gonzalez, R. C. (2005). The role of work in people's lives: Applied career counseling and vocational psychology (2nd ed.) Toronto, ON: Nelson.

Peterson, J. V., & Nisenholz, B. (1999). *Orientation to counselling* (4th ed.). Toronto, ON: Allyn and Bacon.

Sanford-Moore, E. E. (2009). Jackson Vocational Interest Survey (JVIS) (2nd ed.). In E. A. Whitfield, R. W. Feller, & C. Wood (Eds.), *A counselor's guide to career assessment instruments* (5th ed., pp. 268–273). Broken Arrow, OK: National Career Development Association.

Sattler, J. M. (2008). *Assessment of children: Cognitive foundations* (5th ed.) La Mesa, CA: Author.

Schmidt, C. K., & Nilsson, J. E. (2006). The effects of simultaneous developmental processes: Factors relating to the career development of lesbian, gay, and bisexual youth. *The Career Development Quarterly, 55,* 22–37.

Shepard, B. (2004). In search of self: A qualitative study of the life-career development of rural young women. *Canadian Journal of Counselling, 38,* 75–91.

Spreen, O., & Strauss, E. (1998). *A compendium of neuropsychological tests: Administration, norms and commentary* (2nd ed.). New York, NY: Oxford University Press.

Stebleton, M. (2009). NEO Personality Inventory-Revised (NEO PI-R). In E. A. Whitfield, R. W. Feller, & C. Wood (Eds.), *A counselor's guide to career assessment instruments* (5th ed., pp. 407–412). Broken Arrow, OK: National Career Development Association.

Stewart, J. (2010). Assessment from a contextual perspective. In N. Arthur & S.

Collins (Eds.), *Culture-infused counselling* (2nd ed., pp. 189–208). Calgary, AB: Counselling Concepts.

Super, D. E. (1995). Values: Their nature, assessment, and practical use. In D. E. Super & B. Sverko (Eds.), *Life roles, values, and careers*. San Francisco, CA: Jossey-Bass.

Swanson, J. L., & Fouad, N. A. (2010). *Career theory and practice: Learning through case studies* (2nd ed.). Thousand Oaks, CA: Sage Publications, Inc.

Whiston, S. C. (2009). *Principles and applications of assessment in counseling* (3rd ed.). Belmont, CA: Brooks/Cole, Cengage Learning.

Zunker, V. G. (2006). *Career counseling: A holistic approach* (7th ed.). Toronto, ON: Thomson Nelson.

Glossary

Abilities refer to the power to perform a specified act or task, either physical or mental. Such powers can be learned or innate.

Aptitude is an ability, tendency, or capacity that is inherited or is the result of environment and life experiences. Aptitudes can be used to predict how likely a person is to succeed in certain environments.

Career maturity is the attitudinal and cognitive readiness to cope with the developmental tasks of finding, preparing for, getting established in, pursuing, and retiring from an occupation.

Career readiness refers to how developmentally ready (in terms of level of exploration, awareness of implications, and maturity) students are for making these initial career decisions.

Content validity (also known as logical validity) refers to the extent to which a measurement represents all facets of a given social concept. For example, depression scales may lack content validity if they only look at the affective dimension of depression but fail to assess the behavioural dimension.

Cross-cultural fairness requires verifying that the test is appropriate for use with a particular population and includes investigation of validity, reliability, and appropriate norm groups to which the population is to be compared. Validity and reliability take on additional dimensions in cross-cultural testing as does the question of the appropriate norm group. The instrument must be validly adapted, the test items must have conceptual and linguistic equivalence, and the test items must be bias free.

Diagnostic instrument is an assessment instrument that identifies areas of concern with an individual's career development.

Face validity is related to **content validity**, but instead of assessing what the test measures, face validity pertains to whether the test "looks valid" to all participants.

Interests are preferences for activities that are expressed as likes or dislikes.

Norms are standard scores for a group as measured by a test. Norms may be local, regional, or national group scores. Test-takers' scores are compared to the average (norm) scores of a defined group.

Personality is the combination of an individual's personal, social and emotional traits, and behaviours.

Personality traits are relatively enduring patterns of thoughts, feelings, and behaviours that distinguish individuals from one another.

Reliability refers to how stable the results are over time and how free the test is from error. Reliability is the "consistency" or "repeatability" of your measures.

Sampling techniques are used to form a subset of the population that can be used as representative of the entire population.

- **Random sampling** (probability sampling) is a sample that is chosen randomly from the population so that each item in the population has the same probability of being chosen.
- **Non-probability sampling** does not involve random selection and can be a quick way to collect and analyze data but can not be used to determine probability.

Self-system is a psychology term that refers to the set of attitudes and behaviours that affect how people perceive and respond to situations to reduce anxiety. The concept was first developed by Harry Stack Sullivan.

Validity is how well a test measures what it is intended to measure.

Values are qualities that are important to the individual. They are fundamental beliefs that drive the decision-making process. Work values, such as helping society, influencing people, and working alone are essential to consider in career planning. When expressed in the work setting, work takes on purpose and meaning.

Vocational interests are personal likes, preferences, and aspects of work that people enjoy.

Work values are learned or may grow out of needs and are assumed to be a basic source of human motivation.

Discussion and Activities

Discussion

Discussion Questions

1. Given the changing demographics in Canada, how do you see standardized tests evolving over the next 20 years? What cultural issues do you think need to be considered in the development of standardized instruments?

2. Which instrument would you choose to measure the following constructs: personality, interests, values, vocational identity? Why?

3. The Case of the Senior High School Student
    A high school student entering her senior year sees the guidance counsellor to discuss plans after high school. She entered senior high school with passing grades. She had low passing grades in mathematics and science but achieved average grades in English and her other subjects. The student indicated that she spent considerable time doing homework and studying in the previous grade. She is interested in the health professions and wants to know what occupations would be suitable for her to pursue.

    (a) What information would you like to know about this student before you respond to her concern?
    (b) What tests might you administer and why?

Personal Reflections

1. Are you drawn to formal or informal assessments? Why?
2. Find report cards from elementary, middle/junior high school, and senior high school and consider how assessment has affected you. Note patterns based on comments (informal assessment) as well as patterns in formal assessments (grades). What interpretations can you make based on the "data" collected? Would you be in agreement? Does this information constrain your perception of self or does it open up new possibilities?

Career Practitioner Role

1. Building Strengths in Clients
    Campbell (1974) believed that nine assets (talents, intelligence, motivation, friends, education, family, experience, appearance, and health) can act as seeds that career practitioners can nurture with their clients. These "seeds" can have a great impact on future choices.

Questions to reflect on:

- How would you access these "seeds" while conducting and debriefing an assessment?
- What seeds can I nurture right now?
- What seeds currently exist that need a little watering?
- What seeds do you still need to purchase?

2. You are working with two clients and you have been given their Myers-Briggs assessment results. Both clients have the same type – INFP. How do similar results translate into action? What additional information would you seek from each client?

Activities

1. The task of understanding assessments and the process of providing results is best learned by experiencing the process firsthand. Make an appointment at your college or university career centre and consider taking the Strong Interest Inventory and the Myers-Briggs Type Indicator. Write a short reflection paper on your experience. What did you learn as a "client" about yourself and career development? What did you find surprising? What did you learn about assessment and how that may impact your work with others?

2. Case of Sonia
   Sonia is a 55-year-old South Asian woman who sought help at a women's centre in her rural community located outside a large urban centre. Naveen, her husband, recently filed for divorce after 25 years of marriage, and Sonia is devastated and not sure what to do next. Sonia and Naveen have two boys, one aged 24 who attends university and one aged 16. Sonia married Naveen while they were in college and gave birth to their first son shortly after. Sonia completed two years of nursing training. Naveen's career as a top

A Place for Quality of Life Career/LifeSkills Resources

Career/Life Skills provides assessment and resources for career and work counselling. Its mission is to promote life skills and career development by providing the highest quality resources, services, and training to meet the needs of career counsellors, human resources professionals, psychologists, educators, and their clients. Career/Life Skills provides:

1. Innovative, practical solutions and assessment tools such as Personality Dimensions®, the Majors PTI™ (Majors Personality Type Inventory), Jackson Vocational Interest Inventory®, the COPSystem, SkillScan, and the Career Exploration Inventory.
2. A variety of career and lifestyle books
3. Certification and professional development training programs.

For more information, visit <http://career-lifeskills.com/>.

researcher at the university was demanding, and while Sonia contemplated finding work outside the home, she felt it was more important to focus her attention on her children and household responsibilities. Sonia is put in touch with you.

1. What are central issues that need to be addressed?
2. What initial types of information would you need to begin working with Sonia?
3. What types of assessments would you start with?
4. Interview a professional in your community who conducts career assessments. Sample questions might include: What assessments do you use? How do you determine which type of assessment to use with a particular client? What types of challenges have you encountered and how have you managed? How do you keep the working relationship intact while providing assessment results?

3. Career Genogram is a "family career tree." For ideas on how to use and create a career genogram go to <http://work.chron.com/career-counseling-genogram-18191.html>. Include three generations (grandparents, parents/aunts/uncles and you/siblings). Identify family members whom you know or know about.

- Identify each family member's education and work.
- What is your perception of that person's success/failure as a spouse, parent, employee, friend, and relative?
- Did that person experience increased/decreased mobility as result of career choices?
- Was the person balanced in his/her life roles? Were the roles integrated or in conflict?
- Whom did the family admire? (Who were the "successful" people in your family's point of view?) Why?
- Whom did you admire or think was successful? Why?
- What advice did or would this person give you about work, career, and family?

Resources and Readings

Resources

Websites for Career Assessments

Career Decision Making Difficulties Questionnaire (CDDQ) <http://kivunim.huji.ac.il/cddq/>.
The U.S. Occupational Information Network (O*NET) offers SkillsSearch as a tool for matching skills to occupation. <http://www.onetonline.org/skills/>.
Career Key — portal with quizzes and resources. In Canada <http://www.careerkey-ca

.org/> and the U.S. <http://www.careerkey.org/>.

Self-Directed Search — career interest test based on John Holland's theory <http://www.self-directed-search.com/>.

Campbell Interest and Skill Survey <http://profiler.com/>.

Kuder Career Assessment <http://www.kuder.com/>.

Vocopher (contains many inventories for career professionals) <http://vocopher.com/>.

Career Resource Page: Self-Assessments, University of South Florida. <http://careerresource.coedu.usf.edu/selfassessment/selfassessment.htm>.

Career Assessments Do's and Don'ts, Quintessential Careers <http://www.quintcareers.com/career_assessment-dos-donts.html>.

Videos

YouTube video: Where will you be?
<http://www.youtube.com/watch?v=vrpC0pZHUe4>.

Self-Assessments for Choosing a Career Path Video
<http://education-portal.com/videos/Self-Assessments_for_Choosing_a_Career_Path_Video.html>.

Other Resources

Buros Mental Measurement Yearbook. Retrieved from <http://buros.org/mental-measurements-yearbook>.

Knowdell, R. Card Sort Assessment Tools
<http://career-lifeskills.com/career-assessments-79/knowdell-card-sorts-153/>.
<http://www.youtube.com/watch?v=R3zJ4vs6gNs>.

Turning Information into Personal Assessment
Sample card sorts can be seen at <http://careerresource.coedu.usf.edu/linkteachingtools/examplesoflessonplans.htm>.

Self-assessment resources <http://www.rileyguide.com/assess.html>

Supplementary Readings

Amundson, N. (2002). *Food for thought. Career development: Employability dimensions.* Ottawa, ON: Canadian Career Development Foundation <http://www.iaevg.org/crc/files/Communication_Strategy_No. 1_Amundson691_2.pdf>.

Amundson, N. (2009). *Active engagement* (3rd ed.). Richmond, BC: Ergon Communications.

Career/LifeSkills Resources. (2010). *Career exploration and job search: A comprehensive collection of assessments to guide job seekers through each step of the job search process.* Concord ON: Author. <http://clsr.ca/pdf/2010careerassessments.pdf>.

Chope, R. C. (2005). Qualitatively assessing family influence in career decision making. *Journal of Career Assessment, 13,* 395–314. doi: 10.1177/1069072705277913

Chope, R. C. (2006). *Family matters: The influence of the family in career decision making.* Austin, TX: Pro-Ed.

Gibson, D. M. (2005). The use of genograms in career counseling with elementary, middle, and high school students. *Career Development Quarterly, 53,* 353–362. <http://sccn645middle.wikispaces.com/file/view /The+Use+of+Genograms+in+Career+Counseling.pdf>.

Inkson, K., & Amundson, N. E. (2002).Career metaphors and their application in theory and counseling practice. *Journal of Employment Counseling, 39,* 98–108. <http://www.virtualhabitats.com/Students/CareerCounselorWebquest /Career%20Metaphors.pdf>.

Malot, K. M., & Magnuson, S. (2004). Using genograms to facilitate undergraduate students' career development: A group model. *Career Development Quarterly, 53*(2), 178–186.<http://www.thefreelibrary.com/ Using+genograms+to+facilitate+undergraduate+students'+career...-a0127052323>.

Neault, R. (2009). *Use of assessment processes, models, and tools in career development services* (Final Report). Coquitlam, BC: Life Strategies. Retrieved from <http://www.flmm-fmmt.ca/CMFiles/FLMM%20Archive%20-%20Document% 20Archive/Use%20of%20Assesment%20Process%20Models%20and%20Tools /Assessment%20Project%20Final%20Report.pdf>.

Pryor, R., & Bright, J. (2009). Game as a career metaphor: A chaos theory career counselling application *British Journal of Guidance & Counselling, 37*(1), 39–50.

eighteen

CareerCycles

A Holistic and Narrative Method of Practice

MARK FRANKLIN
CareerCycles

PRE-READING QUESTIONS

As you read this chapter, keep the following questions in mind and jot down ideas as you read:

1. How is a narrative method of practice different from traditional test-and-tell assessments?
2. What is a career counselling framework and why is it valuable to both client and career practitioner experiences?
3. What are the key practitioner skills required to successfully facilitate this narrative method of practice?
4. What benefits and challenges do you foresee when attempting to use this narrative method in your career development practice?

Introduction and Learning Objectives

This chapter describes a holistic, narrative framework and method of practice for career counselling (Zikic & Franklin, 2010) in which clients tell their career and life stories and transform the meaning from those stories into choices for their future. Career stories reveal important, valuable, and personally relevant clues to uncover possibilities that have been shut down, ignored, or dismissed by others. By carefully tuning into clients' stories, career practitioners help clients gather and organize what they want in their career and life: what's important now, the strengths they want to use, and other key components to empower career and life choice making.

This chapter begins with an overview of the framework for the CareerCycles (CC) method of practice followed by a description of its two main processes: (a) the career and life clarification process, and (b) the intentional exploration process. The case of Charlotte illustrates the two processes. In the notes to the career practitioner section, a narrative definition of career is presented along with information on how to include assessments into the CC method. This section concludes with information on how to use the CC method in multiple sessions and how to bring closure to the sessions. The chapter closes with a five-step summary of the CareerCycles method of practice.

In this chapter you will learn:

1. How the CareerCycles method of practice integrates narrative, happenstance, cognitive approaches, and positive psychology.
2. How to initiate a collaborative, narrative client experience that engages client as expert, and reframes dissatisfaction into career and life desires.

A Canadian Metaphor

Tap each maple tree, collect sap, refine into syrup, eat and be strengthened!

Picture a maple forest in the spring time during "sugaring off" when sap is collected, and boiled down to make maple syrup. One's early years, high school and postsecondary experiences, jobs, and travel, can each be considered one maple tree in a forest of trees that is one's life. The narrative process of career counselling is like tapping each tree for the sap or the relevant desires, strengths, personal qualities, assets, influences, and possibilities. Once all the sap has been collected, it is boiled down to make maple syrup, which in our metaphor, is a succinct statement of the client's present situation and future desires. Eating the maple syrup that one makes is similar to becoming strengthened and empowered in one's career and life choices or the concentrated knowing drawn from one's life and career experiences.

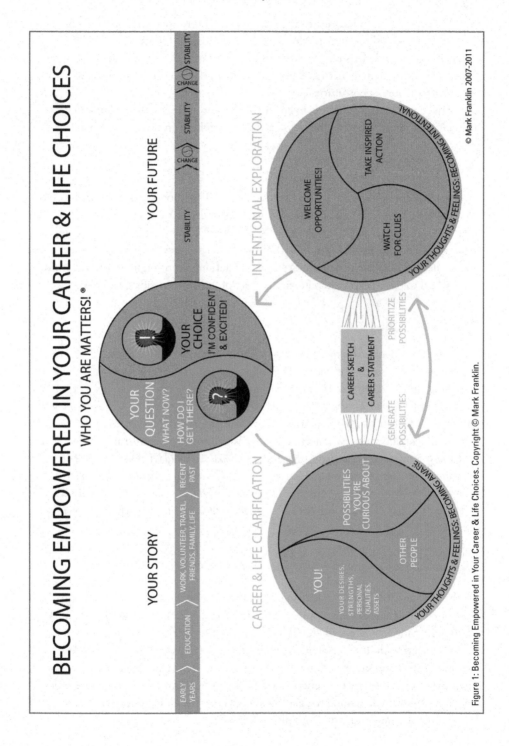

Figure 1: Becoming Empowered in Your Career & Life Choices. Copyright © Mark Franklin.

3. How to gather and organize client desires, strengths, personal qualities, assets, influences, and possibilities, from a client's career and life story.
4. The role that beliefs play in an emergent, narrative career counselling context, and how to align a client's plan with their mindset so they take inspired action and welcome opportunities.
5. Specific exercises and tools to enact the CareerCycles method of practice.
6. How to identify which client groups most benefit from this approach.

CareerCycles (CC) Method of Practice

The overall framework for the CareerCycles (CC) method of practice is illustrated in Figure 1, which graphically depicts its two main processes: (1) career and life clarification and (2) intentional exploration. The CC method of practice comprises over 40 documented interventions within those two processes. It also includes working tools, client handouts, and a training program. Each intervention includes a description as to when to use it, expected outcomes, career practitioner actions, and resources.

The Case of Charlotte

Charlotte, age 33, was working as an advertising account manager in the health and beauty sector. She had been back in the workforce for two years after a year of maternity leave, but found herself dissatisfied. "I'm not going to save the world one bra at a time," Charlotte says, referring to the work she did on a bra account. "I knew there was something else out there but I didn't even know where to go to figure it out." When we began working together, Charlotte stated her career question: "What now, given that I now have a family and my priorities have changed? I have a few ideas ... should I pursue one of them or something else?" Like most people in career pain, Charlotte wanted a quick answer. She wanted to move forward in her career. The paradox is that to move forward in a satisfying direction, she first needed to step back. Let's walk with Charlotte through the CareerCycles framework.

Career and Life Clarification Process

In this process, the career practitioner elicits the client's story and from it gathers and organizes the relevant components (the sap), which are put into a working document called a Career Sketch. Once the Career Sketch is completed, the client is encouraged to draft a personal Career Statement (the maple syrup). Analogous to becoming strengthened by consuming the energy in maple syrup, clients who have a written Career Statement are encouraged to "live their Career Statement" in order to become empowered, making the gap between where they are and where they want to go seem smaller and more manageable.

The client and practitioner begin by collaboratively drafting a key career question, for example, "What should I do next in my career?" or "How can I be more effective in exploring my options?" (See Figure 1.) The client and career practitioner frequently return to this question as a way to ensure that the discussion is moving in a direction that best fits the client's self-defined needs.

The approach involves looking at the client's life as narrative chapters. (See "Your Story" in Figure 1.) After completing the segments entitled "Early Years and Education" on the timeline, the client will list life and career experiences, jobs, volunteer, travel experience, parenting, and so forth. This segment is congruent with Super's (1980) holistic lifespan, life-space approach. The final segment of Your Story represents the recent past — this may be a current or recent period of education, employment, or unemployment. Clients are given the task of drafting their own annotated timeline, showing years, ages, likes and dislikes, and lessons learned in each chapter of their life. Typically clients feel a certain amount of relief and comfort as they realize that this method of practice can help them "connect the dots" from their career story.

The next step in this process is to build the client's Career Sketch (Table 1).

CAREER SKETCH

Desires: What you want and what's important to you (DD) = deeper desires • •	**Strengths**: Skills and knowledge you want to use (D) = want to develop • •	**Natural interests**, emerging passion, evolving identity • •	Possibilities you are curious about: 1. Internal to your organization: • 2. External with another employer: • 3. Self-employment: •
Personal qualities: Personality and how others describe you • •	**Assets**: Education, credentials, experiences, additional skills, & knowledge • •	**Other people's** influence and your life roles • •	4. Volunteer/Service: • 5. Lifelong learning/ Education: • 6. Travel/live elsewhere: • 7. Leisure, family, friends, personal: •
Your thoughts, feelings, and insights.			

Table 1: Career Sketch. Copyright © Mark Franklin.

This simple table is used to gather and organize the client's important information. The client's relevant information relates to Bridges' (1998) D.A.T.A. (desires, abilities, temperament, assets), which is expanded in the CC method to include desires, strengths, personal qualities, assets (education, credentials, and other skills), natural interests, influences of other people, possibilities the client is curious about, and the client's named thoughts and feelings. Drawing from narrative therapy, the career practitioner works with the client to "thicken their story" and undo the negative effects of problem-saturated experiences, and focuses the client on re-authoring a more positive future (White, 2007). Getting feedback is a powerful intervention with a variety of possible outcomes, including confirmation that the client is on the right track with one or more career possibilities. As much of the feedback is usually more favourable than the client expects, the feedback increases the client's confidence in being able to achieve a career goal. These new career and/or training possibilities and any additional input are incorporated into the Career Sketch.

Therefore, ask the client to identify a handful of trusted allies and request career-related feedback. To debrief the feedback, ask for the most meaningful feedback first.

- How was the experience for you, to get this feedback? How did you feel about it?
- Were there any surprises? If so, how do you account for this?
- Let's go through this in enough detail so that we can really see what they said. I need you to be somewhat selective about what we talk about here.

A key outcome of this process is the creation of the Career Statement. This distillation of the Career Sketch is a brief, positively worded crystallization of the client's emerging self-awareness of her/his career possibilities. For many clients, writing and reading aloud their Career Statement is the first experience they have in articulating what is truly important to them, what they authentically want to do, who they really are, and the possibilities they are most curious about and want to explore.

Charlotte's Career and Life Clarification Process

Charlotte's first task was to draw a timeline of her life, highlighting what she liked, choices she made, and what she learned in each chapter of her story.

"Walking through my story gave me the freedom to see that anything was possible," said Charlotte. "There were no bad or impossible ideas. Even talking about what I wanted to be when I grew up — a teacher — was an eye eye-opener. Because I was so deeply into my advertising career, with 7 years of experience, I couldn't see how I could make a good change. I didn't realize that skills can be transferred into other places." Charlotte possessed strong managing, coaching, and mentoring skills. "I didn't realize that using these skills, I could do something really different." Charlotte approached a few trusted allies including acquaintances, co-workers, and friends. "The feedback reminded me about what I like and took me out of the negative place I was in. It reminded me of what I liked about what I was doing."

She continued, "It made me feel great hearing what others said about me, and knowing there were options. I didn't realize there were so many possibilities. I had the power within me to do those things and didn't have to go back to school. Going through a list of skills, looking at past jobs, things I did in college, I gathered skills in all experiences, not just my job." This is a perfect example of how skills and knowledge may come from earlier chapters of your life.

The next step was for Charlotte to draft her Career Statement, a brief statement highlighting seven key outputs from the narrative process: desires, strengths, personal qualities, assets and demonstrated interests, influences of other people, and possibilities.

- *Here's what I want ...* (Desires). I am working with people and loving it; I'm having a reasonable workload, and job advancement. I'm teaching, mentoring, supporting other people; I'm doing good and giving back. I've decided to have more stability and more time for my family.
- *Here's what I want to do or use ...* (Strengths). I want to teach, coach, mentor, and manage. I want to use interpersonal and verbal communication. I want to develop relationships, use conflict-resolution skills, and serve clients. I want to organize and co-ordinate, do strategic thinking, generate ideas, and use my advertising knowledge.
- *Here's the kind of person I am ...* (Personal qualities): I am a person with a tremendous sense of responsibility. I'm reliable, though a bleeding heart. I'm a reader, introspective, and either really on or really off.
- *Here's what I bring with me* (Assets): 6+ years of experience in advertising, wedding planning experience, university courses, director of student advocacy at college, cosmetician — loved it, diploma in advertising.
- *Other people*: I'm mindful of how my role as a parent of a young child continues to influence my career and life choices.
- *Here are the possibilities I'm most curious about and want to explore*: ad agency with a focus on non-profit clients; fundraising and event co-ordinator; self-employment in the form of a website for new mothers; a position in a postsecondary institution such as teaching or student services.

For Charlotte, after years of working on advertising accounts for corporate clients, part of her Career Statement included: "What's important to me is doing good and giving back."

Intentional Exploration Process

In this process, the career practitioner guides the client to use his or her Career Statement to notice clues about new and exciting possibilities, to take inspired action related to those clues, and to "welcome relevant opportunities." (See Figure 1.) Next the client reads the Career Statement, and the career practitioner immediately affirms the Career Statement and introduces the notion of "living your Career Statement." The career practitioner, by showing a positive mindset, furthers the intentional exploration process — the practitioner is showing the client how it feels to have a completed Career Statement. From this place, the client is ready to be introduced to the components of the intentional exploration process.

Using the CC framework as a visual aid, the career practitioner asks the client to "watch for clues" as the first step, so that the client's now positive mindset will shift the focus onto evidence that supports the client's desires. This approach is different from focusing on the negative clues one often notices when placing emphasis on obstacles, hearing "bad news" in the media, or experiencing career or goal anxieties. Positive clues that a client notices make it easier to take inspired action, which is the second step. The third step of welcoming opportunities supposes that clients remain open to both planned and unplanned opportunities. Because clients are watching for clues, career practitioners using the CC method will see an increased likelihood of clients taking advantage of planned happenstance and generating more "beneficial unplanned events" (Mitchell, Levin, & Krumboltz, 1999).

Helping clients become intentional with their thoughts and feelings is also an explicit component of the framework. During the intentional exploration process, clients often experience emotional highs and lows. During low emotional periods, it is particularly important for career practitioners to guide clients to return to their positive mindset by focusing on positive thoughts and challenging negative ones.

Other interventions used here include *Choice Map* (Adams, 2004), *Wouldn't It Be Great* (Hicks & Hicks, 2004), selections from the "happiness activities" found in *The How of Happiness* (Lyubomirsky, 2007), and many others drawn from the burgeoning field of positive psychology. Introducing clients to the notion that they can choose better-feeling thoughts and allow opportunities to appear contributes to their positive mindset and builds their confidence that it may be easier than they initially believed to attract satisfying opportunities.

To keep track of a client's intentional exploration, the career practitioner works with the client to create a Possibility and Exploration Plan or PEP (Table 2). This working document gathers and organizes in one place the client's career exploration information. Each career and life possibility the client wants to explore is listed in a separate row of the PEP. The practitioner guides the process and creates a fun context by encouraging the client to picture each opportunity using the metaphor of playing in a sandbox to generate ways of taking inspired action. Next to each possibility in the

PRIORITY POSSIBILITIES I'M CURIOUS ABOUT	WATCH FOR CLUES: *Internal, External, and Environmental*	TAKE INSPIRED ACTION	POSSIBLE REQUIREMENTS
	Why I think I'd like it. How it fits with my Career Statement.	To find out more: On my own; e.g., Internet research. With other people, e.g., field trip/field research.	Examples: skills, degree, experience.
E.g., Pharmacist	Internal clue: want responsibility for patients. External clue: first day working as pharmacy tech. Desires: help people, more authority. Strengths: lead, interpersonal. Personal qualities: quiet, like one-to-one. Assets: PT experience, interest in chemistry, languages.	Research admission criteria to 3 Ontario universities. Field research with friend who is studying biochemistry. Field trips to universities.	University undergrad in sciences, good grades. High school credits to apply to university.

Table 2: Possibility and Exploration Plan — Copyright © Mark Franklin.

PEP, the client lists internal and external clues, inspired actions they intend to take, and skills and credentials that might be needed to achieve the newly identified career possibilities.

For example, consider a female client working as a pharmacy technician who wants to explore becoming a pharmacist as a career possibility. The career practitioner metaphorically jumps into the sandbox with the client, asking, "What are some clues you've noticed?" and then, "What do you want to do to explore this further?" The client reveals an internal clue that she wants responsibility for the patient. An external clue occurred her first day at work as a pharmacy technician when she saw the pharmacist in action and realized she wanted that role. Inspired actions the client wants to do include researching admission criteria to three universities, conducting field research interviews with a friend of a friend who is studying biochemistry at university, and "field trips" to postsecondary institutions.

Charlotte's Intentional Exploration Process

During the "your story" intervention, Charlotte discovered, among many other desires and strengths, that she wanted to combine her desire "to do good" with her knowledge of the advertising world. This desire formed part of her Career Statement. When Charlotte reads her Career Statement aloud in session, that moment marks the beginning of the intentional exploration process.

Like many clients, Charlotte was hopeful though unsure whether she could bring her Career Statement to life. The career practitioner has to "hold the space" and share the belief with the client that she can and will move towards what she wants. After this important shared experience, the career practitioner shows the client the intentional exploration graphic in Figure 1, and introduces and explains the components of this process: watch for clues, take inspired action, welcome opportunities, and become intentional with your thoughts and feelings.

SPOTLIGHT: *WHO YOU ARE MATTERS! A CAREER AND LIFE CLARIFICATION GAME*
by Mark Franklin

When it comes to becoming empowered in your career and life choices, who you are matters! This message surfaces through an innovative career and life clarification game, designed for youth and adults. By playing this discovery game with like-minded people, participants identify strengths, learn from each other, and recognize who and what influences them. The resulting Career Sketch and Career Statement provide participants with concrete evidence of their growing self-awareness and desired direction, resulting in confidence to engage in meaningful career-planning dialogue. Designed as an alternative to traditional career assessments, the game brings to life the "career and life clarification" process of the CareerCycles method of practice.

The career practitioner then introduces the Possibility and Exploration Plan as the working document to keep track of the client's intentional exploration. Each possibility the client is curious about is entered into the first column. In Charlotte's case, one possibility was an ad agency with a focus on non-profit clients. The next column contains clues that the client has noticed. An external clue came in the form of a suggestion from her mother that Charlotte speak with an acquaintance who worked at a marketing and fundraising agency that worked exclusively with non-profit clients. Their tagline, "marketing for a better world" seemed a good fit for Charlotte.

Charlotte's first internal clue was that she felt excited and inspired about taking action. Her inspired action was to summon the courage to call her mother's acquaintance at the agency. Much to Charlotte's surprise, she was offered a job interview. Several days later, the newly confident Charlotte received a job offer from the company, which she accepted.

The effectiveness of Charlotte narrating her career story is evident in the rekindled energy, good feelings, and positive mindset that flowed from the engaging process of telling her story and then writing her Career Statement. Her intentional exploration was made easier, and almost effortless, compared to the dread so many people attach to traditional job searches, especially in a down job market.

How does Charlotte feel about leaving the old company and joining a new one, more aligned with what's important to her? "I'm really excited. Leaving my old company was bittersweet. They gave me a really nice sendoff. But it wasn't working for me — I'd lost my passion for it. I wanted to do something that gave back, and would be more fulfilling. Now I am."

Key Concepts for Career Practitioners
Using the CC Method of Practice

Working With the Definition of Career

Within the CC framework, career is defined as: *"The full expression of who you are and how you want to be in the world, which keeps on expanding as it naturally goes through cycles of stability and change."* Sharing this definition with clients is a novel way of instilling relief because it veers away from career as a job and introduces a more holistic view of one's career. Let's break it down into component parts.

- *"The full expression"*: Think life, not job! "Full expression" goes beyond work to include volunteering, education and training, activities based on your interests, parenting, eldercare ... it's all you do.
- *"Of who you are"*: Your desires, strengths, personal qualities, demonstrated

interests, education and credentials, additional skills, life roles, influences of other people, and your own thoughts and feelings about who you are, and how you're expressing yourself in the world.

- *"And how you want to be"*: Most people know what they don't want and spend too much time thinking about that. What do you want? What's important to you? These are the questions that reveal your desires. Negative experiences are valuable in helping you translate your "don't wants" into "wants."
- *"In the world"*: Where your deepest wishes meet your daily reality.
- *"It keeps on expanding"*: If you've ever thought your career is contracting, think again. There are no mistakes: only expanding clarity about what you really want emerging from what you now know you don't want.
- *"As it naturally goes through cycles"*: It's perfectly natural that who you are changes. Think cycles, circles, and spirals, rather than a study-work-retire straight line.
- *"Of stability"*: Whatever the duration — 6 months, 6 years, 16 years? — stability gives you the basis for making a difference by doing things you're proud of.
- *"And change"*: Whether self- or externally generated, many people reflect back on periods of change as a blessing in disguise as they provide opportunity for career and life clarification.

❖ *Stop and Reflect*

Consider your own situation in light of this definition. What do you think of this definition? Does it apply to your career and life? Did you equate job with career? If you now recast your career using this definition, how does it change your sense of yourself and your identity?

Incorporating Assessments Into the CC Method

The narrative approach in general, and the CC method of practice in particular, positions the client as expert. The client is the storyteller and arbiter of what to include in his or her Career Sketch and Career Statement. This is in contrast to what often occurs when career practitioners rely on career tests and standardized assessments. Even with competent interpretation and good intentions on the part of the career practitioner, the fact that assessments have been created by experts moves the locus of control of a client's career choices away from the client and into the hands of the assessment authors. In contrast, positioning the client as expert storyteller empowers the person and conveys the message that all they need to make a good career and life choice exists within.

That is not to say that assessment results cannot be integrated into the CC method of practice. For example, Myers-Briggs Type Indicator, True Colors, Temperament, and Personality Dimensions results can be included in the personal qualities section of the Career Sketch. Interest inventories such as the Strong Interest Inventory or the Jackson Vocational Interest Survey can be integrated into the Natural Interests section of the Career Sketch. Career possibilities that clients are curious about that emerge from assessments can also be integrated into the possibilities section of the Career Sketch. Clients themselves determine whether or not to include this information in the Career Statement they write, using the content of the Career Sketch as input.

Sessions and Termination

Clients typically utilize four to seven sessions to work through the CC method of practice. In shorter engagements, clients may reach the beginning of the intentional exploration process and be satisfied with that progress. In a seven-session program, sessions are split between the two processes in the CC method, with a middle session as a transition between the two processes in which the Career Statement is read aloud. Even a one-session narrative intervention can yield a very positive outcome, showing clients that their stories contain much of the essential components required to make good career and life choices. Some clients may want to engage the career practitioner in additional sessions of intentional exploration.

When career sessions are terminated, clients will have completed several working documents of the CC method: the Career Sketch, Career Statement, and the Possibility and Exploration Plan. These tools, as well as the learning gained from the process and through the narrative, can be used by clients as they continue their career journeys on their own.

An important personal attribute outcome of the overall experience for clients is greater confidence and excitement than before for their careers. This is accompanied by a sense of hope and empowerment by which clients' lives are improved, enhanced, and deepened (see "Outcome Study Results" below). They discover how their mindset, thoughts, and feelings help or hinder their ability to move forward, and in this way they are better able to integrate the past, present, and future. While some clients make career changes, others realize they have much of what they want in their present career situations. Clients who choose to stay in their existing careers may still find enrichment by introducing into their lives activities, volunteer opportunities, further education, or travel, in keeping with the broader definition of career. In this way clients create new meanings and achieve a sense of well-being in their careers, which in itself is a positive long-term outcome.

Client Populations Successfully Served Using the CC Method

The CC approach has been successfully used with thousands of clients: youth nearing the end of high school, postsecondary students and recent graduates, those in early career, mid-career professionals, second career seekers, and those exploring late career and retirement scenarios. Clients with troubling or traumatic personal histories may require special sensitivity when using a narrative approach. Informed consent for a narrative approach is also especially important. Difficult life periods can be skipped, or the career professional can simply ask for an overall lesson learned from troubling or traumatic experiences. It is important to respect the client's boundaries of what he/she would like to share (i.e., what the client would consider too personal) and to inform the client that if he/she is in need of individual counselling or psychotherapy, a referral can be made.

Alignment With the Standards and Guidelines

The CC framework aligns with competency S3.2 described in the *Canadian Standards and Guidelines for Career Development Practitioners* (National Steering Committee, 2004), "To Demonstrate Method of Practice in Interactions with Clients." The specific competency S3.2.1 says "to develop a method of practice that is grounded in established or recognized ideas." In keeping with this competency, the CC method of practice is "a personally held model or theory" which is "a combination of models or a personally evolved model" and allows the practitioner to "conduct practice guided by theory." It also complies with the competency objective "to ensure consistency and flexibility in your counselling approach." As such, the CC method can be described and documented. However, to allow for flexibility, especially across clients and practitioners, the CC method may be adapted or refined in collaboration with Associates and Licensees, and is therefore a living entity requiring periodic changes and refinements. Additionally, not all interventions within the approach will be appropriate to all client situations, and therefore career practitioners will have to rely on their training and skills to utilize only the interventions that suit the client needs.

Five-Step Summary of the CareerCycles Method of Practice

1. **Name your question**: Is it a "what now?" question, or more of a "I know what I want, now how do I get there?" Be specific.
2. **Timeline your story**: What did you like and learn in each chapter of your story? Chapters can be early years, education, career portfolio, or the recent past.
3. **Gather and organize**: Examine everything from your story and categorize all elements into seven categories of desires, strengths, personal qualities,

assets, natural interests, other people's influences, and possibilities.

4. **Write your Career Statement**: Highlight the most important elements of your story that you've gathered and organized. Summarize in a succinct paragraph.

5. **Live your Career Statement**: Use it like a compass to direct your intentional exploration by watching for clues, then using the clues to lead you to take inspired action. Then, welcome meaningful opportunities, from wherever they may come.

Outcome Study: Results of CareerCycles Method of Practice

An outcome study of CareerCycles narrative method of practice has shown that individuals in "career pain" who went through the CareerCycles program experienced statistically significant increases in the six key measures of hope, optimism, confidence, resilience, curiosity and exploration, and personal growth.

Mark Franklin and evaluation consultant Basak Yanar designed and carried out a study in 2012 to explore the effect of the CC approach on clients. The researchers found that both of their hypotheses were correct — firstly, that a narrative approach to career management would have a positive impact on individuals' personal attributes including hope, confidence, resilience, optimism, and personal growth; and secondly, that these key personal attributes would be correlated with important career measures including career clarity, job satisfaction, job fit, and alignment between job and career expectations.

The outcome study collected data from 68 past clients, 72% female, 28% male, who experienced on average five sessions with a career professional from among CareerCycles' team of associates, all of whom used the narrative method of practice designed by practice leader Mark Franklin. After completing the CareerCycles program, subjects were asked to compare the extent to which they thought, felt, and behaved before and after the program. The Psychological Capital Questionnaire (Luthans, Norman, Avolio & Avey, 2007) was used to measure hope, optimism,

Career Buzz Radio
by Mark Franklin

"Welcome to Career Buzz, Canada's unique radio conversation that empowers lives, enriches careers, and energizes organizations," begins our weekly career radio show on CIUT, heard in Southern Ontario at 89.5 FM and available worldwide online at <www.ciut.fm >. Launched in 2006, the hour-long show hosted by Mark Franklin and five guest hosts has featured over 300 career stories and experts. Listeners hear ordinary Canadians share their extraordinary and inspirational stories. Career development expert guests have included Norm Amundson, John Krumboltz, and Barbara Moses. The show aims to uncover the intentional actions that our guests have taken and hopes to inspire our listeners to find their own "luck"!

Podcasts are available at <http://www.careercycles.com/category/radioshow>.

resilience, and self-efficacy (confidence). Two additional measures were "Curiosity and Exploration Inventory" and "Personal Growth Initiative Scale."

Summary

The use of the narrative approach at the core of the CC positions clients as experts in their own career and life choices. Each story within a client's career and life is metaphorically like a maple tree that can be "tapped" by the career practitioner for important elements. The "sap" gathered in this way can be refined into a concise Career Statement, like maple syrup, which empowers the client in their career exploration.

The CC method of practice is a cohesive and expanding repertoire of interventions to guide career practitioners to help their clients become empowered in their career and life choices. It is a truly holistic approach that aims to incorporate all facets of a person's life experience and then translates those into viable career options and increased career awareness. First developed by Mark Franklin, the CC approach has benefited greatly from the insights and additions of the many career practitioners who have used it and the intention is to continue to collaborate, refine, and expand the CC method in the future collaboratively with CareerCycles Associates and Licensees, and other career practitioners who choose to use it.

References

Adams, M. G. (2004). *Change your questions, change your life.* San Francisco, CA: Berrett-Koehler Publishers.

Bridges, W. (1998). *Creating you & co.: Learn to think like the CEO of your own career.* Cambridge, MA: Perseus Books.

Hicks, E., & Hicks, J. (2004). *Ask and it is given.* Carlsbad, CA: Hay House.

Lyubomirsky, S. (2007). *The How of happiness: A new approach to getting the life you want.* New York, NY: Penguin.

Mitchell, K. E., Levin, A. S., & Krumboltz, J. D. (1999). Planned happenstance: Constructing unexpected career opportunities. *Journal of Counseling & Development, 77,* 115–124. doi: 10.1234/12345678

National Steering Committee. (2012). *Canadian standards and guidelines for career development practitioners.* Retrieved from <http://career-dev-guidelines.org/career_dev/>.

Super, D. E. (1980). A life-span, life-space, approach to career development. *Journal of Vocational Behavior, 13,* 282–298.

White, M. (2007). *Maps of narrative practice.* New York, NY: Norton.

Zikic, J., & Franklin, M. (2010). Enriching careers and lives: Introducing a positive, holistic, and narrative career counselling method that bridges theory and practice. *Journal of Employment Counseling, 47,* 180–189.

Additional References Supporting the Outcome Study

Kashdan, T. B., Gallagher, M. W., Silvia, P. J., Winterstein, B. P., Breen, W. E., Terhar, D., & Steger, M. F. (2009). The Curiosity and Exploration Inventory-II: Development, factor structure, and initial psychometrics. *Journal of Research in Personality, 43,* 987–998.

Kashdan, T. B., Rose, P., & Fincham, F. D. (2004). Curiosity and exploration: Facilitating positive subjective experiences and personal growth opportunities. *Journal of Personality Assessment, 82,* 291–305.

Luthans, F., Avolio, B. J., Avey, J. B., & Norman, S. M. (2007). Positive psychological capital: Measurement and relationship with performance and satisfaction. *Personnel Psychology 60,* 541–572.

Luthans, F., Norman, S. M., Avolio, B. J., & Avey, J. B. (2008). The mediating role of psychological capital in the supportive organizational climate–employee performance relationship. *Journal of Organizational Behavior, 29,* 219–238.

Robitschek, C. (1998). Personal growth initiative: The construct and its measure. *Measurement and Evaluation in Counseling and Development, 30,* 183–198.

Robitschek, C., & Cook, S. W. (1999). The influence of personal growth initiative and coping styles on career exploration and vocational identity. *Journal of Vocational Behavior, 54,* 127–141.

Discussion and Activities

Discussion

Discussion Questions

1. "Career is from the Latin carrus meaning passage, course, or wheeled chariot. One's career is one's life. In this sense, all counselling is career counselling, since all counselling is about one's life" (Peavy, 2004, p. 44). Discuss.

2. The task of career counselling is to help people construct and enact more meaningful career narratives. Accomplishing this task requires an understanding of narrative resources for making meaning, criteria for adopting a narrative as one's own, and the relationship between narrative construction and enaction, between the reflective spectator on life and the active participant in life (Cochran, 1997, p. x).

    • How is a narrative approach different from more traditional approaches to career development (e.g., Super or Holland, etc.)?
    • What client issues might best be addressed by narrative approaches?
    • What is your opinion of assisting clients from multiple theoretical perspectives?

Personal Reflections

1. Imagine yourself engaging in the CC method as a client. What do you imagine the process would look like between you and the counsellor? What qualities would you expect from a narrative-focused counsellor?
2. Narrative career counselling is underpinned by constructs such as reflection, meaning making, story, and personal agency. It takes a holistic view of individuals and their career concerns. A particular emphasis is placed on the counselling relationship. How would you explain narrative career counselling to a client? How might those from other non-European American cultures respond to this approach? What would the challenges be for you in working with clients from a narrative perspective?

Career Practitioner Role

In what ways does the narrative approach described in this chapter address competency S3.2.4 in the Standards and Guidelines, which states: develop and implement a process for achieving clients' goals that are consistent with your own method of practice? Does this approach to career counselling raise any questions for you?

Activities: Using the CareerCycles Framework

Session One: Getting Started

Find a partner who would like to have a first session with you. Use the interventions below to guide your first session.

1. **What's on the radar screen?**
    Find out what possibilities the client has been thinking about. These may be self-generated ideas or ideas that have been provided by significant others. Eventually, you will enter them into the Career Sketch. Try statements and questions such as:

    *   Sometimes, people with a question about what they should do, have some preliminary or vague ideas. I like to use the metaphor of a "radar screen." What's on your radar screen of possibilities right now? What have you been thinking about, however vague it may be?
    *   What else?

2. **Initial Desires Clarification**
    Find out what the client wants in his/her career life and use these initial desires when drafting the Career Sketch. When the client talks about a negative experience, reframe negative statements by reversing negative experiences into positively worded desires. For example, in response to the question, *"What didn't you like about that job or experience?"* client may say things like: the boss was a

micromanager; it was very repetitive; too much dealing with customers; terrible shifts; et cetera. Your response might be:

> *You know what's great about negative work experience? It helps you clarify what's important to you in making work or career choices. Let's take each one of the aspects of that job you're telling me, and let's turn it into a statement of what's really important to you. So if the boss was a micromanager, what would be important to you in a manager?*

The client may say things like: *Boss gives me space to do my work.*

> *Great! Let's take the next one… if that job was really repetitive, what would be ideal? Is it variety? Or challenge?*

You can use these initial desires when drafting the Career Sketch (optional). Other activities could include introducing the CareerCycles framework and processes and continuing your story as described below.

3. **Introduce the CareerCycles framework and processes.**
   Reframe the client's question in the context of the CC framework using the model in Figure 1. Use a Career Sketch (Table 1) and draft a question from the client's own words that he or she is inspired to answer. Use all information gathered so far and use it to introduce the rest of the Career Sketch, as you fill in what you know already.

   - *Let me take a just a few minutes to step back and reframe everything you've told me so far so we can move forward. I'd like to start with this framework. Please have a look as I walk you through it briefly.*
   - *Now, let me use a Career Sketch and show you what I mean.*
   - *First of all, let's draft your question.*

Write the version of the client's question from your notes. Work with the client to draft a good question.

   - *That's a good question, and I don't know the answer to it! Do you want an answer to this question? Great! This is our goal—answering your question. Research shows that outcomes of counselling are better from a client's perspective when there is a stated goal. This question will be our goal. Okay?*

Now look at the tabular part of the Career Sketch. Go back and forth between Career Sketch and framework so client gets a firm connection between the career and life clarification process and the sections of the Career Sketch.

I'm going to fill in what I heard from you so far.

Now, go through each section of Career Sketch and enter from your notes what you heard from the client.

> TIP: as you write each item in the Desires section, you can say…
>
> *Wouldn't it be great if you [fill in with each of the client's desires]? Wouldn't it be great if you have a commute that was less than half hour? Wouldn't it be great if you had more creativity in your role? (Hicks & Hicks, 2004)*

4. **Work with the narrative:**
    Continue into Your Story directly from the previous intervention, and get started on the narrative while still in the first session. You will likely not finish, but getting started on this intervention shows client how this process works and engages them deeply so that they will want to return for follow-up sessions.

    *   *Your question is really important. As much as clients want career professionals to wave a magic wand over their head and answer questions like this, it just doesn't work that way. However, what I do know is that a question like yours yields answers when we walk through this process.*

Ask for consent.

> *Your question is related to how you got here, how you got to this point in your life and in your story. Would it be okay for me to take you back in time and ask you some questions about how you got to this point in your life? This tends to be very useful, to uncover ideas about who you were and what you wanted to do, before other realities settled on top of you. It's really good to start in the early years and walk forward from there. I'd like to start in your early years, before high school, up to age of 14 or 15. Okay?*

Below are questions you can use. While you are walking through the client's story, be sure to pause each time a desire, strength, personal quality, or asset (demonstrated interest, other skill, and/or credential) arises and debrief it. Ask if it's okay to write it down. Use their language, not yours!

Be curious. Here's your chance to probe, wonder aloud, and ask questions about what you're hearing. But stick with the story and be careful not to get lost in a tangent. Remind yourself and the client where you stepped away from the story and return to that point …

> *We were just talking about your transition from high school to postsecondary, so let's go back there now.*

When a new possibility comes to mind, ask if it's okay to add it to the Possibilities You are Curious About. Be sure to explain that here you're in brain-storming mode.

We're exploring new territory here, so if something comes up, let's see if it passes the bar. If you're curious about it, then let's write it down. If you're not, no problem, we'll just let it pass. Don't worry, my feelings won't be hurt if you discard any ideas of mine!

You likely won't complete the story in the first session. At the end of your time together, review where you are and let the client know you will send them an email for a between-session task to create their own timeline.

Let me hold the story here. We're progressing really well. I'd like to ask you to complete the story using a timeline. I have some notes about this which I will send you. It asks you to timeline your story and annotate it with comments about what you liked and learned. The purpose is to remind yourself of your own story, to bring it all to mind, and also to act as a visual aid for us as we continue to walk through your story next session.

This may take you into the next session or beyond depending on the age of the client, the depth and breadth of their story, and your own probing.

Session Two: Continuing Your Story

Questions to begin the elicitation of the story:

What's changed since we began talking about your career question? Would it be okay to continue where we left off last time?

Here are some questions to walk the client through the chapters of their lives …

- *When you were a child and parents or other important adults asked, What do you want to do, or be, when you grow up? What kind of answers did you give?*
- *What kind of child were you? What did you like doing in your free time?*
- *As a child what work roles did you see and what was your reaction to them? Your parents? Other important adults like grandparents or aunts or uncles? What opinions do they still hold about your future?*
- *What advice or other messages did you receive about the world of work when you were a child?*
- *Let's move to high school… What did you like in high school? Courses? Is that still an interest of yours? What about activities you did outside school? Are you still interested in that?*
- *Did you work during school? What did you like about it? What skills did you gain? What knowledge did you gain?*
- *What was your state of mind as you approached the end of high school? What*

possibilities did you consider? What possibilities did you reject? What led you to reject that?

- *What led you, ultimately, to decide to do what you did? (e.g., apply to university)*
- *What led you to major/specialize in _____? What did you find fascinating during your postsecondary education? What else?*
- *How did your interests change or evolve during your education?*
- *What was your state of mind as you approached the end of your undergrad degree/ college diploma? What possibilities were you considering?*
- *What did you do next? What did you like about it? What strengths did you enjoy using? What skills did you develop? What knowledge did you gain?*

For each period of education, work, parenting, travel, et cetera, ask:

What did you like? What strengths did you enjoy using? What skills did you develop? What knowledge did you gain? What led to your leaving?

Your Story is a significant intervention in which many of client's challenges and personal stories may arise. The CareerCycles method of practice lets personal information emerge in its own time rather than asking for it directly.

Readings

Supplementary Readings

Amundson, N. E. (2010). *Metaphor making: Your career, your life, your way*. Richmond, BC: Ergon Communications.

Brott, P. (2001). The storied approach to a postmodern perspective for career counseling. *The Career Development Quarterly, 49*, 304–313.

Campbell, C., & Ungar, M. (2004a, Sept.). Constructing a life that works: Part 1, Blending postmodern family therapy and career counseling. *The Career Development Quarterly, 53*(1), 16–27.

Campbell, C., & Ungar, M. (2004b, Sept.). Constructing a life that works: Part 2, An approach to practice. *The Career Development Quarterly, 53*(1), 28–40.

Chen, C. (1997). Career projection: Narrative in context. *Journal of Vocational Education and Training, 49*(2), 311–326.

Chope, R. C. (2005). Qualitatively assessing family influence in career decision making. *Journal of Career Assessment, 13*, 395–314.

Chope, R.C., & Consoli, A. J. (2006). A storied approach to multicultural career counseling. In K. Maree (Ed.), *Shaping the story: A guide to facilitating career counseling* (pp. 83–96). Pretoria, South Africa: Van Schaik

Cochran, L. (1997). *Career counseling: A narrative approach*. Thousand Oaks, CA: Sage.

Colley, H. (2004). *Do we choose careers or do they choose us?* Vejleder Forum No 4. Retrieved from <http://www.vejlederforum.dk/page3.apsx?recordid3=228>.

Hansen, J. T. (2002, Summer). Postmodern implications for theoretical integration of counseling approaches. *Journal of Counseling and Development, 80,* 315–321.

Hansen, K. (n.d). *Plotting the story of your ideal career.* Retrieved from <http://www.quintcareers.com/story_of_ideal_career.html>

Payne, M. (2006). *Narrative therapy* (2nd ed.). Thousand Oaks, CA: Sage.

Peavy, R. V. (2004). *Sociodynamic counselling: A practical approach to meaning making.* Chagrin Falls, OH: Taos Institute Publications.

nineteen

Community Capacity Building as a Model for Career Development Planning

SCOTT FISHER
City of Greater Sudbury, Ontario
WAYLON GREGGAIN
University of Toronto
BLYTHE C. SHEPARD
University of Lethbridge

PRE-READING QUESTIONS:

1. What do you think is meant by community capacity building?
2. How might community capacity building apply to career development?

Introduction and Learning Objectives

Community Capacity Building (CCB) may seem a little foreign, or out of place, when discussing career development, yet it is very relevant to the field. More and more, **community capacity building** is being used to develop structures that bring about systematic change. Like the related concepts of community development and empowerment, community capacity building is about increasing the capabilities of people to articulate and address community issues and to overcome barriers to achieving improved outcomes in the quality of people's lives (Chaskin, 2001). More specifically, "[c]ommunity capacity is the interaction of human capital, organization resources, and social capital existing within a given community that can be leveraged to solve collective problems and improve or maintain the well-being of that community" (Chaskin, Brown, Venkatesh, & Vidal, 2001, p. 7). This view is vastly different from prior models that focused on a community's weaknesses and deficits and largely ignored resources and assets.

In this chapter we describe the community capacity building approach by which communities are empowered to address local problems, and show how this holistic approach is better at fortifying a community's resources than delivering social programs based on specific needs. We review the assets that are to be considered in building capacity with particular attention on the importance of the capabilities of individuals and the roles of local organizations. Specific techniques and methods of how to build community capacity will also be explored. We will then examine the context of career development and how the community capacity building model may be applied by career practitioners in their work with individuals and in developing career development programs.

The learning objectives for this chapter are to enable you to do the following:

1   Define community capacity building.
2. Explain how community capacity building is proactive and empowering.
3. Identify the range of potential community assets.
4. Outline the importance of human and social capital as community assets.
5. Outline the steps involved in building community capacity.
6. Clarify the link between individual career planning and community capacity building.
7. Develop awareness of the ethical implications and limitations associated with community capacity building.

What Is Community Capacity Building and Why Is It Important?

Needs-based programs typically focus on what communities lack (a deficit approach) as opposed to what they have (an assets approach). The Nutrition North Canada Program (NNC) is an example of a needs-based program. In 2012, UN Special Rapporteur on the right to food Olivier De Schutter, after consulting with a wide range of Aboriginal groups and communities in Canada, reported on the disproportionate vulnerability of Indigenous peoples in Canada (about 3% of the population) to food insecurity, diet-related illness, and lack of access to land and traditional foods (De Schutter, 2012). The Nutrition North Canada Program is a subsidy program run by the Government of Canada with the aim of improving access to perishable healthy foods in isolated northern communities. De Schutter noted that the NNC program was insufficiently monitored to ensure that retailers pass on appropriate subsidies to recipient communities. However, more fundamentally, he was "concerned that Nutrition North Canada was designed and is being implemented without an inclusive and transparent process that provides Northern communities with an opportunity to exercise their right to active and meaningful participation" (p. 18). He would have preferred an assets-based approach.

A legacy of the needs-based approach is that those receiving aid learn to define themselves and their communities by their needs and their deficiencies. They come to believe that only a state of degradation will enable them to attract resources from expert-based, top-down approaches. In the case of the NNC program, De Schutter maintains that continued and concerted measures are needed to "develop new initiatives and reform existing ones, in consultation and in real partnership with indigenous peoples with the goal toward strengthening indigenous peoples' own self-determination and decision-making over their affairs at all levels" (De Schutter, 2012, p. 19).

Recently, policy makers and local residents have explored asset-based alternatives to community development. Asset-based approaches seek to identify and capitalize on the tangible and intangible assets available to the community, rather than on what the community and its members lack. For example, community members in Port Alberni, BC, enhanced their ability to be self-sufficient in food knowledge, collection, and preservation methods using an Indigenous approach that relied on local knowledge and resources. Here we compare the two approaches and present the benefits of community capacity building.

The Needs-Based Approach

Most social assistance programs are needs-based, that is, they are designed to produce an outcome for a specific and urgent need. In the past, programs related to immigration, health services, social assistance, and housing relied heavily on expert-driven approaches that delivered outcomes to their "clients" or "customers." For communities devastated by natural disasters, the most common path taken has been that of addressing the needs, deficiencies, and problems faced by the community (Kretzmann & McKnight, 1993). For example, in response to the 2011 Slave Lake wildfire that destroyed roughly one third of the community, the Canadian Red Cross stepped in to provide assistance to families, individuals, and community groups. As is the case in emergencies, the Red Cross first conducted client needs assessments and then provided services and materials to meet people's immediate needs for safety and comfort, and to expedite their return to normal daily activities. Over the long term the Red Cross continued to work in the community to identify unmet community needs and to provide appropriate support.

This needs-driven approach uses up most of our financial and human resources today, and has led to situations where the greater the need, the more money the community receives. People become consumers of services, increasingly dependent on outside funding, rather than being producers and creators of solutions. The needs-based approach tends to create and perpetuate the cycle of dependence.

The needs-based approach further weakens the community by pulling in "experts" from outside to advise and guide rather than using and developing local expertise. This use of outside experts is a common practice when we consider the myriad of governmental employment programs aimed at assisting people of wide and diverse backgrounds. Many employment programs, due to the legislated areas of education and training, fall under provincial control. These programs are developed in the provincial capital and representatives are sent to the far reaches of the province to implement them. This deploying of outside experts weakens relationships within the community and loosens the glue that binds the community together. This needs-based strategy perpetuates a type of "maintenance" or "survival" mindset targeted at isolated individuals, rather than developing the energies of the entire community. This type of attitude contributes to feelings of hopelessness that pervades struggling communities (Kretzmann & McKnight, 1993).

The Community Capacity Building (CCB) Approach

Community capacity, in contrast, is the degree to which a community can develop, implement, and sustain actions that allow it to exert greater control over its physical, social, economic, and cultural environments (Littlejohns & Thompson, 2001). Community capacity building has been conceptualized as a holistic representation of capabilities (those the community is endowed with and those the community has access to), plus the facilitators and barriers to the realization of those capabilities in the broader social environment (Littlejohns & Thompson, 2001). In comparison to needs-based models, a greater emphasis is placed on producing resolutions to collective problems as well as accessing and bolstering hidden and overlooked resources (Chaskin, 2001). CCB has been described as a grassroots process that aims to bring together and enhance existing skills and abilities of communities (Atkinson & Willis, 2004). The focus is on finding solutions to problems from existing resources and individuals, and using relationships to leverage the collective knowledge of the community to create solutions.

CCB can also be viewed as being intimately related to outcomes and government policy. As indicated by Dodd and Boyd (2000), "A community's capacity is directly linked to its ability to act effectively to influence change, and to engage government officials and elected representatives in meaningful, collaborative policy dialogue" (p. 9). The emphasis, in this context, is very much based on outcomes and how the community performs against certain measures. Building a community's capacity must be focused on results in order to keep community members engaged by producing concrete changes. The purpose of the CCB process should, therefore, be determined by the collective members of the community in order to create something that is meaningful for everyone involved (Coyne and Associates Limited, 2006). Community support is critical in ensuring that the CCB initiative is accepted, adhered to, and allowed to flourish. In fact, the lack of community support could be used as a measure of the effectiveness of a CCB initiative. If it is succeeding, community members will be active and engaged — even questioning, challenging, and/or debating the issues with a focus on what should be done rather than complaining about what can't be done (Frank & Smith, 1999).

A local approach fosters better co-ordination and understanding within a community. Significant community development takes place only when local community people are committed to investing themselves and their resources in the effort. Moreover, with continuing budget constraints and lack of funds, community capacity building is often the only viable option for some communities (Kretzmann & McKnight, 1993). As pointed out by Atkinson and Willis (2004), there are many internal (within the community) benefits to consider such as civic engagement, the strength of local networks, increased levels of trust, and pride of place. For many battered communities, where the local economy has struggled, a lack of pride and self-worth may make it very difficult to "sell yourself" effectively in a tough job market. CCB can provide tangible outcomes such as increased number of community-based work opportunities and increased competency in setting and achieving goals (Atkinson & Willis, 2004).

What Are the Assets of the Community?

Individual Capacities and Resources

Community capacity building involves all of the community assets, its buildings and natural resources, and its people — its "human capital" or member capacity. To build capacity, community members need to be skilled in working collaboratively, building effective programs, and building effective coalition infrastructures. Members' attitudes and motivations are also crucial. They must: (a) value collaboration; (b) have a strong commitment to the targeted problem; (c) hold positive attitudes about the other stakeholders (e.g., viewing them as capable and needed, and valuing their diversity); and (d) have a positive perception of one's own role and competence (Foster-Fishman, Berkowitz, Lounsbury, Jacobson, & Allen, 2001).

The community may use a mapping technique (described later in the chapter) to inventory the individual talents and skills of its members. As well, the community may gather local stories and knowledge to uncover hidden or overlooked resources (Atkinson & Willis, 2004). Through storytelling, a community may be able to detect root problems impeding its advancement, identify assets and starting points, as well as motivate and enthuse members. It is important to put an emphasis on the potential of all community members to have the ability to contribute, especially if some of them are finding themselves marginalized, such as the elderly, the disabled, and the young.

When the community of West Carleton in Ontario began to experiment with capacity building in their youth mental health promotion, they experienced difficulty, initially, in identifying human assets because community members did not feel they had the skills and understanding to deal with the situation (Austin, 2003). This is a common theme and a challenging aspect of successful community capacity building. Acknowledging that every individual has the potential to contribute to the progress of the overall community is essential; however, many communities will experience the same fate as West Carleton in that some individual members will downplay or not acknowledge their own skills and abilities. In a community whose assets are being mobilized, marginalized people and those who feel inadequate play an integral role in the process — not as recipients of services, but as full contributors to society.

Capacities of Associations, Organizations, and Institutions

Although the capacities of larger groups and institutions may be obvious, they are equally important when it comes to CCB. Private businesses and public institutions, such as schools, libraries, parks, police/fire stations, hospitals, and service agencies make up the most visible part of a community's fabric. Associations are less formal and less dependent on paid staff than institutions and organizations. The largest part of the asset base of any community is composed of its individuals, associations, organizations, and institutions — this is where the **social capital** and sense of community can be found (Kretzmann & McKnight, 1993). The capacity of these larger groups to mobilize a community's resources plays a key role in determining the positive or negative change within the community.

Organizational capacity is the degree to which institutions can organize their members in a productive manner and involves having the following five fundamental aspects:

1. Leaders with good communication, conflict resolution, and administrative skills, and a strong vision.
2. Formalized procedures that clearly identify members' roles and provide clear guidelines for making decisions.
3. Well-developed internal communication systems that allows for effective information sharing and problem solving.
4. Human and financial resources, including those that are required to implement new programs and maintain daily operations.
5. An open learning orientation that seeks and responds to both internal and external feedback.

These five types of organizational capacities are necessary in order to adapt to changing contexts, overcome barriers, and promote accountability (Foster et al., 2001).

Outside organizations can play a key part in forming institutional structures and in identifying challenges that need to be addressed and/or resolved from a community perspective. With a holistic approach such as CCB, these organizations often carry a more favourable position within the community because they have established strong connections and trust among the wider population (Torres & Barnet, 2002). Community networks and "bridges" can be built that allow for wider community involvement and participation in developing systematic policy change.

How to Build Community Capacity

The components required to build community capacity will vary depending upon the terminology used and the approaches taken. There are, however, some common elements that appear when we look at the literature on this topic. Common themes or elements include participation, leadership, communication, skills and knowledge, resources, and sense of community (Aref, Redzuan, & Gill, 2010; Bopp, GermAnn, Bopp, Baugh Littlejohns, & Smith, 2001; Labonte & Laverack, 2001; Maclellan-Wright et al., 2007). Although these "ingredients" will mean different things to different people, they are all necessary to some degree in order to effectively build community capacity. Although we will not go into detail regarding the various elements and their definitions, it is important to keep these themes in mind as they are interwoven throughout the following steps.

Step 1: Map Assets

A thorough map of a community's assets should start with an inventory of the talents, skills, and capabilities of the community's residents. Working household by household, building by building, block by block, the capacity mapmakers will find a surprising array of individual talents and skills; but oftentimes few of these talents and skills have been mobilized for community-building purposes (Kretzmann & McKnight, 1993). Local knowledge that may have been hidden is extremely beneficial for a community to share and learn from in order to advance its goals. When outside experts are utilized to provide solutions to community problems, the lack of local knowledge can be a barrier to obtaining trust and gaining a fuller understanding of the issues at hand. For example, upon further review, a career practitioner may gain a much better understanding as to why there may be hostility to a new governmental program. Working with the community in a collaborative manner can help produce a much more dynamic and accurate map of the community that will allow its members to move forward together. As pointed out by Atkinson and Willis (2004), it is essential to engage as much of the population as possible to identify the full community and not just the vocal members.

Creating an environment of equality is also important in achieving this goal. An environment in which every voice is given equal importance and each person's opinion can be heard will help to keep the community's vision for the future strong. Individuals who can participate in creating a shared vision for their community help validate that everyone involved has innate knowledge and solutions to the issues being discussed (Austin, 2003). Another benefit of community engagement is that people and organizations who normally do not work with one another are brought together for a common purpose, resulting in new relationships and a better capacity to collaborate (Ramirez, Aitkin, Galin, & Richardson, 2002).

Communities are rarely homogenous; thus the need to cast a net far and wide through various methods of engagement in order to capture as much of the capacities of the community as possible. Some methods that can be used include forums, focus groups, surveys (online and paper-based), telephone interviews, and association newsletters. This could include scheduling meetings at different times of the day/ different days of the week, using different survey designs (narrative versus fact-based), or providing information in another language format. By using as many of these methods as possible, a better inventory of the community's assets is obtained. It is also important to stay current as communities change over time, sometimes abruptly. For example, a mill closing down in a single-industry town would have a high impact on the capacity assessment. By regularly assessing a community, there is a much better chance of ensuring that the assumptions and understanding of the community's capacity are accurate (Frank & Smith, 1999).

Non-economic institutions, such as churches, schools, police departments, libraries, hospitals, and parks, can be overlooked in terms of their potential in positively rebuilding their local economies. Yet they have the potential to be key players in building stronger and healthier communities depending on how they spend their money. Although the end result is not of a pure economic benefit, it is still an important part of the community map and may have greater potential in long-term planning than some immediate economic outcomes.

Examples of using non-economic institutions to help rebuild a community's economy include: libraries purchasing from local vendors; hospitals hiring neighbourhood residents; and schools employing students through entrepreneurship training programs. There are several methods that institutions can use to build the local economy: local purchasing, developing new businesses, developing human resources, hiring locally, freeing potentially productive economic space, adopting local investment strategies, mobilizing external resources, and creating alternative credit institutions (Kretzmann & McKnight, 1993). For example, a school board that decides to purchase second-language textbooks from a local supplier may, in turn, provide an opportunity for a local bookstore to expand and provide more services, which then can add to the linguistic and cultural capabilities of the community.

Step 2: Develop a Vision and a Plan

Once a community's assets and capabilities have been identified through mapping, it is important to develop a shared vision and plan that the community can act upon. Without a commonly held vision, the hard work of regenerating a community is difficult to sustain. The process of building community capacity must involve a representative mix of participants and not be limited to the visible civic leaders. It is vitally important that the voices of all community members be heard. An active approach to the management of CCB is needed in order to achieve a broader representation of the community and to eliminate the dominance of representatives from previous power-holding groups such as entrenched families or community elites (Atkinson & Willis, 2004). Past history may have had the effect of "silencing" a group and, without that group's input, the community will suffer in its quest to build capacities. If the vision or plan does not represent the majority of members, the community's problem-solving potential will not be fully realized.

This is often the case with young people who usually have very little voice or influence in the community, and lack the skills and support to participate fully. A rural community in British Columbia succeeded in promoting youth capacity and strengthening the voice of youth by matching each young person with an adult for each position on the local Youth Council, Restorative Justice Committee, and Town Council (Shepard, 2005).

In order to keep residents connected to the here and now, future planning should be tied to problem solving. Members should be committed to mobilizing capacities to deal with current problems; otherwise planning can become a future-oriented and abstract exercise (Kretzmann & McKnight, 1993). The vision and plan should not be focused solely on short-term goals or treated as a "quick fix" to a problem, but should include long-term goals and a vision (Atkinson & Willis, 2004). Developing a shared vision, however, is not always a harmonious process and individuals may have differing opinions as to where the community should be headed.

Institutions and organizations will likely have different priorities and the existing bureaucratic structure may be cumbersome and counterproductive to the community's goals. If members can work together, however, having a unified goal can increase personal investment, creativity, hope, and control (Kretzmann & McKnight, 1993). There may be a tendency to align the process with community elites and/or vocal individuals to lessen conflict and friction. Such an approach may result in increased harm and distress to community members over time. The key is to ensure that leaders in the CCB process possess the ability and skills to negotiate and resolve small-group conflicts (Atkinson & Willis, 2004).

CCB should also allow adequate time and resources to develop inventories and maps that reflect the community in question. However, it should not be an infinite process that impedes the community's ability to achieve its goals. A balance needs to be struck, one that is different for every community. CCB must be systematically addressed and developed. Community member fatigue, or burn-out, is another consideration to take into account when developing a shared vision and plan (Atkinson & Willis, 2004). Some community members may be over-involved as far as time and energy commitments or may be taking the place of other, more suitable members.

Step 3: Leverage Outside Resources to Support Local Development

Once a community's assets and resources have been identified and a shared vision and plan have been developed, the community can seek outside alliances, partnerships, and networks to provide additional assets and resources to create change. A community needs to feel engaged and capable before outside resources can be put to good use; therefore, enlisting outside resources should occur only after all the community's capacities have been thoroughly inventoried and a broad representative group of citizens have begun to solve problems together (Kretzmann & McKnight, 1993). By leveraging outside resources after these steps have been taken, communities are often left with better employment and economic opportunities.

Step 4: Evaluate

Evaluation is an important step to ensure that the community has been able to meet its goals in an efficient and useful manner. Part of this process involves establishing measurements that will result in tangible results that the community can later use to evaluate themselves. Some of the ways in which capacity can be measured include stronger community relationships, new and/or increased community-based opportunities, enhanced communication among members, increased competency in communal goal setting, enhanced respect for limited resources, skilled leadership, and an increased ability to handle stressors (Frank & Smith, 1999). Unfortunately, this step is often neglected or overlooked due to lack of resources and/or support, resistance in the community, or a lack of understanding. However, every CCB initiative should include evaluation and should aim to answer four basic questions:

- What worked and why?
- What did not work and why?
- What could have been done differently?
- What adjustments and changes are required now? (Frank & Smith, 1999).

Answering these throughout the CCB process will ultimately allow for the community to make adjustments as needed.

Using the CCB Framework for Career Development

The community capacity building model can be applied to career development planning and yield many of the same benefits. Increasingly, career development professionals are asked to identify strategic community partnerships in order to develop programs that make the most of limited community resources.

CCB — A Canadian Perspective

CCB has been incorporated into the Canadian career development landscape from work influenced by the *Canadian Standards and Guidelines for Career Development Practitioners* (S&Gs). The S&Gs' community capacity building competencies are linked to maximizing community resources, connecting clients with those resources, and better co-ordinating services for clients within the community (National Steering Committee, 2004).

The idea for linking individual career planning to community capacity building was first proposed for those living in rural environments or in developing nations (Aisensen, Bezanson, Frank, & Reardon, 2002). Researchers have suggested that counsellors in rural and remote communities focus on community sustainability and economic growth as part of individual career development in order to be relevant and effective. In support of this idea, Aisensen and colleagues provided several examples of innovative career-community development projects in which career guidance specialists, teachers, and experts in economic development collaborated to support young people in unpredictable economies. Aisensen and colleagues suggested that such an integrative approach helps address relationships between (a) personal development and employability, and (b) the sustainability and vitality of a community. It is essentially a reciprocal process, whereby the community benefits when its members benefit and vice versa.

The traditional needs-based model requires the career practitioner to "fix" the client's problem of not knowing what career to pursue. The career practitioner becomes an "expert" who is there to give direction and advice.

Community Capacity Building and Career Development

by Waylon Greggain

Paulo Freire once wrote, "...to alienate human beings from their own decision-making is to change them into objects" (Freire, 1970, p. 85). Communities and parents hold a wealth of expertise in life choices and career-path decision making. However, parents and community members are often excluded from the formal career development process because there are no mechanisms for involving them. Community capacity building is about including parents and community members in the dialogue with youth and the process for career development.

As we have seen, the use of an expert can have a negative effect on the ability of the group or an individual to advance collective and individual goals. For example, the career practitioner expert may be mistrusted due to past experiences with other outsiders or be out of touch with local knowledge and events. An asset-based strategy, on the other hand, offers a fresh point of view to assess career choice and intervene for career facilitation purposes (Ebersöhn & Eloff, 2003).

Viewing the receiver of career development services as having inherent or accumulated assets changes the lens through which assistance is offered. Using an **asset-based approach** means moving away from a focus on the expert knowledge and skills of the career practitioner to the skills and abilities of the client. An asset-based approach suggests that helping can be a pluralistic effort where career development becomes a process of facilitation (Savickas, 1997). All of these efforts increase the likelihood of the community's individual members to achieve meaningful goals of their own.

Promoting Community Partnership to Increase Self-Sufficiency and Productivity

Professionals in the career development field must initiate and maintain effective relationships with key community partners. Doing so serves to maximize community resources, co-ordinate services for clients better, and help bring the community together. Career development practitioners must attend regular community gatherings, visit with people new to the community, and share information openly. Other options include seeking out natural helpers, establishing advisory groups, and maintaining relationships with past clients (National Steering Committee 2004). It is vitally important for career practitioners to collaborate with community partners to assess a client's need for community service in areas like training, education, careers/ employment, family support, and finances. In addition to gathering knowledge by formal methods, it also involves informal methods such as narrative accounts from community members. It is the quality of connections between individuals and their community that will help develop a sustainable career development landscape.

Working With the Community to Develop a Vision

The career practitioner should take a key role in helping a community develop its capacity building plan and vision. It is the career practitioner's job to help the community create a common understanding of the preferred vision. Career development workers must participate in a wide array of community organizations and businesses. In doing so, they will help to define parameters for working together by establishing roles and responsibilities. It is also necessary to conduct interviews with a variety of community members in order to facilitate discussions and establish vision statements (National Steering Committee, 2004). This step is especially true of small, rural, or remote communities that have perceived limited resources. Career practitioners should help the community and individuals identify employment and lifestyle alternatives through such mechanisms as building an adaptable workforce, increasing employability and basic skill levels, and improving life and leadership skills.

Working With the Community to Assess and Implement Action Plans

The final two crucial steps in community capacity building that career practitioners can help with are the implementation and evaluation of action plans. Career practitioners can assist in establishing an action plan, promoting an environment that encourages sharing, and helping individuals in defining their roles. An evaluation process is necessary as it encourages accountability and helps to determine what is working and what is not. Career practitioners can help the community to establish evaluative criteria and work with the community to collect and analyze data. One must remember that addressing economic, social, educational, and employment goals is the community's work. Career development practitioners provide support by acting as a resource — they are not meant to take the lead on such activities (National Steering Committee, 2004).

Case Study: Miziwe Biik Aboriginal Employment
and Training Community Capacity Building Project
Miziwe Biik Aboriginal Employment and Training was created in 1991 to meet the unique training and employment needs of Aboriginal peoples in Toronto. The project helps to provide the Greater Toronto Area's Aboriginal community with training initiatives and employment services (Miziwe Biik Aboriginal Employment and Training, 2002). Long-term goals for this community were incorporated into the design and implementation at the outset of the Community Capacity Building Project. Miziwe Biik Board and staff were invited to think how they might fit into the Aboriginal community in the future and were asked to consider how this community might become more self-sustaining. Members were able to identify and consider in more detail some of their inherent skills, abilities, and assets as well as some of the inherent gaps in reaching future goals.

The agency undertook a mapping exercise of existing programs and services available to its clientele, which was meant to serve not as an evaluation of the agency but rather as a snapshot of the agency from the perspective of clients and community members (Miziwe Biik Aboriginal Employment and Training, 2002). The agency identified some of the perceived gaps in services and program delivery facing their community. Other methods for finding available community assets included surveys, various focus groups, and meetings with Elders, employers, management, employment counsellors, and clients. The agency was then able to gather more knowledge of their assets, existing and potential, for their community. One such example involves the Elders and their ability to act as mentors to young Aboriginal people.

One participant in the Elders' focus group spoke extensively about the benefits of having mentors in schools. Elders pointed out that they could be an example to youth by speaking on panels about their own experiences of employment. They said they saw a role for themselves in talking with young people and building connections with the younger generations. Such a link would allow inexperienced, younger people to see how Elders have travelled their own career paths. There is no direct economic benefit to such a mentoring relationship, but the exchange may help to increase social capital as well as highlight the individual capacities needed to achieve the community's goals.

Elders who took part in the research stressed that emotional wellness, self-confidence, and assertiveness are necessary components to improving the status of the Aboriginal workforce. These components, however, are capacities that require efforts beyond a career practitioner-client relationship. These capacities need to be developed through a community capacity building lens. This project was an example of shifting from a deficit (needs-based) approach to an asset-based one that had a broader goal and included all of the community members. The project provided a shift in vision from that of a small agency offering standard employment services (e.g.,counselling and basic training) to an agency with a much broader perspective on how to address the employment needs of Aboriginal people.

Ethical Implications and Limitations

CCB is an organic process that can differ according to the community. We have outlined some key components to using CCB effectively to assist the community in achieving its goals. However, there are some limitations. For example, there are not always local solutions to local problems, regardless of the strength of a community's capacity. Some problems require changes in policies, political approaches, or resource allocations at a provincial or national level (Chaskin, 2001). Education and training, and in many cases employment support programs, are largely dictated by provincial bodies. These "outside" entities can have a severe disconnect to other areas of the province.

Canada is becoming more and more urbanized, with a few key areas gaining the benefit of the growth. In the same vein, many of the decision-making authorities are centralized in these large urban areas. There is a tendency to develop programming that works well for one region (such as urban), but does not work well for another (such as northern or rural communities). When these structures are put into place in

SPOTLIGHT: *THE MEDICAL CAREERS EXPLORATION PROGRAM (MCEP)*
by Frank Deer

The Medical Careers Exploration Program (MCEP), a partnership in Winnipeg between Pan Am Clinic and Children of the Earth School, created a four-year secondary program for Aboriginal students in 2007. The program encourages students to consider entering the medical field.

Every year, a cohort of 12 students is selected to learn core academic competencies related to health. Through internship experiences, they also gain exposure to a variety of areas in health care (MRI, X-ray, physiotherapy, research, and the surgical centre).

The goals are:

- in grade 9, to demystify health care professions;
- to provide a progressive curriculum commensurate with the requirements of the health care sector;
- to provide students the opportunity to participate in varied internship experiences between grades 10–12;
- to foster interest to pursue postsecondary study in health education.

A 2011 study revealed that all the students who took part in this program graduated and that they were interested in pursuing a health-related career.

Read more at <https://www.winnipegsd.ca/schools/childrenoftheearth/programs/medical-careers-exploration/pages/default.aspx>.

a systematic and province-wide manner, it becomes difficult for communities outside of certain areas to effectively "plug into" programs.

Another important consideration is the health of the community networks. An ill-conceived or poorly executed CCB strategy could have disastrous effects and could damage the social networks and community relationships that previously existed (Atkinson & Willis, 2004). There may be a strong aversion to participating in any further CCB projects, or any project that may be perceived as being attached to the previous failure. When conducting an inventory or community map, these negative experiences with prior projects can become crystallized into major concerns. Convincing community members that the issues have been addressed and will not interfere with current or future CCB projects may be necessary to regain the community's trust.

Homogeneity, or the lack thereof, could affect CCB's success as well. Different perspectives and approaches usually result in more creative outcomes and allow a community to progress; however, defining "community" can sometimes be difficult, especially when there are many differing and conflicting views. The views may be so conflicting as to cause harm or distress to other community members and impair their ability to work as a team and reach their goals. Without the majority of members agreeing upon what to do and where they are headed, building community capacity becomes very difficult.

As with any program that involves human subjects, there are many ethical considerations around issues such as privacy, consent, and transparency. A flawed process may undermine results and cause further conflict within the community. For example, according to the Canadian Code of Ethics for Psychology (2000), the Canadian Psychological Association identified ethical conduct when working with marginalized groups as "seeking an independent and adequate ethical review of human rights issues and protections for any research involving members of vulnerable groups, including persons of diminished capacity to give informed consent, before making a decision to proceed" (p. 12). Issues that may arise include privacy and/or consent of the individual or organization, and transparency in the process. The CCB process may be adversely affected if an individual or an organization feels that privacy has been violated or consent not obtained. Not only is the desired goal(s) of the community in danger of not being realized, but there may be lasting effects that will impede the development of any new initiatives.

Conclusion

CCB is a process that allows communities to set and achieve goals that move the entire community forward. Career practitioners can use this approach to assist individuals with the skills, abilities, and capacities that allow them to gain autonomy and interact with the community at large in a more productive manner. Doing so allows the networks and partnerships of a community to become better intertwined. If managed and nurtured properly, this environment benefits both the individual and the community. As career practitioners who adopt a CCB perspective, we engage ourselves in a more meaningful learning process and either directly or indirectly pass along this valuable information to our clients. By choosing to focus on the capacities of the community and therefore the individual, career practitioners can help to reorient clients to a more hopeful and empowered vision of themselves and the future.

References

Aisensen, D., Bezanson, L., Frank, F., & Reardon, P. (2002). Building community capacity. In B. Hiebert & W. Borgen (Eds.), *Technical and vocational education and training in the 21st century: New roles and challenges for guidance and counselling* (pp. 27–47). Paris: United Nations Educational, Scientific and Cultural Organization.

Aref, F., Redzuan, M., & Gill, S. (2010). Community capacity building: A review of its implications in tourism development. *Journal of American Science, 6*(1), 172–180.

Atkinson, R., & Willis, P. (2004). *Community capacity building: A practical guide: Housing and Community Research Unit* (Paper No. 6). Hobart, AU: School of Sociology, University of Tasmania. Retrieved from <http://www.chs.ubc.ca /archives/files/Community%20Capacity-Building%20A%20Practical %20Guide.pdf>.

Austin, P. (2003). *Community capacity building and mobilization in youth mental health promotion: The story of the community of West Carleton* (Cat. No. H39-4/23-2003E-PDF). Ottawa, ON: Minister of Health Canada. Retrieved from <http://www.phac-aspc.gc.ca/mh-sm/mhp-psm/pub/community-communautaires /pdf/comm-cap-build-mobil-youth.pdf> .

Bopp, M., GermAnn, K., Bopp, J., Baugh Littlejohns, L., & Smith, N. (2001). *Assessing community capacity for change.* Cochrane, AB: David Thompson Health Region, Red Deer, AB and Four Worlds Centre for Development Learning. Retrieved from <http://www.loribaughlittlejohns.com/download/ACCC.pdf>.

The Canadian Psychological Association. (2000). Canadian Code of Ethics for Psychologists (3rd ed.). Ottawa, ON: Canadian Psychological Association. Retrieved from <http://www.cpa.ca/cpasite/userfiles/Documents /Canadian%20Code%20of%20Ethics%20for%20Psycho.pdf>.

Chaskin, R. (2001). Building community capacity: A definitional framework and case studies from a comprehensive community initiative. *Urban Affairs Review, 36*(3), 291–323. doi: 10.1177/10780870122184876

Chaskin, R. J., Brown, P., Venkatesh, S., & Vidal, A. (2001). *Building community capacity.* New York, NY: Walter de Gruyter.

Coyne and Associates Limited. (2006). Ripples of change: Community capacity in Vancouver's Downtown Eastside. Report prepared for the City of Vancouver. Vancouver.

De Schutter, O. (2012). Report of the special rapporteur on the right to food. Addendum- mission to Canada. (GE12-18956). Geneva, CH: United Nations. Retrieved from <http://www.ohchr.org/Documents/HRBodies/HRCouncil /RegularSession/Session22/AHRC2250Add.1_English.PDF>.

Dodd, J. D., & Boyd, M. H. (2000). *Capacity building: Linking community experience to public policy.* Halifax, NS: Health Canada, Population and Public Health Branch, Atlantic Regional Office. Retrieved from <http://www.phac-aspc.gc.ca/canada /regions/atlantic/Publications/Capacity_building/capacity_2000_e.pdf>.

Ebersöhn, L., & Eloff, I. (2003). *Life skills and assets.* Pretoria: Van Schaiks Publishers.

Foster-Fishman, P. G., Berkowitz, S. L., Lounsbury, D. W., Jacobson, S., & Allen, N. A. (2001). Building collaborative capacity in community coalitions: A review and integrative framework. *American Journal of Community Psychology, 29*(2), 241–261.

Frank, F., & Smith, A. (1999). The community development handbook: A tool to build community capacity (Cat. No. MP 33-13/1999E). Ottawa, ON: Minister of Public Works and Government Services Canada. Retrieved from <http://www.healthincommon.ca/wp-content/uploads /Community-Development-Handbook-HRDC.pdf>.

Kretzmann, J., & McKnight, J. (1993). Building communities from the inside out: A path toward finding and mobilizing a community's assets. Chicago, IL: ACTA Publications.

Labonte, R., & Laverack, G. (2001). Capacity building in health promotion. Part I: For whom? and for what purpose? Critical Public Health, 11(2), 111–117.

Littlejohns, L. B., & Thompson, D. (2001). Cobwebs: Insights into community capacity and its relation to health outcomes. Community Development Journal, 36(1), 30–41.

Maclellan-Wright, F., Anderson, D., Barber, S., Smith, N., Cantin, B., Felix, R., & Raine, K. (2007). The development of measures of community capacity for community-based funding programs in Canada. Health Promotion International, 22(4), 299–306. doi: 10.1093/heapro/dam024

Miziwe Biik Aboriginal Employment and Training. (2002). Community Capacity Building Project. Retrieved from <http://www.miziwebiik.com/project /applications>.

National Steering Committee (2004). Canadian standards and guidelines for career development practitioners. Retrieved from <http://career-dev-guidelines.org /career_dev/>.

Ramirez, R., Aitkin, H., Galin, K., & Richardson, D. (2002). Community engagement, performance measurement and sustainability: Experiences from Canadian based networks. Canadian Journal of Communication, 30(2), 259. Retrieved from <http://www.cjc-online.ca/index.php/journal/article/viewArticle/1463/1585>.

Savickas, M. L. (1997). Career adaptability: An integrative construct for life-span, life-space theory. The Career Development Quarterly, 45(3), 247–259.

Shepard, B. (2005). Embedded selves: Co-constructing a relationally based career workshop for rural girls. Canadian Journal of Counselling, 39(4), 231–244.

Torres, G. W., & Barnet, K. (2002). Health as community builders. Health Forum Journal, 45(6), 12–17.

Glossary

Asset-based approach involves identifying and tapping all of the potential assets in a neighborhood or community. An asset-based approach to community level planning encourages a shift from "needs" and "problems" toward "assets" and "opportunities" for a sustained livelihood.

Community capacity "is the interaction of human, organizational, and social capital existing within a given community that can be leveraged to solve collective problems and improve or maintain the well-being of a given community. It may operate through informal social processes and/or organized efforts by individuals, organizations, and the networks of association among them and between them and the broader systems of which the community is a part" (Chaskin, 1999, p. 7).

Community capacity building is an approach to strengthening the skills and abilities of people and groups to empower them to contribute effectively in the development of their communities.

Social capital "refers to the institutions, relationships, and norms that shape the quality and quantity of a society's social interactions ... Social capital is not just the sum of the institutions which underpin a society — it is the glue that holds them together" (The World Bank, 1999).

Discussion and Activities

Discussion

Discussion Questions

1. Is community capacity building distinct from community activity generally?
2. What steps would you take to identify where relationships exist naturally in the community?
3. Imagine that you are working in the community to develop an Aboriginal Education Centre. Brainstorm the key features of the program (e.g., to foster Aboriginal identity) and proposed outcomes (e.g., increased self-esteem).

Personal Reflection

Reflect on the following key competencies identified as necessary for engaging in community capacity building. What are areas of strengths? What are areas that you need to develop? These may include:

- analysis of community perspectives,
- analysis of community maps
- able to elicit "thick" descriptions,
- use of creative and empowering language,
- active listening,
- reflection and introspection,
- respect for differences,
- storytelling,
- strategic questioning,
- teamwork,

- tolerance and respect for others.

Career Practitioner Role

1. According to the S&Gs what skills are required to become specialized in community capacity building?
2. Which of these skills do you see as the most challenging?
3. Where would you obtain further training in this area?

Activities

1. Community capacity building is composed of three main types of activity:

   (a) Developing skills — learning and training opportunities for individuals and groups, and sharing through networks and mutual support, to develop skills, knowledge, and confidence.
   (b) Developing structures — developing the organizational structures and strengths of community groups, communities of interest, and networks.
   (c) Developing support — developing the availability of practical support to enable the development of skills and structures.

   Thinking about a community you live in, look for and describe specific examples of those three activities.
   One example of developing skill is seen in the work of the Alberta Ministry of Aboriginal Relations to develop a Community Economic Development Toolkit as a resource for First Nation staff and decision makers, and others interested in promoting Aboriginal community economic development. As a result of the toolkit, in collaboration with Keyano College, courses in Aboriginal economic development were created.

2. The Community Futures Network in British Columbia works with rural communities to assist in their socioeconomic development. As described on its website, "Community Futures focus on building local capacity as a means of facilitating growth from within communities. In addition to assisting with business development, Community Futures practice and promote community Economic Development and Community Economic Adjustment Initiatives. In carrying out these roles, Community Futures act as facilitators, bringing together diverse groups to develop a locally driven vision for their future and integrate community resources into a long-term sustainable strategy." (Retrieved from <http://www.communityfutures.ca/>.) Use the website to answer the following:

   (a) What types of programs are available through Community Futures?
   (b) Provide an example of one successful program funded in any province by Community Futures Network of Canada.

Resources and Readings

Resources

Websites and Videos

Asset-Based Community Development Institute (ABCD), School of Education and
    Social Policy, Northwestern University <http://www.abcdinstitute.org/>.
The Community Toolbox — practical resources <http://ctb.ku.edu>.
Vital Signs, Community Foundations of Canada <http://www.vitalsignscanada.ca
    /en/home>.

Supplementary Readings

Bezanson, L., & Kellett, R. (2001). Integrating career information and guidance
    services at a local level. Ottawa, ON: Canadian Career Development
    Foundation. Retrieved from <http://www.oecd.org/education/country-studies
    /2698200.pdf>.
Chaskin, R. (1999). *Defining community capacity: A framework and implications from a
    comprehensive community initiative.* The Chapin Hall Center for Children at the
    University of Chicago. Retrieved from <http://www.chapinhall.org/sites/default
    /files/old_reports/41.pdf>.
Coleman, J. (1998). Social capital in the creation of human capital. *American Journal of
    Sociology, 94,* 95–120.
Cox, R. S., & Espinoza, A. (2005). Career-community development: A framework
    for career counseling and capacity building in rural communities. *Journal of
    Employment Counseling, 42*(4), 146–159.
Dobson, C. (2007). The citizens' handbook. Vancouver Citizens Community. Retrieved
    From <http://www.citizenshandbook.org/>.
Fedi, A., Mannarini, T., & Maton, K. (2009). Empowering Community Settings
    and Community Mobilization. *Community Development, 40* (30), 275–291.
    doi: 10.1080/15575330903109985
Fletcher, F., McKennitt, D., & Baydala, L. (2008). Community capacity building:
    An Aboriginal exploratory case study. *Pimatisiwin: A Journal of Aboriginal and
    Indigenous Community Health, 5*(2), 9–24.
Frank, F., & Smith, A. (1999). *The community development handbook.*
    Ottawa, ON: Human Resources Development Canada. Retrieved from
    <http://www.healthincommon.ca/wp-content/uploads
    /Community-Development-Handbook-HRDC.pdf>.
Green, M., Moore, H., & O'Brien, J. (2006). *ABCD in action: When people care enough
    to act.* Toronto, ON: Inclusion Press.
Kretzmann, J. P., McKnight, J. L., Dobrowolski, S., & Puntenney, D. (2005) *Discovering
    community power: A guide to mobilizing local assets and your organization's capacity.*
    Asset-Based Community Development Foundation (ABCD). Retrieved from

<http://www.abcdinstitute.org/docs/kelloggabcd.pdf>.

Labour Market Learning and Development Unit. (2000). *Community capacity building: A facilitated workshop. A facilitator's guide.* Ottawa, ON: Human Resources Development Canada. Retrieved from <http://www.cawi-ivtf.org/sites/all/files /pdf/community_development_facilitator_guide.pdf>.

O'Meara, P., Chesters, J., & Han, G. (2004). Outside-looking in: Evaluating a community capacity building project. *Rural Society, 14*(2), 126–141.

Rans, S. A. (2005). *Hidden treasures: Building community connections by engaging the gifts of people on welfare, people with disabilities, people with mental illness, older adults, and young people.* The Asset Based Community Development Institute. Retrieved from <http://www.sesp.northwestern.edu/docs/abcd/hiddentreasures.pdf>.

Simpson, L., Wood, L., & Daws, L. (2003). Community capacity building: Starting with people not projects. *Community Development Journal, 38*(4), 277–286.

Section 7

New Directions and
Emerging Trends in
Career Development Practice

twenty

The Power of Evidence

Demonstrating the Value of Career Development Services

BRYAN HIEBERT
University of Calgary, University of Victoria
KRIS MAGNUSSON
Simon Fraser University

PRE-READING QUESTIONS

1. What do you think is meant by evidence-based practice?
2. What constitutes acceptable evidence of success in evaluating programs and providing services?
3. How can practitioners link the outcomes with the services that are provided?

Introduction and Learning Objectives

The main purpose of this chapter is to demonstrate how an agency, a department, or an individual providing career development services can avoid being a casualty of budget cuts and changed priorities and instead be one of the success stories that receives further support and funding. At its simplest, it is a matter of collecting the necessary evidence to demonstrate the value of the career development services. The key is in being able to demonstrate the connection between the program and positive outcomes for the client.

There is substantial evidence indicating that career counsellors, generally speaking, do not evaluate the impact of their work with clients. For example, in a major national study of career and employment counselling, Conger, Hiebert, and Hong-Farrell (1994) found that 40% of practitioners reported never evaluating their work with clients. Of those who claimed to evaluate their work, the most common method for doing so was simply to ask clients if they found the session useful. In a more recent study, more than 90% of managers and practitioners working in agencies providing career services to youth and adults agreed that it was important to evaluate the outcomes of the services they offered (Lalande & Magnusson, 2005, 2007). However, when asked about their evaluation practices, only about 35% of practitioners reported ever doing so. The data most frequently reported pertained to change in employment status. Funders found this useful, but practitioners lamented that the data were not very relevant to much of the work they did, and did not connect directly to the types of services they offered. In general, very few counsellors collect data on the impact of their services, and when they do, the types of data collected make it difficult to link the services that an agency offers to the outcomes that are achieved. The focus in this chapter is on providing an alternative.

Consider the following question: "Would you invest in something that has no documented track record of success, little certainty about what outcome you could expect, and few promises for how any outcome would be achieved?" Most people would say no! Yet in career services, this is what most service providers expect funders to do. Simply put, it does not make much sense to invest in an intervention if we don't know where we are going with it, we don't know how we're going to get there, and we don't know if we've arrived at the final destination. It is neither professional nor ethical to set about to do things with clients with no evidence base to support what we are doing.

We in the career development field need to reconceptualize how we think about evaluation. Often evaluation is seen as an activity that is conducted after the primary service has been designed, thereby relegating it to the status of an "afterthought." All too often, the main role of career practitioners is seen in terms of the provision of services, not the evaluation of the effectiveness of those services. When evaluation is done, an outsider is usually contracted to take a look at the program and provide feedback. Typically such external evaluators have had little involvement with the program and may not be familiar with the goals and intended outcomes. The assumption is that the outside expert can provide an objective look at the program.

As an alternative to external postservice evaluations, we propose an approach where evaluation is infused into the day-to-day practices of service providers and where service provision and service evaluation are completely intertwined. It is an approach where service providers will always ask themselves two questions:

1. What intervention would be appropriate for this client?
2. How will the client and I determine how well the intervention is working?

Thus, this chapter is about creating a marriage between service provision and outcome. First, we provide a conceptual background for approaching the merger of service and outcome. Then we provide some practical tools to help implement the idea. Finally, we provide suggestions for implementing evaluation into practice, and discuss the policy implications and infrastructure needs that will help support the perspective we advance.

The learning objectives for this chapter are to enable you to do the following:

1. Grasp the importance of evaluating the impact of client services.
2. Understand the importance of infusing evaluation into the day-to-day practices of service providers.
3. Acquire some practical tools to help implement the merger of service and outcome.
4. Understand the steps involved in integrating evaluation into practice.
5. Become familiar with the policy implications and infrastructure needs to demonstrate the value of career development services.

We have used case examples to illustrate the points we make; they have been sufficiently disguised so that the identities of the agencies and the service providers are protected, but all of the stories are real-life examples. Examples of forms that can be used to conduct the evaluation and measure results and sample reports are provided in the appendices to this chapter.

Need for Evaluation

The following two stories from the field illustrate two situations where evaluation helped strengthen and save programs.

Stories From the Field (1): It Seems Our Program Is No Longer Effective

A few years ago one of the authors was contracted by an agency to conduct a program evaluation. The program was very well developed; had a strong rationale, detailed facilitator guide, and explicit expectations about client outcomes; and had been operating very successfully for several years. However, the results of the program had become uneven and the program seemed to be less effective than it was initially. Therefore, the agency wanted an objective third party to evaluate the program.

The program guide, the facilitator manual, and the participant materials were reviewed as the first step of the evaluation process. Next, a few group sessions were observed to see how the written materials were translated into practice. In some cases, it was clear from watching the session exactly where the group was in the intervention program. However in other cases, it was difficult to identify where

---

the group was in the overall program plan. It turned out that some facilitators were adhering strictly to the program guide, while others departed from it substantially. On closer analysis, it turned out that the people who were following the program guide were achieving consistent and effective results, but the people who had modified the program guide in an attempt to make it more "effective" were in fact achieving less consistent and less effective results.

The solution was to educate staff about the program, and for supervisors to monitor session objectives and the processes the counsellors used to conduct the sessions. Within a short time, the program seemed to be working equally well for all facilitators, and a higher degree of success was achieved more consistently across all staff members. As it turned out, the program was excellent and the results were consistently positive as long as the program was being implemented as intended.

Stories From the Field (2): Survivor Stories in Times of Budget Cutbacks

Budget reductions are a common experience for service providers across Canada. A few years ago, this was particularly true in one Canadian province where student service departments in many colleges and universities were severely reduced or eliminated entirely. There were two or three exceptions where the student service departments were left intact and, in one case, even expanded. This raised the question: "Why were these departments not affected negatively by budget cuts?" It turns out that in every case where the department was not reduced, a concerted effort had been made to gather evidence attesting to the positive impact that the student services department was having on students and on the institution as a whole. Evaluating the impact of services on clients, it seemed, provided good job security.

Conceptual Framework

In 2003, a *National Symposium on Career Development, Lifelong Learning and Workforce Development* was held. The symposium brought together service providers, educators, employers, and policy makers working in the career development field. In the plenary session, a senior federal policy maker shocked the Canadian career development community when he said: *"You haven't made the case for the impact and value of career development services, so why should government continue to fund them?"*

In response to that challenge, the **Canadian Research Working Group on Evidence-Based Practice in Career Development (CRWG)** was formed. The CRWG is a consortium of 10 researchers from six Canadian universities and one private foundation (CRWG, n.d.).

Evaluation Practices

One of the first questions facing the CRWG was, "What is the best way to evaluate the effectiveness of career development interventions?" A first step in addressing this question was to obtain a snapshot of current evaluation practices in the field (see Lalande & Magnusson, 2005). One of Lalande and Magnusson's findings was that differing needs and expectations existed between those who funded services and those who provided services. On the one hand, funders were generally more interested in broad social outcomes, such as how many of the people who accessed services found employment. On the other hand, service providers were typically more interested in indicators such as client satisfaction or counsellor reports of service delivery, neither of which addresses the concerns of policy makers. Service providers also expressed frustration that client outcomes they deemed important (such as personal growth, empowerment, optimism about their career futures, and confidence

---

SPOTLIGHT: *THE CANADIAN RESEARCH WORKING GROUP (CRWG) ON EVIDENCE-BASED PRACTICE IN CAREER DEVELOPMENT*
by Lara Shepard

The CRWG is made up of francophone and anglophone independent researchers from six Canadian universities (University of Victoria, University of British Columbia, Simon Fraser University, University of Calgary, Université Laval, and Université de Sherbrooke) who are collaborating to demonstrate the effectiveness of career development programs and services

The mandate is described at the CRWG-GDRC website <http://ccdf.ca /crwg/> as follows:

- to develop an evaluation framework to gather evidence-based data on career development programs and services;
- to promote the implementation of an evaluation culture in the career development field;
- to conduct research to test the framework and build a bank of evidence-based data on the impact of career development programs and services.

in their ability to manage their careers) were not considered to be important by funders. To be fair, policy makers had a point: Frequently, service and funding requests were based on a "moral obligation" argument, which assumed that people needed help in making career decisions and it was the responsibility of a "just society" (or organization or government) to provide that help. Justification for funding services was often based on how busy the service providers were. More often than not, no assessment of the effectiveness of those services was conducted.

Given the milieu described above, the CRWG decided to focus on client change as the primary indicator of the effectiveness of career development interventions, because it was seen as central to the challenge issued by policy makers. We drew on two trends that had become prominent in recent years: **evidence-based practice** and **outcome-focused intervention** (Charles, Ernst, & Ponzetti, 2003; Morago, 2006; Taylor & White, 2002; Webb, 2001).

Evidence-based practice focuses on providing services that have predictable positive effects. Evidence-based practice is important because, ethically speaking, clients deserve to receive interventions that have a positive track record for producing change. Furthermore, when that evidence is provided, job security for service providers is enhanced. The central question in evidence-based practice is: *What would be the best program or intervention to use with this client?*

Outcome-focused intervention involves demonstrating the added benefit of the services that are offered to the client or to society at large. Outcome-focused intervention is important because successful programs are frequently discontinued for lack of convincing evidence that clients have changed as a result of the services they received. Moreover, funders, clients, and agency managers, as well as service providers themselves, want evidence that the services in question have tangible, positive impacts on clients as well as on society at large. The central question in outcome-focused intervention is: *What evidence will tell me how well interventions are working?*

Frequently, the foundation for evidence-based practice comes from **randomized controlled trials** (RCTs). However, several authors have described the substantial problems associated with using RCTs as the sole basis for addressing efficacy concerns (e.g., Hiebert, 1997; Hiebert & Charles, 2008; Hiebert, Domene, & Buchanan, 2011; Horan, 1980). Thus, in this chapter, we offer an alternate approach that combines both evidence-based practice and outcomes-focused intervention. An alternative, and equally viable approach to RCTs, is to incorporate the notion of local clinical scientist (Tricrweiler & Stricker, 1998) into service delivery practices. Local clinical scientists (or our preferred term *professional practitioners*) are practitioners who adopt a scientific attitude towards the work they do. They are clear about the nature of the change client's desire and clear about what they will do to meet client goals. They document what they do and how well it works. **Professional practitioners** are rigorous observers, operating in their everyday reality: They emphasize theory and evidence-based practice, rather than merely technique (DeAngelis, 2005; Levant, 2005).

Professional practitioners treat their work with clients as investigations, tracking the various factors that might influence client change, documenting the client changes that are observed, and looking for patterns that connect contextual factors, processes used to initiate client change, and outcomes achieved. Each client becomes an "n = 1" experiment. Over time and multiple iterations of an intervention, patterns emerge and predictions can be made about treatment effectiveness. We are not suggesting that observations made by professional practitioners are better than, or should replace, observations deriving from RCTs. However, we do argue that such an approach is an equally viable alternative methodology for demonstrating the effectiveness of career development interventions. As Barlow (1981) points out, this will encourage practitioners to become more responsive to research evidence, and help them produce some of that evidence themselves.

To implement this philosophy, we needed an approach to evaluation that would be relevant enough that practitioners in the field would use it, yet comprehensive enough to cover the most important factors affecting client change. The resulting framework was a simple Inputs > Processes > Outcomes approach. The framework has been described extensively elsewhere (e.g., Baudouin, et al., 2007; Lalande, Hiebert, Magnusson, Bezanson, & Borgen, 2006) and therefore it will be only summarized briefly here (see Figure 1).

In the framework depicted in Figure 1, Framework for Evaluating Client Change, on the next page, you'll note that:

- Inputs are the resources that are available to help clients change (i.e., pursue the outcomes).
- Processes are the mechanisms that are involved in achieving the outcomes (i.e., what counsellors and clients do to facilitate client change).
- Outcomes are the client changes that result from the inputs enacting the processes (i.e., the knowledge and skills that a client acquires, the attitudes and other personal attributes that a client develops, and the impact of those on a client's life).

The three elements are interconnected, but the relationship is not linear. Inputs feed processes and processes result in outcomes. However, outcomes are also influenced by the inputs (resources) available, and the nature of the inputs (especially the competencies of the staff) influence the process (interventions) that can be enacted. Thus, even though the framework may look linear, in reality, the three elements are very interactive.

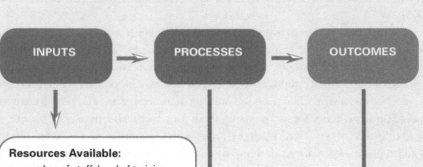

Resources Available:
- number of staff, level of training, type of training;
- funding;
- service guidelines/agency mandate;
- infrastructure and facilities;
- community resources.

Activities and process that link to outcomes or deliverables
1. Generic interventions:
- working alliance, microskills, relationship skills, et cetera.

2. Specific interventions:
- interventions used by service providers,
- skills or strategies used by service providers,
- home practice completed by clients,
- programs offered by agency,
- involvement by third parties.

Indicators of client change
1. Learning outcomes:
- knowledge and skills that can be linked directly to the program or intervention being used.

2. Personal attribute outcomes:
- changes in intrapersonal variables (e.g., attitudes, self-esteem, motivation, etc.).

3. Impact outcomes:
- impact that the learning outcomes or the personal attribute outcomes have on the client's life,
- social and relational impact,
- economic impact.

Figure 1:
Framework for
Evaluating
Client Change.

Integrating Evaluation and Intervention

The evaluation framework described above integrates nicely with an intervention framework that is typically used in career counselling and career development services. The intervention usually begins by examining the client's context with a view to identifying the specific goals that a client wants to accomplish. The client's needs and the outcomes that are identified are integrated with available resources to develop a service plan. The service plan will include specific tasks that service providers and clients will need to engage in to meet the client's goals. These goals can be thought of as containing several specific outcomes and indicators of change that will determine the extent to which the outcomes have been achieved. The dynamic relationship between these factors (intervention, evaluation, and service delivery) is depicted in Figure 2.

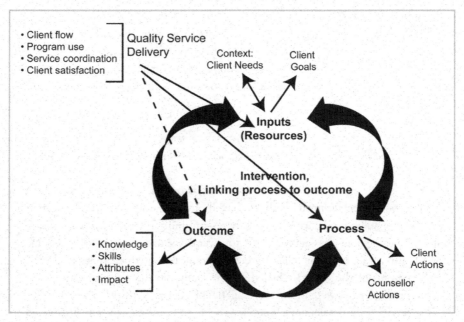

Figure 2: Interconnection Between Intervention, Evaluation, and Service Delivery.

It is important to note that Figure 2 contains an additional group of variables named *Quality Service Delivery*. This category includes factors that are important to agency managers, funders, and policy makers but do not relate directly to client change or intervention planning. Variables such as ease and timeliness of access, service utilization, and number of clients served, and so on, are important when evaluating the overall quality of services available, but by themselves, they do not speak to the impact of services on clients or on society. Simply put, quality service delivery goals are insufficient for professional practice because they do not directly address client change or the effectiveness of the processes used to effect that change.

One final point deserves mention. When providing services, and especially when evaluating services, it is important to begin by identifying the types of client changes that are being sought. The client context and client goals need to be at the forefront of service provision to ensure that the expected outcomes are realistic. Practitioners and clients need to be in agreement regarding all aspects of the work they will do together.

Once the outcomes are clear, indicators of success and of progress towards success must be identified. Next, the processes needed to produce the outcomes can be developed and the resources needed to implement those processes can be recruited. There is a strong need for planning these two processes together. Each of the factors identified in Figure 2 need to be taken into account and the interactive nature of the factors needs to remain central in the planning and implementation of both the intervention and evaluation plan.

To summarize, in order for the evaluation to be effective, evidence must be documented regarding the resources used, the processes implemented, the client competencies (i.e., the knowledge, skills, and personal attributes) that were acquired, as well as the impact of those outcomes on the client's life or any larger societal or economic impacts.

Stories From the Field (3): **The Importance of Monitoring Process Variables**

A number of years ago a major agency, whose primary mandate was to help injured workers to return to work, contacted one of the authors to review their Job Finding Club programs. The primary responsibility for conducting Job Finding Club programs was subcontracted to several agencies and one troublesome observation was that some clients were returning two or three times to do the program. All of the agencies had the same facilitation guide, and the success rates for all agencies were in the range of 80% placement within 2–3 weeks.

In the initial telephone interviews with the agencies, it was discovered that some agencies were explicitly following the facilitation guide; however, about one third of the agencies had also hired a job marketer to help the clients find jobs. In those programs, clients were not learning job search skills; they were relying on the job marketer to find them jobs and thus did not develop job search strategies. If they found themselves unemployed again, they simply returned to the program for more help.

To address the problem, the funding agency introduced a program audit, where part of one staff member's time was devoted to conducting unannounced site visits to see how closely the vendors were following the program. The service providers were all given a program-audit checklist in advance, and were told that there would be unannounced visits to see how closely the prescribed program was being followed. In actual fact, the site visits only happened once or twice, but the belief that they could happen was enough to get all providers following the program, and the rate of clients seeking to repeat the job club dropped to zero. The conclusion was that when the Job Finding Club program was followed the clients learned job search skills, and were able to use those skills independently to manage future career transitions. Setting up a system to monitor a program will make the program more focused and effective in terms of client change.

Tools and Resources

We believe that virtually all clients are capable of answering the question: *How useful are you finding the career development services you are accessing?* We further believe that in very few cases, perhaps no cases at all, would the client's answer be based on standardized test scores. Thus, it is important to develop (a) an alternative way to assess client change, and (b) other means for linking client outcomes to the services that are being accessed in ways that incorporate how clients actually think, act, and feel. Members of the CRWG have been experimenting with several new processes, most of which are informal assessment tools. A compendium of these tools is provided at CRWG (n.d.). Two of those tools are described in this section.

Evaluation as a Decision-Making Process

Frequently, evaluation is approached from a judgemental perspective: An evaluator passes judgement on the topic under examination. Let us say you are interested in the extent to which participants found a workshop useful. To find out, you might use a **Likert-type rating scale**, where participants are given a sentence stem such as, "I found the workshop really useful," and asked to select from five options: Strongly Disagree; Disagree; Neither Agree nor Disagree; Agree; Strongly Agree. One problem with this approach is that there is often considerable discrepancy between individual raters in interpreting the rating options — this is called **inter-rater discrepancy**.

Instead of using a judgement model, we suggest approaching evaluation from a decision-making perspective, where an evaluator examines the evidence and decides on the level of acceptability on the topic under examination. Approaching evaluation as a decision-making endeavour involves a two-step process, as depicted in Table 1,

Evaluation as a Decision-Making Process. In guiding people through the decision-making process, we use common language to describe various steps. We do this in the belief that using common language increases the relevance of the process, is easily understood by participants, and therefore increases the consistency of interpretation and reliability of participant responses.

Step A, decide if the competency (degree of preparation, level of engagement, level of knowledge, etc.) **is acceptable** (employable or adequate at a beginning level) **or unacceptable** (unlikely to result in continued employment in a work setting).

Unacceptable	Acceptable

Then, in Step B, decide:

If the level of competence is unacceptable, is it:
    really quite poor (= 0), or
    almost okay (= 1).
If the level of competence is acceptable, is it:
    just barely okay (= 2) [but still acceptable, otherwise it would be 1],
    really very good (= 4), or
    somewhere in between (= 3) [better than minimally acceptable, but not yet excellent].

The resulting rating scale is presented below.

Unacceptable		Acceptable		
0	1	2	3	4

Table 1: Evaluation as a Decision-Making Process.

Consider, as an example, the self-evaluations (or supervisor evaluations) of practicum students on factors such as knowledge, skill, level of competence, degree of preparation, and so on. In such situations, we have found that using the decision-making approach depicted in Table 1 results in high inter-rater agreement. When several raters look at the same performance, there is high agreement among the raters on what should be the appropriate rating.

We have also found that for the individual rater the decision-making approach results in higher consistency in ratings over time. When the same rater looks at the same performance on different occasions, there is high agreement on the rating from Time 1 and Time 2. Thus, many of the "judging issues" (e.g., what is the difference between "Agree" and "Strongly Agree") are reduced, and we have a higher degree of consistency and more trustworthy ratings (i.e., higher reliability).

Retrospective Assessment

One difficulty with using self-assessments to determine changes in skill or knowledge is that people don't know what they don't know. To illustrate, people enrolled in a program to improve interpersonal communication might be asked to rate their communication skills at the beginning of the program and again at the end of the program. At the beginning, many people think that their communication skills are reasonably good and they rate themselves quite high. During the program, as they get to know more about what constitutes good communication, they realize that their knowledge and skills are not as good as they initially thought. At the end of the program they are asked to rate themselves again, and the ratings are often lower than they were at the beginning, even though they have learned a lot and have an increased level of skill (see Hiebert et al., 2011; Posavac, 2011; Robinson & Doueck, 1994; Spiro, Shalev, Solomon, & Kotler, 1989). This is because their measuring stick changed as their learning progressed.

A form of retrospective assessment, which we have named Post-Pre Assessment, is often used to address this problem, as it creates a consistent measuring stick for both preassessments and postassessments (see Rockwell & Kohn, 1989). This process is used ONLY at the end of a program. It asks people to use their current level of knowledge to create a common measuring stick for preprogram and postprogram assessments. For example, when a workshop or program is finished, participants are asked: *Knowing what you know now about interpersonal communication, how would you rate yourself before the workshop, and how would you rate yourself now?* The self-assessment is done only at the end of the workshop or program, but it asks people to self-assess their preprogram competencies (hence the name **"post-pre assessment"**), along with their postprogram competencies, using the same measuring stick (i.e., "Knowing what you know now...").

The process for creating a post-pre assessment usually begins by listing the explicit outcomes that are being sought, and then using these outcomes as the item stems in a questionnaire. The mindset provided in the preceding paragraph is described (i.e., knowing what you know now about topic X), followed by the item stems (i.e., the explicit outcomes being sought).

An example of a post-pre assessment form is provided in Appendix A and also Appendix B of this chapter. Using the example of a workshop for facilitating student transition from university to the workplace, Appendix A shows how post-pre assessment can be used to evaluate knowledge and skill gains, and identify changes in personal attributes from participating in the workshop.

Appendix B, Sample Summative Evaluation Results, shows the evaluation data that can be obtained from one of these workshops and illustrates the types of conclusions that can be derived from this approach. These data provide strong support for the learning changes that have occurred as a result of the workshop (Pothier, Robertson, Hiebert, & Magnusson, 2008).

It is important to note that even though the example provided in Appendix A and Appendix B is for a workshop, the same process can be used to work with an individual client. In this case you will be viewing the client as a program of one participant, and working through a program tailor-made to address his or her needs. In our field research, we have worked with service providers to help them use these five steps with their clients:

1. Identify typical client goals.
2. Identify what they would use as indicators of success, indicating that the goal was being achieved.
3. Design the experiences (processes) needed for the client to learn the knowledge and skills, as well as acquire the personal attributes needed to achieve the goals.
4. Identify the skills that the service provider would use in guiding the client through the processes.
5. Identify the resources that would be used throughout the process to implement the intervention and evaluation plans.

Working through these steps typically takes about an hour the first time, but the planning process becomes substantially shorter the second and third time as the practitioners get the hang of doing it. With practice, the planning process takes no more time than a practitioner usually would take to prepare for an individual client interview.

The procedure described above provides useful data for linking the client change outcomes to the services that have been accessed and for developing summative evaluation.

A similar process can be used to obtain formative feedback for improving a program or an intervention. To do that, simply list all of the topics that have been part of the workshop or the intervention plan, and ask the client to use the decision-making approach to indicate how useful they found each item. The same list can be used to indicate how engaged a client was in the intervention: simply list the topics and ask the client (or workshop participants) whether they "completed that item," "sort of completed that item," or "did not complete it at all." Appendix C, Sample Formative Feedback Results, contains a sample of a form used to obtain participant engagement data, and an example of the collected data and formative feedback on usefulness of workshop to the participants.

The approach described above will provide data on many aspects: (a) how engaged the participants were in the process, (b) how useful they found each of the topics, (c) the knowledge and skills participants learned, (d) the personal attributes they acquired, (e) the impact on the participants' lives, and (f) the participant attributes for the changes they experienced. Thus, we have a clear link between client change and the service provided, and we can say with confidence whether or not the program was responsible for the changes participants experienced.

❖ *Stop and Reflect*
An exhaustive collection of forms and checklists can be obtained from the website of the Canadian Research Working Group on Evidence-Based Practice in Career Development, at <http://www.crwg-gdrc.ca/>. Navigate to Resources > Evaluation Tools > Compendium of Evaluation Tools. These tools adopt the approaches outlined above and extend the areas of application to include numerous informal (non-standardized) procedures for gathering evidence of client change and intervention effectiveness.

Taking the Next Step: Integrating Evaluation Into Practice

So far, we have provided a framework for integrating evaluation into your practice, and provided some examples of tools and resources that can be used within this framework. We now turn our attention to integrating evaluation into practice. We suggest seven general stages to follow regardless of the scope of practice — whether you are considering evaluating large-scale interventions such as programs, or small-scale interventions such as individual counselling sessions. We see these stages not as hard and fast rules, but rather as a means of conceptualizing the process.

Stage 1: Understanding Service Foundations and Client Context

The guiding question in Stage 1 is, *What factors outside of the intervention might have an impact on the results?*

Services, whether consisting of individual counselling, workshops, or intervention programs, are embedded within unique contexts and circumstances. Before engaging in effective evaluations, we must consider the environment in which we are working. Although that may sound trite, we have repeatedly found examples of "mismatches" between the intention of the service and the needs of the client. If we want to properly evaluate our services, we need to clearly identify the nature of those services, the contexts in which they are provided, and the needs of the clients accessing them. A more complete discussion of the alignment of service delivery with client needs can be found in Magnusson (1992) and Magnusson, Day, and Redekopp (1993).

Stories From the Field (4): **Making Sure the Intervention Is Appropriate**

One of the authors was invited to help a government agency understand why a funded program was doing so poorly. The goal of the program was to help women receiving Social Allowance to make the transition to employment. The program was a well-regarded employability skills program where participants were taught how to prepare résumés, develop contacts and job leads, and present themselves effectively in interviews. However, most of the participants were not ready to use such skills. They were on welfare because of a host of social and personal issues: Many had been (or were currently) victims of emotional and/ or physical abuse; most had young children to care for; and most lacked formal education beyond high school. The problem was not so much that the program was ineffective, but that the program was inappropriate for the types of needs the participants experienced.

Nature of Services

The nature of a service can be thought of in terms of "what gets done, with whom, by whom." When people lose sight of any of these three components, it becomes difficult to determine what are the most effective services for clients. When examining the nature of service, it is important to consider service focus (i.e., the broad goals for service provision). Employment services typically focus on helping clients consider and/or find a particular kind of job. Vocational services help clients to link talents, interests, and passions in considering what kinds of work are best suited to them as individuals. Career services help clients with personal/lifestyle decisions and the balancing of multiple life roles (including occupational) across their lifespan. In the example we provided earlier, clients with career-service needs were put into an employability-focused program, with unfortunately predictable results.

Hiebert and Borgen (2002) describe types of services in terms of advising, guiding, and counselling. Advising services typically focus on providing general information (such as Labour Market Information or LMI) that may assist clients. Guidance services attempt to match information about clients with information about the world of work so that clients can make sound work-related decisions. Counselling services engage in interpersonal processes for exploring life issues. Using these descriptions, we can see that the participants in *Stories From the Field (4)* primarily received advising services when most of them would have benefitted more from counselling services.

In determining the nature of services it is also important to consider the primary audience and the form to be used in delivering the services. The primary audience may be a specific age group (e.g., adolescents, older adults, etc.), gender, or segment of society (e.g., recent immigrants). The form of intervention is frequently embedded within an agency mandate, and includes services such as individual, group, psycho-educational, or self-directed. It is always important to ask if a particular client fits the primary audience and would benefit from that form of service. Three questions are useful when examining the nature of services:

1. Who is the primary recipient of our services?
2. What is the nature of our services? and
3. How are our services provided?

Context of Service

If the nature of the services you provide is the reason for your evaluation, then the factors external to your services form the context. We mentioned earlier that contextual factors do not indicate client change as a result of your services, but they certainly do provide a backdrop for understanding and explaining your results. For example, suppose you offered a job-finding service aimed at helping trained workers find employment within a specialized industry. Let's further suppose that 75% of the participants were able to find suitable employment. Is that a good result or not? If the unemployment rate in that sector was less than 5% in your region, then the people funding your service might conclude that you did not do very well. On the other hand, if the unemployment rate consistently hovered around 30%, your funder would probably think this was a terrific program. The answer to the question, "How good is this?" often depends on contextual factors.

A number of contextual factors may come into play in the evaluation of any service delivery. Table 2, Taking Stock of the Context for Service Evaluation, contains a sample checklist of items that could be used to identify unique or special circumstances that might have an impact on the results you are able to attain. It is also important to clearly describe the nature of your client group for, as we saw in *Stories From the Field (4)*, it is possible to deliver a good program, but to the wrong clients, and get disappointing results.

NAME OF PROGRAM OR SERVICE	
Context	Factors that may affect results
Social	
Cultural	
Political	
Economic	
Spiritual	
Gender	
Other	

Table 2 : Taking Stock of the Context for Service Evaluation.

Taken together, examining the nature of the service, the contextual factors in which the service operates, and the needs of the clients, will help you design a more effective evaluation and better understand your results. This will put you in a stronger position to argue for the efficacy of your program.

Stage 2: Describing Desired Outcomes

The core question to be asked in Stage 2 is, *What do we want to achieve?* Lalande and Magnusson (2005) found that many Canadian service providers were frustrated by the fact that the only measure of success funders considered important was employment status. The service providers believed they were accomplishing far more with their clients than what they were being asked to report on.

Agency and Funder Goals

When integrating evaluation and service delivery, it is imperative to understand the goals of the agency and funder, and then work to establish links between your services and their goals. For example, if you are working in an educational setting, the goals of your institution will likely include improving retention rates, improving academic performance, reducing program completion times, and ensuring successful transition to either employment or further studies. However, there are many steps along the way to achieving these goals. Thus, it is important to negotiate desired outcomes with the funders (i.e., what will count as success). In *Stories From the Field (2)*, the departments not only measured the outcomes of their services, but they also showed the impact of those services on broader institutional goals. It was that linkage that made the services valuable to the institution.

It is also important to keep an open mind regarding the nature of the ultimate impact of services. For example, Conger and Hiebert (2007) developed "employment equivalence" as a metric that could equate the completion of psychoeducational workshops to employment status, and Peruniak (2010) builds a convincing argument for viewing "quality of life" as an ultimate impact of career services.

Stories From the Field (5): Increasing College Students' Skills for Learning

An instructor in a trades program at a large technical institution approached one of the counsellors over coffee and complained about how poorly prepared his students were for dealing with the academic components of their program. The counsellor offered to provide a brief study skills session for the students and the instructor agreed to give two, 2-hour blocks of class time for the sessions. The counsellor asked for a copy of the grade book, with names removed, so that a performance baseline could be established and then met with the class for 15 minutes to see what problems they had with their learning. Based on the class feedback, a short program was designed and delivered. After the second session, students reported that they had tried many of the suggestions and found them very useful. The counsellor then obtained the grades on the next class assessment, compared them with the baseline academic performance, and discovered a substantial improvement in academic performance. The results of the evaluation, including initial academic performance, student ratings of the workshop, and subsequent changes in academic performance, were described in a brief report, and distributed to the instructor, the department head, and the director of the division, who were impressed to see the substantial gains made by one of their most difficult student groups. The director went on to advocate for the retention of the student services department during budget cuts that came the following year. The results were also communicated to the students, with the message, "see what happens when you use the learning techniques to your advantage?" Reports from the instructor suggested that the students maintained and even improved on their performance for the rest of the term, and that there were far fewer behavioural and discipline issues, as well as a much lower rate of absenteeism

---

Type of Client Change

A second important factor to consider when integrating evaluation and service delivery is the type of client change that is being sought (i.e., the outcomes). Although these changes are client-determined, they also may need to be supplemented by counsellor experience. For example, there may be developmental sequences that counsellors know the clients will need to go through before they can reach their ultimate goal. These developmental sequences need to be included in the list of client-change outcomes. A client may be aware of the need to craft a good résumé, but the service provider will know the necessary sub-goals involved (e.g., a list of educational accomplishments, a chronology of prior employment, how to describe job duties in behaviour terms, etc.), and will build these into the evaluation plan.

In addition to the above, it is important to remember that clients are not always able (or willing) to articulate their goals. A presenting problem often masks a deeper issue. In such cases, it is necessary to revise the goals and deal with the deeper issue before resolution of the presenting problem is possible.

At this point, we want to address a common barrier that people face when trying to integrate evaluation into practice, namely, trying to do too much and making the outcome list too long. Recently, one of the authors was assisting a colleague to evaluate the impact of one of her courses. When asked to think about the kinds of student changes that she wanted to see as a result of the course, the outcome list contained more than 70 items. At some level, each of the 70 outcomes may have been useful, but the resulting form for data collection would have taken at least 30 minutes to complete and the data analysis would have been onerous. If the goal had been to conduct a one-time comprehensive evaluation, then perhaps such a strategy would have been fine. However, if the goal is to obtain evidence of the impact of a service by incorporating evaluation into everyday practice, it is more realistic to identify a few (5 to 10) major outcomes that are measured consistently, rather than a long list of items that rarely get evaluated. The decision-making and post-pre approaches described earlier are useful for obtaining such data. Appendix D has further examples of client-change outcomes.

Stories From the Field (6): **Translating Outcomes Into Measures**

Magnusson (1992) described career counselling in terms of working towards a general set of outcomes, which included:

- a dream or vision of a preferred future (the installation of hope),
- a specified goal (a target for action),
- a list of alternatives (options),
- a plan for goal attainment (the means),
- an acceptable career fit (satisfaction and resolution),
- self-sufficiency (adaptability and interdependence).

Each of these can be translated into a sentence stem that clients could rate:

- I am confident that I will have a meaningful place in the future.
- I have a clear sense of my future career direction.
- I have alternatives in mind if my first choice does not work out.

- I have a plan for reaching my preferred future.
- I have found work (or other life roles) that fit my needs and aspirations.
- I am confident that should other changes happen in my life, I will be able to make new plans.

Stage 3: Describing Core Activities

Once you have clearly articulated a set of desired outcomes, the next question to ask is, *What do we (service provider and client) need to do to achieve the outcomes?* Addressing this question helps link the core processes to the desired outcomes. In career counselling, core activities can be thought of in three broad categories: generic interventions, specific interventions, and programs (Figure 1, Framework for Evaluating Client Change). Generic interventions represent the sorts of counselling skills and processes that are used in virtually all situations. They include activities such as forming a working alliance with the client, exploring and defining client issues, goal setting, problem solving, action planning, and so on. Specific interventions are geared towards meeting specific individual client needs. They include those activities that have defined sequences of interactions with clients, such as the administration and interpretation of assessment instruments, the use of structured exercises (e.g., pride stories), or skill training (e.g., relaxation techniques or interpersonal communication skills). Programs are sets of activities that are structured in a particular sequence (e.g., job clubs or career-exploration workshops).

To provide a link between services and outcomes, it is important to be able to identify what is actually done with clients for the purpose of effecting client change. The service provider or counsellor may use the **professional practitioner** approach described earlier to obtain a strong level of intentionality. The professional practitioner engages in activities in the belief that the activity is most likely to produce desired change. It may be helpful to use an intervention grid that links outcomes with processes as illustrated in Table 3 (on the next page), Intervention Planning Grid. Each cell in the matrix invites a question about what will be done to achieve the desired outcome.

Stage 4: Selecting Measures and Scales

After planning the activities (processes) that link to the intended outcomes, the next important question is, *What will be the indicators of success?* Here it is necessary to find ways to measure both what you do, as well as what happens when you do it.

OUTCOMES				
	Learning	**Attributes**	**Impact**	**Other**
Processes Career decision making				
Work-specific skills enhancement				
Work search				
Job maintenance				
Career-related personal development				
Other				

Table 3: Intervention Planning Grid.

Let us first consider how to measure the process factors (i.e., what you do). Keep in mind that we need to address two important and related questions: How well did the service provider deliver the service as intended?, and How well did the participants follow the program as intended?

It is relatively easy to construct a process checklist for specific interventions and programs by listing the required steps or components of the program and attach a rating scale to each item. You probably want a measure of the extent to which participants did an activity, and you also may be interested in finding out how interesting or useful they found each activity.

We use two rules to guide the selection of measures. The first rule is to keep the scales simple. The second rule is to use common language, instead of technical language, to reduce misinterpretation of what a rating might mean. For example, on a homework assignment that participants were supposed to do as a part of an intervention, we might ask each participant if they "Didn't Do It" (rating of 0), "Sort of Did It" (rating of 1) or "Did It Thoroughly" (rating of 2). To obtain usefulness ratings, we have found that the decision-making approach described earlier in Table 1 is useful. The client engagement and the usefulness information measures often can be combined in the same form, as is depicted in Table 4, Sample Activity and Usefulness Participation Rating Sheet.

There are a variety of ways to evaluate the outcomes of an intervention. Measures of impact are commonly used by funders or agencies to determine the effectiveness of an intervention. These measures frequently reflect economic goals (e.g., employment), or goals that have direct impact on an organization's economic status (e.g., retention rates at educational institutions) and/or reputation (e.g., academic performance). Standardized tests may be used in a pretest/posttest design to indicate change

MODULE 1, UNIT 1

IN WORKING THROUGH MODULE 1, to what extent have you completed the following activities?

HOW USEFUL DID YOU FIND THE EXERCISES?
In responding, please use a two-step process:
(A) decide on whether the degree of usefulness was *acceptable* or *unacceptable*, then
(B) assign the appropriate rating:
(0) unacceptable,
   (1) not really acceptable, but almost there,
   (2) minimally acceptable (but still okay, otherwise it would be 0 or 1),
(4) exceptional,
   (3) somewhere between minimally acceptable and exceptional.

Activity	Didn't do it	Sort of did it	Did it thoroughly	Unacceptable 0	1	Acceptable 2	3	4
Unit 1 Exercises								
• *The Big Picture* worksheet	☐	☐	☐	☐	☐	☐	☐	☐
• *List of De-motivators*	☐	☐	☐	☐	☐	☐	☐	☐
• *List of Possible Career Options*	☐	☐	☐	☐	☐	☐	☐	☐
• *Core Motivators* worksheet	☐	☐	☐	☐	☐	☐	☐	☐
• *Reality Check Brainstorm*	☐	☐	☐	☐	☐	☐	☐	☐
• *Career-building Framework* (career vision and current situation)	☐	☐	☐	☐	☐	☐	☐	☐

Table 4: Sample Activity and Usefulness Participation Rating Sheet.†

attributed to an intervention. For example, a counsellor evaluating an intervention to reduce anxiety may administer the State-Trait Anxiety Inventory before and after the intervention: If the intervention was effective, there should be a decrease in the "state anxiety" scores in the latter test.

However, other measures that follow the professional-practitioner model also provide useful information linking intervention to client change. Observational measures, self-report measures, and other "informal" measures often provide the most interesting and useful indicators of client change. Data collection tools such as behavioural checklists and observation grids are particularly useful for this purpose. Self-report measures are used to gain client perspectives on their experiences. Although the reliability of any single self-report may be low, the reliability of combined self-reports across individuals and/or across instances of an event is very high (Gilbert, 2006).

In addition to the above, we have found it useful to ask participants to what extent did the change they experienced arise from the intervention or from other factors. After participants have assessed themselves along each of the desired intervention outcomes, we ask: "To what extent do you attribute changes you reported to the intervention (or program)?" and "To what extent do you attribute these changes to other factors in your life?" The participant attribution for change provides a convincing link between intervention and outcome.

Stage 5: Collecting Evidence

The core question that guides stage 5 is not simply, *How do we collect data (evidence)?* but rather, *How do we collect evidence most efficiently?* When evaluation is included as part of the initial design of an intervention, a good part of the work of collecting evidence will be done before a client walks through the door. When you specify the sorts of client changes you are trying to influence and identify the indicators of success for each, you have created your primary-outcome-assessment plan. When you plan intentional interventions to produce those client changes and develop the accompanying process measures, you have created a process-assessment plan.

All that is left is to decide when and how often to administer the evaluation tools you have developed. The process measures are typically collected after each "natural" phase of the intervention. If you are running a psycho-educational group that meets weekly for 5 weeks, you will probably administer a process assessment after each session (often, this is done at the start of the next session, which has the side benefit of serving as an excellent transition to the new material). These process assessments should not take more than 5 minutes to complete (and often can be completed in a minute or so). You will most likely administer the outcome assessment at the end of the intervention; a good rule of thumb is that it should not take more than 10 to 15 minutes for a participant to complete the outcome assessment.

Stage 6: Working With the Data

The guiding question for Stage 6 is *How do I make sense of the data I have collected?* For the most part, addressing this question need not involve complex statistical analyses. We suggest that there are alternative ways to organize the evidence such that the information helps improve practice and creates compelling arguments about the impact of services.

The informal assessments we have described lend themselves well to presenting accessible data that speak directly to the issues that are important to funders and practitioners alike. A useful beginning point is to compile frequency counts and percentages (e.g., 23 out of 25 (92%) of the participants in your program were able to find employment). Each of the process and outcome variables that we have described can be reported in this way and Appendix B, Sample Summative Evaluation Results, provides a sample of how these sorts of data can be analyzed and reported. In some cases, such as process checklists, it is also possible to report measures of central tendency, such as mean scores (e.g., participants went from a mean score of 1.4 to a mean score of 3.2 on their self-ratings of personal confidence before and after the program). However, we have found that it is often more useful to simply report frequencies, especially for process data.

Sometimes people are interested in knowing if the relationships in the data are statistically significant. In such cases, Chi-square tests can be used to determine if differences in the frequencies of categorical data are significant and t-tests or other inferential statistical analyses can be used for data that are more continuous in nature. However, in most cases, frequency counts, percentages, and mean scores will be sufficient to provide convincing evidence linking intervention and outcome. While a full description of the appropriate statistic to use for your data analysis is beyond the scope of this chapter, we do want to emphasize that the use of formal and/ or traditional program evaluation techniques are compatible with the approach we describe.

Stage 7: Reporting Results and Marketing Your Services

One of the most important questions you will ask throughout the evaluation process is, *How do we use the data to convince others?* If we want to influence how others value our services, then we must be accountable for our work. A few reporting or marketing principles may help guide you.

The first principle of marketing services is to work from the macro to the micro. How do your interventions impact core agency or institutional needs and values (i.e., the big picture outcomes)? You may be more interested in the micro level of client change (e.g., increased sense of self, increased hope, etc.), but your first task is to express those changes in terms that are meaningful to other decision makers.

The second principle is to demonstrate movement in your results. Most client change is not done in a single step, nor is it an "all or nothing" phenomenon. It is possible to show movement towards a larger impact (such as higher job placement) by reporting increases in a client's level of hope or confidence, a better self-understanding, an increased ability to describe the local job market, an ability to demonstrate self-marketing skills, or any number of other intermediary steps.

We have found one of the best ways to demonstrate such movement is through the post-pre assessments described earlier. For example, in one program, we asked participants to use the post-pre strategy to assess their understanding of how to move forward in their careers. The data showed that, before the intervention, 15 of the 29 participants rated their understanding as being "Unacceptable," and no participants rated it as being "Exceptional." After the intervention, no participants rated their understanding as "Unacceptable" or even "Minimally Acceptable," and 14 had moved to self-ratings of "Exceptional." As a group, self-ratings went from an average of 1.45 before the intervention to 3.48 (maximum score = 4) after. The accountability picture becomes even more convincing when the data are aggregated across several desired outcomes, as is illustrated more extensively in Appendix B, Sample Summative Evaluation Results. These data provide powerful indicators of movement in the desired direction. How you use the data to inform your own practice will be as important as how you use them to convince others. In most cases, the act of designing an evaluation process at the same time that you design the intervention will help you to be more intentional in your practice. You can also look at the process data you collect to see how the participants in your intervention view the activities. Practitioners and clients often have differing perspectives on what is important in the services they access (Manthei, 2006).

Recently, we were part of the team exploring the impact of Labour Market Information (LMI). In that project, we developed a protocol for assessing client needs to make sure that clients received an intervention that matched need. We also developed protocols for delivering the intervention. At first, the counsellors felt constrained by adhering to strict protocols. However, later they reported that their practice improved greatly by adhering to the intervention protocols and that they would continue to use the protocols after the study was completed. Counsellors also discovered that many clients did not need all of the help they usually provided. Once client needs were correctly identified, clients demonstrated a high level of self-sufficiency in meeting their needs, thereby freeing counsellors to spend more time with those clients who really needed a deeper level of service. In reporting the results, we were able to say that (a) clients received the intervention that matched their needs, (b) counsellors delivered the programs as intended, (c) clients were engaged in the program, and (d) substantial gains were made in knowledge, skills, personal attributes and employment status. The data permitted us to make the link between the services provided and the outcomes obtained.

The final principle in communicating results is to ensure that decision makers actually get to see the results of your work. A few years ago, we conducted an evaluation of an innovative new program offered by a university career service. The results of the evaluation were exceptionally positive. The program was shown to have far more impact than even those delivering the program had hoped for. Unfortunately, the results of the evaluation were not conveyed to senior administration. Soon after, the institution needed to make budget cuts and the program was cancelled. Even if it is necessary to use "guerrilla techniques" (i.e., finding ways to get around the system), you need to get your results in front of the people who make the decisions for allocating resources. Many excellent programs are terminated because the people making the decisions are not aware of the evidence attesting to the effectiveness of the program. Stated bluntly, the results don't matter much if no one knows about them. The bottom line in evaluation is to tell the people who need to know in language they can understand, what the data say about the outcomes of the services you provide.

Conclusion

Often evaluation is seen as an activity done by an external expert who passes judgement on the effectiveness of a program. As an alternative, we propose an approach where evaluation is infused into the day-to-day practices of service providers and where service providers always ask themselves two questions: (1) What intervention would be appropriate for this client? and (2) How will the client and I tell how well the intervention is working?

If I were a funder, my reasoning might be something like this: *You think you have a program that will help clients attain "X." I am willing to fund such a program. What evidence will you show me that my investment in your agency has been worthwhile?* In most cases, client flow data will not be enough, nor will documentation of all the skills and competencies of the service providers. A clearly articulated set of goals and objectives will help convince me to fund the program, because I can see the potential positive impact of what you are promising the clients. However, I am unlikely to fund it a second time if you can't show me that the client goals you promised have been met. The bottom line is that I need evidence to support my decisions.

Our focus throughout this chapter has been on encouraging practitioners to reformulate their professional identity, so that their view of self-as-professional includes a union between process and outcome. Most practitioners do not see relationship building as separate from intervention. Relationship building is part of the intervention. In a similar way, evaluation must be seen as being integral to the intervention. Reformulating one's view of self-as-professional will take time; however, we believe that doing so will raise the profile of career development and provide evidence for the effectiveness of career services. As people begin to work with these ideas, they will develop creative ways to demonstrate the value of the services they provide.

Evaluating services is a never-ending process. We encourage practitioners to start that process as soon as possible. Do not worry about getting it 100% right; just do it. Then share your results with others, so that collectively we can begin to more adequately demonstrate the value of career services.

Stories From the Field (7): **The Economic Value of Career Services**

A community agency received a contract to provide career development services to welfare recipients with the goal of helping them integrate into the labour market. The contract included a targeted outcome of 200 jobs at a total project cost of $260,000.00. Based on these figures, the average cost per client job was $1,300. This represented the government investment in career services for the project. Return on investment came from three sources: (a) welfare savings for the clients who found employment, (b) project staff employed to deliver the program and paid income tax on those earnings, and (c) taxes paid by clients who gained employment during the period of the project. Clients in the program were requested to provide a copy of their welfare pay stubs at the beginning of the program. This request was not a required condition for them receiving services; however, most clients complied with the request.

As clients obtained employment, the organization documented the client's starting wage and hours of work. Clients were then provided follow up services to help them stay employed. The organization tracked the duration of employment, and used this information to estimate the taxes paid by the clients and the project staff. When the program finished, clients were again asked to provide a copy of their pay slip, regardless of whether or not they had found a job. Then the organization calculated the increase in earnings for each client, as well as the increase in income tax paid by clients. The earnings of the service providers was used to determine the per-client income tax paid by those employed to deliver the program.

The return on investment was somewhat variable, depending on factors such as employment barriers, job availability, and so forth. However, over the two 1-year projects that were completed, the return on investment was in the range of $1.14. In other words, for each dollar the government spent on delivering career services programs to these clients, they received $1.14 within the same year. This 14% return would continue to grow as long as the client remained on the job, and provides clear economic support for viewing career services as an investment and not an expense.

References

Barlow, D. H. (1981). On the relation of clinical research to clinical practice: Current issues, new directions. *Journal of Consulting and Clinical Psychology, 49*, 147–155.

Baudouin, R., Bezanson, M. L., Borgen, W., Goyer, L., Hiebert, B., Lalande, V., … Turcotte, M. (2007). Demonstrating value: A draft framework for evaluating the effectiveness of career development interventions. *Canadian Journal of Counselling, 41*, 146–157.

Canadian Research Group on Evidence-Based Practice in Career Development (CRWG). (n.d). Homepage <http://www.crwg-gdrc.ca/crwg/>.

Canadian Research Group on Evidence-Based Practice in Career Development (CRWG). (2009). *Compendium of sample evaluation (evidence gathering) tools.* Ottawa, ON. Retrieved from <http://www.crwg-gdrc.ca/crwg/wp-content /uploads/2010/11/COMPENDIUM_EvaluationTools_EN.pdf>.

Charles, G., Ernst, K., & Ponzetti, J. (2003). Ethics and outcome measures. *Canada's Children, Canada's Future: The Journal of the Child Welfare League of Canada, 10*(2), 5–11.

Conger, S., & Hiebert, B. (2007). Employment and educational equivalence outcomes as measures of employment and career counselling. *Canadian Journal of Counselling, 41*, 186–193.

Conger, D. S., Hiebert, B., & Hong-Farrell, E. (1994). *Career and employment counselling in Canada.* Ottawa, ON: Canadian Labour Force Development Board.

DeAngelis, T. (2005). Shaping evidence-based practice. *APA Monitor on Psychology, 36*(3), 26. Retrieved from <http://www.apa.org/monitor/mar05/shaping.html>.

Gilbert, D. (2006). *Stumbling on happiness.* New York, NY: Random House.

Hiebert, B. (1997). Integrating evaluation into counseling practice: Accountability and evaluation intertwined. *Canadian Journal of Counselling, 31*, 112–126.

Hiebert, B., Bezanson, M. L., Magnusson, K., O'Reilly, E., Hopkins, S., & McCaffrey, A. (2011). *Assessing the Impact of Labour Market Information: Preliminary Results of Phase Two (Field Tests).* Final report to Human Resources and Skills Development Canada. Retrieved from <http://www.crwg-gdrc.ca/crwg/index.php /research-projects/lmi> (select Phase 2 Report).

Hiebert, B., & Borgen, W. (2002). *Technical and vocational education and training in the 21st century: New roles and challenges for guidance and counselling.* Paris: UNESCO Section for Vocational and Educational Training. Retrieved from <http://unesdoc.unesco.org/images/0013/001310/131005e.pdf>.

Hiebert, B., & Charles, G. (2008). *Accountability and outcomes in health and human services: Changing perspectives for changing times.* Calgary, AB: Canadian Outcomes Research Institute. Retrieved from <http://people.ucalgary.ca/~hiebert/research /files/CORI_Issue1_web.pdf>.

Hiebert, B., Domene, J. F., & Buchanan, M. (2011). The power of multiple methods and evidence sources: Raising the profile of Canadian counselling psychology research. *Canadian Psychology, 52*(4), 265–275. doi: 10.1037/a0025364

Horan, J. (1980). Experimentation in counselling and psychotherapy: New myths about old relations. *Educational Researcher, 9*, 4–10.

Lalande, V., & Magnusson, K. (2005). *The state of practice in Canada in measuring career service impact: A CRWG report.* Ottawa, ON: CRWG (Canadian Research Group on Evidence-Based Practice in Career Development). Retrieved from <http://www.crwg-gdrc.ca/>.

Lalande, V., & Magnusson, K. (2007). Measuring the impact of career development services in Canada: Current and preferred practices. *Canadian Journal of Counselling, 41*, 146–157.

Lalande, V., Hiebert, B., Magnusson, K., Bezanson, L., & Borgen, B. (2006). Measuring the impact of career services: Current and desired practices. In R. Neault, N. Arthur, & L. Edwards (Eds.). *Natcon Papers 2006.* Ottawa, ON: Canada Career Consortium. Available at <http://www.natcon.org/archive/natcon/papers/natcon_papers_2006_e5.pdf>.

Levant, R. F. (2005). Evidence-based practice in psychology. *APA Monitor on Psychology, 36*(2), 5. Retrieved from <http://www.apa.org/monitor/feb05/pc.html>.

Magnusson, K. (1992). Transitions to work: A model for program development. *International Journal for the Advancement of Counselling, 15*, 27–38.

Magnusson, K., Day, B., & Redekopp, D. (1993). Skills are not enough: Innovative strategies and services for youth in transition. *Guidance and Counselling, 8*(4), 6–20.

Manthei, R. J. (2006). What can clients tell us about seeking counselling and their experience of it? *International Journal for the Advancement of Counselling, 27*, 541–555.

Morago, P. (2006). Evidence-based practice: From medicine to social work. *European Journal of Social Work, 9*, 461–477.

Peruniak, G. S. (2010). A quality of life approach to career development. Toronto, ON: University of Toronto Press.

Posavac, E. J. (2011). *Program evaluation: Methods and case studies* (8th ed.). New York, NY: Prentice Hall.

Pothier, P., Robertson, I., Hiebert, B., & Magnusson, K. (2008). *Measuring career program effectiveness: Making it work.* Paper presented to CANNEXUS: Canada's annual career development conference, April 14–16, Montréal, Québec.

Robinson, E. A. R., & Doueck, H. J. (1994). Implications of the pre/post/then design for evaluating social group work. *Research on Social Work Practice, 4*, 224–239.

Rockwell, S. K., & Kohn, H. (1989). Post-then-pre evaluation. Journal of Extension, 27(2), 1–5.

Spiro, S. E., Shalev, A., Solomon, Z., & Kotler, M. (1989). Self-reported change versus changed self-report: Contradictory findings of an evaluation of a treatment program for war veterans suffering from post-traumatic stress disorder. *Evaluation Review, 13*, 533–549.

Taylor, C., & White, S. (2002). What works about what works? Fashion, fad and EBP. *Social Work & Social Sciences Review, 10*(1), 63–81.

Trierweiler, S. J., & Stricker, G. (1998). The scientific practice of professional psychology. New York, NY: Plenum.

Webb, S. A. (2001). Some considerations on the validity of evidence-based practice in social work. *British Journal of Social Work, 31,* 57–79.

Glossary

Canadian Research Working Group on Evidence-Based Practice in Career Development (CRWG) was formed to address two important issues in the field of career development:

- Increase pan-Canadian sharing of research and promising practices, with an emphasis on sharing French and English research.
- Strengthen the overall evidence base for career development practice with an emphasis on informing policy.

The CRWG website can be found at <http://www.crwg-gdrc.ca/>.

Evidence-based practice (EBP) is the use of mental and behavioural health interventions for which systematic empirical research has provided evidence of effectiveness as treatments for specific problems. EBP promotes the collection, interpretation, and integration of valid and applicable patient-reported, clinician-observed, and research-derived evidence.

Inter-rater discrepancy is the degree of agreement among raters concerning the content validity of test or inventory items.

Likert-type rating scale is a survey response scale that asks respondents to indicate their attitude by rating their level of satisfaction or degree of agreement with a statement. The scale usually ranges from 1–5; 1–7; or 1–9 points. Degrees of agreement may be substituted for numeric points on a scale.

Outcome-focused intervention is based on results that have had demonstrable indicators of success or outcomes.

Post-pre assessment is a retrospective approach to measuring client change. Participants are asked to use their current frame of reference to create a common measuring stick for assessing their competence before and after a workshop. For example, participants in a workshop on how to understand and use labour market information might be asked: *"Knowing what you know now about using labour market information for career decision making or job search, rate yourself before the workshop and rate yourself now."*

Professional practitioners, as a term used in this chapter, have the following attributes: their practice is based on a significant body of theory; they have appropriate qualifications from a recognized body of peers; they are committed to undergoing continuous professional development; they consult best practices before undertaking work; and they are held to a code of conduct. Professional practitioners are clear about the nature of the change client's desire, clear about what they will do to meet client goals, and they document what they do and how well it works. Professional practitioners focus equally on providing appropriate services for clients and providing evidence that the service is resulting in a positive impact on the lives of clients.

Randomized controlled trial (RCT) is an experiment in which investigators randomly assign eligible subjects into groups to receive or not receive one or more interventions that are being compared. RCTs help to eliminate effects of extraneous variables that may confound experimental results, which helps to establish external validity and generalizability.

Discussion and Activity

Discussion

Class Discussion Questions

1. Based on your understanding of the importance of assessing career development services, what are the key ingredients for career practitioners to be aware of and to monitor over time?
2. Suppose you followed an evaluation game plan similar to the one suggested in this chapter, using a combination of some of your current evaluation practices and ideas you got from this chapter. Suppose further that the evidence ended up being exceedingly positive. How would you go about making sure that the people who need to hear about this success actually do hear about it; i.e., telling the people who need to know, in language they can understand, that your program was an amazing success?

Personal Reflection Questions

1. Why is it important to evaluate the impact of client services? What concerns do you have about integrating evaluation into your everyday practice? What benefits do you see associated with integrating evaluation into your everyday practice?
2. In considering the "power of evidence," what further skills, supports, and resources do you need to be effective in evaluating the effectiveness of interventions used with clients?

Career Practitioner Role Questions

1. Free self-directed career interventions and assessments are available on the

Internet. Find four online resources and determine what criteria you would use to assess whether the resources would be suitable for use with clients. How would you evaluate their effectiveness with clients?

2. Identify a community-career partnership that exists in your province and discuss the work-related and job-specific skills needed to monitor the benefits of the program to individuals, to the employer, and to the community?
3. Some target outcomes of a career program may not occur until well after the completion of the program. What informal assessment would you create for longer term follow-up intervals?

Activity

There is a growing consensus that ethical and social values should be addressed when evaluating career services. How would you elicit ethical and social values from clientele that use these services to include in evaluations of services provided? Create a citizens panel with a small group in your class and discuss what central values you deem important (for example: access to the organization, choice of services, and quality of interventions).

Appendices: Sample Forms, Analysis, and Reports

Appendix A. Sample Post-Pre Evaluation Form

The Applied Career Transitions Program *Evaluation Form*

Program Goals

The goals of Module 1 are that participants will:

1. Formulate a clear understanding of what they want to build in their career (career vision).
2. Gather and analyze information about themselves and their past experience in relation to their career (career portfolio).
3. Identify and research career options that align with their career vision (research portfolio).
4. Identify emerging career goals and make decisions about the next steps they will take to move forward in their career.

First, Some General Questions

In answering these general questions, we would like you to compare yourself now and before you completed the ACT program. **Knowing what you know now**, how would you rate yourself before the ACT program, and how would you rate yourself now?

In responding to the questions, please use a two-step process: (A) decide on whether the characteristic in question is **acceptable** or **unacceptable**, then (B) assign the appropriate rating:

(0) unacceptable,

(1) not really acceptable, but almost there,

(2) minimally acceptable (but still okay, otherwise it would be 0 or 1),

(3) somewhere between minimally acceptable and exceptional,

(4) exceptional.

Graphically, the scale looks like this:

Unacceptable		Acceptable		
0	1	2	3	4

REGARDING THE PROGRAM GOALS FOR MODULE 1, and knowing what you know now, how would you rate yourself before the program, and how would you rate yourself now?	BEFORE WORKSHOP	NOW
	Unacceptable / Acceptable 0 1 2 3 4	Unacceptable / Acceptable 0 1 2 3 4
1. A conceptual understanding of the processes involved in moving forward in your career.		
2. An articulation of the core motivators (e.g., your career vision) that describe what you want to build in your career.		
3. An articulation of how your career is impacted by your current situation (supports and challenges) in the different contexts of your life.		
4. An assessment of your past work, education, and life experiences.		

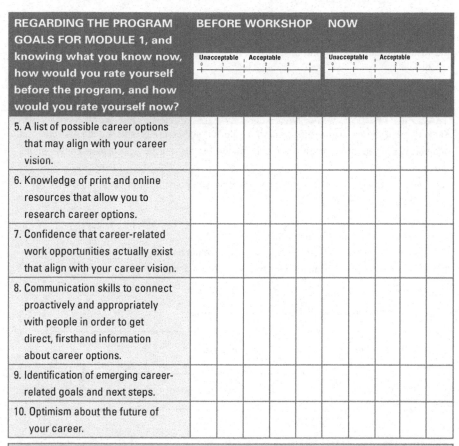

REGARDING THE PROGRAM GOALS FOR MODULE 1, and knowing what you know now, how would you rate yourself before the program, and how would you rate yourself now?	BEFORE WORKSHOP (Unacceptable 0-1 / Acceptable 2-3-4)					NOW (Unacceptable 0-1 / Acceptable 2-3-4)				
5. A list of possible career options that may align with your career vision.										
6. Knowledge of print and online resources that allow you to research career options.										
7. Confidence that career-related work opportunities actually exist that align with your career vision.										
8. Communication skills to connect proactively and appropriately with people in order to get direct, firsthand information about career options.										
9. Identification of emerging career-related goals and next steps.										
10. Optimism about the future of your career.										

11. To what extent would you say that any changes depicted above were the result of completing the ACT program, and to what extent were they a function of other factors in your life?

Mostly Other Factor	Somewhat Other Factors	Uncertain	Somewhat This Program	Mostly This Program
0	0	0	10	19

12. Are you currently working?	Yes __	No __

13. If you answered yes to the above question, to what extent is this work related to your career vision?

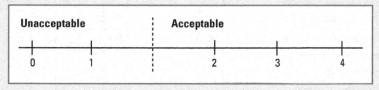

Table 5.

Appendix B. Sample Summative Evaluation Results

The results pertaining to completing the ACT program are summarized in the table below.

In answering these general questions, we would like you to compare yourself now and before you completed the ACT program.

Knowing what you know now, how would you rate yourself before completing the ACT program, and how would you rate yourself now? In responding to the questions, please use a two-step process.

(A) decide on whether the characteristic in question is acceptable or unacceptable, then (B) assign the appropriate rating:

(0) unacceptable,

(1) not really acceptable, but almost there,

(2) minimally acceptable (but still okay, otherwise it would be 0 or 1),

(3) somewhere between minimally acceptable and exceptional,

(4) exceptional.

Graphically, the scale looks like this:

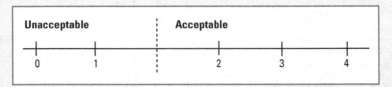

REGARDING THE GOALS FOR THE ACT program, and knowing what you know now, how would you rate yourself before the program, and how would you rate yourself now?	BEFORE WORKSHOP						NOW					
	0	1	2	3	4		0	1	2	3	4	
1. A clear understanding of the processes involved in moving forward in your career.	7	8	8	6	0	1.45	0	0	0	15	14	3.48
2. A clear understanding of the core motivators (i.e., your career vision) that describe what you want to build in your career.	3	10	11	5	0	1.62	0	0	2	10	17	3.52

REGARDING THE GOALS FOR THE ACT program, and knowing what you know now, how would you rate yourself before the program, and how would you rate yourself now?	BEFORE WORKSHOP						NOW					
	Unacceptable		Acceptable				Unacceptable		Acceptable			
	0	1	2	3	4		0	1	2	3	4	
3. A clear understanding of how your career is impacted by your current situation (supports and challenges) in the different contexts of your life.	1	9	9	9	1	2.0	0	0	4	12	13	33.1
4. An assessment of your past work, education, and life experiences.	1	9	10	8	1	1.97	0	0	2	11	16	3.48
5. A list of possible career options that may align with your career vision.	4	9	14	2	0	1.48	0	0	2	12	15	3.45
6. Knowledge of print and online resources that allow you to research career options.	4	13	9	2	1	1.41	0	0	2	13	14	3.41
7. Confidence that career-related work opportunities actually exist that align with your career vision.	6	11	6	6	0	1.41	0	0	6	16	7	3.03
8. Communication skills to connect proactively and appropriately with people in order to get direct, firsthand information about career options.	7	7	7	6	2	1.64	0	1	2	15	10	3.21
9. Identification of emerging career-related goals and next steps.	5	12	8	4	0	1.39	0	0	4	11	13	3.32
10. Optimism about the future of your career.	8	10	5	5	1	1.34	0	2	2	14	11	3.17
						Avg						Avg
Cumulative Mean All differences in mean scores are statistically significant (p < .01)						1.57						3.34

Table 6.

Description of the Evaluation Results

The data in the summary table provide a clear picture of the dramatic effects accompanying completion of the ACT program and indicate that it was highly successful in achieving the intended outcomes. More specifically, we draw attention to the following:

- All together there were 29 (participants) x 10 (items) = 290 ratings.
- Regarding the participants' assessment of their competencies before the workshop, there were 144 ratings (almost 50%) in the Unacceptable category and 6 ratings of Exceptional.
- At the end of the workshop, there were 3 ratings in the Unacceptable category and 130 (45%) ratings of Exceptional. All 3 ratings of Unacceptable were in the "almost there" category.
- Stated another way, at the end of the workshop, Module ratings of "acceptable" changed from 50% to 99%, with 86% (249 of 290) of those responses being greater than minimally acceptable, and 45% of the responses being Exceptional (up from 2% before the workshop).
- In 8 of the 10 outcome measures, all participants who rated themselves as "Unacceptable" at the beginning rated themselves as having "Acceptable" levels of competence at the end. Moreover, there was a very strong movement into the upper categories of Acceptability with the predominance of responses being at level 3 or 4.
- The mean scores also indicate a substantial shift, from Unacceptable (mean score less than 2) to Acceptable (mean score greater than 2). The increases in mean scores on all 10 items were statistically significant. In other words, the activities included in Module 1 produced significant change in the desired direction on all of the outcome measures.

The impact of the changes described above was that 23 out of 29 participants were employed at the end of the program and for 10 of those 23 participants their jobs were directly in line with their career vision.

In any real-life situation, there are many factors that can influence an outcome. To determine the extent to which the ACT program was influential in creating the outcomes, we asked participants for their attributions of what caused any changes they noticed. Specifically, we posed the following question and received the responses indicated (see next page).

Overall the evaluation results for the ACT program indicate that it is highly successful in helping participants meet the outcome objectives of the program and in producing a noteworthy impact on employment status. Furthermore, in the minds of participants, the impacts achieved were largely the result of their participation in the program and were not due to other factors operating in their lives.

To what extent would you say that any changes depicted above were the result of completing the ACT program, and to what extent were they a function of other factors in your life?

Mostly Other Factors	Somewhat Other Factors	Uncertain	Somewhat This Program	Mostly This Program
0	0	0	10	19

Table 7.

Appendix C. Sample Formative Feedback Results

For each of instructional activities that were part of ACT program, we would like you to address two questions:

1. To what extent have you completed each of the activities in the program?
0 = Didn't do it.
1 = Sort of did it.
2 = Did it thoroughly.

2. How useful did you find the exercises?
   In responding to the questions regarding usefulness, please use a two-step process: (A) decide on whether the degree of usefulness is acceptable or unacceptable, then (B) assign the appropriate rating:
(0) unacceptable,
(1) not really acceptable, but almost there
(2) minimally acceptable (but still okay, otherwise it would be 0 or 1),
(3) somewhere between minimally acceptable and exceptional,
(4) exceptional.

Graphically, the scale looks like this:

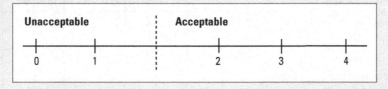

Table 8.

The data presented above indicate that overall, participants found the activities to be very useful. The mean scores for each unit met or exceeded values of 3.0, meaning that participants found the activities more than minimally useful. The completion ratings across the four units of ACT program indicate that participants were highly engaged at the beginning of the module and became progressively less engaged as they progressed. Generally, participants dropped from thoroughly completing activities in Unit 1, to sort of completing activities in Unit 4. The most likely reason for this is that as participants found employment, they were less motivated to continue completing the workshop activities. The usefulness data also flag a few items that likely should be revised to make them more engaging (e.g., items 1.2.b, 1.2.g, and 1.4.a).

REGARDING THE ACTIVITIES IN THE ACT Program, please indicate the extent to which you completed each activity, and also how useful you found the exercise.	COMPLETION			USEFULNESS					
	0	1	2	Unacceptable 0 1		Acceptable 2 3		4	
Unit 1 Components									
1.1.a The Big Picture	0	2	27	0	0	2	15	11	3.32
1.1.b List of Demotivators	0	3	26	0	0	1	16	11	3.36
1.1.c Possible Career Options	1	10	18	0	1	4	17	6	3.00
1.1.d Core Motivators	0	2	27	0	0	1	11	16	3.54
1.1.e Reality Check	1	8	20	0	1	1	16	9	3.22
1.1.f Career-Building Framework	1	4	22	0	0	5	7	15	3.37
Overall Means for Unit 1 —		**1.80**							**3.30**
Unit 2 Components									
1.2.a Master Experience List	1	8	20	0	2	2	9	14	3.30
1.2.b Table of Contents	13	6	9	2	2	6	10	2	2.62
1.2.c Career Vision (all exercises from Unit 1)	0	4	24	0	1	3	8	15	3.37
1.2.d Experience and Skills (Master Experience List and current résumés)	0	9	19	0	1	1	14	12	3.32
1.2.e References and recognition (list of references, reference letters, etc.)	4	8	16	0	2	6	8	12	3.07

REGARDING THE ACTIVITIES IN THE ACT Program, please indicate the extent to which you completed each activity, and also how useful you found the exercise.	COMPLETION			USEFULNESS					
	0	1	2	Unacceptable 0	1	Acceptable 2	3	4	
1.2.f Educational credentials (copies of degrees, certificates, and transcripts)	4	8	16	2	0	1	14	11	3.14
1.2.g Work samples (papers, projects, reports, etc.)	6	11	10	0	2	6	12	8	2.93
Overall Means for Unit 2 —		1.44							3.11
Unit 3 Components									
1.3.a Career options research list	0	8	21	1	0	2	13	13	3.28
1.3.b Career options summary sheet	7	14	8	0	0	8	10	8	3.00
1.3.c Information and notes for each career option being researched	2	16	10	0	0	3	14	10	3.26
Overall Means for Unit 3 —		1.35							3.18
Unit 4 Components									
1.4.a Career option decision grid	10	10	9	2	0	3	9	8	2.95
1.4.b Emerging career goals worksheet	12	12	7	2	0	2	9	9	3.05
Overall Means for Unit 4 —		0.94							3.05

Table 8.

Appendix D. Examples of Client-Change Outcomes

Examples of Learning Outcomes (from Blueprint for Life/Work Designs)

1. Personal management outcomes:

   - build and maintain a positive personal image,
   - interact positively and effectively with others,
   - change and grow throughout one's life.

2. Learning and work exploration outcomes:

   - participate in lifelong learning supportive of life/work goals,

- locate and effectively use life/work information,
- understand the relationship between work and society/economy.

3. Life/work building outcomes:

- secure, create, and maintain work,
- make life/work-enhancing decisions,
- link decision making to life/work,
- maintain balanced life/work rules,
- understand the changing nature of life/work roles,
- understand, engage in, and manage one's own life/work process.

Examples of Personal Attribute Outcomes

1. Attitudes:

- belief that change is possible,
- internal locus of control.

2. Intrapersonal factors:

- confidence,
- motivation,
- self-esteem,
- stress,
- depression.

3. Client independence:

- client self-reliance and initiative,
- independent client use of tools provided in career services.

Examples of Client-Impact Outcomes

1. Employment status (placement rates).
2. Participation in training.
3. Engaging in job search.
4. Client ability to fit in at the workplace.
5. Reduction of negative or self-defeating personal behaviours.
6. Increase in positive or self-asserting behaviours.
7. Increased job stability.
8. Natural job progression occurs for clients.
9. Societal impacts.
10. Relational impacts.
11. Economic impacts.

twenty-one

The Professionalization of Career Development in Canada in the 21st Century

LYNNE BEZANSON
SAREENA HOPKINS
ELAINE O'REILLY
Canadian Career Development Foundation

PRE-READING QUESTIONS

1. What is meant by the career development sector in Canada?
2. What is career development?
3. Why is it important for career development practitioners to belong to professional associations? To become certified?

Introduction and Learning Objectives

Career development practitioners must respond to the ever-changing career needs of individuals and, at the same time, handle ongoing labour market shifts and challenges. As the global recession of 2008–2009 has shown, labour markets can move from relative stability to instability very quickly and unexpectedly. The nature of work and the nature of the employment contract have shifted significantly in recent years, creating both opportunities and challenges for individuals, and shaping career development theory, policy, and practice.

This chapter highlights transformations in the career development sector in Canada over the past 15 years to the present day. Some transformations are responses to external influences — these are "outside-in transformations" — and include such forces as economic restructuring, demographic changes, globalization of the economy, external markets, and technological changes. Education and employment play an overarching role in these external influences. Other transformations come from within the sector itself — "inside-out transformations" — such as initiatives that support the career development profession in Canada and increase coherence in training throughout the sector.

Studies done by the **Organisation for Economic Co-operation and Development (OECD)** have strongly influenced the outside-in transformation. The OECD report, *Career Guidance and Public Policy: Bridging the Gap* (2004), examined later in this chapter, highlighted the important exchange between public policy and the delivery of career guidance services in the context of these external influences. Policy makers in OECD countries expect career services to "improve the efficiency of educational systems and the labour market and to contribute to social equity" (OECD, 2004, p. 8). The new emphasis on lifelong learning and active labour market policies has heightened the challenges. The report noted that there needs to be wider access to these services in ways that are more flexible and which do not strain "the public purse" (OECD, 2004, p. 8).

One of the strongest, inside-out transformations has been the professionalization of the sector. The 2011 Survey of Canadian Career Service Professionals conducted by CERIC found that 68% of respondents felt that being professionally certified was important or very important to them. They also listed 37 provincial, national, and international associations through which they were presently certified or pursuing certification (CERIC, 2011). In the *Pan-Canadian Mapping Study of the Career Development Sector* (2009), researchers found that career development practitioners place a high priority on access to professional training, and they want more professional recognition in the form of certification and/or licensing. Québec (career counsellors) had licensing and Alberta had voluntary certification in place prior to this mapping study; British Columbia added voluntary certification; as of 2013, New Brunswick, Ontario and Nova Scotia are in the process of developing certification.

This chapter provides several references to influential reports and websites where more information can be reviewed. The reader is encouraged to explore these additional resources to obtain a more comprehensive perspective and to become aware of career development issues and progress in Canada and internationally.

By the end of this chapter, our aim is that you achieve the following learning objectives:

1. Understand the difference between outside-in and inside-out transformations that are taking place in the career development sector in Canada.
2. Outline the ways in which our understanding of career development has changed over time.
3. Explain why it is important to have meaningful dialogue between the career development sector and policy makers.

4. Grasp the importance of research and evaluation in the development of the profession.
5. Explain the reasons for the professionalization of the career development sector.
6. List the organizations, associations, and other bodies that support career development in Canada.

Transformation From the Outside-In

There have been three significant "outside-in" transformations to the career development profession arising from external forces: (a) an expanding scope of practice, (b) a stronger connection between policy and practice, and (c) the necessity for an evidence base for practice.

An Expanding Scope of Practice

Until the latter part of the 20th century, career development was seen as focusing primarily on preparing people for the world of work. While career development encompassed the development of the whole person, a critical emphasis was placed on gaining the skills and experience to qualify for, secure, and sustain work (The Counselling Foundation of Canada, 2002). The primary goal of career development in those years was directed at improving one's employability for obtaining meaningful work.

Career development was, at its simplest, (a) job matching for unemployed adults, and (b) aptitude/interest testing for some high school students near the end of their schooling. In the latter part of the 20th century, the scope of career development widened to include such activities as managing career transitions, balancing various life roles, addressing the need for lifelong learning, and responding to issues of social equity and inclusion.

Career development is no longer job matching, but a holistic discipline that encompasses an individual's lifespan. Career development has come to embrace not only

A Quality of Life Approach to Career Development

In the book *A Quality of Life Approach to Career Development*, Geoff Peruniak explores the meaning of work, and highlights a model of quality of life as an integrative and holistic framework for career development. Within this framework, the concept of career includes not only paid work but also other aspects of life experience and learning. The book emphasizes the importance of looking at the person as a whole within an important network of roles and experiences.

Going beyond theoretical discussion, he presents a number of case studies to illustrate the concepts introduced. Peruniak also considers the influence of nature and community in relation to career development that make up the fabric of personal and social meaning.

(University of Toronto Press <http://www.jstor.org/stable /10.3138/9781442686885>)

job information, labour market information, and interest and aptitude testing, but also values, skills development, work environment preferences, passion and talents, and cradle-to-grave life/work competencies. Career development today is seen as a lifelong process of acquiring the knowledge, skills, and attitudes to explore and discover, make plans and decisions not only about education, training, and employment, but also about personal management, life/work skills, and life/work quality. Career development is considered part of lifelong learning, in that personal and vocational skills constantly change and expand during a lifetime in response to career changes and emerging opportunities.

While there is no universal definition of career development, recent definitions reflect this much-expanded view (and, thus, much-expanded expectations) for the sector:

- Career development refers to activities that enable citizens of any age, at any point in their lives, to (a) identify their capacities, competencies, and interests; (b) make meaningful educational, training, and occupational decisions; and (c) manage their individual career paths in learning and work (OECD, 2004, p. 19)
- "Career development is the lifelong process of managing your living, learning and earning in order to move to where you want to be." (CCDF <http://www.ccdf.ca>)
- Career development is the pattern of one's total life and all of its roles, not just work; many forces mold one's choices, especially spirituality and meaning found in work. (Hansen, 2001)

Graham Lowe, in his book *The Quality of Work* (2000), discusses the indicators of quality work and argues that, in a highly developed economy such as Canada's, work must include more than a means of survival: It must include "the opportunity to do personally meaningful, socially useful work that promotes a sense of security and well-being" (p. 6). According to Lowe, the basic pillars of quality work are tasks that are meaningful to workers personally and include:

- a decent standard of living that affords a sense of economic security,
- employment relationships that are respectful,
- healthy and safe work environments,
- worker participation in decision making.

As the career development field has grown through new discoveries, inventions, and real-world experiences there has been an adjustment in thinking in Canada and globally:

- from intervention at key points in life to a lifelong perspective,
- from psychological testing to tasting the world of work,
- from external expert support to career (self)-management skills,
- from individual guidance to group and self-help approaches. (Zelloth, 2009)

The scope of practice for career development practitioners expanded to include disciplines and jurisdictions previously thought to be outside the realm of career development: (a) elementary, secondary, and postsecondary classroom curricula; (b) labour, business, and government; (c) sector councils; (d) social agencies and mental health; (e) industries; and (f) economics .

This expansion has important implications for practitioners in terms of their professional identity, their qualifications, and their ongoing professional development. Providing a service with a lifelong perspective to cover many life roles requires a very different and much more expansive skill-set than is the case for a service focused primarily on a client's employability. The career development agenda becomes very holistic, multidimensional, and complex as issues of quality of work and quality of life are added to the lifelong perspective. A quote by the late Dr. R. Vance Peavy (2001) captures this well: "When one asks, 'What kind of career should I have?' one is really asking, 'How should I live my life?'" (p. 6).

❖ *Stop and Reflect*
After having read the chapters in the textbook, how has your understanding of the role and responsibility of the career practitioner shifted?

The Connection Between Policy and Practice

In Canada, as in many other countries, career and employment services are public services provided free of charge through schools, career and employment centres, and community-based organizations. Career services in postsecondary institutions are generally funded through student fees. There is also a private practice sector in career development and career counselling, but it is relatively small compared to public provision. This means that career and employment services are largely dependent on public funds and the priorities of politicians and senior policy makers. It is therefore critical that career development be well understood by funders, and that ongoing dialogue and consultation take place between the career development sector and appropriate policy bodies. Regrettably, this has not been the case in most countries, Canada included.

One reason for the insufficiency of consultation between the career development sector and policy bodies is the lack of a common language. Public policy boards and policy makers tend to speak in two languages. "One discussion uses terms such as analysis, outcomes, accountability, costs and benefits, and evidence based decision making. The second [discussion] includes terms such as influence, popularity, power, alliances, interest groups and change processes" (International Symposium 2001, p. 197). The career development field uses a third and very different language: *process, culture and context, collaboration, and client centred*. It is therefore not surprising that the final report of the OECD Study of Career Guidance Policies (2004) is titled *Bridging the Gap*. The movement towards building stronger connections between policy and career development practice has been strongly influenced by this study.

OECD Study Into Career Guidance Policies

The OECD, located in Paris, began a study in 2002 of Career Guidance Policies in 14 OECD countries, including Canada. This study has been duplicated in over 55 countries thereby providing an immense database of career development policies, models, and practices. *Career Guidance: A Handbook for Policy Makers* (OECD, 2002a) recognized the need for lifelong career development services as part of effective lifelong learning and active labour market policies. There was widespread consensus across participating countries that a highly developed, lifelong career-information and career development system is central to: (a) supporting a competitive, knowledge-based economy; (b) advancing active employment and welfare policies; and (c) promoting social inclusion. There was also widespread consensus that a transformation of career development systems is needed in order for career development policy and services to play this central role effectively. Four overall conclusions emerged from the study (OECD, 2002a):

1. Career development is both a private and public good. However, career development, lifelong learning, and sustained employability need to be better connected and reflected in policies that focus on access to information and career services across the lifespan.
2. Career development is essential in laying the foundations for lifelong learning. Within the K–12 formal educational system, access is far from universal, and career and educational planning is often submerged by personal and social counselling issues. In most countries, services within postsecondary education are particularly inadequate.
3. While services are lifelong in principle, in practice access is primarily targeted towards youth — most frequently marginalized at-risk youth — and on the unemployed. Large percentages of the population do not have access.
4. In all the countries in the study, components of a quality career development system were identified. To date, no one country has put all the quality pieces together.

The OECD *Review of Career Guidance Policies* report on Canada (2002b) high-lighted some Canadian strengths, notably:

- the quality of labour market information;
- the development of strategic instruments such as *The Real Game Series*, the *Blueprint for Life/Work Designs*, and the *Canadian Standards and Guidelines for Career Development Practitioners* (S&Gs);
- creative support for public-private partnerships and third-sector initiatives.

The report also highlighted weaknesses, including:

- emphasis on producing information resources rather than their effective utilization;
- lack of a coherent framework for career development services within the educational system;
- services for adults based largely on a crisis-oriented deficit model rather than on a proactive developmental model engaging all Canadians;
- the lack of adequate quality assurance across the career development field;
- lack of strategic leadership capable of co-ordinating the breadth of career development provision. (OECD, 2002, p. 25)

The OECD recommendations for Canada and its reviews of guidance services in other countries offer Canada important guideposts for strengthening the career development sector (Bezanson & Renald, 2003). The OECD Report merits periodic revisiting to evaluate levels of progress in all of the areas cited.

OECD *Bridging the Gap Report*
In their final *Bridging the Gap Report* (OECD, 2004), the components of an effective lifelong career development system were outlined. The features are:

- transparency and ease of access over an individual's lifespan, and the capacity to meet the needs of a diverse range of clients;
- particular attention to key transition points during an individual's lifespan;
- flexibility and innovation in service delivery to reflect the differing needs and circumstances of diverse client groups;
- processes to stimulate regular review and planning of services;
- access to individual guidance by appropriately qualified practitioners for those who need such help, available at times when they need it;

- programs to develop career management skills;
- opportunities to investigate and experience learning and work options before choosing them;
- assured access to service delivery that is independent of the interests of particular institutions or enterprises;
- access to comprehensive and integrated educational, occupational, and labour market information;
- involvement of relevant stakeholders.

These features provide a kind of "quality assurance" framework against which effective career development systems can be assessed. They, too, merit revisiting as a checklist for assessing the extent to which Canadian career development services have adopted these features.

Another key outcome of the OECD 2004 study was the establishment of the **International Centre for Career Development and Public Policy** (ICCDPP) whose role is to promote global collaboration in career guidance policy (<http://www.iccdpp. org>). This centre is now firmly established as a repository of international policy, research, and practice documents. The OECD study has been hugely influential in making the necessity for stronger connections between career development practice and public policy transparent and concrete.

International Symposia
A secondary, but equally transformational, effect of efforts to bridge policy and practice has been the development of reciprocal international partnerships. Canada has played a substantial role in this development. The International Symposium movement began in 1999 in Ottawa, Canada. In recognition of the tremendous gaps in the communication, vision, and understanding between professionals in the career development field and policy makers, a small team of career development leaders from Canada, the United Kingdom, and New Zealand met to determine a way forward.

They proposed a symposium that would bring together internationally career development professionals and government policy makers to discuss how they could best work together to promote and support a field capable of furthering individual career development as well as overall economic development. From 1999 to 2011, six international symposia have been held; the first two in Canada (funded by Human Resources and Skills Development Canada (HRSDC); led by CCDF), followed by Australia, Scotland, New Zealand and Hungary. Participating countries have ranged in numbers from 14 to 34. Canada was instrumental in developing the working format of the meetings, which has been maintained, with minor adjustments, for all symposia. A crucial outcome of the symposia has been the formation of teams in each country to bring together, as much as possible, equal numbers of senior policy makers in relevant portfolios, recognized career development researchers, and representatives of career development practitioners. Each symposium has had specific themes for development including: (a) career development structures/policy models, (b) quality outcomes, (c) costs/benefits, (d) professional qualifications, (e) transformational technology. There have also been sessions on: (a) Prove It Works, (b) Role of the Citizen, and (c) Culture Counts. The expectation is that each country develop an action plan to implement before the next gathering (see <http://www.iccdpp.org> for all Country Papers and Symposium Proceedings).

Canada's team began by modeling a strong collaborative and collegial spirit that continues today in the symposium movement. The members have been able to return to their respective provinces and organizations and, with different levels of success, follow through with their commitment for change. Relationship building and collaboration, willingness to learn from other points of view, sharing resources, approaches, and ideas — these are the hallmarks of the movement so far, and they keep getting stronger, providing an increasingly firm foundation for improving national and international career development.

International co-operation has expanded Canada's views of career development models and has inspired professionals to explore new methods to improve services and professional development. It has allowed career development practitioners, researchers and policy makers in Canada to assume a leadership role on global topics such as evidence-based research. Canada's formation of the **Canadian Research Working Group on Evidence-Based Practice in Career Development (CRWG)** and the federal government's investment in rigorous evidence-based research has positioned Canada to contribute internationally in this area.

Participation in the symposia also stimulated Canadian study and pursuit of what is now an emerging global "trend" to provide all-age career services in lieu of specific or narrow criteria for service. In this, Canada has benefitted from model examples such as Scotland's all-age career services (Brown, Dent, Galashan, Hirsh, & Hughes, 2006).

The first Pan-Canadian Symposium on Career Development, Lifelong Learning and Workforce Development in 2003 was inspired by the OECD findings and Canada's participation in the International Symposium movement, again funded by HRSDC and hosted by the **Canadian Career Development Foundation (CCDF)**. Representing a wide range of interests in policy, research and practice, teams from all provinces and territories, except the Northwest Territories, participated. Out of the 15 issues identified as important to the advancement of career development in Canada, delegates agreed on three urgent priorities:

1. A comprehensive vision for a coherent delivery system that includes those most often excluded from accessing services (i.e., employed and underemployed adults).
2. A long-term comprehensive strategy to instill a lifelong learning and career

development culture in education and workforce development policies.
3. Positioning career development in the context of social, economic, and community development. (Pan-Canadian Symposium, 2003)

In 2007, the **Forum of Labour Market Ministers (FLMM)** formed the **Career Development Services Working Group (CDSWG)** to strengthen the connection between policy and practice. The intent of this federally co-ordinated body was to bring together representatives of the provincial and territorial government departments responsible for career and employment services so as to: (a) ensure co-ordination across jurisdictions, (b) share information on areas of mutual interest, and (c) influence the access, quality, and quantity of services available to the Canadian public. Because Canadian career and employment services are highly decentralized, there had been no pan-Canadian policy body that could address shared concerns. The CDSWG funded and led a number of specific projects including a mapping study of the career development sector and a review of quality service standards. Unfortunately, the CDSWG was disbanded in the summer of 2011 when HRSDC discontinued funding.

Dialogue between the career development sector and policy makers has increased substantially in the last decade. However, there remains much work to be done to formalize the connections and make them much more transparent. In many countries, career development themes are part of the political discourse, but this is rare in Canada, both federally and provincially. Additionally, career development practitioners have not embraced the role of advocates for policy change. Professional training programs rarely include policy issues and many practitioners are simply not exposed sufficiently to them. This is deserving of attention on several fronts. As noted earlier, most career services are publically funded and services that are not well understood by policy makers become vulnerable to funding cuts. At least equally important is advocacy for policies that support access to quality and comprehensive services over the lifespan.

The Necessity for an Evidence-Based Practice

As funding for all forms of public services is subjected to increased scrutiny and accountability, career development service providers face growing pressure to prove that their services are beneficial and cost-effective. In 2004, Magnusson and Roest stated that, despite an increased awareness of the need to better understand how and why career services are effective, we still possess very little concrete evidence that career interventions actually work; the evidence that we do have tends to reflect very specific interventions for specific populations. Hughes, Bosley, Bowes, and Bysshe (2002) stated that one of the challenges in efficacy research in career development was the lack of common outcome measures. Other researchers have suggested the development of cost-benefit analyses to document the results of career services, and the creation of national research databases to collect and distribute such information (Herr, 2003; International Symposium on Career Development and Public Policy, 1999, 2001); and increased efficacy research to link career practices to economic efficiency, social equity, and sustainability (Killeen, White, & Watts, 1992).

The CRWG has been a leader in advancing the evidence base for career development services. This group was formed in 2002, following the Pan-Canadian Symposium, in response to a challenge by senior policy makers to "prove that career and employment services work." The CRWG is a partnership among six Canadian universities (anglophone and francophone) and CCDF. Researchers are independent, but collaborate on projects that fit within the group's mandate, which is:

- to develop an evaluation framework for gathering evidence-based data on career development programs and services,
- to promote a culture of evaluation in the career development field,
- to conduct research that tests the evaluation framework and builds a bank of evidence-based data on the impact of career development programs and services.

To date, the group has developed an evaluation framework and has tested it in workplaces where career development programs were offered to employees and in employment centres where clients need labour market information to assist them in decision making or in searching for work. The workplace research took place over 3 years in which three different programs were implemented in a range of workplaces, and the impacts of these programs on employees were tracked at 3 months, 6 months and, in one program, 12 months after program completion. All programs had positive results with significant impacts (p < .01) on personal self-efficacy, career self-management, self-esteem, skills development, and job retention. All research reports are accessible at <www.crwg-gdrc.ca>.

The CRWG and CCDF have continued to conduct leading-edge research to further refine and apply the evaluation framework and extend the sector's evidence base. Members of the CRWG and CCDF are also contributors to an international working group on evidence-based practice, established after Symposium 2009 by the executive director of the ICCDPP. The working group collaborates on sharing research and on joint projects to advance the evidence base. Advancements are reported at each symposium. Information on additional international developments can be found at <http://www.iccdpp.org>.

There is also indirect evidence that persuasively supports the positive impact of career development on participation in postsecondary education. For example, the Canadian 2004 Youth in Transition Survey (YITS) tracked movement of youth between high school, postsecondary education, and the labour market. It found that those who continued in postsecondary education had achieved higher levels of both academic and social engagement in high school than those who did not continue to a postsecondary institution (Statistics Canada, 2006). Academic engagement and achievement are influenced by the extent to which learners believe their learning is relevant to their personal future direction. A key goal of career development in the education sector is to help learners make relevant connections between what they are learning now and what they might pursue in the future. The number one reason given for leaving school was "lack of fit" or the need to change programs. The available evidence on behalf of career development is thus positive and expanding. However, research gaps remain, and most research has been short term and focused on immediate results. Longer-term and longitudinal research is needed, as is research on broader and more representative samples of the population.

The CRWG would argue that the professional practitioner needs to evaluate career development processes and outcomes constantly and be able to make direct links between what they do as practitioners and the results they achieve with individuals and groups. Evaluation needs to be part of everyday professional practice. However, evaluation is usually a very small component of professional preparation programs at both the diploma and degree levels.

To some extent, the catalysts for these three significant transformations — expanding practice, connection of polity to practice, and growth of evidence-based practice — have come from outside the sector. But significant transformations have also been occurring from inside the career development sector as the practitioners define and expand their field of practice.

Transformation From the Inside-Out

The OECD in its study of several countries found that the career development sector was "weakly professionalized." Membership in professional associations, standards for practice, licensing and certification of practitioners, a clear and enforced code of ethics, and clear and consistent professional training routes for qualification were all areas that were inconsistent at best and non-existent at worst. There has been huge progress towards a more "highly professionalized" career development sector in Canada since 2000. Many of the key foundations necessary to support and sustain a profession have been developed and are now in place.

The Canadian Standards and Guidelines for Career Development Practitioners (S&Gs) and the Movement Towards Certification

Having a framework of standards and guidelines is key to formalizing a practice and advancing the profession. As can be seen from the emphasis on the S&Gs in this textbook, a clear framework to regulate entry and progression pathways is essential in defining a profession and is a key aspect of its effectiveness. The S&Gs allow enough capacity to "mix and match" to reflect many delivery settings, while still maintaining a professional standard. The S&Gs have been highly influential in increasing professionalism in the field. They have been used as the basis for establishing career practitioner certification in the provinces of Alberta and British Columbia and developing procedures moving towards certification in Ontario, New Brunswick and Nova Scotia. The S&Gs were updated in 2011–2012 and will continue to be reviewed periodically to ensure that they remain a current and relevant resource.

There is a unique situation in the province of Québec with respect to standards and certification. Career counselling (i.e., orientation professionelle) has been a regulated profession in Québec for many years. Career counsellors must have a master's degree and be licensed by L'Ordre des conseillers et conseillères d'orientation du Québec (OCCOQ). Career development practitioners without master's degrees also practise in Québec but cannot legally call themselves career counsellors. Despite these differences, the S&Gs have been recognized by the OCCOQ and validated against their own competency framework.

It is noteworthy that in Québec, where career counselling is a licensed profession, undergraduate and graduate programs specializing in career counselling exist in most universities. This is generally not the case in other provinces, where graduate programs typically provide a small number of career development courses within an education or counselling psychology program. Many community colleges offer specialized diplomas or certificates in career development and such programs are increasing in number. Offerings at the university level are also slowly expanding (Burwell & Kalbfleish, 2010). Depending on the province, certification may be as a Canadian Career Development Practitioner or a Canadian Career Development Professional, both with the acronym CCDP. Certification is a growing trend across Canada, and a very positive development for increasing the professionalism of the career development sector as well as promoting greater consistency in training programs.

Professional Membership and Professional Development

Membership in a professional association is an important component of professional identity in many fields. Professional associations maintain oversight of their field, protect the public interest, and are usually a source of professional development and networking for its members. In the provinces with certification or licensing in place, it is the association's role to manage these processes.

Unlike many countries, Canada does not have a national career development association, although there is a small, vibrant, Career Counsellor Chapter within the national Canadian Counselling and Psychotherapy Association (CCPA), and CERIC plays a convenor role among the many sectors that intersect career development in Canada. At the provincial level, career development associations exist in eight provinces and there are signs of associations beginning to form in other provinces and territories. This is a significant increase since year 2000.

In 2008, the Canadian Council for Career Development (CCCD) was created as an alliance of provincial career development associations and other key sector stakeholders (government, postsecondary, private, and non-profits). CCCD members work collaboratively on common priorities and share promising research and practice in the hope of positioning itself as a point of contact for policy issues.

A critical component of a professional identity is keeping abreast of current research and promising new practices.

Professional conferences are the most common way for professionals to stay current. Many provincial associations host their own annual conferences. From 1975 until 2006, there was an annual national conference titled NATCON (National Consultation on Career Development) funded in part by the federal government and **The Counselling Foundation of Canada**. Funding ceased and for a period of time, the field was adrift without a pan-Canadian professional development opportunity. Support came from the **Canadian Education and Research Institute for Counselling** (CERIC), a national organization dedicated to promoting career-counselling-related research and professional development opportunities across Canada. CERIC, with support from The Counselling Foundation of Canada, launched Cannexus in 2007, a national career development conference designed to promote the exchange of information and explore innovative approaches in the areas of career counselling and career development. This conference is now firmly established as "the" national conference of choice for the sector.

CERIC has also provided the profession with *The Canadian Journal of Career Development*, an academic peer-reviewed journal that began in 2002 through support from The Counselling Foundation of Canada, and *Careering*, a free magazine for career development professionals. As well, CERIC has encouraged professional development for many years though awards and bursaries to support students in their education. Connect with these programs and resources at the CERIC website <http://ceric.ca>.

A new interest in professional development and training has also emerged for provincial government employees who provide career and employment services. Comprehensive training programs now run in five provinces and one territory. The courses are fully aligned with the S&Gs and preapproved for the **Educational and Vocational Guidance Practitioner (EVGP)** credential, an international certification through the **International Association for Educational and Vocational Guidance (IAEVG).** Please visit <http://www.iaevg.org> for more on IAEVG and their EVGP certification.

If career practitioners in the field are to be active members of a career development community, motivated to experiment with new ideas and contribute to the field, they need to be proud of their profession and feel recognized as important contributors to society. A large part of that will come from the availability and uptake of professional and personal development options. Professional membership, training, and certification are potent aids in public recognition and credibility. The career development profession has been greatly strengthened over the past few years through the work of these organizations and associations. There remains much work to be accomplished but the "train to increased professionalism" has left the station.

The Professional Career Development Roadmap

Any ongoing movement towards professionalism in any sector greatly benefits from a roadmap that lays out where a sector is, its strengths and weaknesses, and priorities for continued progress. The Pan-Canadian Mapping Study in 2008 (Bezanson, O'Reilly, & Magnusson, 2009), funded by the Career Development Services Working Group (CDSWG), provided such a roadmap for the career development sector. The study was an online survey completed by nearly 1,000 agency managers and practitioners in 10 provinces. The analysis of responses revealed that respondents were quite representative of their relative provincial populations.

This study confirmed that the sector is highly diverse in types of workplaces and service delivery arrangements. Career development practitioners work in community-based agencies, public and private schools, educational institutions/departments, employment agencies, special interest group and settlement agencies, private career guidance businesses, insurance companies, business, unions, apprenticeship boards, co-op education, sector councils, government, business organizations, media, companies, government department career centres, private counselling practice, human resource offices in large corporations, career guidance centres, career libraries, human resource departments, research organizations (business, economic, labour market, education) government (human resources, economics, labour market information), and foundations. And they have many titles, including: career counsellor, employment counsellor, career coach, career practitioner, human resources practitioner, vocational rehabilitation counsellor, job search practitioner, labour market information specialist, trainer, adult educator, work developer, and settlement counsellor.

The following are the key findings from the study:

- Career development practitioners (CDPs) and their agencies appear to operate within a well-defined scope of practice. They have a clear employment, career, and labour market mandate. This is an interesting and encouraging finding in the context of the "outside-in" transformation noted earlier in this chapter of an expanding scope of practice.
- The career development practitioner population is, in a sense, self-made. CDPs come from a wide range of work settings and educational

backgrounds, and they come to career and employment services as a second or third occupational stop in their careers. They are a well-educated population, predominantly female, with a very high level of job satisfaction. At the same time, specialized training in career development is rare and haphazard, achieved through either preservice or on-the-job training. In terms of directions the sector needs to take in the near future, access to professional training was ranked highest by CDPs, and second highest by managers.

- Professional identity and recognition emerge as recurring, important issues for the practitioner community; specifically, practitioners want more professional recognition in the form of certification and licensing processes.
- There is little to no consistency in the requirements for career development jobs. Some respondents are of the view that this permits generalists into the field, which is essential given the diverse public served; others are of the view that more rigorous and consistent standards for recruitment are necessary. This lack of clear standards presents a major challenge in solidifying the professional identity of the sector.
- There is very little consistency in job titles, particularly among English-language practitioners. This creates confusion for the public, who must discern what services are being offered and where, and compromises the professional identity and coherence of the career development sector.
- There does not appear to be an established training and professional development culture within the sector whereby practitioners regularly participate in training to remain up to date with new developments, tools, and skills
- There are a relatively small number of direct service providers; it is difficult to imagine that the numbers are adequate to the need. A survey of how the public perceives its career and employment needs and services would be a very informative study.

Five priorities for action from the study were suggested as follows:

1. Promote and enhance a training and development culture within the sector.
2. Promote increased understanding and use of competency frameworks such as the *Standards and Guidelines for Career Development Practitioners* (S&Gs) and the *Blueprint for Life/Work Designs* or their equivalencies as tools to increase coherence in the sector.
3. Support provincial and territorial initiatives to introduce certification programs for Career Development Practitioners and a mechanism to support their compatibility and ensure cross border mobility.

4. Conduct a policy review of criterion-based career development and employment services.
5. Conduct a survey to assess public need for, access to, and satisfaction with current career and employment service provision.

As the profession addresses these issues and continues to grow, its professional roots will deepen. Recognition of the value of the profession — seen from within the field and from without — reflects a growing professional identity. As this identity becomes stronger and government and business sectors recognize the value of career development to the whole of society, a wide range of disciplines will begin to work towards similar goals for the preferred future of individuals and a healthy labour market. This in turn broadens the range of work and placement options for the career profession.

Conclusion

The career development community in Canada has made great strides in the years since 2000. There is an unprecedented investment in targeted research, a significantly stronger evidence base, and a renewed commitment to training/professional development, accountability, collaboration, and cohesion across the field. The sector has the tools, supports, and structures needed to continue to grow as a profession. There is a spirit of collaboration among associations and organizations across the country and an international movement in which Canada is a key partner, with career development, lifelong learning and the interface between policy and practice high on its agenda. The career development landscape is transforming in dramatic and exciting ways. Hopefully, the three P's — Policy, Proof, and Professionalism — will dominate the coming decade and further transform the career development sector.

References

Bezanson, L., O'Reilly, E., & Magnusson, K. (2009). *Pan-Canadian mapping study of the career development sector*. Canadian Career Development Foundation. Retrieved from <http://www.ccdf.ca/ccdf/wp-content/uploads/2011/01/PAN-CANADIAN-MAPPING-STUDY-OF-THE-CAREER-DEVELOPMENT-SECTOR.pdf>.

Bezanson, L., & Renald, C. (Eds.). (2003). *Working connections: A pan-Canadian symposium on career development, lifelong learning and workforce development: Papers and proceedings*. Ottawa, ON: The Canadian Career Development Foundation. Retrieved from <http://www.iaevg.org/crc/files

/Pan_Canadian_Symposium%202003_Proceedings820_2.pdf>.

Brown, V, Dent, G, Galashan, L., Hirsh, W., & Hughes, D. (2006). Country Papers for the International Symposium on Career Development and Public Policy held in Sydney, Australia.

Burwell, P., & Kalbfleisch, S. (2010). *Directory of career development education programs in Canada: Updated January 2010*. Toronto, ON: CERIC. Retrieved from <http://www.ceric.ca/documents/CDEP_Directory.pdf>.

Canadian Education and Research Institute for Counselling (CERIC) (2011). Survey of Career Service Professionals. Retrieved from <http://www.ceric.ca/?q=en /node/466>.

The Counselling Foundation of Canada. (2002). *A coming of age: Counselling Canadians for work in the twentieth century*. Toronto, ON: Author.

Hansen, S. L. (2001). *Integrative life planning: Critical tasks for career development and changing life patterns*. New York, NY: John Wiley and Sons Ltd.

Herr, E. L. (2003). The future of career counseling as an instrument of public policy. *The Career Development Quarterly, 52*, 8–17.

Hughes, D., Bosley, S., Bowes, L., & Bysshe., S. (2002) *The economic benefits of guidance*. Derby, UK: Centre for Guidance Studies, University of Derby.

International Symposium on Career Development and Public Policy (1999). *Making waves: Career development and public policy*. International symposium Ottawa: CCDF. Retrieved from <http://web.archive.org/web/20020222050628/> <http://www.ccdf.ca/MakingWaves.html>.

International Symposium (2001). *Making waves: Volume 2 connecting career development with public policy*. Ottawa: CCDF.

Killeen, J., White, M., & Watts, A.G. (1992). *The economic benefits of careers guidance*. London, UK: Policy Studies Institute.

Krumboltz, J. D. (1994). Improving career development theory from a social learning perspective. In M. L. Savickas & R. L. Lent (Eds.), *Convergence in career development theories* (pp. 9–31). Palo Alto, CA: CPP Books.

Lowe, G. (2000). *The quality of work*. Don Mills, ON: Oxford University Press.

Magnusson, K., & Roest, A. (2004). *The efficacy of career development interventions: A synthesis of research*. Retrieved from <www.iaevg.org/crc/files /magnusson-CareerEfficacy-synthesis829_2.doc>.

Organisation for Economic Co-operation and Development (OECD). (2002a). *Career guidance: A handbook for policy makers*. Paris: Author. Retrieved from <http://www.oecd.org/dataoecd/53/53/34060761.pdf>.

Organisation for Economic Co-operation and Development (OECD). (2002b). *OECD Review of career guidance policies — Canada Country Note*. Paris: Author. Retrieved from <http://www.oecd.org/education/country-studies /1963039.pdf>.

Organisation for Economic Co-operation and Development (2004). *Career guidance and public policy: Bridging the gap*. Paris: Author. Retrieved from <http://www.oecd.org/education/country-studies/34050171.pdf>.

Peavy, R. V. (2001). *A brief outline of SocioDynamic Counselling: A*

co-constructivist perspective on a helping. Retrieved from <http://www.sociodynamic
-constructivist-counselling.com/documents/brief_outline.pdf>.

Statistics Canada (2006). Youth in transition survey: *Update of the education and
labour market pathways of young adults.* Ottawa, ON: Statistics Canada
<http://www.statcan.gc.ca/daily-quotidien/060705/dq060705a-eng.htm>.

Zelloth, H. (2009). *In demand: Career guidance in EU neighbouring countries.*
Luxembourg City, LU: European Training Foundation. doi: 10.2816/78201.
Retrieved from <http://www.etf.europa.eu/pubmgmt.nsf/%28getAttachment
%29/8559E4566D38A6E3C12576020050A7BC/$File/NOTE7UELKN.pdf>.

Glossary

Canadian Council for Career Development (CCCD) is an umbrella group that
promotes collaboration on career development issues among provincial/territorial
and national career development associations, action groups, and related
organizations (<http://cccda.org/cccda>).

Canadian Career Development Foundation (CCDF) is a recognized leader both
nationally and internationally in the field of career development. Established in
1979 as a non-profit charitable foundation, CCDF works on projects that advance
career development and the capacity of the profession to respond with compassion
and skill to all clients and stakeholders in an ever-changing work environment
(<http://ccdf.ca/>).

Canadian Education and Research Institute for Counselling (CERIC) is a
charitable organization dedicated to promoting career-counselling-related
research and professional development opportunities across Canada
(<http://www.ceric.ca>).

**Canadian Research Working Group on Evidence-Based Practice in Career
Development (CRWG)** strengthens career development by improving the
overall evidence base for career development practice "with an emphasis on both
informing policy and building a evaluation culture in the sector," and increasing
"pan-Canadian and international sharing of research and promising practices,
with an emphasis on sharing French and English research." (Quoted from
<http://www.crwg-gdrc.ca/crwg/index.php/about-us>.) Main website is at
<http://www.crwg-gdrc.ca/crwg/>.

Career Development Services Working Group (CDSWG) was created by the
FLMM in 2007 to ensure co-ordination across services and to share information
on areas of mutual interest and concern related to the development and delivery of
career development services at the regional and pan-Canadian levels.
　　The goals of the CDSWG were to:

- identify and promote best practice,
- increase the Career Development Services knowledge base through research,
- facilitate access to Career Development Services,
- enhance the quality and effectiveness of Career Development Services, establish and strengthen domestic and international networking opportunities.

The CDSWG was disbanded in 2011. There is, however, continued interest across the career development sector to secure a renewed mandate and funding for this body.

The Counselling Foundation of Canada is a family foundation established by Frank G. Lawson in 1959 to create and enrich career counselling programs and improve the technical skills of career counsellors. The object of the Foundation is to engage in charitable and educational activities for the benefit of people, thus enabling them to improve their lifestyles and make a more effective contribution to their communities.

Educational and Vocational Guidance Practitioner (EVGP) is an international certification program for career practitioners offered by the International Association for Educational and Vocational Guidance (EVGP). The certification is built around a set of international competencies that practitioners need in order to provide quality service. The EVGP competencies were developed from and are closely aligned with the *Canadian Standards and Guidelines for Career Development Practitioners* (S&Gs) were validated with a pool of 700 practitioners working in a variety of different jobs across 38 countries. Like the Canadian S&Gs, the EVGP competencies are made up of a set of core competencies that focus on the knowledge, skills, and attributes needed by all practitioners and a set of specialized competencies required for some practitioners depending on the nature of their work. Courses may be "preapproved" as eligible towards the EVGP and/or individual practitioners may apply directly to the Center for Credentialing in Education to have their qualifications reviewed for the EVGP certification. Additional information and application forms for the EVGP can be found at <www.iaevg.org>.

Forum of Labour Market Ministers (FLMM) is composed of provincial and territorial ministers, and the federal minister responsible for the labour market. The forum of Labour Market Ministers was created in 1983 to promote discussion and co-operation on labour market matters.

International Association for Educational and Vocational Guidance (IAEVG) is a worldwide guidance and counselling association, whose mission is to promote the development and quality of educational and vocational guidance. IAEVG's mission is also to ensure that all citizens who need and want educational and vocational guidance and counselling can receive this counselling from a competent and recognized professional. The association publishes a newsletter three times a year. Furthermore IAEVG publishes the *International Journal for Educational and Vocational Guidance*, a refereed journal publishing articles related to work and leisure, career development, career counselling, guidance, and career education. The website is at <http://www.iaevg.org/>.

International Centre for Career Development and Public Policy (ICCDPP) facilitates international sharing of knowledge and information concerning public policy and career development issues. ICCDPP is a base for knowledge and information including proceedings from international symposia, and reports and news provided to the site by the users and by other international contacts. ICCDPP is supported by organizations such as the OECD, individual country donations and a collaborative relationship with Kuder, Inc. See <http://www.iccdpp.org>.

Organisation for Economic Co-operation and Development (OECD) is an international economic organization that promotes policies that will improve the economic and social well-being of people around the world. The OECD provides a forum in which governments can work together to share experiences and seek solutions to common problems and to assist governments in understanding what drives economic, social, and environmental change. The OECD is found at <http://www.oecd.org>.

Discussion and Activities

Discussion

1. Review the three definitions of career development given in the chapter.

    (a) Identify any features/themes that are common across all three definitions.
    (b) Identify any features/themes that are not common across all three definitions.
    (c) Which definition comes closest to how you would define career development?

    Give your rationale.

2. Policy makers increasingly require "evidence" of positive impacts for the services they fund. What "evidence" do you think would convince policy makers? What is your rationale? How easy or difficult do you think it would be to gather this "evidence"? Why?

3. Prioritize the findings of the *Pan-Canadian Mapping Study* from your perspective (i.e.,those issues which you think are the highest priorities for Canadians). Give your rationale.

4. *"Discussions on public policy have two languages. One uses terms such as analysis,*

outcomes, accountability, costs and benefits, and evidence based decision making. The second includes terms such as influence, popularity, power, alliances, interest groups and change processes" (International Symposium 2001, Papers and Proceedings, p. 197). Imagine you are in a meeting with career development peers in a services agency. Have a discussion (15 minutes) on career development that uses these two languages. After 15 minutes, discuss how easy/difficult it was to talk about career development in policy language and how important you think it is.

Personal Reflection

As you have progressed through this textbook, what new innovative ideas have emerged for you in regards to career development? How would you address experimenting and/or implementing your innovative ideas in the community or your workplace? Outline and describe the steps you would take.

Career Practitioner Role

What does it mean to be considered an active member of the career development community? How does being part of a career development community influence your understanding of professional identity? What are the key elements which constitute professional engagement in the field? Explain each element.

Activities

1. The OECD (2002) lists features of an effective lifelong career development system. Using this background document, conduct a short (20-minute) interview with an individual who provides career development services (a guidance counsellor/ guidance head/career development practitioner/career services manager/ employment counsellor, etc.) and get their assessment of the extent to which these features are in place in their specific work setting. Find out as much as you can about where the individual you interview thinks the current system is weak or strong and why. Write a short report on your findings.

2. The Canadian Research Working Group on Evidence-Based Practice in Career Development (CRWG) was formed to address two important issues in the field of career development:

    *   strengthening the overall evidence-base for career development practice with an emphasis on both informing policy and building an evaluation culture in the sector;
    *   increasing pan-Canadian and international sharing of research and promising practices, with an emphasis on sharing French and English research.

Conduct a web search on "evidence-based practice in career development." Review various web resource's to identify the most helpful websites, resources, and articles. Share the list with the class.

Resources and Readings

Resources

Websites

Association of Career Professionals (ACP) — global organization <http://www.acpinternational.org/>.
Canadian Career Development Foundation (CCDF) <http://www.ccdf.ca/>.
Canadian Council for Career Development (CCCD) <http://cccda.org/cccda>.
Canadian Education and Research Institute for Counselling <http://ceric.ca>.
The Canadian Journal of Career Development — academic, peer-reviewed journal <http://ceric.ca/cjcd/>.
Canadian Research Working Group on Evidence Based Practice in Career Development <http://www.crwg-gdrc.ca/index.html>.
Canadian Standards and Guidelines for Career Development Practitioners <http://career-dev-guidelines.org/career_dev/>.
Cannexus — National Career Development Conference <http://www.cannexus.ca/>.
ContactPoint <http://www.contactpoint.ca/> and OrientAction <http://www.orientaction.ca> — multisector online communities for career development professionals.
International Association for Educational and Vocational Guidance (IAEVG) <http://www.iaevg.org/iaevg/index.cfm?lang=2>.
International Centre for Career Development and Public Policy <http://www.iccdpp.org/>.
Organisation for Economic Co-operation and Development (OECD). About OECD <http://www.oecd.org/about/>.
OEDC Canada <http://www.oecd.org/canada/>.

Supplementary Readings

Bell, D., & O'Reilly, E. (2008). *Making bridges visible: An inventory of innovative, effective or promising Canadian school-to-work transitions practices, programs and policies*. Ottawa, ON: Work and Learning Knowledge Centre and the Canadian Career Development Foundation. Retrieved from <http://www.ccl-cca.ca/pdfs /WLKC/CCDFENMakingBridgesVisibleFINAL.pdf>.
Burwell, R., & Kalbfleisch, S. (2007). Deliberations on the future of career development education in Canada. *Canadian Journal of Career Development*, 6(1), 40–49.

Burwell, R., Kalbfleisch, S., & Woodside, J. (2010). A model for the education of career practitioners in Canada. *Canadian Journal of Career Development, 9*(1), 44–52.

Canadian Career Development Foundation. (2005). *The state of practice in Canada in measuring career service impact: A CRWG report.* Author. Retrieved from <http://www.crwg-gdrc.ca/>.

Organisation for Economic Co-operation and Development (2002). Rethinking human capital (pp. 117–132). In OECD (Eds.), *Education policy analysis.* Paris: Author. Retrieved from <http://www.oecd-ilibrary.org/education /education-policy-analysis-2002/rethinking-human-capital_epa-2002-7-en>.

Watts, A. G., & Sultana, R. (2004). Career Guidance in 37 countries: Contrasts and common themes. *International Journal and Vocational Guidance, 4*(2–3), 105–122. doi: 10.1007/s10775-005-1025-y

Watts, A.G. (2005). The role of information and communication technologies in integrated career information and guidance systems: A policy perspective. *International Journal for Education and Vocational Studies, 2*(3), 139–155. doi: 10.1023/A:1020669832743

twenty-two

Emerging Trends

Canadian Perspectives on
Career Development Practice in the 21st Century

NATASHA CAVERLEY
Turtle Island Consulting Services Inc.
SEANNA QURESSETTE
Creating Intentional Change Inc.
BLYTHE C. SHEPARD
University of Lethbridge
PRIYA S. MANI
University of Manitoba

PRE-READING QUESTIONS:

1. What do you see as the key themes emerging in career development practice in Canada?
2. What are the challenges and opportunities for career professionals in the next 10 years?
3. What are some of the challenges and opportunities facing today's Canadian workforce (from an individual, organizational and/or societal perspective)?

Introduction and Learning Objectives

To find a career to which you are adapted by nature, and then to work hard at it,
is about as near to a formula for success and happiness as the world provides.
One of the fortunate aspects of this formula is that, granted the right career has been found,
the hard work takes care of itself. Then hard work is not hard work at all.
— Mark Sullivan

Acknowledgement: The authors of this chapter would like to thank all of the authors in this textbook for their contributions to this closing chapter.

The practice of career development in Canada is continually expanding and changing to meet the needs of individuals and employers working within a diversified economy and labour force. Increased global competition, the financial crisis of 2008, the effects of government debt and deficit pressures, and changing demographics are creating greater demand for career development programs, services, and supports.

Emerging trends in career development present new challenges and opportunities. Major directions today are: (a) multidisciplinary roles of career counsellors and career development practitioners; (b) the utilization of integrated, holistic career services and resources (**one-stop employment services**); (c) career search strategies that rely heavily on social media; and (d) the need for socially just strategies to serve diverse communities. Rather than viewing these as daunting challenges, we present these trends as opportunities for career development practitioners to become more resilient and adaptable in a changing work environment and to develop new competencies and strategies to assist individuals in addressing their career needs

Overview of the Chapter

In this closing chapter, we will review some of the key topics covered in this textbook. We start by reflecting on emerging career development theories, models, and strategies. Then, the diversified roles of career counsellors and career development practitioners are discussed with pointers to implications for economic development, career planning, and labour market trends. Next to be highlighted are emerging work search strategies and integrated employment services, followed by a review of career development issues facing marginalized groups (i.e., individuals of low socioeconomic status, Aboriginal people, and immigrants). This section highlights the inherent need for counsellors and practitioners to work with all facets of Canadian society — particularly, our most vulnerable populations. The chapter will conclude with an examination of current and future shifts in career development services.

At the conclusion of this chapter you will be able to:

1. Explain the expanding roles of career counsellors and career development practitioners in Canada's economy and labour force.
2. Identify emerging career development theories, models, and strategies and their implications in the 21st-century Canadian workforce.
3. List work search strategies, career resources, and related supports that can aid individuals in advancing their career planning.
4. Describe career development issues facing marginalized groups in Canadian society.
5. Describe aspects of the shifting landscape of career development services in Canada.

In response to Canada's diversified workforce and economy, career counsellors and career development practitioners are adapting their skills, strategies, and interventions to work with individuals and employers who are experiencing both micro- and macro-level changes. They may be working with individuals coping with mental health issues in the workplace (e.g., depression, addiction, etc.), or employers managing rapid organizational and operational changes (e.g., reduced workforce, globalization of products and services, diverse/multicultural work environments, etc.). Therefore, a multidimensional understanding of career development as a culturally congruent, contextualized, client-driven, and strengths-based approach is important to ensure that career development programs and services are providing the necessary supports to individuals and employers now and in the future. Career is a large part of self-identity. It shapes our values, our lifestyles, and the affiliations we have with individuals, groups, and society (including the broader labour market); in sum, it shapes how we define ourselves.

Developing Inclusive, Contextually Sensitive, Theoretical Models

Career development has been explained by a number of theories, none of which on its own is adequate to explain the complexity of the field. Arising from the ideas of Peavy (1997), Young and Valach (2004), and Cochran (1997), there is a trend towards a constructivist worldview with a focus on holism, connectedness, context, and the active role of individuals in the construction of their careers. In this paradigm, the career development of individuals may only be understood in relation to their environments.

According to Savickas and colleagues (2009):

(t)he core concepts of 20th century career theories and vocational guidance techniques must be reformulated to fit the postmodern economy. Current approaches are insufficient. First, they are rooted in assumptions of stability of personal characteristics and secure jobs in bounded organizations. Second, they conceptualize careers as a fixed sequence of stages. Concepts such as vocational identity, career planning, career development, and career stages each are used to predict people's adjustment to work environments assuming a relatively high stability of the environments and people's behavior. (p. 240)

In the complex and rapidly changing world of work, responsibility for career development has been increasingly divested from organizations to individuals. In this new world of globalization and constant technological advancement, individuals are expected to transition several times in their lifetime between learning and work.

Consequently, career management has become an important task for individuals as they navigate their way in society and the new world of work. In order to find new meaning and understanding in the future, career practitioners must learn from and acknowledge the past.

Theories should be flexible enough to accommodate ongoing and unexpected change. We have moved far beyond seeing individual careers as following predictable paths or believing that individuals will choose one career and stay with it for life. In recent years, we have witnessed the emergence of Krumboltz's (2009) planned happenstance learning theory of careers, Bright and Pryor's (2011) chaos theory of careers, Patton and McMahon's (2006) systems theory framework, and Savickas' (2005) focus on constructing careers and career adaptability.

The interconnection of work and life issues needs to be acknowledged and recognized. Increasingly, human resources management professionals are now dealing with counselling-related issues such as career planning, work-life balance, and strengthening employer and employee relationships. Hansen's (2011) work on integrated life planning is an example of a holistic theoretical approach, while Magnusson and Redekopp's (2011) coherent career practice is another model that incorporates several interrelated elements. Neault and Pickerell (2011) have also bridged the silos of individual and organizational career development perspectives with their career engagement and employee engagement models. With the advent of mobile technologies, the struggle to achieve work-life balance is exacerbated as more and more people are working anywhere and anytime, thereby blurring the lines between work and other life roles and responsibilities.

Culture should be integrated into our understanding of career development, career choices, and life roles. Most counsellors and career practitioners recognize the complexity of culture and try to incorporate cultural considerations into their work with clients. Arthur and Collins' (2010) culture-infused approach, Leong and Lee's (2006) cultural accommodation model, and Pope's (2011) recent work on career counselling with underserved populations are broadening the range of career development theories and models that are available to counsellors and practitioners in providing culturally congruent structures and frameworks for working with diverse clients.

Career counsellors and career development practitioners need to strategically utilize theories as tools and supports. Rather than teaching a single theory as the "right way" to conceptualize career issues, the emerging trend is to introduce several theories and models that professionals can draw upon to assist with "case conceptualization," and from which they may select appropriate interventions and assessment tools. New theories based on notions of constructivism and contextual understanding, such as the developmental-contextual theory (Vondracek, Lerner, & Schulenberg, 1986) and the systems theory framework (Patton & McMahon, 2006), lend themselves less easily to the assessment processes of trait and factor counselling.

These newer theories are focused on client actions, strengths, and complexity, not on client passivity, problem solving, and simplicity. As Savickas (1996) asks, "How do counsellors apply theories that are partial and simple to clients who are complex and whole?" (p. 193). Additionally, these theories approach assessment in new ways, drawing on informal qualitative assessments that are flexible, open ended, and holistic. They allow clients to tell their own career stories and to unpack life themes and patterns (Peavy, 1997). Practitioners act as "biographers who interpret lives in progress rather than as actuaries who count interests and abilities" (Savickas, 1992, p. 338). A future trend will be the infusion of multiple assessments integrated into individual career planning using a combination of formal and informal assessments.

There is a growing movement to unify existing theories of career development in terms of promoting an eclectic approach towards vocational issues. Such an approach involves collaborating across disciplines (e.g., counselling, human resources management, developmental psychology, industrial and organizational psychology, and sociology) to renew, revitalize, and integrate traditional and emerging theories to clarify their constructs and purpose. For example, the systems theory framework (Patton & McMahon, 2006) of career development is one attempt to unify theory and practice through a focus on individuals and their system of influences. Information is incorporated into an individual's existing frameworks of experience and knowledge in a relational and associative way through which new meaning and new knowledge are created.

❖ *Stop and Reflect*

1. What do you think of the idea of "metatheories" to integrate and combine current career theories?
2. How would you implement them practically?

Recommended Readings
_____

Articles by multiple authors (2010). *Journal of Employment Counseling*, 48(4), 146–190. Special Issue: Thoughts on Theories.

Savickas, M. L. (2012). Life design: A paradigm for career intervention in the 21st century. *Journal of Counseling and Development*, 90, 13–19.

Responding to the Continuously Changing World of Work

Career development is the art (not science) of constructing a fulfilling and prosperous life. In turn, economic development and prosperity for provinces, territories, and Canada as a nation, is an aggregate of the success of every Canadian citizen. It is incumbent upon individuals, career development practitioners, and strategic partners (e.g., educational institutions, government, and employers) to work together to advance career opportunities and foster competencies that will be in strong demand in the coming decades in order to strengthen Canada's economy. For individuals, and for our nation as a whole, subscribing to the notion of "business as usual" in the area of career development is not an option. With the race for talent in an ever-expanding knowledge economy, a harmonized, whole-community approach to career and workforce development is needed to help youth and adults: (a) develop informed career dreams for their future; (b) meet individuals who can help them achieve their career dreams; and (c) obtain the necessary resources and supports to fulfill those dreams.

Career planning is developmental in nature and encompasses work, family, and lifestyle. It provides the means to manage change, which allows greater opportunity for fulfillment of one's life from youth to adulthood. Career planning develops skills that individuals can utilize for decision making in current and future work/life issues as they arise. In recognition of multidimensional career models in the Canadian labour market, schools are incorporating career planning and guidance into earlier grades (including elementary school) and involving members of the community and parents to engage in this journey with their children. Specifically, emerging trends in guidance and career planning focus on fostering and promoting personal competence at all ages. Managing personal finances and leadership skills are addressed. Attention is paid to lifelong learning and diversifying workforce skills and abilities. Co-ops, internships, work placements, and apprenticeships, all known as work-integrated learning (WIL), are becoming standard practice in today's colleges and universities. Career practitioners are required to understand and transmit knowledge about employment and labour market demands for communities and industries in Canada (i.e., via labour market surveys and occupational outlook projections).

Therefore, a holistic approach to career development requires now, more than ever, the proactive involvement of educators, families, communities, employers, and government agencies. Investing in skills, strategies, training, employment programs, and workforce development initiatives will help address labour market shortages and enhance collective participation of Canadians in the social and economic life of their communities.

Due to changes in demographics and anticipated shortages of trained skilled workers, the historical model of a one-dimensional career path where individuals "work until they drop or make it to the top" no longer seems to be a viable lifestyle choice. Instead, multidimensional career models have become the norm in Canadian society as a means of addressing current and future labour market needs. Therefore, career planning and associated strategies need to be flexible and adaptable to assist individuals in coping with both life and career transitions.

It is important to consider the necessity of lifelong learning when developing and rejuvenating individuals at different points along their life-cycles. Learning over one's lifespan is crucial for acquiring skills needed to ensure long-term employability. Increasingly, people are working past the "normal" retirement age of 65 in part because of financial need, and, for some, because they enjoy their work and the social and intellectual stimulation of the workplace (Pignal, Arrowsmith, & Ness, 2010). By 2025, the projected population of pensionable age in North America is predicted to expand to 20% (University of Ottawa, n.d.).

Career practitioners are shifting their practice to a lifelong learning perspective in order to help older workers consider new ways to contend with the transition to retirement. The emerging trend is for career practitioners to encourage potential retirees to continue building their personal assets and develop individual resiliency. In the event of an uncertain future, older workers are also encouraged to consider how they can increase their employability and continue to consider their options to adapt to a volatile educational and labour market. Many individuals may need to further their education and update their skills or change career paths entirely. Older workers will need to take more responsibility for their economic security at this stage of their life. Education and further training will enable older workers to maintain their labour market flexibility. The career practitioner will need to assess how able the older worker is to take responsibility and construct a life-career plan. Influences of gender, culture, and social class could prevent clients from pursuing opportunities of further education and training. Career practitioners will need to consider the intersections of diversity with the new emerging demographic of the older worker.

Assisting Clients to Develop the Skills and Knowledge to Effectively Manage Their Careers

Career search strategies, interview skills training, and instructions on résumé writing continue to be important career development skills in the 21st-century labour market. The demand for work-experience-based programs for students in high school and at postsecondary institutions is increasing, as students strive to gain international job market experience to diversify their competencies. Through the expansion of resources on the Internet and the creation of social media sites (i.e., Facebook, Twitter, LinkedIn, and others), job seekers are turning to the Internet to find work by posting online résumés, establishing or enhancing their professional reputation, and obtaining more information about employers. Additionally, employers are using social media to find and screen candidates. Career practitioners need to discuss social media etiquette and privacy issues with clients to ensure that what they post online will not hinder their career success.

As social media networks continue to grow and influence the labour market, some career development practitioners are predicting the end of the traditional paper résumé. Instead, an emerging trend is the design and use of virtual résumés where candidates upload their résumés to the Internet, attach them to their social media accounts, or even have a Quick Response (QR) code or related barcode on a business card that can be scanned to view the virtual résumé. The virtual résumé can be industry or career specific. For example, a graphic designer or photographer can utilize a virtual résumé to show interactive and photo-heavy documents to prospective employers. Moreover, Skype "interview rooms" can be used for the interview process as opposed to incurring costs for candidates and employers travelling to and from the interview site.

Career practitioners need to monitor these trends carefully and their associated protocols as some trends may prove to be a bust rather than a boom.

Recommended Reading

Career Thought Leaders. (2012). *Findings of 2011 global career brainstorming day: Trends for the now, the new and the next in careers.* <http://www.careerthoughtleaders.com/wp-content/up /CTL-Brainstorming-WhitePaper-2011.pdf>.
Watts, A. (2011). Sixth international symposium on career development and public policy in Budapest, Hungary: Reflection note. <http://eletpalya.munka.hu/c/document_library /get_file?uuid=43060b2f-7ce4-4a9b-8f24-04f07f453192&groupId=10418>.

Achieving Outcomes That Are Socially Just

Globalization and rapid societal and workplace change have contributed to increasing diversity in Canada. However, career development has not adequately addressed the needs of some groups such as people with disabilities, culturally and linguistically diverse people, Aboriginal peoples, individuals of low socioeconomic status, and people with mental illness.

One challenge has been to encourage career counsellors and career development practitioners to assume a greater role in fostering diversity and supporting social justice in Canadian society. Professional education programs need go beyond knowledge about social justice to that of supporting professionals in developing related skills. Career development practitioners may be interested in incorporating social justice into their professional practice, but organizations may resist this change for reasons such as racism, sexism, stereotyping, oppression, and ageism. The challenge then becomes how to implement organizational reforms that support practitioners in performing the work for which they were trained — it may mean challenging organizational practices.

As responsible professionals, career development practitioners need to be accountable for the impact of their work. As measures and methods are developed to assist clients with their work and life changes, it will be important to consider how career development practitioners measure the impact of interventions across multiple dimensions (i.e., organizational, social, and other levels of change). If career development practitioners are encouraged to address systemic barriers in Canadian society for marginalized populations, they will need tools to show that their efforts are making a positive difference.

In a social justice context, effective practitioners have knowledge of and are sensitive to diversity when establishing career development relationships. Input from such groups could assist practitioners in better understanding their needs and encouraging the development of services that are culturally and context sensitive.

Bridging Two Worlds: Aboriginal Career Development

The social justice mission of enhancing equity and changing systems is a hallmark of the psychology of working (Blustein, 2006). Blustein challenges career practitioners and theorists to reconsider the world of work as a system. Work can have many functions including: (a) as a means for survival and power, (b) as a means of social connection, and (c) as a means of self-determination. How do Aboriginal peoples construct notions of work? Until we can better understand Aboriginal cultural beliefs about working, education, and training, Aboriginal career programs and services will be hit and miss in their effectiveness. Career practitioners need to continue to examine the boundary of work and social oppression in developing practices and policies that will promote greater equity and access to opportunities.

Aboriginal-specific role modeling and mentoring, and educational achievement awards and related financial support, can greatly assist in meeting Aboriginal peoples' personal and community career needs. The proactive engagement of community and family to support and witness the journey of Aboriginal peoples as they pursue their given career path is considered a best practice for Aboriginal-specific training, employment, and other career-related programs. The potential exists for Aboriginal peoples to provide the next generation of **human capital** in Canada.

Celebrating Cultural Diversity: Immigrants to Canada

Immigrants greatly enrich the social, cultural, and economic fabric of Canada. In turn, we have a duty to ensure that Canada's laws and policies assist immigrants in settling successfully in this country. The barriers to employment cannot be solved by one sector alone; rather, we need to engage government, business, and the community if we want Canada to be a place where newcomers thrive. In addition to seeking employment, some immigrants deal with social loss such as possible dislocation from their family and home country, loneliness and powerlessness in a new country, and low self-confidence as it relates to English proficiency. Discussion and research are now emerging in the career development field to design processes such as PLAR (prior learning assessment and recognition) to better recognize the competencies immigrants have gained through formal and informal learning. Similar processes are being developed and implemented that assist immigrants in demonstrating their competencies to employers, regulatory bodies, and educational institutions.

Mentorship programs for immigrant professionals are being developed in Canada as a means of fostering workplace integration and increasing diversity. For example, the Edmonton Region Immigrant Employment Council's (ERIEC) Career Mentorship Program involves occupation-specific mentoring where mentors assist immigrants with networking and finding relevant jobs. Most major Canadian cities have this type of program. In Toronto it is the Toronto Region Immigrant Employment Council (TRIEC).

Through the Provincial Nominee Program, immigrants who already possess the skills, education, and work experience needed to make an immediate economic contribution to their province or territory are nominated. Since this program is provincial, it often involves newcomers moving to areas of Canada not traditionally settled by immigrants.

Recommended Readings

Prior learning assessment and recognition (PLAR) in Canada <http://www.cicic.ca/412/prior-learning-assessment-and-recognition-in-canada.Canada>.
Edmonton Region Immigrant Employment Council's (ERIEC) Career Mentorship Program <http://www.eriec.ca/mentor-stories/>.
Provincial Nominee Program <http://www.cic.gc.ca/english/immigrate/provincial/index.asp>.
Toronto Region Immigrant Employment Council (TRIEC), Stories <http://triec.ca/stories/>.

Career Development for Individuals of Low Socioeconomic Status

For millions of Canadians, the economic crisis is far from over. Hundreds of thousands of the unemployed are exhausting their EI coverage, and discovering a provincial social assistance system that is a shadow of what it was in the recession of the early 1990s. Those in desperate need of income support, due to the loss of a job, the loss of a spouse, the loss of good health, old age, or any number of other life circumstances, find that the social safety net meant to catch them has been shredded. (Seth Klein, British Columbia Director from the Canadian Centre for Policy Alternatives in The Missing Issues File: Poverty,

Reduction, 2011)

Low socioeconomic status can have a negative effect on a variety of aspects of an individual's life such as mental and physical health, education, and career achievement. Career-related challenges often experienced due to poverty and income inequality centre on high unemployment rates, low labour force representation, low wage earners, and low educational attainment. Unfortunately, Aboriginal peoples are one of Canada's most vulnerable populations. Rates of poverty for Aboriginal women are double that of non-Aboriginal women. Aboriginal peoples in Canada are also four times more likely to experience hunger as a direct result of poverty than the rest of the population (McIntyre, Connor, & Warren, 1998).

An emerging trend in the field is to take a social constructionist perspective on class, a topic that is often ignored when studying human behaviour (Blustein, 2006). It may be productive to explore how **classism** is perpetuated in overt and covert ways. What is the role of self-stigma in understanding the worldview of clients of low socioeconomic status? Internalized classism is the "negative emotional and cognitive consequences experienced by the individual resulting from that individual's inability to meet the demands of his or her economic culture" (Liu et al., 2004, p. 10). Classism is a topic that will be brought to the forefront over the next decade as practitioners work with clients to overcome the powerful ways that society's structural attributes privilege one group of people over others.

Recommended Reading

Raphael, D. (2007). *Poverty and policy in Canada: Implications for the health and quality of life*. Toronto, ON: Canadian Scholars Press.

Shifting Landscape for Employment Services

Provincial governments are adopting new ways to provide employment services. In British Columbia, for example, in 2012 the government opened 85 new "storefront" WorkBC Employment Services Centres across the province (Government of B.C. 2012). The new model, introduced in 2012, integrated 10 existing employment programs into one. In the past, clients had to go to different agencies to access these different employment programs and services; now they can come to one place to have all their needs met. For job seekers, this will mean having access to a variety of services under one roof. This includes self-serve job search services, as well as client needs assessment, case management, and other employment service options for those needing individualized services. In Ontario, the Employment Service Delivery framework, introduced in 2010, is customer centred and provides integrated, quality employment services to job seekers and employers seeking to hire across Ontario.

One-stop employment centres are viewed as a business service with a focus on results and on the employment and career development goals of the job seeker. The services are provided in a businesslike environment, and the job seeker is treated as a valued customer. Quality one-stop employment services require an individualized, customer focus that considers the level of services and supports needed for the client to achieve and maintain employment, achieve educational and career development objectives, and sustain the economic well-being of their family. To be successful, these services must also consider the human-resources needs of the employers in the local job market, the community resources available, and the trends and economic considerations in the labour market.

The movement from social service to business service is the result of shifts in three key areas of employment services: (a) perspectives on clients, (b) professional identity, and (c) the financing of service delivery, as we will learn in the following sections.

Perspectives on the Client

In the mid-1980s, when unemployment insurance was widely available and programs and employment services were housed in Canada Employment Centres (CECs), it was the job of a federal government employee to ensure that each individual had the tools needed to navigate his or her unemployment. The starting point was to identify the individual's needs and the specific employment-related services that could meet those needs. In complex cases, the federal employee would help the client deal with needs according to the stage in the job-loss cycle. However, when employment services were moved out of government offices, service delivery changed to one focused on solutions, and staff members were trained to work with clients to overcome barriers to employment success. It is not surprising that many of these practitioners saw themselves as providing a social service to the less fortunate.

While the job-loss cycle provided a good framework at the beginning of the employment services industry, it did not adequately address the changing labour market. Increasing numbers of program participants were experiencing employment that included short-term, part-time, and "intermittent labour market attachment" as a consequence of economic changes in the early years of the 21st century. The problem identification (or needs determination) approach also did not address the other side of the labour market equation, namely the employer. Employment services, in order to support an active client-and-employer interdependency, needed to shift into assessing a client's readiness for the labour market; the employment services needed to build upon a client's existing foundation to strengthen employment success, while also accumulating knowledge and experience in the current labour market.

The most direct process of measuring client readiness for the labour market was to assess clients using the same basic criteria employers use. For example, in

British Columbia, the employment readiness criteria includes: (a) previous labour market attachment; (b) skills, experience, and education; (c) abilities, strengths, and aptitudes; (d) capacity for job search; (e) personal and practical factors; and (f) the outcome objective (Ministry of Social Development (MSD), 2011, p. 372).

Assessing client readiness assumes all clients have some level of readiness that can be built upon to achieve an outcome result. The language and tone of service delivery in a readiness perspective mirrors the Appreciative Inquiry model of identifying what is working in a system (i.e., client readiness) and building capacity from those identified strengths (i.e., intervention steps; Hammond, 1996). This framework assumes clients are at different levels of employment readiness and can become attached to the labour market or the community through incremental intervention (MSD, 2011).

For this framework to be effective — that is, to create labour market or community attachment outcomes — career development practitioners have incorporated employer perspectives about what precise skills and criteria are used to determine employment readiness within a particular working environment. Therefore, to ensure that client readiness matches employer readiness, an increasing number of career development practitioners are venturing beyond serving only the unemployed client to also gathering data from employers within their communities. These labour market investigations are broadening the picture of possible paths for client readiness and inspiring new attachment opportunities.

Professional Identity

Early employment programs were first staffed by professionals from other fields of social service, or by para-professionals who aspired to work as counsellors or social workers. Work teams were composed of: (a) those with degrees, (b) those who had completed secondary school education along with some college, and (c) those who had other industry-specific training (Kalbfleisch & Burwell, 2007). In the early years of service delivery, job postings in the field rarely required training specific to career development, particularly as such training was largely unavailable outside of Québec (Kalbfleisch & Burwell, 2007). Many career practitioners had entered the profession by accident or through a related field.

It was not uncommon for program staff to have been participants of the programs they ended up working in. In the early days of non-government service delivery, program staff needed to have the right attitude, be willing to learn the procedures, and be open to help any client who walked through the door. For many years, those providing employment services used a wide range of job titles to describe the same service. For example, a person who sat in an office and met with clients individually may have been called an employment counsellor, an employment consultant, a career counsellor, or an employment specialist. All of these titles had the potential of being misleading about the nature of the intervention and/or the qualifications of the person providing the intervention. The range of entry points, educational and experiential backgrounds, and job titles also made it difficult for practitioners to be easily identified by the broader community.

Once the *Canadian Standards and Guidelines for Career Development Practitioners* (S&Gs) were established, it became possible to test individual competency levels of program staff. With the development of the S&Gs came the ability to design training programs to enhance areas where competency skill sets were absent or below standard requirements. Today, specific training in the core competencies is available at a wide range of educational levels ranging from postsecondary diplomas to advanced degrees.

The development of a competency profile for the profession also made it easier for career development practitioners to forge a clear career identity. According to Chope (2000), a career identity is the "kernel of all that you hope to be or become, the nucleus of your workplace confidence. It represents the accrual and integration of your experience, skills, interests, values, and personality characteristics" (p. 58). A career identity fosters a commitment to, and a passion for, one's career as well as increased **career decision self-efficacy**. The affirmation of career identity can also give direction to new learning or continuing education and training that can reinforce or enhance identity (Chope, 2000). Adopting the practice of **clinical supervision** by career practitioners will help in establishing career identity and recognition of the competencies. The work of skilled and experienced career practitioners trained in the techniques of effective supervision will assure the public and employers of the ethics and value of the profession.

Across Canada, professional certification bodies are using the S&Gs as the benchmark for certifying practitioners within their region. The credentialing process provides clients, employers, and the general public with an assurance that the individuals providing employment services meet a nationally recognized competency level. Credentialing means practitioners must become lifetime learners, continually upgrading their career development skills, whether through formal or informal learning environments. Credentialing also enables program funders to be successful in monitoring programs for consistent service standards and results.

From Social Agency to Business Service

Delivery of employment services has been shifting from a social agency approach to a business model. The following table shows the differences between the two approaches. Pre-2005, services tended to focus on helping the distressed job seeker and were funded by the federal government; today, employment services, now under provincial management, must be accountable and self-supporting and designed to meet the needs of a wide range of clients.

	FROM SOCIAL AGENCY	TO BUSINESS SERVICE
Clients	• Clients have employment needs that can be satisfied through employment programs. • Services are provided through a solution-focused helping model that serves primarily job seekers.	• Clients can be rated on levels of employment readiness and labour market strengths. • Services are based in Appreciative Inquiry and strengths-based approaches that serve job seekers and employers.
Services	• Services provided by people with a wide range of professional qualifications. • People drawn to helping professions.	• Services are provided by Certified Career Development Practitioners (CCDPs) who have demonstrated competencies based on the S&Gs. • Professionals are committed to creating accountable results.
Payment	• Paid up front to deliver programs. • Funder: Government, Employers, and Employees.	• Reimbursed for services delivered after targets are achieved. • Funder: Employers and employees.
Managed	• Federally.	• Provincially.
Primary Measuare of Success	• Client satisfaction	• Incremental labour market benchmarks.

Table 1: Key Shifts from Social Agency to Business Service.

This shift is described further in the next section about financing.

Financing Employment Services

When employment services were first contracted to non-government agencies and organizations, the funds disbursed for programs and services came from government revenues and employer/employee contributions. Unemployment insurance funds were designated for both direct benefits paid to the unemployed individual (UI) and for extended benefits and employment programs and services, known as "Part II Dollars" (Markenko, 2009).

During this time, organizations with a wide range of mandates and missions created employment projects that provided services to unemployed individuals within their community using Part II funds. The funds were disbursed in intervals based on project-proposal forecasted cash flows and projected program outcomes. Essentially, programs were paid up front for services delivered over the duration of the contract, with only a small hold-back between the end of service delivery and final report submission. Organizations that ran projects during these years did not require a substantial outlay of their own capital funds in order to host projects, as the dollars were disbursed from the extended benefits shortly after agreements were signed, and often before service delivery began.

When unemployment insurance became employment insurance (EI) in 1996, the federal government was no longer a contributor to the fund. It now became the sole responsibility of those involved in the labour market (i.e., employers and employees) to fund the re-employment system for job seekers (Lin, 1998). With this shift came the need for employment services to behave in a more business-like manner; that is, the EI system, including benefits paid to the unemployed and to employment services, had to be financially self-sustaining.

Since the late 1990s, the process of funding employment services has undergone major shifts to make these services more accountable including: (a) disbursement of funding dollars has become a provincial responsibility; (b) benchmark payments are tied to outcomes; and (c) project budgets are much leaner and data tracking systems are in place to create more precise reporting mechanisms. By 2005, the management of employment service dollars had moved from the federal government to provincial governments through Labour Market Development Agreements (LMDAs). These agreements enable provinces and territories to design, deliver, and manage skills and employment programs for unemployed Canadians, particularly for those who are eligible for Employment Insurance (EI) benefits (HRSDC, 2013).

With the signing of LMDAs across Canada, employment services are now results driven. Where in the past benchmark payments were made based on a forecast document at the time of project proposals, now project results are tracked on a moment-by-moment basis. It is now the responsibility of service providers to develop innovative tools to accurately and precisely measure the effectiveness of their services within a community.

The government's role in this framework is to provide financial oversight and to ensure that programs meet stipulated service requirements. Under provincial management, contracts are granted by large service regions, reducing the amount of infrastructure funding required to run programs. Consequently, there is much less duplication of management and overhead than in the previous funding model. Additionally, programs and services are connected to integrated case management systems that generate intervention-specific invoices once services have been delivered. Service providers are rewarded for earlier and greater client success with larger benchmark payments. Services that do not generate measurable outcomes are not funded. In this model, it is essential that service providers have a clear understanding of the real return on investment of the service they are providing.

Likely the most powerful emerging trend in financing employment services is a continuing increase in emphasis on demonstrating the value of career development services. Policy makers often refer to it as "proving it works," whereby evidence-based analysis is needed to sustain flexible, innovative, and cost-efficient career development program design and delivery. Furthermore, it is important to develop a professional career development identity that includes providing a strategic balance between core career services (i.e., accessible to all Canadians) and specialized career services (i.e., for marginalized populations in Canada) and evaluating the effectiveness of said services. Currently, when asked what career development practitioners do, most individuals use words or phrases that pertain to processes such as listening, facilitating, supporting, and empowering. There seldom is any mention of client change or evaluating service effectiveness.

In order to survive in the future, career practitioners must see their roles as providing services that include assessing the degree of client change. This requires a shift in professional identity so that career practitioners see themselves as having multiple roles and functions. These emerging trends are embedded in a larger context of professionalism in career services and, ultimately in the recognition that services are a function of professional preparation and evidence-based practice.

Conclusion

For career development practitioners in the 21st century, counselling, guidance, and related interventions require adaptation to emerging trends and responsiveness to individual needs and societal change. As responsible professionals, career practitioners will be called upon to utilize career development strategies that are adaptable to Canada's diverse population, and will include everything from reconstructing career theories and models to advocating for social change for marginalized groups. Over the coming decades, the diversified and changing role of career development practitioners will contribute to the overall transformation of economic development and career planning in Canada by identifying emerging workforce issues and designing complementary career services to build capacity for the socioeconomic benefit of all Canadians.

References

Arthur, N., & Collins, S. (Eds.). (2010). *Culture-infused counselling: Celebrating the Canadian mosaic* (2nd ed.). Calgary, AB: Counselling Concepts.

Blustein, D. L. (2006). *The psychology of working: A new perspective for career development, counseling, and public policy.* Mahwah, NJ: Lawrence Erlbaum Associates.

Bright, J. E. H., & Pryor, R. G. L. (2011). The chaos theory of careers. *Journal of Employment Counseling, 48*(4), 163–166.

Chope, R. C. (2000). *Dancing naked: Breaking through the emotional limits that keep you from the job you want.* Oakland, CA: New Harbinger Publications.

Cochran, L. (1997). *Career counseling: A narrative approach.* New York, NY: Sage.

Government of British Columbia. (2012). WorkBC employment centres now open in B.C. Retrieved from <http://www2.news.gov.bc.ca/news_releases_2009-2013/2012SD0004-000410.htm>.

Hammond, S. A. (1996). The thin book of appreciative inquiry. Plano: TX; Thin Book Publishing.

Hansen, S. (2011). Integrative life planning. *Journal of Employment Counseling, 48*(4), 167–169. doi: 10.1002/j.2161-1920.2011.tb01105.x

Human Resources and Skills Development Canada (HRSDC). (2013).*Labour market development agreements.* Retrieved from <http://www.hrsdc.gc.ca/eng/jobs/training_agreements/lmda/index.shtml>.

Kalbfleisch, S., & Burwell, R. (2007). Report on the Canadian career counselling educator survey. *Canadian Journal of Career Development, 6*(1), 4–20.

Klein, S. (2011). *The missing issues file: Poverty reduction.* Retrieved from <http://www.behindthenumbers.ca/2011/04/16/from-the-missing-issues-file-poverty-reduction/>.

Krumboltz, J. D. (2009). The happenstance learning theory. *Journal of Career Assessment 17*, 135–154. doi: 10.1177/1069072708328861

Leong, F. T. L., & Lee, S. H. (2006). A cultural accommodation model of psychotherapy: Illustrated with the case of Asian-Americans. *Psychotherapy: Theory, Research, Practice, and Training, 43*, 410– 423. doi: 10.1037/0033-3204.43.4.410

Lin, Z. (1998). *Employment insurance in Canada: Policy changes.* PERSPECTIVES Statistics Canada (Catalogue no. 75-001-XPE, pp. 42–47).

Liu, W. M., Ali, S. R., Soleck, G., Hopps, J., Dunston, K., & Pickett, T. (2004). Using social class in counseling psychology research. *Journal of Counseling Psychology, 51*, 3–18.

Magnusson, K., & Redekopp, D. (2011). Coherent career practice. *Journal of Employment Counseling, 48*(4), 176–178. doi: 10.1002/j.2161-1920.2011.tb01108.x

Markenko, J. (2009). *Employment insurance in Canada: History, structure and issues.* Retrieved from <http://www.mapleleafweb.com/features/employment-insurance-canada-history-structure-and-issues>.

McIntyre., L., Connor, S., & Warren, J. (1998). *A glimpse of child hunger in Canada.* Ottawa, ON: Applied Research Branch, Strategic Policy, Human Resources

Development Canada.

Ministry of Social Development. (2011). *Request for proposals number ELMS-004*, (Appendix H: 4). Victoria, BC: Government of British Columbia.

Neault, R. A., & Pickerell, D. A. (2011). Career engagement: Bridging career counseling and employee engagement. *Journal of Employment Counseling, 48*(4), 185–188. doi: 10.1002/j.2161-1920.2011.tb01111.x

Patton, W., & McMahon, M. (2006). *Career development and systems theory: Connecting theory and practice* (2nd ed.). Rotterdam, NL: Sense.

Peavy, R. V. (1997). Sociodynamic counselling: A constructivist perspective. Victoria, BC: Trafford.

Pignal, J., Arrowsmith, S., & Ness, A. (2010). *First results from the survey of older workers, 2008*. Statistics Canada, Special Surveys Division. Retrieved from <http://www.statcan.gc.ca/pub/89-646-x/89-646-x2010001-eng.htm>.

Pope, M. (2011). The career counseling with under-served populations model. *Journal of Employment Counseling, 48*(4),153–155. doi: 10.1002/j.2161-1920.2011.tb01100.x

Savickas, M. L. (1992). New directions in career assessment. In D. H. Montross & C. J. Shinkman (Eds.), *Career development: Theory and practice* (pp. 336–355). Springfield, IL: Charles C Thomas.

Savickas, M. L. (1996). A framework for linking career theory and practice. In M. L. Savickas & W. B. Walsh (Eds.), *Handbook of career counseling theory and practice* (pp. 191–208). Palo Alto, CA: Davies-Black.

Savickas, M. (2005). The theory and practice of career construction. In S.D. Brown & R.W. Lent (Eds.), *Career development and counseling: Putting theory and research to work* (pp. 42– 70). Hoboken, NJ: John Wiley & Sons.

Savickas, M. L., Nota, L., Rossier, J., Dauwalder, J-P, Eduarda Duarte, M., Guichard, J., ... van Vianen, A. E. M. (2009). Life designing: A paradigm for career construction in the 21st century. *Journal of Vocational Behavior, 75*(3), 239–250.

Sullivan, M. (n.d.). [Quote]. Retrieved from <http://www.finestquotes.com/quote_with-keyword-Career-page-1.htm>.

University of Ottawa. (n.d.). *Facts and figures: Aging in Canada and the world.* Retrieved from <http://www.med.uottawa.ca/sim/data/Aging_e.htm>

Vondracek, F. W., Lerner, R. M., & Schulenberg, J. E. (1986). *Career development: A life-span developmental approach*. Hillsdale, N.J.: Erlbaum.

Young, R. A., & Valach, L. (2004). The construction of career through goal-directed action. *Journal of Vocational Behavior, 64*, 499–514. doi: 10.1016/j.jvb.2003.12.012

Glossary

Career decision self-efficacy is an individual's degree of belief that he or she can successfully complete tasks necessary to making significant career decisions.

Classism is differential treatment based on social class or perceived social class.

Classism is the systematic oppression of subordinated class groups to advantage and strengthen the dominant class groups.

Clinical supervision occurs when the supervisor concentrates on training and evaluating the practitioner (supervisee) and the quality of services provided to individual clients.

Human capital is the collective skills, knowledge, or other intangible assets of individuals that can be used to create economic value for the individuals, their employers, or their community.

One-stop employment services provide comprehensive services to job seekers through service centres, in person, and online. The centre obtains appropriate information from job seekers, including resources and services needed to meet their identified needs, and offers an array of services for job search, assessment, workplace counselling, and much else.

Discussion and Activities

Discussion

Discussion Questions

1. As highlighted in this chapter, in order to stay current, practitioners will need to develop new competencies. Discuss the following competencies developed by the American Society for Training and Development (<http://www.astd.org/Publications/Magazines/TD/TD-Archive/2013/01/Training-and-Development-Competencies-Redefined>):

   - Stay abreast of new and emerging technologies and matching the appropriate technology.
   - Foster a culture of connectivity and collaboration via mobile and social technology.
   - Leverage the learning styles and preferences of new generations entering the workforce and capture the knowledge of those leaving it.
   - Anticipate and meet the training and development needs of an increasingly global workforce and contribute to talent development.
   - Demonstrate the value and impact of learning by using data analysis to measure the effectiveness and efficiency of services.

2. In the past, the metanarrative of career development has been characterized as a progress story. The key metaphor has been one of progressing up an

occupational ladder and establishing a sense of security over time. However, there are many individuals who conceptualize career development in different ways and whose experiences do not fit the metaphor of the "occupational ladder." There are many individuals who encounter barriers and drift, get sidetracked, or flounder in their career development. What new metaphors come to mind to encompass the various narratives of career development for individuals that also incorporate our current culture and societal expectations?

Personal Reflection

As a novice career development practitioner, what concerns you most about these emerging trends?

- The expanding roles of career practitioners?
- Implementing "metatheories" in working with clients?
- Working with marginalized groups from a social justice framework?
- Using social media as part of the client's work search strategy?
- Providing services based on evidence-based practice?

Career Practitioner Role

1. In career construction theory, it is often suggested that four key aspects are important to consider in career adaptability: (a) being concerned about your future, (b) feeling a sense of control over your future, (c) considering possible selves, and (d) fostering a sense of confidence in pursuing one's aspirations. How would you assess and foster career adaptability in a client who posed the following questions?

- "Do I have a future?"
- "How much control do I have over my future choices?"
- "What do I want to do with my future?"
- "Can I do it?"

2. Free self-directed career interventions are being developed for users and are available on the Internet. Find a few online resources and create criteria and assess whether the resources being developed are helpful for people.

Activities

Summarize the chapter by writing a paragraph on each of the five points below.

1. Explain the expanding roles of career counsellors and career development practitioners in Canada's economy and labour force.

2. Identify emerging career development theories, models, and strategies and their implications in the 21st-century Canadian workforce.
3. List work search strategies, career resources, and related supports that can aid individuals in advancing their career planning.
4. Describe career development issues facing marginalized groups in Canadian society.
5. Describe aspects of the shifting landscape of career development services in Canada.

APPENDICES

Appendix A

Code of Ethics

Canadian Standards and Guidelines
for Career Development Practitioners

2004

Editors' note: This Code of Ethics was developed by the *Canadian Standards and Guidelines for Career Development Practitioners* (S&Gs) in 2004.* The Canadian Career Development Foundation has granted CERIC permission to reproduce the *Code of Ethics* in this textbook as an appendix for quick reference. The official and most current version of this "living" document is available from S&Gs' website, <http://career-dev-guidelines.org/career_dev/>. (Publication Information: ATEC (2004). *Canadian Standards and Guidelines for Career Development Practitioners*. Ottawa, ON: Human Resources Development Canada.)

Code of Ethics

Preamble

Career development practitioners are engaged in a wide spectrum of activities in many fields. They work in a wide range of organizational settings and provide a spectrum of services and programs to a diverse population. This Code of Ethics is intended as a platform for the Canadian Standards and Guidelines for Career Development Practitioners.

This Code of Ethics is designed to reflect the breadth of the field as a companion to the core competencies that are being developed nationally. Therefore this Code of Ethics is purposely broad and quite general. Further detailed and focused ethical guidelines may be developed for the specialization areas identified. These specialized guidelines will then be considered as an adjunct to this Code of Ethics, not a replacement for this Code. The Code of Ethics does not supersede legislation and regulations that you as a practitioner are required to follow according to the jurisdiction you work in and the services you provide.

The purpose of the Code of Ethics is to provide a practical guide for professional behaviour and practice for those who offer direct service in career development and to inform the public which career development practitioners serve. Ethical principles help career development practitioners to make thoughtful decisions to resolve ethical dilemmas. The Code of Ethics when combined with the Canadian Standards and Guidelines for Career Development will protect the consumer and the public when receiving the services of career development practitioners.

Definitions for the purpose of this Code

Client: means the person(s) or organization to whom the career development practitioner provides services. This may include individuals, groups, classes, organizations, employers and others.

Customer: means the person(s) or organization that is paying for the career development service. A customer may or may not be the client.

Field: refers to practitioners involved in career development services.

1. **Ethical Principles for Professional Competency and Conduct**

1.a. Knowledge/Skills/Competency
Career development practitioners value high standards of professional competence and ensure they are able to offer high standards of professional knowledge, skills and expertise.

1.b. Self-Improvement
Career development practitioners are committed to the principle of lifelong learning to maintain and improve both their professional growth and the development of the field in areas of knowledge, skills and competence.

1.c. Boundary of Competency
Career development practitioners recognize the boundaries of their competency and only provide services for which they are qualified by training and/or supervised experience. They are knowledgeable of and arrange for appropriate consultations and referrals based on the best interests of their clients.

1.d. Representation of Qualifications
Career development practitioners do not claim nor imply professional qualifications or professional affiliations that may imply inaccurate expertise and/or endorsement. Career development practitioners are responsible for correcting any misrepresentations or misunderstandings about their qualifications.

1.e. Marketing
Career development practitioners maintain high standards of integrity in all forms of advertising, communications, and solicitation and conduct business in a manner that enhances the field.

1.f. Relations with Institutions and Organizations
Career development practitioners assist institutions or organizations to provide the highest calibre of professional service by adhering to this Code of Ethics. Career development practitioners will encourage organizations, institutions, customers and employers to operate in a manner that allows the career development practitioner to provide service in accordance with the Code of Ethics.

1.g. Respect for Persons
Career development practitioners respect and stand up for the individual rights and personal dignity of all clients. Career development practitioners do not condone or engage in sexual harassment. Career development practitioners promote equality of opportunity and provide non-discriminatory service. Clients who fall outside the mandate of an organization should be referred to appropriate services.

1.h. Abide by the Code of Ethics and Provincial and Federal Laws
Career development practitioners abide by all of the by-laws outlined in this Code of Ethics and furthermore comply with all relevant provincial/territorial and federal legislation and regulations.

Career development practitioners inform others (such as colleagues, clients, students, employers, and third party sources) about the Code of Ethics and relevant laws as appropriate and any mechanisms available if violations of the Code of Ethics or laws are perceived to have taken place.

Career development practitioners take appropriate action to try to rectify a situation if ethical, moral or legal violations are perceived to have taken place by a colleague, whether a career development practitioner or not.

1.i. Use of Information and Communication Technology

Career development practitioners using information and communication technology which involves a client and service provider who are in separate or remote locations, are aware that all aspects of the Code of Ethics apply as in other contexts of service provision.

Career development practitioners provide clients with relevant information about themselves, as is appropriate for the type of relationship and service offered.

2. Ethical Principles for Career Development Practitioner-Client Relationship

2.a. Integrity/Honesty/Objectivity

Career development practitioners promote the welfare of clients by providing accurate, current and relevant information.

Career development practitioners assist clients to realize their potential and respect clients' rights to make their own informed and responsible decisions.

Career development practitioners are aware of their own personal values and issues and avoid bringing and/or imposing these on their clients.

2.b. Confidentiality

Career development practitioners respect the privacy of the individual or third party referral source and maintain confidentiality of information as is appropriate for the type of relationship and service offered.

Career development practitioners will inform clients and customers of the limits of confidentiality.

Career development practitioners offering services in a group, family, class or open setting (such as a Career Resource Centre) take all reasonable measures to respect privacy.

Career development practitioners are cautioned that the issues of confidentiality apply to the use of information and communication technology, e.g., voice mail, faxes, e-mail.

2.c. Releasing Private Information

Career development practitioners release confidential information in the following circumstances:

- with the express permission of the client
- where there is clear evidence of imminent danger to the client*
- where there is clear evidence of imminent danger to others*
- where required by law, such as in reporting suspected child abuse or upon court order

(* When the situation allows, action should be taken following careful deliberation and consultation with the client and other professionals. The client should be encouraged to take personal responsibility as soon as possible.)

Career development practitioners attend to privacy and security in the maintenance and release of all records, whether records are written, on audiotape, or videotape, computerized or electronically stored.

2.d. Informed Consent

Career development practitioners honour the right of individuals to consent to participate in services offered, dependent upon the rights the individual does have, such as in being legally required to attend school.

Career development practitioners fully inform clients as to the use of any information that is collected during the offering of service. Career development practitioners ensure that information collected will only be used for its intended purpose or obtain the consent of clients for any other use of the information.

Career development practitioners inform clients and customers about the types of service offered and the limitations to service, as much as is reasonably possible given the type of service offered, including information about the limits to confidentiality, legal obligations, and the right to consult with other professionals.

Career development practitioners who work with minors or dependent individuals who are unable to give voluntary, informed consent, take special care to respect the rights of the individual and involve the parents or guardians wherever appropriate.

2.e. Multiple Relations

Career development practitioners are aware of the ethical issues involved in having personal relationships with clients. Career development practitioners avoid having conflicting relationships whenever possible. If such a relationship cannot be avoided the career development practitioner is responsible to monitor the relationship to prevent harm, ensure that judgement is not impaired and avoid exploitation. To this end career development practitioners utilize informed consent, consultation, supervision and full disclosure to all parties involved.

2.f. Conflict of Interest

Career development practitioners avoid and/or disclose any conflicts of interest which might influence their professional decisions or behaviours. Career development practitioners do not exploit any relationship to further their personal, social, professional, political, or financial gains at the expense of their clients, especially if the situation would impair the career development practitioner's objectivity.

Career development practitioners work to resolve any conflicts of interest with all parties involved giving priority to the best interests of the client.

3. Ethical Principles for Professional Relationships

3.a. Consultation

Career development practitioners reserve the right to consult with other professionally competent persons ensuring the confidentiality of the client is protected.

3.b. Respect for Other Professionals

Career development practitioners make full use of the resources provided by other professionals to best serve the needs of the client, including professional, technical, or administrative resources. This means understanding and respecting the unique contributions of other related professionals. Career development practitioners seek to avoid duplicating the services of other professionals.

As career development practitioners have a responsibility to clients, they also have a responsibility to fellow service providers.

When a complaint is voiced about other service providers, or inappropriate behaviour is observed, the career development practitioner will follow the appropriate channels to address the concerns.

Ethical Decision-Making Model

This is a model of ethical decision making to complement the Code of Ethics developed for the Canadian Standards and Guidelines for Career Development. This model is offered to assist career development practitioners with a process to follow and with cues, such as emotional reactions, which may assist in making better ethical decisions and resolving ethical dilemmas.

Steps in Ethical Decision Making

1. *Recognize that an ethical dilemma exists.*

    An emotional response by a career development practitioner is often a cue to the need to make an ethical decision, such as feeling uneasy about a situation, questioning one's self or the actions of a client, or feeling blocked or uncomfortable in a situation with a client or colleague.

2. *Identify the relevant ethical issues*, all of the parties involved, and the corresponding pertinent ethical principles from the Code of Ethics.

    The career development practitioner can check his/her feelings of discomfort and what these may tell about the situation. The feelings of the client or a third party involved in the dilemma could also be explored.

    In some situations following one of the Codes of Ethics will offer enough guidance to resolve the situation. In situations where more than one Code is relevant or there is more than one course of action, the career development practitioner will need to proceed further with this model. Examine the risks and benefits of each alternative action.

    The examination should include short-term, ongoing and long-term consequences for each person involved, including the Practitioner, when more than one Code of Ethics is relevant or alternative courses of action seem to be suggested by the Code of Ethics. In such situations gathering additional information and consulting with a trusted colleague is highly recommended.

    The career development practitioner can check his/her own emotional reactions to each solution and those of others involved in the decision. The career development practitioner also needs to determine if he/she has allowed enough time for contemplation of the situation. Projecting the various solutions into the future and envisioning the possible scenarios as each decision is enacted can be helpful.

4. **Choose a solution, take action and evaluate the results.**
    The career development practitioner needs to act with commitment to one of the solutions, checking that the solution continues to feel the best that can be done in the situation, for all involved. The practitioner will need to assume responsibility for the consequences of the decision and be willing to correct for any negative consequences that might occur as a result of the action taken. This means determining that the outcome feels right and re-engaging in the decision-making process if the ethical dilemma remains unresolved.

5. **Learn from the situation.**
    The career development practitioner will examine each ethical situation to consider the factors that were involved in the development of the dilemma and to see if any future preventative measures could be taken. Examining what he/she has learned from the situation and how the experience might affect future practice are also important activities for the career development practitioner.

Ethical Decision-Making Models Consulted

Canadian Psychological Association (1991). Canadian code of ethics for psychologists. Ottawa, ON: Author.

Hill, M., Glaser, K., & Harden, K. (1995). A feminist model for ethical decision making. In E. J. Rave, and C. C. Larsen (Eds.), Ethical decision making in therapy: Feminist perspectives. New York, NY: Guilford Press.

Sheppard, G., Schulz, W., & McMahon, S. (1999). Code of ethics for the Canadian Counselling Association. Ottawa, ON: Canadian Counselling Association.

Acknowledgements for Code of Ethics

The Canadian Standards and Guidelines for Career Development Ethics Subcommittee would like to acknowledge the following resources that were consulted in preparing the Code of Ethics.

Code of Ethics for:

Canada
Alberta Teachers Association – Teacher's Code of Professional Conduct
Canadian Association of Career Educators and Employers

Canadian Association of Pre-Retirement Planners
Canadian Association of Rehabilitation Professionals
Canadian Association of Social Workers
Canadian Counselling Association
Canadian Psychology Association
Career Development Association of Alberta
International Association of Career Management Professionals
Ontario Alliance of Career Development Practitioners Ethical Standards (DRAFT)
Ontario Society of Psychotherapists
Personnel Association of Ontario
The Educational Association of Networking, Education and Training for Workers in
    Employment, Rehabilitation and Career Counselling (British Columbia)
The Professional Corporation of Guidance Counsellors of Québec

United States
American Counseling Association
Career Development Facilitator
National Association of Colleges and Employers
National Career Development Association
National Board for Certified Counselors, Inc. — Standards for the Ethical Practice of
    Web Counseling

International
Institute of Careers Guidance (Britain)

Papers and Documents

Creed, K. (1999). Ethical Issues for Online Counselling. Unpublished document.
Schultz, W. (1996). Career and employment counsellors' code of ethics. In J. Kotylak &
    D. Welch (Eds.). Building Tomorrow Today: Proceedings from the Third Annual
    Consultation for Career Development in Alberta. Edmonton, AB: Alberta Career
    Development Action Group.
Schultz, W. (1998). An integrated approach to ethical decision-making. Paper
    presented to the annual conference of the Canadian Guidance and Counselling
    Annual Conference, Montreal, Québec.
Schultz, W. (1998). Some ethical guidelines for group counsellors. Paper presented
    to the annual conference of the Canadian Guidance and Counselling Annual
    Conference, Montreal, Québec.
Simard, S. (1996). A guide to criterion-based assessment of employability skills
    including sample performance criteria. Paper presented to the 3rd International
    Partnership Conference of the Conference Board of Canada. Toronto, Ontario.
Stewart, J. (1999). Ethical issues in career counselling. Guidance and Counselling,
    14(2), 18–21.

Ward, V. (1998). Training career development facilitators in ethical decision-making. In M. Van Norman (Ed.). Natcon Papers 1998. Toronto, ON: University of Toronto Guidance Centre

Appendix B

Professional Resources for Career Practitioners

Canadian National Associations and Foundations

Canadian Association of Career Educators and Employers (CACEE)
   <http://www.cacee.com/>. The Canadian Association of Career Educators and
   Employers (CACEE) is a national non-profit partnership of employer recruiters
   and career services professionals. Our mission is to provide authoritative
   information, advice, professional development opportunities and other services to
   employers, career services professionals, and students.

Canadian Career Development Foundation (CCDF) <http://ccdf.ca/>. CCDF is
   a recognized leader both nationally and internationally in the field of career
   development. Established in 1979, as a non-profit charitable foundation, CCDF
   works on projects that advance career development and the capacity of the
   profession to respond with compassion and skill to all clients and stakeholders in
   an ever-changing work environment.

Canadian Career Information Association (CCIA) <http://www.ccia-acadop.ca/>.
   The Canadian Career Information Association / L'Association canadienne de
   documentation professionnelle was formed in 1975. It brings together individuals
   who share a common interest in the development, distribution and use of career
   resources.

Canadian Coalition of Community-Based Employability Training (CCCBET) <http://
   www.ccocde-cccbet.com/>. Members of CCCBET, a national, non-profit

organization, are from provincial and national non-profit employment and training associations and organizations. CCCBET's vision statement is, "That Canada's employment and training sector offers recognized, professional services and that all people have access to community-based services that support their pursuit of meaningful employment and social inclusion."

Canadian Council for Career Development (CCCD) <http://cccda.org/cccda>. An umbrella group for career development groups and their partners to promote collaboration. For a list of members, see the Directory of Members at CCCD <http://cccda.org/cccda/index.php/members/directory-of-members>.

Canadian Education and Research Institute for Counselling (CERIC) <http://www .ceric.ca>. CERIC is a charitable organization dedicated to promoting career counselling-related research and professional development opportunities across Canada. It is directed by a volunteer board of directors reflecting a broad sectoral representation in the field of career counselling. CERIC funds both research as well as learning and professional development in Canada. Several programs support and benefit career professionals including: ContactPoint/OrientAction online communities, Cannexus National Career Development Conference, *The Canadian Journal of Career Development* (CJCD), and a Graduate Student Engagement Program.

Canadian University and College Counselling Association (CUCCA) <http://www.cacuss.ca/divisions_communities_CUCCA.htm>. The Canadian University and College Counselling Association is a national group of counsellors and counselling psychologists in postsecondary institutions, counselling educators and graduate students in counselling-related programs.

Career Development Chapter, Canadian Counselling and Psychotherapy Association (CCPA) <http://www.ccpa-accp.ca/en/chapters/details/?ID=9>. The mission of the CCPA Career Development Chapter is to support career practitioners in the field, to provide materials for quality service for consumers, and to create and recognize new initiatives in the field.

Career Professionals of Canada <http://www.careerprocanada.ca/>. Members represent all sectors and regions across Canada and include employment consultants, career coaches, résumé writers, interview coaches, outplacement consultants, recruiters, and a wide variety of other career professionals.

The College Sector Committee for Adult Upgrading <http://www.collegeupgradingon. ca>. The College Sector Committee for Adult Upgrading is committed to providing leadership in promoting the continuous improvement of the delivery of academic upgrading programs to meet the needs of adult learners in the Ontario Community College system. The CSC Coordinates communications, conducts research, provides practitioner training, and develops learning materials intended to promote excellence at all colleges. The CSC is also responsible for the development and distance delivery of the Academic and Career Entrance (ACE) program.

Provincial Organizations

Alliance of Manitoba Sector Councils <http://www.amsc.mb.ca/>. The Alliance of Manitoba Sector Councils (AMSC) is a formal group of 18 sector councils with common goals:

1. Promote productivity, competitiveness, and community economic development through innovative and leading-edge collaborative projects.
2. Encourage entrepreneurship and small and medium business start-up programs creating future opportunities for growth and development.
3. Strengthen the skills of our Manitoba workforce and economy to allow an increase in production and competitiveness locally, nationally, and internationally.
4. Respond to the labour market changes through strategic initiatives related to Human Resources and Training to retain and recruit workers to Manitoba.
5. Strengthen the skills of our current and future sector leaders in the area of human resources and training.
6. Encourage joint and co-operative projects between sectors, with education, with industry and with government.

Association des conseillers d'orientation du collegial (ACOC) <http://www.acoc. info/Accueil/affichage.asp?B=342>. ACOC, an association of counsellors in Québec, meets the needs of its members by providing college-related professional development activities, supporting the growth and development the expertise of college counsellors, and disseminating career resources.

Association of Service Providers for Employability and Career Training (ASPECT) <http://www.aspect.bc.ca/>. ASPECT is an organization for British Columbia`s community-based trainers. It provides leadership, education, advocacy, and public awareness in support of its members who provide community-based workforce development services.

Career Development Association of Prince Edward Island (CDAPEI) <http://cdapei. wordpress.com/>. CDAPEI promotes networking of professionals, community partners, and individuals seeking to strengthen career development initiatives on PEI.

First Work <http://www.firstwork.org/>. First Work aims to help young people find and maintain meaningful employment that will help improve the quality of their lives by supporting the network of local youth employment centres across Ontario. Association members receive help with knowledge transfer, public policy, professional development, and strategic communications.:

Ontario Alliance of Career Development Practitioners <http://www.oacdp.on.ca/>. The Ontario Alliance of Career Development Practitioners is an inclusive organization that provides strategic leadership to the Ontario partners in career development. It promotes best practices through the communication of information and the adoption of common standards and guidelines to enhance client-centred service delivery.

Ontario Network of Training Skills Project (ONESTEP) <http://www.onestep.ca/>. ONESTEP is a province-wide non-profit umbrella organization for the community-based training and employment (CBET) sector. More than 450 programs are provided by their member agencies, with over 250,000 clients served each year. Services include but are not limited to: career and personal counselling; literacy, ESL and numeracy programs; job-finding clubs; computer courses; sector-specific training (finances, tourism, health care); and job placement.

Regroupement québécois des organismes pour le développement de l'employabilité (RQuODE) <http://www.savie.qc.ca/rquode2/>. The Québec Coalition of Development of Employability (RQuODE) is a non-profit organization formed in 1987. The RQuODE is composed of 61 members, located in 12 of the 17 regions of Québec. Its objectives are to:

- Improve methods of intervention that contribute to successful organizations;
- Increase the efficiency of working with disadvantaged clients in terms of employment;
- Promote a forum of expertise in integration to work;
- Facilitate communication between agencies;
- Represent all members to governmental, social, economic, and community.

Réseau des services spécialisés de main'd'oeuvre (RSSMO) <http://rssmo.qc.ca/>. The RSSMO is the Québec association of non-profit organizations that provide employability services to help people with special difficulties.

International Organizations (Sample)

International

Association of Career Professionals International (ACPI) <http://www. acpinternational.org/>. The Association of Career Professionals International is a "global organization dedicated to advancing public awareness of the career management profession, as well as in promoting the international profile and credibility of its varied membership."

Career Industry Council of Australia (CICA) <http://www.cica.org.au/>. CICA is a collaboration of non-profit career practitioner associations in Australia, providing a voice for the career industry. It facilitates liaisons and promotes awareness.

International Association for Educational and Vocational Guidance (IAEVG) <http://www.iaevg.org/IAEVG/>. IAEVG advocates that all citizens who need and want educational and vocational guidance and counselling can receive this counselling from a competent and recognized professional; recommends the basic nature and quality of service that should typify the service provided to students and adults; and recommends the essential training and other qualifications that all counsellors in educational and vocational guidance should have.

United States

National Association of Colleges and Employers (NACE)<http://www.naceweb.org/>. "The National Association of Colleges and Employers connects campus recruiting and career services professionals, and provides best practices, trends, research, professional development, and conferences."

National Career Development Association (NCDA) <http://associationdatabase.com/aws/NCDA/pt/sp/Home_Page>. The National Career Development Association provides professional development, resources, standards, scientific research, and advocacy. NCDA is a founding division of the American Counseling Association (ACA).

Appendix C

Primer on Aboriginal Peoples and Canadian Law

In order to better understand career development from an Aboriginal perspective, it helps to appreciate the consequences of Canadian legislation and government policies on Aboriginal peoples (**First Nations, Métis,** and **Inuit**). Career practitioners should have a sense of what Aboriginal peoples have experienced over time so that they can better empathize with their clients' situation and understand the social and economic barriers they continue to face. Without such awareness, practitioners may end up offering ineffective or inappropriate services to their Aboriginal clientele.

The history provided below highlights some of the more significant political and legislative events in the history of Aboriginal peoples in Canada. We hope that through this review, career professionals will have a greater understanding of the Aboriginal struggle for recognition of their rights.

Acts, Accords, and Policies

Royal Proclamation of 1763

As settlers moved in to occupy British North America, the British government proclaimed that the interests of Aboriginal peoples and their lands must be protected under the Crown. Specifically, the Royal Proclamation of 1763 states that only the Crown may buy land from the First Nations people. To date, this proclamation has and continues to be significant in terms of recognizing Aboriginal title and rights (First Nations Studies Program, 2013a).

Constitution Act, 1867 — Section 91(24)

This section of the Constitution Act (originally known as the British North America Act) describes how the Government of Canada has exclusive legislative authority for Indians and lands reserved for Indians (i.e., reserves; Government of Canada, 2013a).

Constitution Act, 1982 — Section 35

In the amendment to the Constitution Act in 1982, Section 35 provides constitutional protection to the rights of Aboriginal people in Canada. Examples of Aboriginal rights that Section 35 has been found to protect are fishing, logging, hunting, Aboriginal title (i.e., the right to land) and the right to enforce treaties (Government of Canada, 2013b).

Indian Act

This statute was first passed in 1876. It gave the Government of Canada exclusive authority over Indian people living on reserves. The Act defines who are Indians and their associated rights. The Act previously denied First Nations people the right to vote unless they gave up their Indian status and associated rights. In 1960, First Nations people received the right to vote in federal elections without giving up their Indian status. At present, the Indian Act remains in effect. Though amendments were made to the statute from approximately 1881 to 2000, the Act remains fundamentally unchanged since 1876. The most recent amendment in 2000 allows First Nations band members living off reserve to vote in band elections and referendums. The Indian Act is administered by the Minister Responsible for Aboriginal Affairs and Northern Development Canada (Government of Canada, 2013c).

The White Paper 1969

Former Minister of Indian Affairs, Jean Chretien, prepared a policy document (The White Paper 1969) that proposed the elimination of the Indian Act and Aboriginal land claims. In addition, the White Paper supported the assimilation of First Nations people into the Canadian population as "other visible minorities" rather than being recognized as a distinct racial group (Government of Canada, 1969). In response to the 1969 White Paper on Indian Policy, Harold Cardinal and the Indian Chiefs of Alberta countered by preparing the "Citizens Plus" policy document (the Red Paper). The Red Paper and the Calder v. British Columbia (Supreme Court of Canada, 1973) decision were contributing factors for the Liberal Party of Canada (the governing party of Canada at the time) to step away from the policy recommendations described in the 1969 White Paper.

Calder versus British Columbia (1973)

The Calder v. British Columbia decision by the Supreme Court of Canada concerning Aboriginal title to lands in British Columbia was the first time that Canadian law acknowledged that Aboriginal land title existed prior to European contact or colonization (Supreme Court of Canada, 1973). Subsequent legal decisions such as Delgamuukw, Nisga'a, Gitxsan, Wet'suwet'in, Haida, Taku River Tlingit, Musqueam, Heiltsuk, Sto:lo, and Tsilhqot'in Nation are making significant contributions in the protection and advancement of Aboriginal title and rights — affirming that First Nations people exist and they have laws and governments.

Bill C-31: Act to Amend the Indian Act

This is the 1985 pre-legislation name of the Act to Amend the Indian Act. This legislation removed discriminatory clauses against women and restored status and membership rights. Aboriginal people who have been reinstated as status Indians under this Act are often referred to as "Bill C-31 Indians" (First Nations Studies Program, 2013b).

Powley Case

On September 19, 2003, the Supreme Court of Canada acknowledged the existence of Métis as a distinct Aboriginal people in Canada with existing rights that are protected by section 35 of the Constitution Act, 1982 (Métis National Council, 2013).

Kelowna Accord

Under the leadership of former Prime Minister Paul Martin, Aboriginal leaders, various provincial and territorial governments, and the federal government gathered on November 24–25, 2005 at the "First Ministers and National Aboriginal Leaders Strengthening Relationships and Closing the Gap" meeting in Kelowna, British Columbia. At this meeting, the First Ministers (the Prime Minister and Provincial/ Territorial Premiers) and National Aboriginal leaders made a commitment to work together and strengthen their relationships across jurisdictional boundaries (Aboriginal, provincial, territorial and federal levels of government). This dialogue session resulted in the development of a 10-year agreement entitled "The Kelowna Accord" — a working paper that addressed closing the socioeconomic gap between Aboriginal people and other Canadians. Major themes of the Kelowna Accord included economic development, education, and health. These were reflective of issues that cut across all Aboriginal populations. The Accord presented tailored recommendations for First Nations, Métis and Inuit people. (Kelowna Accord, 2005). The plan included $5 billion over five years to improve the lives of all Aboriginal people (CBC, 2006). In 2006, the new federal government of Prime Minister Stephen Harper decided not to follow through on the agreement.

First Nations-Federal Crown Political Accord on the Recognition and Implementation of the First Nations Governments
Signed in May 2005, this national agreement between First Nations and the Government of Canada focused on the reconciliation, collaborative review, and development of policies relating to First Nations' rights and self-government (Assembly of First Nations, 2005).

Statement of Apology to former students of Indian Residential Schools
On June 11, 2008, Prime Minister Stephen Harper officially apologized on behalf of the Government of Canada for the harm inflicted by the Indian Residential School System. In operation for over a century (from the 1840s into the 1990s), the Indian Residential School System took over 150,000 Aboriginal children from their families and communities and placed them in non-Aboriginal operated residential schools across Canada. The intention was to isolate Aboriginal children by separating them from their languages, families, communities, and cultures — and thereby assimilating them into mainstream Canadian culture. In addition to the negative effects of assimilation, there were allegations of abuse (psychological, physical, and sexual), overcrowding, lack of medical care, and poor sanitation that many Aboriginal children were exposed to during their attendance at residential schools (Aboriginal Affairs and Northern Development Canada, 2008). The Statement of Apology, 2008, was to begin a process of reconciliation between Aboriginal people (particularly, former residential school survivors) and the Government of Canada, and ensure that government systems and processes like the residential schools are never repeated.

United Nations Declaration on the Rights of Indigenous People
This UN declaration covers a wide range of human rights and fundamental freedoms related to Indigenous peoples, including the right to preserve and develop their cultural characteristics and distinct identities as well as ownership and use of traditional lands and natural resources. The declaration also covers rights related to religion, language, education, and the rights to participate in the political, economic, and social life of the society in which Indigenous peoples live. On November 12, 2010, the Government of Canada officially endorsed this declaration (United Nations Declaration of the Rights of Indigenous Peoples, 2007).

Bill C-3 Gender Equity in Indian Registration Act
On December 15, 2010, Bill C-3: Gender Equity in Indian Registration Act received Royal Assent and came into effect on January 31, 2011. This Act ensures that eligible grandchildren of women who lost status as a result of marrying non-Indian men are entitled to registration (Indian status) (Gender Equity in Indian Registration, 2010). Because of this legislation, approximately 45,000 persons will become newly entitled to registration.

Bill C-45 and the Idle No More Movement

The Government of Canada introduced Bill C-45 on October 18, 2012, entitled, A Second Act to Implement Certain Provisions of the Budget Tabled in Parliament on March 29, 2012, and Other Measures. Bill C-45 was an omnibus budget bill that changed legislation contained in over 60 acts or regulations (Government of Canada, 2013d). As it pertains to Aboriginal issues and rights, changes to legislation that included the Indian Act, Navigation Protection Act (former Navigable Waters Protection Act) and Environmental Assessment Act served as a catalyst for the Idle No More Movement in the fall of 2012 (Rabson, 2013).

The Idle No More Movement saw Aboriginal people at the grassroots level from across Canada gather in solidarity through rallies and social media (on Twitter at #IdleNoMore) raising awareness about Aboriginal issues in response to Bill C-45. Organizers and supporters of The Idle No More Movement saw Bill C-45 as an erosion of treaty and Aboriginal rights, and a lack of consultation with Aboriginal people on changes to federal legislation. On December 10, 2012, a National Day of Solidarity and Resurgence was held. Despite the actions of the Idle No More Movement, Bill C-45 was passed and received Royal Assent on December 14, 2012. Bill C-45 is now referred to as Jobs and Growth Act, 2012 (Government of Canada, 2013d).

References

Aboriginal Affairs and Northern Development Canada. (2008). Statement of apology to former students of Indian residential schools. Retrieved from <http://www.aadnc-aandc.gc.ca/DAM/DAM-INTER-HQ/STAGING/texte-text/rqpi_apo_pdf_1322167347706_eng.pdf>.

Assembly of First Nations. (2005). A First Nations-Federal Crown political accord on the recognition and implementation of the First Nations governments. Retrieved from <http://64.26.129.156/cmslib/general/PolitcialAccord-May2005Eng&Fr.pdf>.

CBC (2006). Undoing the Kelowna Agreement. Retrieved from <http://www.cbc.ca/news/background/aboriginals/undoing-kelowna.html>.

First Nations Studies Program. (2013a). Royal Proclamation, 1763. Retrieved from <http://indigenousfoundations.arts.ubc.ca/home/government-policy/royal-proclamation-1763.html?type=123&filename=Royal%20Proclamation%2C%201763.pdf>.

First Nations Studies Program. (2013b). What is Bill C-31? Retrieved from <http://indigenousfoundations.arts.ubc.ca/home/government-policy/the-indian-act/bill-c-31.html?type=123&filename=Bill%20C-31.pdf>.

Gender Equity in Indian Registration. (2010). Retrieved from <http://www.parl.gc.ca/HousePublications/Publication.aspx?Language=E&Mode=1&DocId=4901865>.

Government of Canada. (1969). Statement of the Government of Canada on Indian policy. Retrieved from <http://epe.lac-bac.gc.ca/100/200/301/inac-ainc/indian_policy-e/cp1969_e.pdf>.

Government of Canada. (2013a). Constitution Act, 1867. Retrieved from
    <http://laws.justice.gc.ca/PDF/CONST_E.pdf>.
Government of Canada. (2013b). Constitution Act, 1982. Retrieved from
    <http://laws.justice.gc.ca/eng/Const/page-15.html>.
Government of Canada. (2013c). Indian Act. Retrieved from
    <http://laws-lois.justice.gc.ca/eng/acts/I-5/>.
Government of Canada (2013d). Omnibus Bill C-45. Retrieved from
    <http://parl.gc.ca/HousePublications/Publication.aspx?DocId=5765988>.
Kelowna Accord. (2005). First Ministers and National Aboriginal leaders strengthening
    relationships and closing the gap. Retrieved from
    <http://www.health.gov.sk.ca/aboriginal-first-ministers-meeting>.
Métis National Council. (2013). R. v. Powley: A case summary and frequently asked
    questions. Retrieved from <http://www.metisnation.org/media/51918
    /r_v_powley.pdf>.
Rabson, M. (2013). A guide to the Idle No More Movement, treaties and legislation.
    Retrieved from <http://www.winnipegfreepress.com/opinion/fyi
    /movers-and-shakers-188470781.html?device=mobile>.
Supreme Court of Canada. (1973). Calder et al. v. Attorney-General of British
    Columbia [1973] S.C.R 313. Ottawa, ON: Author.
United Nations Declaration of the Rights of Indigenous Peoples. (2007). Retrieved
    from <http://www.un.org/esa/socdev/unpfii/documents/DRIPS_en.pdf>.

Glossary

First Nations is the term used today instead of Indian. Status Indians are registered under the Indian Act, and Non-Status are not. Many communities also use the term "First Nation" in the name of their community.

Inuit are Indigenous peoples who reside in the Arctic regions of Canada, Denmark, Russia, and the United States.

Métis are Aboriginal people who can trace their parentage to First Nations and European descent. Métis means a person who self-identifies as Métis, is of historic Métis Nation Ancestry, is distinct from other Aboriginal peoples, and is accepted by the Métis Nation.

Note: Aboriginal Affairs and Northern Development Canada provides an extended list of terminology for Aboriginal peoples at <http://www.aadnc-aandc.gc.ca/eng/1100100014642/1100100014643>.

Knowledge Champions

A very special thank you to the Knowledge Champions
for career development who helped to support
the publication of this educational resource.

BC Career Development Association

BC Career Development Association is a non-profit professional association of career development practitioners. BCCDA offers training and practitioner resources and hosts the annual Career Development Conference. BCCDA administers the CCDP designation — Certified Career Development Practitioner. Be part of a vibrant community of practice — visit BCCDA at <http://www.bccda.org>.

CareerCycles

CareerCycles empowers career professionals through open-enrollment and on-site training in our evidence-based, narrative method of practice, featuring online storytelling tools for blended delivery so you can reach more clients, more effectively! Also, get certified to facilitate our Who You Are MATTERS!® career clarification game, which dovetails with the methodology. We've helped 3,500+ individuals develop careers for the future. <http://careercycles.com>

Career Development Association of Alberta

The Career Development Association of Alberta (CDAA) has been a proud participant in the career development community since 1997. CDAA serves career practitioners with professional development, certification, and advocacy and contributes leadership, resources, and professionalism to the field. CDAA is your partner in career development: current, connected, committed. <http://www.careerdevelopment.ab.ca/>

CAREER LEADER

CareerLeader LLP

CareerLeader is an integrated approach to business career self-assessment built on the premise that interests, motivators, and skills will drive future career success and satisfaction. Based on over 50 collective years of scientific research and experience, CareerLeader is the market leader used by educational institutions, corporations, and counsellors worldwide since 1994. <http://careerleader.com>

Centre of Excellence in Financial Services Education

Centre of Excellence in Financial Services Education

The Centre of Excellence in Financial Services Education works to strengthen Toronto's talent pool and elevate the region's stature as a financial services capital by aggregating research on talent and educational strengths, working with educators to improve the focus of education programs, and showcasing the sector's strengths and career opportunities. <http://www.explorefinancialservices.com/>

CERIC

CERIC — the Canadian Education and Research Institute for Counselling — is a charitable organization that advances education and research in career counselling and career development. We support the creation of career counselling–related research and professional development for a cross-sectoral community through funding project partnerships and our strategic programs. These programs are Cannexus, ContactPoint/OrientAction, and *The Canadian Journal of Career Development*. <http://www.ceric.ca>

CES Career Education Society

The CES Career Education Society is a non-profit organization in British Columbia of people in education, business, industry, labour, government, and private organizations who work together to champion career and learning management as an essential life skill, with special emphasis on career education initiatives that benefit the province's youth. <http://ces.bc.ca/>

Concordia University College of Alberta

Concordia University College of Alberta has been at the forefront of career practitioner training since 1987, specializing in the development of principles and practices that guide both the practitioner and his/her clients to manage careers in the face of recurring changes. As Canada's first provider of career development training, Concordia continues to be recognized as a leader in the field. <http://concordia.ab.ca/>

Dalhousie University College of Continuing Education

Dalhousie University College of Continuing Education offers a wide range of innovative educational programs to diverse populations across Canada. Our online courses for career development professionals provide both new and experienced practitioners with an opportunity to deepen their knowledge of the field, build professional competencies, and enhance service to clients. <http://www.dal.ca/faculty/cce/programs/career-development.html>

Information and Communications Technology Council (ICTC)

Information and Communications Technology is a not-for-profit organization that conducts research and develops and implements solutions to help Canadians take advantage of the digital economy. Through our primary focus on Talent Innovation, Research, and Policy Development, ICTC strives to ensure Canada has the right skills and competencies in a diverse and inclusive workforce. <http://www.ictc-ctic.ca> and <http://www.newcomersICTcareers.ca>

Kathleen Johnston Consulting

Kathleen Johnston is a Career Strategist who helps high-achieving women imagine and create their ideal work. She has helped hundreds of women take charge of their careers and their lives with self-belief and confidence. Kathleen is also a published author and a sought-after speaker on topical career-related issues. <http://www.kathleenjohnston.com/>

Knightsbridge

Knightsbridge is a human capital solutions firm that truly integrates the expertise of finding, developing, and optimizing an organization's people to deliver more effective solutions that maximize investments in people and deliver better performance. Knightsbridge works with clients across North America, the UK, and Australia. <http://www.knightsbridge.com/>

Life Strategies Ltd.

Life Strategies Ltd., an award-winning, project-based organization, is home of the fully online Career Management Professional Program. With expertise in career development, e-learning, training, facilitation, speaking, coaching, psychometrics, research, writing, and curriculum development, we contribute to maximized potential and engagement, supporting individuals and organizations to be the best they can be! <http://www.lifestrategies.ca/>

Marine Institute of Memorial University

MARINE INSTITUTE

It's a big world. Be at the center of it. Welcome to the Marine Institute of Memorial University. We're a world-leading centre for marine and ocean-related career education and research. A cutting-edge education from the Marine Institute is one of the most affordable in Canada and gives you credentials that are recognized around the globe. <http://www.mi.mun.ca>

Memorial University of Newfoundland

Memorial University of Newfoundland has four campuses and over 19,000 students. The Memorial University experience goes beyond pure academics and invites a discovery of self, community, and place. We celebrate our unique identity through the stories of our people — the work of our scholars and educators, the ingenuity of our students, the achievements of our alumni — and the impact we collectively make in our province, our country, and our world. <http://www.mun.ca>

MixtMode

We know what it takes to bring technology and career practice together. We are pioneers in online career guidance and makers of eVolve Learning Technology. We can help you build a web-based solution, develop online career materials, and expand your practitioning skills. MixtMode is the consulting division of Training Innovations. <http://www.mixtmode.ca>

Ø Psychometrics   Psychometrics

Help your clients find careers they love! Psychometrics Canada is the Canadian source for the Myers-Briggs Type Indicator®, Strong Interest Inventory®, and other quality personality, interest, and values assessments. We have been supporting career guidance professionals in education, government, and business with tools and training for over 35 years. <http://www.psychometrics.com/>